Rick Merrill
Spring 1978
Municipal Finance

Financial Markets and the Economy

CHARLES N. HENNING

WILLIAM PIGOTT

ROBERT HANEY SCOTT

University of Washington

Prentice-Hall, Inc., *Englewood Cliffs, New Jersey*

Library of Congress Cataloging in Publication Data

HENNING, CHARLES N.
  Financial markets and the economy.

  Includes bibliographical references.
    1. Finance—United States. 2. Banks and
banking—United States. 3. Money—United States.
4. Financial institutions—United States. I. Pigott,
William, joint author. II. Scott, Robert
Haney, joint author. III. Title.
HG 181.H37   332′.0973   74-8479
ISBN 0-13-315424-6

Printed in the United States of America

10   9   8   7   6   5

PRENTICE-HALL INTERNATIONAL, INC., *London*
PRENTICE-HALL OF AUSTRALIA, PTY. LTD., *Sydney*
PRENTICE-HALL OF CANADA, LTD., *Toronto*
PRENTICE-HALL OF INDIA PRIVATE LIMITED, *New Delhi*
PRENTICE-HALL OF JAPAN, INC., *Tokyo*

Contents

III Financial Markets   185

IV The Level and Structure of Interest Rates   271

Foreword

This appears to be the volume that teachers of money and banking and financial institutions have been waiting for.

It has long been recognized that the student is short-changed when his first, and frequently only course in macrofinance concentrates on money and banking to the exclusion of the other financial institutions and the operation of the financial market place. Up to now, however, it has been difficult for the teacher to find a volume that integrates financial institutions and markets and that also indicates the relevance of these institutions and markets to the economy in general.

Financial Markets and the Economy does the job. It explains money and banking in simple terms, it gives a good picture of the other financial institutions, and it shows the workings of the money and capital markets in terms the student can not only understand but can also examine with interest.

The topics covered in this volume are the topics covered in the financial press and in the financially related committees in the halls of Congress and the various state legislatures.

A student will leave this text with a good dose of theory, but he will also understand why financial institutions are modifying their functions today, why the Federal Reserve is under pressure to refine its goals, and why the tax-exempt bond is being threatened with extinction.

Frequently text writers get so wrapped up in their own studies that they lose perspective as to what a student should really be required to retain. This volume is not subject to that criticism. Rather it shows thorough research of both the academic as well as the institutional literature of finance and places topics in good perspective without emphasis to extreme on pet topics of the authors.

Professors Henning, Pigott, and Scott have found the prime void in the availability of textbooks on finance. They appear to have filled this void to a degree that will merit appreciation not only from professors, but also from the full gamut of students—ranging from the newest to those reviewing for perspective in preparation for Ph.D. orals.

Paul S. Nadler
Professor of Finance
Graduate School of Business Admin.
Rutgers University

Preface

This book presents an overview of our financial system and the role it plays in the economy. It is designed for use in courses in financial institutions and markets. The only prerequisite for students is a course in the principles of economics. The book may also be used in courses in money and banking, especially by instructors who wish to stress the manner in which financial institutions and markets play a role in the transmission of macrofinancial policy actions to various sectors of the economy and to GNP. The book is of moderate length and is especially suited to one-quarter courses, or to one-semester courses, especially if additional readings are assigned.

We hope that the book fills a void which we believe exists because purely descriptive texts give insufficient attention to financial markets, the intermediary process, and the role and the determination of interest rates. Moreover, such texts do not give students a sense of the importance of the financial system for the economy. Traditional money and banking texts usually focus on banks only as creators of money. They often ignore other functions of banks and the other financial institutions, both of which are important in the process of financial intermediation.

The book can be used in conjunction with a book of readings, or with readings selected by instructors. To aid in selection, an extensive and up-to-date bibliography, with annotations indicating the significance of various readings, follows each chapter. Many readings are available on request from the Federal Reserve System and sometimes from other sources, in classroom quantities.

The book is policy oriented because of the significant impact which macrofinancial policies have on financial markets. A discussion of goals and monetary theory is provided as a review for some students. Since schools of business administration and departments of economics are requiring fewer specific prerequisites for courses beyond the introductory level, instructors cannot assume a uniformity of background among their students.

International aspects of finance could have been treated by themselves in one or more chapters, but we chose to discuss such aspects where appropriate. Chapters 8, 9 and 10 include discussion of the influence exercised by foreign demand for and supply of loanable funds, the Eurodollar market, and the Eurobond market, and matters relating to the international balance of payments are included in the chapters dealing with policy.

An effort has been made to include recent important developments such as progress toward an electronic funds transfer system, the Hunt Commission report, and the Administration's proposals for financial reform. In the area of international finance attention is given to recent developments in foreign exchange markets and to measures to reform the world monetary system. Similar effort has been made to discuss controversial areas in theory and policy such as the term structure of interest rates, the high employment budget, and the appropriate guides to Federal Reserve policy.

At the same time, we must recognize that change is a hallmark of the financial system. Institutions and markets are in a continual state of flux; monetary and credit conditions change over time; the policy questions of today may not be those of tomorrow. We urge the reader, therefore, to view this textbook only as an introduction to the study of financial markets and the economy, and to keep abreast of financial developments by perusing current issues of financial publications such as those listed in the Selected References at the end of each chapter. Such a practice will not only keep the reader "up to date," but will provide the excitement and flavor of the financial world that a textbook can only suggest.

The authors wish to acknowledge many helpful comments made by three reviewers—Professor Paul Nadler, Rutgers University; Dr. Paul Horvitz, Director of Research, Federal Deposit Insurance Corporation; and Professor George H. Hempel, Washington University, St. Louis. These reviewers are, of course, not responsible for any errors or omissions. Several colleagues in the faculty of the Graduate School of Business Administration, University of Washington, also helped by reading and commenting on certain chapters: Peter Frost, Alan Hess, and Charles W. Haley. Finally, the careful typing of several drafts of the manuscript by Joanne Beaurain merits the authors' appreciation.

Charles N. Henning

William Pigott

Robert Haney Scott

Seattle, Washington

1

Introduction

In a modern economy, income is partly spent for consumption and partly saved, and much of the saving is channeled into investment via a variety of financial institutions and markets. An efficient financial system assures the flow of such loanable funds into their most desired uses. These institutions and markets provide borrowers with funds needed *now*, while at the same time providing lenders with a variety of financial assets (bank deposits, pension claims) with varying degrees of safety, liquidity, and yield.

The process of the flow of saving into investment is complex in a modern economy because of the many types of financial institutions and markets, whose principal role is to act as intermediaries between borrowers and lenders. The financial markets establish the interest rates—the prices—at which present funds are exchanged for future funds. The right to have funds in the future is indicated by financial assets or claims, held by lenders.

Changes in financial markets and in activities of financial institutions affect both the total level of economic activity and the allocation of funds to various sectors and types of activity. Part I introduces the analysis of the financial system: Chapter 1 presents an overview of the institutions and markets involved in this process and a brief introductory discussion of the determination of interest rates. Chapter 2 includes more detailed discussion of relationships between saving and investment and explanation of flow of funds accounting, which provides an organized framework for data on flows of funds among financial institutions and financial markets.

1

Introduction to our Financial System: an Overview of Markets and Institutions

The term "market" usually brings to mind a geographic place where people exchange commodities or claims (such as bonds). Typically, in economics, terms are defined more narrowly than in everyday use, but the reverse is true of "market." Economists use this term to refer both to the place in which an exchange occurs and to the mechanism, such as a telephone conversation. A market is simply a place or mechanism of exchange; it *may* be located in a specific place.

A financial market is simply a place or mechanism for the exchange of financial assets.[1] As in most markets in modern industrialized countries, these financial assets are purchased and sold for money. Unlike goods and services, financial assets are not consumed; they are *claims* that enable their holders, upon disposing of the claims, to obtain consumable goods and services. A financial institution is simply any institution most of whose assets consist of claims rather than inventory and plant and equipment. Financial institutions serve as intermediaries in financial markets. They provide borrowers with "loanable funds" in exchange for bonds, promissory notes, and other financial assets. Because financial assets are not consumed, what is bought and sold is their *use for a period of time.*

The price for the use of loanable funds is the interest paid and received. The amount of interest paid on a loan depends upon many factors, including size of the loan, length of time of the loan, and risk of default. The price of funds is usually stated as a rate of interest—an amount paid per dollar per annum. By using the *rate* of interest rather than an amount, one can readily compare different prices for different lengths of time and different face amounts of loans.

Thus the rate of interest is the rate charged to obtain present funds in exchange for future funds; alternatively, it may be regarded as the rate of

[1]Money is a financial asset, but because of its special characteristics and special importance, it is usually classified separately.

discount on future funds required in order to obtain them now. That is, $100 lent now for $106 to be repaid one year from today means $6 in interest, and the rate of interest paid by the borrower is 6 percent. Alternatively, $106 to be repaid to the lender a year from now must be discounted by approximately 6 percent to find the $100 that the lender lends today in order to receive $106 a year from today.

The rate of interest is usually expressed as an annual rate, which may be simple or compound; in the latter case the interest payment is added to the principal amount, and both continue to earn interest (are compounded) at regular intervals—annually, quarterly, monthly, or even continuously. The frequency of compounding, of course, affects the total amount received (paid) at maturity of the loan. The various ways of stating the rate of interest and the diversity of interest rates both in forms of statement and in amount make interest rate regulation difficult and sometimes confusing, and make it difficult for borrowers to know the precise rate they are paying. Effective "truth in lending" legislation requiring that borrowers be informed of the precise interest rates they are paying is not nearly as easy to draw up as it might seem.

INTEREST RATES AND SECURITIES PRICES

Transactions in financial markets may be viewed in two ways: (1) borrowing and lending of funds, and (2) selling and buying of securities. The price of a loan, or the "cost" of loanable funds, is the rate of interest, as noted above. The purchase price of a security, on the other hand, is the amount paid by a lender for a security—it is approximately the same as the amount of the loan supplied by the lender. Figures 1–1 (a) and (b) contain supply and demand curves for loanable funds and for securities, respectively.

The supply curve in Figure 1–1 (a) contains the same information as

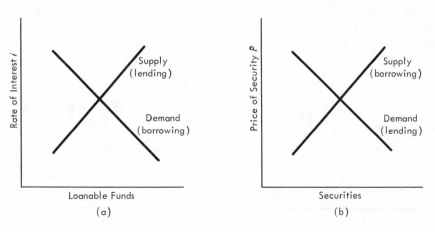

FIGURE 1–1

the demand curve in Figure 1–1 (b). That is, the "supply of funds" would be equivalent to the "demand for securities" if all financial assets were bought and sold. Similarly, the "demand for funds" would be equivalent to the "supply of securities" under that condition.

Interest rates vary inversely with the prices of securities. If Y is a given annual dollar income return, if PV is the price of a security, and if i is the rate of interest, then $PV \times i = Y$, and $PV = Y/i$. Equivalently, $i = Y/PV$. The formula $PV = Y/i$ is often referred to as the "discount formula." If we think of Y as an amount of future income and i as a rate at which this amount is to be "discounted," then PV is the present value or price of the security, and PV varies inversely with i.

If, in Figure 1–1 (a), the demand for funds shifts to the right (increases), then the rate of interest should increase, if no other changes occur. People who demand funds offer securities for sale. Thus, in Figure 1–1 (b), the supply of securities increases as the supply curve shifts to the right, and the price of securities falls. For example, when the federal budget runs into deficit, government demand for loanable funds increases and the rate of interest rises as the demand curve shifts to the right in Figure 1–1 (a). Similarly, the government offers a larger supply of securities in the market and the price of securities falls as the supply curve shifts to the right in Figure 1–1 (b). Both parts of Figure 1–1 illustrate the same event.

FUNCTIONS OF FINANCIAL MARKETS

Financial markets perform an *economic* function. They facilitate the transfer of real economic resources from lender to borrower. Lenders have earned money incomes and wish to save part of their earnings for future use. They can earn interest on their savings by lending their purchasing power to someone who wishes to obtain command over real resources (purchase labor services, plant and equipment, land, and so on). Thus, real resources flow to borrowers and away from lenders. Lenders have reduced their present consumption and will have higher income (and a higher consumption level if desired) in the future when the loan matures. Borrowers will have used the borrowed funds productively; if invested in new machines, these will produce a larger income—raising the real standard of living not only of borrowers, but of others in the economy.

By facilitating transfers of real resources, financial markets serve the economy and the welfare of its citizens. Under a free enterprise pricing system, profit-seeking entrepreneurs provide people with commodities they are willing and able to pay for. As consumer desires change over time, it is necessary that factors of production flow readily into the hands of producers who respond to those changing desires. Because financial markets permit shifts of real resources far more efficiently than the barter agreements that would be necessary in their absence, such markets are highly productive; in a modern highly developed economy they are essential.

Financial markets also perform a *financial* function. They provide borrowers with funds (purchasing power) they want or need to have *now* to carry out their plans. Also, they provide lenders with earning assets so that a lender's wealth may be held in a productive form without the necessity of direct ownership of real assets. There is, of course, no sharp dichotomy between *economic* and *financial* functions of financial markets, and it is only for analytical purposes that economists draw such a distinction. In general, when real resources are affected we refer to economic functions, but many financial transfers have only slight effects upon real resource allocation and in these cases economists refer to *financial* functions.

THE DIVERSITY OF FINANCIAL MARKETS

When we speak of "the financial market," we treat funds or securities exchanged as if they were homogeneous—as if there were only one type of fund or one security. This is, of course, an oversimplification; there are, in fact, dozens of financial markets in which a wide variety of securities are exchanged, and "loanable funds" covers the funds supplied for many different types of loans. Among more important differences are differences in purposes of loans, in time period or maturities of loans, in credit risks involved, and in collateral required. Some loans to consumers are made for housing or other durables; business loans finance the purchase of inventory or plant and equipment; loans to governmental units supplement their tax receipts. In the case of most borrowers, there are various degrees of risk of default, which lenders are willing to assume only if the promised interest rate is high enough to compensate for the additional exposure. Some loan transactions require borrowers to pledge specific assets, which can be sold to protect lenders, and so forth. There are mortgage markets, markets for corporate bonds, government securities, tax exempt bonds, foreign securities, and many others. The markets in which these securities are traded reflect differences in purposes, maturities, and risks.

Loan markets also differ geographically. Local loans may be made by banks, retail firms, and finance companies. Mortgage markets are mostly local or regional, with mortgage money for local construction supplied by local savings institutions. In larger localities there are often regional securities exchanges. The securities of large well-known corporations are traded nationally or even internationally. United States government securities are bought and sold by individuals and firms located around the world. National and international exchanges of funds occur in telephone and telegraphic markets, with principal connections in headquarters in such major markets as New York, London, Frankfurt, Tokyo, and Zurich. These centers handle orders from nearly everywhere on earth.

THE CLASSIFICATION OF FINANCIAL MARKETS

Financial markets may be classified in a variety of ways. To describe and analyze their diversity, we may employ a set of different classification schemes. First, there are new issues markets (*primary* markets), in contrast to *secondary* markets for securities that are already outstanding. A strong and active secondary market gives "liquidity" to a financial asset. Someone may buy a security, planning to sell it before maturity. The ease and convenience with which it can be sold prior to maturity without large risk of capital loss is a measure of a security's liquidity. Second, a distinction is sometimes made between markets for *loans* and markets for *securities*, although buying securities is, of course, lending. A "loan" is usually negotiated face to face, while ultimate buyers and sellers of securities are usually unknown to each other. Banks lend to business firms and individuals, while business firms and governments issue securities. Consumers in a sense issue securities in the form of promissory notes and mortgages, but there is little market for such promissory notes, and the market for mortgages is not as fully developed as the markets for stocks and bonds. Third, there are markets for securities that are *debts* (bonds) and for those that are *ownership shares* (stock certificates). Many technical differences between stocks (called shares in England) and bonds (called stock in England) are sometimes emphasized so strongly that observers are apt to overlook the basic role and function that each plays—to provide funds to business managers. Both represent sources of funds, albeit acquired on quite different terms. Fourth, securities may be traded on the "floor" of a stock *exchange*, or "*over-the-counter*" by telephone contact with dealers or brokers. Fifth, securities markets may be classified as to whether they are "*money*" markets or *capital* markets. The term "money market" is a bit misleading in its popular usage. The term does *not* mean a market where different national currencies are exchanged for each other—that is called the foreign exchange market. Rather, by "money market" is meant the market for short-term loans or securities, usually those that mature in one year or less. Because such loans are very "close" to money, inasmuch as they will be exchanged for money (mature) in the very near future, they are called "money market" loans, and short-term securities are called "money market" instruments. In this sense they differ from the "capital" market for longer-term instruments of indebtedness or shares of ownership. There is, of course, no fine dividing line between these two market classes, nor indeed among any of the five classification schemes mentioned. Given the diversity of financial markets, any classification scheme can be only broad and imprecise.

Although financial markets are distinct and diverse, they are closely interconnected. Transfer costs—costs involved in effecting an exchange of securities between market participants—are quite low in comparison with those attached to exchange of real commodities. Although new issue flotations and the processing of new loan applications may have significant transfer costs, the processing of outstanding paper certificates or notes is not expensive; therefore, connections between various financial markets may be maintained without great cost per dollar of lending. Interconnections are also strengthened by the ease with which information about market prices and terms becomes available. A potential used car buyer is confronted with time-consuming and costly visits to a variety of shops, and a sore toe from kicking tires, but a lender or a borrower may obtain quotations by phone readily.

Security price and yield information flows rapidly and freely throughout financial markets. Also, borrowers and lenders are nearly always involved in several markets at the same time. A bank diversifies its portfolio of loans and investments among many types of financial instruments. Many financial managers can easily switch from one market to another. A private citizen often "lends" to more than one financial institution at a time. He may own an insurance policy, a savings account, a demand deposit in a commercial bank, some government bonds, and other financial assets. Borrowers also typically use a variety of sources of funds. Again, financial markets are interconnected because borrowers and lenders have many options and alternatives in both sources and uses of funds.

In an efficient market funds flow freely and rapidly among its various sources and uses. Insofar as financial instruments are substitutable for each other, changes in supply and demand in one sector of a market have a rapid spillover effect into adjacent markets. Rapidity and strength of such spillover effects depend, of course, upon the degree of substitutability—the greater the degree of substitutability, the stronger and more immediate the transmission of effects. When markets are closely linked, interest rates in the linked markets move up and down together as supply and demand conditions change.

THE MONEY AND CAPITAL MARKETS

We could divide financial markets into primary and secondary markets, loan and securities markets, debt and equities markets, exchange and over-the-counter markets, or money and capital markets. In this text we emphasize the distinction between money and capital markets, money markets being those in which traded instruments have an original maturity of one year or less, while capital markets are those for longer-term securities. Intermittently, references are made to primary and secondary markets, to the differences between loans and securities markets, to debt versus equities, and to securities exchanges in comparison with over-the-counter markets. However, differences between markets for short-term loans and securities and those for long-term financial assets are emphasized in separate chapters.

The Money Market

In the money market, short-term loans are negotiated and short-term securities are issued; these securities are also, in most cases, traded in a secondary market. However, both the rates for primary issues of short-term securities and the rates established by their sale in the money market are important. Thus a short-term security such as a Treasury bill may be issued at a particular rate, and may be traded at a slightly different rate in the money market after issue. Because rates in the secondary market are widely reported, more attention may be given them. Short-term loans are made at specified interest rates; since promissory notes for these loans are not traded, they are not mentioned in connection with the secondary money market, but interest rates on such loans are closely related to interest rates in the secondary money market. The money market is largely an "over-the-counter" or more properly "over-the-telephone" market.

A list of principal money market instruments includes United States Treasury bills, Federal funds, negotiable certificates of deposit (CDs), bankers' acceptances, Eurodollars, and commercial paper. It should be noted that most of the money market instruments are liabilities of banks and the government, and thus the risk of default is very low.

At mid-1973, total gross public debt of the United States government was $458 billion. Of this amount, $263 billion consisted of marketable securities —the remainder being savings bonds and special issues held only by United States government agencies and trust funds. Of the marketable portion of the debt, $100 billion consisted of Treasury bills. These bills are sold at auctions. Principal bidders include some twenty government securities dealers, many banks and corporations, and individuals who wish to invest at least $10,000 at a time. Noncompetitive bids are filled at the average price of those competitive bids that are awarded. Some $2 billion of ninety to ninety-two day (3-month) bills are usually "rolled over" each week. There are also an assortment of 6-month bills outstanding and subject to periodic refunding, and some one-year issues. Some issues of bills are designated as TABs—tax anticipation bills. These are attractive to corporations as an earning asset in which to hold idle funds in anticipation of tax obligations, inasmuch as the Treasury accepts maturing TABs for direct payment of taxes.

"Federal funds" represent a unique money market instrument. Federal funds are *deposits* that member banks (banks that are members of the Federal Reserve System) and others hold at Federal Reserve Banks. Member banks with reserves *in excess* of those required by the Federal Reserve may lend their excess reserves to other banks simply by arranging by phone (or telegraph) a transfer of funds from the lending bank's account at the Fed into the borrower's bank account at the Fed. The transfer of funds is generally reversed the following business day, so that loans of this type are usually for one day (or three days over weekends, four days if a long weekend). During the last week of June 1973 average daily gross purchases of Federal funds for a sample of forty-six reporting banks were over $14 billion. The volume of funds traded during a week reflects the importance of this market in a better way than the amount outstanding on any one day because only excess reserves are traded and there is a large volume of Federal funds (deposits in Federal Reserve Banks) that is not traded.

Negotiable certificates of deposit are now an important money market instrument. This type of security is a relative newcomer to the money market scene—rising to importance in the early 1960s. At mid-1973, some $62 billion of negotiable CDs in denominations of $100,000 or more were outstanding. Commercial banks accept demand deposits and time deposits. Time deposits are divided into savings deposits, special time deposits, such as Christmas Club accounts, and time deposits placed with a bank for a specified time period and evidenced by a certificate issued by the bank. Some time deposit certificates (CDs) are *negotiable*. The depositor may hold the certificate until "maturity," the date specified on the certificate. But because the certificate is negotiable, if the depositor wishes, he can sell the certificate at a discount in the secondary market for CDs by signing it over to a buyer. Then, when the certificate becomes due, the bank repays the new holder rather than the original depositor.

Commercial paper consists of short-term corporation I.O.U.s that are sold either directly or through dealers to a variety of investors. Commercial and finance company paper outstanding at mid-1973 amounted to $36 billion. Funds acquired from the sale of commercial paper are used largely as "working capital"; that is, they provide funds necessary to carry on day-to-day activities of businesses. In the case of finance companies, funds are needed to support the advance of funds to sellers of durable goods and automobiles, under installment plans. Commercial paper is an old form of money market instrument that has renewed importance recently.

Eurodollars are another recent addition to the list of money market instruments. For illustrations, let us suppose that they are created in the following way. Assume that a British exporter receives a check drawn in dollars, on an American bank, in payment for goods he has sold. He may wish to keep the dollars in anticipation of a need to make dollar payments in six weeks. Rather than exchange the dollars for pounds sterling now and then re-exchange the pounds sterling for dollars next month, he may deposit the dollar check in his bank. His bank in England is willing to accept the dollars and keep a dollar amount for him; that is, they are prepared to repay him with dollars whenever he wishes repayment. Assume he makes his dollar deposit as a time deposit for six weeks (or even as a demand deposit, because some banks in Europe pay interest on demand deposits). The bank now has dollars available to lend to customers who may wish to borrow them. Thus, the bank earns interest on the loan and pays interest to the depositor in the normal fashion. In essence, European banks handle some accounts denominated in currencies other than their own. "Eurodollars" is a narrow term, for the English bank may also handle accounts in Swiss francs, French francs, or German marks. Sometimes the term "Eurocurrencies" is used. Eurodollars may be *borrowed* by business firms, individuals, or banks. It is interesting to note that *American* banks have *borrowed* large sums of Eurodollars at certain times, causing the Federal Reserve System to establish regulations for control of such borrowing. Also, recent Eurocurrency regulation by the British government now restricts activities of London firms in this market. The market may not continue to flourish if governments move to restrict it, although at present it is a significant market having wide effects on international finance.

Other smaller and less significant money markets exist, such as the market for bankers' acceptances. These are simply drafts drawn on and accepted by banks—short-term bank obligations.[2]

---

[2]The distinction between a promissory note and a draft or bill of exchange is that a promissory note is signed by the debtor or buyer (the drawer or maker) and is a *promise* to pay, and a draft is signed by the creditor or seller, and represents an *order* to pay—often to a third party, termed the payee. A draft is drawn on the debtor (termed

The Capital Markets

The capital markets include those for long-term government securities, for corporate bonds, for stocks, for "municipal" bonds issued by state and local government units, and for mortgages.

At mid-1973, about $163 billion of marketable United States Treasury bonds and notes were outstanding.[3] These, along with all other elements of the national debt, come into existence when federal expenditures exceed tax revenues; the deficit is financed through the sale of debt instruments. The government must decide how much of the deficit is to be financed by the issue of bonds and notes, how much by Treasury bills, and how much from other minor sources.

At the end of 1972, it was estimated that the total of corporate bonds outstanding was $452 billion, and the value of corporate stock outstanding was estimated at $1,228 billion. During 1972, net new issues of all corporate bonds and notes amounted to $19 billion. Another $13 billion of new stock (net) was also issued, and the total net addition to outstanding notes, bonds, and stock was $32 billion. Incidentally, this was a relatively large amount; the amount of *new* stock issued in most years is very small. Corporate stock, of course, represents "ownership" in a legal sense, and stocks normally have no maturity dates. They are, then, essentially long-term financial instruments,[4] and corporations must decide how much long-term funds to obtain by sale of bonds, how much by sale of new stock, and how much from retained earnings and other sources.

Municipal bonds are issued by state and local governments, usually to finance capital expenditure projects—streets, sewers, buildings, and the like. Often, provision is made in tax laws for repayment of principal and interest. Municipal bonds have a unique federal tax characteristic in that interest income received by the bondholders is exempt from federal taxation. This rather strange legal provision stems from the doctrine of separation of powers of the federal government from those of state and local governments, and is still a subject of controversy among students of constitutional law. Tax

---

the drawee), or on some other party who is to pay—for example, the debtor's bank. Of course, arrangements must be made in advance to draw such drafts; the debtor or buyer may arrange for the bank to issue a letter of credit or an acceptance agreement for this purpose.

[3]Technically, "bonds" may be issued with any maturity, but generally they mature in not less than five years. Government obligations which generally have shorter maturities than bonds (but longer than Treasury bills) are Treasury notes and certificates of indebtedness. Treasury notes may be issued with maturities up to seven years (prior to 1967, the maximum was five years). No certificates of indebtedness were outstanding in 1973.

[4]Relatively little direct attention is given to the stock market as such in this book. Many excellent books have been written about it. Our purpose is to examine financial markets from a broader-based point of view, and we wish to avoid extensive direct concern with this particular market, especially the details of pricing, trading, and measuring stock market activity.

exemption enables state and local governments to borrow at lower rates of interest than they would otherwise have to pay and, therefore, represents a form of subsidy. These securities are attractive to some lenders, especially those in high income tax brackets, because of their special tax status. The amount outstanding at the end of 1972 was estimated at $173 billion.

Mortgages represent long-term financial commitments secured by liens on real estate.[5] Mortgage debt outstanding on all properties in the United States at mid-1973 was estimated to be $600 billion—a sizable figure by any standard—and seasonally adjusted net mortgage debt formation reached an annual rate of over $69 billion in 1972. Of the total of $600 billion, some $480 billion was held by financial institutions, including banks, insurance companies, savings and loan associations, and others. About $71 billion was held by individuals. Some $49 billion was held by United States government agencies or United States-sponsored agencies, including the Federal National Mortgage Association, the Veterans Administration, and others.

THE ROLE OF GOVERNMENT IN FINANCIAL MARKETS

Government affects virtually every aspect of financial activity in the United States. Government's role is important and widespread, as borrower, insurer, regulator, and ultimate source of liquidity.

The United States government is the largest single borrower in the world. With federal budget deficits varying widely from year to year, it is difficult to say how rapidly United States debt will increase, but no doubt it will continue to rise. The paper dollar bills that we carry in our pockets are promises to pay issued either by the Federal Reserve System or in some cases by the United States Treasury. In other words, these are noninterest bearing I.O.U.s. One type was originally issued directly by the government to finance government expenditures. In any event, our circulating medium of exchange is a form of government debt, if the Federal Reserve System is considered to be a part of the government.[6]

State and local governments also issue large amounts of debt, and such debt seems to increase rather steadily at a rate of about 8 percent per year. With continued urbanization, the role of state and local governments in the economy is bound to expand steadily in the foreseeable future, and state and local taxes are not likely to be sufficient to meet desired expenditures.

Besides the various types of government debt, there exist a large number of debt issues of federal agencies (and of agencies originally sponsored by the federal government) that have credit programs of various sorts. Among these are the Veterans Administration, Federal Housing Administration, Federal National Mortgage Association, Small Business Administration, and Federal Home Loan Banks. Some of these agencies insure private loans, some lend

[5]Sometimes corporate bonds are secured by real estate mortgages. These issues are not counted as mortgage debt.

[6]There has been much discussion of the "independence" of the Federal Reserve System, but for present purposes we may treat the System as part of the government.

directly, and some purchase private marketable securities. To finance their loans and purchases of securities, they issue debt instruments of their own (or "participation certificates" that give the buyer "ownership" of a part of a package of mortgages, say, that the agency holds). Through such agency activities the federal government again has significant effects on financial markets from both the supply side and the demand side.

But government involvement does not stop here. Besides participating directly in markets, government agencies regulate financial institutions. Commercial banks and most other financial institutions are regulated by either the federal government or the state that granted their charters. Three federal agencies—the Federal Reserve System, the Comptroller of the Currency (Treasury Department), and the Federal Deposit Insurance Corporation—are significant in regulating commercial banks.[7] Thus one or more government agencies control the chartering of new banks, approve branching and merging of banks, insure deposits, set maximum interest rates that banks can pay on various types of time deposits, and to some extent control rates that banks charge customers for various services offered. Mutual savings banks, savings and loan associations, credit unions, insurance companies, and small loan companies are also regulated. The Federal Savings and Loan Insurance Corporation insures share accounts (similar to deposits) in savings and loan associations in a manner similar to the insurance of demand and time deposits and savings accounts in commercial banks by the Federal Deposit Insurance Corporation. Through the Securities and Exchange Commission, the government also regulates the sale of new securities to the public and the operations of brokerage firms and securities exchanges.

Finally, government agencies have responsibility for implementation of monetary, fiscal, and debt management policies in the interest of economic stabilization. In carrying out these policy programs, they exercise tremendous influence on the cost and availability of credit; this influence is felt throughout the entire structure of financial markets and institutions. Of special importance is the role of the Federal Reserve System as the ultimate source of liquidity for the banking system. The Federal Reserve has power to make funds available to banks and other government agencies on an almost unlimited scale if it were essential to do so in the public interest.

SUMMARY

There are many interrelated markets for loanable funds. The principal borrowers are business, government, and consumers; the principal lenders, consumers, government, and business. These market participants buy and sell both new and existing financial assets at prices determined in the markets. Borrowers have outstanding debt, and lenders have earning assets; debt and credit are two sides of the same coin.

[7]Many other government agencies, of course, regulate banks along with other firms —for example, there are regulations concerning hours of work, employment of minorities, and so forth.

For securities that vary in price, interest rates vary inversely with the prices of the securities. An increase in demand for funds leads to an increase in interest rates and at the same time a decline in prices paid for securities.

Financial markets perform both an economic and a financial function. Real economic resources are transferred to their most desired uses through provision of funds to borrowers and acquisition of earning assets by lenders, and funds are provided to borrowers *when needed*, at the same time providing claims for lenders, to be exercised later if desired.

Financial markets are diverse, with many types of loans and securities for many different purposes. But these markets are also closely interconnected; transactors move easily into and out of various market segments.

The role of government in financial markets is pervasive because of (1) direct government participation in the markets, (2) government regulatory activities, and (3) government responsibility for high employment and economic stability, because attainment of these goals involves direct and indirect manipulation of financial markets for policy purposes. The government's influence extends beyond institutions and markets to all those who participate as borrowers or lenders and to individuals and businesses as buyers of goods and services, taxpayers, and citizens seeking a higher standard of living.

QUESTIONS FOR DISCUSSION

1. List a number of different types of financial assets. Which would you classify as money? Why?

2. Make an attempt to define the term "loanable funds." Try to make your definition carefully, to include precisely what is meant.

3. Distinguish between the economic function and the financial function of financial markets.

4. Distinguish between the "money market" and the "market for money" that is referred to in economic theory when the theory of the supply of and demand for money is discussed. Continue your analysis by distinguishing between "tight money" in the money market, and a small or decreasing money supply. It may be helpful to draw diagrams of supply and demand in the money market, and of the supply of and demand for money.

5. Among money market instruments, which do you think would usually have the highest interest rates, and which the lowest interest rates (Treasury bills, negotiable CDs, Federal funds, commercial paper, bank acceptances, or Eurodollars)? Is it possible for interest rates on some of these to fluctuate so widely that they may be among the highest at times and among the lowest at other times? If so, give an example or two, and explain.

6. Distinguish between bonds and mortgages. Some firms issue bonds secured by mortgages. In which category should these be classified? Why?

7. What grounds can you suggest for government participation in financial markets—for the establishment of agencies that make loans and issue bonds?

8. When the United States Constitution states that "Congress shall have the power to create money and regulate the value thereof," why is monetary policy in the hands of the central bank (the Federal Reserve System)?

9. Try to think of some institutions that are borderline, in that they might be classified as financial or as nonfinancial institutions. Indicate the basis for classification.

10. A very basic idea in finance is the discounting of future earnings or income to obtain the present value of that income. Does this discounting imply that people prefer present rather than future income?

SELECTED REFERENCES

The following texts provide extensive coverage of financial markets and institutions: *Financial Institutions and Markets* by Murray E. Polakoff et al. (Boston: Houghton Mifflin, 1970), is an unusual reference work (twenty-eight authors) that is a complete study of the loanable funds markets. The text includes sections on measuring and forecasting financial flows and interest rates, as well as numerous public policy topics. Paul F. Smith's *Economics of Financial Institutions and Markets* (Homewood, Ill.: Richard D. Irwin, 1971) integrates descriptive materials on financial markets and institutions into economic theory and emphasizes the nature of financial decisions and portfolio policy. For a rather sophisticated "introduction" to finance that integrates portfolio policy into the analysis of financial intermediation see Basil J. Moore, *An Introduction to the Theory of Finance* (New York: Free Press, 1968). Of special interest are the sections on the dynamics of monetary disturbances and monetary policy.

Walter G. Woodworth's *The Money Market and Monetary Management*, 2nd ed. (New York: Harper & Row, 1972) is limited to short-term (money) markets. It covers in detail the objectives, instruments, and history of monetary, fiscal, and debt management policies. As its title implies, *Function and Analysis of Capital Market Rates* by James C. Van Horne (Englewood Cliffs, N.J.: Prentice-Hall, 1970) provides an intensive analysis of interest rates, including their role and determination, the term structure, and factors responsible for rate differences (paperback). In the field of money and capital markets, Roland I. Robinson and Dwayne Wrightsman, *Financial Markets: The Accumulation and Allocation of Wealth* (New York: McGraw-Hill Book Company, 1974) is a revision of the book by Roland I. Robinson, *Money and Capital Markets* (New York: McGraw-Hill Book Company, 1964); it deals at greater length than our text with the money and capital markets, and devotes a final section to evaluation of the performance of financial markets.

Financial Institutions, 5th ed., by D. P. Jacobs, Loring C. Farwell, and Edwin Neave (Homewood, Ill.: Richard D. Irwin, 1972) and *The Financial System*, 2nd ed. by James B. Ludtke (Boston: Allyn and Bacon, 1967) both furnish a wealth of data and supplemental information on the institutions that supply funds to consumers and businesses and facilitate international trade.

Many interesting empirical questions and theoretical issues are difficult to include in a conventional text. Moreover, there is no substitute for original writing in conveying to the serious student the flavor of debates and the importance of policy issues that have arisen in the last two decades. Many important original articles are included in the following collections of readings:

Banking and Monetary Studies, ed. Deane Carson. Homewood, Ill.: Richard D. Irwin, 1963.

> *Money, Financial Institutions, and the Economy,* James A. Crutchfield, Charles N. Henning, and William Pigott, eds. Englewood Cliffs, N.J.: Prentice-Hall, Inc., 1965.
>
> *Money and Economic Activity* (3rd ed.), ed. Lawrence S. Ritter. Boston: Houghton Mifflin Company, 1967.
>
> *Monetary Economics: Readings,* ed. Alan D. Entine. Belmont, Calif.: Wadsworth Publishing Company, 1968.
>
> *Readings in Money, National Income, and Stabilization Policy* (Rev. ed.), ed. Warren L. Smith and Ronald L. Teigen. Homewood, Ill.: Richard D. Irwin, 1970.
>
> *Monetary Economics: Readings on Current Issues,* ed. William E. Gibson and George G. Kaufman. New York: McGraw-Hill Book Company, 1971.

The Federal Reserve System is a continual source of data, published monthly in the *Federal Reserve Bulletin.* In addition, the twelve Federal Reserve Banks offer the public free subscriptions to their reviews (usually monthly) that report on staff studies, contain original articles on economic and financial affairs, and outline current developments in the economy.

Journals and monographs of special interest to students of the area covered in this book are the *Journal of Finance,* the *Journal of Money, Credit, and Banking,* and *Savings and Residential Financing* (annual conference proceedings of the United States Savings and Loan League). On a day-to-day or week-to-week basis, the best coverage of financial developments is found in the *Wall Street Journal,* the *Journal of Commerce,* the *Commercial and Financial Chronicle, Barron's,* and the weekly issues of *Comments on Credit* issued by Salomon Brothers, New York. The weekly *Business and Financial Letter,* inaugurated in late 1972 by the Research Department of the Federal Reserve Bank of San Francisco, is also very useful. For regular coverage of developments in the international aspects of macrofinance, two very useful sources are the weekly *International Letter* issued by the Federal Reserve Bank of Chicago and the semimonthly *IMF Survey* issued by the International Monetary Fund.

2

Saving and Investment and the Role of Financial Intermediaries

One of the most important concepts in economics and the study of financial affairs is the relation between saving and investment. Whether we are examining the causes of business fluctuations, the process of economic growth, or the role played by financial institutions in these developments, we must always be concerned with the meaning and significance of saving and investment and the relation between them. Of special interest are the process by which saving and investment take place in a modern enterprise economy and the role played by financial institutions that act as intermediaries between lenders and borrowers.

In a modern economy, the process of investment is carried out by one group of individuals and institutions, while much of the saving is done by another group. Financial institutions and instruments mediate between the saver and the producer who invests. These facts make it necessary, in examining the roles of saving and investment, to draw clear distinctions between (1) "real" and "financial" investment, and (2) "ex ante" (planned) and "ex post" (realized or actual) saving and investment.

SAVING, INVESTMENT, AND FINANCIAL INVESTMENT

Saving and investment are "flow" concepts as opposed to stock concepts.[1] Just as one may observe the water level in a lake at any point in time, or the flow of water into and out of a lake over a period of time, so one may measure the stock of capital goods existing in an economy at a point in time or the flow of investment spending over a period of time. Investment is the process of capital formation. The existing stock of capital depreciates over time as it is used in producing consumer goods or other investment goods,

[1] It is useful to distinguish the flow concept, "saving," from a stock concept, "savings." Savings are holdings of wealth in some form, usually claims. Savings thus are equivalent to financial capital.

so that _net investment_ is the net addition to the stock of capital (gross investment less depreciation and other capital consumption allowances) occurring over a period of time. These additions to the stock of capital are "real" investment.

Saving is a residual concept. It is that part of the output of an economy that is not consumed. Output (equal to income) is produced over a period of time; part of that output is consumed, another part is not consumed, but saved. That part that is saved is added to the stock of wealth (capital goods including inventories) and presumably is available for use in the future. Thus, _by definition_, saving is identical with "real" investment. Both are flow concepts and refer to the addition to the stock of capital (wealth) that occurs over a period of time.

Most "real" investment is undertaken by business firms. Businessmen order newly produced capital goods—equipment, machinery, construction items, inventories. These capital goods are used in producing consumers' goods and other capital goods in the future. Similarly, consumers invest in housing. Saving decisions, on the other hand, are made by consumers and government as well as by business managers. Consumers spend less than their income, and thus save. Governments may spend less than the amount of tax revenue collected, and thereby save (usually, when this occurs, they pay off previous debt). Business firms may hold undivided profits (retained earnings) or set aside, from earnings, depreciation allowances, and save in these ways.[2] The actions of those who save result in real investment. They may also result in financial investment through the purchase of claims, or in an increase in holdings of money (provided the central bank allows the money supply to increase).

"Financial" investment refers to acts of acquiring claims to wealth or liquidation of debt (redemption or repayment). In the acquisition of a claim to wealth (an earning asset) there is no immediate change in the stock of wealth of the economy. An asset formerly held by one person is simply transferred to another person's ownership. Purchase of a stock or a bond may precede or accompany real investment, but the purchase itself does not represent real investment. When saving and investment occur, there is an addition to the stock of wealth of the economy at large.

The term "financial investment" relates to individual consumers or firms (or the government) and their daily decisions about the forms in which they hold their claims to wealth (earning and nonearning assets). When referring to "real" investment, the analyst always has in mind the creation of productive tools or inventories of goods and materials that will be used in the production of consumers' goods or other investment goods.

Ex Ante and Ex Post Saving and Investment

The difference between ex ante and ex post saving and investment is that ex ante refers to plans or expectations about saving and investment,

---

[2]Technically, saving is the earnings set aside rather than the depreciation allowances, but, with some liberty, analysts pool the two accounting concepts under the heading of savings.

while ex post refers to actual, realized, past levels of saving and investment. In a modern economy, in which saving decisions are made principally by consumers and investment decisions are made principally by businessmen, it would be rare indeed to find ex ante saving equal to ex ante investment—that is, to find planned or expected saving on the part of consumers to be the same in value as planned or expected investment by businessmen. On the other hand, ex post saving must always equal ex post investment for the entire economy if all sectors of the economy are properly accounted for; this equality is a matter of definition.

In simple equation form we may write:

Planned (ex ante) investment + unplanned investment = actual (ex post) investment

and $I \equiv S$

Planned (ex ante) saving + unplanned saving = actual (ex post) saving.

Although by definition actual saving must equal investment, it is clear that planned (ex ante) saving and investment can differ. That is, there may be *unplanned* elements of saving and/or of investment which, when combined with planned elements, make the actual or realized levels of saving and investment equal during a given period of time. Investment in inventory may be used as an example of how there may be a discrepancy between ex ante saving and investment even though ex post saving and investment are necessarily equal.

Let us assume that managers of a firm plan to increase inventories by 100 units. However, buyers purchase less than expected so that actual inventories rise by 150 units, 50 of which are unplanned. At the same time, assume that buyers had planned saving of 150 units. Actual and planned saving are equal in this example.

In the example, ex post saving and investment are both 150; ex ante saving is 150, but ex ante investment is 100, and unplanned investment in inventories is 50. The unplanned element—the discrepancy between ex ante saving and investment—is entirely on the investment side. Other examples could be given in which unplanned saving, perhaps because of changes in income, would occur rather than unplanned investment. In any event, whether ex ante saving and investment differ because of unplanned elements in saving or in investment, it is likely that subsequent adjustments by consumers or business firms will produce changes in spending and output. For this reason, the analysis of ex ante saving and investment is useful in explaining why there are fluctuations in economic activity. This explanation, and the role of financial institutions in the process, are discussed in a subsequent section.

Saving and Investment and the National Income Accounts

National income accounts are designed for classification and measurement of the total value of goods and services produced for *final* use in a country during a given period.[3] The gross amount is usually referred to as gross national product (GNP). After deducting depreciation and other capital consumption allowances and certain other items from GNP, the resulting amount is termed national income. It is useful to consider briefly the relation between expenditures for GNP and the income received in the form of wages, rent, interest and profits. Then the relationship between saving and investment can be examined in more detail because our discussion of financial markets is directly concerned with saving and investment.

Figure 2–1 shows these relationships in simplified form. One may view expenditures for final output as consumer expenditures, government spending, gross investment spending, and net spending by foreigners for exports. The same total amount may be viewed as income received by those who receive wages, rent, interest, and profits before depreciation allowances (earnings before depreciation allowances).

As noted on the lower left side of the figure, income may be used for consumption spending or may be saved. Saving may be used for direct investment, as for example when the owner of a single proprietorship business uses funds he has saved to add new equipment to his store; it may also be used for financial investment, in the purchase of financial assets (stocks, bonds, promissory notes, and so forth); or it may simply be held in the form of additional money (assuming that the total money stock has been allowed to increase during the period).

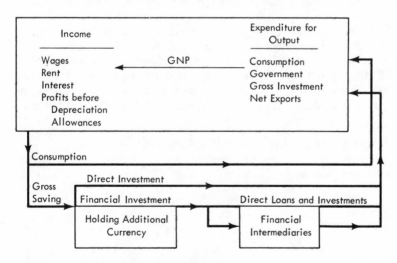

FIGURE 2–1   GNP, Saving, and Investment

Net exports (net foreign investment) is often ignored, since, for the U.S., it is relatively small, and in recent years sometimes negative. Technically, saving equals total investment—domestic plus net foreign investment.

[3]The largest part of the gross value of transactions in an economy is not for the exchange of "final" goods, but rather for (1) the exchange of "intermediate" goods and (2) the exchange of existing assets such as houses or financial claims. These latter transactions do not represent output, and our description of saving and investment is not directly concerned with them.

Financial investment may go directly into loans and investments (purchase of corporate bonds, government bonds, stocks, and so on) or may be channeled through financial intermediaries such as banks, savings and loan associations, life insurance companies, and others. Funds received by such institutions may be channeled into business loans and investments, investments in government securities, or consumer loans. Amounts loaned to consumers may be used by them for consumption. Similarly, amounts loaned to government provide funds for the government to use for current spending.

Money is more carefully defined in Chapter 4, but at this point it may be noted that money is separated from other financial assets because of its special characteristics and importance. Moreover, in the United States, although interest or dividends are received at some point in time by almost all of those who own other financial assets, those who hold money do *not* receive interest when they hold coins, paper money, or demand deposits (checking accounts). In some countries interest is paid on demand deposits, and thus this criterion for distinction—the presence or absence of interest payments—cannot always be used to divide money from other financial assets.

Table 2–1 contains figures on saving and investment in billions of dollars for the year 1972 in the United States. The measures are taken from national income accounts prepared by the U.S. Department of Commerce and published in the *Survey of Current Business* (and also republished in several places, including the *Federal Reserve Bulletin* and *Economic Indicators*).

In 1972, as in any other year, gross investment in the economy equaled gross saving. Gross investment is the amount spent, in current dollar values, both for replacement of investment goods that have become obsolete or otherwise depreciated and for net new additions to the capital stock. Addition to business inventories is treated as investment; reduction in inventories is treated as disinvestment. In addition to private domestic invest-

TABLE 2–1   U.S. Gross Saving and Investment, 1972 (billions of dollars)

Gross private domestic investment		178.3
Fixed investment	172.3	
Net change in business inventories	6.0	
Net foreign investment		−7.6
Gross investment		170.7
Personal saving		49.7
Gross corporate saving		123.8
Undistributed profits	29.3	
Inventory valuation adjustment	−6.9	
Depreciation allowances	101.4	
Government surplus or deficit (−)		−2.8
Gross saving		170.7

SOURCE: *Survey of Current Business*, August 1973.

ment, there is a positive or negative amount of United States net foreign investment, which is measured by the excess of exports over imports of goods and services, including net transfer payments to foreigners.

The gross saving figure includes saving of the household, business, and government sectors during the year. Government surplus (deficit) is the saving (dissaving) of federal, state, and local governments, as defined to fit the national income accounts. It is not the same as the amount of surplus (deficit) reported by the President each year in the annual government budget, because state and local government saving or dissaving is included and because of some differences in definitions of expenditures and receipts used in different budgets. Saving and investment in Table 2–1 is *ex post*.

The Economic Significance of Saving and Investment

Economists use the concepts of saving and investment to help analyze two important aspects of macroeconomics: (1) fluctuations in economic activity between prosperity and recession, and (2) the process of economic growth. Ex ante amounts are frequently used in analysis of causes of fluctuations that occur in the level of business activity; ex post saving and investment are significant factors affecting rates of economic growth. Both ex ante and ex post amounts, of course, vary cyclically and may affect long-run growth.

Why do business enterprise economies experience periods of expansion in output and employment, frequently accompanied by inflation, followed after some months or years by declines to levels we describe as "recessions"? Why, in other words, do we have business fluctuations? One approach suggests that discrepancies between what businessmen plan to invest in capital goods and the amounts they and members of the other sectors plan to withhold from the spending stream usually differ; that is, ex ante investment usually exceeds or falls short of ex ante saving. The level of income and spending rises when planned I > planned S, and declines when planned S > planned I. In this view, changes in economic activity occur when investment spending is greater or smaller than the amounts that would be saved at a given level of income. These discrepancies or differences between saving and investment may occur because of unplanned changes in sales and inventories or unplanned changes in income and spending. If planned investment and planned saving are not equal, it is because savers have different plans from those who determine the amount of investment or because of unplanned elements on either side that lead to subsequent changes in investment plans or saving plans and further increases or declines in spending and income.

The amount of capital formation—the level of saving or investment—is also important because of its relationship to economic growth. Here we refer to the resources going into productive processes that either widen the application of capital or intensify its use. Our capacity to produce more goods and services over time—our growth in economic activity—may result from supplying a larger, better-educated and trained labor force with more capital (capital widening) or from utilizing more capital per unit of labor or output (capital deepening). Although there are clearly many physical, social, and psychological factors responsible for the differences in growth rates among countries or within a country over time, the ratio of capital to GNP seems empirically to be highly significant. Countries with high growth rates have high saving/gross national product ratios. An economy with capital-intensive production processes, therefore, is likely to grow faster in terms of physical output than other countries. But because of the need to provide fairly continual investment outlets of high magnitude, such an economy is also likely to expand or decline as investment spending fluctuates relative to the nation's saving.[4]

SAVING AND INVESTMENT IN
BARTER AND MONETARY ECONOMIES

A "barter" economy is, by definition, one without money; nor are there any other financial assets or liabilities. Hence, there are no financial institutions. All trade of economic goods takes place "in kind." Because trade of goods must take place "in kind," only small amounts can be traded on any one occasion. Barter markets are almost always two-person markets, and there is no system of money prices. In theory, a system of relative prices could exist, but only if everyone engaged in trading knew the amounts of each good that could be traded for amounts of each and every other good—an unlikely state of affairs.

Equally important, from our point of view, all saving and investment decisions would be simultaneous: *if* one saved, he would thereby invest in real goods, and if he invested he would save to provide the real resources. Not only would saving be identical with investment in this sense, but all economic units would have balanced budgets at all times; there would be no external financing. Barter economies provide a single type of asset for savers to acquire, real capital goods; the saver-investor has but one source of finance, his own saving. Not only would the level of income and capital formation be low, but quite likely the economy would be inefficient. Investment-saving would be tied rigidly to the distribution of current income and would not be subjected to a yardstick of profitability. Capital formation would take place or not, depending upon the level of current income and the decision to consume or save.

In a barter economy, saving equals investment in the ex ante sense as well as in the ex post sense. The decisions or plans to save and invest occur simultaneously: they are both made by individuals.

The most elementary type of monetary economy is one with money as the sole financial asset (debt).[5] Fiat money (issued by the government in

---

[4]Because ex post $S = I$ at all times, the realized levels of S and I are always equal, but rise or fall during cyclical swings.

[5]Except for gold (and silver or similar monetary metals), all financial assets are also debt. Hence if financial assets increase, debt increases. It should be noted that stocks are not technically debt, but they are evidences of *claims* held by stockholders.

order to acquire goods and services from the private sector) may consist of coins and paper money that the community accepts as legal tender. It is a debt of the government and an asset of households and business firms.

The importance of money in the economy is twofold: first, money serves as a medium of exchange and helps circumvent the restrictions on exchange imposed by the system of barter. Goods and services are exchanged for money, which in turn may be exchanged for goods and services. This promotes the development of markets, wider exchange, and specialization in production and distribution.

Second, money provides an additional asset for savers and an additional means of financing expenditures of investors. Savers may acquire real assets *or* accumulate cash balances; investors may finance expenditures from current saving *or* by drawing down previously accumulated money holdings. The rigid link between saving-investment and the distribution of current income is broken, and although all expenditures are financed internally, some flexibility has been introduced into the saving-investment process.

More complex and sophisticated financial systems simply extend the range of choices and alternatives available to suppliers and demanders of loanable funds. By increasing the number and variety of savings media (uses of funds) and the techniques and means of raising funds (sources of funds), more sophisticated financial systems facilitate transfer of real resources from lenders (surplus units) to borrowers (deficit units).

A sophisticated financial system is an essential feature of a highly industrialized economy. The mass production and distribution of goods and services and the high degree of specialization in product and factor markets are mirrored in the financial sector of the economy by a similar degree of complex interaction: an elaborate system of markets and institutions provides the mechanisms for bringing suppliers and demanders of funds together. The saving-investment process is facilitated by numerous institutions that offer savers a wide variety of substitutes for real capital or money, thus encouraging the flow and diversification of saving, and many methods of providing borrowers with funds to meet their requirements, thus promoting investment spending.

The transfer of real resources is made possible by a flow of funds from lenders through financial intermediaries to borrowing or deficit units. These funds are then available to bid for resources that are released from present consumption into the output of capital goods.[6]

Figure 2–2 depicts the process of intermediation.[7] In effect, Figure 2–2 is a blow-up of the part of Figure 2–1 that relates to transfers of funds rather than to real income. On the one hand there are the borrowers, who wish to supplement their current income and savings by acquiring funds to finance their expenditures. On the other hand there are the lenders, whose

---

[6]At full employment, saving makes investment possible by releasing resources. At less than full employment, investment spending may raise the level of real income and make more saving possible and hence available.

[7]This diagram is based on that of John G. Gurley, *Liquidity and Financial Institutions* in the Postwar Period, Study Paper No. 4, Joint Economic Committee, 86th Cong., 1st sess., January 25, 1960, p. 21.

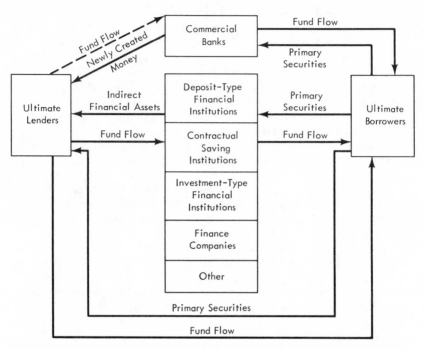

FIGURE 2–2

income and savings are in excess of their own internal needs. Positioned between these two groups are the financial institutions that serve as intermediaries ready to accommodate simultaneously both deficit and surplus sectors. The arrows indicate the direction of flow of securities and the net flows of loanable funds in the opposite direction. The nonbank financial institutions are discussed in detail in Chapter 5, but at this point it should be noted that the deposit-type financial institutions include mutual savings banks, savings and loan associations, and credit unions; the contractual saving institutions include insurance companies and pension funds; the investment-type institutions include mutual funds and trust departments of commercial banks; and "other" consists chiefly of government agencies or agencies that were originally government agencies such as farm credit agencies and housing or mortgage market agencies (for example, the Federal National Mortgage Association).

We see that several sources of funds are available to borrowers. Households, business firms, or government units in need of funds may either borrow directly from savers, by selling their securities directly to them, or indirectly, by selling securities either to commercial banks (monetary intermediaries) or to nonmonetary intermediaries such as mutual savings banks, life insurance companies, or pension funds. The term "indirect borrowing" or "financing" thus implies the use of intermediaries as proximate lenders. However, the ultimate source of funds is the original lender because, as the diagram shows, the intermediaries acquire loanable funds from lenders and make them available to borrowers.

What is the process by which these financial intermediaries acquire loanable funds? Primarily it is by offering savers a more attractive alternative to the direct purchase of the borrower's debt. That is, by providing savers with assets that are either safer, more liquid, or have a higher net return—or, more likely, some attractive combination of these features—intermediaries induce lenders to exchange their loanable funds for claims against financial institutions rather than against primary borrowers. In essence, intermediaries buy borrowers' debt and sell their own liabilities to surplus units in exchange for loanable funds. An alternative way of viewing this process of intermediation is to visualize intermediaries as borrowing at one level of interest rates—those paid to lenders—and lending at another—the rates charged borrowers. The costs of serving as intermediaries, including a profit, are met by the excess of the lending rate over the borrowing rate.

Intermediation affects the saving-investment process in several ways. First, it facilitates the separation of the investment decision from the saving decision. Investment decisions can be made with no direct tie to any single saving decision. Second, intermediation encourages saving by providing diversification of assets available to lenders, diversified according to risk, yield, and liquidity. Third, intermediation encourages investment by providing a variety of available sources of funds that differ in regard to maturities of loans, interest charges, repayment provisions, and so on. Fourth, and of great importance, use of intermediaries reduces the risk of default to lenders and also assures borrowers that funds are generally available, whereas availability from individuals might be difficult to ascertain. Both of these are cost-reducing functions that mean lenders receive higher net return and borrowers pay less for funds than in the absence of intermediaries. Specialization of activities increases productivity. Some individuals can specialize in the *management* of real resources, borrowing funds when necessary, while *owners* of such resources may continue their chosen activities. Labor and other resources involved in activities of intermediaries contribute to real productivity of the economy and to improving the standard of living because intermediaries are able simultaneously to satisfy portfolio preferences of borrowers and of lenders.

The reader may note that in Figure 2–2 there is a solid line from commercial banks to ultimate lenders showing creation of money, but a dotted line showing fund flows. This is to indicate that commercial banks receive deposits of currency from ultimate lenders and pay out currency to depositors, but they also create new deposits when they make loans to borrowers, or they may pay out additional currency in this process. Although these funds go to borrowers, the line is drawn to ultimate lenders because most of the funds are spent by borrowers, and those who receive them, perhaps after several transfers, are ultimate lenders. Creation of money, either in the form of additional deposits or currency, makes possible additional lending by ultimate lenders, which in turn makes possible increased production of goods and services. For this reason commercial banks are set apart from other financial institutions. Other financial institutions must generally reduce their assets when they make loans, but commercial banks often need not do so. Although the public affects money creation indirectly, banks are the proximate agent for money creation. They may maintain the level of the money supply, subject to controls imposed by the central bank and the government, even in a recession in which borrowing by business firms and consumers is much reduced; banks may simply buy securities if loans decline, and thus maintain the total level of demand deposits. The implications of the important role of commercial banks in money creation are indicated in the next chapter and at many points throughout the book.

Debts, Assets, and Financial Intermediation

Three important points are the subject of this section: (1) for every debt there is an asset; (2) most external financing is through debt issue rather than equity issue;[8] and (3) the greater the reliance on debt and external finance, the more important is the role to be played by financial intermediaries.

1. It is well known that income and expenditures are two sides of the same coin; spending of one sector is income of another. Similarly, debts and assets are two sides of the same coin—one's debt is another's asset. This element of interdependence is often overlooked; for example, we look favorably upon growth of assets but disapprovingly upon growth of debt. Individuals, firms, or governments may deficit spend (borrow) to finance expenditures. Such spending units issue debt instruments—government securities, corporation notes and bonds, mortgages, and so on—which are all assets purchased either by ultimate lenders or by financial intermediaries.

Note, however, that while all debts are also assets, the reverse is not true; all assets are *not* debts. Some assets are real assets (real capital or land or other earning source). In the United States, all *financial* assets are debt—even coins may be regarded as debt of the government. At this point no distinction is made between bonds (debt) and stock (equity) because their functions are basically the same.

Both assets and debts are created when credit is extended; "to obtain credit is to incur debt."[9] Although an individual may incur excessive debt, it is recognized that during prosperous economic times there is always a rapid increase in overall indebtedness, and during economic recessions there is always a slowdown in the rate of growth of outstanding debt. Debt performs a desirable function in any economy, and one should hesitate to condemn debt simply because, on some occasions, it is misused.

2. Most spending in our economy is financed out of current income. That is, it is financed "internally." The remaining spending is financed "externally" through debt creation or equity issue. Most "external" financing

---

[8]However, the existing *stock* of equity issues is very large because of the fact that most equity issues continue to be outstanding indefinitely.

[9]*The Two Faces of Debt*, Federal Reserve Bank of Chicago, 1972, p. 2. This pamphlet contains an excellent description of the role of debt in the economy.

is undertaken by acquiring funds through issuance of debt instruments rather than equity (ownership) claims. For a variety of reasons both borrowers and lenders in recent years have preferred debt instruments to equities when engaged in external financing.

First, holders of debt instruments have prior claim to income and assets rather than the residual interest of ownership. Thus, debt instruments provide greater "safety" of principal (less risk of loss) than equity instruments.

Second, current taxation rules give debt a privileged position. Interest charges on debt are deductible as business expenses. Even interest on most personal loans and home mortgages is deductible from personal income for tax purposes. In this way, borrowing is "subsidized" by the government's system of taxation, and this alone gives great impetus to borrowing as opposed to equity issue as a means of financing expenditures.

Third, managers of business firms are often reluctant to dilute existing stockholders' equity because to do so will not only reduce control but also reduce earnings available to existing owners. If a firm is growing, current owners stand to share in the growth. If the growth is financed by debt, each shareholder retains control and ownership proportional to his number of shares of stock. On the other hand, if additional shares are sold, then each proportional interest in the growth is diminished. Thus, stockholders often do not approve of dilution of their pro rata share of ownership. Managers do not wish to offend existing shareholders because shareholders can vote to replace management if disillusionment is strong enough.

3. The third point to be emphasized in this section is that the greater the amount of spending financed externally through debt or equity issues, the greater will be the role played by financial institutions. If all our spending were financed out of current income, there would be no need for the services of such institutions. At the other extreme, if all spending were financed by issuance of debt or equity, then all increases in spending would have to be accompanied by concomitant changes in debt or equity, and the role of financial institutions would be maximized. In the United States economy, of course, internal financing out of current income is by far the most important source of funds, and we can say that on average budgets are far closer to being balanced (income-financed) than they are to being totally debt financed. Nevertheless, during recent decades the average net increase in debt outstanding has amounted to approximately 10 percent of GNP. Thus in the early 1970s net additions to the nation's debt have been on the order of $100 to $125 billion per year. We can expect this figure to rise over time as the economy continues to grow.

Growth of Debt and Equity Claims

Under present institutional arrangements that favor the use of debt instruments as a vehicle for transferring loanable funds, growth of debt is the financial side of growth in national income and output. Indeed, historically the ratio of debt to GNP in the United States has generally risen during prosperous times and declined during recessions. But it has averaged about

1.85; that is, $185 of debt is outstanding during the year for every $100 worth of gross national product produced during an average year.[10] Continued expansion of economic activity would seem to require a continuation of the growth of debt, barring unforseseen institutional changes favoring (say) increased reliance upon international financing or equity financing.

Because for many purposes debt (such as bonds) and equity claims (stock) are substitutes, it is useful to consider the growth of total primary securities—those issued by ultimate borrowers, not by intermediaries—including both debt and equity. Primary securities have increased, on the average, 2.3 to 2.7 times as rapidly as GNP; thus, for every $100 billion rise in GNP (approximately the rise from 1971 to 1972), primary securities in an average year increase by from $230 to $270 billion. Implications of this increase are most significant in the capital markets. There will be increases in the various types of bonds and mortgages outstanding, and, unless legal and other changes adversely affect the trend, stock market values will rise significantly. The depressed level of stock market prices in the early 1970s meant that the total value of stocks outstanding was substantially below the trend level of the value of this form of primary security. Of course, even if trends continue, rise in stock prices may be delayed, and such actions as tax changes affecting capital gains might even cause a change in the long-term trend in equity values.

Real economic growth almost always requires growth in real capital. Financial growth accompanies growth in real capital. This is not to say that every sector of the economy must grow. Some sectors grow at higher rates than the average for the economy. These sectors typically include large borrowers who rely extensively on external financing as well as on large amounts of internal financing. The introduction of new technology requires venturing into unknown and untested areas of research, which help us to realize higher standards of living. Financing such ventures requires a viable group of diverse financial institutions; thus financial institutions may have a special importance for economic growth.

SAVING AND INVESTMENT AND THE FLOW OF FUNDS

We already noted that although aggregate saving and investment must be equal, ex post, for the entire economy, it is unlikely that saving will equal investment for any particular sector of the economy. For a given sector, saving may exceed investment. But this means that this sector must have funds that are used for purposes other than financing its own investment spending. If a sector has investment greater than saving, then this requires sources

---

[10]Marshall A. Robinson reported that in an average year during the period 1916–1957 new net primary securities (additions to government, and business and consumer debt) equaled about 10 percent of the current gross national product. At the same time, the economy has experienced an average rate of growth in nominal gross national product (*not* real product) of about 5.5 percent per year. Thus, $10/5.5 = 1.85$ approximately. See his paper: "Debt in the American Economy," The Brookings Institution, Reprint No. 31, June 1959.

other than its own saving to provide the necessary funds. Saving of all sectors together is one source of funds, and investment is one use of funds. The accounting system that includes *all* the sources and uses of funds for the various sectors and, in summary, for all sectors, is the "flow of funds" accounts.[11] We turn now to a brief description of these accounts and some applications of flow of funds analysis.[12]

The flow of funds accounts are derived as follows. First, divide the economy into relatively homogeneous groups or sectors—for example, households, business firms, and governments—and then prepare a statement of sources and uses of funds for each sector. Next, sum these sectoral accounts and place them side by side to form a table or matrix. Third, relate the various flows to the several sectors.

To simplify the construction of sector accounts, it is useful to lump all households into one category or sector, all nonfinancial business firms into a second, governments into a third, and so on until we have divided all the nation's economic units into sectors. Depending upon the data available, the purpose of the analysis, and the degree of disaggregation necessary, we may develop a small or large number of sectors.

The next step is to examine the balance sheets of the various sectors at the beginning and end of a quarter or a year and note the *net* changes in the stock of assets, liabilities, and net worth that occurred during the period.[13] Certain assets may have increased in value, others declined; some liabilities may be greater and some smaller than at the beginning of the period. If the total of assets or liabilities has changed, so will the net growth of a particular sector. This comparison of two balance sheets shows the sources and uses of funds as changes in various accounts over the period, as for example:

January 1, 1972 to December 31, 1972

Uses	*Sources*
Δ real assets (investment or disinvestment	Δ liabilities (borrowing or debt repayment)
Δ financial assets (lending or sale of securities)	Δ net worth (saving or dissaving)

[11]Although flow of funds accounts include all flows, the emphasis is on nonincome flows, especially those shown in Figure 2–2. The flow of funds accounts may be compared with source and application of funds statements in private accounting, just as national income accounts may be compared with income (profit and loss) statements. Unfortunately, the third type of financial statement, balance sheets, are available for the national economy only in the form of tentative estimates. Work on national balance sheets progressed much more slowly than work on national income accounts.

[12]For an excellent but succinct description of this topic see: Lawrence S. Ritter, "The Flow of Funds Accounts: A Framework for Financial Analysis," *The Bulletin*, No. 52, August 1968, New York University, Graduate School of Business Administration, Institute of Finance.

[13]Capital gains are not counted, however; an increase in stock values, for example, occurs only as a result of net new issues of common or preferred stock.

A simple source and use statement for a given sector shows intersectoral flows on a *net* basis. That is, it does not record intrasector transactions; for example, those among nonfinancial business firms. Also, a net increase in assets is treated as a *use*, while a net increase in liabilities (or net worth) is considered a *source* of funds. That is, debt repayment or dissaving, which are in fact uses of funds, are treated as *negative sources* of funds; and disinvestment in real assets or the sale of securities, which are in fact *sources* of funds, are treated as *negative uses*. This characteristic of the accounts faciltates handling the data uniformly, but unfortunately may also obscure some changes both within sectors and among different sectors.

Households, firms, and other economic units acquire funds by rearranging their assets and liabilities or by current saving. Funds may be used to acquire assets, including investment goods, or they may be used to reduce liabilities. The conventional accounting practice is to treat an increase in assets as the only use and an increase in liabilities or net worth as the only sources of funds.

For a given sector, and, by summing all sectors, for the economy as a whole, the following equalities obtain:

$\triangle$ net worth + $\triangle$ liabilities = $\triangle$ real assets + $\triangle$ financial assets, or saving + borrowing = investment + lending.

It follows that if a sector's $S > I$, then $L > B$, while if $I > S$, then $B > L$; surplus sectors are net lenders and deficit sectors are net borrowers. In our simplified accounts we have not shown the variety of assets such as bonds, notes, deposits, money, and so forth that lenders may acquire, nor the different kinds of debts that a deficit sector may issue to finance its spending. The accounts used by the Federal Reserve System and other sources of data provide for a higher degree of differentiation by disaggregating both the assets involved in flows of funds and the sectors.

In principle, an account is easily established for each of the several sectors that make up the economic system. Sources and uses of funds are identified as in the case of our hypothetical sector. If we place these statements side by side, we form a matrix to describe an interconnected system of flow of funds for, say, a year. As is shown in the hypothetical matrix in Table 2–2, not only does each sector's sources match its uses but, by summary, total sources equal total uses. Furthermore, while $S \neq I$ for any sector individually, for the economy as a whole, $S = I$.

Table 2–2 is a simplified, hypothetical flow of funds matrix for an economy that has been divided into four sectors. Items in the cells of the matrix represent dollar flows that occurred during a period of time. In general, U stands for uses of funds and represents acquisitions or additions to assets, while S stands for sources of funds and represents additions to liabilities or to net worth.

We find that households saved 60 of their income during the period and used 10 of this to purchase real investment goods and the remaining 50 of this saving to purchase financial assets from financial intermediaries. The business sector saved 40, but also invested 80 during the period. This required

TABLE 2–2   Flow of Funds Accounts for a Given Time Period

	Households		Business		Government		Financial Intermediaries		All Sectors	
	U	S	U	S	U	S	U	S	U	S
Saving (net worth)		60		40		−10				90
Investment (real assets)	10		80						90	
Net change in financial assets	50						50		100	
Net change in financial liabilities				40		10		50		100
TOTALS	60	60	80	80	0	0	50	50	190	190
Sector surplus or (deficit)	50		(40)		(10)		−0−		−0−	

Note: *U* stands for uses and *S* stands for sources of funds.

business to obtain 40 in additional funds from financial intermediaries in order to have a total of 80 for investment spending. The government, by running a deficit in its budget, dissaved 10 and had to issue 10 of financial liabilities to cover this excess of spending over tax revenues. Finally, financial intermediaries experienced an increase in both assets and liabilities. They accepted deposit liabilities to the households in the economy in the amount of 50. At the same time, they used these deposits to purchase the debt of 40 that business offered in the market.

The column totals show equality of *S* and *U* for each sector, in keeping with the requirements that flow of funds statements always balance, so that net changes in uses equal net changes in sources for each sector.

The row totals show the overall equality of uses and sources of funds in the aggregate, for all sectors. Saving by households, business, and government totalled 90, since the government actually dissaved 10. This total saving also equals total investment of 90, of which, in this simplified example, 80 was undertaken by business firms and 10 by households. The government's dissaving figure (−10) probably results from the fact that government spending is treated as being entirely for goods and services and not as representing additions to the stock of capital. In the United States, the federal government does not maintain a separate set of "capital" budget accounts as some other countries do. This is an arbitrary procedure. If, in fact, the government spent 10 on long-lived dams, perhaps it would be more appropriate to replace the −10 under sources with a +10 under uses in the investment row. Then total investment would be 100 and again equal to total saving. However, this is not the convention in the United States.

Households increased their holdings of financial assets by 50, and this is reflected in the *sources* side of the Financial Intermediaries column, showing a 50 increase in financial liabilities. This 50 might be considered, for example, as consumer demand and time (savings) deposits at banks and savings and loan associations—liabilities of financial institutions. The 50 under uses reflects the holding (purchase) of government securities and business bond issues. Overall, we see that financial assets increased by a total of 100, and financial liabilities also increased by 100. Thus, in the "all sectors" column the total of 190 reflects the equality: S + Borrowing = I + Lending. In our simple example, saving and investment were both 90, while borrowing and lending were both 100.

Along the bottom of Table 2–2 there is a row indicating the surplus or deficit that each sector realized in its budget. Households had a surplus of 50, while business firms and government both engaged in deficit financing (debt financing) of part of their expenditures, 40 and 10 respectively.

In this simplified table we did not include a separate row for money; rather we pooled money as an asset in the row with other financial assets. Furthermore, we did not assume that financial intermediaries created money, whereas we know that commercial banks *do* create money. We have kept the example simple in order to give the reader a feeling for the nature of flow of funds accounts without the complexity actually to be found in the accounts as published. The *Federal Reserve Bulletin*, for example, contains quarterly data on flows of funds in considerable detail. One table provides a summary of funds "raised and advanced in United States credit markets" and another shows "principal financial transactions" with a breakdown of money supply holdings, time and savings account holdings, United States government securities, private securities, and so on, all of which constitute an elaborate breakdown of our single category "net change in financial assets." Once a year, tables show balance sheet values of the various financial assets held by the various sectors.[14]

APPLICATIONS OF FLOW OF FUNDS ANALYSIS

Economic forecasters often use the flow of funds frame of reference in analyzing trends in interest rates and credit flows. Each February, Bankers Trust Company issues an *Investment Outlook* in the form of a sources and uses statement with a breakdown of mortgages, corporation stocks, corporation bonds, government securities, and so forth, and their ownership among a variety of financial intermediaries such as life insurance companies, pension funds, and savings and loan associations. This statement is more simplified than tables published by the Federal Reserve System. The Life Insurance Association of America and Salomon Brothers also prepare flow of funds tables on a regular basis.

By looking at flows of funds matrices over time, analysts can speculate

[14]In these tables, values of stocks are shown at market prices, including capital gains, with reduced figures when capital losses occur.

about future trends and the possible impact on fund flows as a result of ex ante (expected) shifts in the demand for or supply of funds, and the relevance of these shifts for segments of the market. Of special interest to banks and savings and loan associations, for example, is the process of "disintermediation." If interest rates rise on United States Treasury bills, relative to rates obtainable at savings institutions, households may purchase Treasury securities instead of placing their funds in financial institutions. Thus, savings deposits may be withdrawn from financial intermediaries and funds may flow directly from households, the ultimate lenders, to government, the ultimate borrower in this case. Disintermediation generally results in less activity and therefore less profit for financial intermediaries, at least in the short run; it also results in a smaller flow of funds to activities financed by such institutions. With the flow of funds accounts one can trace and perhaps predict the results of the process of disintermediation.

Projections of the flows of funds are used within the Federal Reserve System to aid in anticipating results of monetary policy actions. For example, if projections of flows of funds indicate that disintermediation is likely, actions may be taken to prevent it from being too pervasive. Perhaps the best example is disintermediation that results in a smaller flow of funds to those institutions that are mainly active in financing housing. If Federal Reserve System officials are concerned about the need for housing finance, they may take actions to avoid a large reduction in funds available for this purpose.

In addition to the use of projections of flows of funds as an aid in making monetary policy decisions, flow of funds data are becoming more widely used as sources for studies of portfolio choices of sectors of the economy. Questions such as the relative preferences of a particular sector for money versus other financial assets may be studied, using these data. The data also provide an alternative measure of elements in total saving, although there are significant differences between saving figures developed from various sources.

A significant problem arises from the fact that flows do not include capital gains, whereas annual data on assets and liabilities are valued at market prices, and hence for such items as common and preferred stocks, they include capital gains.

Unfortunately, a simple analytical framework comparable to that used in analysis of changes in national income has not been developed for the flow of funds. Complexity of the data and the lack of obvious or easily found causal relationships tend to make the data more valuable as a source of empirical information to be used in testing hypotheses than as a conceptual framework from which economists develop important hypotheses quickly. However, appropriate monetary policy actions should be based on a knowledge of the transmission process through which such actions ultimately affect real national income and prices; it is therefore to be expected that research will continue and research effort will increase.

Detailed examination of flow of funds accounts is beyond the scope of this book, but the reader is encouraged to examine one or more of the sources mentioned above in order to familiarize himself with details contained in them.

SUMMARY

Saving and investment are essential concepts in economics and finance. It is important, however, to distinguish among the various ways the terms are used. "Real" investment refers to capital formation and includes expenditures for plant and equipment, residential and other construction, and additions to inventories. "Financial" investment means purchases of stocks, bonds, and other claims to wealth. Economists also distinguish between actual (ex post) and planned (ex ante) saving and investment. The former refers to amounts of saving and investment that actually occur during a given period of time. Measured this way, the nation's saving necessarily equals the nation's investment in capital during a given period. Ex ante saving and investment, on the other hand, are likely to differ because consumer (and other) plans to save or spend need not match business plans to invest in plant, equipment, and inventories.

In barter economies, the decision to save is a decision to invest in real capital. Financial investment is nonexistent because there are no financial assets. All current saving must be invested, and all investment is financed solely from current saving, out of current income. More sophisticated economies which use money and other financial assets have available a wider set of sources and uses of funds. Savers are not forced to invest in real capital, and investors are not limited to current saving as a source of funds.

In a modern economy, financial institutions act as intermediaries between ultimate lenders and borrowers. They facilitate the flow of real resources from surplus to deficit spending units. In essence, intermediaries buy borrowers' debt instruments with funds they acquire from lenders who choose to hold claims against these institutions. To the extent that intermediation promotes the flow of saving into efficient investment outlets, it makes possible a higher and more productive rate of capital formation than would otherwise obtain.

Historically, most spending has been financed internally rather than through debt creation or equity issues. The role of financial intermediaries has, therefore, been more limited than would be the case if most expenditures were financed externally. Most external financing has been through debt rather than through equity issue because of concern on the part of lenders for "safety" of principal, tax considerations, and managements' desire not to dilute stockholder equity.

The flow of funds accounts provide a useful framework for classifying and measuring the sources and uses of both internal and external funds. This framework shows clearly the relationships among various sectors of the economy, and among each sector's saving, investment, lending, and borrowing. The data are a useful tool in predicting financial flows and interest rates, and are being more frequently used to test hypotheses concerning behavior of consumers and other groups in holding and acquiring various types of assets.

QUESTIONS FOR DISCUSSION

1. If saving is income that is not consumed, what about income held in the form of additional currency? What about holdings of additional demand deposits in banks? Relate to the "S = I" discussion.

2. Show how ex post saving and ex post investment *must* be equal, by using balance sheets for individuals, totaling these for the economy, and eliminating items which are equivalent because one is the reverse of the other.

3. Indicate why items shown at the left side of the box in Figure 2–1 may be termed "gross national income." If profits after depreciation allowances were negative, what would be the situation of the economy?

4. Why does a country with a rapid rate of growth in income almost always have a high ratio of saving/GNP?

5. What comment can you make about those who argue that "debt is bad"? Comment on the relationship between this view and the view that credit is desirable.

6. On the basis of the ratios of debt securities and primary securities as a whole (debt plus equities) to GNP, project total debt to 1980, on the basis of projection of GNP. Show how you derive the projections.

7. Why do business firms in the United States rely more heavily on debt issues than on equity issues for external financing?

8. What is meant by "disintermediation"? When or under what conditions is it likely to occur?

9. Name as many individual types of financial institutions as you can, and classify each within the classification used in Figure 2–2.

10. Are the flow of funds accounts comparable to income statements, balance sheets, or "source and use of funds" statements? Why?

SELECTED REFERENCES

Among the many texts that discuss the role of saving and investment in economic analysis and their place in the national income accounts, see Warren L. Smith, *Macroeconomics* (Homewood, Ill.: Richard D. Irwin, 1970) or Edward Shapiro, *Macroeconomic Analysis*, 3rd ed. (New York. Harcourt, Brace, Jovanovich, 1974).

The pioneering work of John Gurley and Edward Shaw in developing a theoretical framework that shows how ". . . debt, financial assets, financial institutions and financial policies shape, and are in turn shaped by, general levels of prices and output" is found in their *Money in a Theory of Finance* (Washington, D.C.: The Brookings Institution, 1960), and numerous articles, including their "Financial Aspects of Economic Development," *American Economic Review*, September 1955, pp. 515–538; "Financial Intermediaries and the Saving-Investment Process," *The Journal of Finance*, May 1956, pp. 257–276; and "The Growth of Debt and Money in the United States, 1800–1950;

A Suggested Interpretation," *The Review of Economics and Statistics,* August 1957, pp. 250–262.

Our simple presentation of the flow of funds accounts, like that of most recent texts, draws substantially upon the work of Lawrence S. Ritter in his *The Flow of Funds Accounts: A Framework for Financial Analysis,* New York University, *The Bulletin,* No. 52, August 1968. The Board of Governors of the Federal Reserve System publishes quarterly flow of funds data in the *Federal Reserve Bulletin;* once a year the data include estimates of financial assets and liabilities for each sector, by types of assets and liabilities.

II

The Supply of and Demand for Loanable Funds

Supply and demand for loanable funds are important because they determine interest rates and affect the allocation of funds to various sectors of the economy.

The supply of loanable funds is largely channeled through commercial banks and nonbank financial institutions, which are discussed in Chapters 3–6. Commercial banks are especially important because they create money, a type of financial asset of special significance, indicated by the correlation between changes in the stock of money and changes in the level of business activity.

Demand for loanable funds comes largely from the business sector, from the demand for mortgage credit, from consumers, state and local government units, the federal government, and foreigners. Private domestic demand for loanable funds, the first three of these sources of demand, is discussed in Chapter 7; government and foreign demands for loanable funds, in Chapter 8.

3

Commercial Banks
in the
Financial Markets

Commercial banks are the most important intermediaries participating in the financial markets. First, they are, with few exceptions, the only financial institutions legally entitled to accept demand deposits—deposits transferable by check by depositors. The significance of this is that these deposits are commonly used as a medium of exchange and account for the bulk of the nation's money supply. Second, commercial banks are a major holder of the savings of the public. Business firms and individuals hold time and savings deposits, which along with demand deposits, compete with other financial assets in their portfolios.[1] Third, banks are the largest single source of loanable funds to business firms, consumers, and the government sector. Bank credit is used to finance investment expenditures, the purchase of consumer durables, and the spending of federal, state, and local governments.

In this chapter we examine the portfolio policies of banks: the objectives and practices that determine the kinds of assets and liabilities banks hold. Of special interest is the management of a bank's liquidity position and the innovative responses of bankers to dynamic changes in the financial markets during the past decade. The chapter concludes with a brief discussion of government regulation and supervision of the commercial banking industry.

COMMERCIAL BANKS AS BUSINESS FIRMS

Bank objectives and policies are similar to those of other financial institutions: all seek long-run profits by lending and investing funds at their disposal

---

[1]Because only commercial banks accept demand deposits, there is no competition between banks and other institutions for these deposits. However, banks compete vigorously with each other in local and, in some instances, national markets for depositors. Also, in the competition for savings deposits banks compete with other institutions whose liabilities are close substitutes for bank deposits. These include savings and loan associations, mutual savings banks, and to a lesser degree, life insurance companies, pension funds, and mutual funds.

at as high a rate of return as is consistent with an appropriate degree of safety of principal. But unlike many other lenders, banks must be prepared to meet the withdrawal of these funds virtually on demand.[2] The need for liquidity is therefore of utmost importance, and the central problem facing the bank's management is how to reconcile these often conflicting demands upon the bank's resources—safety, earnings, and liquidity. To put the problem in perspective, let us examine the business transactions of banks as recorded in the balance sheet and the income statement.

The Bank Balance Sheet

The balance sheet displayed in Table 3–1 shows the major accounts of commercial banks that belong to the Federal Reserve System. These banks are referred to as *member banks*. Membership in the Federal Reserve System entails certain rights and requirements with important implications for the bank's holdings of assets and liabilities. We discuss the implications when appropriate, but it suffices now to say that most of the nation's banking business is conducted by member banks.[3]

In the table, the assets represent the uses of funds, and the liabilities and capital accounts are the sources of funds. On the asset side of the balance sheet are (1) cash assets, (2) earning assets, consisting of loans and securities, and (3) other assets. Liabilities are mainly demand and time deposits (including savings deposits), although borrowings are also important. The remaining item is the capital account, consisting of owners' equity and subordinated long-term debt.

Bank Cash Assets

Cash assets include vault cash and reserve balances at Federal Reserve Banks (so-called *legal reserves* of member banks), balances at other commercial banks, and cash items in the process of collection. At the end of 1972, cash assets totalled $96.6 billion, 17 percent of total assets, and were about equally divided between legal reserves and balances due from other commercial banks on the one hand, and cash items in the process of collection on the other. Vault cash and deposits at Federal Reserve Banks serve

---

[2]With the exception of certificates of deposit, which banks usually redeem only at maturity, most time deposits may in practice be withdrawn at any time even though, legally, notice of intent to withdraw may be required. Demand deposits are, of course, payable in currency or transferable on demand.

[3]At mid-1973, there were 14,048 commercial banks in the United States. Although less than half were members of the Federal Reserve System, these member banks held almost 80 percent of the assets or deposits of the banking system. However, there has recently been some tendency for banks to withdraw from the Federal Reserve System, and many newly chartered banks do not join the System. One reason is the attractiveness of state reserve requirements, which are not necessarily less percentagewise, but permit holding reserves in more attractive forms. See Thomas O. Waage, "The Need for Uniform Reserve Requirements," Federal Reserve Bank of New York, *Monthly Review*, December 1973, pp. 303–306.

TABLE 3–1   Balance Sheet, Member Commercial Banks, December 1972

	Billions of $	Percentage of Total	Percentage of Subcategory
Assets			
Cash assets	96.6	17	
Reserves at FRB	26.1		27
Vault cash	6.6		7
Due from banks	19.4		20
Cash items in process of			
collection	44.5		46
			100
Loans	329.5	56	
Commercial and industrial	112.1		35
Real estate	73.1		23
Consumer	64.5		21
Agricultural	8.5		3
Securities	14.8		5
Financial institutions	27.8		8
Other	9.2		4
			100
Investments	136.2	23	
U.S. Treasury	48.7		36
Municipal securities	69.6		51
Corporate bonds and notes	17.9		13
			100
Miscellaneous	22.8	4	
Total assets	585.1	100	
Liabilities and capital			
Demand deposits	238.7	41	
Private	174.8		73
Interbank	31.9		13
U.S. Treasury	9.0		4
State and local governments	13.5		6
Certified checks	9.5		4
			100
Time deposits	243.8	42	
Private	211.1		86
Interbank	3.6		2
U.S. Treasury	.5		—
State and local governments	28.6		12
			100
Borrowings	36.4	6	
Capital accounts	41.2	7	
Miscellaneous	25.0	4	
Total liabilities and capital	585.1	100	

SOURCE: *Federal Reserve Bulletin*, May 1973, pp. A18–22.

to meet daily transactions needs of banks and legal reserve requirements. Cash items in the process of collection are essentially checks that will soon be presented to other banks for payment either through facilities of the Federal Reserve System or those so-called "correspondent banks."

The correspondent system is a unique feature of United States banking, acting as a linking mechanism among banks across the country.[4] Small banks associate with larger city banks, especially those in major financial centers, which provide them with a wide variety of services such as check collection facilities, investment advice, access to data processing equipment, the opportunity to participate in syndicated loans, and so on. Smaller banks would find it expensive and difficult to provide these services for themselves. In return, the smaller banks agree to carry deposits with their correspondents; these deposits provide the correspondent banks with additional funds. This network reduces the information and transactions costs of credit and is essential in the United States, where the banking system consists of about 14,000 separate banking firms, the majority of which are quite small. Both the asset, due from banks (balances at other commercial banks), and most of the liability account, due to banks (interbank deposits), are the result of correspondent banking relationships.

Bank Loans and Investments in Securities

Most of banks' funds are used to acquire earning assets, which provide the bulk of revenue and enable them to cover expenses, including the cost of capital. Earning assets are classified as (1) loans or (2) securities; the former are usually negotiated on an individual basis with borrowers, whereas the latter are the obligations of governments and large, well-known corporations, which are usually sold on the open market and are available to a wide variety of prospective buyers. In general, bankers prefer loans to securities because of the higher interest return and, more important, because a loan today usually opens the door to "repeat business" in the future, once the banker-borrower relationship is established.[5]

Types of Bank Loans

Bank loans may be classified as: (1) commercial and industrial, (2) real estate, (3) consumer, (4) agricultural loans, (5) loans for purchasing or carrying securities, (6) loans to financial institutions, or (7) other loans. The first three are by far the most important, making up about 75 to 80 percent of member banks' loan portfolios at the end of 1972. The preferred loan for most banks is to business firms for working capital purposes. It is typically a short-term credit, subject to renewal, used by the business firm to carry accounts receivable and to purchase inventories; loans having an original maturity of one year or more ("term loans") are, however, a substantial part of business loans.

Loans for the purchase of residential property and consumer durables

---

[4]See "Correspondent Banking: Part I, Balances and Services," Federal Reserve Bank of Kansas City, *Monthly Review*, November 1970, pp. 3–14.

[5]See Edward J. Kane and Burton G. Malkiel, "Bank Portfolio Allocation, Deposit Variability, and the Availability Doctrine," *Quarterly Journal of Economics*, February 1965, pp. 113–34.

are the next largest categories, and for some "retail" banks located in small or medium-sized cities, may be as important as business loans. The real estate loans are either insured or guaranteed by the federal government (Federal Housing Administration or Veterans Administration) or are so-called conventional loans. They are secured by residential property as provided for in mortgages, which call for amortization of the loan over a period of, say, twenty or thirty years. Consumer loans help finance the purchase of automobiles, appliances, or other durables; in most cases larger loans of over $1,000 are secured by durable goods such as automobiles or other acceptable property. Needless to say, the specific provisions as well as the relative importance of various loan categories vary from bank to bank.

Investments

Banks also extend credit when they purchase securities, and this category of assets may be especially attractive when loan demand is slack, as a way of employing loanable funds. A very high percentage of these securities represents the obligations of governmental units; the remainder is corporate notes and bonds. Over the past twenty-five years, banks have added significantly to their holdings of the tax exempt obligations of state and local governments (municipals), while their holdings of United States Treasury securities have remained quite stable in amount. The major reasons for the reduced importance of Treasury securities are the substantial increase in bank loans, the improved marketability of municipals, and the increasing number of alternative sources of liquidity available to larger banks, which has reduced the need for holding United States government securities. These changes in bank loans and investments are shown in Table 3–2.

Deposit Liabilities

The most important source of bank funds is deposits, which at the end of 1972 made up 83 percent of total liabilities and capital, and were about equally divided between demand and time accounts. Banks accept deposits from individuals, partnerships, and corporations and also from state and local governments and the United States Treasury. Banks also hold deposits of other banks, as noted earlier in connection with correspondent banking.

TABLE 3–2 Member Bank Loans and Investments

	Percentage of Total Loans and Investments	
	December 31, 1952	*December 31, 1972*
Loans	45	71
U.S. Treasury securities	44	10
Municipal securities	7	15

TABLE 3–3

Amount of net demand deposits	Reserve percentages
First $2 million or less	8
Over $2 million—$10 million	10½
Over $10 million—$100 million	12½
Over $100 million—$400 million	13½
Over $400 million	18

SOURCE: *Federal Reserve Bulletin*, November 1973, p. A–9.

Demand Deposits

Under Federal Reserve regulations, net demand deposits of member banks are subject to reserve requirements that are applied under a set of graduated reserve ratios. As of October 31, 1973, these ratios were as shown in Table 3–3.

The amount of reserves a member bank must hold in vault cash plus balances with the district Federal Reserve Bank—only these two items count as legal reserves—is based upon the average daily net demand deposits of the second week preceeding, that is, two weeks earlier than, the statement week, plus the reserves required against time deposits held during that earlier period. The time deposit reserve requirements are different from those on demand deposits and are shown in Table 3–4 (rates in effect October 31, 1973).

Determination of the amount of net demand deposits requires calculation of total demand deposits (including such items as officers' checks and certified checks, because these are bank obligations that normally will become deposits shortly). From gross demand deposits, as thus determined, two items are subtracted: (1) cash items in process of collection, because these are included in gross deposits, but because they are in collection, they have not been subtracted from the deposits of other banks, although they soon will be; and (2) demand deposits held *by* the bank in *other* United States domestic banks because these interbank deposits are *not* deposits held by the public or by the government. Sometimes (for example, in World War II) government

TABLE 3–4   Reserve Requirements for Time Deposits

Savings Deposits	Other Time Deposits	
	Under $5 million	Over $5 million
3%	3%	5%

SOURCE: *Federal Reserve Bulletin*, November 1973, p. A–9.

deposits could also be deducted—they were not subject to reserve requirements. This encouraged banks to buy government securities and, in turn, to
give the government deposit credits.

The bank officer responsible for managing the bank's reserve position,
sometimes referred to as its "money position," knows in advance what his
daily average legal reserves must be during the weekly reporting period,
because of the fact that they are based on deposits of the second preceding
week, as described above. And because his vault cash *actually held*, as well
as his reserve *requirement*, is based upon the period two weeks earlier, he
knows what his average daily balance at the Federal Reserve Bank must be
during the weekly reporting period. In short, he must hold an average daily
balance at his regional Federal Reserve Bank during a given statement week
equal to the required percentage of his bank's net demand deposits during
the second preceding week, less the average daily amount of vault cash held
during that same earlier week.

Time Deposits

The time/demand deposit ratio is important because it influences the
amount of loans a bank may make and the amount of deposits it may hold.
We should note also that the cost to the bank of funds acquired by accepting
time deposits is higher than the cost of demand deposits. The difference is
somewhat less than the amount of interest that must be paid on time deposits,
inasmuch as the administrative costs of handling demand deposits are somewhat higher than those of handling time deposits. The payment of explicit
interest on demand deposits is prohibited. Because of these different costs, the
deposit "mix" is an important factor affecting banks' profitability.

The term "time deposits" includes (1) savings deposits, (2) nonnegotiable
time certificates, (3) negotiable certificates of deposit, and (4) open account
time deposits. Savings deposits may be added to or withdrawn when the
depositor presents himself with his passbook at the bank or makes his request
through the mail. Although a thirty-day notice of withdrawal may be required, banks ordinarily waive this requirement and pay such deposits on
demand to the depositor, but not to a third party.

Nonnegotiable time certificates consist of a variety of instruments such
as savings bonds, savings certificates, investment certificates, and so on. As
the name suggests, these time deposits are not transferable; they are also not
redeemable prior to maturity under usual circumstances. This category is
often referred to as "consumer" time deposits, especially those in denominations of less than $100,000, to differentiate them from "business" time de-
posits, which are typically in denominations of $100,000 or more and usually
negotiable as well.

Negotiable certificates of deposit (CDs) are issued by large banks and
bought mainly by nonfinancial corporations. At times, state and local governments, foreign interests, and nonbank financial institutions also purchase
these short-term securities. The instrument is negotiable because it is payable
either to the bearer or to the order of the depositor, and its negotiability has
encouraged the development of a secondary market that has become one of
the most important money markets. Most CDs, especially those traded in the

New York market, are issued in minimum denominations of $100,000 with the most common denomination being $1,000,000. These and other aspects of CDs are discussed in Chapter 9.

The remaining category of time deposits is open account time deposits. These time deposits are "open" in that they do not, as a general rule, have a definite maturity date, but are automatically renewed unless the issuing bank or the depositor gives written notice of intent to terminate the contract. Such notice is usually required ten to thirty days prior to termination. Mostly, these deposits are owned by business firms which agree to maintain them as a condition of acquiring a line of credit from the bank; they are similar in this respect to a "compensating balance," which is discussed shortly. In some cases, open account time deposits are interest-bearing, as, for example, when the deposit serves in lieu of a performance bond posted, say, by a contractor to ensure that he meets certain contractual requirements, or in the case of a Christmas account, which provides a means of setting aside funds for a definite time and need.

As we have seen, time deposits may be classified in different ways, such as in terms of ownership, reserve requirements, or type of deposit. For purposes of Federal Reserve Regulation Q, which establishes ceiling rates of interest on time and savings deposits, a different classification system is used: time deposits are either (1) savings accounts, (2) multiple maturity time deposits, or (3) single maturity time deposits. Multiple maturity deposits include those that are automatically renewable at maturity without action by the depositor and deposits that are payable after written notice of withdrawal. Single maturity time deposits are classified by size of deposit and maturity time. For example, deposits of less than $100,000 with a maturity of thirty days to one year, one to two years, two years and over; deposits of $100,000 and over with a maturity of thirty to fifty-nine days, sixty to eighty-nine days, and so on. Under Regulation Q, banks are allowed to pay higher rates on time deposits than on savings deposits, and at the time this was written there was no limit on the interest rate on deposits of $100,000 and over with a maturity of thirty to ninety days. This provision allows banks to compete for short-term funds that might otherwise be used to purchase money market instruments such as United States Treasury bills or commercial paper.

Both multiple and single maturity time deposits are usually evidenced by a certificate, and hence are often referred to as CDs; those of less than $100,000 may be nonnegotiable or negotiable CDs. For larger denominations, negotiable CDs over $100,000, a secondary (resale) market has developed in recent years, which is discussed later.

Because other aspects of a bank's deposit liabilities are examined in Chapter 4, when we look at different measures of the money supply and deposit creation, our remaining comments on deposits in this section are limited to (1) U.S. Treasury Tax and Loan Accounts and (2) the "compensating balances" of business firms.

United States Treasury Tax and Loan Accounts

The United States Treasury holds its working balances at the twelve Federal Reserve Banks and pays for goods and services purchased by drawing down these deposits, which in recent years have averaged about $2 billion. Deposits are also held in thousands of commercial banks across the country that have qualified as special depositories; these are called Tax and Loan Accounts because funds flow into them from two sources: (1) when individuals and businesses pay taxes (or withhold from employees' pay checks), these proceeds are deposited into Tax and Loan Accounts of the various banks in the Federal Reserve district, and (2) banks are sometimes allowed to pay for most of their purchases of United States Treasury securities or purchases on behalf of their customers by crediting their Tax and Loan Accounts. The Treasury's working balances at Federal Reserve Banks are augmented by "calling" these deposits out from time to time and transferring them to the Treasury's General Account at Federal Reserve Banks.[6] Usually the "calls" are scheduled to coincide with Treasury payments so as to minimize the impact on the banking system's reserves. Even so, individual banks experience sharp changes in deposits and reserves as the result of discrepancies between Treasury expenditures and receipts.

Compensating Balances

Many large regional or national business concerns prearrange a "line of credit" with a bank that agrees to provide loan funds over a period of several months or more, and up to a certain limit, upon request. The line of credit is not a legally binding contract, but banks do not change the amounts agreed upon unless significant change occurs in relevant conditions. In return for this assurance of credit, the borrower usually is obliged to maintain an appropriate average level of deposits, often 10 to 20 percent of the line of credit, which "compensates" the bank for the costs of providing ready funds and any services associated with the credit agreement.[7] If, for example, the borrower must maintain deposits of 20 percent of a line of credit of $100,000 and loans have a 6 percent interest rate, full use of the line means $80,000 are available at an annual cost of $6,000, raising the effective interest rate to 7½ percent.

On the other hand, the "true" cost of the loan *to the borrower* may be lower than in this simple example if the balances the borrower would have held in the absence of the line of credit agreement were the same as or higher than with the agreement, if the rate of interest charged were lower because of the additional average balance held, or if additional services were provided to the borrower without further charge—if the bank considered itself to be compensated for these services by the balances held by the borrower. As is true of most bank practices, the compensating balance requirement is applied flexibly and the specific provisions vary from bank to bank and with respect to different borrowers under different sets of credit conditions. Com-

---

[6]For a more complete description of this mechanism, see Federal Reserve Bank of Richmond, "Treasury Tax and Loan Accounts," *Monthly Review*, January 1966, reprinted in Paul F. Jessup, ed., *Innovations in Bank Management: Selected Readings* (New York: Holt, Rinehart, and Winston, 1969) pp. 129–34.

[7]See Jack M. Guttentag and Richard G. Davis, "Compensating Balances," Federal Reserve Bank of New York, *Essays in Money and Credit*, 1964, pp. 57–61.

pensating balances are usually part of the deposits held by business firms; usually they are demand deposits, but they may be time deposits, especially in cases of "link financing," in which a borrowing firm finds a financial institution that will deposit the compensating balance so that the borrowing firm may utilize the entire amount of the line of credit.

Banks may gain several advantages from compensating balances: they are assured of keeping a certain amount of deposits and they *may* obtain a higher effective interest rate. They also have leeway in allowing borrowers to obtain additional funds, if needs were underestimated, by permitting the compensating balance to decline.

Borrowings and Capital Accounts

The term "borrowings" in Table 3–1 refers to the nondeposit liabilities of member banks and includes (1) borrowing from Federal Reserve Banks, (2) purchases of Federal funds, (3) borrowing of Eurodollars, (4) sale of bank promissory notes, and (5) sale of loans and securities under repurchase agreements. Long-term notes and debentures (capital debts) are, strictly speaking, also liabilities, but under certain restrictions governing minimum maturities, banks are allowed to include them as part of bank capital. Thus, bank capital is defined somewhat differently than the capital accounts of non-financial business firms.

Borrowings

The only categories under "borrowings" that are of quantitative importance today are the first three; bank sales of commercial paper and assets under repurchase agreements were significant in the 1960s for a brief period, but have been largely discontinued because of changes in Federal Reserve regulations which rendered them uneconomical sources of funds. Borrowing from the Federal Reserve, in the Federal funds market, or overseas in the Eurodollar market remain important sources and are discussed in Chapter 9.

Capital Accounts

The principal capital accounts are (1) capital stock, (2) surplus and (3) undivided profits. Capital stock is mostly common shares which were sold when the bank was newly organized, issued later to raise additional long-term funds, or increased through stock dividends. The initial offerings of stock (at a required 20 percent or more premium over par value in the case of national banks) created the surplus account. The surplus subsequently increases through retention of earnings and their transfer to this account. Undivided profits is the account which is credited with each year's earnings and subsequently debited when cash dividends are declared, when (or if) asset shrinkage occurs, or when the bank's directors increase the surplus account, thus earmarking earnings as permanent capital rather than amounts available for dividend payments.

The amount and structure of the capital accounts are important to commercial banks because the amount of capital is a measure of the cushion available to protect depositors against loss in the event of shrinkage in asset values and possible insolvency. The almost uninterrupted decline in the banking system's capital/deposit ratio during the period for which data are available has led to increasing concern with the question of the "adequacy of bank capital."[8] Whether a particular bank's capital is sufficient, however, depends upon much more than the capital/deposit ratio. Additional factors such as the risk structure of assets, the volatility of deposits, the overall liquidity position, and ultimately the quality of a bank's management are also important. But if a bank's capital is deemed inadequate after an examination of these items, the regulatory authority may suggest to the bank's management that it increase the capital stock or surplus by following a more conservative dividend policy or by other means.

In recent years, the relative decline in capital accounts has heightened bankers' interest in senior securities as a source of long-term funds. Preferred stock and capital debt (capital notes and debentures), little used since the depression period of the mid-1930s, have been gaining favor, especially among bankers anxious to avoid possible dilution of the existing common shareholders' equity. Rulings by the Comptroller of the Currency have permitted national banks to include long-term capital debt as capital, for purposes of calculating lending limits. The most important limit relates to the size of a loan that may be made on an unsecured basis to an individual borrower—no more than 10 percent of its unimpaired capital and surplus. There are a number of exceptions to this rule for loans secured by suitable collateral. Similar restrictions apply to real estate loans, which are limited to a certain ratio of a bank's capital and surplus or a certain proportion of its time deposits. Also, because they are exempt from reserve requirements and interest rate ceilings, capital debts may prove, under certain conditions, a more profitable source of funds than time deposits.[9]

Bank Income and Expenses

Our cursory examination of the balance sheet for member banks shows that, as a dealer in debt, most of a bank's income and expenses result from use of borrowed funds. This is confirmed by the income statement for member banks for 1972, presented in abridged form in Table 3–5. It shows the principal sources of revenue and expenses, most important of which is the

[8]A summary of a study conducted by the Association of Reserve City Bankers, Chicago is found in Roland I. Robinson and Richard H. Pettway, *Policies for Optimum Bank Capital: Summary*, February 1971, reprinted in *Innovations in Bank Management*, ed. Paul F. Jessup (New York: Holt, Rinehart and Winston, Inc., 1969), pp. 183–86. However, the solvency of the banking system and protection of depositors depend on the maintenance of a prosperous economy, the insurance coverage provided by the Federal Deposit Insurance Corporation, and the ultimate source of liquidity, the Federal Reserve System.

[9]See Paul S. Nadler, *Time Deposits and Debentures: The New Sources of Bank Funds, The Bulletin*, No. 30, New York University Graduate School of Business Administration, July 1964, pp. 24–30.

TABLE 3–5 Income and Expenses of Member Banks, 1972

	Billions $	Percentage of Subcategory
Operating income—total	31.3	
Interest from:		
Loans	20.8	67
Securities	6.1	19
Trust department	1.3	4
Service charges, fees, and other	3.3	11
		100
Operating expenses—total	25.6	
Interest on:		
Time and savings deposits	10.5	41
Federal funds and other borrowing	1.7	8
Salaries, wages, and benefits	6.0	24
Other operating expenses	6.5	26
		100
Income before taxes and securities	5.7	
gains or losses	.5	
Gains or losses (−)	1.4	
Income taxes	4.4	
Net income		

SOURCE: *Federal Reserve Bulletin*, May 1973, p. 330.

interest received from loans and securities and interest paid on time and savings deposits, respectively.

By far the largest income item is interest from loans. This varies in importance from year to year as the composition of earning assets changes and as the general level of interest rates rises and falls with the level of business activity. Since the early 1950s, loans have exceeded securities and have increased at a faster rate of growth.[10] Interest rates have also risen during this twenty-year period; hence, interest from loans has become an increasingly important source of revenue, especially during periods of recovery and expansion of economic activity.

In 1972, as in most recent years, interest paid on time deposits exceeded each of the other operating expenses, including wages and salaries. The amount of interest paid depends, of course, on the amount and composition of time deposits, level of competing market rates, and structure of interest rate ceilings imposed by the Federal Reserve under Regulation Q. Though not treated as an operating item, bank gains or losses on securities sold affect net income, and reflect conditions in the securities markets during the year. In 1972 banks took net gains on securities as prices firmed from the lower level of 1969–70; net losses were incurred in some earlier years as banks

[10]During World War II, banks gradually came to hold more securities than loans. Loan demand was not great because firms that produced to sell to the government were largely financed in other ways, and government securities were plentiful as the national debt was increased to help finance the war.

liquidated securities on a large scale in order to provide funds for loan purposes.

The Elements of Portfolio Policy

Let us turn to the central problem facing managers of commercial banks: how to manage their assets and liabilities so as to provide an adequate rate of return to stockholders, consistent with an appropriate degree of safety and liquidity. Earlier we expressed this goal in terms of reconciling the conflicting needs for safety, earnings, and liquidity. But safety and liquidity are not ultimate goals in themselves; they are necessary to achieve the long-run goal of managers, profitable operation of the firm. The bank must at least remain solvent (the realizable value of its assets must equal its legal liabilities plus the value of the "capital stock" account) in the long run, and able to ensure convertibility of deposits into currency in the very short run, if the expectation of profit is to be realized. There would, of course, be no "problem" if there were no risks or uncertainties. If the behavior of deposits were manageable, or at least predictable, and if there existed a collection of assets that were at the same time eminently safe and profitable, the banker's life would be simple indeed. But unfortunately, such is not the case. Assets are risky in varying degrees, deposits are volatile, and the promised rate of return on loanable funds varies directly with the degree of risk and inversely with its liquidity.

In short, safety of assets is of paramount importance because of the low capital/deposit ratio—that is, the thinness of the equity cushion; liquidity is necessary to meet the double-barreled demands of depositors and borrowers; earnings are essential if the bank is to compete successfully for customers, employees, and stockholders. In terms of managing the portfolio of assets, the banker must think in terms of "trade-offs" and recognize (1) that no single asset meets all of his requirements and (2) that the cost of improved earnings is increased risk and reduced liquidity.

Safety and Management of Bank Assets

Banks are required to seek safety in the choice of assets for their portfolios because bank failures have serious implications for the entire community. This is an important reason why banks in the United States are prohibited from investing in stocks and why stocks acquired as collateral for defaulted loans must be disposed of within a specified length of time. Another reason why banks are not allowed to own stocks is to prevent the undue concentration of financial power in the economy that such ownership may provide. Thus this prohibition is not simply a matter of reducing risk but is deeply rooted in the aversion to monopoly power. There are certain relatively minor exceptions to the prohibition. A member bank is obliged to buy stock in the Federal Reserve Bank of its district, and member banks are allowed to own, cooperatively, stocks in companies operating data processing facility centers. Banks may also own stock in bank-related subsidiaries such as safe deposit companies and in certain cases, those engaged in foreign banking.

Similarly, relatively high standards of safety are imposed by law and/or tradition on loans and investments. Loans were for many years supposed to be "self-liquidating" assets, convertible into cash through sale of the short-term assets acquired by the borrower, using the loan proceeds.[11] Recognizing that not all bank assets were self-liquidating assets, it was later suggested that assets were safe if they were shiftable—if they could be sold, without significant loss, to another financial institution. Still later, it was recognized that loans might be relatively safe if anticipated income of the business firm seemed likely to be sufficient to repay the loan with interest.

Standards of safety in the acquisition of investment assets have been improved by regulations that in general prohibit banks from acquiring any but the highest grades of bonds and similar securities.

Liquidity and Management of Bank Assets

Until the 1960s, the problem of bank liquidity was usually analyzed within the framework of adjusting the bank's asset portfolio. Accordingly, deposits were treated as an undependable source of funds subject to unexpected withdrawal and beyond the control of the bank's management. The maintenance of adequate liquidity was achieved by holding assets that had short-term maturities or that could be sold quickly and at minimum loss to meet these currency drains. From the time of Adam Smith (circa 1776) until the Great Depression of the 1930s, the "real bills" doctrine was prominent in the literature concerning appropriate bank behavior. According to this doctrine, because banks borrow short-term funds (deposits), they should also lend short-term funds. Their earning assets should be restricted to short-term self-liquidating business loans, for what we referred to earlier as working capital purposes. Thus, bank loans would not only be profitable and safe, but would provide a continual source of liquidity.

The "real bills" doctrine was eventually abandoned both in practice and in principle. First, under this doctrine bank lending policy often failed to accommodate the needs of bank customers. Business firms' investment programs required long-term as well as short-term financing, and consumers required installment loans and mortgage loans to finance their expenditures for durable goods and housing. Second, in accommodating the legitimate "needs" of business and commerce, the banking system contributed to business fluctuations by increasing business loans and deposits during prosperity and reducing them during recession. Even for the individual bank, the loans were often not "self-liquidating," especially during times of crisis. The "real bills" doctrine presumed that bankers could and would judge the appropriate amount of loans to meet the needs of increasing output, but would not make loans that would result in a potentially inflationary increase in demand. This judgment is difficult to make, and if a recession occurs, "sound" loans may no longer be sound. Moreover, central banks began to be more active in efforts to control the economy, expanding bank reserves when they desired an in-

---

[11]The prime example of the self-liquidating loan is one made to enable a firm to increase its inventory above normal levels for peak sales, such as at Christmas. Sales during the period provide funds to repay the loan plus profits for the business firm.

crease in credit and money, and reducing bank reserves when they felt this was necessary. Under these circumstances, commercial banks were subordinated to the central banks as controllers of the level of credit and thus of the level of economic activity. Most economists now accept the role of central banks as controllers of the money stock or of credit, and the "real bills" doctrine as a prescription for commercial bank behavior is no longer accepted.

During the period following World War II, the resurgence of loan demand made it profitable for financial institutions, including banks, to reduce their substantial holdings of United States Treasury securities and replace them with loans to business and consumers. This was facilitated by the Federal Reserve's policy of buying government obligations at par, and large amounts of federal debt were shifted into the Federal Reserve's portfolio. Under these conditions "shiftability" became the hallmark of asset liquidity, and the provision of a protective or secondary reserve became the first line of defense in meeting the bankers' liquidity needs.

The Schedule of Priorities

The secondary reserve is an important part of the concept of the "schedule of priorities," a significant development in the theory and management of bank assets.[12] Using this approach, the banker reviews the past behavior of his accounts, and from this information prepares estimates of his near-term requirements. He then allocates his assets in such a way as to satisfy his most urgent prospective needs, according to his schedule of priorities:

1. First priority—Primary reserves: Cash and cash items necessary to meet the legal and operating demands of the bank, that is, reserves and correspondent balances.
2. Second priority—Secondary reserves: Short-term Treasury securities, commercial paper, and other readily marketable assets available to meet liquidity requirements.
3. Third priority—Customer loans: Loans to business and individuals that usually provide the major part of the bank's earnings.
4. Fourth priority—Investment for income: United States Treasury, municipal, and corporate securities to supplement income from loans or to provide an element of diversification, if necessary.

The obvious value of establishing the schedule of priorities is that it encourages the banker to quantify his anticipated requirements and at least implicitly to take them into account when making decisions about the allocation of the bank's funds. It also permits clear recognition of the fact that most of the assets with the highest degree of liquidity (vault cash and balances with other banks) are not available to meet the possible demands upon the bank associated with deposit withdrawals and loan requests. That is, a member bank must *maintain* legal reserves in an amount depending upon the size and composition of its deposits and the required reserve ratios applicable to

---

[12]The "schedule of priorities" is presented in Roland I. Robinson, *The Management of Bank Funds*, 2nd ed. (New York: McGraw-Hill Book Co., 1962), pp. 13–18.

these liabilities. Hence, in the event of deposit withdrawals, only a small portion of the legal reserve can be made available to meet withdrawals. In addition, as an operating bank, correspondent balances must be treated as relatively frozen assets insofar as availability is concerned. Of course, reserves may be drawn down temporarily, and in an emergency balances due from other banks may be called upon to meet currency requirements, but they must be restored to "normal" levels within a very short time if the bank is to continue to function as it did before the emergency arose. The primary reserve is not a long-run source of liquidity. Furthermore, the schedule-of-priorities concept rightly subordinates the need for current earnings to the short-run liquidity needs of the bank, while treating investment for income as a residual claim upon the bank's resources.

Liquidity and Management of Bank Liabilities

In the 1960s, certain developments in financial markets shifted bankers' attention to sources of funds, especially deposits. First, relatively slow growth in demand deposits and continued reduction in the commercial banks' share of savings deposits forced banks to compete aggressively for savings and to reevaluate their loan policies.[13] Increased expenditures on advertising, higher interest rates paid on savings deposits, and solicitation of real estate and consumer loans were the major steps taken to help reverse the outflow of funds and to attract new customers.[14] Second, many of the larger regional and money market banks were experiencing withdrawals by corporate depositors, who found that money market instruments such as Treasury bills and commercial paper, which offered safety and liquidity plus an interest return, made demand deposits an undesirable form in which to hold short-term funds. In early years, business firms had been satisfied to hold excess demand deposits because the opportunity costs were very low and negotiable time deposits were unavailable to them. The gradual upward trend of market rates and the loss of business deposits posed a serious problem, and several of the larger banks responded to this disintermediation by issuing negotiable time certificates of deposit, an important new money market instrument. In early 1961, a market developed for these negotiable CDs, and the number of banks issuing certificates increased as business firms found them profitable for their excess funds.

Although the CD was an instant success and provided a new means of tapping the money market, for many banks it proved to be a mixed blessing: liquidity could be purchased by issuing CDs, but if rising market rates later made them unattractive, the holder would invest the proceeds at maturity in other instruments, and the issuing bank faced a loss of deposits.

[13]The circumstances are discussed more fully in Chapter 15, but it may be noted that, especially in the later 1950s, the rate of growth of bank reserves and of money was slow, presumably because of Federal Reserve policy.

[14]It should be observed that unless currency is requested, deposits are not withdrawn from the banking system but are transferred between individual banks. Nonetheless, these losses may impose significant losses of liquidity upon a particular bank and force an adjustment in its deposit and asset position.

The volatility of deposits intensified the search for other sources of liquidity. Bankers explored other markets and turned to Eurodollars, commercial paper, and older sources of funds—the Federal funds market and borrowing from the Federal Reserve—as alternative ways of meeting the loss of deposits. These sources are described in Chapter 9. Suffice it to say here, their management of liabilities represented a creative response by bankers to the changing financial environment in which they operate. Since the mid-1960s assets, liabilities, and to a lesser extent, capital accounts have been "managed" by bankers in their attempts to provide an optimum combination of safety, liquidity, and earnings.

Recent Expansion of Banking Services

The banks' search for profitable opportunities has not been limited to improving the management of assets and liabilities. They have also acted aggressively to serve new markets and to supply new services both domestically and abroad. Three developments during the period since 1960 deserve special mention: the formation of bank holding companies, the growth of "retail banking," and the expansion of international banking.

Bank Holding Companies

Shortly after the banks turned to nondeposit sources of funds, the Fed countered these efforts to avoid monetary restraint by requiring banks to hold certain reserves against such nondeposit liabilities as borrowings of Eurodollars. This and other factors encouraged banks to form bank holding companies, which could issue commercial paper exempt from any reserve requirement. This technique provided banks, indirectly, with additional funds.

Bank holding companies also were formed to enable banks to expand and diversify their services. Multibank holding companies made it possible to establish multiple office banking in states that limited branching by a single bank. In the late 1960s banks made widespread use of the one-bank holding company to diversify into nonbanking activities such as financial management advisory service, factoring, mortgage banking, and some types of insurance.

Federal Reserve regulations, which did not cover one-bank holding companies until 1970, have in some ways limited this type of diversification. However, holding companies remain free to diversify geographically; they may establish businesses (subsidiaries) providing financial services "closely related" to banking in any area of the country where state law permits. Today, the Fed's list of approved activities is fairly lengthy.

However, financial institutions are much more closely regulated than most industrial and retailing firms. Consequently, nonfinancial companies that offer financial services may have advantages in the breadth of services they may offer, their freedom to experiment with new services without first seeking regulatory permission, their nationwide service capabilities, ease of entry into markets, and flexibility in means of financing their service activities. Bank holding companies have some of these capabilities to some extent, but are limited by regulation in many ways. Thus a major nationwide retail firm can engage in life insurance underwriting, but a bank holding company presently cannot. In the long-run outlook, bank holding companies may obtain a less restrictive regulatory environment, and thus be able to engage successfully in financial services that are more profitable, and have greater growth potential, than deposit services. Or, they may feel that such flexibility is unlikely to be obtained, and some may divorce other financial service activity from deposit and closely related services.

Retail Banking

In domestic markets the period since 1960 has been one of continued growth in "retail banking." Commercial banks, especially those outside money market centers, have moved aggressively into consumer lending and have expanded their financing of housing. More recently, banks of all sizes have increasingly participated in credit card plans that have enabled them to penetrate into new consumer and retailer markets and to promote fuller utilization of the banks' wide range of financial services. Some economists believe that rising per capita income, and the growth of certain types of consumer spending, make retail banking an attractive area for expansion of services.

Extension of International Banking

Expansion into foreign markets has also become a major activity, especially for the nation's leading banks. International banking activity has been spurred by the growth of banks' multinational business customers and, recently, by opportunities presented by more flexible exchange rates. An increasing portion of many banks' revenue derives from international banking departments and subsidiaries. Edge Act authority, little used until 1955, has been the basis in recent years for establishment of a substantial number of Edge Act subsidiaries, which operate only in foreign countries (although they may have an office in the United States). Large banks have also acquired foreign subsidiaries in order to serve customers *in* foreign countries.

THE REGULATION OF COMMERCIAL BANKS

In terms of government regulation and control, business firms in the United States fall into one of three categories. At one end of the spectrum are firms in the utilities and transportation areas, which are "vested with a public interest," accorded certain rights and responsibilities by government, and regulated as public utilities. At the other end are the vast majority of business enterprises that are in many ways relatively free of government control, subject only to the broad guidelines and constraints imposed by the antitrust laws. Somewhere in between are the financial institutions, the banks and nonbank intermediaries, all regulated and supervised to one degree or another. The location of the banking industry in this spectrum of control has changed from one time period to another as new laws were passed governing its activities, or new interpretations of existing laws were handed down by the courts or by the regulatory agencies.

Regulation over commercial banks is exercised at both the federal and state level, a historical result of our system of "dual banking," under which a bank is chartered by either the federal or a state government. A federally chartered bank is a "national" bank, subject to regulation and supervision by the Comptroller of the Currency; and because its charter entails compulsory membership in the Federal Reserve System and insurance coverage by the Federal Deposit Insurance Corporation, it is, in effect, governed by these three federal agencies as well as to some extent by the banking authority of the state in which it does business. State-chartered banks have the option of membership in the Federal Reserve System and insurance coverage by the FDIC. As shown in Table 3–7, most banks are state-chartered, nonmember, insured banks. In practice, and to avoid duplication, the responsibility for the regulation of commercial banks is divided insofar as possible (see Table 3–6).

The scope of government regulation is very broad and affects both the *structure* of the banking industry and the *practices* of the individual banks. The number of banks and banking offices, their relative sizes, the geographical distribution of banking facilities—the structure of the industry—is partly the result of government decisions concerning proposed entrants, mergers, or branching of existing banks. Practices and policies of banks are also subject to a wide range of proscriptions that limit or prohibit certain types of assets or liabilities in bank portfolios or rates of interest charged borrowers or paid to depositors. It was observed earlier, for example, that certain types of loans are restricted to a percentage of capital and that maximum rates of interest on time deposits are imposed under Regulation Q. Other regulations prohibit banks from buying stocks of private business firms and from holding corporate bonds which do not meet certain standards of quality.

TABLE 3–6

Type of Bank	Major Regulatory Agency
National banks	Comptroller of the Currency
State member banks	Federal Reserve System
Insured nonmember banks	Federal Deposit Insurance Corp.
Uninsured banks	State banking authorities

TABLE 3–7   Commercial Banks, June 30, 1973

Total	Member		Nonmember	
	National	State	Insured	Noninsured
14,048	4,631	1.076	8,137	204
Member Banks 5,707			Insured Banks (member plus nonmember insured) 13,844	

SOURCE: *Federal Reserve Bulletin*, August 1973, p. A–96.

The Basis for Regulating Banks

The history of the regulation of money is as old as the history of money itself. Concern over the gold content of coins led Archimedes to discover the principle that, "a body, while wholly or partly immersed in fluid, loses in weight by an amount equal to that of the fluid displaced." Lighter metals could be mixed with gold so that coinage was "debased." In his day coins were put directly into circulation by governments. Legal control over lending practices also has a long history. Usury, the charging of interest for a loan, was considered a sin by St. Augustine, and governments prohibited it. Even today, laws of doubtful social desirability prohibit "usurious" charges by lenders—that is, charges in excess of those that legislatures believe to be "fair" rates. Thus, in money and lending, activities have always been regulated by law.

The particular set of laws now impinging upon financial institutions in the United States is the outgrowth of a long and interesting history.[15] Three very general observations can be made. First, the Constitution gives authority for control over the supply of money to the federal government.[16] For the several states to allow such power to rest in a central government was probably no less of a relinquishment of authority than that allowing the federal government control over the army and navy. But the several states retained their rights, among them the right to charter corporations and regulate financial practices, inasmuch as these rights were not specifically vested in the federal government. Thus, the struggle between federal and state governments for power and control has helped fashion the diversity of regulatory authority.

Second, United States history is replete with episodes of financial panic. Attempts to provide the country with a central bank after 1836 failed repeatedly to receive Congressional sanction (from 1791 to 1811 and from 1816 to 1836 the First and Second Banks of the United States had carried out some of the activities usually associated with central banks). Hence, the Treasury exercised erratic control over the money supply by purchase of gold and silver and coinage of these metals, and later by issue of paper money in the form of silver, and later, gold certificates. Banks were chartered by states with little restraint and inadequate regulations, and a period preceding the Civil War is now referred to as the "Age of Wildcat Banking." Banks in nearly every small community in the West began issuing their own notes, liabilities that circulated as currency. Failure was frequent, and public trust was shattered. After establishment of the national banking system at the time of the Civil War, a federal tax was levied on notes issued by state banks in order to

---

[15]See the interesting chapter by H.E. Krooss and M.R. Blyn on "The Evolution of U.S. Money and Capital Markets and Financial Intermediaries" in Murray E. Polakoff et al., *Financial Institutions and Markets* (Boston: Houghton Mifflin and Company, 1970), pp. 62–82.

[16]Article I, Section 8 of the Constitution reads "The Congress shall have Power To . . . coin Money, regulate the Value thereof, and of foreign Coin and fix the Standard of Weights and Measures; . . ."

stop their issue, and states began to exercise greater control over bank activities.

Third, a large set of regulatory controls grew out of the disaster of the Great Depression of the 1930s. The general failure of the economy and widespread failures of financial institutions led to a proliferation of laws and regulations and the establishment of a variety of supervisory agencies and government operated financial intermediaries.

With this background of federal-state power maneuvering, a history of repeated financial panic, and finally a depression of gigantic proportions, it was easy to provide a rationale for the establishment of regulations and controls. It was argued that the public should have a failure-proof banking system. Experience seemed to show conclusively that an unregulated banking system was unstable and subject to repeated breakdown as a result of overbanking and bad management. Because of its central importance to the economy, the system should be made failure-proof by whatever regulatory devices could be found. A "safe" banking system would have to prevent "cutthroat competition." The term is ill-defined, but in general it means that restrictions should be placed on the freedom of one bank to compete with or undersell its competitor. For example, out of the anxiety over excessive competition came the prohibition of interest payments on demand deposits and ceilings on interest rates paid on time deposits. If a new bank opens its doors and offers a higher rate for deposits, then deposits would, according to this argument, immediately flow out of the existing bank and this could occasionally cause failure of existing banks.

Whatever merits this argument may have had in an earlier day, it is difficult to accept today. Nothing prevents the victim bank from matching the rate offered on demand deposits and thereby stemming the tide of funds outflow. Nevertheless, regulations of this sort are deeply imbedded in our banking system. Only a few years ago, savings institutions in California appealed to the state regulatory commission to impose regulation to restrict the value of a gift offered for opening a new account to two dollars or under—a clear example indicating that businessmen often press for regulation if they feel that it is in their short-run best interest, and that government regulations designed to "protect the public" often protect the industry and neglect the public.

Another type of regulation following from the intent to construct a failure-proof banking system restricts banks from holding "risky" assets. In general, banks may not invest in the stock market. Only certain high-quality corporate bonds are eligible for bank ownership. Regulations are many and diverse and are justified as necessary for the "protection of the depositor's money."

Finally, restrictions on the entry of new banks or financial institutions limit competition and protect existing institutions from failure. Anyone wishing to establish a new bank, financial intermediary, or branch must argue persuasively that the "convenience and needs" of the community will be served if the license to operate is granted.

In addition to the argument that we need a failure-proof system, there is another argument providing a rationale for bank regulation. This argument concerns bank efficiency, the provision of service at minimum cost to the public. Competition promotes efficiency and therefore bank mergers and bank branching are controlled to ensure that one bank does not obtain monopoly power. Holding companies often own controlling interests in banks, and holding company activities are also closely regulated to ensure that competition remains.

Purposes and Effects of Regulation

Thus, regulations are designed (1) to provide safety for depositors, (2) to limit excessive competition, (3) to limit risk-taking on the part of banks, and (4) to ensure that adequate services are provided at low cost to the public by restricting mergers and holding company activities that might eliminate competition and lead to monopoly.

It should be obvious that these goals of bank regulation may frequently be inconsistent with one another. A "safe" banking system means one free of failure, but occasional failure is the logical outcome of a competitive structure, for only by failure is the inefficient firm removed from the industry. The establishment of the Federal Deposit Insurance Corporation has perhaps done the most toward reaching the goal of protecting the depositor. Many economists now argue that this protection is sufficient and that more liberal chartering of banks is now desirable in order to promote competition.[17]

But competition resulting from existence of many firms may not promote efficiency. If there are significant "economies of scale" in the production of banking services, then larger banks are able to provide services at lower unit costs. Some observers believe that significant economies of scale do exist. The manager of a branch of a large bank may offer more services to a customer than the manager of a unit bank the same size as the branch office. This is because a branch can tap the resources of its head office. Thus, to insist on an all-unit bank system, as is the case in the state of Illinois, for example, may deny customers the services they otherwise might have obtained. Allowing banks to penetrate their rivals' markets may be the best way of promoting competition. At present, most unit banks are small, *and* most communities are served by fewer than three banks; therefore, merging of small banks and allowing large banks to branch into each other's territory (perhaps by branching across state lines), but not allowing large banks to expand inside of their own market areas, might be the best way to increase competition among banks.

The question of how a growing economy is to provide growth of banking services—through *more* banks, or through banks of *larger size*—depends primarily upon the stance taken by regulatory authorities.

---

[17]Eli Shapiro suggests having banks free to choose risky assets, but subject to a variable insurance premium in his "Credit Controls and Financial Intermediaries," *Conference on Saving and Residential Financing*, 1965 Proceedings, U.S. Savings and Loan League, Chicago, pp. 59–74. For an excellent review of the issues see: Kenneth E. Scott and Thomas Mayer, "Risk and Regulation in Banking: Some Proposals for Federal Deposit Insurance Reform," *Stanford Law Review*, Vol. 23, May 1971, pp. 857–902.

Issues concerning safety and efficiency and just how to obtain the optimum banking system are unresolved. Many economists and financial market observers agree that certain changes in our regulatory framework are desirable. Some argue that many parts of the present system of regulation are disruptive of banking practices, expensive in terms of wasted resources, and tend to promote a misallocation of resources. They are disruptive of banking practices because they arbitrarily interfere with bank portfolio policies and there is often an implicit assumption that banking supervisory personnel know better than bankers what income-risk positions are best. But the job of the supervisory personnel is difficult when regulations interfere with other free choices of portofolio managers. Regulations are often expensive in terms of resources, not only because of direct costs of conforming to them, but also because they induce banks to devote labor effort in search of alternative sources and uses of funds.

Finally, regulations often promote a misallocation of resources by preventing market forces and relative cost considerations from determining the final allocation. Regulations that restrict interest payments on time and savings deposits clearly distort the flow of savings into and sometimes out of the mortgage market. As a result, residential construction is often severely affected by this type of interference with the market mechanism.

THE HUNT COMMISSION REPORT

In 1970 President Nixon appointed Reed O. Hunt as Chairman of a Commission on Financial Structure and Regulation.[18] The Commission's report to the President was published in December 1971 and contains a large number of recommendations for changes in regulatory procedures. Among these was the recommendation that the power to set ceilings on interest rates paid on time and savings deposits be abolished gradually over a ten-year adjustment period. (The Commission recommended that the current prohibition against the payment of interest on demand deposits be retained for the time being.) In another sweeping proposal, the Commission recommended that ". . . under specified conditions, savings and loan associations and mutual savings banks be permitted to provide third party payment services, including checking accounts and credit cards to individuals and nonbusiness entities only," and that the thrift institutions be allowed to convert their charters to allow them to become full commercial banks if they wish to offer facilities to the full range of customers, including business.

These recommendations are designed to introduce a greater degree of competition in the financial industry and to reduce some difficulties experienced by thrift institutions because of their restricted asset mix and their inability to increase yields on assets when either yields on their liabilities increase or they lose funds as market rates rise and attract funds from savers.

---

[18]Prior to the Commission Report, the February 1971 issue of *Journal of Money, Credit, and Banking* carried a symposium on the subject, with articles by Karl Brunner, George H. Borts, John M. Culbertson, Thomas Mayer, Henry C. Wallich, and Thomas R. Atkinson. Since the report many review articles have appeared.

In addition, the Commission made many recommendations for reorganization of the system of controls over banks, including, for example, the establishment of a new agency, the office of the Administrator of State Banks, and to remove the Office of the Comptroller of the Currency from the Treasury Department and make it an independent agency with the title, Office of the National Bank Administrator.

On August 3, 1973, the Treasury Department released *Recommendations for Change in the U.S. Financial System,* followed by a later release in September. In general, the recommendations followed the thrust of the Hunt Commission report but did not cover a number of Commission recommendations and in a few cases went somewhat further, such as in recommending permission for NOW accounts in both commercial banks and thrift institutions (mutual savings banks and savings and loan associations). Although no recommendation was made to permit payment of interest on demand deposits, the existence of NOW accounts (accounts on which negotiable orders of withdrawal may be issued, payable to third parties) could, in the words of the release of August 3, "blur the difference between demand and savings accounts to such an extent that the prohibition will become meaningless" (p. 9). It seems apparent that the progress of technology in the use of electronic funds transfer systems (EFTS), combined with the innovation of NOW accounts, is likely to result in significant changes in practices, competitive positions, and legislation.

SUMMARY

Commercial banks are the most important intermediaries in the financial markets. They provide a wide range of deposit and loan facilities to more customers than any other types of financial institution.

Banks hold cash assets to meet legal reserve requirements and daily transaction needs, and because of "correspondent" relationships with other banks. Most bank funds, however, are used to acquire earning assets. The most important of these are loans to business firms and to consumers. Banks also hold government securities for both liquidity and income reasons.

Demand and time deposits are the most important sources of funds. Under Federal Reserve regulations, both types of deposits held by member banks are subject to reserve requirements and to interest rate ceilings. In recent years, time deposits have grown faster than demand deposits, as savings accounts and time certificates of deposit have proved to be attractive to consumers and to business firms.

Most of a commercial bank's income and expenses result from its use of borrowed funds. Interest earned on loans is the major source of revenue; interest paid on time deposits is the major expense. Thus a bank's net income depends upon the size and composition of its assets and liabilities, the level and structure of interest rates, and various government regulations.

Long-run profitability is the main objective of a bank's portfolio policy. But to be profitable a bank must maintain an appropriate degree of safety and liquidity. Safety of assets is of paramount importance because banks have a relatively low capital/deposit ratio (equity/debt ratio). Liquidity is necessary because of the short-term nature and volatility of many bank liabilities.

Over the years there have been changes in banking theory and practice concerning the management of a bank's liquidity position. The "real bills" doctrine, widely held prior to the 1930s, was replaced by the "shiftability" theory of liquidity which stressed the marketability of assets. Since the 1960s banks have found it profitable to manage their liabilities as well as their assets in meeting liquidity needs and in attempting to increase profits. Several new techniques and markets have developed, among them the market for negotiable CDs, Eurodollars, commercial paper issued by bank holding companies, and others.

Regulation of commercial banks is exercised at both the federal and state levels. Regulations affect the structure of the banking industry and the practices of individual banks. Some of the restrictions and controls were imposed to assure a "safe" banking system; others were imposed to promote efficiency, mainly by encouraging competition among banks. Many believe that these goals may at times be inconsistent with one another. Although views differ as to *what* changes ought to be made in bank regulation, many favor more liberal regulation of branching, mergers, and portfolio practices, including the payment of interest on deposits.

Commercial banks have become "department stores" of finance, engaging in many types of lending, some types of investing, and many activities closely related to lending and investing. In some previous decades, government regulation limited these activities. But bank innovations in recent years, including the issue of negotiable CDs, broadened the role of banks in the U.S. financial structure. The development of the one-bank holding company, with the holding company owning the bank and also number of subsidiaries engaging in different activities closely related to banking, has caused further change. Amendments to the Bank Holding Company Act passed in 1970 may have seemed restrictive. But the fact that Congress gave the Board of Governors of the Federal Reserve System the authority, subject to court review, to determine permissible activities of bank holding companies and their subsidiaries has opened the possibility of a broadening scope of activities. Few new or innovative services have as yet been declared permissible, but the fact that one-bank and multibank holding companies controlled over 60 percent of all commercial bank deposits at the end of 1972, and the breadth of their activities, are already significant.

QUESTIONS FOR DISCUSSION

1. Would you expect causes of the growth of time deposits to be different from causes of the growth of demand deposits? If so, what differences do you see?

2. Do banks prefer to make business loans (if possible) rather than consumer loans, mortgage loans, other loans, or investments? If so, what reasons can you suggest for this preference?

3. What reasons can you suggest for the higher reserves required for deposits in excess of certain amounts? Is the difference between the reserve requirements for the first $2 million of deposits (8 percent) and that for deposits over $400 million (18 percent) justified? Explain.

4. The negotiable CD was "invented" in the early 1960s. Indicate the reasons for this development and the effects it had on banks—their balance sheets, their earnings, their costs, and their competitive position vis-à-vis other institutions.

5. How would you determine the "true cost" of a compensating balance to the borrower?

6. Of the three major sources of nondeposit debt funds (borrowing from the Federal Reserve System, purchasing Federal funds, and borrowing Eurodollars), which do you think banks prefer? Why? Does it depend on conditions? If so, what conditions?

7. In 1946, banks had far more investments in United States government securities than loans. Why? Is it "natural" that banks gradually increased the share of loans in their portfolios since that time? Under what conditions might investments again become more important?

8. Why is safety more important for bank portfolio selection than for most other institutions?

9. How has liquidity changed as a determinant of bank portfolio selection with the increase in nondeposit sources of debt funds?

10. Bank regulation appears to have shifted from time to time from regulation approaching the type applied to public utilities to regulation approaching the type applied to competitive industries. What reasons can you suggest for this shift in public policy? Cite some examples of the shift in the direction mentioned. Then cite some examples of shift in the reverse direction at other times.

SELECTED REFERENCES

An excellent introduction to commercial bank portfolio policy is presented in Roland I. Robinson, *Management of Bank Funds*, 2nd ed. (New York: Mc-Graw-Hill, 1962). This traditional view of banks as relatively passive lending institutions has been modified in recent years as the competition for funds has become more intense and as new markets and techniques have developed. The newer view of banks as "profit maximizers," eager to exploit any sources or uses of funds open to them is outlined in "Sources of Commercial Bank Funds: An Example of 'Creative Response,'" Federal Reserve Bank of Cleveland, *Economic Review*, November 1965, reprinted in Paul F. Jessup, ed., *Innovations in Bank Management: Selected Readings* (New York: Holt, Rinehart, and Winston, 1969), pp. 152–65, and in "An Alternative Approach to Liquidity: Parts I–IV," Federal Reserve Bank of Kansas City, *Monthly Review*, December 1969, February 1970, April 1970, and May 1970. A more sophisticated treatment of some aspects of portfolio policy is found in Howard Crosse and George H. Hempel, *Management Policies for Commercial Banks* (Englewood Cliffs, N.J.: Prentice-Hall, 1973).

A valuable discussion of the relationship between the money supply function and bank portfolio policy is found in Thomas Mayer, *Monetary Policy in the United States* (New York: Random House, 1968), pp. 80–88.

A plethora of articles on the regulation of commercial banks within the past decade has ranged from description and appraisal of the regulatory framework to an evaluation of Regulation Q. The first three suggested readings are broad in coverage and are reprinted in several books of readings. The other articles deal with topics of special interest to students of financial markets.

Almarin Phillips, "Competition, Confusion, and Commercial Banking," *Journal of Finance*, March 1964, pp. 32–45.

Donald Jacobs, "The Framework of Commercial Bank Regulation: An Appraisal," *The National Banking Review*, March 1964; reprinted in *Innovations in Bank Management: Selected Readings*, ed. Paul F. Jessup, New York: Holt, Rinehart, and Winston, Inc., 1969, pp. 402–21.

Paul M. Horvitz, "Stimulating Bank Competition through Regulatory Action," *Journal of Finance*, March 1965, pp. 1–13.

Robert Lindsay, "The Enconomics of Interest Rate Ceilings," *The Bulletin*, New York University Graduate School of Business Administration, December 1970.

George J. Benston, "Interest Payments on Demand Deposits and Bank Investment Behavior," *Journal of Political Economy*, October 1964, pp. 431–49.

One very important development in banking is the growth of bank holding companies and their nonbanking activities. For a concise treatment, see "Bank Holding Companies: An Overview," Federal Reserve Bank of Chicago, *Business Conditions*, August 1973, pp. 3–13.

The September 15, 1973, issue of *Business Week* included a 37-page section on "The New Banking," describing such developments as bank holding companies, new international banking services, foreign banks establishing offices in the United States, electronic funds transfer systems, bank marketing, regulatory problems, and growing activities of trust departments of banks.

The competition between banks and bank holding companies and nonfinancial business firms is discussed in a booklet by Cleveland A. Christophe, *Competition in Financial Services* (New York: First National City Corporation, 1974).

4

Money, Banks, and Monetary Controls

This chapter is concerned with the money supply, the unique role commercial banks play in the payments mechanism, and the monetary controls used by the Federal Reserve System in the conduct of monetary policy. In the first section we present some of the alternative ways of defining and measuring the money supply. We then distinguish between money and credit. In the second section we review the process by which banks create money on the basis of reserves they are required to hold against their deposit liabilities. In the third section we examine the sources of bank reserves, developing the "bank reserve equation" which indicates determinants of the "monetary base" (bank reserves plus currency). In section four, we present an analysis of the relationship of the monetary base to the money supply, indicating the role played in the determination of the money supply by the banks, the public, the Treasury, and the Federal Reserve System. Finally, in section five, we present a brief overview of Federal Reserve policy tools for control of the money supply.

CONCEPTS AND MEASUREMENTS
OF THE MONEY SUPPLY

Traditionally, economists have defined money in terms of its primary function of serving as a medium of exchange. Money might also serve as a store of value, a unit of account, or a standard of deferred payments, but its distinguishing feature is that it is used to pay for goods and services or to liquidate debt.[1] In this view, only currency and demand deposits (checking

---

[1] Although an important part of our spending involves credit instruments—credit cards, open credit account, and receivables—the debts so established are finally settled only by payment of money, unless one debt is offset against another.

accounts) are money; other close substitutes, such as time or savings deposits at commercial banks or thrift institutions, are called "near-money."

In recent years, several economists argued that the medium of exchange criterion is not the proper basis for judging assets that are, or are not, money.[2] Some who favor different criteria would include all deposits at commercial banks; others would extend the list of assets qualifying as money to include savings accounts at mutual savings banks and share accounts in savings and loan associations. At the heart of the matter is the question of what constitutes the money supply for purposes of economic theory, the money supply that should be controlled in the interest of maintaining prosperity without inflation. The choice of the proper definition of money, currently the topic of much debate, is a matter of utmost concern to both policymakers and private participants in the financial markets.

The most commonly used measures of money are:

1. currency in circulation plus private demand deposits adjusted, referred to as M_1, and
2. M_1 plus commercial bank time deposits (other than large negotiable CDs),[3] referred to as M_2.

"Private demand deposits adjusted" means *private* demand deposits (excluding government deposits); the adjective "adjusted" means that interbank deposits and items in process of collection are deducted to avoid duplication. A third measure of money, M_3 (M_2 plus deposits at mutual savings banks and share accounts at saving and loan associations) is not widely used by analysts but is now published with the M_1 and M_2 measures on a regular basis in the *Federal Reserve Bulletin*.

As noted, all three measures of money exclude currency held as vault cash in commercial banks, cash items in process of collection ("float"), interbank deposits, and deposits owned by the federal government. Vault cash is excluded since it is not available for spending by consumers, business, government, or foreigners; interbank deposits and items in process of collection are excluded to avoid double counting. Perhaps government deposits should be included in the money stock. The reason offered for excluding them is that government spending decisions are presumably not related to the amount of deposits held by the government. Some analysts, however, argue that some erratic movements in the money supply would be smoothed out if government

[2]One approach is to define money so as to include only those assets whose marginal changes correlate "best" with certain important economic variables, for example, national income, output, or prices. Others view the elasticity of substitution as the proper selection criterion. These and other empirical criteria are taken up in David Laidler. "The Definition of Money," *Journal of Money, Credit and Banking*, August 1969, pp. 508–25.

[3]Large negotiable CDs are excluded because they are essentially money market instruments, similar to commercial paper rather than to savings accounts; moreover, they vary sharply in amount. See Charles W. Hall, "Defining Money: Problems and Issues," Federal Reserve Bank of Cleveland, *Economic Review*, October 1971, pp. 3–12.

deposits were included.[4] Finally, money supply as defined for these measures *does* include foreign demand deposits at Federal Reserve Banks, on the ground that these deposits may be spent by their holders on the same basis that demand deposits in commercial banks may be spent by their holders.

Table 4–1 contains money supply data for recent years to illustrate the different orders of magnitude for the three measures. The reader will note that Table 4–1 is headed "Measures of the Money Stock." The terms money supply and money stock are often used interchangeably in the literature, and we follow this practice. Technically, "money stock" might be preferred when referring to the amount of money in existence, and "money supply" in cases such as discussion of the interest elasticity of money—for example, how much the money supply might increase if interest rates were higher.

Before turning to the process of money creation by commercial banks we need to distinguish "money" from "credit." Money, as we have seen, consists of *certain* liabilities of financial institutions and government. Credit, on the other hand, refers to the earning assets held by lenders, including financial institutions. Both money and credit may be created when banks buy securities or make loans, but no money creation is directly involved when nonbank lenders extend credit.

THE PROCESS OF MONEY CREATION BY COMMERCIAL BANKS

The student may recall from an introductory course in economics the elements of money creation: when banks make loans or buy securities they typically

TABLE 4–1 Measures of the Money Stock (billions of dollars)[1]

	M_1 (Currency plus demand deposits)	M_2 (M_1 plus time deposits at commercial banks)[2]	M_3 (M_2 plus deposits at thrift institutions)[3]
1968	201.6	382.5	577.2
1969	208.8	293.3	594.0
1970	221.3	425.2	641.3
1971	236.0	473.8	727.7
1972	255.5	525.1	821.6

[1]Seasonally adjusted, end of the year
[2]Excludes negotiable CDs of $100,000 or more
[3]M_2 plus average of the beginnings and end of month deposits of mutual savings banks and saving and loan shares.
SOURCE: *Federal Reserve Bulletin*, February 1973, p. 73.

[4]Paul S. Anderson and Frank E. Morris, "Defining the Money Supply: The Case of Government Deposits," Federal Reserve Bank of Boston, *New England Economic Review*, March/April 1969, pp. 21–31.

credit the demand deposit accounts of the borrowers. That is, they pay for earning assets by creating claims against themselves, deposit liabilities. The money supply, therefore, increases (decreases) when banks acquire (liquidate) assets. Also, changes in the money supply *may* result from shifts by depositors between demand and time deposits. If the public chooses to hold more time deposits, perhaps because of an attractive interest return on savings, M_1 will decline as depositors draw down their checking accounts and transfer the funds into interest-bearing deposits. The M_2 money supply is not immediately changed by such shifts, however, because M_2 includes both types of deposits.[5]

Because bank credit policy is so important in its effects on the money supply, we must emphasize again that when banks extend credit they *create new deposits*; they do *not* simply lend out depositors' funds. From the individual banker's point of view, the ability to lend does depend upon a net inflow of deposits, the major source of funds. Therefore, bankers may object to the assertion that they simply create more deposits whenever they wish to increase their loans. How can we reconcile the two views: that bankers create money—deposits and currency—rather than lending their depositors' funds, even though their ability to create money does depend upon the value of deposits they receive? The first step is to distinguish *primary* from *derivative* deposits. The former arise from deposits of cash or checks drawn upon other commercial banks; the depositors receive credits to their checking accounts or time deposits, and the banks add to vault cash or send the checks to the local Federal Reserve Bank for credit to the banks' reserve accounts.[6] A *primary* deposit is a source of bank reserves, and if the bank's reserves are greater in amount than its required reserves—required against demand and time deposits—the "excess" reserves enable the bank to make loans and grant credit, and "create" deposits in the process. These deposits are derivative deposits, so called because they are derived from extension of bank credit.

Thus, a single bank can create money to the extent of its excess reserves. If it makes loans and creates deposits beyond this amount, it may face an adverse balance of payments (clearing house balance) vis-à-vis other banks when the checks drawn against these deposits are presented for payment, and its reserve position may fall below the level required. If the bank does not expand its loans and security holdings to the extent of its excess reserves, perhaps because of inadequate loan demand or a generally conservative loan policy, the bank will have reserves available for future use. The banking system, the collection of all banks, can also expand its loans and deposits to the extent of its excess reserves. However, when viewing the entire banking system it is important to note that for any given primary deposit, a multiple of that amount in new deposits may be created by all banks. In other words, an increase in excess reserves will permit all banks together to add to loans and deposits by a multiple of the original excess reserves.

A simple example may help clarify this important point. Assume that all

---

[5]Because demand and time deposits are subject to different reserve requirements, these shifts between the two types of deposits may change the volume of excess reserves available to the bank. This point is developed in a later section.

[6]To simplify, we assume at this point that all commercial banks are members of the Federal Reserve System and are allowed to hold their legal reserves as vault cash or as deposits with the Federal Reserve Bank of their district.

banks are members of the Federal Reserve System and that the reserve requirement for demand deposits of member banks is 20 percent.[7] If Mr. Jones deposits $10,000 in currency in his bank in exchange for a demand deposit receipt of $10,000, the bank's total cash reserves have increased by $10,000. Of this amount, if the bank has exactly the required amount of reserves at the time, $2,000 must be held as required reserves because of the 20 percent legal reserve requirement. Thus, excess reserves increase by $8,000 and the bank may make new loans totaling $8,000. When the borrower spends the $8,000, the person or firm receiving the check will deposit it in his account in, say, another bank. The first bank honors the check drawn upon it, and currency, or more likely a reserve balance at the Federal Reserve, is transferred to the second bank, which now has increased deposits of $8,000 and excess reserves of $6,400. If the second bank in turn makes a loan of $6,400 and the funds are transferred to a third bank, further lending and deposit creation may occur until the banking system has no remaining excess reserves: until the additional required reserves total $10,000, new loans total $40,000, and total deposits have risen by $50,000. Each bank has extended credit (made loans) and created deposits to the extent of its excess reserves; and, the system of banks has done so by a multiple of the original excess reserve. This power to create money results from the so-called "fractional reserve" system that permits banks to hold reserves equal to some fraction of their demand deposits. In our example, the theoretical limit to the expansion of deposits, when r is the required reserve ratio, R is total reserves, and D is deposits, is given by $D = 1/r \times R$. Because r was assumed to be .2, $1/r = 5$, so that $D = 5R$. This theoretical "money multiplier" of 5 is only an approximation to the actual value that might obtain; the actual value is smaller because there are some "leakages" in the process of money creation, which we deal with in a later section.

The reader should note that the creation of money does not occur because of the existence of a system of banks, but because deposits do not leave the system. If all checks were redeposited in the same bank, this amount of deposit creation would occur with only a single bank.

Sources of Bank Reserves

We have seen that banks, individually and collectively, must have excess reserves in order to expand their earning assets and create new deposits. How do banks acquire these reserves? What sources of reserves are available to them? In answering these questions we must again distinguish carefully between an individual bank and the banking system, for sources of reserves are different in the two cases.

A Single Bank

How does an individual bank acquire vault cash or balances with the Federal Reserve? On a purely formal level, a bank may increase its reserves

---

[7] Also assume that the public chooses to hold all new money as demand deposits rather than currency.

(a bank asset) by reducing other assets or by increasing its liabilities or net worth. That is, given a certain balance sheet position, the bank may reduce its other assets, such as loans or securities, through repayment or sales. If loans are repaid, borrowers' deposits are reduced as loans are liquidated. Required reserves decline; because total reserves are unchanged, excess reserves increase. (Excess reserves equal total reserves minus required reserves.) When securities are sold, excess reserves rise if the bank's own depositors purchase the securities; if the buyer is not a depositor—for example, if the buyer is either another commercial bank, the Federal Reserve, or a depositor of another commercial bank—total reserves rise by the amount of securities sold.

Changes in liabilities or net worth are also sources of reserves for a single bank. By attracting new or additional demand or time deposits, as deposits of either currency or checks drawn on other banks, an individual bank gains reserves, usually at the expense of another bank. For some banks, borrowing from other banks (Federal funds) and/or from the Federal Reserve (discounts and advances) are methods frequently used to adjust reserve positions. Sales of debentures (unsecured bonds), or capital notes, or net stock in the bank are longer-term sources of reserve balances that increase total reserves or excess reserves, depending upon whether the purchaser is a depositor of the bank or not, as in the case of securities sold from the bank's portfolio of assets. A "source" that increases excess reserves for both the individual bank and the banking system is a reduction in the required reserve ratio. A decline in reserve requirements increases excess reserves by reducing the amount of vault cash or deposits at Federal Reserve Banks that member banks are required to hold against a given level of deposits.

From a banker's point of view, the financial markets, especially those for Treasury securities, Federal funds, CDs, and similar items—the money market —provide the chief mechanism for adjusting his reserve position. Some of these sources provide reserves for one bank while reducing the reserves of others; use of some techniques or markets may increase the reserves of the entire system. In general, shifts of depositors from a bank to another bank, borrowing by one bank from another, or the sale of assets by one bank to another transfer reserves rather than altering the level of reserves available to the banking system.[8]

The Banking System

Some sources of reserves listed above for a single bank cannot be viewed as a source for the banking system as a whole. An obvious example is the case of Federal funds; if one bank borrows reserves from another bank, total reserves available to all banks in the system have not changed. Thus, Federal funds are not a source of reserves for the system.

---

[8]The amount of reserves required depends upon the volume of the deposits, and whether classified as demand or time deposits. In September 1972 the Fed removed the earlier geographical classification of city banks and country banks and brought all member banks under the same scheme. Current reserve requirements are published in the *Federal Reserve Bulletin.*

A misconception sometimes encountered is that the general public can be a source of reserves for the banking system: some may think that people can withdraw their savings from savings institutions and deposit them in banks, thereby providing banks with reserves. But if their savings are in the form of deposits, this merely transfers deposits from one bank to another; and if their savings are in some other institution such as a life insurance company, this merely transfers title to deposits from these institutions to the public (for example, I may obtain a draft from my savings and loan association and deposit it in my bank, but this amount is immediately deducted from the deposit maintained by the savings and loan association in some bank). The only way in which, for the system as a whole, the public can add to bank deposits and bank reserves is to hold less *currency*, depositing some of its currency holdings in banks. This does happen, frequently after holidays, but the flow is a temporary one.

Specifically, then, we wish to understand how the banking *system* obtains those reserves that allow for the multiple creation of money and loanable funds (credit). We also wish to understand clearly those factors that determine the relation between bank reserves and the money supply. Briefly, the banking system's reserves increase or decrease as a result of actions by the Federal Reserve System, the Treasury, the public, and the banks themselves. These sectors determine the relationship between reserves and the money supply. To examine these matters carefully, we need a framework for analysis. There are other ways to proceed, but we have chosen to utilize the so-called "monetary base" and the money multiplier.

Bank Reserves, the Monetary Base, and the Money Supply

Bank reserves are created and destroyed by various Federal Reserve and Treasury actions and by some actions of individuals and business firms. The level of currency in circulation is also the result of decisions by these units. The money supply that exists at any point in time is the net outcome of a variety of policy decisions by monetary authorities and of portfolio decisions by individuals and firms. To capsulize the nature of the interaction of factors that determine the money supply, we use the concept of the monetary base. But first let us review briefly a few of the most significant factors that affect the level of bank reserves and the level of currency in circulation.

Currency and Bank Reserves

Years ago when the Treasury bought silver, it paid for the silver bullion and issued silver certificates, redeemable in silver bullion. These certificates then circulated as currency, and were said to be "backed" by silver. The Treasury no longer issues these certificates, but this is a good example of one way currency entered the economy in the years before the Federal Reserve System was established. During the Civil War, Congress authorized the

Treasury to issue currency without regard to "backing" in bullion; these certificates were called "greenbacks." Some still circulate; for example, they may be found in the form of two-dollar bills popular at race tracks. Issue of greenbacks was authorized in the 1930s, but they were not issued, and gradually most paper currency in the United States has come to consist of Federal Reserve notes issued by the Federal Reserve System.

The Treasury also may buy gold and issue gold certificates or credits payable in gold certificates to Federal Reserve Banks in exchange for deposit credit. To pay for its purchase of gold, it writes a check on its deposit with the Federal Reserve. When the individual selling the gold receives the check, he deposits it with his commercial bank. The bank then collects by sending the check to the Federal Reserve and ownership of the deposit passes from the Treasury to the member bank; hence member bank reserves increase, and again the potential money supply increases as lending power of banks expands. If the gold is purchased from a foreign country, the check is paid to an agency of that country, and deposited in its account in a Federal Reserve Bank, with the same result.

The point is that the Treasury has the power to issue liabilities against itself with certain limits, and these liabilities serve either as currency in circulation (for example, greenbacks) or as reserves of Federal Reserve Banks (such as gold certificates), and also usually result in an increase in reserves of commercial banks. Governments in other countries do the same thing by buying, for example, dollars, in the form of title to deposits in United States banks, and in recent years the Fed has bought marks and some other currencies with similar results.

Federal Reserve Banks also have the power to issue liabilities against themselves. Paramount among the procedures for doing so is the creation of a demand deposit in favor of a member bank. For example, assume that a member bank finds its legal reserve position deficient and goes to the Federal Reserve to borrow funds. The Fed gives the member bank a deposit, or creates a deposit liability, in precisely the same way that a commercial bank creates a deposit liability when it makes a loan to a customer. Member bank deposits with the Fed are, of course, reserves of member banks—sometimes called "high-powered" money because upon the base provided by these reserves, commercial banks can expand loans and deposits and hence the money supply.

When the Fed was first established in 1913 (operations began in 1914), the borrowing mechanism was the principal tool of control over the supply of money exercised by the Fed. As a central bank it was labeled the "lender of last resort," a source of funds available for tapping if ever a financial panic were to threaten.[9] But the borrowing mechanism is no longer the Fed's principal tool of control over the level of bank reserves. Today, "open market

---

[9]Under the National Banking System which preceded the Federal Reserve System, individual national banks around the country had the authority to issue their own notes. These were printed up by the government and were identical except for the name of the individual issuing bank printed on the face of the note. Frequent money panics occurred when there were not enough such notes to meet the demand for currency, and this and other defects of the system led to the creation of the Federal Reserve System.

operations" play this role, as the Fed buys and sells government securities on the open market.

When the Fed buys a government security on the open market, it pays for the security by issuing a check drawn on itself and payable to the seller. When the seller receives the check, he deposits it in his account at a commercial bank and the commercial bank then collects the check by sending it to the Fed for deposit. Thus, the Fed has created a liability against itself in the form of a member bank demand deposit, and this liability is part of the reserves of the banking system.

The Fed also issues circulating currency in the form of Federal Reserve notes, which now constitute over 88 percent of all currency in circulation. If individuals wish to hold more currency, they go to a commercial bank, draw down their deposits, and receive either Federal Reserve notes or Treasury currency. If a commercial bank finds its supply of currency running low, it asks the Fed to reduce its deposit and send either Federal Reserve notes or Treasury currency (now chiefly coin). The Fed acts as agent for the Treasury in distribution matters. Thus, the Fed again has created a liability against itself in the form of a note outstanding, and this currency can be used either as hand-to-hand cash or as reserves in the till of a commercial bank.[10]

It is, therefore, by the creation of deposit and note liabilities against itself that the Fed supplies reserves to banks and currency to the public. The Treasury, too, has limited power to create liabilities against itself, and the combination of the decisions of these two authorities provides the mechanism for control over the "monetary base," which consists of currency in circulation and member bank reserves, high-powered money.[11]

Although decisions of the Fed and the Treasury to issue liabilities together determine the total volume of member bank reserves and currency in circulation[12]—the monetary base—decisions by others in the economy help determine the major part of the money supply (demand deposits) that banks create through their lending activities. The decisions of business firms and individuals in the aggregate help determine the ratio of currency to deposits and thus, the volume of bank reserves.

If an individual holds funds in the form of time deposits rather than demand deposits, this also affects the volume of reserves that can be used to create demand deposits. This is because there is a reserve requirement (although a small one) for time deposits; thus, the larger the volume of time deposits, the larger will be the amount of reserves required for time deposits

[10]If Treasury currency (e.g., coin) is provided, assets of the Federal Reserve System are reduced. When the Federal Reserve System needs more coin, coins are obtained from the mints, and the government's deposit account at the Fed is increased just as you or I may increase our bank accounts by depositing coin.

[11]We ignore the role of nonmember commercial banks in the money supply creation process except to note here that nonmember state banks can use currency and deposits with other banks as reserves. As member bank reserves and deposits increase, reserves (and hence deposits) of nonmember banks can (and do) also increase.

[12]Technically, perhaps the term "currency outside banks" should be used—as it is in tables published in the *Federal Reserve Bulletin*—instead of the term currency in circulation, which technically means all currency issued. Currency held in bank vaults is a part of bank reserves.

and the smaller will be the amount of reserves (out of a given total) left over to use as a base for expansion of demand deposits. Again, decisions of individuals and businesses regarding the proportion of deposits held in time deposits affect the lending power of banks and the volume of money banks create.

Finally, the Treasury makes decisions about the volume of deposits it holds in its Tax and Loan Accounts with commercial banks. United States government demand deposits in commercial banks are referred to as Treasury Tax and Loan Accounts because the funds in them come chiefly from withholding of taxes and balances created when commercial banks make loans to (buy securities of) the government. When the Treasury calls the funds for transfer from commercial banks to its account with the Fed (on which it writes most of its checks), member bank deposits with the Fed fall as the Treasury's account with the Fed rises. If not offset by other changes, the result is a reduction in the volume of bank reserves and in the ability of banks to lend and create money. This action changes the *size* of the base, but it has another effect as well. Banks are required to hold reserves against United States government deposits. For a *given* base, the fewer United States Treasury deposits there are, the greater the amount of reserves that remain available for the expansion of private loans and demand deposits. Thus, Treasury decisions about where to hold its accounts, with commercial banks or the Fed, affect the money supply as defined (money held by the public).

Commercial banks themselves have some leeway in deciding to lend or not to lend. Because excess reserves are not earning assets, most bank managers attempt to keep excess reserves very close to zero. If excess reserves are zero, we sometimes say that the banking system is "fully loaned." In this case the actual reserve ratio is equal to the legally required reserve ratio. If, however, for whatever reason, bank managers maintain excess reserves, then the actual reserve ratio is somewhat greater than the legally required ratio, and the volume of money created by the banking system is somewhat less than it otherwise would be. Because banks must have at least the required amount of reserves or face penalties, and because of the constant flow of funds in and out of reserves, it is almost inevitable that banks hold *some* excess reserves.

To summarize, we wish to emphasize that portfolio decisions of the Federal Reserve and Treasury (the government) determine the size of the monetary base, and that portfolio decisions of commercial banks, individuals and businesses, and the Treasury all have effects on the amount of money—demand deposits and currency in circulation—that rests upon the base that the Fed and Treasury create.

THE BANK RESERVE EQUATION
AND THE MONETARY BASE

To bring together the diverse activities of the Federal Reserve, the Treasury, and the public that affect the money supply, we begin with a look at the Federal Reserve balance sheet. Then we add the relevant Treasury monetary accounts to derive the "bank reserve equation;" this equation is revised for a clear view of the monetary base.

Principal items in the combined balance sheets of the twelve Federal Reserve Banks include the following:

Assets	*Liabilities and Capital*
Currency	Federal Reserve notes outstanding
Gold certificates and foreign exchange	Member bank deposits (reserves)
Government securities	Treasury deposits
Discounts and advances	Foreign and other deposits
(Loans to member banks)	Other liabilities and capital
Float	
(Cash items in process of	
collection less deferred	
availability items)	
Other assets[1]	

[1]Foreign currencies and SDRs ("paper gold" issued by the International Monetary Fund) may be included in other assets. If gold becomes less important as an international reserve asset, SDRs are likely to be larger in amount and in importance. For many central banks in other countries, foreign exchange may also be an important asset.

Federal Reserve Assets

Under assets, "currency" includes chiefly currency issued by the Treasury and held by the Federal Reserve Banks. Gold certificates are issued by the Treasury in the aftermath of a gold purchase in order to replenish the Treasury deposit account that was depleted when the Treasury wrote a check to pay for the gold; the Federal Reserve System buys foreign exchange (marks, and so on) when it wishes to affect exchange rates or needs foreign currencies for other reasons. Government securities are U.S. government securities that the Federal Reserve has either bought outright or holds temporarily under repurchase agreements. Discounts and advances are simply loans to member banks, as discussed earlier.

"Float" arises out of Federal Reserve check-clearing activities. Member banks that deposit checks with the Fed for collection may not receive deposit credit immediately if the checks are drawn on banks some distance away. Instead, the Fed credits a liability account called "deferred availability items," and debits an asset account called "cash items in process of collection." On a scheduled time basis, not more than two days, the Fed reduces the deferred availability account and increases the deposit account of the depositing bank. But the bank on which the check was drawn may not yet have been presented with the check to be paid by it, and so the Fed does not reduce its reserve balance by the amount of the check until the bank receives the check. Thus, for a day or two, depending upon location and transportation conditions, the account "cash items in process of collection" is larger than the account "deferred availability items"; this difference is the "float." The member bank that deposited the check with the Fed has had its reserves increased, but the member bank on which the check was drawn has *not* had its reserves decreased; thus an increase in float represents a *net* increase in reserves available to member banks. Float is not peculiar to the Federal Reserve System; it exists whenever two agencies or individuals keep records and there is a time difference. Thus, if Jones writes a check to Smith, Jones's checkbook shows a lower balance, but Smith's does not show a higher balance until he receives and deposits the check. Federal Reserve float is especially important because of the key role of bank reserves in the economy. In effect, Federal Reserve float is a short-term interest-free loan by the Fed to member banks.[13]

When the check is finally received by the bank on which it was drawn and the Fed is notified, the Fed reduces that bank's deposit with the Fed and also reduces the item "cash items in process of collection" by the same amount; thus float is eliminated. But check clearing is a continuous process, and some float is always outstanding. The float varies widely from day to day and is increased when weather or strikes disrupt normal communication and transportation channels. It also has regular daily, weekly, and monthly variations arising from the regularity in payment procedures institutionalized in the economy.[14]

Federal Reserve Liabilities

On the liability side of the balance sheet, principal items are Federal Reserve notes outstanding and member bank deposits, which are counted as reserves of member banks (along with currency they hold). These two items form the monetary base. The other items are Treasury deposits and other deposits, a few other liabilities such as dividends payable, and capital.

Treasury Monetary Accounts

To this Federal Reserve composite balance sheet, we must add the appropriate Treasury monetary accounts and then rearrange the accounts in order to arrive at the "bank reserve equation." Additions to bring in Treasury actions are:

Assets	*Liabilities*
Gold Stock and Foreign Exchange	Gold Certificates plus Free Gold (gold against which no certificate has been issued)
Treasury Currency Outstanding	Treasury Currency Outstanding
Treasury Cash (except free gold)	Treasury Cash (except free gold)

[13]The reasons for the existence of float is that banks, like individuals, want credit as soon as possible for checks they deposit or send for collection.

[14]See Irving Auerbach, "Forecasting Float," *Essays in Money and Credit*, Federal Reserve Bank of New York, 1964, pp. 7–12.

With these additions we have added equal amounts to both sides of the Federal Reserve balance sheet; hence totals on both sides are still equal. Now we make four changes.

1. Because gold certificates are both Treasury liabilities and Federal Reserve Bank assets, they appear on both sides of the equation and may be deleted from both sides, leaving gold stock on the left.
2. Free gold and Treasury cash (except free gold) may be combined, on the right side, to form total Treasury cash—free gold and currency held by the Treasury.
3. Federal Reserve notes outstanding plus Treasury currency outstanding on the right side of the equation, minus currency and Treasury cash (except free gold) on the left side may be combined to form a single item—money in circulation, or money held outside of the Treasury and Federal Reserve banks.
4. Vault cash of commercial banks may be subtracted from money in circulation and added to member bank deposit balances to form total reserves of member banks (the subtraction of vault cash leaves Currency Outside Banks).

With these changes, the items remaining are:

Gold stock and foreign exchange	Member Bank Reserves
Treasury Currency Outstanding	Treasury Cash
Federal Reserve Credit	Treasury Deposits in Federal
Government Securities	Reserve Banks
Discounts and Advances	Foreign and Other Deposits in
Float	Federal Reserve Banks
Other Assets	Currency in Circulation (currency
	outside banks)
	Other Liabilities and Capital

Increases in Federal Reserve credit, increases in the monetary gold stock, and increases in Treasury currency outstanding are the three principal *sources* of bank reserves; the other items in the question are competing *uses* of reserves. That is, an increase in Federal Reserve credit, in the monetary gold stock, or in Treasury currency outstanding provides funds that *increase bank reserves* unless they are diverted to one of the competing uses of funds (or unless there is a decrease in one of the other sources of funds). Federal Reserve credit is extended through open market operations, discounts and advances, and float. The other major source of funds for bank reserves is an increase in the gold stock; because silver certificates are no longer being issued and are being replaced by Federal Reserve notes, an increase in Treasury currency outstanding is likely to be relatively insignificant.

Thus, the balance sheet items in the bank reserve equation can be interpreted as a statement of sources and uses of bank reserves. By moving all items except member bank reserves and currency in circulation from the right-hand side to the left-hand side, and considering them to be subtractions, we

TABLE 4–2   Sources and Uses of the Monetary Base

Average of daily figures for week ended Wednesday, April 25, 1973

Sources of the Base		Uses of the Base	
Federal Reserve Credit:		Member bank deposits	
Holdings of securities	$75.9	at Federal Reserve	$26.7
Discounts and advances	1.7	Currency in circulation	66.3
Float	2.7		
Other Federal Reserve assets	1.1		
Gold stock	10.8		
Treasury currency outstanding	8.4		
Treasury cash holdings	− .4		
Treasury deposits at Federal			
Reserve	−3.6		
Foreign deposits at Federal			
Reserve	− .3		
Other liabilities and			
capital accounts	−2.6		
Other Federal Reserve deposits	− .7		
Sources of the base	$93.0	Uses of the base	93.0
Reserve adjustment[1]	6.9	Reserve adjustment	6.9
Monetary base	$99.9	Monetary base	$99.9

[1]See footnote 15.

can construct a table of sources and uses of the monetary base. This appears in Table 4–2.[15]

The monetary base—the base on which the money supply rests—consists of two uses, member bank reserves and currency in circulation (outside of banks), which appear on the right. The size of the monetary base is under the control of the Federal Reserve and the Treasury; that is, it is under the control of the nation's monetary authorities.

THE MONETARY BASE AND THE MONEY SUPPLY[16]

Let the money supply, consisting of demand deposits and currency outside banks, which we defined earlier as M_1, be some multiple, m, of the "monetary base," B. Thus, $M = mB$. (In this section we understand M_1 to be the money supply, M.)

The monetary base, B, is the *net* monetary liabilities of government—in

[15]A reserve adjustment item is shown in Table 4–2 because, without this adjustment, figures for the monetary base would not necessarily be comparable from time to time. When reserve requirements are changed, more reserves (or less) are needed to support, as a base, the same amount of deposits.

[16]This section draws substantially on the presentation found in Jerry L. Jordan, "Elements of Money Stock Determination," *Review*, Federal Reserve Bank of St. Louis, October 1969, pp. 10–19.

particular those of the Fed and the Treasury—held by the commercial banks and the nonbank public.

Earlier we discussed how banks are able to create money (demand deposits) up to some multiple of their reserves as determined by the legal reserve ratio. Demand deposits were some multiple of member bank reserves. Here, in contrast, we broaden our perspective somewhat, and attempt to view the entire money supply (demand deposits *and* currency in circulation) as some multiple of the monetary base (rather than some multiple of member bank reserves alone):

$$M = mB.$$

The Money Multiplier

The relation between M and B is m, the money multiplier. The value assumed by m is the result not only of the legally required reserve ratio for commercial banks, but also of the portfolio decisions of commercial banks, the public, the Treasury, and the Federal Reserve System. These decisions may be specified as follows:

$r = R/(D + T + G)$ reserves ÷ total deposits

$k = C/D$ currency ÷ private demand deposits

$t = T/D$ time deposits ÷ private demand deposits

$g = G/D$ government deposits ÷ private demand deposits

where

R = member bank reserves

C = currency in circulation

D = private demand deposits

T = time deposits

G = government deposits

To derive the multiplier, proceed as follows:

1. $M = D + C$
2. $B = R + C$
3. $R = r(D + T + G)$
4. $C = kD$ where k is some fraction
5. $T = tD$ where t is some fraction
6. $G = gD$ where g is some fraction

Substitute 3 and 4 into 2,

7. $B = r(D + T + G) + kD$

Substitute 5 and 6 into 7,

8. $B = r(D + tD + gD) + kD$, or
$B = [r(1 + t + g) + k]D$
9. $D = \{1/[r(1 + t + g) + k]\} B$
10. $C = \{k/[r(1 + t + g) + k]\} B$
11. $M = \{(1 + k)/[r(1 + t + g) + k]\} B$

Equation 9 shows the relation between the level of demand deposits and the base. Equation 10 shows the relation between the volume of currency in circulation and the base. Finally, equation 11 shows the relation between the money supply and the base—the coefficient of B is m;

$$m = \frac{1 + k}{r(1 + t + g) + k}$$

The money multiplier contains all of the factors other than B that affect the money supply. Portfolio decisions of commercial banks are reflected in the value of r, which results from commercial banks' willingness to hold not only legally required reserves but also some excess reserves, and the value of t, which reflects the banks' willingness or ability to attract time deposits, as they might through, say, raising interest rates they pay for time deposits. Portfolio decisions of the nonbank public are reflected in k, which results from decisions to hold cash or demand deposits, and in t, which reflects decisions to hold time deposits rather than demand deposits. Portfolio decisions of the Treasury are reflected in g, which results from decisions to hold deposits with commercial banks rather than at the Federal Reserve Banks. And, of course, the Fed determines B, with some influence from the Treasury (which the Fed may offset if it wishes). A diagram with check marks to indicate which sectors' decisions directly affect the determinants of the money supply follows:

	Sector			
Determinants of M_1	Commercial Banks	Nonbank Public	Treasury	Federal Reserve
B			√	√
r	√			√
k		√		
t	√	√		
g			√	

Empirical Values of the Base and Multiplier

At the end of 1972, the value of B in the United States was roughly $97 billion. Like items in most economic time series, the base fluctuates consid-

erably from month to month, occasionally rising or falling by as much as
$1 billion in a month. But the long-term trend of B over time is upward.
During the 1960s, on the average, the yearly rate of increase in B was 4.09
percent. A growing economy needs a growing money supply and a growing
monetary base to support it. Thus, it is expected that some rate of increase
will continue over the long-term future.

The money multiplier, m, fluctuated in the neighborhood of 2.6 during
most of 1972. (See Figure 4–1.) This ratio is actually computed by observing
M/B. Broken down into its component parts, estimates are:

$$r = .09, k = .28, t = 1.25 \text{ and } g = .04.$$

These values, of course, are subject to change, because each depends upon
portfolio decisions of various sectors. The principal items causing m to vary
from month to month are t and k. Of course, month-to-month changes are
obscured when we take, say, the average for a year and then look at year-to-
year changes.[17] The value of t rose from around .6 for the year 1960 to 1.25

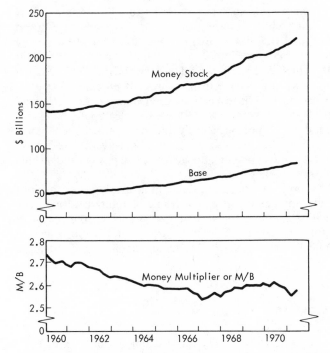

FIGURE 4–1   Money Stock, Monetary Base, and Money Multiplier: 1960–71

SOURCE: Federal Reserve Bank of St. Louis and Federal Reserve Bank of Richmond, *Monthly Review*, March 1972, p. 3.

[17]See Jane Anderson and Thomas M. Humphrey, "Determinants of Change in the
Money Stock: 1960–1970," *Monthly Review*, Federal Reserve Bank of Richmond,
March 1972, pp. 1–8, for a detailed examination of changes in m over the decade of
the 1960s.

in 1970, reflecting increasing use of time deposits by individuals and businesses and the aggressive promotion of time deposit facilities by commercial banks. Annual average values of k also rose during the 1960s from .26 to about .29. This reflects an increased demand for currency, as opposed to demand deposits, on the part of the public.[18] Values of r declined from 1.25 to .085 during this period, as legal reserve requirements were lowered and banks also reduced their holdings of excess reserves. Finally, the value of g showed no consistent trend; as an average for 1962 it was .05, while for 1969 it was about .035.

Can monetary managers of the Treasury and the Fed count on m to be stable; that is, can they control M relatively quickly by policy moves designed to set a particular value for B? The answer to this question is yet to come, and many economists are actively engaged in examination of evidence to see just how stable m is over time.

Lest the reader assume, because we have written a definite formula $M = mB$, that somehow the relation represented by m is established, we urge him to understand that the value m is *not* independent of actions designed to alter B. In other words, the formula is a way to put some pieces of a puzzle together, but it is not the complete picture by far. For example, if B increases when the Fed buys short-term securities and this leads to reduced yields on these securities and the yields on time deposits seem attractive by comparison, then the public may shift into T out of D, causing an increase in t and a decrease in M. Thus, B and M would not be independent of each other: a rise in B would lead to a decline in m as well. If an expansion of B and a subsequent expansion of M leads to increased demand for currency, then k would be affected and so would M. Other examples could be given. Furthermore, $r, k, t,$ and g are not necessarily independent of each other. A change in T and t will affect r, because r is a weighted average of excess and legal required reserve ratios for demand and time deposits, and r falls when t rises, because of the way they are defined.

Thus, the formula should not be interpreted in a mechanistic fashion; rather it should be looked upon as a convenient frame of reference for analysis of a variety of monetary matters. In particular, it points up the necessity of understanding portfolio decisions of individuals, as they choose among instruments of the financial markets, if we are to understand money supply creation fully.

MONETARY CONTROLS

In this concluding section, we review briefly the instruments of control Federal Reserve officials have at their disposal and point up the connections between these instruments and conditions in those financial markets that are the focal points of this book. Our concern with the money supply and the

[18]Why this occurred in a period when inflation was reducing the value of money is somewhat of a puzzle. See "The Growing Appetite for Cash," *Federal Reserve Bank of Chicago, Business Conditions*, April 1971, pp. 12–16.

institutional mechanism for controlling it stems from the belief that changes in the money supply lead to changes in the level of aggregate demand. Economists differ in opinion about the precise mechanism by which changes in the supply of money affect spending. Some believe that an increase in the supply of money will lead directly to spending by consumers and businessmen. Others believe that increases in the money supply lead to purchases of bonds, which drive bond prices up and interest rates down. Lower interest rates, in turn, induce spending on the part of consumers and business. Whichever view one holds about the mechanism, it follows that money supply changes affect demand. If the rate of growth in the money supply over the long run is too great, inflation and its undesirable effects will result. If the rate of growth is too small, the likely result will be reduced demand, deflation, and unemployment. It is important, therefore, to control the money supply so that it grows rapidly enough but not too rapidly. We now examine the policy tools of the Federal Reserve that are used to regulate growth of the money supply.

Open Market Operations

The seven members of the Board of Governors of the Federal Reserve System and five of the twelve presidents of the twelve regional Federal Reserve Banks constitute the twelve-member Federal Open Market Committee (FOMC). Four of the five bank presidents are members on a rotating basis, while the fifth, President of the Federal Reserve Bank of New York, is a permanent member of the committee. Open market operations are carried out by a trading desk in New York, and the Manager of the Open Market Account is an officer of the Federal Reserve Bank of New York. Records of the FOMC are released to the public about ninety days following frequent meetings, and are published in the *Federal Reserve Bulletin*. The FOMC gives instructions of a general nature to the account manager. Instruction may be "to promote ease" or "to maintain prevailing conditions" or "to accommodate greater growth in the monetary aggregates."[19]

If the account manager buys United States government securities, he pays for these with a check drawn on the Fed. When this check is deposited in a commercial bank and then returned to the Federal Reserve, that member bank's account is increased, reserves are increased, and B is increased. Sizable purchases by the Fed may drive up the prices of government securities and drive yields down. Thus, the government securities market is the principal medium for exercising monetary policy. Furthermore, because banks have excess reserves, the immediate impact may be observed in the Federal funds market. Excess reserves of some banks may be lent to other banks that wish to enlarge their reserve positions. With large amounts of excess reserves,

---

[19]For a description of open market operations during 1971 see the report prepared by Alan R. Holmes, Manager of the open market account, "Open Market Operations and Money and Credit Aggregates—1971," *Federal Reserve Bulletin*, April 1972, pp. 340–62. Mr. Holmes' report on open market operations during 1972 appears in the *Federal Reserve Bulletin*, June 1973, pp. 405–16.

supply of Federal funds increases, and yields on Federal funds fall. The market for Federal funds reflects from day to day the extent of ease or tightness of reserves in the banking system.

Open market operations are sometimes termed "defensive" and sometimes "dynamic." For example, if a snowstorm delays forwarding of deposited checks, float may increase dramatically. The manager of the account then sells government securities in order to absorb some of the reserves supplied to member banks by the increased float. Thus, although the manager may wish to *add* reserves to the system, he must nevertheless sell some governments, for otherwise the float will create a large volume of reserves and increase the base by more than the desired amount. "Defensive" operations, therefore, are housekeeping operations designed to offset various influences on reserve positions, while "dynamic" operations are those designed to promote changes in the money supply as dictated by policy.[20]

Similarly, when currency flows out of banks on a large scale, as it does at Christmas or Easter time, and before other holiday periods, the Fed buys securities to replenish what would otherwise be depleted bank reserves. The procedure is reversed as currency flows back into the banks in the aftermath of these periods of high spending. Thus, on a seasonal basis the Fed alters the base in order to offset changes in m that follow from changes in k. When gold flows out of the country, this reduces the base. The Fed offsets the impact on the base by buying an equivalent amount of government securities. Thus, through open market operations the Fed can negate the impact of international gold flows on the base and therefore on the domestic money supply.

Discounting (Borrowing) by Member Banks

Insofar as the Fed lends directly to member banks, the base is increased and so is bank lending power. However, since it is typically the case that the Fed has already created tight conditions by open market sales, reserves are reduced and member banks finding themselves short of reserves may obtain reserves by borrowing from the Fed. Thus, when the Fed lends to banks it is in a sense undoing with its left hand what its right hand did somewhat earlier. The borrowing mechanism is under intensive review. Many economists feel that this tool of policy is an abomination and should be suspended, especially in view of the thoroughly developed market for Federal funds. However, in the tight money period of 1970 total borrowings by member banks reached a level of over $1 billion, indicating that in spite of its uncertain future, the "discount window" of each of the Federal Reserve Banks where member banks borrow is still very active.[21]

Some economists feel that with the United States system of many indi-

---

[20]For a description of "defensive" and "dynamic" responsibilities of the Fed, and a description of activity on the trading desk see Robert V. Roosa, *Federal Reserve Operations in the Money and Government Securities Market*, Federal Reserve Bank of New York, July 1956.

[21]Actually, there is no window as such; borrowings are negotiated in an office.

vidual banks, there is need for the discount window as a "safety valve" for individual banks caught in a difficult position. Effective April 19, 1973, Regulation A, which covers loans to member banks, was revised to allow an estimated 2,000 small banks in agricultural and resort areas to borrow from the discount window on a seasonal basis. Reserve banks will be able to make loans up to ninety days if the member banks apply in advance for the borrowing privilege and prove that they must satisfy a seasonal demand for funds for at least an eight-week period. They must also show that they lack reasonably reliable access to national money markets. This requirement is surely difficult to meet inasmuch as modern communications enable the immediate transfer of funds and immediate borrowing in the market for Federal funds. Nevertheless, the institution of this "seasonal" borrowing privilege indicates that discount window activity will remain strong in the near future.

Changes in Legal Reserve Ratios

The power of the Fed to set legal minimum reserve ratios helps determine the size of r in the money multiplier equation. Of course, r is partially determined by the decisions of managers of commercial banks to maintain excess reserves in greater or lesser amounts. In recent years the Fed has generally lowered reserve requirements from time to time, with an occasional small increase. Reducing reserve requirements and open market purchases are alternative ways of providing additional bank reserves, on which banks can create the additional money needed in a growing economy. Some reasons for preferring one means rather than the other are discussed in later chapters.

Interest Rate Ceilings and Other Controls

Besides the tools that affect reserves, the monetary base, or the money multiplier directly, the Fed has a variety of other powers that can have considerable influence in financial markets. Regulation Q allows Federal Reserve authorities to establish a maximum interest rate that commercial banks may pay depositors on time deposits. Payment of interest on demand deposits was prohibited by the Banking Act of 1933. In other countries banks often may pay interest to individuals holding demand deposits. Banks in the United States are allowed to reduce service charges if individuals maintain deposits of a certain amount or over during the monthly service charge period so that depositors who maintain sufficient balances make little or no payment, directly, for the checking services provided. In effect, such persons are receiving the equivalent of interest on their accounts, in comparison with those who pay service charges.[22]

---

[22]Questions that may be raised are rather complex: for instance, what service charge would just compensate the bank for its cost of handling checking accounts? What does a specified deposit balance (for example, $300) contribute to offsetting the cost of handling the account by providing for the particular bank funds that may be loaned out at interest?

On passbook savings deposits in 1973, the maximum interest rate payable by banks was raised to 5 percent. On time deposits of larger amounts and longer term to maturity, maximum rates ranged from 5½ percent to 7½ percent. However, for the special category of negotiable CDs of $100,000 and over, with maturity from thirty to ninety days, the ceiling was suspended on January 21, 1970. Later, in mid-May 1973, the decision was made to suspend rate ceilings entirely on these large negotiable CDs with maturities of 90 days or more. There is considerable pressure to remove interest rate ceilings altogether and permanently, although some groups have expressed opposition to this. The reasons for the controversy are discussed in later chapters.

Regulations G, T, and U, prescribed in accordance with the Securities and Exchange Act of 1934 and its amendments, limit the amount of credit that a bank, broker and dealer, or others, can extend to someone wishing to purchase and carry securities, by prescribing a maximum loan value that is a specified percentage of the market value of the security at the time credit is extended. These percentages are called margin requirements. In early 1970, on margin stocks the requirement was 80 percent. By December of 1971 it was reduced to 55 percent, and late in 1972 it was raised again to 65 percent. At the end of 1973 it was again reduced, this time to 50 percent. Thus, a purchaser of $100 of stock could borrow $50 from a bank and put up $50 cash, pledging the securities as collateral against his loan. On convertible bonds the ratio was 50 percent. These requirements have a direct impact on the availability of funds in the market for equities and convertible bonds.[23]

During periods of severe economic stress, the Fed has been given direct controls over terms of lending to consumers for mortgages and for all forms of instalment credit. By "terms" we mean the down payment required and the length of time over which repayment must be made. For example, such controls were exercised during World War II and in several periods after that war. The Fed no longer has such power, but could easily be given it again; from time to time the suggestion is made that such power be available on a standby basis.

Moral suasion is also a policy tool. Federal Reserve memoranda sent to commercial banks can induce them to restrict "speculative" or other types of loans, and bank examiners often look at the "quality" of the loan—noting whether it is more or less speculative. Although these procedures are not clearly defined, bank managers are sensitive to the overall examination procedure and the availability of funds for certain types of loans can be influenced. On September 1, 1966, a letter from each Federal Reserve Bank president to member banks in his district stated that the "System believes that the national economic interest would be better served by a lower rate of expansion of bank loans to business" and that "this objective will be kept in mind by the Federal Reserve Banks in their extensions of credit to member banks through the discount window." Occasions like this, when the Federal Reserve System feels impelled to supplement its usual credit control powers

---

[23]A requirement is also imposed on short sales.

with special pronouncements, usually come in times of "crisis," or at least severe strain, in the money market.[24]

SUMMARY

Money is important because in a modern economy almost all purchases involve money; and as shown in Chapter 2, total purchases equal total income. Money is also important because there are significant correlations between rates of increase in the money stock and GNP. Problems in defining and measuring money, however, complicate analysis. Money consists of currency plus liabilities of certain financial institutions. In the present institutional environment, money is usually defined to include only demand deposit liabilities of commercial banks, in addition to currency. Money so defined is labeled M_1. M_1 is important because payments are generally made either in currency or by checks on demand deposit accounts, and not in any other way. Some economists include time deposits in commercial banks, with some adjustment; a major reason is the recent close correlation of money so defined (M_2) with GNP.

Commercial banks create money by making loans and giving borrowers deposit credits or currency. An isolated commercial bank, if it were the only bank in a country, could create money just as well as a system of banks. However, most countries have banking systems consisting of a number of banks, from less than a dozen in some countries to many thousands in the United States. In a banking system, the money-creating process involves creation of deposits on the basis of reserves, with the limitations that banks generally may not hold less than the required amount of reserves; that the public may shift some funds from deposits to currency and vice versa; that the public may shift funds from demand deposits in commercial banks to time deposits and vice versa; and that the government may shift its deposits from commercial banks to the Federal Reserve Banks.

Currency plus bank reserves, with appropriate adjustments, have been termed the "monetary base" on which deposits are created. The "bank reserve equation" shows the factor affecting the monetary base; amounts of items in the equation can easily be ascertained or controlled by the Federal Reserve System.

A formula used recently shows the factors affecting the size of the money stock, given the size of the monetary base. This formula is termed the "money multiplier $\left(\dfrac{M}{B}, \text{ or } m \right)$. Examining this formula, it is seen that the public, the government, and the commercial banks, as well as the Federal Reserve System, play roles in determining the size of the money stock.

However, the Federal Reserve System has the ability to control the size of the money stock over a period of time, although it may not be able to do

---

[24]In May 1973 strong inflationary pressures led Arthur F. Burns, Chairman of the Board of Governors, to send a somewhat similar letter to all banks.

so as quickly as may be desired nor as precisely. The tools it uses include open market operations, discounting for member banks and occasionally for others, changes in legal reserve requirement ratios, and interest rate ceilings and some other control tools. Open market operations are the major tool, other tools serving only supplementary functions.

QUESTIONS FOR DISCUSSION

1. In what ways does the fact that they "create money" make commercial banks different from deposit-type financial institutions such as mutual savings banks and savings and loan associations?

2. List arguments for the use of M_1 as the money supply; then list arguments for using M_2. Which is the better measure? Why?

3. Some economists prefer the term "stock of money" rather than the term "money supply." Why?

4. Would it be possible for a single commercial bank, if isolated, for example, in Alaska, without communications, to create money?

5. Show in skeleton balance sheet form, for the Federal Reserve Banks and for commercial banks, the effects of open market purchases by the Fed.

6. Show how the bank reserve equation is used to examine factors determining the size of the monetary base.

7. Derive the equation for the money multiplier. Why is the money multiplier quite volatile in the short run?

8. Contrast "defensive" and "dynamic" open market operations.

9. Evaluate each of the other tools now used, or used in the past, by the Fed to control the money supply and/or credit. How useful is each? What defects do you find in each?

10. Why is it necessary at certain times to restrain bank loans to business firms? Why has the Fed at certain times indicated that whether banks restrain such loans or not will be kept in mind when banks apply to the Fed for borrowings? At the opposite extreme, the Fed was compared by one writer to a fire department in May 1970: Federal Reserve Bank officers told banks that if they needed to borrow from the Fed in order to accommodate bank customers who needed loans, especially to meet short-term cash needs such as those for maturing commercial paper, the Fed would be happy to lend to them. Why? What was the situation, and what purpose was served?

SELECTED REFERENCES

Several of the many excellent textbooks on money and banking that should serve to supplement the discussion of the role of commercial banks in the money-creating process and the Federal Reserve's monetary controls are listed at the end of Chapter 1.

Because of the importance of money in economic and financial affairs, the student would find it rewarding to survey the controversy over the definition and measurement of money. An excellent introduction is provided in David Laidler's "The Definition of Money," *Journal of Money, Credit, and Banking,*

August 1969, pp. 508–25 (reprinted in *Monetary Economics: Readings on Current Issues*, ed. William F. Gibson and George G. Kaufman (New York: McGraw-Hill, 1971).

The monetary base and multiplier model, which has become widely used to integrate the roles played by the commercial banks, the public, the Treasury, and the Fed in determination of the money supply, is presented in Jerry L. Jordan's "Elements of Money Stock Determination," *Review*, Federal Reserve Bank of St. Louis, October 1969, pp. 10–19 (reprinted in *Monetary Economics: Readings on Current Issues*).

The weekly Federal Reserve statement provides information about the monetary base presented in terms of the sources and uses of member bank reserves. A useful pamphlet is the *Glossary: Weekly Federal Reserve Statements*, published by the Federal Reserve Bank of New York, 1972, which gives full detail on this topic. Current values for the base and the monetary multiplier are published weekly in the Federal Reserve Bank of St. Louis, *U.S. Financial Data*. *Monetary Trends* by the same bank includes data on the rates of change of M_1 and M_2, bank credit, and the base.

Methods used by the Federal Reserve System in developing statistics on the alternative measures of the money supply are described in such articles as "Revision of the Money Stock Measures and Member Bank Reserves and Deposits," *Federal Reserve Bulletin*, February 1974, pp. 81–95. For a less technical discussion, see Federal Reserve Bank of San Francisco, *Business & Financial Letter*, February 15, 1974.

5

Nonbank
Financial Institutions

Much investment is direct, or internally financed; for example, business firms use retained earnings to invest in new plant and equipment. Second, funds are transferred directly from ultimate lenders to borrowers without the intermediation of financial institutions, or with only the aid of dealers or brokers; for example, individuals buy corporate bonds. Finally, a part of the funds obtained by borrowers is channeled through banks or nonbank financial institutions. At times, funds are removed from these institutions by consumers and others for the direct purchase of stocks, bonds, or mortgages; this is termed disintermediation, as mentioned earlier.

The total of all funds transferred directly from ultimate lenders to ultimate borrowers, as in the purchase of stocks or bonds by individuals, plus the funds channeled through bank and nonbank financial intermediaries, is termed "loanable funds."

Total loanable funds may be treated as the sum of three amounts: saving from income available (termed planned saving in Chapter 2),[1] funds available because of an increase in the size of the money supply, and funds already saved and held in the form of money, which people and institutions attempt to lend. They may attempt to lend because they are attracted by relatively high interest rates or by a possible future rise in the prices of stocks, bonds, or other financial assets. Lending from money held idle means that the velocity, or velocity of circulation, of money is increased, since lending re-

---

[1]An analysis based on planned or expected savings was developed by Swedish economists including Bertil Ohlin ("Some Notes on the Stockholm Theory of Savings and Investment," *Economic Journal*, 1937), while Dennis Robertson ("Saving and Hoarding," *Economic Journal*, 1933) developed an analysis based on periods of time, saving at the beginning of a period being derived from the income of the previous period. Neither planned saving (ex ante saving) nor saving from the income of the previous period need equal investment in the present period, whereas saving and investment in the present period (ex post) must be equal.

quires a turnover of money. Increase in velocity of money is termed dishoarding, although this term must be used carefully, for reasons developed later.[2] Velocity of money may also be increased by more rapid spending for goods and services, which may occur, for example, when people expect that prices may rise or that availability of some goods may be reduced. Thus velocity of money is increased by attempts to lend more rapidly and by attempts to spend more rapidly. If the economy is treated as a "three-market" economy—a market for goods and services, a market for loanable funds or for financial assets other than money, and a "market" for money[3]—the three activities of spending, lending, and dishoarding (or attempting to dishoard) are clearly separated. It may be mentioned that the velocity of money may be reduced, which can be termed hoarding; this reduces the total available loanable funds. The money supply can also be reduced, decreasing the total available loanable funds, although this has seldom occurred since World War II.

One of our major concerns with nonbank financial institutions, in this chapter and in Chapter 6, is to examine whether they affect saving, the size of the money supply, or hoarding or dishoarding (change in the velocity of circulation of money). Because only the central bank and the commercial banks create money (ignoring the small amount of coins minted by the government), nonbank financial institutions cannot *directly* affect the size of the money supply. But they may do so *indirectly*, and whether they do so and to what extent are important. Saving may be affected if growth of certain types of nonbank financial institutions causes people to save a larger or a smaller percentage of their income. Size of the money supply may be affected indirectly if, for example, the competition of nonbank financial institutions such as savings and loan associations induces commercial banks to pay higher interest on time deposits, thus increasing, in all probability, the ratio of time deposits to demand deposits (t in the money multiplier formula in Chapter 4) and affecting the size of the money multiplier. Velocity of money is affected because transfers of funds from currency or demand deposits to savings and loan associations, for example, involve a turnover of money when the transfer is made, additional turnover when the savings and loan association places the funds in its deposit account in a commercial bank, and additional turnover when the savings and loan association makes loans. This turnover may involve only an increase in what is termed the *transactions velocity* of money, if only transfers of funds are involved. It may, however, also involve an increase in the *income velocity* of money if, for example, loans made by the savings and loan association result

---

[2]The money supply may be decreased instead of being increased, thus subtracting from the supply of loanable funds, and the public may attempt to hoard instead of dishoard. Thus the total supply of loanable funds may be saving plus the increase in the money supply plus dishoarding ($S + \Delta M + DH$), $S - \Delta M - H$ (hoarding), or another combination of these.

[3]Harry G. Johnson, "Monetary Theory and Keynesian Economics," *Pakistan Economic Journal*, June 1958, pp. 56–70; reprinted in Harry G. Johnson, *Money, Trade and Economic Growth* (London: George Allen and Unwin, Ltd., 1962), and in Warren L. Smith and Ronald L. Teigen, *Readings in Money, National Income, and Stabilization Policy* (Homewood, Ill.: Richard D. Irwin, 1965).

in additional spending by consumers for the purchase of new homes.[4] An increase in income velocity, with a given stock of money, means an increase in GNP. Thus changes in transactions velocity of money resulting from transfers of funds to nonbank financial institutions may be of some significance, and changes in income velocity are of even greater significance.

We are also concerned with the effects of flows of funds through these institutions to the money and capital markets, effects of such flows of funds on interest rates, and effects on the various sectors of the economy that obtain funds for ultimate use. Uses of funds include housing construction, business domestic investment, consumer spending, government spending, and foreign investment. Before proceeding to substantive issues in Chapter 6, it is desirable to have a workable classification of the many nonbank financial institutions (NBFIs) that can serve as a framework for analysis.

Because of the variety of financial institutions, and the possibility of classification based on sources of funds, uses of funds, legal form, and so on, no classification is likely to be perfect in distinguishing those having similar important characteristics. The classification used in this chapter is based primarily on the nature of the liabilities of the institution. An alternative classification could be based on functions performed, and some reference to groupings based on such a classification is necessary at times.

A CLASSIFICATION OF NONBANK
FINANCIAL INSTITUTIONS

In a classification based primarily on the nature of their liabilities, NBFIs may be classified into five groups: (1) deposit-type financial institutions, which have liabilities quite similar to the deposits held by commercial banks—these include mutual savings banks, savings and loan associations, and credit unions; (2) contractual saving institutions, whose liabilities are defined by contracts for future payments under specified conditions—insurance companies and pension funds; (3) investment-type institutions, whose liabilities are shares or trust agreements evidencing ownership or beneficial interest in long-term securities (stocks and bonds)—mutual funds, closed-end investment companies, and personal trust funds and common trust funds managed by

---

[4]Transactions velocity of money is found by dividing total transactions by the average money stock: $V_t = PT/M$. With a simple algebraic change this is $MV = PT$, the well-known equation of exchange, in which M is the stock of money, V is its transactions velocity, and PT is the total volume of goods and services, each good or service being multiplied by its average price and the total summed. (An error in many books is to define T as the total volume of transactions or of goods and services sold; obviously apples and automobiles cannot be added. See Clark Warburton, "Algebra and the Equation of Exchange," *American Economic Review*, June 1953, pp. 358–61. Income velocity of money is found by dividing total income by the average money stock: V_y equals PO/M or GNP/M, where O is output and GNP is gross national product. Because of the importance of income for economic theory, economists usually refer to income velocity rather than to transactions velocity. Income velocity can be measured as GNP/M; transactions velocity is difficult to measure empirically, as no convenient empirical measure of PT is available. Bank debits (the total of all checks drawn on bank deposits plus withdrawals from bank demand deposit accounts) may be used as a proxy for PT, with the understanding that currency transactions are ignored.

commercial banks and trust companies; (4) finance companies, whose liabilities include commercial paper, bank borrowing, and debentures, backed by substantial equity capital; and (5) a miscellaneous group, including government and quasi-government lending agencies whose liabilities are termed "agency securities," investment and brokerage houses that serve a function of facilitating financial investment, and such minor institutions as pawnshops.

Liabilities are important because they are a major factor in determining the nature of the asset portfolio acquired and held by an institution. The legal status, maturity, and other characteristics of liabilities affect the need for liquidity, rate of return, and safety of assets held by the institutions.

Table 5–1 shows the relative size of commercial banks and the five groups of nonbank financial institutions and the major institutions in each group, in 1960 and in 1971. For comparison, it may be noted that total holdings of financial assets of *all* sectors at the end of 1971 were \$4,562.8 billion, excluding holdings of liabilities of financial institutions. Personal trusts are also excluded from this figure because they are included with assets of households,

TABLE 5–1   Total Financial Assets of Major Institutions (in billions of dollars)

	End of 1960	Percentage of Total	End of 1971	Percentage of Total
Commercial banks				
Commercial banks	230.9	30.9	574.5	33.1
Deposit-type financial institutions				
Mutual savings banks	40.6	5.4	89.6	5.2
Savings and loan associations	71.5	9.6	206.3	11.9
Credit unions	5.0	0.7	18.3	1.1
Contractual savings institutions				
Life insurance companies	115.9	15.5	214.5	12.4
Nonlife insurance companies	26.3	3.5	54.6	3.1
Private pension funds	38.2	5.1	128.4	7.4
State and local government				
employee retirement funds	19.6	2.6	64.8	3.7
Investment institutions				
Mutual funds	17.0	2.3	55.0	3.2
Personal trust funds	140.5[a]	18.8	199.4[c]	11.5
Finance companies	24.1	3.2	64.4	3.7
Miscellaneous				
Government-sponsored agencies	11.3	1.5	50.3	2.9
Other[b]	6.6	0.9	14.6	0.8
Total	747.5	100.0	1,734.7	100.0

[a]Estimate for 1964; does not include pension plan funds held by trust departments of banks.
[b]Includes agencies of foreign banks, banks in U.S. possessions, and security brokers and dealers.
[c]Estimate for 1970; does not include pension plan funds held by trust departments of banks.

SOURCES: *Federal Reserve Bulletin*, June 1972; Federal Reserve Bank of New York, *Monthly Review*, October 1972.

TABLE 5–2 Financial Asset Holdings of Financial Institutions and Other Sectors (in billions of dollars, end of 1971)

Sector	Currency and Demand Deposits Amount	%	Share Accounts and Time Deposits Amount	%	Life Insurance Reserves Amount	%	Pension Fund Reserves Amount	%
Commercial banks	45.4ᵃ	7.9	—	—	—	—	—	—
Savings and loan associations	2.2	1.1	—	—	—	—	—	—
Mutual savings banks	0.9	1.0	0.5	0.6	—	—	—	—
Credit unions	0.9	4.9	—	—	—	—	—	—
Life insurance companies	1.8	0.8	—	—	—	—	—	—
Other insurance companies	1.5	2.7	—	—	—	—	—	—
Private pension funds	1.6	1.2	—	—	—	—	—	—
State and local government retirement funds	0.5	0.8	—	—	—	—	—	—
Mutual funds	0.8	1.5	—	—	—	—	—	—
Finance companies	3.9	6.1	—	—	—	—	—	—
Households and non-profit institutionsᵇ	134.9	6.2	496.0	22.9	137.0	6.3	268.1	12.4
Business firms	57.3	13.6	14.1	3.3	—	—	—	—
State and local governments	10.4	11.9	30.4	34.8	—	—	—	—
Federal government	13.5	13.1	0.5	0.5	—	—	—	—
Federally sponsored credit agencies	0.2	0.4	—	—	—	—	—	—
Monetary authorities	—	—	—	—	—	—	—	—
Foreign	6.4	4.2	7.2	4.8	—	—	—	—
Miscellaneous	2.1	14.3	—	—	—	—	—	—
Total	284.3 (238.9)ᶠ	5.3	548.7	12.1	137.0	3.0	268.1	5.9

Dashes indicate either no holdings or negligible holdings.

ᵃOf this amount $10.1 billion were deposits in other commercial banks and $27.8 billion were deposits in Federal Reserve banks.
ᵇIncludes personal trust funds.
ᶜOf this amount, trade credit was $180.5 billion.
ᵈOf this amount, gold and foreign exchange were $10.1 billion, and Treasury currency

in flow of funds statistics. Savings bonds totalled $54.9 billion, and are included in the total holdings of all sectors. A large part of the holdings of the household sector consists of holdings of stocks; household sector ownership of stocks was valued at $878.7 billion at the end of 1971.

Table 5–2 shows financial asset holdings of financial institutions and other sectors at the end of 1971 in amounts and percentages of total holdings of financial assets by each institution or sector. This table gives a convenient summary of the major types of assets held by various institutions and sectors. For example, commercial banks held 44.4 percent of their financial assets in

United States Government and Agency Securities		State and Local Government Securities		Corporate Bonds		Mortgages		Stocks		Loans		Other		Total	
Amount	%	Amount	%	Amount	%	Amount	%	Amount	%	Amount	%	Amount	%	Amount	%
83.5	14.5	82.9	14.6	4.0	0.6	82.5	14.4	0.5	0.1	255.1	44.4	20.6	3.6	574.5 (529.1)ᶠ	100.1
17.5	8.5	—	—	—	—	174.5	84.5	—	—	1.6	0.8	10.6	5.1	206.4	100.0
5.2	5.8	0.4	0.4	12.6	14.0	61.9	69.1	3.0	3.3	2.8	3.1	2.3	2.6	89.6	99.9
2.4	13.0	—	—	—	—	0.9	4.9	—	—	14.2	77.2	—	—	18.4	100.0
4.0	1.9	3.5	1.6	79.3	37.0	75.6	35.2	20.5	9.6	19.8	9.2	10.0	4.7	214.5	100.0
3.9	7.1	19.3	35.3	9.3	17.0	0.3	0.5	15.5	28.3	—	—	4.9	9.0	54.7	99.9
2.7	2.1	—	—	29.0	22.6	3.7	2.9	86.6	67.4	—	—	4.8	3.7	128.4	99.9
6.0	9.2	1.9	2.9	36.2	55.8	7.1	10.9	11.2	17.3	—	—	2.0	3.1	64.9	100.0
0.6	1.1	—	—	4.9	8.9	—	—	47.1	85.6	1.6	2.9	—	—	55.0	100.0
—	—	—	—	—	—	7.0	10.9	—	—	53.4	82.9	0.1	0.2	64.4	100.1
77.1	3.6	52.3	2.4	47.5	2.2	44.9	2.1	878.7	40.5	5.2	0.2	28.8	1.3	2,170.5	100.1
10.1	2.4	3.2	0.8	—	—	—	—	—	—	50.6	12.0	286.1ᶜ	67.9	421.4	100.0
34.3	39.3	2.1	2.4	5.9	6.8	2.2	2.5	—	—	—	—	2.0	2.3	87.3	100.0
—	—	—	—	—	—	9.5	9.2	—	—	49.7	48.1	30.3	29.3	103.4	100.2
2.7	5.4	—	—	—	—	29.9	59.6	—	—	15.6	31.1	1.8	3.6	50.2	100.1
70.8	75.7	—	—	—	—	—	—	—	—	0.3	0.3	22.4ᵈ	24.0	93.5	100.0
46.0	30.4	—	—	2.0	1.3	—	—	21.4	14.1	4.4	2.9	64.0ᵉ	42.3	151.4	100.0
1.8	12.2	1.0	6.8	1.0	6.8	—	—	1.0	6.8	7.8	53.1	—	—	14.7	100.0
368.6	8.2	166.6	3.7	231.7	5.1	500.0	11.1	1,085.5	24.0	482.1	10.7	490.7ᵍ	10.9	4,563.1 (4,517.8)ᶠ	100.0

and SDR certificates were $8.0 billion.
ᵉOf this amount, gold was $33.1 billion.
ᶠExcludes amount of currency and deposits held by commercial banks, since their holdings are chiefly claims on themselves (interbank deposits) or on Federal Reserve banks.
ᵍOf this amount, trade credit (accounts receivable) was $195.9 billion, interbank claims were $49.8 billion, and gold and foreign exchange were $44.4 billion (including gold held by monetary authorities throughout the world).

SOURCE: Flow of funds data, *Federal Reserve Bulletin*, June 1972.

loans, 29.7 percent in bonds, and 14.4 percent in mortgages. Institutions that are major holders of various types of financial assets are readily discerned in this table. As an example, note that the major purchasers of corporate bonds are life insurance companies, private pension funds, state and local government retirement funds, and households, while mutual savings banks, nonlife insurance companies, state and local governments, commercial banks, and foreigners are less important purchasers. As a second example, note that over 90 percent of all of the state and local government securities were held by commercial banks, nonlife insurance companies, and households. These and similar percentage distributions are the important information to be obtained, and these percentages change relatively little from year to year. Thus, the data for 1971 in the table may be considered as a guide to types and percentages of assets held by various institutions with little change in the absence of major reforms.

Deposit-Type Financial Institutions

Deposit-type financial institutions have liabilities that are very similar to the deposit liabilities of commercial banks. Time deposits in mutual savings banks have the same general characteristics as time deposits in commercial banks. Although some object to referring to accounts in savings and loan associations as "deposits," and prefer to term them "share accounts," the term deposits is found in the law in some states. Whether referred to as deposits or share accounts, they are similar to deposits in that they may be withdrawn on short notice (in practice, usually without notice, for the most common type of account). Amounts held in accounts do not vary in value except for the addition of interest or dividends from time to time. The term "fixed-value redeemable claims" has been used to refer to these financial assets, to emphasize these two characteristics. When viewed as assets held by the public, the liabilities of these institutions are characterized by a high degree of safety under present conditions, a high degree of liquidity (the fact that they can quickly be converted into money without loss in value), and a moderate rate of return. These assets (plus time deposits in commercial banks, in some views) have also been referred to as "near-monies," to emphasize that they are very close substitutes for money.[5]

It is clear that a shift from demand deposits to time deposits in a commercial bank, as in a transfer of funds from checking accounts to savings accounts, reduces the money supply if money is defined as M_1 (currency plus demand deposits) but does not change the money supply if money is defined as M_2 (currency plus demand deposits plus time deposits in commercial banks, other than large negotiable time certificates of deposit). A shift of funds from demand deposits in a commercial bank to accounts in deposit-type nonbank financial institutions does not change the size of the money supply, under either definition. Any funds shifted to these institutions in the form of checks or drafts are then deposited by these institutions in demand deposit accounts in commercial banks. Funds in the form of currency are also normally deposited if such funds increase currency holdings of the institutions to higher than desired levels, but the currency would be counted as part of the money supply regardless of where it is, as long as it is held by the public (all sectors except the government, the central bank, and the commercial banks).

Although such shifts do not necessarily cause any change in the money

---

[5]For the view that evidence indicates they are not very good substitutes, see, for example, E. L. Feige, *The Demand for Liquid Assets: A Temporal Cross-Section Analysis* (Englewood Cliffs, N.J.: Prentice-Hall, 1964); for the opposite view, see T. H. Lee, "Substitutability of Non-Bank Intermediary Liabilities for Money: The Empirical Evidence" *Journal of Finance*, September 1966, pp. 441–57.

supply, they do constitute dishoarding, or an increase in the velocity of money and thus an increase in the supply of loanable funds.[6] The hypothesis has been advanced that the growth of NBFIs, by resulting in an increase in the velocity of money, may affect spending and income. An important policy question thus emerges: is it necessary to control the size of the liabilities of deposit-type NBFIs, or will control of the size of the money supply (M_1 or M_2) suffice to control spending and income? Consideration of policies is deferred until later (Part V); at this point we may simply note that activities of deposit-type financial institutions do add significantly to the supply of loanable funds, or credit extended. We now turn to some characteristics of specific deposit-type financial institutions.

Mutual Savings Banks

Mutual savings banks date back to the early part of the nineteenth century, when civic-minded individuals wished to establish institutions to encourage thrift on the part of workers by providing safe depositories for small amounts saved. A mutual savings bank has been defined by the United States Supreme Court as

> . . . an institution in the hands of disinterested persons, the profits of which, after deducting the necessary expenses of conducting the business, inure wholly to the the benefit of the depositors, in dividends, or in a reserved surplus for their greater security.

The "disinterested persons" are trustees, who are self-appointed at the time of organization, and who perpetuate themselves by electing successors to fill vacancies. Large profits are not envisaged in organizing mutual savings banks. Few have been organized in recent years, although some have come into existence as a result of conversion of savings and loan associations into mutual savings banks.

Mutual savings banks are state-chartered and exist in only seventeen states and Puerto Rico. The states are largely in the northeastern part of the United States, although Washington, Oregon, and Alaska are western states in which mutual savings banks exist. Proposals for federal chartering of mutual savings banks have been made in several studies of the United States financial system. Because mutual savings banks and savings and loan associations specialize in real estate mortgage lending, it was felt that federal chartering and the possible resulting spread of mutual savings banks to states where they are not now established would strengthen the residential mortgage market and encourage competition between mutual savings banks and savings and loan associations in states where such competition cannot occur. It is also argued that, on grounds of equity, mutual savings banks should have the privilege of seeking either state or federal charter, as this privilege is available to commercial banks and to savings and loan associations.

Safety of deposits is evident in the historical record of mutual savings

---

[6]The increase in transactions velocity is clearly evident, as money is transferred; an increase in income velocity is probable, if the NBFIs lend the additional funds to borrowers who wish to spend.

banks. Only about 1½ percent of the total number of mutual savings banks in existence suspended operations in the four-year period 1930–33, whereas about 16 percent of the total number of commercial banks in operation at the beginning of 1930 suspended operations in that period. In spite of this excellent safety record, many mutual savings banks have joined the Federal Deposit Insurance Corporation, giving depositors the same protection as insured commercial banks give their depositors. Mutual savings banks in the state of New York organized a commercial bank, the Savings Bank Trust Company, to perform for the mutual savings banks in that state the central function of making loans to them in an emergency. The Savings Bank Trust Company can obtain emergency funds by borrowing from the Federal Reserve System because it is a member bank. Mutual savings banks in Massachusetts have created their own deposit insurance system. Thus about 90 percent of the total deposits in mutual savings banks are insured.

Liquidity of the deposits in mutual savings banks is supported by holdings of cash and government securities, by the ability of those mutual savings banks which are members of the Federal Reserve System to borrow from Federal Reserve Banks, and by other factors such as the regular inflow of amortization payments on mortgage loans.

Mortgage loans normally constitute about two-thirds of the total assets of mutual savings banks, as indicated in Table 5–2. Government and corporate bonds are of some importance in their asset portfolios, and small amounts of state and local government securities, stocks, consumer loans, and other assets are also held.

Savings and Loan Associations

Savings and loan associations, for some time called building and loan associations, date back to before the middle of the nineteenth century. They were originally intended to be associations pooling the funds of members in order to make mortgage loans to members; gradually a difference developed between the borrowing group and the saving group, and the institutions began to solicit savings from the general public. Savings and loan associations may now be either federally chartered or state-chartered. They are managed by boards of directors; the extent to which share account holders actively participate in election of directors varies. Federal savings and loan associations must be members of the Federal Savings and Loan Insurance Corporation rather than of the Federal Deposit Insurance Corporation. Maximum insured amounts and general insurance provisions are similar, but a commercial bank, having demand deposits, must close its doors immediately if it cannot meet depositors' requests for withdrawals. Savings and loan associations, on the other hand, could in the past go "on notice" for a time, and payments to share account holders could be delayed. In practice, this has not often occurred, and under present conditions it is quite unlikely; safety of deposits in a commercial bank and of share accounts in a savings and loan association seem comparable, if both are insured institutions.

Technically, a difference between mutual savings banks and savings and loan associations on the one hand and commercial banks on the other hand is that commercial banks are now almost all incorporated and have stockholders. With the exception of stock savings and loan associations, which exist in some states, savings and loan associations are owned by their depositors or share account holders.[7] A mutual savings bank is not technically owned by its depositors, but its surplus, in the event of its dissolution, would be divided among the depositors after payment of liabilities. Because of the legal status of savings and loan associations, payments to depositors or share accounts holders are legally termed dividends rather than interest in some references, but this technical distinction is largely ignored by the public.

Liquidity of savings and loan associations is provided by holdings of cash and government securities, and by their membership in the Federal Home Loan Bank System. Savings and loan associations that are members of the system may borrow from the Federal Home Loan Banks under specified conditions, just as commercial banks may borrow from Federal Reserve Banks.

Savings and loan associations have an even larger proportion of their assets in the form of mortgage loans than do mutual savings banks, over four-fifths. Although recent legislation has permitted them to diversify somewhat by allowing them to make certain types of consumer loans, the heavy concentration of assets of these two institutions in mortgage loans means that when flows of funds into these institutions are heavy, as in 1971–72, availability of funds for mortgage loans increases. When that flow is reduced, however, the mortgage market tightens, sometimes drastically.

Credit Unions

Credit unions date only from the early twentieth century. They are state- or federally chartered nonprofit cooperative institutions designed to provide credit to members. Members must have a common bond of some type—they must be employees of a given firm, members of a given profession (such as teaching), or in similar associations. The major differences between credit unions and the other institutions just discussed lie in this requirement of a bond of association among members of a credit union, and in the fact that most of the loans made by credit unions are consumer loans rather than mortgage loans.

Cost of operation of credit unions is low because in many cases some work is performed by volunteers and because office space and utility services are often provided by the employer of members of the union. Credit unions are in effect subsidized, to aid in providing credit to members who otherwise might have to pay high interest costs.

For most of the other deposit-type institutions, safety has been assured

---

[7]In early 1972, after almost a decade without any conversions, a federal mutual savings and loan association converted into a state-chartered stock savings and loan association, perhaps with the encouragement of the regulatory authority. Stock associations tend to be more aggressive than mutuals, making more construction and mobile home loans, more loans with high ratios of loan to value, and generally more profits, although they also at times incur sizable losses because of the types of loans they make. For an interesting discussion of recent efforts to stimulate changes that might result in longer-term liabilities and shorter-term assets for savings and loan associations, see Sanford Rose, "The S & Ls Break Out of Their Shell," *Fortune*, September 1972, pp. 152–70.

since the 1930s by deposit insurance, but until recently credit union accounts were not insured (although some credit unions obtained insurance through private agencies). It was recommended in the *Economic Report of the President*, 1956, that Congress "consider the desirability of establishing a self-supporting federal program of share-account insurance for credit unions." In 1970, this was finally implemented by the establishment of a national credit union insurance fund, following the establishment of the National Credit Union Administration as an independent agency. Accounts in federal credit unions are insured to a maximum of $20,000 per account, as bank deposits are, and accounts in state-chartered credit unions may be insured. Some states now require that any state-chartered credit unions that are not insured by the National Credit Union Administration (NCUA) must obtain state insurance.

On the asset side, credit unions compete with commercial banks (consumer loan departments), sales finance companies, personal finance (small loan) companies, and retailers in making loans to finance the purchase of automobiles or appliances, to repay other debts, to pay for medical services or other special expenses, such as those for vacations, or for other purposes.

Cash and government securities provide liquidity; credit unions also sometimes borrow from commercial banks to meet peak loan demand, and may do so to meet part of their liquidity needs.

In a sense, the credit union has two inconsistent goals: to pay high rates to its members who have credit union accounts, and to charge low rates to borrowers, who are part of the same group of people. Savings and loan associations had a similar inconsistency in goals in their early history, but they now aim at paying the highest return consistent with appropriate safety and liquidity to share account holders and do not now feel obligated to serve the interests of borrowers in keeping interest rates low, although this was once an important aim. The credit union is still presumably concerned both with paying high rates to account holders and with charging low rates to borrowers.

United States Savings Bonds

Although not an institution in the brick-and-mortar sense, United States savings bonds should be mentioned at this point because they serve the same purpose as the deposit-type institutions in meeting the desires of individuals for places to put funds with a high degree of safety and liquidity, moderate yield, and no fluctuation in price. They have sometimes been classified with deposits and savings and loan accounts as another form of fixed-value redeemable claim. The nature of the liability is somewhat different, however, because yields are lower if bonds are redeemed early, and the maximum yield is obtained only if the bonds are held to maturity. Relative yields have varied, and at times the yields on savings bonds have compared unfavorably with those paid by the deposit-type institutions, although yields were increased in the early 1970s.

Savings bonds are not marketable, and hence should be considered separately from most of the remainder of the national debt. In fact, one result of growth of the volume of savings bonds was the accumulation of an amount of government debt in nonmarketable form. If it can be assumed that those who buy savings bonds are generally not in the market for marketable government bonds, the result of the growth in the volume of savings bonds may have been a somewhat smaller volume of marketable bonds than would have been issued otherwise. The result is presumably higher prices and lower yields for marketable government securities.

When interest rates paid on savings bonds differ markedly from those paid by deposit-type institutions, shifts in funds occur because safety and liquidity are comparable.

Perhaps the most important issue concerning savings bonds is the question whether "constant purchasing power" bonds should be issued, as has been done in some countries. Commissions that have studied the financial system have recommended against this.[8] It has been argued that issuing such bonds would (1) single out a certain group for protection against the harmful effects of inflation, (2) tend to lead to acceptance of the inevitability of inflation, and (3) compete unfairly with other liquid assets. On the other hand, a number of economists have argued for the issuance of purchasing power bonds in order to provide the consumer sector with a hedge against inflation without incurring the risks involved in purchase of equity instruments. Issue of constant purchasing power bonds would be a significant step, since a major characteristic of the liabilities of commercial banks and of deposit-type institutions is that they do not rise in value as inflation occurs. Issue of purchasing power bonds would undoubtedly be followed by changes in characteristics of some other financial assets.

Contractual Savings Institutions

The contractual savings institutions, life insurance companies and pension funds, are characterized by a steady inflow of funds under contracts or agreements, in the form of insurance policies or pension fund agreements, which require policyholders and pension fund participants to pay regular premiums. Although failure to pay insurance policy premiums can result in cancellation of the insurance, there are relatively few instances of pension participants failing to make payments or insurance policyholders failing to pay their premiums. An exception occurred in the serious depression of the early 1930s. Thus a steady inflow of funds to the contractual saving institutions is guaranteed. Liquidity is not an important problem, although some degree of liquidity is maintained. The major problem is the investment of the large volume of funds received.

Moreover, both life insurance companies and pension funds are able to predict the payments they must make, in any given year, with a relatively high degree of accuracy, and these payments change only gradually from year to year. The growth of "variable annuities," still in its infancy, may

[8]See, for example, the *Report of the Commission on Money and Credit* (Englewood Cliffs, N.J.: Prentice-Hall, 1961), p. 107.

gradually change this situation, because variable annuities provide fluctuating benefits, depending on changing income and changing values of the assets in which the funds are invested. At present, however, both the inflow of funds and the amounts of payments to be made are closely predictable. Moreover, the rate of return guaranteed in insurance policies has been relatively low. Thus insurance companies have less need for a high rate of return than most of the other nonbank institutions.

Life Insurance Companies

The importance of life insurance companies in the money and capital markets arises largely from the fact that much of the insurance sold is in forms other than term insurance. Term insurance is in force for a specified term—one, five, or ten years—and, although often renewable at the end of the term, is not renewable at the same premium rate, but at a higher rate as the risk of death is greater. Premiums are sufficiently high to cover operating expenses of the insurance companies and to provide for an addition to their surpluses, for mutual companies, or dividends to the stockholders for stock life insurance companies, but they would not provide large sums for investment. Most insurance policies, however, are not term policies; they are "whole life" policies on which the same premium is paid until death, limited-payment life policies on which the same premium is paid for a limited term of years, endowment policies in which the same premium is paid for a limited term of years, at the end of which a face amount plus dividends and interest (if left to accumulate) are paid to policyholders. With constant premiums in these and other policies, the premiums must be high enough to meet average payments the companies must anticipate making over the lives of the policies. Thus for any of these policies, higher premiums during the early years provide substantial funds to be invested by the companies. Moreover, term insurance involves no return to those still alive at the end of the term, whereas many of the other types of policies provide for a return to policyholders at some point in time, at retirement age, for example, in the case of many endowment policies. Thus many life insurance policies combine an element of insurance (payment to beneficiaries in the event of death) with an element of saving (payment to the policyholder at some time in the future). Because, under these policies, payments are made at *some* point in time, to someone, policyholder or beneficiary, the life insurance companies must accumulate funds to make these payments. As long as the volume of policies sold exceeds the payments on matured policies, the insurance companies have an increase in funds available for financial investment.

Because guaranteed rates of return specified in insurance policies have been relatively low, insurance companies have generally not needed to seek extremely high rates of return. However, they need higher rates of return than the rates obtained by commercial banks on some of their liquid assets. Commercial banks have accepted low yields in some periods because of their need for liquidity. As life insurance companies need somewhat higher yields but have relatively little need for liquidity, they invest in long-term capital markets. Their investments have been largely in corporate bonds, government bonds, and mortgages, with a trend developing toward investment in common stocks. Some funds are invested in "municipal" securities issued by state and local governments. However, because mutual life insurance companies, which provided more than half of the insurance in force in 1971, are subject to relatively low rates of taxation, they are less interested in the tax-exempt feature of these securities than other groups of investors. During World War II, when government securities were plentiful, insurance companies invested rather heavily in them; then, in the postwar period, their holdings of such securities declined.

Insurance companies have used what is termed "direct placement" for much of their investment in corporate bonds, negotiating directly with the borrowing corporation for purchase of a large block of bonds. Because regular inflows of funds are expected, life insurance companies often make forward or future commitments for investment of substantial sums. Borrowers can avoid some underwriting and registration costs, and terms can be flexible, with special provisions agreed upon by both parties.

Insurance companies were legally restrained from investment in stocks for many years because it was believed that investments in stocks involved greater risks than investment in bonds. Recognition of the higher average yields on stocks and the growth of "variable annuities" has resulted in increased investment in stocks; laws have been liberalized somewhat to permit this.

More than one-third of all financial assets held by life insurance companies consists of mortgages. The largest portion of these are conventional, but a large part also consists of FHA-insured or VA-guaranteed mortgages. Because life insurance companies operate over wide territories and cannot have large offices in every local area, they frequently obtain mortgages by arranging with mortgage companies for purchase from those companies of groups or packages of mortgages, in sizable total amounts. Forward or future commitments of several months are usually made for such purchases, as they often are for purchases of directly placed bond issues. Mortgage companies usually know in advance when mortgages will be sold to insurance companies. Thus, some lag may be anticipated between the time of any change in mortgage rates or regulation and the effect of such change on purchases of mortgages by insurance companies.

Total assets of life insurance companies have grown more slowly since World War II than before that time. The slower growth may be attributed either to the fear that inflation reduces the value of insurance policies or to increased competition by other financial institutions. There has been somewhat more rapid growth in term insurance than in other forms, suggesting that some persons may be buying term insurance but investing the remainder of the funds that would otherwise be paid in higher premiums for other forms of insurance in another type of financial asset. Presumably the assets they invest in would, to some extent at least, provide some hedge against inflation.

Finally, mention should be made of policy loans as a financial asset. Most policyholders have clauses in their policies permitting them to borrow specified amounts at relatively low interest rates compared to rates on other consumer loans. At times, especially when other sources of consumer loans were limited, policyholders have turned in increasing numbers to their life insurance companies for loans. In 1966 and again in 1969, for example, periods of "credit crunches," this resulted in some reduction in the volume of funds available for investment by life insurance companies in the long-term capital markets.

Partly because of continued inflation, the growth of life insurance companies in the period since World War II has been somewhat lower than that of most other financial institutions. Policy benefit amounts are fixed when policies are purchased, and rates of return have not been increased. Thus when other institutions increased their interest rates, they became more attractive for the investment of funds by savers; financial assets that rose in price, such as stocks in the 1960s, were also attractive. Other causes of slower growth of insurance companies are the increased competition for consumers' savings by pension funds and by the required contributions for social security, which have risen sharply in recent years. Because social security benefits have also been increased and social security benefits are to be raised automatically when the consumer price index rises beginning in 1975, social security has perhaps had some favorable effect on life insurance companies. People who anticipate rising social security benefits may be more satisfied with fixed-amount insurance policies.

However, some insurance companies have begun to sell variable insurance policies, benefits rising if there are increases in the prices of equities in which some of the funds are invested. Early in 1973, the Securities and Exchange Commission exempted life insurance on a variable basis from regulation under the Investment Company Act. Such exemption makes it easier for life insurance companies to sell variable insurance policies. Because reserves are based on actuarial calculations and are only a fraction of the face values of the policies, a given percentage of capital gain on invested funds will provide a much smaller percentage of increase in the insurance benefit. Nevertheless, a $10,000 policy purchased in 1935 might have provided from $50,000 to $100,000 in 1972, instead of $10,000, depending on the particular company's policy provisions, if this type of insurance had been purchasable in 1935.[9] If sales of policies of this type increase, life insurance companies, which have been limited buyers of common stock, will become more important in the stock market.

It remains to be seen whether these and other developments will allow an increase in the rate of growth of insurance companies sufficient to maintain their total share in assets held by all financial institutions.

Pension Funds

Pension funds include the funds held by the Old Age, Survivors, Disability, and Health Insurance System (OASDHI, or social security) and by some federally supervised pension funds such as the Railroad Retirement fund and the Civil Service pension fund, corporate pension funds, and the employee retirement funds of state and local governments. Social security

[9]See *Fortune*, March 1973, pp. 51–56.

funds and the federally supervised pension funds are invested in special classes of government securities; this "locks up" a portion of the national debt and reduces the supply of marketable government securities below the levels it might otherwise reach, but in other respects these funds do not affect the capital markets. Primary attention may be given to the corporate pension funds and the employee retirement funds of state and local governments.

Corporate pension funds have become important recently—indeed, largely in the second half of the twentieth century, although some corporate pension funds began as early as World War I. Pension agreements usually provide for a pension of a certain number of dollars each month, often calculated as a multiple of the number of years worked, with variations. Although unions may negotiate for increases in pension amounts, once these are agreed upon the amounts of pension payments are fixed for a period of time. Because contributions are usually made by employers, sometimes solely by employers, and because payments are fixed until terms of the agreement change, it is in the interest of employers to obtain high rates of return on investment of pension funds, so that the same dollar amounts of pensions may be obtained with smaller contributions. As pension funds became more common, the desire for a higher rate of return led to some shift from the bonds most pension funds were first invested in, to stocks on which the combined return of dividends and capital exceeded the average rate of return on bonds.

Because accounting valuation of assets is discretionary and most funds carry assets at cost, fluctuations in market values of stock do not create difficulties. Because pension fund income is exempt from taxation, pension fund managers have little interest in tax-exempt securities.

Assets in pension funds grow over long periods because most of the employees who come under a newly formed pension plan are a number of years from retirement. For many years, contributions made by those who are employed exceed the payments of those who have retired. Moreover, inadequate provisions for "vesting" have meant that many employees who are discharged or who seek other employment lose their pension rights. Thus, pension funds generally can look forward to a long period of growth. Any legislative or other encouragement that would make possible the growth of funds in areas not now generally covered would obviously lead to further growth of total pension fund assets for some period of time. The major area for such growth is that of medium-sized and small business firms.

Many corporate pension funds are managed by trust departments of banks, some by corporations themselves, and some by life insurance companies. Pension funds constitute over 35 percent of the assets of the trust departments of banks, and about 60 percent of this amount is invested in common stocks.[10] There is intense competition among financial institutions for the business of management of these large sums.

State and local government employees retirement funds, in contrast to corporate pension funds, are hedged about by restrictions, and, when re-

[10]Edna E. Ehrlich, "The Functions and Investment Policies of Personal Trust Departments," Federal Reserve Bank of New York, *Monthly Review*, October 1972, pp. 255–70.

strictions are not limiting, the asset portfolio depends on the sophistication of the investment officer. In many jurisdictions his investment training may be very limited. Hence it is not surprising that until recently most of the funds were invested in state and local government and United States government securities.

The chief importance of the contractual saving institutions, both the life insurance companies and the pension funds, is that they are an important conduit through which savings regularly flow into designated parts of the money and capital markets. Although growth rates may change over time, there usually are not wide fluctuations in the inflow of funds, as there have been among the deposit-type institutions. Unlike the deposit-type financial institutions, insurance companies are usually not important in attracting increased funds at certain times; thus insurance companies are generally not important in their effects on the velocity of money.

Property and Casualty Insurance Companies

Property and casualty insurance companies are quite different in their investment policies from life insurance companies and pension funds, but they are discussed here to complete the coverage of insurance companies. Payments that have to be made by such companies are not nearly as easily predictable as those of life insurance companies; if inflation occurs, many payments of property and casualty insurance companies rise because costs of repairs and replacements are greater. Hence property and casualty insurance companies have both a greater need for liquidity and a greater need for higher return than life insurance companies, leading them to invest in government securities for liquidity and in stocks for higher return. Because many of them are stock companies, subject to the regular corporate income tax, they also invest in municipal securities because of the tax-exempt feature. Property and casualty insurance companies invest rather heavily in stocks. When stock market values rise, dividend yields *appear* to decline.[11] Nevertheless, net investment income provides a supplement to net underwriting income (premiums minus underwriting expenses and loss claims paid). In recent years, when net underwriting income has been negative (losses), net investment income has allowed the companies to continue to show profits.

Investment-Type Institutions

The major investment-type institutions include mutual funds, sometimes referred to as "investment companies," and personal and common trust funds managed by trust departments of commercial banks. Specified commitments are agreed upon for payments of income from these funds to beneficiaries, although some mutual funds provide for automatic reinvestment of dividends and capital gains distributions.

Mutual funds regularly sell shares to investors and invest the funds in

[11]Net yields before taxes are relatively low because of the relatively large investments in tax-exempt securities, which have low yields.

stocks. Their advantages to small investors are that they permit diversification, not possible in direct investment of small amounts in individual stocks, and that they may provide more expert management than small investors could generally give to their own portfolios of stocks. Mutual funds grew rapidly after World War II, as stock prices generally rose. Since the market decline of 1969–70, however, mutual funds have experienced excesses of redemptions of shares over new sales. Emphasis on performance—substantial short-term capital gains—in the 1960s led some mutual funds to engage in rapid turnover of stocks held in their portfolios and thus may have contributed to the volatility of the market. The fact that mutual funds concentrated attention on a limited number of favorite stocks may also have caused the prices of such stocks to rise more than would otherwise have been the case. There is disagreement concerning both the effect of mutual funds on volatility of stock prices and the management expertise of mutual funds. Such questions are outside the scope of this book, but the attitude of investors toward mutual funds will be an important factor affecting stock prices. If investors are hesitant to buy mutual fund shares and instead place their funds in other financial institutions, stock prices may remain lower in relation to earnings than they were in the 1960s. Much depends on to what extent investors feel a need to invest in assets that can raise in price, in order to hedge against inflation. Such factors will affect both the rates of growth of various financial institutions and the money and capital markets individuals and institutions supply funds to.

Closed-end investment companies are a special type; they issue shares that are not redeemable; new shares are not sold regularly. Thus for considerable periods of time, no new shares may be sold, whereas mutual funds regularly sell new shares and endeavor to expand. Closed-end investment companies offer the possibility of leverage: investors may obtain higher returns because the fund issues debt instruments, such as debentures, as well as capital shares. Purchasers of capital shares may obtain higher returns if returns on assets funds are invested in are higher than interest rates that must be paid on the debentures. A number of closed-end investment companies were organized before the stock market crash of 1929; their shares have continuously sold at discount in recent years. Thus there is little incentive to form new companies, and closed-end investment companies may continue to be an investment medium for only a small group of investors.

A special type of closed-end investment company, first formed in the United States in 1967, is termed a "dual-purpose" fund. Each fund's portfolio is divided equally into (1) investments made for investors who want income and who have purchased income shares (half of the total shares issued), and (2) investments made for investors who want capital gain, and who have purchased the other half of the total shares issued. Investors who purchase income shares receive all of the dividends on all shares. Investors who want capital gains receive all of the capital gains, which are reinvested instead of being paid out. The funds have specified terminal dates, on which income shares are redeemed at prices specified when the shares were issued. If dividends fall short of guaranteed amounts, the difference is made up; all remaining assets then are divided among the capital gains shareholders. Like other closed-end investment company shares, dual-purpose fund shares have sold at discounts most of the time. Discounts on capital gains shares have been greater than discounts on income shares, but even holders of income shares, if they sold their shares, found their effective yields reduced by discounts. Discounts on income shares have been caused by the rise in most interest rates since the shares were issued, making other interest yields more attractive. Discounts on capital gains shares are caused by declines in stock market prices, by brokers' lack of interest in selling shares of dual-purpose funds because their commissions on such sales are less than on sales of mutual funds, and by adjustment for taxes that must at some point be paid on currently unrealized capital gains. Discounts may also be caused by the fact that, because leverage exists on account of the fixed rates to be paid on the income shares, there is greater risk; leverage means greater returns for the capital gains shareholders if total returns are higher than the yield rates promised on the income shares, but it also means smaller returns for the capital gains shareholders if total returns are less than the promised income share yield rates. To compensate for the risk involved in this leverage, purchasers of shares in dual-purpose funds offer lower prices for them, creating the discounts.[12]

Personal trust funds managed by trust departments of banks are highly safety-oriented, preservation of capital being a major goal. One general guideline for investments in many states is the "prudent man rule," which specifies that managers of trusts must invest "only in such securities as would be acquired by prudent men of discretion and intelligence in such matters who are seeking a reasonable income and the preservation of their capital." There is wide leeway for interpretation of this rule. Most of the funds are invested in common stocks (about two-thirds), corporate bonds (about 15 percent),[13] government securities, state and local government securities, and real estate and real estate mortgages (a little over 5 percent in each category).

Both the contractual saving institutions and the investment-type institutions have a dual importance in the capital markets: they are important because of the inflows of funds to them, which they largely invest in long-term assets; and they are important as holders and managers of large amounts of wealth. Markets for long-term financial assets involve purchases and sales in amounts that, in any given year, are small fractions of the total held by individuals and institutions. Although individuals still hold a majority of the total value of all stocks, individuals as a group have been net sellers for a number of years. Because of this selling pressure, prices of stocks would tend to fall if they were not purchased in sizable amounts by institutions such as pension funds, personal trust funds, and mutual funds. The existence of such institutions provides a substantial demand for stocks, and thus generally has helped stock prices to rise over long periods of time, in spite of temporary declines. Moreover, if corporations had to attract individual investors in larger numbers, they might well have to pay out more funds in dividends.

---

[12]See *Fortune*, April 1973, pp. 25–27.

[13]Corporate bonds constitute a significant percentage of total assets held by trust departments because of their importance in pension funds managed by these departments.

Purchases of stocks by institutions that desire both dividends and capital gains, and for whom capital gains are relatively attractive when the institutions are growing in size, permits corporations to retain large amounts of earnings, rather than seeking a flow of funds for investment financed by sales of newly issued securities in the capital markets.

Investment-type institutions, like contractual saving institutions, have rather long investment horizons. Since their inflows of funds usually exceed their outpayments because they are growing, they need not be concerned about sale of stocks or bonds on account of temporary needs for funds. Temporary fluctuations in values of stocks and bonds can be overlooked. If long-run prospects for higher values for stocks look bright, such institutions can continue to buy and hold them, whereas individuals and institutions with shorter investment time horizons are more concerned about short-term price fluctuations.

Thus the investment-type financial institutions are important participants in the capital markets. They provide funds that have helped maintain the general long-term rise in stock prices, and they make it possible for corporations to retain large amounts of earnings for use in investment.

Finance Companies

Finance companies include three types of institutions: sales finance companies, which finance purchases of automobiles and other durable goods on the installment plan; consumer finance of small loan companies, which specialize in making small loans to consumers; and business or commercial finance companies, which specialize in loans to business firms, usually loans that could not be obtained from commercial banks because banks regard the risks as higher than they wish to incur at the rates of interest they are permitted to charge. Finance companies have a quite different liability and capital structure from that of other financial institutions. Unlike banks and other deposit-type institutions, they have a relatively large proportion of equity capital, averaging about one-third of their total funds. To obtain the rest of the funds they need, they borrow in the short-term money market and in the long-term capital market, by obtaining bank loans and by issuing commercial paper (promissory notes) and debentures (bonds not secured by specific assets). A large part of the outstanding commercial paper has been issued by finance companies; often they place this commercial paper directly with institutions such as life insurance companies and banks. Life insurance companies need *some* liquid assets, and banks often wish to invest some funds in commercial paper because of its unusually high degree of safety and high liquidity.[14] Commercial paper is not renewed at maturity, and its maturity is relatively short—never more than 270 days, because longer maturity would

---

[14]It was most unusual, in 1970, that the Penn Central Transportation Co. had $82 million in commercial paper outstanding when the Penn Central went into bankruptcy, because prior to that time there had been almost no defaults on commercial paper since 1936. For an interesting story of the 1970 crisis and how it was met, see Carol J. Loomis, "The Lesson of the Credit Crisis," *Fortune*, May 1971, pp. 141–43; 274–86.

necessitate its issue in compliance with the rather burdensome regulations governing the issuing of long-term securities. Liquidity results from the short maturity, often tailored to investors' desires, although there is some repurchase of commercial paper by issuers, which provides some additional degree of liquidity.

Finance companies, because they borrow in both the short-term money market and the long-term capital market, provide one of the links between these markets, and are thus important in the relationship between long-term and short-term interest rates.

With the exception of business finance companies, which provide short-term business credit, finance company funds go into consumer finance. Thus, sales finance companies and personal finance companies compete with the consumer loan departments of commercial banks and credit unions. They assist nonfinancial institutions such as retailers in extending consumer credit for the purchase of goods and services. Utilities and professional men such as doctors and dentists are other sources of consumer credit.

Miscellaneous

The most important group of financial institutions not previously discussed is one that originated as government agencies, many of which are now privately owned but still subject to some government control. Other miscellaneous financial institutions include investment (brokerage) houses and pawnshops. Investment houses aid in the sale of corporate securities by acting as brokers for customers and/or by aiding in the underwriting and distribution of new issues of such securities; they extend some credit to consumers in the form of brokers' loans on margin accounts for purchase of stocks and bonds, and they receive some credit from consumers in the form of idle customers' balances. The government and quasi-government agencies are largely in the fields of credit for housing and agriculture; the government has entered the field of business credit only in a limited way, the chief agencies being the Small Business Administration for credit to small business firms, and the Export-Import Bank for credit to finance exports (and, theoretically, imports).

The first government institutions were established in agriculture; the Federal Land Banks were organized to provide agricultural mortgage credit. Much later Federal Intermediate Credit Banks and Production Credit Associations were formed.

In the field of housing, the first significant effort of the government was directed toward insurance of mortgage loans, to encourage private lending institutions to make such loans. The insurance and guarantee programs of the Federal Housing Administration (FHA) and the Veterans Administration (VA) have significantly aided the mortgage market. The government also established agencies to provide housing for low-income groups; the Public Housing Administration (PHA) and the Farmers' Home Administration are evidence of the government interest in subsidizing such housing. The Rural Electrification Administration (REA) was very important in subsidizing the distribution of electricity. Finally, a group of agencies have been created to aid in developing a secondary market for mortgages—the Federal National Mortgage Association (FNMA, or Fanny Mae), the Government National Mortgage Association (GNMA, or Ginny Mae), and the Federal Home Loan Mortgage Corporation (Freddy Mac).

The historical details of the establishment of these and other agencies are not of great interest, but the existence of a number of privately owned agencies that were formerly government agencies is significant in the money and capital markets. Securities of these agencies compete with Treasury securities and private securities, and some significant effects in yield fluctuations result from such competition. The fact that most of these agencies (those that are privately owned) are not now included in the federal government budget removes them from scrutiny when the budget is being curtailed—in effect influencing the flow of funds into the housing and agricultural credit fields.

SUMMARY

Nonbank financial institutions may be described and classified in such a way as to group together those with significant similarities in types of liabilities, those that have similarities in the nature of the flow of funds they receive, and those that most directly compete with each other.

Deposit-type financial institutions have demand or short-term liabilities and fluctuating inflows of funds; they compete directly for savings to be held in liquid form with a high degree of safety.

Contractual saving institutions have long-term liabilities and quite regular inflows of funds under contractual arrangements.

Investment-type institutions have generally long-term liabilities and place their funds in long-term financial assets such as stocks, bonds, and real estate.

Finance companies have both long-term liabilities in the form of debentures and short-term liabilities in the form of bank borrowings and commercial paper. They are able to shift funds from short-term to long-term investment and vice versa.

Finally, the most important miscellaneous institutions are the government-sponsored agencies that were established to aid in granting credit, especially in the fields of housing and agriculture, in situations where it was believed that private credit was inadequate.

QUESTIONS FOR DISCUSSION

1. Cite reasons for classifying deposit-type financial institutions in one group. What similarities do they have other than the short-term character of their liabilities?

2. Is deposit or share-account insurance equally needed for deposits in commercial banks, deposit in mutual savings banks, share accounts in savings and loan associations, and accounts in credit unions? Why or why not?

3. Why do commercial banks invest such small amounts of funds in corporate bonds?

4. Why do savings and loan associations invest almost no funds in corporate bonds?

5. Why is there no change in the size of the money supply (M_1) when funds are shifted from demand deposit accounts in commercial banks to accounts in or claims on nonbank financial institutions?

6. What are the arguments for permitting federal charters for mutual savings banks? Are there any arguments against this change?

7. Would you expect life insurance companies to grow as rapidly in the next decade as commercial banks or nonbank deposit-type institutions? Why or why not?

8. What factors may permit greater growth of private pension funds in the next decade, and what factors may tend to restrict such growth?

9. Why are finance companies such important issuers of commercial paper? What factors may tend to affect the rate of growth of commercial paper in the next decade?

10. Why did government sponsored financial institutions become important in the fields of agriculture and housing?

SELECTED REFERENCES

Financial institutions discussed in this chapter are described in more detail in a number of books; mention may be made of the books by Ludtke and by Jacobs, Farwell, and Neave, listed at the end of Chapter 1.

Statistics concerning growth of major financial institutions may be found in the *Federal Reserve Bulletin*, the *Life Insurance Fact Book* (annual), in the *Savings and Loan Fact Book* (annual), in the *International Credit Union Yearbook* (annual), and in the *Finance Facts Yearbook* (annual, published by the National Consumer Finance Association). The *NCUA Quarterly*, published by the National Credit Union Administration, provides more current information on credit unions, and the *Journal* published by the Federal Home Loan Bank Board provides current information monthly on housing finance institutions.

An extensive discussion of the growth of savings and loan associations is that of Arnold W. Sametz, ed., *Cyclical and Growth Problems Facing the Savings and Loan Industry—Policy Implications and Suggested Reforms*, New York University Institute of Finance, *The Bulletin*, Nos. 46–47, March 1968.

Many useful analytical studies are found in the proceedings of the *Conference on Savings and Residential Financing*, published annually by the United States Savings and Loan League from 1958 through 1970.

An interesting history of various types of financial intermediaries is that of Herman E. Krooss and Martin R. Blyn, *A History of Financial Intermediaries* (New York: Random House, 1971).

Information on personal trust funds is available in Edna E. Ehrlich, "The Functions and Investment Policies of Personal Trust Departments," Federal Reserve Bank of New York, *Monthly Review*, October 1972, pp. 255–70 and January 1973, pp. 12–19.

For a comprehensive study of mutual funds, see Irwin Friend, Marshall Blume, and Jean Crockett, *Mutual Funds and Other Institutional Investors: A New Perspective* (New York: McGraw-Hill, 1970).

A historical study of mutual savings banks is that of Weldon Welfling, *Mutual Savings Banks: The Evolution of a Financial Intermediary* (Cleveland, Ohio: Case Western Reserve University Press, 1968).

Analytical materials on credit unions are relatively scarce, but see John T. Croteau, *The Economics of the Credit Union* (Detroit: Wayne State University Press, 1963).

6

Some Current Issues Concerning Financial Institutions

Many questions concerning banks and nonbank financial institutions could be discussed, but this chapter is limited to five issues currently of considerable interest: (1) the uniqueness of commercial banks, (2) competition among financial institutions, (3) the problem of handling payments and records of payments, (4) the effect of the growth of financial institutions on saving, and (5) the appropriate place of government lending and government lending agencies.

THE UNIQUENESS OF COMMERCIAL BANKS

Textbooks vary in the degree of importance they assign to the uniqueness of commercial banks. Many discuss only commercial banks, thus leading readers to infer that other institutions are of little importance; some, on the other hand, deemphasize the uniqueness of commercial banks, stating that the line of demarcation between commercial banks and other financial institutions is less distinct than might be assumed.

The uniqueness of commercial banks may be evaluated on the basis of answers to three related questions: (1) Do banks alone, and no other financial institutions, create money? (2) Once money has been created, is it true that the nonbank public has no means of reducing or increasing the money stock? and (3) Do commercial banks have a greater effect on spending and velocity of money than other institutions? If so, whether or not their money-creating power is unique, they may be sufficiently more important than other institutions in the financial process of spending, lending, and income creation to be regarded as unique.

The Issue of Money Creation

Whether commercial banks alone create money depends upon one's definition of money. Because most economists define money as either M_1 (currency plus demand deposits) or M_2 (currency plus demand deposits plus time deposits in commercial banks, excluding large negotiable certificates of deposit), it is clear that among private financial institutions commercial banks, and only commercial banks, can create money.

The strongest position in opposition to this view was taken by the authors of the British Radcliffe Report; they argued that in the long run of economic development, what has been regarded as money has changed. Moreover, they argued that what is important is not the amount of the money supply, but the degree of liquidity in an economy, because the degree of liquidity determines the extent of spending. Spending may occur, they pointed out, not only because people hold money, but because they have other liquid assets—and even because they have assurance that, up to certain limits, they can borrow.

The view expressed in the Radcliffe Report is not widely held among economists at present, because such a view leads to general reluctance to assign importance to any specific group of assets that may be labeled as money. Yet the importance of the money supply—whether defined as M_1, M_2, or M_3—has been substantiated in a sufficiently large number of studies that it must be concluded that money has special significance. In most studies, the definition of money has been either M_1 or M_2; hence, it may be concluded that commercial banks have unique importance in their ability to create money. That the line of demarcation between commercial banks and some other financial institutions might be changed in the future by legislative and institutional changes does not alter the present significance of the classification.

The "Hot Potato" Issue

A second aspect of the argument is the contention that once banks have created money, the public cannot reduce the stock of money. Money is like a "hot potato," shifted from one party to another. It is of course recognized that the public can shift demand deposits into time deposits, thus reducing M_1 but at the same time increasing the time deposit component of M_2 (thus leaving total M_2 unchanged. But except for this, some argue, the public cannot significantly change the size of the money stock. An element of truth in this argument must be recognized: transfer of funds to savings and loan associations, or other NBFIs, does *not* reduce demand deposits; it merely transfers their ownership to NBFIs. Shifts from demand deposits into currency (or vice versa) change the *form*, not the size, of the money stock. This is easily understood if it is assumed that the person wishing to transfer funds from his demand deposit account to a savings and loan account does so by writing a check and depositing the check in the savings and loan association. That institution sends the check for payment to the bank, and accepts payment in the form of an increase in its own deposit account in the bank. If the transfer is made in currency, it may be assumed that additional currency would not be held by the savings and loan association but would be deposited in its account in a bank.[1] Moreover, it must be noted that more saving means less consumption, not necessarily any change in the stock of money; in fact, saving is usually temporarily embodied in money holdings, but then is transferred to other assets—thus transferring the ownership of the money to others, but not changing the money stock held by the public.

Is it, then, correct to argue that the public has little or no control over the size of the money stock? Some economists have proposed a "new view." They argue that if the public prefers other financial assets such as corporate or government bonds to money, they will bid up the prices on such assets. As yields decline, banks may find it necessary to reduce their asset holdings because assets may not yield enough to cover costs. Thus, banks would reduce the money stock by reducing demand deposits as their assets declined.

In an extreme example, the argument that the public could induce a decline in the money stock might be correct; but it must be recognized that this is not likely to occur. Although actions of the public *can* cause banks to reduce the money supply, banks are not likely to do so. This is illustrated by the fact that in recent recessions banks have not reduced the money stock. When business and consumer loans declined, they substituted mortgage loans and investment in government securities, thus maintaining their asset portfolios and their deposits at approximately the same levels as before. We conclude that under most conditions the public has relatively little direct influence on the size of the money supply, especially if it is defined as M_2; if it is defined as M_1, the public can influence its size by shifting from demand deposits to time deposits and vice versa. Indirect influence exists, of course, through the effect actions of the public may have on the money multiplier, as explained in Chapter 4.

The Issue of Degree of Effect on Spending

Do commercial banks have a greater effect on spending than other financial institutions?[2] If bank reserve requirements are reduced, banks can make loans (or add to their investments) and thus expand credit. But when they expand loans, banks do not as a group lose reserves; they simply create deposits. NBFIs, on the other hand, *do* lose reserves, at least initially, when

[1] A qualification must of course be made to the extent that withdrawals of currency reduce bank reserves and thus may reduce the amount of money that *can be* created by banks. At present, anticipated seasonal withdrawals of currency are usually met by central bank actions to provide additional reserves to the banks.

[2] For a more detailed discussion than is possible in this text, see Jack Guttentag and Robert Lindsay, "The Uniqueness of Commercial Banks," *Journal of Political Economy*, September–October 1968, pp. 991–1014.

they make loans. NBFI reserves are held in cash on hand and deposits in commercial banks. When NBFIs make loans, they transfer title to deposits, which they held, to borrowers or designated payees. Thus, the initial effect of loans is a loss of reserves. Subsequently, the public may decide to hold additional amounts in share accounts and other forms in NBFIs; but these decisions depend upon the attractiveness of such financial assets, whereas, except for amounts withdrawn in the form of currency, both borrowers from commercial banks and those to whom such borrowers make payments continue to hold money.

A reduction in bank reserve requirements—or an increase in bank reserves as a result of open market operations by the Federal Reserve System—permits additional credit and money creation by banks. If the public then shifts funds to savings and loan associations, for example, to restore the previous ratio of savings and loan account holdings to demand deposit holdings, it permits additional credit creation by the savings and loan associations. But now assume that savings and loan associations have reserve requirements and that these are reduced. Additional credit creation by the savings and loan associations is then possible. But this does not lead to any further credit creation by banks. Borrowers receive title to deposits in commercial banks, and transfer such title to those to whom they make payments. Velocity of money increases, but there is no reason to anticipate a change in the size of the money stock. Even if the amount of share accounts in savings and loan associations was much larger than the amount of demand deposits in banks, the credit creation by banks *and* by savings and loan associations, resulting from a reduction in reserve requirements for banks, would be larger than the credit creation by savings and loan associations *alone*, resulting from a reduction in reserve requirements for savings and loan associations. Of course, the larger the NBFIs become, the less important the difference is, for the ratio of bank credit creation plus NBFI credit creation to NBFI credit creation alone will fall as the importance of NBFIs increases.[3] But the principle remains—banks have a greater importance for credit creation than NBFIs, as long as NBFIs keep deposits in banks as a major part of their reserves and such bank deposits are money—means of settlement of debts exchanged among sectors of the public, including the NBFI sector, but usually neither increased nor decreased in amount by such exchange.

This conclusion hinges on the fact that NBFIs hold reserves largely in the form of deposits in commercial banks, and these deposits are payments media for them as well as for the general public. Thus the foundation of the greater importance of commercial banks in credit creation is the special status of banks resulting from the practice of using money (and only money) for *final* settlement of debts.

[3]Thus if the ratio of deposits in deposit-type NBFIs to total deposits (demand plus time) in banks were 1:1 (fairly close to the present ratio), bank credit creation plus NBFI credit creation would be about ten times as great as NBFI credit creation alone, on the basis of the same percentage reduction in reserve requirements for both types of institutions. If the ratio were 10:1, bank credit creation plus NBFI credit creation would be about twice as great as NBFI credit creation alone.

COMPETITION AMONG FINANCIAL INSTITUTIONS

Even those who emphasize the uniqueness of commercial banks do not deny that commercial banks compete with other financial institutions, especially the nonbank deposit-type institutions. Competition occurs both in efforts to attract funds of savers and in the investment of such funds. Effects of this and other competition among financial institutions may be viewed from the perspective of the institutions themselves, the effects on velocity of money and total spending, and the effects on various types of loans and spending.

Competition among Deposit-Type Institutions

Competition among deposit-type institutions has been widely discussed. Liabilities of all institutions in this group are held as liquid assets by the public, and characteristics of the various assets are sufficiently similar to induce shifts from one to another with changes in yields.

Recent Competitive Trends

In the 1950s, growth of savings and loan associations was relatively rapid, and some concern was expressed over the competition of these institutions with commercial banks. Growth of savings and loan associations in this period was more rapid than that of commercial banks, in part because slow growth of the money supply (a result of Federal Reserve policy) did not permit rapid growth of demand deposits of banks. In part, however, the slower growth of commercial banks occurred because they did not take sufficient initiative in seeking new sources of funds in additional time deposits and other forms. In the 1960s, the position was reversed; commercial banks entered a period of rapid growth as they were permitted to raise interest rates paid on time deposits, and they actively sought and attracted large amounts of deposit funds plus nondeposit funds obtained by borrowing.

In this competition, commercial banks have one major advantage and several small disadvantages. Their major advantage is that they need not pay as high a rate of interest (by about ¾ percent, according to one study)[4] as savings and loan associations. Their disadvantages which are less significant, include the following: (1) They must keep slightly more funds in nonearning assets as reserves. (2) They may have a slight disadvantage in net return on loans because savings and loan associations specialize in higher-interest conventional mortgage loans, and they have a disadvantage because they must pay somewhat higher rates of income tax than savings and loan associations. (3) They must pay a return to stockholders, which mutual savings and loan associations need not do. Both types of institutions must, of course, add to capital accounts as their deposits and share account liabilities grow, in order

[4]Jack R. Vernon, "Competition for Savings Deposits: The Recent Experience," *National Banking Review*, December 1966, pp. 183–92.

to maintain an appropriate capital/deposit ratio or capital/share account ratio.

Although total commercial bank profits rose in the 1960s, commercial bank profit margins narrowed as higher marginal costs were incurred when rates of interest paid on time deposits rose. The average "spread" between rates paid by savings and loan associations and those paid by banks fell from 1½ percent or more in the early 1950s to about ½ percent in the mid-1960s, while the ratio of bank net income to bank capital accounts—a measure of the rate of total profit on capital—did not fall significantly. This reduction in interest rate spread led to a rapid rise in savings accounts in commercial banks; from the end of 1965 to the end of 1971, household savings accounts in commercial banks nearly doubled, while household share accounts and deposits in savings and loan associations and mutual savings banks increased by only about 60 percent. Concern over welfare of the commercial banks in the 1950s was replaced by concern over the welfare of the nonbank deposit-type institutions in the late 1960s and again in 1973. In view of this situation, the time never seemed ripe for complete removal of the ceilings on interest rates paid on commercial bank time deposits; in fact, in 1966, when money was "tight," Congress extended interest rate ceilings to the savings and loan associations and mutual savings banks. However, regulations permitted the thrift institutions to pay higher interest rates than those which could be paid on savings accounts held by commercial banks. In 1966 and 1969, the gap between market instruments such as bonds and the ceiling rates on time deposits widened to such an extent that both commercial banks and thrift institutions were "disintermediated." Both suffered sharp reductions in the inflow of savings. The thrift institutions were especially hard hit; they were caught in a profit squeeze because of the nature of the maturity structure of their portfolios. As short-term rates rose relative to long-term rates, the cost of obtaining new savings exceeded the return on new assets including mortgages. Furthermore, higher costs in the form of higher rates on savings accounts applied to most of their liabilities, whereas earnings on assets were lower because of lower rates on mortgage loans still held, which had been made at lower rates. As earnings failed to keep pace with rising costs, the income position of thrift institutions was adversely affected. This development was a major factor in the changing competitive position of commercial banks vis-a-vis savings and loan associations in the late 1960s. Although banks lost savings, their income was not so adversely affected because earnings on many assets rose with the general upward shift in interest rates.

Competition and the Effectiveness of Monetary Control

Concern over the competitive position of the different institutions is not the only reason for examining the competition in this field. There is also concern that nonbank deposit-type institutions, by attracting funds from commercial banks, might expand credit even when monetary policy was restrictive on commercial banks. Gradual long-run growth did not give rise to concern, as this could be allowed for in policy decisions; the concern was that cyclical fluctuations might create a problem.[5]

Evidence in the studies of Milton Friedman and others that velocity of money generally rose when the money supply increased and fell when the money supply declined, in cyclical fluctuations, threw some doubt on whether changes resulting from shifts of funds to and from nonbank financial institutions might change velocity in a direction contrary to that desired for monetary policy.[6] The possibility was still open that control of bank credit might not be sufficient to control credit expansion by the nonbank deposit-type institutions, or that, if it were, restraint on bank credit might have to be unduly restrictive. Some argued, however, that the commercial banks, as shown above, contribute far more to changes in velocity than do the nonbank financial institutions because of commercial bank shifts from investments—which may involve purchase of existing securities and hence no rise in income velocity of money—to loans—which provide funds for the purchase of goods and services, and hence, usually a rise in income velocity. Moreover, in the credit crunches of 1966 and 1969, it became evident that the nonbank deposit-type institutions might suffer much more than the commercial banks when tight monetary policy caused interest rates to rise sharply. Thus concern over control of the nonbank deposit-type institutions diminished. The gradual rise in income velocity of money since 1960, and the more rapid rise in periods of rising business activity (1961–66 and 1971–73) is shown in Figure 6–1.

Proposals to Permit Increased Competition

Concern over competitive advantages of nonbank deposit-type institutions, which had been significant in the 1950s, shifted to concern whether

---

[5]This problem was emphasized in the writings of John G. Gurley and Edward S. Shaw (see, for example, *Money in a Theory of Finance*, Washington, D.C., The Brookings Institution, 1960), although it is not clear to what extent they concurred in the policy recommendation that could be inferred—that nonbank financial institutions as well as commercial banks should be subject to controls by the monetary policy authorities.

[6]Friedman found that in the period prior to World War II, when the trend of velocity was downward, velocity sometimes declined both in recovery phases and in declining phases of business activity. However, since World War II velocity has increased in periods of business expansion, and declined slightly in recessions. Since periods of business expansion have been longer than periods of recession, the trend of velocity has been upward. These empirical data are not in dispute. There are, however, different interpretations. Friedman's interpretation is given in Milton Friedman and Anna J. Schwartz, "Money and Business Cycles," *Review of Economics and Statistics*, February 1963, Supplement. They argue that demand for money rises when business activity increases, but not as much as current income. Henry Latané has argued that the rise in velocity is caused to a much greater extent by changes in interest rates. Rising interest rates cause the public to minimize money holdings in order to obtain higher-interest income. Since Friedman defines money as M_2 (as explained in Chapter 4), while Latané defines it as M_1, their views do not necessarily conflict greatly. M_2 includes time deposits in commercial banks, which earn interest; hence M_2 may rise either because people wish to hold more money (M_2) in periods of rising business activity, or because people wish to economize on money (M_1) but hold more time deposits.

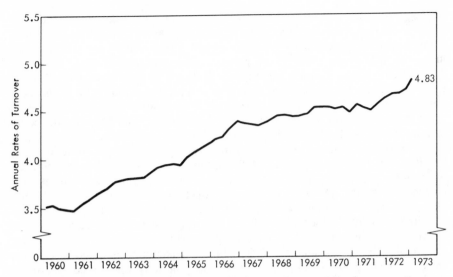

Annual rates of turnover computed with quarterly GNP (current dollars) at seasonally adjusted annual rates, and seasonally adjusted monthly averages of daily money stock. Latest data plotted: 1st quarter 1973.

FIGURE 6–1   Income Velocity of Money (GNP/Money Stock)

SOURCE: The Federal Reserve Bank of St. Louis.

they would be able to compete effectively with the commercial banks, as well as to the question of their ability to meet outflows of funds caused by "tight money" conditions. In 1970, the Hunt commission appointed by the President and mentioned briefly in Chapter 3 began a study of changes in the private financial system that might be necessary to maintain and extend effective competition. Unlike the report of the Commission on Money and Credit, issued in 1961, the Hunt Commission report, completed and issued in 1971, did not consider the problem of goals, monetary and fiscal policies, and international relations, but focused almost entirely on the private financial system.

The major thrust of a number of proposals in the Hunt Commission report is to permit greater competition between deposit-type nonbank financial institutions and commercial banks, and to allow them to compete on equal grounds. The Commission emphasized that the various proposals were to be viewed, not singly, but as a package. Thus, implementing one proposal might help the competitive position of commercial banks, while another would help the NBFIs. By implementing both at the same time, they would both be on more nearly equal footing.

Major proposals favorable to nonbank deposit-type financial institutions would permit them to make more consumer loans, to acquire more corporate bonds and allow them to use variable rate mortgages. The extent some of these activities, if widely permitted, would enable thrift institutions to increase their share in financial activity is difficult to estimate. Mutual savings banks already are permitted to handle demand deposits in three states (Indiana, Maryland, and New Jersey), and one mutual savings bank handles such deposits in Connecticut. However, the highest proportion of demand deposits in any such bank in 1972 was 7 percent, while the overall share was only 1.7 percent. Even if thrift institutions attracted their share of *individual* demand deposit accounts, they could not necessarily acquire the important demand deposit accounts of business firms. The smaller number of offices of thrift institutions, the resulting lack of convenience as compared with commercial banks, and the inability of thrift institutions to make business loans (unless given permission to engage in this activity as well) are disadvantages.

It is not clear how significant the disadvantage of lack of convenience will continue to be. Changes are occurring in both thrift institutions and commercial banks that will significantly affect the competitive outlook. One change is revised regulations for thrift institutions permitting establishment of "limited facility" offices that differ from branches in that there are specific restrictions on personnel, size, capital investment, and/or activities. Another is provision for establishment of "satellites" that may be manned (a counter in a retail store, for example) or unmanned—a fully automated electronic device, operated by a special card given to customers, located almost any place, and operating 24 hours a day, 7 days a week, 365 days a year, to receive deposits, accommodate cash withdrawals to limited amounts, and perform some other services. Legislative restrictions on these types of services are in process of revision, and clearly the convenience differential is likely to change.

Demand deposits do not necessarily rise in periods of tight money, to provide an offset to the loss of time deposits drained away by the attractiveness of high interest rates in market instruments. Flow of funds data indicate that demand deposits of households rose only 1 percent in 1966 and in 1969 (periods of tight money), but rose 12 percent, 17 percent, and 16 percent in 1965, 1967, and 1968 respectively. Of course, both commercial banks and nonbank deposit-type institutions are adversely affected by the outflow of time deposits, but commercial banks have other alternative sources of funds —for example, borrowing Eurodollars, which was done extensively in 1969.

Finally, demand deposits are costly. Special checking accounts (small accounts that average $300 or less per account) cost commercial banks about 5 cents per year, per dollar of such deposits, in excess of service charge income. If service charges were not imposed, the cost would be almost 10 cents a year per deposit dollar. If commercial banks compete by offering "no service charge" accounts, it will be difficult for savings institutions to compete on a cost basis. Moreover, entry costs are high. The cost per dollar of deposit for an institution handling 1,000 accounts is about 50 percent higher than for an institution handling 50,000 accounts.[7] Because thrift institutions entering the business of handling demand deposits are likely to have only a small

---

[7] See Paul S. Anderson and Robert W. Eisenmenger, "Structural Reform for Thrift Institutions: The Experience in the United States and Canada," Federal Reserve Bank of Boston, *New England Economic Review*, July–August 1972, pp. 3–17. See also *Policies for a More Competitive Financial System*, Proceedings of a Conference held in June 1972, Federal Reserve Bank of Boston.

number of accounts initially and for some time, their entry costs will be substantial.

One method of providing nearly an equivalent of demand deposits is the so-called NOW accounts offered by mutual savings banks in two New England states. Depositors holding such accounts may write negotiable orders of withdrawal (NOW orders) which recipients can cash like checks.[8] Whether this practice will be permitted to continue and will spread widely is still uncertain, but its existence is evidence of interest by some mutual savings banks in providing what amounts to checking services. Savings and loan associations can now offer a limited type of third-party payment plan designed principally for payment of such recurring expenses as utility bills, but they do not have the authority to issue generally negotiable payments media such as NOW orders. Although the Hunt Commission recommended that under certain conditions thrift institutions be permitted to handle third-party payments, it also recommended that those doing so be required to join the Federal Reserve System and to maintain the same reserves required for other institutions handling demand deposits, and that taxes on all institutions that handle demand deposits be uniform. The use of NOW orders appears to involve handling third-party payments, although this may be debatable if the orders are orders on commercial banks for transfer of funds.

At the same time, the Commission suggested that prohibition of payment of interest on demand deposits should be removed over the long run, being retained for a transition period during which its other recommendations are put into effect. The NOW orders appear to constitute a means of, in effect, paying interest on demand deposits. In effect, NOW accounts extend clearing house privileges to institutions that do not bear their share of the costs of handling such transfers.

On these grounds, the Federal Reserve Board of Governors has opposed NOW accounts in their present form.[9] Opposition rests in part on the lack of equity involved in permitting thrift institutions, which pay lower taxes generally and have lower reserve requirements, to offer payments mechanism services to depositors. More importantly, the issue is the need of monetary control authorities to control all institutions that provide payments mechanism services and the desire to make all such institutions share in costs of improving, as well as providing, the necessary service facilities.

Consumer loans would help to diversify the asset portfolios of thrift institutions, thus making them less vulnerable to withdrawals of short-term deposit liabilities than they now are (because their assets are now nearly all long-term assets). But consumer loans, although they have high gross yields, have processing costs that total about 4 percent per year, in contrast to processing costs of only about ½ percent for mortgage loans. Thus mortgage loans at 7½ percent may be just as profitable as consumer loans at 11 percent.

Permitting thrift institutions to acquire more corporate bonds would simply substitute one long-term asset for another. Corporate bonds might

---

[8]*Wall Street Journal*, March 19, 1973, p. 10.

[9]*Federal Reserve Bulletin*, April 1973, pp. 276–80.

be somewhat more attractive than mortgages at certain times, but the advantage would be relatively small. Fundamentally, diversification through additional holdings of corporate bonds does not reduce the basic difficulty—that thrift institutions have relatively short-term liabilities but long-term fixed-rate assets.

Savings institutions might protect themselves against periods of tight money by increasing their capital reserves to a point that they could pay high current market interest rates on their deposits when necessary, without being technically insolvent, as some of them were in the liquidity crisis of 1970. Unfortunately, this would require reserves much higher than at present. To meet the standard used by the Federal Reserve System to measure adequacy of bank capital, for example, savings and loan associations would need to have reserves approximately twice as high (in relation to share accounts) as at present.

Variable-rate mortgages, widely used in some foreign countries, such as Finland, Great Britain, The Netherlands, and Sweden, clearly benefit the thrift institutions. Use of variable-rate mortgages with appropriate safeguards was one of the recommendations of the Hunt Commission. It was suggested that borrowers should be offered fixed-rate alternatives, the variable rate should be fully explained, the maximum movement for any 5-year period should be only 3 percent, the index that determines rate changes should be agreed upon, and mortgages should be given the option of continuing or of arranging new financing after 5 years. Combined with some incentive, borrowers might then accept variable-rate mortgage loans. Whether the "returns" to thrift institutions would be large enough to warrant incurring these costs to strengthen their position in times of rising interest rates is questionable. In conclusion, it appears that most measures to help savings institutions in periods of tight money are not very likely to be of significant value, with the possible exception of variable-rate mortgage loans.

More than a decade ago, Paul Samuelson raised the questions, at a meeting sponsored by the United States Savings and Loan League, whether the relatively high yield, with a high degree of safety, on funds deposited in thrift institutions could be predicted from economic theory, and if not, whether it can be said that mortgage financing is unable to get its "fair" share of available capital.[10] Reflecting on these questions, some, although perhaps a minority, might conclude that if thrift institutions are able, because of various regulations and conditions, to obtain *more* funds from savers than might be predicted from economic theory, perhaps housing is obtaining more funds than it would in an economy where the assumptions of classical economic theory were more nearly valid. A very important question of policy goals can be raised: how important is "better" housing as a goal? The view might be held, again perhaps by a minority, that a high-priority goal is a

---

[10]Paul A. Samuelson, "The Current State of the Theory of Interest Rates, with Special Reference to Mortgage Rates," *Proceedings of the 1960 Conference on Savings and Residential Financing*, May 1960, p. 25; reprinted in James A. Crutchfield, Charles N. Henning, and William Pigott, *Money, Financial Institutions, and the Economy: A Book of Readings* (Englewood Cliffs, N.J.: Prentice-Hall, 1965).

rapid increase in the growth of per capita real income, and that if income rises rapidly, consumers can spend on housing if they wish, or at the other extreme they may live in very modest homes and devote much more funds to travel and other forms of recreation or to various types of consumer goods and services other than housing.

On the other hand, it is possible that the inflation accompanying the Vietnam war and the wide fluctuations in interest rates that occurred in the late 1960s created special stringencies for the thrift institutions—stringencies that may not recur for some time. The sizable housing boom that began in 1970 made the problem of adverse effects on housing of the impact of monetary policy less urgent, and the tight money conditions reached in 1973 did not at first cause such severe disintermediation. In the summer and early fall, loss of funds by thrift institutions was sizable because of a change removing interest rate ceilings for a period on certain time deposits.[11]

Government regulates both commercial banks and NBFIs. Often there are inequities, and the removal of these should improve the financial structure, as well as lead to increased competition and a more efficient allocation of resources in providing financial services to the general public. Whether the package of changes proposed by the Hunt Commission will help or hurt commercial banks relative to other deposit-type institutions and whether they will help the mortgage and housing market relative to other loan markets are questions which cannot be answered definitely with available evidence.

Competition among Other Financial Institutions

In a sense, although they may not compete as directly as the various deposit-type financial institutions, all financial institutions compete for the saving generated in the economy. However, business firms use most of their savings for investment in plant, equipment, and inventories, and borrow additional funds in most years. The government also, although it could save by having budget surpluses, usually has a deficit, and must borrow. Thus financial institutions compete principally for the saving of consumers. Consumers allocate their saving among real estate, durable goods, near-monies, insurance, pension fund contracts, long-term investment in bonds and equities (either directly or through mutual funds or trust funds), and investment in liquid assets such as government securities.

The share of saving allocated to housing has gradually declined as mortgage debt has rapidly increased. In recent years, saving invested in housing (cost minus depreciation minus debt) has been nearly zero. (When capital gains are taken into account, the amount of gain in housing value minus depreciation and debt is of some significance, but it must be remembered that capital gains are not treated as saving in national income accounting.) The allocation of saving to durable goods has increased, but the major increas over the long run has been in the allocation of saving to financial

---

[11]For a savings and loan association view of this episode, see *Savings and Loan News*, November 1973, pp. 16–17.

investment in the various financial intermediaries. The more rapidly growing holdings have been deposits and accounts in deposit-type institutions, time deposits in commercial banks, pension funds, and (during some periods) mutual funds. Slower growth has been experienced in holdings of equities, life insurance, and demand deposits. Future trends are difficult to predict, but some insight into factors affecting projections may be gained by consideration of a few important influences.

Perhaps the most pervasive influence affecting the allocation of saving has been inflation. From the end of the Civil War until nearly the beginning of the twentieth century, the trend of prices was downward, and from the beginning of the twentieth century until 1914 the trend of inflation was very mild. After the inflation during and after World War I, prices declined again, were quite stable during the 1920s, and declined again in the Depression. However, since World War II inflation has been a pervasive and continuing influence, with several periods of more rapid inflation, the most severe being in the late 1960s. Although it is true that, with the exception of the period 1968–69, inflation in the United States has generally been less than in any other major industrialized country (and this is true again in 1972), inflation has been significant enough to cause concern about any future income in fixed dollar amounts. A small beginning has been made in developing variable annuities and some pension plans—notably the CREF plan for college professors—which vary in amount because they are based on underlying values of equities. Provision has been made for social security benefits to vary with price level changes beginning in 1975. From time to time, individuals suggest issuing purchasing power bonds, which would provide an alternative to fixed-value redeemable claims. Insurance claims have been somewhat adversely affected by these trends, and the growth rate of insurance company assets has slowed somewhat.

Another influence on the allocation of saving is the longer period of time that people live, on the average, after retiring. Gradual decline in death rates has been one cause of this; a trend toward somewhat earlier retirement has been another. The result has been increased emphasis upon saving for retirement: pension funds and near-monies have been beneficiaries of this trend.

Third, the rate of growth of commercial banks is an important factor affecting the allocation of saving. This growth rate may depend on two factors: (1) if the Federal Reserve System focuses its attention on control of the long-term growth of M_2, this is the major factor; (2) however, if they focus primarily on M_1, the efforts of banks to achieve growth in total assets by attracting time deposits and increasing other liabilities is of importance. In this case, banks can grow more rapidly than the rate permitted by the Federal Reserve System for growth in M_1. The rate of growth in the money supply depends significantly upon the rate of inflation that is anticipated and regarded as acceptable; if inflation at a 3½ percent rate, compounded, were regarded as acceptable, and if full employment is a major goal of policy, then the combination of about 4½ percent long-term trend rate of increase in real output and a 3½ percent rate of inflation would produce about an 8 percent rise in spending. Some of this rise might be accounted for by a rise in the velocity of money, but a 6 percent or more increase in the money supply (defined as M_1) would be a reasonable projection. If saving continues at a relatively constant ratio to income, funds available for financial investment will rise approximately proportionately with income, and the relatively slower rate of growth of the money supply will permit continued and more rapid increases in other financial assets.[12]

Finally, the position of various groups of institutions and other channels for financial investment is not entirely the result of fluctuations in demand. It is also partly the result of variations in the supply of various financial assets. In the 1960s it was widely anticipated, for example, that relatively slow growth in the supply of government securities would reduce the amount of saving going into this form of financial investment. The large deficits in recent years and anticipated future deficits cast some doubt on this projection. Growth of government debt will—because government borrowing has priority —leave somewhat less saving available from any given level of income for other types of financial investment.

THE PROBLEM OF HANDLING PAYMENTS

The threat that the growing volume of checks to be cleared will swamp the banks' payments-handling mechanism has prompted many efforts to find a means to reduce paperwork connected with payments. Some have anticipated rapid progress toward a less-check (not a checkless) society, in which a system of automatic payment transfers will reduce the paperwork load substantially. Steps toward this goal are tentative—consumer acceptance of automatic payment transfers must be obtained, and problems of computerization must be solved. Experiments under way in 1973 give some indication of the success of this effort. The SCOPE (Special Committee on Paperless Entries) project is designed to permit California banks to exchange preauthorized paperless credits and debits. A business firm sends to its own bank a magnetic tape with data on items paid frequently, such as payroll checks. The bank extracts information for its own deposit accounts and sends the magnetic tape to a central clearing facility that extracts information for all other California banks. In New York and Ohio experiments are being conducted in which bank depositors are asked to authorize banks to process payments immediately to selected merchants, based on information received from the merchants. In these experiments, problems of errors by store clerks, or re-

---

[12]Inflation seems, in recent experience, to have increased saving as a percent of personal disposable income, even if only temporarily. Concern for sufficient financial assets to maintain living standards in the future seems thus far to have outweighed concern about acquisition of assets to avoid the continued depreciation in the value of money holdings. If inflation can be held below the point where depreciation in the value of money becomes the paramount concern—the point at which people begin to buy any type of real asset, simply to buy it before prices rise—saving may be at least as high as the past trend.

conciliation of bank balances, and of payments from accounts with insufficient funds are being evaluated.[13] In Atlanta, Georgia, a similar payments project is under way. In the Atlanta project, it is also proposed to provide "bill-checks," machine-processable documents that customers can endorse and stipulate the amount and date on which their banks are to debit their accounts to pay vendors or creditors. Consideration has been given to installing point-of-sale (POS) computer terminals in retail stores, with direct connection to bank computers for authorization of charges against deposits.

Although experiments take time, it seems likely that during the next decade substantial progress will be made in handling many types of payments through "checkless" transfers. To the extent that commercial banks act more swiftly than nonbank financial institutions in providing such facilities, banks may be able to increase their advantage. They may also find it less necessary to provide additional fully equipped banking offices, as customers will be able to obtain many services by telephone, in retail stores, or in "satellites" (automated facilities).

Aside from the mechanical elements involved and the psychological factors related to consumer acceptance, this change is significant for financial markets and the economy because it will bring a substantial increase in the transactions velocity of money. Instead of the usual several days or more of "float" time, payments will be made more quickly, and changes in money balances held will occur promptly. The increase in transactions velocity will probably be accompanied by an increase in income velocity of money, as more rapid transactions generate income more quickly. Thus, a slower rate of growth of the money supply may be required to attain a given increase in total spending without significant inflation.

Questions arise in connection with the access of commercial banks and thrift institutions to electronic funds transfer systems (EFTS) or means of "checkless" transfers. If commercial banks have access and thrift institutions do not, one can visualize paychecks being automatically deposited by such transfer into commercial banks; if so, the placement of funds by consumers in thrift institutions might be much reduced, especially if Regulation Q ceilings on payment of interest on time deposits are removed and commercial banks are permitted to pay as much interest on such deposits as thrift institutions. On the other hand, if thrift institutions have access to an efficient system for "checkless" transfers, and commercial banks, or some of them, do not, the situation might be reversed. If "satellite banking," in the form of unmanned automated teller stations, either in retail establishments or in such places as parking lots, is engaged in extensively by one type of institution and not by the other, significant changes can be envisaged, especially if in some way the public comes to have a preference for carrying out as many financial transactions as possible through such stations rather than in banking or thrift institution regular offices. Use of such developments as the "In-Touch" system offered for a time by Seattle-First National Bank may permit customers

---

[13]See *The World Banking Challenge*, Lectures and Proceedings at the 25th International Banking Summer School, held at Brown University, Providence, Rhode Island, August 1972 (Washington, D.C.: American Bankers Association, 1972), pp. 132–35.

who have touch-tone telephones to pay bills and complete other transactions from any place in the country. Significant implications for branch banking, for branching by thrift institutions, and for the limitation of activities of a bank to a single state are also apparent.

EFFECT OF GROWTH OF FINANCIAL INSTITUTIONS ON SAVING

Thus far it has been assumed that the ratio of saving to income will continue to be relatively constant in the long run. The question may now be asked, is there any evidence that the growth of financial institutions tends to affect the ratio of saving to income? If so, such influence would be significant, for a small change in the ratio of saving to income would produce a large change in the amount of saving within a few years.

The Income/Saving Relationship

With the general acceptance of Keynesian theory, it was widely agreed that income is the major factor affecting consumption. Because saving equals income minus consumption, if income is the major factor affecting consumption, it must also be the major factor affecting saving. If so, there is little room for any effect on saving resulting from changes in rates of growth of financial institutions. And in fact, many financial institutions are conduits for financial investment of saving already resulting from decisions concerning the disposition of income.

The long-run stability of the ratio of personal saving to personal disposable income, found in empirical studies, led to a general belief that this ratio would not change significantly in the long run, although it might vary during business fluctuations.[14] On this basis, it was generally presumed that factors such as growth of financial institutions would not significantly affect the volume of saving—that their major effects would be on the velocity of money and the sectors into which loanable funds were channeled.

Effect of Growth of Pension Funds on Saving

One study, however, found that persons covered by pension plans saved higher fractions of their income than persons of comparable income levels who were not under pension programs. Not only did they save more in the

---

[14]Incidentally, it also raised some questions about the consumption function, or relationship of consumption to income. For if in the long run saving/income is a relatively constant ratio, the long-run consumption function must be a straight line rising from the origin (income zero, consumption zero) at less than a 45° angle. Thus it cannot intersect the 45° line, as the short-run consumption function was presumed to do. There are various ways of reconciling this divergence; one is to assume that the short-run consumption function shifts upward over time.

form of pension contributions, but they saved more in other forms as well.[15] In a period of rapid growth of pension plans, this should have resulted in a rise in the long-run ratio of saving to income, but there was little evidence that this occurred.[16] However, the growth of pension funds is recent, and some evidence of their effect may show up as time passes.

Several plausible hypotheses may be advanced to account for the increase in savings when individuals participate in pension programs. People may not regard the funds contributed to pension plans as available for other purposes, and hence may save in other forms in order to provide for planned expenditures. Or, the expectation of pension income may create an awareness of the need for other saving. These hypotheses have neither been proved nor disproved with present evidence.

THE PROPER PLACE OF GOVERNMENT LENDING

A final topic for consideration in our review of nonbank financial institutions and their growth is the proper place of government lending, a particularly appropriate topic because of the recent rapid growth of government and quasi-government agencies and of agency securities.

Reasons for Government Lending

Government lending has generally been justified on one or both of two grounds: (1) government lending will improve the allocation of resources; (2) government lending will aid in redistributing income in a desired manner. Misallocation of resources may occur if there is a degree of monopoly in lending, if there is less than sufficient information available concerning borrowing opportunities, if there are legal restrictions that distort lending, or if there are external economies and/or diseconomies in lending (because external economies or diseconomies may not affect lenders—they affect society as a whole or groups other than the lenders). Thus, student loans may not be made in sufficient amounts because private lending agencies do not recognize the benefit to society arising from a better-educated population.

The government agencies mentioned earlier were established largely on the basis of arguments that special conditions existed in certain fields—that agriculture could not obtain sufficient credit, especially because legal restrictions prevented the long-term lending necessary for farmers to buy land and pay for it out of income; that special agencies were needed to provide loans

[15]Phillip Cagan, *The Effect of Pension Plans on Aggregate Saving* (New York: National Bureau of Economic Research, 1965).

[16]For example, in the decade 1955–65, saving averaged 6.7 percent of disposable personal income, and there was no discernible tendency for the ratio to rise. At the same time, pension saving as a fraction of total personal saving rose from 30 percent to over 40 percent. Data for years after 1965 are not very useful because they are distorted by the effects of the inflation during the Vietnam conflict.

to small business firms and to exporters; and that institutions were needed to create a secondary market for mortgages to improve their liquidity and thus aid in free movement of funds into this field. It was also argued that special agencies were needed to make housing loans to low-income persons on a subsidized basis.

The special needs of agricultural credit (long-term mortgage loans and relatively large amounts of credit, for the sizes of the communities involved, at certain times in the agricultural production cycle), and the desire for more adequate housing led to establishment of most of the government agencies in these two fields.

Results of Government Lending

Because housing and farming are markedly sensitive to changes in credit conditions, it should perhaps not be unexpected that the government has attempted to moderate the effects of changes in cost and availability of credit on these sectors.

The direct lending activity of government agencies in these fields does not seem to have prevented growth of private lending. For example, farm mortgage credit extended by life insurance companies and banks has grown rapidly, in spite of the existence of Federal Land Banks. *Perhaps* private institutions would have played a more active role in the absence of government activity, but this remains debatable. If widely accepted social goals do not seem to be adequately served by private financial institutions, government agencies are likely to be established to shift the flow of funds in the desired direction.

The growth of the government lending agencies has resulted in growth of what are termed "agency securities," bonds and other securities issued by these agencies in the capital markets. Interest rates (yields) in these securities are usually somewhat higher than on comparable Treasury issues (since the agency issues have somewhat less liquidity), but somewhat lower than yields on corporate bonds. The result of this process is a larger flow of funds to the mortgage market and the field of agricultural credit, a preempting of funds that otherwise might go to other sectors. Investors prefer agency securities over purely private securities because of their status as securities of quasi-government agencies; yet they do not obtain the full advantage of the lower rate of interest on Treasury borrowing. Those who favor these programs argue that the funds supplied through these agencies mitigate the effects of credit stringency on housing and to some extent on agriculture. Those who question these programs argue that the desired actions could be accomplished at less cost through direct Treasury borrowing and that agency borrowing means this activity escapes budget scrutiny—thus changing the allocation of national resources without explicit consideration in the budget decision process. Basically, proponents argue that funds obtained through the issue of agency securities are helping protect the mortgage and agricultural credit markets from the effects of credit stringency; opponents argue that this is being done at the cost of creating programs subject to review neither by the private credit market mechanism nor by the budget decision process.[17] The agencies have become major factors in the capital markets, and continue their activities whether they are vitally needed or not. In fact, there is some evidence that they may lower mortgage rates relative to other long-term rates; thus increasing the difficulties of savings and loan associations in earning rates high enough to pay rates on their share accounts sufficient to attract savings.[18]

SUMMARY

This chapter has been concerned with five current issues concerning financial institutions: the uniqueness of commercial banks, competition among financial institutions, the problem of handling payments and records of payments, the effect of financial institutions on the growth of saving, and the appropriate place of government lending and government lending agencies.

Commercial banks *are* to some degree unique because they have liabilities that constitute money—means of final settlement of debts—and because they have greater importance for credit creation than nonbank financial institutions have, as long as nonbank financial institutions keep deposits in banks.

Competition among financial institutions could be improved by less regulation, greater freedom to change interest rates, and more freedom for various institutions to hold a variety of financial assets. But whether this freedom, and the resulting competition would alleviate problems of monetary stringency, which have affected housing and certain other economic sectors when interest rates are high, is questionable.

The long-run stability of the ratio of personal saving to personal disposable income, found in empirical studies, is very significant for the level of economic activity. One study indicated that pension plans may cause an increase in the saving/income ratio. Although this hypothesis cannot be proved at this time, it would be very significant, if correct, for long-run growth of the economy.

Government lending and the government-sponsored lending agencies were established to aid in attaining widely accepted social goals that did not seem to be adequately served by private institutions, and they have attained an important place in the capital markets.

A major concern, that nonbank financial institutions, especially deposit-type institutions, might significantly affect velocity of money and perhaps even offset monetary policy actions, has largely disappeared. Recent attention

---

[17]See, for example, the views of R. Bruce Ricks and of Murray Weidenbaum in the *Federal Home Loan Bank Board Journal*, September 1971, pp. 7–16.

[18]Continued subsidization of mortgage borrowers may eventually lead to requests by other borrowers in other subsectors of the economy for the privilege of borrowing at the lower rates which are possible when funds are generated by federally sponsored agencies. See Kenneth J. Thygerson, *The Effect of Government Housing and Mortgage Credit Programs on Savings and Loan Associations*, Occasional Paper No. 6 (Chicago: United States Savings and Loan League, 1973).

has been focused on the allocative effects of NBFIs, especially their effects in channeling funds into housing and other special areas. Concern over distributive effects has replaced concern over effects on economic growth. In 1973, some questions were again beginning to be raised concerning growth, and it is possible that such questions may be given greater emphasis in the future. An appraisal of financial institutions should be partly in terms of an answer to the question: "What are our major economic goals, what priorities do they have, and what type of financial system will best aid in promotion of these goals?"

QUESTIONS FOR DISCUSSION

1. What are the arguments for and against the view expressed in the British Radcliffe report—that what is important is the liquidity of the economy, not the size of any single type of financial assets, such as M_1 or M_2?

2. Develop a numerical example to show how banks have a greater effect on spending than other financial institutions. Show how your conclusions depend on the fact that nonbank financial institutions hold deposits in commercial banks; that is, deposits in commercial banks are payments media for NBFIs as well as for individuals, business firms, and government.

3. Why have NOW accounts been opposed by some authorities?

4. Develop arguments for and against variable-rate mortgage loans.

5. Trace the effects of inflation on financial institutions, financial assets, and interest rates.

6. What are the major factors determining the growth rate of commercial banks? Do the same factors affect the rate of growth of other financial institutions?

7. What are some of the factors that must be considered in introducing a system of paperless entries for payments recording?

8. Why is the possible effect of pension funds on the ratio of saving to personal disposable income such an important question for research?

9. If financial institutions (with the possible exception of pension funds) do not significantly change the ratio of saving to disposable personal income, why are the growth and development of financial institutions essential in the process of economic development of less developed countries?

10. Do you believe that government lending agencies should be included in the federal government budget in order to facilitate a consideration of the desirability of their activities in relation to other possible uses of funds? Have the agencies gained a special position by being government-sponsored agencies, yet not subject to government budget scrutiny?

SELECTED REFERENCES

The potential importance of nonbank financial institutions in affecting spending economic growth and development was emphasized in a series of writings by John G. Gurley and Edward S. Shaw. For relevant works, see the selected reference list following Chapter 2.

Evidence that money and so-called near-monies were not very good substitutes was provided by Edgar L. Feige, *The Demand for Liquid Assets: A Temporal Cross-Section Analysis* (Englewood Cliffs, N.J.: Prentice-Hall, 1964). Feige's conclusions were criticized by Tong Hun Lee, "Substitutability of Non-Bank Intermediary Liabilities for Money," *Journal of Finance*, September 1966, pp. 441–57.

The "new view" that there is no very clear line of demarcation between commercial banks and other financial institutions was set forth by James Tobin, "Commercial Banks as Creators of 'Money,' " in Deane Carson, ed., *Banking and Monetary Studies* (Homewood, Ill.: Richard D. Irwin, 1963). The view that money is important has been espoused by Milton Friedman in many writings, and because he defines money as currency plus liabilities of commercial banks, he presumably regards commercial banks as uniquely important.

See also Joel M. Yesley, "Defining the Product Market in Commercial Banking," Federal Reserve Bank of Cleveland, *Economic Review*, June–July 1972, pp. 17–31. This article examines opposing viewpoints in economic literature, court decisions, and statistical studies concerning the question whether commercial banks compete significantly with other financial institutions.

The study by Phillip Cagan, *The Effect of Pension Plans on Aggregate Saving* (New York: National Bureau of Economic Research, 1965) provides evidence of the effect of pension plan saving on total saving.

The article by Donald Shelby, "Some Implications of the Growth of Financial Intermediaries," *Journal of Finance*, December 1958, pp. 527–41, was significant in showing the multiplication of credit (and thus the increase in velocity of money) concomitant with growth of various types of financial institutions.

The recommendations of the Hunt Commission are detailed in *The Report of the President's Commission on Financial Structure and Regulation* (Washington, D.C.: Government Printing Office, 1971). They may be compared with the recommendations of the Commission on Money and Credit in 1961: *Money and Credit: Their Influence on Jobs, Prices, and Growth* (Englewood Cliffs, N.J., Prentice-Hall, 1961). A very useful review of issues raised by the Hunt Commission report is found in *Policies for a More Competitive Financial System*, Proceedings of a Conference held in June 1972 (Boston: Federal Reserve Bank of Boston, 1972). For a critical view of the Hunt Commission report, see Roland I. Robinson, "The Hunt Commission Report: A Search for Politically Feasible Solutions to the Problems of Financial Structure," *Journal of Finance*, September 1972, pp. 765–77.

The many changes currently taking place in improvement of the payments mechanisms and new competitive thrusts by both banks and nonbank financial institutions are discussed in scattered articles in various journals. For one general review, see John J. Balles, "Competitive Outlook in Banking," Federal Reserve Bank of San Francisco, *Monthly Review*, November 1972, pp. 3–10.

7

Private Domestic Demand
for
Loanable Funds

One theory of interest, to be discussed in detail in Chapter 12, regards "the" interest rate—the average of all interest rates or a "representative" interest rate—as being determined by the supply of and demand for loanable funds. The *supply* of loanable funds is the sum of money that would be made available during a period of time, at various interest rates, for purchase of financial assets other than money itself: that is, for loans and investment. This supply comes from individuals and from the financial institutions discussed in Chapters 3–6. The *demand* for loanable funds is the sum of money that business, government, consumers, and others wish to borrow at various interest rates. The demand comes chiefly from business, government, and consumer sectors.

With these facts in mind, we take up the analysis of demand for loanable funds as it is evidenced by the issuance of "primary securities"—those issued by ultimate borrowers. Business firms issue primary securities, such as bonds and promissory notes, to borrow from individuals and from banks. Banks, in turn, issue savings passbooks and time certificates of deposit to depositors. Such passbooks and certificates are not primary securities because they are issued by intermediaries rather than by ultimate borrowers.

An analysis of the demand for loanable funds should begin with the factors affecting the issue of primary securities. The factors that cause borrowing are generally grounded in "real" economic changes, and hence at this point we relate our analysis of financial markets to causes of changes in the real level of economic activity. The chief question discussed in this chapter is, what are the factors that create a demand for loanable funds by the various parties who wish to borrow?

The demand for loanable funds comes from the business sector, the consumer sector, the state and local government sector, the federal government sector, and the foreign sector. Although financial institutions lend to each other—for example, commercial banks lend to credit unions and finance companies—this type of lending is mentioned only briefly.

For convenience, demand for loanable funds is analyzed in terms of business demand, demand for mortgage credit, consumer demand, government demand, and foreign demand. Businesses demand funds for plant and equipment spending, inventory increases, and increasing the liquidity ratios of business firms. Demand for mortgage credit arises both from residential construction and other construction. Consumer demand for loanable funds is chiefly for the purchase of automobiles and other durable goods, but also to some extent for current consumption.[1] State and local government demand for loanable funds is chiefly for construction purposes, schools, other institutional buildings, sewers, utilities, bridges, and highways. Federal government demand is based on need to meet deficits that arise when expenditures exceed taxes and other revenues by more than the amount that can be met by drawing down cash balances. Finally, foreign demand for loanable funds arises from foreign business and government spending in excess of their own available domestic funds. The first three sources of demand for loanable funds are discussed in this chapter; federal government, state and local government, and foreign demand for loanable funds are discussed in Chapter 8.

BUSINESS DEMAND FOR LOANABLE FUNDS

Business firms demand loanable funds because they expect to earn, from investment in various assets, more than the cost of the loanable funds, including an allowance for the risk involved in investment in real capital assets. The assets of business firms consist largely of plant and equipment, inventories, accounts receivable, and a relatively small amount of liquid assets to meet current payments. When business firms believe that an increase in any of these assets—but especially plant and equipment and inventories—will yield enough return to warrant the allocation of funds, they will allocate either funds already available or funds obtained by borrowing or selling equities.

The fundamental rate of return, or interest rate, is therefore the expected return on assets held by business firms, chiefly real capital assets. Business firms, by investing funds in a type of activity in which they have acquired or can develop expertise, can earn enough in an average year to pay the cost of borrowed funds and still obtain a margin of net profit sufficient to compensate them for the risks they take. At the margin, business firms can afford to pay in interest the same rate they are earning on their investment of funds in real capital assets. Firms that have higher rates of return than the marginal firm earn an additional amount, which compensates them for risks they incur.[2]

---

[1]Spending for automobiles and other durable assets is treated as consumption spending in the national income accounts, but is treated as investment in the flow of funds accounts described in Chapter 2. If the flow of funds treatment were followed, it could be stated that most consumer borrowing, as well as most business borrowing, is for investment.

[2]It is assumed at this point that the relative shares of labor, capital, and land in total national income (or GNP) remain the same. If the share obtained by capital falls,

In this analysis, the basic rate of interest is related to the productivity of capital. If productivity increases by 3 percent and if inflation is 4 percent, so that GNP in nominal terms increases by 7 percent a year, with the same assumptions the return to business firms also increases by 7 percent a year. Business firms at the margin can pay up to 7 percent as interest for borrowed funds. The nominal rate of interest is thus based upon the "real" rate of interest; it may increase by an "inflation premium" when the price level is rising.[3]

During any given period, business firms need funds for investment in plant and equipment. The amount of such investment depends on expected yields. Investment, in turn, leads to an increase in income, an increase in consumption, and a further increase in income. The concept of the investment multiplier (often termed simply "the" multiplier) should already be familiar; it is the relation of the increase in income to the increase in investment.[4] If the multiplier is, for example, 2½, then the increase in GNP would be 2½ times the increase in investment. It should be recognized that this direct multiplier is augmented by an indirect effect, or feedback, from consumption to investment; this is often termed the accelerator. The two effects together give the net result in increasing GNP. In any calculations, investment must be measured on a net basis—that is, depreciation and other capital consump-

---

business firms may not be able to pay quite as high a rate of interest as is mentioned. Based upon the assumption that real GNP increases by 3 percent a year, capital, labor, and land can each receive returns which increase 3 percent a year without causing inflation. This was the basis of the wage-price guidelines, given some publicity by the government in the early 1960s; thus capital can receive interest or profits of 3 percent, and labor can receive its current wage rate plus an increase of 3 percent, without danger of causing further inflation. For further details on the guideposts, see *Economic Report of the President*, January 1962, pp. 185–90.

[3]This view is based upon Irving Fisher's analysis. It must be recognized that there is another view: that the yield on assets that fluctuate in price (such as real capital assets and stocks) is based upon the yield on assets such as bonds, money, and near-monies, which have a fixed value (at some point in time) in money terms. In this view, when inflation occurs, prices of assets that fluctuate in price rise, and yields on such assets therefore decline. Thus yields on such assets decline relative to yields on fixed-value assets, such as bonds. The view adopted in the text assumes that the yield on real capital assets is the basic yield, from which other yields are derived; the alternative view assumes that the zero yield on money is basic, and that the relative demand for and supply of money versus the demand for and supply of bonds determines the rate of interest on bonds. The data do not firmly support one view as opposed to the other, but the authors prefer the view that the productivity of real capital assets is fundamental and provides the basis for paying interest. For a recent review of the evidence, see Stephen F. LeRoy, "Interest Rates and the Inflation Premium," Federal Reserve Bank of Kansas City, *Monthly Review*, May 1973, pp. 11–18.

[4]To refresh the reader's memory, the multiplier is $\Delta Y/\Delta I$. Because Y (income, or GNP) equals I (investment) plus C (consumption) if government and foreign spending is ignored, Y/Y equals I/Y plus C/Y (dividing all items in the equation by Y). Thus I/Y equals 1 minus C/Y, or $Y/I = \dfrac{1}{1 - C/Y}$. The multiplier is equally related to increases in income, investment, and consumption, so that $\dfrac{\Delta Y}{\Delta I} = \dfrac{1}{1 - \dfrac{\Delta C}{\Delta Y}}$. As is apparent, if consumption were a stable fraction of income, the multiplier would be a constant. Since consumption varies to some extent as a fraction of income, the multiplier also varies.

tion allowances must be deducted from gross investment (often referred to in the statistics as gross private domestic investment, or GPDI, to obtain net investment.[5]

Because the use of capital increases output, investment in plant and equipment is obviously related to growth of GNP. It has been estimated that business fixed investment must be approximately 9 percent of GNP in order to result in a growth of 3½ percent per year in GNP.[6] Attempts have been made to estimate how much higher than 9 percent the ratio of fixed investment spending to GNP must be in order to achieve higher rates of growth, but this leads us into the theory of economic growth, which is not our concern at this point. Moreover, factors other than the amount of investment—for example, technological improvement, education of workers, and application of technological advances—are determinants of the rate of growth.

Business firms must also invest in additions to their inventory holdings. Inventory is held because sales do not coincide with output, and sufficient stock must be kept in inventory to avoid losses in sales and costs of frequent reordering. The optimum amount of inventory is that which balances the costs of holding inventory (capital costs, warehousing or storage costs, service costs, and costs arising from risks involved in holding inventory when styles may change) with the costs of lost sales and frequent reordering. Quantitative models have been developed to determine the cost-minimizing levels of inventories, and the widespread use of computers may permit a lower ratio of inventories to sales than was possible when it was more difficult to calculate amounts needed at various places. In any event, some ratio of inventory to sales is desirable, and as sales increase, inventories must generally increase also. In aggregate terms, this is why figures for "final" total demand (GNP minus additions to inventories) are an indicator of the projected trend in GNP—as final demand rises, inventories must also rise, and hence GNP will rise even if it has been falling because of reductions in inventories.

Finally, business firms borrow at certain times to add to their liquid financial assets. Business firms must hold some liquid assets in order to meet excesses of current payments over current receipts, which may occur from time to time. At times the liquidity of business firms may be of critical importance, as in the "liquidity crisis" in the spring of 1970, when some firms could not pay promissory notes, or commercial paper, as they came due, and those who evaluate credit began to wonder whether many firms had enough liquidity to meet other current liabilities. Fortunately, at that time the Federal Reserve System made additional reserves available to banks, and banks were able to extend loans to many business firms that were in some difficulty. In the period that followed, business firms rebuilt their liquidity positions to some extent.[7]

---

[5]GPDI includes additions to inventory and to the stock of housing as well as investment in plant and equipment, but in this and the following paragraph, the reference is to investment in plant and equipment.

[6]Robert M. Solow, "Technical Progress, Capital Formation and Economic Growth," *American Economic Review*, Papers and Proceedings, May 1962, pp. 76–87.

[7]The ratio of corporate financial assets to short-term liabilities fell from 1.025 in early 1966 to approximately 0.85 in late 1970, as banks continued for some time to

Internally Generated Funds

Business firms generate a sizable amount of funds internally because they make depreciation and other capital consumption charges against earnings but do not make corresponding cash outlays, and because they retain a sizable portion of their earnings after depreciation and taxes. The ratio of dividends paid to total earnings after taxes, termed the payout ratio, is usually about 50 percent on the average, although ratios vary, being considerably higher for most utilities and lower for new and rapidly growing firms. Internally generated funds remaining after dividends have been paid are available for investment; they constitute gross business saving. They are likely to be used for internal investment purposes because they are not likely to have any alternative use that can produce a higher yield. Normally, rates of return on real capital assets are higher than bond yields and other yields on financial assets, and presumably the firm could not invest its money in some other line of business at a higher yield, since the firm has expertise in its own field.

What is the cost of such funds? Investors presumably invested in a given firm because it was earning, say, 10 percent on its capital, and investors could not find other companies with comparable risk that earned a higher rate. Thus the company must earn, or expect to earn, at least 10 percent on its capital in order that those who purchased stock will be satisfied with their investment. If stock prices reflected accurately the discounted expected earnings of the firm, one could say that the firm should earn a high enough rate of new investments to maintain the price of its shares at the current level. If such prices fall, it means that investors expected a lower rate of return, and holders of stock in that firm would suffer in comparison with other investors. Thus the cost of equity capital in the form of funds from depreciation[8] and retained earnings is the same 10 percent rate that the company has been earning on its capital.[9] Growing firms whose earnings are increasing tend to retain much or all of their earnings after taxes; utilities, which are permitted to earn a specified rate of return by the regulatory agencies, may pay out most of their earnings and borrow funds as needed.

---

borrow in order to finance investment. Efforts to improve the ratio resulted in a rise to nearly 0.9 by late 1972. See "Corporate Financing and Liquidity, 1968–72," Federal Reserve Bank of Richmond, *Monthly Review*, November 1972, pp. 12–15.

[8]The reader probably recognizes that the term "funds from depreciation" is a shorthand expression and not precisely accurate. Funds are, of course, not supplied by depreciation, but by earnings against which depreciation was charged. In some cases, earnings may not be sufficient to cover these charges, and hence less funds are supplied in such cases.

[9]Essentially this is an opportunity cost concept; if investors received all earnings in the form of dividends, they would be free to reinvest or not; presumably they would reinvest in firms with comparable risk that earn comparable rates of return. For further discussion, see any standard text on corporate finance; for example, J. Fred Weston and Eugene F. Brigham, *Managerial Finance*, 3rd ed. (New York: Holt, Rinehart, and Winston, 1969), pp. 344 ff.

In a country where economic growth is occurring, it is not likely in most years that funds available because of depreciation charges and from retained earnings will be sufficient to meet investment needs. As is known in macroeconomic theory, investment fluctuates more widely than the level of general business activity.[10] Hence it usually happens that although internally generated funds may be sufficient in the early months of a period of rising business activity to provide for investment for many firms, the need for external funds rises as business activity continues to increase. Some firms, such as utilities, pay out a large part of their earnings in dividends and engage in a large volume of construction on a regular basis. They borrow significant amounts even in years of relatively low total business demand for loanable funds, and hence some firms are borrowing even during recessions. On the other hand, borrowing may continue to be heavy near the end of a period of rising business activity, as firms find that they have used up most of their excess capacity and must build new facilities. Thus borrowing was especially heavy in the years 1969–70, even though business activity began to turn down in late 1969, and profits had begun to decline earlier.

The Marginal Cost of Funds

In a growing economy investment normally exceeds the amount of internally generated funds. When prices rise in inflation, funds available from depreciation and other capital consumption allowances are generally not sufficient to cover replacement cost of worn-out plant and equipment.[11] Some and perhaps all of retained earnings have to be used to maintain the current level of the stock of capital. Thus some borrowing is likely to occur, and the relevant marginal cost of funds is that of borrowing (or issuing equity) in the money and capital markets, as indicated in schematic form by the rising part of the marginal costs of funds curve (ab) in Figure 7–1.

The flat portion of the marginal cost of funds curve in Figure 7–1 indicates the cost of internally generated funds; the portion of the curve designated as ab indicates the cost of borrowed funds and of funds raised through new issues of equity securities. This cost is presumed to rise as additional amounts are borrowed because additional amounts of loanable funds will be supplied, it is generally assumed, only at higher interest rates. The marginal

[10]In part, this is simply because of the fact that real capital assets are used for long periods of time. Because of this fact, only 1/10 or 1/20 of their value may be lost by depreciation in a single year. If in that year demand should increase by 10 percent, it may be necessary to invest enough funds to replace worn-out equipment (10 percent of the equipment, say) and also to add enough new equipment to produce 10 percent more output (perhaps 10 percent more equipment), to meet the additional demand. This "acceleration" principle, as it is known, is a "feedback" from consumption to investment.

[11]If firms used replacement cost values for fixed assets in their accounting records, depreciation charges could approximately equal replacement costs. This is done by some firms in some countries, for example, in The Netherlands. See Gerhard G. Mueller, *Accounting Practices in The Netherlands* (Seattle: Graduate School of Business Administration, University of Washington, 1962) and Abram Mey, *On the Application of Business Economics and Replacement Value Accounting in The Netherlands* (Seattle: Graduate School of Business Administration, University of Washington, 1970).

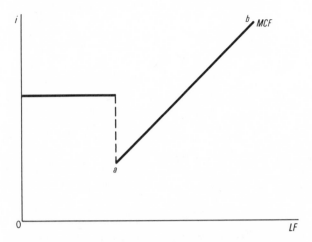

FIGURE 7–1   Marginal Cost of Funds for Business Firms

cost of funds could fall temporarily if, for example, the central bank created a large amount of additional money, but such exceptions are likely to be rare.

Borrowing for Plant and Equipment Spending

The borrowing by business firms may provide funds for investment in plant and equipment, for additions to inventory, or for increase in liquidity of firms. In a period of inflation, internally-generated funds may be less adequate for inventory replacement, just as depreciation charges may be less than the cost of replacing worn out plant and equipment. Firms that use first-in, first-out (FIFO) inventory accounting may show profits that are in part illusory, because the inventory used up (and shown as a cost) is less expensive than that which must be acquired to replace it. Use of last-in, first-out (LIFO) inventory accounting shows much smaller profits. The inventory valuation adjustment made in the national income accounts results in reduced profits, closely approximating the reductions that would occur if all firms used LIFO. Retained earnings shown in the national income accounts are thus a more accurate indication of funds available for additional investment than are retained earnings reported by firms that use FIFO inventory accounting.

In theory, the amount of funds borrowed should be the amount needed for that quantity of investment at which the marginal efficiency of investment equals the marginal cost of funds. The total amount of investment is indicated by the point where marginal efficiency of investment equals marginal cost of funds; the amount borrowed is the *additional* amount needed to supplement internally generated funds. A considerable amount of the internally generated funds—usually more than the amount of funds equal to depreciation charges, and perhaps in some cases more than total internally generated funds—are needed simply to replace worn-out or obsolescent plant and

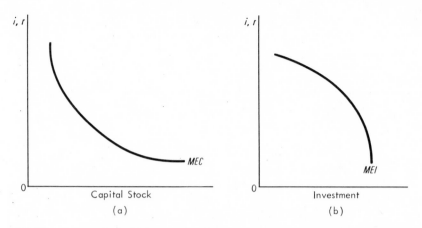

FIGURE 7–2 Marginal Efficiency of Capital and Marginal Efficiency of Investment

equipment. Additional investment, beyond that amount, is *net* investment (see Figure 7–3).

The term "marginal efficiency of investment" requires brief explanation. The term "marginal efficiency of *capital*" is frequently used, and is found in Keynes' famous work, *The General Theory of Employment, Interest and Money*. But more accurately, what is significant is the marginal efficiency of *investment*—not the return on a marginal addition to the country's stock of capital, regardless of time, but the return on a marginal addition to investment in the current time period.[12] The difference between the marginal efficiency of capital and the marginal efficiency of investment is illustrated in Figure 7–2. The value of the stock of capital is the total value of real capital assets in the economy. At the present time, this is roughly equivalent to GNP for one year. Investment in plant and equipment in a year, however, is normally not more than 9 percent or 10 percent of the value of the capital stock; total investment is about 14 percent, adding inventory and housing investment.

The term "efficiency" is used rather than marginal rate of return on investment (or capital) because two different investments might have the same average rates of return, but one may have a higher "efficiency." As explained earlier, income to be received in the future is discounted by some rate of interest in obtaining the present value of such income. Thus the present value of a bond is found by the formula

$$PV = \frac{Y_1}{(1 + r)} + \frac{Y_2}{(1 + r)^2} + \frac{Y_3}{(1 + r)^3} + \ldots + \frac{Y_n}{(1 + r)^n} + \frac{F}{(1 + r)^n}$$

[12]Some of the considerations involved are presented clearly in Gardner Ackley, *Macroeconomic Theory* (New York: The Macmillan Company, 1961), pp. 481 ff. See also Abba P. Lerner, *The Economics of Control* (New York: The Macmillan Company, 1944), Chapter 25, for a much earlier presentation.

in which PV is present value, $Y_1 \ldots Y_n$ are the interest payments to be received in the future, and F is the final maturity value to be paid to the bond-holder. Similarly, the present value of a real capital asset is found by the same formula. In this case, F represents the scrap or resale value of the capital asset at the end of whatever period is being considered. Use of this formula does not imply that people prefer present goods to future goods, but simply that because a return is obtained over a period of time, the value of a capital asset at the beginning of any period is less than the value at the end of the period by the amount of return to be obtained.

Using this formula, suppose that one investment were expected to yield nothing the first year, 5 percent the second year, and 10 percent the third year, while another investment was expected to yield 10 percent the first year, 5 percent the second year, and nothing the third year. The two investments would have the same average rate of return (5 percent), but the second investment would have greater efficiency, because the first year's return (10 percent, compared to nothing on the first investment) would be discounted for only one year to obtain its present value. The 10 percent yield in the third year, returned by the first investment, would have to be discounted for three years to obtain its present value.

The marginal efficiency of investment curve is likely to be concave toward the axes and the marginal efficiency of capital convex toward the axes because an attempt to make a very large amount of investment in a *single*

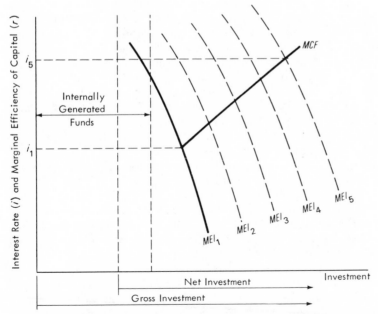

FIGURE 7-3 Marginal Efficiency of Investment and Marginal Cost of Funds with Rising Business Activity

period is likely to cause the rate of return to fall sharply, whereas additions to the country's stock of capital over a longer period of time are likely to be at rates of return only slightly less than those obtained on previous additions to the stock of capital. In a short period of time it is not possible for necessary additional labor to become available except at rising costs, and additional investments are likely to yield sharply lower rates of return if investment spending is unusually great. There are barriers to an extremely large amount of investment in a given period that probably do not exist for additions to capital stock over long periods of time.

The Role of the Debt/Equity Ratio

If investment continues to increase over a number of periods of rising business activity business borrowing usually increases, although there may be some rise also in internally generated funds and therefore some increase in investment that can be financed without borrowing.

As business borrowing increases, it is likely that at some point corporations begin to have debt/equity ratios that are higher than desired. Some corporations may encounter this point relatively quickly, others after a longer time. Suppose that the marginal efficiency of investment curve shifts to the right, as innovations or prospects of higher rates of return for other reasons result in higher expected marginal efficiency of investment at given levels of investment; there is, therefore, an increase in investment. This situation is diagrammed in Figure 7–3. In such a situation, more firms find, as time passes, that in order to maintain what is believed to be an appropriate debt/equity ratio, they must obtain additional equity. As more firms reach such a point, the volume of new issues of stock increases, and the mix of funds obtained by business firms may shift somewhat in the direction of a higher proportion of funds obtained through issues of stock.

The debt/equity ratio is important because it is one measure of the risk incurred by those who lend funds to business firms. If the debt/equity ratio is low, the firm has a relatively large amount of its own funds with which to repay debt if necessary. Such a firm can easily repay debt by liquidating assets and reducing its equity. As the debt/equity ratio rises, the risk incurred by lenders increases. Firms must liquidate larger fractions of their total assets to repay debt, and the resulting reductions in their equities become larger relative to the remaining equity.

Cost of capital obtained through stock issues is generally higher than that for debt issues because new stock must yield the same return that is now being obtained on investment, or higher, plus the cost of issuing new stock (flotation costs). Moreover, earnings from which dividends are paid are taxable income, whereas interest is paid on bonds before taxable income is calculated. Hence the marginal cost of funds generally may be assumed to continue to rise. At some point the *MEI* curve may cease to shift to the right —higher returns for additional investments are no longer expected. If at such a point conditions lead to lower expected returns, the *MEI* curve may shift to the left, and a business recession may follow.

The average period of a business upturn since World War II has been about 30 months, or about 7½ quarters. Some recoveries, however, have continued as long as 8 years—for example, the recovery from the first quarter of 1961 to the last quarter of 1969 continued for approximately 35 quarters, if the "minirecession" of early 1967 is ignored.

An amount of investment less than the amount needed to replace worn-out and obsolete assets could occur only in a declining economy. An amount of investment less than the amount provided by internally generated funds is not likely. If the marginal cost of funds were high enough to discourage retention of earnings, bond yields would be nearly as high as, or possibly higher than, returns on some real capital assets. This would mean that little or no return, or perhaps a negative return, was being obtained for the additional risk involved in holding real capital assets rather than financial assets such as bonds. If bond yields were as high as or higher than common stock dividend yields plus capital gains, investment in real capital assets through retention of earnings would be discouraged, and industries would be contracting rather than expanding. This may occur for an individual firm, and some firms may go out of business, but it is unlikely for the economy as a whole. Thus, except for temporary periods, dividends plus capital gains must be higher than bond yields in a growing economy. If, for example, average bond yields are 7 percent, dividends plus capital gains must be higher; if dividends average 3 percent, capital gains must average *at least* 4 percent, in the long run.

Borrowing to Finance Additions to Inventories

In addition to borrowing for plant and equipment spending, business firms need to borrow funds in order to increase their inventories when this is necessary. Basically, inventories are required in a certain ratio to sales, this ratio depending upon the efficiency with which inventories can be supplied to the points of sale, the time required for obtaining additional inventories, and the degree of fluctuations in sales. When inventory/sales ratios are relatively low, business firms need to add to inventories, especially if sales are rising. Borrowing for this purpose is likely to be short-term borrowing, largely from commercial banks, or from commercial finance companies for some marginal firms or firms that have borrowed as much as they can from banks.

Percentage fluctuations in inventory borrowing are likely to be very great, as in some years business firms reduce inventories and may need no funds for inventory purchases on a net basis. In other years, with rapidly rising sales, business firms need large additions to inventories. For this reason, demand for short-term borrowing is likely to fluctuate more (in percentage terms) than long-term borrowing. This is a second reason why short-term interest rates are likely to fluctuate more than long-term interest rates. They also fluctuate more with a given change in demand for securities because a very small change in the price of a short-term financial asset causes a large change in its yield, since the yield is obtained over a short period.

There is no absolute dividing line between short-term inventory borrowing and long-term borrowing for plant and equipment spending. Even plant and equipment spending may at times be financed by short-term borrowing, especially in the early stages of a business recovery. Until a business recovery has proceeded for some time, business managers may not clearly perceive that a significant increase in investment and hence in long-term borrowing will be needed, and they may attempt, for a time, to meet needs for replacement of equipment and maintenance through short-term borrowing. Moreover, short-term borrowing often becomes longer-term borrowing as loans are renewed by banks. At times, moreover, loans may be negotiated with banks in the form of term loans with an original maturity of more than one year, at lower interest rates than those that would have to be paid on bond issues or even on short-term loans.[13]

Moreover, although there are certain normal inventory/sales ratios that may serve as guidelines in forecasting inventory accumulation or reduction, these ratios are not fixed, and inventory changes may not occur as expected. An example is the recession of 1969–70, in which inventory ratios were not reduced for some time; for this reason, buildup of inventories was also delayed as business activity rose in 1971 and 1972. The inventory/sales ratio declined rather slowly in 1971 and did not fall to the 1968 level until early 1972; hence only moderate inventory buildup occurred during 1972. Fluctuations in the inventory/sales ratio are shown in Figure 7–4; note that inventories have usually fluctuated between 1.4 and 1.6 times monthly sales.

Borrowing to Increase Liquidity

Finally, business firms may borrow, either short-term or long-term, in order to improve their own liquidity ratios if these are relatively low. One reason for such borrowing is the concern that low liquidity ratios (low ratios of liquid financial assets to current liabilities) may be looked upon unfavorably by lenders, or may lead to situations in which payments due on current liabilities cannot be met. Another reason is the fear that if borrowing should become necessary, there might be occasions when commercial banks might not lend: they might already have become "loaned up," reaching a loan-to-deposit ratio as high as they wish to maintain. Businessmen might foresee, or think they foresee, actions by the Federal Reserve System to tighten credit. Memories of such actions—for example, in 1966 and again in 1969—might reinforce their beliefs.

Such borrowing is most likely to occur after a long period of business expansion, in which the need for funds for investment in plant and equipment may have caused a reduction of liquid assets to minimum levels at the same time that current liabilities were being increased through borrowing from banks and increases in accounts payable.

---

[13]During the period 1948–64, the rate charged on term loans by New York City banks was often lower than the rate charged on even the largest short-term loans; see Albert M. Wojnilower and Richard E. Speagle, "The Prime Rate," in *Essays in Money and Credit*, Federal Reserve Bank of New York, 1964, pp. 47–56.

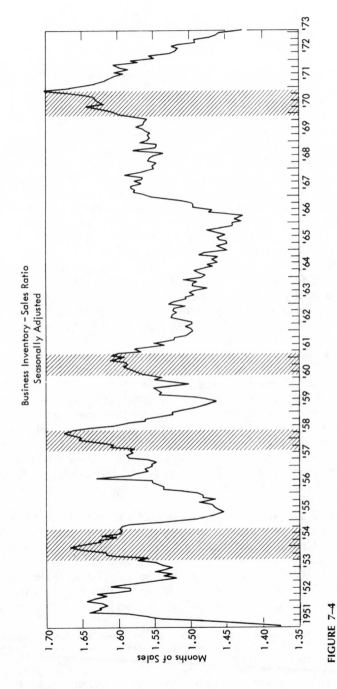

FIGURE 7-4

SOURCE: United States Department of Commerce, Bureau of Economic Analysis.

147

Forecasting the Demand for Loanable Funds by Business Firms

The demand for loanable funds by business firms is the sum of their borrowing and issue of new equity securities for investment spending, for increases in inventories, and for improvement of their liquidity position. Surveys of the investment spending plans of business firms, made by government agencies and by private firms, aid in forecasting borrowing for investment in plant and equipment;[14] analysis of trends in inventory/sales ratios, their current level, and the forecast level of sales aids in forecasting borrowing to finance increases in inventories; and analysis of liquidity ratios aids in forecasting liquidity borrowing.

The amount of borrowing for these purposes cannot be adequately forecast, however, until an estimate has been made of the amount of funds likely to be available from depreciation and other capital consumption allowances and from retained earnings, as these funds will generally be used before borrowed funds are sought. Of course, in every year there are firms that need funds, but more firms begin to borrow as internally generated funds become insufficient to meet planned investment. The amount of depreciation may be affected by any changes in rules governing depreciation rates, and the amount of retained earnings may be affected not only by profit margins but also by any change in corporate tax rates.

With these estimates made for total funds needed and for internally generated funds, the analyst is ready to estimate the demand for loanable funds by business firms. In general, because amounts for the preceding period are known, the task of the analyst is to estimate *changes* in plant and equipment spending, inventory accumulation, liquidity, and internally generated funds. Although borrowing for plant and equipment spending is generally long-term borrowing, and other funds are generally obtained through short-term borrowing, there is no precise dividing line, and the separation of borrowing into long-term and short-term may be difficult; thus it may be difficult to forecast effects in the short-term market in comparison with effects in the long-term market.

In conclusion, it may be noted that fluctuations in loans by banks to business firms are determined largely by demand. One recent study showed that when demand fell, loans declined, even though the supply of funds banks could have used to make loans remained ample. In the late 1950s and in the early 1960s, New York banks had sufficient funds to make a substantial additional volume of business loans, but loans increased only 2½ percent a year; on the other hand, loans increased at over 20 percent a year

---

[14]The Commerce Department-Securities and Exchange Commission (usually referred to as the Commerce-SEC) surveys and the McGraw-Hill surveys of intentions to spend for business fixed investment have been quite successful in forecasting expenditures. Errors have been substantially less than the average annual variations in expenditures. See Arthur M. Okun, "The Predictive Value of Surveys of Business Intentions," *American Economic Review*, Papers and Proceedings, May 1962.

in the mid-1950s and in the mid-1960s, when demand was strong. The most significant demand factors were capital expenditures and internal saving of business firms. The fact that business firms borrowed to finance capital expenditures was reflected in the high proportion of term loans, nearly two-thirds of all business loans outstanding. Bank loans are also obtained as interim financing in the early stages of capital projects, when the amount of funds that will ultimately be needed is not necessarily known. The second major factor affecting loan demand was the availability of internal financing relative to fixed investment and changes in inventories. When cash flows were less than these needs for funds, bank borrowing increased sharply. Inventory financing was less significant in this particular study than it might have been in other studies because it was conducted in New York City; in that city, the concentration of financing by banks of utilities and petroleum companies, neither of which carry large inventories relative to their size, means that inventory financing is less important than in most centers.[15]

Agricultural Demand for Credit

Farms are usually both homes and business operations, and agricultural credit could be treated as both business and consumer credit. As there are only a relatively small number of corporations engaged in agriculture, most farmers must borrow from financial institutions or individual lenders rather than in the bond market. The need for credit has become increasingly important with more extensive use of farm machinery, chemical fertilizers, and other manufactured products. Because farmers have *relatively* heavy debt—largely as a result of their need to purchase long-lived assets in the form of farm land and machinery—and relatively few liquid assets, their demand for credit fluctuates rather widely with the need for purchases of equipment, seed, feed, fertilizers, and land. At the same time, risks of lending in agriculture are greater than in business, generally because of the small size and usually noncorporate form of farm businesses, the sometimes inadequate record-keeping, and the risks generally peculiar to agriculture: crop and livestock diseases, weather changes, insect pests, and other sources of risks, plus the risk of widely fluctuating prices because of relatively inelastic demand for many farm products and relatively wide fluctuations in supply.

The demand for credit in agriculture has the same origin as the demand for credit in other business, recognition of the productivity of land and capital. The agricultural revolution since the mid-1930s led to great increases in output per man-hour, with increased use of equipment and fertilizer. The increased return permitted borrowing. (Increase in output per man-hour is often referred to as productivity of labor; it can also be referred to, as in this paragraph, as productivity of capital. Perhaps the best phraseology would be "the increase in productivity of labor using more (or better) land and capital.")

[15]George Budzeika, *Lending to Business by New York City Banks*, New York University, Institute of Finance, *Bulletin*, Nos. 76–77, September 1971.

One significant problem in demand for agricultural credit has been that of gaining access to institutions and markets that could provide credit at rates comparable to those charged to other forms of business, with perhaps some adjustment because of the risks peculiar to agriculture. The establishment of government-sponsored agricultural credit agencies, mentioned in Chapter 5, gave farmers an improved position. First, it gave them alternative sources of borrowing, and in some cases *a* source of borrowing, by creating credit agencies that could supplement lending by commercial banks, life insurance companies, and individuals. Second, by establishing institutions that could obtain funds for loans to agriculture by issuing bonds, it gave noncorporate farms access to the bond market. Incidentally, the bond could be issued at relatively low rates of interest because the agencies were government-sponsored and government-regulated, and the securities, as agency securities, had nearly the same status as Treasury securities.

Demand for agricultural credit is a relatively small factor in an economy such as that of the United States, in which a very small percentage of GNP is produced by the agricultural sector. Nevertheless, the need of agriculture for loanable funds has increased rapidly since the mid-1930s, and the importance of credit for agriculture in providing the marginal funds needed cannot be overlooked.

Most of the long-term demand by the agricultural sector for credit is for mortgage credit, used in buying land and sometimes to obtain funds on the security of land already owned. Although the direct demand is for mortgage credit, if the funds are obtained from a government agency—for example, a Federal Land Bank—the Federal Land Bank obtains its funds primarily from the issue of bonds. Thus the level of bond interest yields has relevance for farmers, and high bond interest rates may indirectly affect farm credit.

Most of the short-term and intermediate-term demand for credit by the agricultural sector is met by commercial banks and by government-sponsored agencies such as the Production Credit Associations, which in turn can obtain funds from another government-sponsored agency, the Federal Intermediate Credit Banks. These institutions, in turn, issue bonds to obtain funds, so that both long-term credit and short-term credit depend to some extent on bond interest rates.

THE DEMAND FOR MORTGAGE CREDIT

Mortgage credit means credit secured by mortgages on real estate. Most housing is constructed and purchased with the aid of mortgage credit, and a substantial amount of nonresidential construction also makes use of mortgage credit. Construction by public utilities and by many industrial firms, however, is usually financed by bond issues, and such demand is not considered as mortgage credit even if the bonds are secured by mortgages. Construction undertaken by nonprofit institutions, such as college buildings, hospitals, and religious structures, and some commercial and industrial buildings, including office buildings, is often financed by loans secured by mortgages on buildings being constructed, and is a factor in mortgage credit demand. Thus mortgage credit demand comes from consumers, nonprofit institutions, and to some extent from business firms.

A substantial amount of mortgage credit is used to finance purchases of existing houses, existing offices, and other buildings. As inflation has occurred, prices of homes have frequently risen by more than enough to offset depreciation, and as mortgages were paid off, new purchasers found that larger mortgages were needed to buy them. Demand for such credit does not depend directly on the current volume of construction, and hence may be more difficult to forecast than the volume of mortgage credit needed to finance new construction. Sometimes homeowners borrow by increasing the amounts of existing mortgages, or by obtaining new mortgages, to use the funds for other purposes.

Nature and Growth of Mortgage Credit

Mortgage debt differs from other debt because the collateral consists of mortgages on land and buildings. Hence, although attention should always properly be given to ability of borrowers to repay, some weight is inevitably placed on property values. Emphasis is given to such things as loan-to-value ratios, and to methods of appraising values of properties on a cost basis, on a market sales basis, or on a capitalization of prospective income basis. None of these bases is completely satisfactory, as costs cannot be accurately adjusted to reflect current values, sales prices of similar properties are not entirely accurate indexes of potential sales prices of particular properties because properties vary, and prospective income cannot be accurately foreseen.

Mortgage debt also differs from certain other debt because mortgages are heterogeneous. They differ in amounts, properties differ in descriptions and characteristics, and they differ in quality in terms of assurance of clear title and other factors. Hence, unlike corporate and government bonds, which have broad secondary markets based on continuous sale of homogeneous securities, mortgages have a much less adequate secondary market and much less liquidity. It should be noted, of course, that mortgage loans are not as heterogeneous as other business loans, and that there is some secondary market for mortgages, while there is almost no secondary market for business loans. Liquidity of mortgages is intermediate between that of bonds and of business loans.

Mortgage credit (mortgage debt outstanding) has increased very rapidly; the increase in mortgage credit since World War II has been greater than the increase in government and corporate securities combined. Even this comparison understates the volume of mortgage lending; because repayment of mortgage debt is usually on an amortized basis, such mortgage debt is repaid every year, and the funds are normally loaned out again.

Mobile homes—which some say are neither mobile nor homes—are not yet included in national income accounts under the heading of construction, but are classified as consumer durables. Their purchase is generally financed by finance companies or commercial banks, and in some ways the mobile-home dealer operates like an automobile dealer. Nevertheless, mobile homes must be considered as part of the housing picture; they are financed by what is termed consumer credit rather than mortgage credit, however.[16]

Sources of the Demand for Mortgage Credit

Demand for mortgage credit depends on the volume of residential and nonresidential construction, just as business demand for credit depends on spending for plant and equipment and inventories. It may be argued that the volume of construction depends in part on availability of mortgage credit. If mortgage credit is readily available, builders may be induced to expand operations more than they otherwise would. It is difficult to determine whether availability of mortgage credit is a significant independent factor determining the volume of construction. Maisel has included the interest rate on conventional mortgages as one factor in a regression equation used to predict the number of housing starts.[17] Certainly, high interest rates and restricted availability of credit frequently have curtailed an increase in housing starts.

Demand for mortgage credit for residential construction also depends upon the number of housing units being constructed, the land and building costs involved, and the loan-to-value ratios used by lending institutions or individual mortgage lenders. The number of housing units being constructed depends in turn on the number of new households being formed and the number of houses demolished for slum clearance, highway construction, and so on. Both the number of households to be formed and the number to be demolished are relatively accurately predictable, although at times certain factors may create problems for those who attempt to analyze housing demand; for example, after a wartime period in which many families were forced to live together, newly married couples often living with their parents, there may be a demand for new housing arising out of "undoubling," the amount of which may be difficult to estimate. Construction costs vary with price levels, number of rooms per house, and features included in construction (built-in appliances, etc.). Land costs also vary with price levels, but depend to some extent on the relative numbers of single-family and apartment dwellings being built; land on which apartment houses are built is

[16]See the interesting article by Lawrence A. Mayer, "Mobile Homes Move into the Breach," *Fortune*, March 1970, pp. 126–30; 144–46.

[17]See Sherman Maisel, *Financing Real Estate* (New York: McGraw-Hill, 1965). Housing starts may be assumed to be a function of interest rates on conventional mortgages, vacancies, the ratio of rental costs to housing construction costs, the change in the number of houses and apartment buildings under construction, and the number of removals. Housing starts may be related to some of these variables with lag, for example, they may be related to the average level of mortgage interest rates in several previous quarters. Removals may be related to the previous period's stock of housing. With estimates of the lags involved, the regression equation can be developed. Such a forecasting equation is not suitable for continued use without modification because conditions change. However, like computer models used in forecasting general business activity, such a partial model of one sector of the economy has definite usefulness.

usually more expensive per square foot, but the number of square feet per household is smaller. Finally, loan-to-value ratios depend partly upon the amount of financing being handled by particular types of institutions. The major types of institutions making mortgage loans are commercial banks, savings and loan associations, mutual savings banks, and life insurance companies (which frequently purchase mortgage loans already made by mortgage companies). Each of these institutions is subject to regulations that limit maturities of mortgage loans and in many instances limit loan-to-value ratios. Loan-to-value ratios have been raised in recent years; they are usually higher on FHA-insured or VA-guaranteed loans than on so-called conventional mortgage loans. FHA-insured and VA-guaranteed loans are insured or guaranteed by a federal government agency, the Federal Housing Administration (FHA) or the Veterans' Administration (VA), in return for payment of a specified premium. Although financial institutions may suffer some losses because of repossession and other costs, they are insured against loss of principal and interest on such loans. FHA-insured and VA-guaranteed loans are more common when funds are more readily available because lending institutions make them at such times, although at other times they prefer the higher rates and less red tape of conventional loans.

The demand for nonresidential mortgage credit is based largely on the amount of construction of commercial, religious, educational, and hospital buildings. The amount of such construction is more difficult to forecast and is likely to be a source of error in any forecast of demand for mortgage credit. Although almost all increases in residential construction are financed by mortgage credit, a substantial part of an increase in nonresidential construction may be financed by other means. Utilities finance construction through bond issues, and this is frequently true for other industrial firms. Construction by state and local governments is usually financed by municipal bond issues. Hence even an accurate forecast of the trend in total nonresidential construction does not assure an accurate forecast of the nonresidential demand for mortgage credit.[18]

Short and Long Cycles in Construction Activity

Construction activity is cyclical, exhibiting both short-term cycles and long cycles. Short-term cycles in construction activity tend to exhibit a pattern different from that of cycles in general business activity; construction activity generally rises during the latter part of a decline in general business activity, continues to rise as general business activity begins to rise, and begins to decline some time before the peak in general business activity. Like most

[18]Robinson Newcomb has emphasized the impact of the acceleration principle on construction: because construction may add only perhaps 3 percent to the total stock of buildings and other structures in a year, small variations in demand for utilization of structures can cause large changes in the amount of construction; see Robinson Newcomb, "Construction Forecasting," in William F. Butler and Robert A. Kavesh, eds., *How Business Economists Forecast* (Englewood Cliffs, N.J.: Prentice-Hall, 1966), pp. 186–220.

forms of investment, construction activity tends to fluctuate more widely than general business activity. One factor causing the difference in pattern is the sensitivity of construction activity to interest rates and availability of credit. Interest rate costs constitute a large part of total costs of financing construction, and hence a rise in interest rates during an upswing tends to inhibit construction, especially residential construction. As general business activity declines, and interest rates fall, the lower interest costs and greater availability of credit encourage an increase in construction activity.

Long cycles are also found in construction activity; these long cycles have typically been about twenty years from trough to trough, the most recent clearly identifiable trough being in the period 1942–44, probably because of the war. Shorter cycles are superimposed on the long cycles, and both must be kept in mind in forecasts of cyclical activity. The evidence for the existence of long cycles and the length of long cycles is not entirely satisfactory. Thus, after the trough in 1942–44, the next trough should have occurred in the late 1950s or the early 1960s. No clear trough at that time is identifiable, although housing activity did not rise significantly.

It is generally presumed that there is a "normal" level of vacancies in housing, related to size, mobility, income level, and rate of growth of the population, and to tax and other costs of holding property vacant. There is also presumed to be a "normal" demand for housing, composed of the number of net households formed, the increase in "normal" vacancies, and demolitions. As construction activity rises and housing starts begin to exceed the level of normal demand, vacancies begin to rise. When builders begin to recognize that their activities are outrunning demand, the number of housing starts begins to fall, but the number of vacancies may continue to rise as long as housing starts still exceed the normal demand for houses. When they fall below that level, vacancies begin to fall; they may continue to fall as long as housing starts are below the level of demand. Fluctuations in the number of housing starts are generally rather wide because of the time required for developing real estate subdivisions and because of the large number of small builders, many of whom have relatively little knowledge concerning general market conditions.

Flow of Mortgage Funds

Because the amount of mortgage loans demanded in any area does not usually equal the amount of mortgage lending available in the area, mortgage market facilities are needed to permit funds to flow in greater volume to areas in which there is greater demand, and to permit resale of at least some mortgages when lending activity is greater than the inflow of funds permits. Many lending institutions, especially in recent years, have been active in lending in areas outside of their own localities, and government agencies have been established to increase the market for mortgages by being ready to buy and sell mortgages. Institutions located in areas where mortgage loan demand is heavy have solicited savings deposits from out-of-state savers, although restrictions have been imposed on the extent of such solicitations. Such deposits may be more volatile than other share accounts, as they are often made in response to advertising of interest rates higher than those paid in other states. In recent years thrift institutions have not been very successful in attracting such funds from other areas. The Federal Home Loan Bank system has sometimes restricted savings and loan associations that have obtained more than a specified proportion of their savings from other states.

Forecasting the Demand for Mortgage Credit

Forecasting the demand for mortgage credit involves combination of a forecast of the demand for residential mortgage credit with one for the demand for nonresidential mortgage financing. Maturities of mortgages are limited, although the number of years to maturity has been increasing in recent years. Although some increase in maturity may be possible, to keep the annual interest rate from rising too much, when demand for mortgage loans is heavy, the rate of interest rises rather sharply. Above certain interest rate levels, demand for mortgage credit may be responsive to changes in interest rates. Borrowers find that high interest rates cause monthly payments to be much greater, and normally their income is not rising sufficiently to enable them to make such payments easily. When interest rate ceilings are imposed, as they have been on FHA-insured and VA-guaranteed loans, demand cannot be satisfied at rates above the ceilings. Unless mortgages are discounted to the sellers, such mortgage loans cannot be made. Thus the burden of interest cost may be shifted in part to sellers.

CONSUMER DEMAND FOR LOANABLE FUNDS

Consumer demand for loanable funds could be ignored by treating the supply of loanable funds from consumers as a net supply, subtracting consumer borrowing from gross saving. However, it is preferable to begin with the gross supply of loanable funds by consumers, and to treat consumer demand for loanable funds as a part of total demand. This is in accord with the reality of the market for loanable funds, and facilitates analysis because it separates consumer saving from consumer borrowing.

Consumer Saving and Borrowing

At least since the advent of Keynesian theory in the 1930s, it has been generally assumed that consumer saving depends on consumer income. Whether the correlation was made between personal saving and GNP or between personal saving and disposable personal income, relatively high correlations were obtained with annual data. This led to the presumption that consumer saving is not very sensitive to interest rate changes. Because saving by business firms (depreciation and retained earnings) is also not very sensitive to changes in interest rates, the conclusion was reached that saving could be treated as a function of income, not a function of interest rates. Whatever the factors that determined how much income was saved, it seemed that interest rates played a small role.

However, there was some variation in the rate of saving out of income over the course of a business cycle. Moreover, the marginal rate of saving did not (with the possible exception of a year or two in the Great Depression) become negative for the population as a whole, as might have been expected from a long-run consumption function of the same form as the original formulation of short-term Keynesian theory.[19] These facts led to the elaboration of more sophisticated theories of the relationship between saving and income.

Arthur Smithies suggested that the shift might be related to changes in the proportions of certain groups in the population and to the continual introduction of new commodities that competed for consumer spending. Cross-section studies show that farmers save more than urban residents with the same levels of income; the shift of population from farms to cities might tend to raise consumption and reduce saving. Older persons consume more and save less of their income; the relatively greater proportion of older persons in the population thus might also tend to raise consumption. Finally, the introduction of new commodities might tend to have the same effect.[20]

James Duesenberry suggested that cyclical fluctuations in the rate of saving might be explained by the fact that income fluctuates over the cycle; as income rises, consumption rises, but with a lag, so that at high levels of business activity, there is more saving. Then as business activity declines in a recession, consumers reduce their spending, but not as much as the decline in income; they are reluctant to reduce consumption from the peak attained in the period of peak income. Hence the rate of saving declines.[21]

Milton Friedman introduced the somewhat different view that consumption is proportional, not to measured income (as measured in GNP accounts), but to "permanent" income—long-run expected income, which may be estimated by extrapolation of a weighted average of past incomes, the most recent income being given the greatest weight. He argued that consumption is not related to "transitory" income, unexpected windfalls. A considerable number of attempts have been made to test the permanent income hypothesis, with varying results. Both Kuznets' data on GNP and Friedman's hypothesis

[19]In the original formulation of Keynesian theory of the consumption function, based on his statement that "men are disposed, as a rule and on the average, to increase their consumption as their income increases, but not by as much as the increase in their income," $\Delta C/\Delta Y$ was assumed to be greater than zero but less than one. It was usually presumed, moreover, that $\Delta C/\Delta Y$ was sufficiently less than unity that at some low level of income, consumption would equal income, and there would be no saving. If it were assumed that the long-run consumption function had the same form, the implication was that at some time in the past there was no saving. The fact that in the long run C/Y was relatively constant (instead of falling as income rose) led to reconsideration of the relationships.

[20]Arthur Smithies, "Forecasting Postwar Demand: I," *Econometrica*, January 1945, pp. 1–14.

[21]James Duesenberry, *Income, Savings, and the Theory of Consumer Behavior* (Cambridge, Mass.: Harvard University Press, 1949).

suggested that $\Delta C/\Delta Y$ was approximately equal to C/Y (not less, as had been assumed).[22] However, some tests found that $\Delta C/\Delta Y$ was less than C/Y, although the difference was not as great when permanent income was used for Y as it was when income as measured in GNP was used.[23]

With any of the theories other than that of Friedman, there was no basis for a theory of consumer borrowing, except borrowing that might be done by those with low incomes, who might spend more than their total incomes. Such borrowing does occur, but it does not constitute the major portion of present-day consumer borrowing. Most present-day consumer borrowing is done by middle-income consumers and is related to purchases of automobiles or appliances, or to the remodeling and improvement of homes.

A theory of consumption similar to Friedman's, that can account for this common type of consumer borrowing quite easily, is that developed by Modigliani and Brumberg, and further amplified by Modigliani and Ando.[24] This theory hypothesizes that in any year consumption is proportional to the present value of total resources accruing to the individual or head of household over the rest of his life. Total resources accruing to him over the rest of his life are the sum of net worth from previous periods plus the present value of income the person expects to earn. Expected income could be measured in a manner similar to that used by Friedman, but Modigliani and Ando preferred to hypothesize that expected income is the same as current income except for a possible scale factor, or that the figure should be adjusted by a different scale factor for employed and for unemployed. With this hypothesis, young married couples, because they can look forward to a long period of discounted expected income, could be expected to spend much of their total income, and perhaps more than the total. If the previous peak income is regarded as a proxy for wealth or net worth, the Ando-Modigliani formulation is similar to that of Duesenberry, mentioned above.

The theory of the consumption function is still in the process of development, and no firm final conclusion can be reached at this point. A related question is the impact of stock market prices on consumption, as rising prices of stocks and resultant capital gains add to net worth. of those who invest in stocks.[25] The evidence to date is consistent with the life cycle hypothesis

[22]Kuznets' data were reported in Simon Kuznets, *National Product Since 1869* (New York: National Bureau of Economic Research, 1946), and the permanent income hypothesis was presented in Milton Friedman, *A Theory of the Consumption Function* (Princeton: Princeton University Press, 1957).

[23]See, for example, Thomas Mayer, "The Propensity to Consume Permanent Income," *American Economic Review*, December 1966, pp. 1158–77.

[24]Albert Ando and Franco Modigliani, "The 'Life Cycle' Hypothesis of Saving: Aggregate Implications and Tests," *American Economic Review*, March 1963, pp. 55–84. For a review of recent developments in the theory of consumer spending, saving and borrowing, see Robert Ferber, "Consumer Economics, A Survey," *Journal of Economic Literature*, December 1973, pp. 1303–42, esp. pp. 1304–12.

[25]See Robert H. Rasche, "Impact of the Stock Market on Private Demand," *American Economic Review*, Papers and Proceedings, May 1972, pp. 220–28. See also Kul B. Bhatia, "Capital Gains and the Aggregate Consumption Function," *American Economic Review*, December 1972, pp. 866–79.

and the presumption that changes in prices of assets such as stocks can significantly affect consumption; but the evidence is not such that there is a consensus of agreement on these points.

The Growth of Consumer Credit Demand

Consumer credit has grown rapidly in the twentieth century, as new institutions have developed in this field, and existing institutions such as commercial banks have been attracted to it. The growth of consumer debt has two significant effects: (1) it permits increased consumer spending and thus indirectly tends (through a feedback effect) to increase business investment spending; and (2) it creates a volume of liabilities that compete with liabilities of other sectors, thus causing interest rates to be somewhat higher than they would be otherwise. To some extent, therefore, it may also tend to reduce investment spending based on borrowing; it is difficult to evaluate the overall effect on investment.

The growth of consumer debt, especially consumer installment debt, is largely the result of the growth of the automobile and appliance industries. Borrowing to purchase these types of assets, especially automobiles, can be justified on the ground that the assets provide services for a number of years, and it is therefore reasonable to pay for them over a period of years.

Since 1920, consumer credit has increased very rapidly in three periods: in 1920–29, it grew at 15 percent per year; in 1936–41, it grew at 11 percent per year; and in 1947–55, it grew at 19 percent per year. It decreased in the depression of the 1930s and during World War II, but it did not decline significantly in the postwar recessions. Growth of the various forms of consumer installment credit is shown in Figure 7–5. Installment credit constitutes over 80 percent of total consumer credit; the remainder, noninstallment credit, is composed of single-payment loans (chiefly from banks), charge accounts (including bank credit cards), and service credit from utilities and professional men such as doctors and dentists.

As the ratio of consumer credit to personal income rose, some concern developed that continued rise in this ratio might create problems. One economist attempted to explain the trend of this ratio. He assumed that a "life cycle" theory of saving and borrowing was valid, and that most borrowing would be done by young household heads acquiring durable goods. Therefore he argued that the increase in the number of households and the increase in average income per household would be the major determinants of the size of consumer installment debt. From this reasoning he derived the result that the ratio of consumer installment credit outstanding will tend to approach a limiting constant equal to $\dfrac{k\,(1 + r)}{r}$, in which k is the increase in consumer installment debt as a fixed proportion of personal income and r is the annual rate of growth of personal income.[26] A later study used personal income, the

[26]Alain Enthoven, "The Growth of Installment Credit and the Future of Prosperity," *American Economic Review*, December 1957, pp. 913–29. See also his later supplementary article, in response to criticisms, "On a Debt-Income Model of Consumer Installment Credit Growth: Reply," *American Economic Review*, June 1964, pp. 415–17.

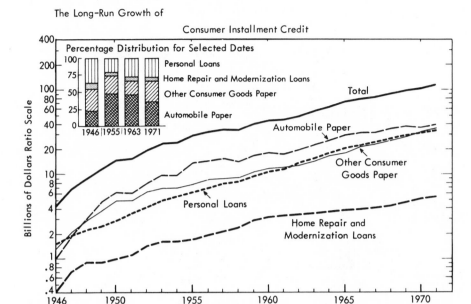

FIGURE 7–5   Consumer Installment Credit

SOURCE: Federal Reserve Bank of Kansas City, *Monthly Review*, February 1973, p. 4.

square of personal income, the number of income-receiving units, and the level of liquid assets held by the household sector of the economy as the determinants of the ratio.[27] The two models predicted, or explained, the growth of consumer installment credit rather well, as indicated in Figure 7–6. The second model may have been slightly more accurate, but this model assumed an inverse relationship between liquid asset holdings and consumer debt, which seems to be incorrect. Probably it is best to assume the simplest case—the rapid rise in consumer debt in the decade after World War II was caused largely by the shortage of durable goods during the war, and after the war consumers tried to "catch up."

Neither model explained very well the deceleration in the growth of consumer installment credit relative to personal income in the late 1960s and early 1970s. It is quite possible that the factors responsible were the general rise and wide fluctuations in interest rates, and the onset of relatively rapid inflation. Although it might be assumed by some that inflation would tend to increase consumer installment credit by inducing people to buy more before prices rise, within certain limits inflation seems to have the opposite effect.

[27]Helen M. Hunter, "A Behavioral Model of the Long-Run Growth of Aggregate Consumer Credit in the United States," *Review of Economics and Statistics*, May 1966, pp. 124–31.

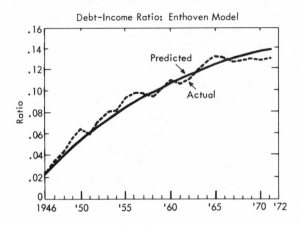

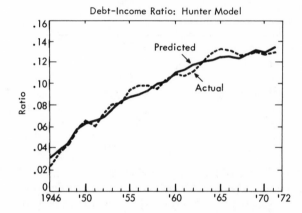

FIGURE 7–6   Ratio of Consumer Installment Debt Outstanding to Personal Income

SOURCE: Federal Reserve Bank of Kansas City, *Monthly Review*, February 1973, pp. 6, 7.

One hypothesis is that consumers try to save more and borrow less because they feel that asset holdings may not be sufficient to provide for future expenditures. Liquid assets held by families in the $5,000 to $15,000 income bracket, which do most of the installment credit buying, dropped in 1965–70, and it may well be that the future trend in the consumer installment debt/personal income ratio depends on the trend in interest rates and inflation.[28]

[28]Michael J. Prell, "The Long-Run Growth of Consumer Installment Credit—Some Observations," Federal Reserve Bank of Kansas City, *Monthly Review*, February 1973, pp. 3–13. Prell regarded the factors restraining the growth of consumer credit in the late 1960s and early 1970s as chiefly cyclical factors.

Consumer Credit Demand and Economic Stabilization

The question has been raised many times whether consumer credit contributes to increasing the amplitude of business fluctuations. With the possible exception of the period 1954–55, consumer credit was not the *main* factor in business upswings, but such credit has amplified fluctuations. Cases can be found, however, in which cash sales fluctuated more than credit sales—for example, automobile sales in 1950–53.

Selective regulation of consumer credit may be necessary if consumer credit is destabilizing and if general control of money and bank credit does not significantly affect consumer credit. It has been argued that consumer credit is slow to react to general control of money and credit, or perhaps is little affected, because (1) consumers are not sensitive to changes in the interest rates they must pay, and such rates do not change much; and (2) banks and other consumer lenders are slow to restrict consumer credit because they have sizable staffs and do not wish them to be idle, and because they find consumer lending quite profitable. Profitability of consumer lending, of course, varies with the level of other interest rates; when other interest rates are high, consumer lending may have a smaller advantage, or possibly no advantage, in profit potential.

Evidence from the period 1955–56, a period of credit restraint by the monetary authorities, indicates that both large banks and medium-sized banks restricted consumer credit in this period when their deposit experience was unfavorable—when they either lost deposits or had a smaller increase in deposits than the average bank.[29] There was some evidence that medium-sized banks in the sample, banks with deposits of $10 million to $50 million, were somewhat slow to restrict consumer credit, but both groups of banks restricted consumer loans more than commercial loans. Large banks, especially those with unfavorable deposit experience, sold government securities in order to continue to expand business loans.

Evidence also indicates that tightening credit leads banks to increase compensating balances required for finance companies, to apply general restrictions on lines of credit to such companies, and to reduce purchases of

[29]Paul Smith, "Response of Consumer Loans to General Credit Conditions," *American Economic Review*, September 1958, pp. 649–55. Smith's data were obtained from banks that had more than one-third of their total loans in the form of consumer loans. Data from this period are used because the policy of restraint after the 1957–58 recession prevented output from again reaching its potential level until 1965, and the credit crunches of 1966 and 1969 provide somewhat different conditions. More recently, Thomas Mayer, "Financial Guidelines and Credit Controls," *Journal of Money, Credit, and Banking*, May 1972, pp. 360–73, argued that tight monetary policy has a direct impact on consumer installment credit; he simply observed a positive correlation between rates of nominal money stock growth and installment credit or debt/income ratio growth. It should be remembered that, although most interest rates rose in the late 1960s, consumer installment loan rates did not, in general, because they are limited by statutory ceilings.

commercial paper offered by finance companies. Finance companies are able to offset such restriction to some extent by shifting from bank borrowing to capital market borrowing through the issuing of debentures and through directly placed commercial paper, commercial paper sold directly to insurance companies and other institutional lenders. Such borrowing in these circumstances may be at relatively high cost, and hence there is some restraint. To the extent that business firms and other institutions are willing to reduce their liquidity in the form of cash and to purchase commercial paper, velocity of money may increase and consumer credit may be less affected by restraint.

"Tight" money has comparatively little effect on terms of loans to consumers, but rates charged to dealers are raised and floor-plan credit used to finance dealers' inventories of automobiles and appliances is tightened.

Selective control of consumer credit was used during three recent periods —during World War II, for a brief period in 1948–49, and again in 1950–52 as a part of emergency measures for the Korean war period. Regulation W, issued by the Federal Reserve System, specified minimum down payments and maximum loan maturities. Enforcement involved many administrative problems: it was difficult to control installment sales credit without controlling consumer installment loan credit; the use of the device of large "balloon payments" at the ends of repayment periods, used as a device to extend maturities, had to be guarded against; and regulations had to be very carefully worded to prevent escape from control by breaking sales into parts. Objections were raised by some who argued that Regulation W discriminated against lower-income consumers. The Federal Reserve System has desired to avoid such controls unless they seemed essential, as they did during World War II when automobiles were not being manufactured. After extensive study, the Board of Governors of the Federal Reserve System did not recommend that they be given even a standby power to impose such control, and concluded that fluctuations in consumer installment credit, with some exceptions, were "generally within limits that could be tolerated in a rapidly growing and dynamic economy."[30] The arguments leading to the conclusion that consumer credit control is not needed except in emergencies may be summarized as: (1) consumer credit may not again grow as rapidly as it did just after World War II, when consumers made large purchases of durable goods; (2) changes in consumer credit have not been *significantly* destabilizing, as they have amounted to only about 1/7 of total changes in GNP in recent years; (3) pressure for credit control can be exerted through other means; (4) there is no assurance that money not spent on durable goods would be spent in "better" ways; and (5) consumer credit control may not prevent loan delinquencies because reasons for such delinquencies are many, delinquencies often occurring when consumers are young, transient, and inexperienced, rather than when down payments are too small and maturities too long.[31]

[30]*Federal Reserve Bulletin*, June 1957, p. 648.
[31]These conclusions were reached in a study by Paul W. McCracken, James C. T. Mao, and Cedric Fricke, *Consumer Installment Credit and Public Policy* (Ann Arbor, Michigan: Bureau of Business Research, Graduate School of Business Administration, University of Michigan, 1965).

SUMMARY

This chapter has analyzed the demand for credit by the business sector, the demand for mortgage credit, and consumer demand for loanable funds. Attempt has been made to indicate the reason, or summarize a theory explaining why a particular demand for credit arises, and then to examine the manner in which this demand appears in the market for loanable funds.

Consideration has been given, where appropriate, to interest sensitivity of the various categories of demand, and to means of forecasting demand. Cyclical changes accompanying the general fluctuations in business activity and the real estate cycle were described.

Business demand for loanable funds, based upon rates of return that businessmen believe they can earn by investment in real capital assets, constitutes the major source of fluctuations in demand. These fluctuations have significant impact on interest rates. Because of relatively high productivity of capital, demand for business loans tends to persist in periods of high economic activity, even when interest rates rise sharply. Because of the profitability of business loans, commercial banks and occasionally some other financial institutions tend to satisfy business loan demand if they can, even at the expense of other types of loans.

The demand for mortgage credit is based primarily on factors such as household formation and demolition of houses, and does not necessarily increase at the same time as business loan demand. Thus financial institutions that supply mortgage credit (primarily commercial banks, mutual savings banks, savings and loan associations, life insurance companies, and mortgage companies) may expand such credit when business loan demand is slack.

Economists have gradually come to accept a permanent consumption or life cycle hypothesis of consumer spending and saving, rather than the early Keynesian explanation that spending by consumers was based on current income. Young married couples, looking forward to a long period of discounted expected income, may spend their total income and go into debt. Thus consumer credit demand is likely to be increasing when the population in the twenty to forty-four year age bracket is increasing. Consumer credit demand is also affected by the desire to purchase durable goods that have long useful lives, providing service over many years. Consumer credit may also contribute to increasing the amplitude of business fluctuations because consumers are not very sensitive to increases in interest rates and banks are somewhat slow to restrict consumer credit. Nevertheless, evidence has led most economists to conclude that the overexpansion of consumer credit in boom periods is not likely to be serious enough to justify special controls on consumer credit. Fluctuations in consumer credit are generally within limits that can be tolerated in a dynamic, growing economy. Except in wartime, there does not seem to be enough justification for consumer credit controls.

QUESTIONS FOR DISCUSSION

1. Present the argument that relates the interest rate which can be paid by business firms to the rate they expect to obtain by investment in real capital assets.

2. Why is it generally presumed that business firms use internally generated funds for investment purposes before they borrow external funds for such needs?

3. What is the role of the debt/equity ratio in determining the extent of business borrowing for investment purposes?

4. Is long-term investment ever financed by short-term borrowing? Under what conditions may this occur?

5. Why is borrowing to finance investment in inventories likely to be from commercial banks or business finance companies? Show how commercial bank lending is important in inventory fluctuations.

6. Why may business borrowing for liquidity purposes occur even after a long period of increasing capital investment has ended?

7. Why were government-sponsored financial institutions that obtained funds by selling bonds important in providing additional credit for agriculture?

8. Evaluate the argument that, in contrast to business demand for loanable funds, the demand for mortgage credit may be a dependent variable, the independent variable being the *supply* of mortgage credit.

9. How does the life cycle theory of the consumption function differ from the theory of the consumption function originally presented by John Maynard Keynes and early Keynesian economists?

10. Why are measures to control the availability of credit generally relied upon to control expansion of business and mortgage credit, whereas direct control of consumer demand for loanable funds is sometimes urged?

SELECTED REFERENCES

This chapter involves some integration of the theory of business finance with part of macroeconomic theory. Hence a text on business finance, such as Stephen H. Archer and Charles A. D'Ambrosio, *Business Finance: Theory and Management*, 2nd ed. (New York: The Macmillan Company, 1972) may be a useful reference.

Relevant macroeconomic theory is discussed in detail in Gardner Ackley, *Macroeconomic Theory* (New York: The Macmillan Company, 1961).

Much more detailed coverage on some points relative to demand for loanable funds is provided by Polakoff and others, *op. cit.*, Chapters 12–15.

An interesting discussion of corporate borrowing and the "liquidity crisis" of 1970 is found in Carol J. Loomis, "The Lesson of the Credit Crisis," *Fortune*, May 1971, pp. 141–43; 274–86.

Whether the rise in business spending for plant and equipment in the latter part of the 1960s was a temporary deviation or the beginning of a long-run trend is the subject of an interesting article by Lawrence A. Mayer, "Capital Goods May Get A Growing Share," *Fortune*, June 1971, pp. 97–99; 150–54.

For statistical data and projections, see the annual *Supply and Demand for Credit* (Salomon Brothers) and the *Investment Outlook* (Bankers Trust Company) as well as the *Federal Reserve Bulletin*.

For comments on the illusory nature of part of retained earnings in a period of inflation, see Henry C. Wallich and Mable I. Wallich, "Profits Aren't As Good as They Look," *Fortune*, March 1974, pp. 126–29, 172.

8

Government and Foreign Demand for Loanable Funds

Government demand for loanable funds includes both demand by state and local government units and demand by the federal government. State and local government units borrow because, like private sectors of the economy, their planned or unplanned expenditures frequently exceed their receipts, at least temporarily. State and local government units have no way of creating money to meet their needs; hence their demand is similar in many respects to that of the private sectors discussed in Chapter 7. The federal government can, however, if it wishes, create money. Moreover, although the Federal Reserve System is to some degree "independent" of the government, it has an obligation to take some appropriate actions to facilitate government borrowing. Thus demand for loanable funds and supply of loanable funds are not entirely independent, and especially in wartime and in other emergency periods, a central bank must create money when governments require it.

Foreign demand includes borrowing by foreign firms and official agencies from United States individuals and financial institutions, marketing of foreign securities in United States money and capital markets, and also the direct investment made by United States firms and individuals in branches and subsidiaries abroad. Because direct foreign investment, like domestic direct investment, does not channel funds into a money or capital market, direct investment may be excluded when the market for loanable funds is discussed.

Foreign countries constitute sources of supply of loanable funds as well as sources of demand. Foreign individuals, institutions, firms, and governments invest in the United States money and capital markets, and supply funds to certain types of financial institutions. Because neither foreign demand nor foreign supply of loanable funds has been discussed thus far, both are treated in this chapter.

Government and foreign demand for loanable funds are important because they frequently fluctuate widely, sometimes tripling in one or two years, and then declining again to small fractions of the peak amounts. For example, in

1969 it was estimated that government and foreign demands for loanable funds totaled only $9.9 billion, whereas in 1971 it was estimated that they totaled $44.4 billion and in 1973 it was estimated that they totaled $31 billion. (These figures exclude foreign demand in the form of sales of equities, for which data are not readily available.) Thus they are important elements in demand, having a more than proportionate effect upon interest rates because of their wide fluctuations.

STATE AND LOCAL GOVERNMENT DEMAND FOR LOANABLE FUNDS

Like other sectors, state and local government units borrow because available receipts are not sufficient to meet desired expenditures, and future receipts can be expected to provide the funds to repay debt over a period during which assets purchased with the aid of borrowing will continue to provide services.

Why State and Local Government Units Borrow

State and local government units have provided in increasing amounts services that require capital expenditures—highways, schools, water supply facilities and sewers, electric utilities (except where these are supplied by private companies), airports, parks, and others. Of course, in connection with these facilities there are also current expenditures: highway maintenance, salaries of teachers and school administrators, and so on. The ratio of capital expenditures to total expenditures of state and local government units has been quite stable, approximately 26 percent since World War I; both have grown at an annual rate of about 9 percent. This is somewhat higher than the average annual growth of GNP because the growth of the automobile and airplane industries, the trend toward urbanization, and the trend toward a greater number of years of education for the average person have caused state and local government expenditures to increase at a rapid pace.[1]

In the long run, the ratio of borrowing by state and local government units to their capital expenditures has averaged about 55 percent. This ratio has declined somewhat since World War II, as federal government aid has replaced, to some extent, local financing. Thus state and local government debt outstanding has increased at a slightly slower rate (about 8 percent per year) than state and local government expenditures.

During World War II, state and local government units borrowed very small amounts, as resources were diverted to wartime purposes. As receipts continued to flow in at normal and sometimes higher rates, state and local government units built up their holdings of liquid assets to such an extent that by the end of World War II they were, on a net basis, out of debt—their liquid assets exceeded their debts.

---

[1]Occasionally, expenditures other than construction expenditures—such as veterans' bonuses, welfare benefits, and disaster relief—have been financed by borrowing, but the long-run average of such borrowing is small.

Since World War II, state and local government units have borrowed more heavily, to finance construction of facilities mentioned above. State and local governments usually borrow all funds needed for planned construction before beginning a project. Such funds, borrowed at relatively low cost, because of the exemption of interest payments from federal income tax, can be invested in federal government securities at higher returns. Sometimes state and local government units have issued securities to provide funds to retire an older issue of securities on the first available call date. Some states also issued industrial aid bonds, to construct plants to specification for industrial firms, to which the plans were then leased. The lease payments are used to amortize the bond issue. Congress limited the amounts of such bond issues in 1968, and subsequently they have been less important.

There have been other changes in the purposes of state and local government borrowing, but some of these changes tend to offset others. For example, as state and local government borrowing for construction of toll highways declined, subsequent to passage of the Interstate Highway Act of 1956 that provided substantial federal government funding for major interstate highways, state and local government spending for other highways rose. Similarly, as spending for local school construction declined, spending for higher education increased.

Debt Limitations

State and local government units defaulted on debts on a number of occasions in depressions in the 1830s, 1870s, 1890s, 1930s, and on some other occasions. In many cases there was poor planning of capital expenditures. These defaults resulted in limitations on bases for borrowing, amounts of debt, and/or terms and conditions of borrowing; frequently these limitations were incorporated in state constitutions and other basic legislation.

Efforts to avoid the debt limitation provisions, as they could not easily be eliminated from state constitutions, were made by creating special agencies to construct and operate certain facilities. Revenues from use of these facilities were to constitute the source of repayment of the debt and payment of interest on the debt. Nonguaranteed debt has also been issued, partly to avoid debt limitations, since courts often ruled that the limitations applied only to fully guaranteed debt, and partly to avoid the need for taxpayers to provide the funds to meet debt service payments if user charges on the facilities fail to do so. In many cases, however, nonguaranteed debt is in effect guaranteed: the state is likely to provide aid for a facility before the agency defaults on its debt, or it is likely to make good on defaulted issues. Thus, the use of agency debt and nonguaranteed debt has resulted in higher interest costs, but the debt could be issued in this manner whereas it could not otherwise be issued because of the debt limitation provisions.[2]

[2]See William E. Mitchell, *The Effectiveness of Debt Limits on State and Local Government Borrowing, Bulletin,* New York University, Institute of Finance, No. 45, October 1967.

Interest Elasticity of Borrowing by State and Local Government Units

Recent periods of high interest rates have provided some evidence that borrowing by state and local government units is sensitive to changes in interest rates. The borrowing process is rather lengthy. After an initial decision to borrow, it may be necessary to have a vote by the legislature or a referendum vote by the citizens, and thereafter bids may be sought from investment bankers for the authorized issue of securities. These are cumbersome procedures that take considerable time. Credit crunches in 1966 and again in 1969 resulted in reduction or abandonment of planned borrowing in a number of cases, although it is not entirely clear whether financing of the projects was prevented or simply delayed by these conditions.[3]

Demand for loanable funds by state and local government units may be influenced by anticipated availability of the supply of loanable funds. State and local government securities have the almost unique feature that the interest income on them is exempt from federal income tax.[4] Because of this feature, their yields are relatively low, and hence they are sold almost exclusively to those who pay relatively high rates of federal income tax—high-income individuals, commercial banks, and property and casualty insurance companies constitute the major sources of demand for these securities. Thus, to some extent the demand for borrowing by state and local government units may be varied somewhat in accordance with anticipated availability of funds from these sources. When interest rates are high, usually because of relatively high demand for funds from the business sector, commercial banks and perhaps some of the other groups are likely to be relatively short of funds for purchase of state and local government securities.

After 1969, state and local governments found themselves with budget surpluses. Tax rates were increased and additional· funds were raised from fees at public hospitals and student tuition fees. At the same time, greatly increased federal aid provided a dramatic increase in funds after 1965 (see Figure 8–1).

There has been a slowdown in construction activity by state and local governments. Partly this can be traced to demographic factors, as declining population in school-age groups made it unnecessary to construct many additional schools. Partly it can be traced to voter rejection of some school and other bond issues. Partly, also, it is the result of high interest rates.

---

[3]John E. Petersen, "Response of State and Local Governments to Varying Credit Conditions," *Federal Reserve Bulletin*, March 1971, reported surveys indicating that about one-third of planned state and local government long-term borrowing was canceled because of tight money in 1969–70. However, more than half of the funds they had planned to raise through long-term borrowing was raised through short-term borrowing, not subject to legal interest rate ceilings.

[4]For special reasons, stocks issued by some private utilities have this characteristic, in whole or in part, but this situation is changing and the number of such stocks on which dividends are not fully taxed is declining sharply.

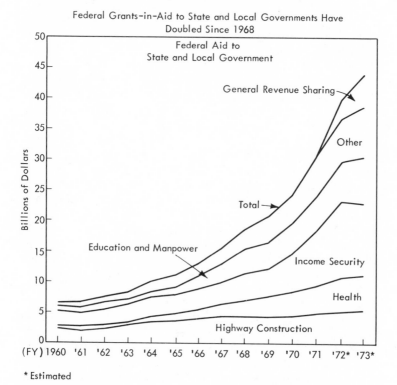

FIGURE 8–1   Federal Grants-in-aid to State and Local Governments

SOURCE: Federal Reserve Bank of Philadelphia, *Business Review*, March 1973, p. 23.

Until recently, state and local governments as a whole did not vary more than $1 or $2 billion from a balanced budget position, as shown in Figure 8–2. Thus, whether the government budget position was stimulative or restrictive depended on the situation of the federal government budget. However, with the growing surpluses in state and local government budgets after 1969, the net budget position of total government activity began to approach a balance by 1973. Thus total government fiscal impact on the economy was not a major factor in continued business expansion.

FEDERAL GOVERNMENT DEMAND FOR LOANABLE FUNDS

Government lending agencies were mentioned in Chapter 5, in discussion of the various institutions that act as intermediaries in *supplying* loanable funds. The major impact of the government, however, is in its role as a *demander* of loanable funds. There is presumed to be no interest elasticity in government demand; government does not vary its borrowing as interest rates rise and fall, but borrows whatever is needed to meet any gap between spending based on authorizations and appropriations and revenues based on current tax rates. Government borrowing is based on budget plans that combine decisions to continue present government programs, decisions based on the desirability of new programs as viewed by Congress, and fiscal policy decisions to spend more or less than is expected to be received in tax and other revenues. Because tax and spending decisions are not fully coordinated, results may be less than optimum. Questions of fiscal policy are explored in Chapter 17. The present concern is with how the process works and how the amount to be borrowed is determined.

The Budget Process

The budgetary cycle in the United States is far from simple. It has been estimated that the total time elapsing from budgetary planning in agencies and departments to the final development of the budget is about twenty-seven

The Near Balancing of State and Local Budgets Before 1970 Meant that the Federal Budget Position was a Close Approximation of the Total Government Surplus or Deficit

FIGURE 8–2   Government Budget Positions

SOURCE: Federal Reserve Bank of Philadelphia, *Business Review*, March 1973, p. 25.

months.[5] The President's budget message is usually delivered to Congress in late January of each year, presenting the proposed budget for the fiscal year beginning the next July 1.

Any new activity for which spending is proposed must be authorized by legislation, passed by appropriate committees of the House and Senate and approved by the President or allowed by him to become law without his signature. Legislation authorizing an activity is customarily followed by a bill appropriating money for the activity, although authorization and appropriation may be included in the same legislation. Tax bills must, under the Constitution, originate in the House of Representatives, and by custom appropriation bills also originate there. They are first considered by the Appropriations Committee of the House. Some programs are long-term or permanent and do not require annual authorization, while others require authorization and appropriations each year. Sometimes authority is given to spend money from borrowed funds. Authority to spend money, enter into contracts, or borrow money is given in legislation providing what has been termed "new obligational authority." If the authorization is to spend borrowed money, no further legislation is needed. Some government loan programs operate in this way. It is expected that the funds used will be borrowed and will then revolve as loans are made and repaid. Often Congress authorizes spending greater amounts than are actually spent in a given year, and there is often a carryover of obligational authority.

Authorizations and appropriations are considered singly or in groups, but there has been no mechanism to force Congress to consider the entire process and its result. Bills to require this were under consideration in early 1974, and rational consideration of total spending may gradually develop. Meanwhile, approval of specific authorizations sometimes makes it difficult or nearly impossible to approve other types of spending without sizable deficits in the final budget. For example, Social Security benefits were increased approximately 20 percent in 1972 and another 11 percent in 1974. The accompanying increase in Social Security contributions meant, in effect, an increase in taxes, the proceeds to go for increased Social Security benefits.

Government departments and agencies make expenditures, subject to controls established in the legislation. Actual payment is often made after goods have been delivered and found to meet specifications, although progress payments are also common. Departments and agencies, in purchasing goods and services, usually award contracts; this is termed "incurring obligations." There may be a substantial time lag, after funds are authorized and appropriated, before funds are spent or obligations incurred. There may be another time lag before such spending affects spending by other sectors of the economy. Thus the importance of cash flow data as well as budget data is evident.

Almost all government spending takes the form of issuance of checks on the government's General Account, maintained in Federal Reserve Banks. Thus government spending reduces government deposit balances in those banks and increases private deposits in commercial banks. Because these latter

[5]Jesse Burkhead, *Government Budgeting* (New York: John Wiley and Sons, 1956), p. 106.

are part of the money supply, the stock of money is thereby increased. Of course, it may have been reduced when funds were transferred from government deposits in the commercial banks to the government's General Account, to provide enough funds for expenditures.

Measurement of the Need for Borrowing: The Unified Budget

A preliminary measure of the need for borrowing may be gained from the unified budget that is presented to Congress, modified by congressional action, and reviewed thereafter in the mid-year review.[6] Several different budget concepts have emerged as means of measuring the government's fiscal position. The concepts differ because of differences in inclusion or exclusion of certain receipts or spending, differences in accruals and cash flows, and some differences in timing. In the late 1960s, the President's Commission on Budget Concepts recommended the usage of what was termed the unified budget, and the budget is now presented to Congress in this form.[7]

The unified budget includes all government receipts and spending, including those of the trust funds such as the social security fund. These had not previously been included in the old administrative budget, and their exclusion meant that the administrative budget provided a very incomplete picture of the fiscal situation. Lending activities are shown in a separate section of the unified budget, but only lending by government-owned agencies is included; the agencies originally established by the government but now privately owned are not included.[8] Third, it was planned that after a transitional period the unified budget would, insofar as possible, be on an accrual basis, receipts and expenditures being recorded when the obligation to pay taxes is incurred or when the obligation to spend funds is incurred. Although this procedure is in accord with generally accepted accounting procedures, it makes the unified budget less than fully satisfactory as an indicator of need for borrowing because accrued receipts do not provide a current inflow of funds, and the timing of actual spending and of actual receipts may differ. For some purposes, therefore, it may still be necessary to refer to figures for government cash flows, and for some comparisons with other parts of the national income it may be necessary to refer to what has been termed the NIPA budget—national income and product account budget. Nevertheless, the unified budget figures provide a starting point for evaluating the demand for loanable funds by the federal government.

[6]The mid-year review (actually late in the summer, usually), although not nearly as much publicized as the January budget, is a better indicator of the fiscal situation of the government, because it incorporates both the actions by Congress (or most of them) and the changes that occurred in the economic situation, which may not all have been anticipated.

[7]Not all of the recommendations made have been incorporated at the time of writing this book, but the differences are relatively minor.

[8]These privately owned credit agencies represent another category of institutions constituting a demand for loanable funds, but they are not separately discussed in this chapter.

Cash Flows, Cash Balances, and Debt

When a cash-flow deficit occurs, the Treasury may draw down its cash balances or it may borrow. Historically, the government could print money (noninterest-bearing government debt), but this power is now restricted.[9] Because spending of receipts from borrowing from the Federal Reserve System has effects similar to those resulting from printing and spending of money, this type of borrowing also is restricted to special circumstances. Thus the government generally must borrow either from the general public, including nonbank financial institutions, or from commercial banks. Effects may differ. If the Treasury sells new securities to commercial banks, commercial banks may be permitted to pay for the securities by crediting Tax and Loan Account deposit balances of the government, rather than by reducing their own cash holdings. The banks may even be excused in wartime from holding reserves for the increased deposits. In such cases, an automatic supply of loanable funds exists to meet the demand for loanable funds by the government, and effects in the loanable funds market on interest rates and on other borrowers do not occur directly. If the Treasury sells new securities to commercial banks, but they must pay for these by reducing cash balances, the ultimate effects depend upon the monetary policy of the central bank, to be discussed in Chapter 16. Excluding these special cases, Treasury borrowing from the general public means that an additional demand is added to the demand of the private sectors, or perhaps causes some shifts in their demand. Because the Treasury must borrow what is needed to meet the budget deficit, except for such adjustments as it may make in its cash balances, it is presumed that the amount of borrowing by the federal government is not affected by interest rates.

The Debt Ceiling and the Interest Rate Ceiling

In an effort to control the volume of federal debt, Congress has imposed a ceiling on the public debt. This has had little effect, however; unlike the ceilings on debt of state and local governments, which forced them to use other means of raising funds, the ceiling on the federal debt has simply been raised by Congress when necessary. This is because Congress recognizes that it is responsible for tax receipts and appropriations and therefore also responsible for any deficit that arises when receipts fall short of expenditures. The chief effect of the ceiling has been to increase the burden on the Treasury, since action to raise the debt limit is seldom taken until the limit is nearly reached, and the Treasury may have problems in determining amounts and types of debt to be issued at such times. The closeness of actual debt to the ceiling is shown in Figure 8–3.

Congress also imposed a ceiling on the coupon interest rate on bonds at the time of World War I. At first 3½ percent, it was raised to 4¼ percent in

[9]The last time the government was authorized to print flat money was in the Thomas amendment to the Agricultural Adjustment Act in 1933; this act authorized the issue of a maximum of $3 billion in "greenbacks," but the power was not used.

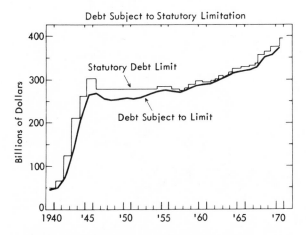

FIGURE 8–3   Debt Subject to Statutory Limitation

SOURCE: Federal Reserve Bank of Kansas City, *Monthly Review*, April 1971, p. 10.

1918.[10] Bonds may be of any maturity, but are typically issued with a maturity of at least five years. The maximum permissible coupon rate, 4¼ percent per year, has been too low in recent years to permit issue of such bonds, unless they were to be sold below par so that the effective yield could be more than 4¼ percent. The rise in yields on long-term bonds above the 4¼ percent ceiling rate beginning in 1965 is shown in Figure 8–4. Some, including Robert Kennedy when he was Attorney General, argued that bonds could be issued at a discount, but in general the Treasury has preferred not to do this because it would be against the spirit, if not the letter, of the law. Thus the practical effect of the interest rate ceiling was to cause the Treasury to issue types of securities other than bonds. In 1971, Congress authorized the Treasury to issue $10 billion in bonds without regard to the 4¼ percent ceiling. The first issue under this authorization was a 10-year 7 percent offered in July, 1971. By mid-1973, $7.7 billion of outstanding bonds carried coupon rates exceeding 4¼ percent, but total bonds outstanding constituted less than one-fifth of total marketable government debt, in contrast to nearly half such debt in 1965. The major effect of this interest rate ceiling has been to shift more borrowing to short-term securities.

FOREIGN DEMAND FOR AND SUPPLY OF LOANABLE FUNDS

Foreign demand for and supply of loanable funds remain to be considered. In the absence of barriers to international capital movements, funds would presumably flow into foreign financing on the same basis that they flow into do-

[10]On the details of the debt and bond interest rate ceilings, see Michael J. Prell, "The Treasury Debt and Bond Rate Ceilings," Federal Reserve Bank of Kansas City, *Monthly Review*, April 1971, pp. 9–16.

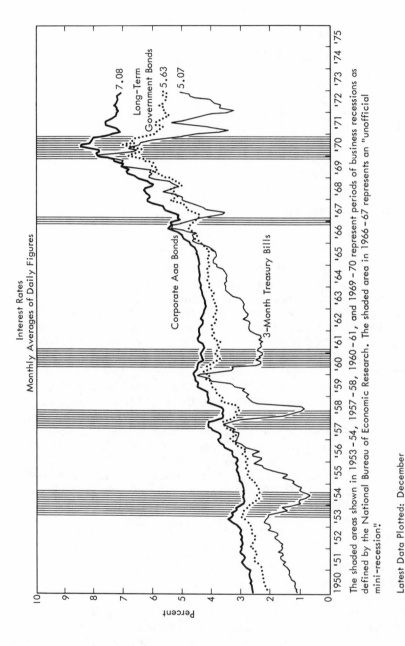

Interest Rates
Monthly Averages of Daily Figures

7.08

Long-Term
Government Bonds

5.63

5.07

Corporate Aaa Bonds

3-Month Treasury Bills

1950 '51 '52 '53 '54 '55 '56 '57 '58 '59 '60 '61 '62 '63 '64 '65 '66 '67 '68 '69 '70 '71 '72 '73 '74 '75

The shaded areas shown in 1953–54, 1957–58, 1960–61, and 1969–70 represent periods of business recessions as defined by the National Bureau of Economic Research. The shaded area in 1966–67 represents an "unofficial mini-recession."

Latest Data Plotted: December

FIGURE 8–4 Yields on Selected Long-Term Securities, 1946–73

SOURCE: Federal Reserve Bank of St. Louis, *Review,* January 1973, p. 3.

mestic uses: relative yields in relation to safety and liquidity. Thus foreign countries and their residents compete for loanable funds on the same basis as sectors of the domestic economy; that is, interest rates paid or rates of return earned must be comparable with United States domestic rates, commensurate with the degrees of risk and liquidity in the types of loans and investments made in foreign securities and industries.

Much foreign investment is direct investment. An American firm builds a branch plant abroad, buys a controlling interest in a foreign country or establishes a new foreign subsidiary by direct investment. In a sense this may be considered to be a foreign demand for loanable funds, and certainly it is likely to reduce the supply of loanable funds otherwise available in the United States domestic markets. However, such investment is usually made at the initiative of the investing firm, which sends funds overseas in making the investment. Such flows of funds are not directly reflected in supply or demand in the loanable funds market in this country. Although the volume of direct investment is significant and has important effects, it is not part of foreign supply of and demand for loanable funds in the U.S. money and capital markets.

Foreign demand for long-term loanable funds is expressed directly in sales of foreign stocks and bonds in the American market. Purchases of these securities represent long-term portfolio investment by American investors; part of the supply of loanable funds is thus diverted to meet foreign demand.

If, for the moment, it is assumed that imports and exports of goods and services are equal in value, it is evident that any net direct or portfolio investment in foreign capital assets or securities provides funds to foreign countries or their residents. They hold these funds for the moment in the form of short-term dollar balances. An increase in such balances represents an increase in current liabilities in the United States balance of payments. Such an increase and/or loss of international reserve assets such as gold is termed a deficit in the balance of payments because it represents a reduction in the ratio of reserve assets held to current liabilities that must be met. A decline in this ratio, or deficit in the balance of payments, has been regarded as undesirable, and measures have usually been taken to limit such deficits when they continue or are sizable.[11]

Controls on Foreign Loans and Investments

Because both direct and portfolio investment increased rapidly in the 1960s, foreigners acquired large amounts of dollar holdings. Because foreign individuals and private foreign institutions were not permitted to convert their dollar holdings into gold, official holdings of dollars were deemed more significant as a potential claim on United States gold holdings. During the 1960s, efforts were made to reduce foreign demand for loanable funds (or alternatively the supply of loanable funds to foreign investment) by, (1) placing an

---

[11]The precise nature of a deficit must be specified, however, and it must be shown that that particular deficit is detrimental before there is justification for such actions. See John Pippenger, "Balance-of-Payments Deficits: Measurement and Interpretation," Federal Reserve Bank of St. Louis, *Review*, November 1973, pp. 6–14.

interest equalization tax (IET) on purchases of foreign securities in order to reduce the amount of such investment; (2) introducing a voluntary program of controls on bank loans to foreign companies and residents; and (3) starting a mandatory program of control to limit direct investment by American firms.[12]

These controls remained in effect for some time, but in early 1974 they were all eliminated. Thus the United States returned to its traditional position of relative freedom from controls on international loans and investments. The action followed readjustments of currency values, discussed in the following paragraphs, and was expected in the long run to encourage both an outflow of loans and investment from the United States and investment in the United States by foreigners. With removal of controls, foreigners would have less need for concern that at some time controls might prevent them from withdrawing funds that they had invested.

Adjustment of Currency Values

In spite of these programs, foreign holdings of dollars continued to rise, and as these holdings were transferred to foreign governments, United States gold holdings declined when foreign governments converted dollar holdings into gold. A sharp outflow of gold in August 1971 and a concomitant rise in foreign official dollar holdings triggered the closing of the "gold window," the announcement by President Nixon that gold would no longer be available to foreign official holders of dollars.[13] Foreign governments, therefore, as well as foreign individuals and private institutions, had to decide whether, in view of this action, they wished to continue to accumulate dollar balances. As individuals sold unwanted dollar balances, foreign official holdings of dollars increased. The only solution was the refusal to purchase dollars—which meant that the values of foreign currencies, in countries in which this occurred, rose relative to the value of the dollar. Thus the result was the upward revaluation of a number of European currencies and of the Japanese yen.

The United States, at the same time that it closed the "gold window," imposed a 10 percent surcharge on duties on imports, except where such duties were limited by agreements. It was understood that this additional duty would be eliminated after foreign currencies had been revalued upward; for the time being, the additional duty tended to reduce United States imports relative to exports.

Agreement on revised values of a number of currencies was achieved at a meeting at the Smithsonian Institution in Washington, D.C., in December 1971, and the import surcharge was eliminated shortly thereafter. It was also

[12]The IET was enacted in 1964, the VFCR (voluntary foreign credit restraint) program was begun in 1964, and the mandatory control on direct foreign investment was instituted in 1968.

[13]Mention should be made of the role played in this episode by the holdings of Eurodollars abroad. Eurodollars are dollar balances held outside the United States, for example, in the form of Eurodollar deposits in European banks. Those who held such deposits, including multinational firms, could quickly and easily transfer them into a currency they felt might appreciate in value, and those who received dollars in excess of desired holdings sold them to central banks.

agreed that currencies might fluctuate somewhat more widely than had been permitted under previous rules. Thus, temporarily, the problem created by deficits in the United States balance of payments was alleviated.

When total U.S. foreign spending for goods, services, loans, and investments exceeds similar spending by foreigners in the United States, foreigners accumulate liquid assets in the form of dollar balances. Under some circumstances, such as those existing for a time after World War II, foreign countries may desire to accumulate additional dollar balances, because they may feel that their reserves of such assets are insufficient. When liquid balances exceed desired amounts, however, foreigners either spend such balances for United States exports, use them to make long-term investments in the United States, or try to convert them into some basic international reserve assets such as gold, or into other currencies such as marks.

Early in 1973, dollar balances held by foreigners again were used to purchase marks, gold, and other assets which seemed likely to rise in value. After acquiring a substantial amount of dollars, the German central banks felt that further effort to hold down the mark was not warranted. After international consultations the dollar was again devalued, the price of gold being raised to $42.22 per fine ounce. The German mark was revalued upward, in terms of gold, by 3 percent, and major currencies were permitted to float in relation to the dollar. The pound sterling and the lira were also permitted to float relative to other major currencies, but the other Common Market currencies were to be kept within limits of 2¼ percent relative to each other.

Further reform of the international monetary system was obviously needed, and plans were to be drafted for a group of nations prior to the September 1973 meeting of the governors of the International Monetary Fund. Without discussing in detail the many specific problems, it is clear that arrangements were needed with respect to coordination of financial polices of major nations, the degree of flexibility to be permitted in exchange rates, the need for surplus nations as well as deficit nations to make adjustments, the specific events that might trigger such adjustments, the role of gold and "paper gold" as international reserve assets, and the question of convertibility of dollars into gold, paper gold, or some other asset.[14]

The Long-Run View

Direct controls on foreign loans and investments, like direct controls on consumer demand for loanable funds, are difficult to enforce and may in the long run adversely affect processes that might reverse the flow. Foreign loans and investment cause a return flow of dividends, interest, and profits, which may in time equal and exceed the outflow, as the outflow is likely to be a de-

---

[14]"Paper gold," or "special drawing rights" (SDRs), were created in 1970–72 by the International Monetary Fund (IMF) and distributed to member countries in accordance with quotas. SDRs were guaranteed in terms of gold, and were to be used only by central banks, to settle balances. They added to world liquidity, which was believed to be insufficient in view of the rapid rise in world trade and payments and the slow rise in monetary gold holdings.

creasing percentage of the total amount invested abroad, while the percentage return on investments may remain relatively stable. Of course, the situation is more complex: an outflow of capital frequently requires some outflow of parts for maintenance; establishment of additional subsidiaries abroad may reduce United States exports or increase United States imports, or both; additional investment in foreign countries increases their income, and hence their consumption, including imports from the United States (United States exports); and there may be other less direct effects.

Loans to foreigners plus the flow of investments to foreign countries plus imports may exceed borrowing (other than through addition to short-term liquid liabilities) plus exports; the difference must be settled in internationally acceptable reserve assets. Otherwise, governments impose controls on capital flows, and because capital flows are difficult to separate from trade, controls on trade follow. Foreign demand for loanable funds and a foreign contribution to the supply of loanable funds are legitimate parts of the loanable funds market. But an excess of one over the other creates problems not easily solved. In the long run, actions to promote foreign spending in the United States and/ or a foreign supply of loanable funds to the United States constitute the best means of solution of the problem. Control of inflation in the United States relative to inflation abroad is one means of increasing foreign spending in the United States; lower prices for securities and higher yields in the United States relative to yields abroad are one means of stimulating a supply of loanable funds from foreign countries.

SUMMARY

State and local government units borrow primarily to finance capital expenditures for construction. At the end of World War II, state and local government units were, on a *net* basis, out of debt. Past defaults resulted in strict limitations on state and local government borrowing. The limitations, in turn, led to efforts to evade them, by creating special agencies to operate facilities and to borrow funds for construction. The borrowing process is lengthy, and increase in interest rates may prevent both planned borrowing and borrowing already decided upon.

Because interest income on state and local government securities is exempt from the federal income tax, these securities are bought chiefly by high-income individuals, commercial banks, property and casualty insurance companies, and some other less important groups. When interest rates are high, commercial banks and some other purchasers are likely to be relatively short of funds.

Federal government borrowing, unlike that of state and local government units, is presumed *not* to be interest elastic. Government borrowing need not weigh cost versus expected return, although the Treasury may try to reduce cost of debt. A preliminary measure of the need for government borrowing is to be found in the unified budget. Cash flows are a more accurate indicator of need, but even so, may not be precise, as the government may to some extent vary its cash balances. Congress imposed a ceiling on federal debt, but this has simply been raised when necessary. It has had little effect except to create inconveniences when debt approached the ceiling. Congress also imposed a ceiling on the coupon interest rate on bonds, although later a small amount was exempted from the ceiling. This ceiling could be evaded by selling bonds at a discount, but the Treasury has disliked this alternative. Instead, the Treasury has issued some intermediate-term debt at rates higher than the ceiling rate on bond interest and has financed heavily through short-term issues.

Foreign demand for *loanable funds* has generally been a relatively small part of total demand, although much *direct* investment by American firms abroad has occurred. Because the investment outflow was not matched by corresponding increase in net U.S. exports nor by net foreign long-term investment in the United States, foreign countries accumulated large dollar balances and substantial amounts of gold until President Nixon "closed the gold window" on August 15, 1971. Increases in gold and dollar balances held by foreigners are termed a "deficit" in the U.S. balance of payments. Various measures were taken in the 1960s to reduce deficits by restricting investment and payments abroad. Two devaluations of the dollar followed, raising the official price of gold. The free market price of gold in foreign countries soared far above the official price level. Major foreign industrialized countries permitted values of their currencies to "float" upward, to reduce dollar balances held by their central banks. In 1973, fundamental reform of the international monetary system was under discussion. Reform plans involved better coordination of financial policies of major nations, greater flexibility in exchange rates, adjustments in exchange rates by surplus nations as well as by deficit nations, agreement on roles of gold and "paper gold" (drawing rights in the International Monetary Fund, guaranteed in value in terms of gold and available only for payments among central banks), and agreement on convertibility of dollars into gold, "paper gold," or some other asset.

It was anticipated that changes in exchange rates and international monetary reform would result in increased U.S. exports and increased long-term investment in the United States by foreign countries. Increase in supply of loanable funds in the United States would follow. Slower increase in liquid dollar balances held by foreign countries would permit a more orderly functioning of the international monetary system. Large accumulations of gold and dollars by oil producing nations, arising from the energy crisis and actions of such nations, added a complicating factor. Major central banks agreed that they were free, beginning in late 1973, to sell gold, thus potentially reducing the role of gold in the international monetary system. However, adverse effects of the energy crisis on Europe and Japan and resulting declines in values of their currencies made gold and dollars again seem to be of continuing importance.

QUESTIONS FOR DISCUSSION

1. Why does the federal government depend heavily on short-term borrowing, while state and local government units use short-term borrowing only rarely?

2. Why are commercial banks so important as purchasers of state and local government securities?

3. What are the arguments for and against the exemption of income on state and local government securities from the federal income tax?

4. Households and commercial banks are the major purchasers of federal government debt. Why?

5. Show how divergence between federal government receipts and expenditures has an impact on bank reserves.

6. What might be the effects if Congress repealed the ceiling on interest rates on government bonds?

7. Evaluate the program of controls on United States foreign lending and investment; did it eliminate the problem it was designed to solve?

8. Show how the United States government actions of August 15, 1971 forced an upward "float" of major foreign currencies.

9. Do you think that "floating" of major foreign currencies (the situation in late 1973) is desirable in the long run? Why or why not?

10. Why is it apparently necessary for the United States to have less inflation (a lower rate of inflation) than other major industrialized countries?

SELECTED REFERENCES

A historical review of the desirability and value of the income tax exemption for income from municipal bonds may be found in Roland I. Robinson, *Postwar Market for State and Local Government Securities* (Princeton, N.J.: Princeton University Press, 1960).

The unified budget concept is discussed in the *Report of the President's Commission on Budget Concepts* (Washington, D.C.: U.S. Government Printing Office, 1967). See also Joseph Scherer, "The Report of the President's Commission on Budget Concepts: A Review," Federal Reserve Bank of New York, *Monthly Review*, December 1967, pp. 231–38.

On federal debt and interest rate ceilings, see Ira O. Scott, Jr., *Government Securities Market* (New York: McGraw-Hill, 1965) and his bibliography on these topics, pp. 192–93.

For a relatively nontechnical discussion of the balance of payments and the international monetary mechanism, see Leland B. Yeager, *The International Monetary Mechanism* (New York: Holt, Rinehart, and Winston, 1968). For a discussion of the role of short-term capital movements in creating or escalating international monetary crises, see Donald L. Kohn, "Capital Flows in a Foreign Exchange Crisis," Federal Reserve Bank of Kansas City, *Monthly Review*, February 1973, pp. 14–23. Proposals for reform of the international monetary system are discussed in Norman S. Fieleke, "International Economic Reform," Federal Reserve Bank of Boston, *New England Economic Review*, January–February 1973, pp. 19–27, and in Chapter 5, "The International Economic System in Transition," *Economic Report of the President*, January 1973. The United States proposals for reforms, presented to the IMF in September 1972, are set forth in a supplement to Chapter 5, *Economic Report of the President*, January 1973, pp. 160–74. A convenient, relatively nontechnical discussion of the situation in the early 1970s is Francis Cassell,

International Adjustment and the Dollar, rev. ed., April 1973, Ninth District Economic Information Series, Federal Reserve Bank of Minneapolis.

For a thoughtful consideration by a leading economist of the longer-run outlook for international transactions, see Paul A. Samuelson, "International Trade for a Rich Country," *Morgan Guaranty Survey*, July 1972, pp. 3–11.

Changing interpretations of the data shown in balance of payments accounts may be appreciated by reading three successive articles: Norman S. Fieleke, "Accounting for the Balance of Payments," Federal Reserve Bank of Boston, *New England Economic Review*, May/June 1971, pp. 2–15; Christopher Bach and Anatol Balbach, "The New Look for the Balance of Payments," Federal Reserve Bank of St. Louis, *Review*, August 1971, pp. 8–11; and John Pippenger, "Balance-of-Payments Deficits: Measurement and Interpretation," Federal Reserve Bank of St. Louis, *Review*, November 1973, pp. 6–14.

III

Financial Markets

Financial markets exist for initial issue and purchase of financial assets and for secondary trading. Although the term "market" may suggest trading of assets, some loans and investments are not traded or are seldom traded after the initial transaction. Interest rates on such loans and investments are interrelated with secondary market rates and both are analyzed in this part of the book.

The money market in which short-term funds are obtained by borrowers and in which many types of short-term financial assets are exchanged is discussed in Chapter 9. Short-term interest rates are determined in this market, and most intervention of the central bank for the purpose of implementing monetary policy also occurs in this market.

The capital markets in which bonds, mortgages, and stocks are issued and traded are discussed in Chapters 10 and 11. Chapter 10 is devoted to debt issues—bonds and mortgages—that have important primary and secondary markets. Chapter 11 is devoted to the market for stocks, or equities, where the focus must be on the important secondary market, as addition to the outstanding supply of equities in any year is relatively very small.

9

The Money Market

Individuals and institutions supply funds to the money market and the capital markets where borrowers obtain funds they desire. Primary markets enable borrowers to obtain funds, while secondary markets provide liquidity for lenders and thus induce them to lend at lower rates than they would probably require if they knew they would be forced to hold securities or promissory notes to maturity. Not all types of financial assets have secondary markets, but in general, secondary markets are important. In some cases, development of a primary market would be difficult if a secondary market were not developed simultaneously.

Capital markets facilitate investment and provide a degree of liquidity for financial assets that, being long-term, would not otherwise be liquid. The money market facilitates short-term financing and assures the liquidity of short-term financial assets. The money market is also the main focus of central bank activities in implementing monetary policy, although central banks do occasionally deal in the long-term government securities market. Finally, the money market is significant in indicating changes in short-term interest rates, monetary policy, and availability of short-term credit.

DEFINITION AND NATURE OF THE MONEY MARKET

The money market is the place or mechanism whereby funds are obtained for short periods of time (from one day to one year), and financial assets representing short-term claims are exchanged. As with the capital markets, there is a primary money market, where short-term funds are obtained at varying rates, depending on the source of funds, the credit standing of the borrowers, and so on. There is also a secondary market, where financial assets representing short-term claims are traded, at rates determined by demand for and supply of short-term financial assets.

The money market has no specific place of operation; it consists simply of the total activity of all those who lend and borrow short-term funds. Often, "money market" refers primarily to the secondary market in these assets, but interrelationship between the secondary market and rates established in the primary market for short-term loans cannot be ignored.

The money market, at least in terms of the secondary market, is largely an over-the-telephone market. The heart of the market machinery consists of about forty-six "money market" commercial banks, which trade heavily in money market instruments; nearly two dozen government securities dealers, some of which are banks; a few commercial paper dealers and a few bank acceptance dealers; some brokers who specialize in aiding borrowers to obtain funds and placing funds for lenders; and the Federal Reserve Bank of New York, which intervenes in the market to implement monetary policy.

Money market obligations traded in the secondary market are characterized by a very high degree of safety and are issued by borrowers of very high credit standing. Although the secondary market has no specific location, its ready accessibility by telephone makes it possible for lenders and borrowers in all parts of the country to lend and borrow funds quickly. Thus both safety and liquidity are nearly always assured. In a liquidity crisis, of course, safety and liquidity may come into question, as some types of money market instruments may not be paid at maturity, leading to questioning of the liquidity and safety of others.

The "average" or "representative" short-term interest rate on money market instruments is significant in several ways: (1) it indicates the return obtainable on those funds lenders feel they must keep in liquid form, and its fluctuations may affect the flow of funds into liquid assets; (2) it indicates the cost of borrowing for those who need short-term funds, and although fluctuations may not be as vital as fluctuations in the long-term rate, because short-term borrowing may be possible even at high interest rates, the cost of short-term borrowing is of some significance as an indicator of borrowing ease or difficulty; and (3) conditions in the money market are of some significance for monetary policy, discussed in detail in Chapter 16.

Rates in the money market fluctuate much more widely than capital market rates. Figure 9–1 shows the movement over time of both the average of corporate Aaa bonds (a representative capital market rate) and the average rate on three-month Treasury bills (a representative money market rate). Short-term rates usually fall when business activity declines; even in the "mini-recession" of early 1967, Treasury bill rates fell sharply, as shown. However, short-term rates do not always follow closely the changes in business activity. Business activity was rising slowly in 1971 and more rapidly in 1972, but short-term interest rates fluctuated widely.

ROLE OF THE MONEY MARKET

Both risk of capital losses and risk of default are minimized in the money market. Risk of capital losses is often termed *money* risk. Money risk is minimized

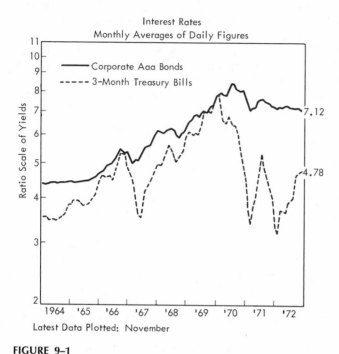

Interest Rates
Monthly Averages of Daily Figures

Corporate Aaa Bonds
----- 3-Month Treasury Bills

Ratio Scale of Yields

7.12

4.78

1964 '65 '66 '67 '68 '69 '70 '71 '72

Latest Data Plotted: November

FIGURE 9–1

SOURCE: Federal Reserve Bank of St. Louis, *Review*, December 1972.

because the financial assets are short-term; hence a change in interest rates cannot affect their prices very much because the assured maturity value is discounted for only a short period. Risk of default, often termed credit risk, is minimized because instruments in the market, especially in the secondary market, are for the most part liabilities of the government, the central bank, and commercial banks—credit risk is small.

The importance of the money market, however, arises from two facts: (1) the existence of an efficient money market means that short-term financial assets can almost instantly be converted into money, to make payments; and (2) the central bank operates in the money market to increase or reduce bank reserves, and incidentally affects short-term interest rates. It may also affect long-term rates, either indirectly or by direct dealing in long-term financial assets.

The money market assures borrowers that they can, generally, obtain short-term funds quickly, and it assures lenders that they can convert their short-term financial assets into money.

Major borrowers include the Treasury, commercial banks, securities dealers, and some nonbank financial institutions and business firms. The Treasury can obtain funds easily and often inexpensively in the short-term market.[1]

---

[1] An extreme example is the low cost of short-term government financing during World War II; the yield on Treasury bills was pegged at ⅜ percent per annum.

Finance companies and some business firms can issue commercial paper at relatively low rates in many cases, to obtain funds for operations and inventory accumulation. Commercial banks can issue CDs and thus obtain funds for lending. Federal Reserve Banks are not borrowers, but have deposit liabilities that are traded by those owning such deposits. Government securities dealers must borrow to finance their holdings of securities. Those who borrow on bank acceptances because they need funds for short periods of time can usually obtain funds relatively cheaply in this manner, although high rates may be paid when it is difficult to obtain funds in other ways, such as by direct loans. Finally, commercial banks may need to borrow, temporarily, from Federal Reserve Banks.

Major lenders are commercial banks, corporations and other business firms, nonbank financial institutions, state and local governments, foreign governments, central banks, private institutions, and the Federal Reserve System. Commercial banks place funds temporarily not needed, but which may be needed to meet deposit withdrawals or bank loan demand, in money market instruments. Corporations and other business firms hold money market instruments to meet payments such as taxes, to provide for unexpected payments, or to hold temporarily funds borrowed in long-term markets for later use for investment. Nonbank financial institutions hold such instruments for the same purposes. State and local governments may have funds from taxes or borrowings that are temporarily not needed. Foreign governments, central banks, and private institutions accumulate funds from sales to United States firms and resident individuals and from other sources, such as sales of their own currencies to purchase dollar instruments in the foreign exchange market. Finally, the Federal Reserve System holds short-term securities, chiefly Treasury bills, but also government agency securities and bank acceptances, as a result of open market purchases.

Individuals usually did not lend significant amounts in the money market, partly because it was inconvenient for them to buy money market instruments and partly because rates frequently dropped far below long-term rates (see Figure 9–1). In the 1970s, because of the very high return on money market instruments and their high degree of safety, individuals found them attractive. Most of the instruments must be purchased in relatively large amounts, but several mutual funds made it possible for small investors to purchase money market instruments indirectly by buying shares in those mutual funds (see *Fortune*, April 1974, pp. 81 ff.).

Each instrument in the secondary money market is created in primary market negotiations, with the exception of Federal funds—deposit liabilities of Federal Reserve Banks—which are created by the Federal Reserve System through policy actions. A major primary short-term asset for which there is generally no secondary market is the short-term loan made by banks and to some extent by a few nonbank financial institutions such as finance companies.

A large part of total payments for dealings in the money market is made in Federal funds, funds on deposit in Federal Reserve Banks. The speedy transfer of such funds from the account of one bank or one customer's bank to another bank or participant in the money market is a useful feature.

INSTRUMENTS AND RATES IN THE
SECONDARY MONEY MARKET

Instruments in the United States secondary money market include United States Treasury bills, short-term government agency securities, Federal funds, bank acceptances, negotiable CDs, commercial paper, and Eurodollar liabilities. Rates on these, except agency securities and bank acceptances, are shown for a three-month period in Figure 9–2. Note the volatility of most money market rates in comparison with capital market rates. In addition to a rate of yield on each of these instruments, several other rates are significant to the money market: the prime rate on short-term bank loans to customers with high credit ratings, the dealer rate on loans to United States government securities dealers, the discount rate on discounts and advances obtained from Federal Reserve Banks, and the rate on repurchase agreements—agreements to sell government securities and to repurchase them later, at agreed prices.

Government Securities: Treasury Bills

In both Great Britain and the United States, the bulk of the short-term debt of the government (sometimes called "floating debt") is in the form of Treasury bills, an instrument invented at the suggestion of the famous financial economist, Walter Bagehot, in 1887. When federal government debt was small in the United States, Treasury bills were not used, but in 1929 they were issued because it was believed (1) that their use could eliminate errors of judgment in pricing bond or certificate issues, and (2) that their use could permit closer matching of maturities with fund needs, thus avoiding the payment of interest on funds not needed. In 1972, the amount of Treasury bills outstanding reached $100 billion, and their total has continued to rise;[2] Treasury bills now constitute more than one-third of the total outstanding marketable public debt. However, if there is no war for a number of years, need for government borrowing may lessen, and Treasury bills and other forms of government debt may constitute a smaller fraction of total securities in the money and capital markets. If the economy continues to grow, private debt must increase concomitantly, and thus private financial instruments are likely to become relatively more important.

Treasury bills have been issued with maturities of three months, six months, nine months, and one year.[3] There are also issues referred to as Tax Anticipation Bills, or TABs, designed to attract funds held temporarily for payment of income taxes; TABs are set to mature one week after a quarterly tax pay-

---

[2]The Treasury used to issue marketable certificates of indebtedness, which carried interest coupons instead of being sold at auction at discounts. With the introduction of one-year bills, certificates of indebtedness became less useful, and there were none outstanding in 1972.

[3]The 6-month bill now provides the greatest amount of funds. Nearly $2 billion of 3-month bills and a little over $1 billion of 6-month bills mature each week.

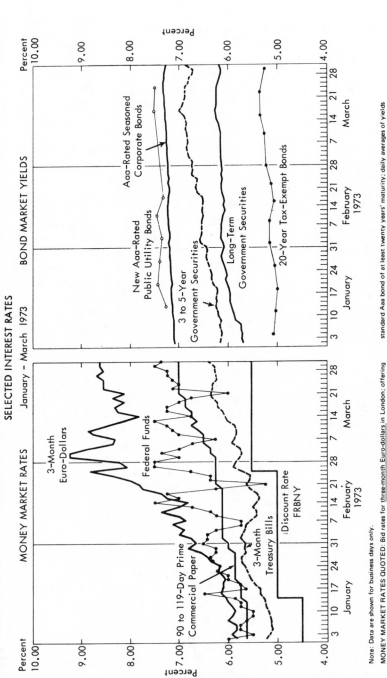

SELECTED INTEREST RATES
January – March 1973

MONEY MARKET RATES   BOND MARKET YIELDS

Note: Data are shown for business days only.

MONEY MARKET RATES QUOTED: Bid rates for three-month Euro-dollars in London; offering rates (quoted in terms of rate of discount) on 90- to 119-day prime commercial paper quoted by three of the five dealers that report their rates, or the midpoint of the range quoted if no consensus is available; the effective rate on Federal funds (the rate most representative of the transactions executed); closing bid rates (quoted in terms of rate of discount) on newest outstanding three-month Treasury bills.

BOND MARKET YIELDS QUOTED: Yields on new Aaa-rated public utility bonds are based on prices asked by underwriting syndicates, adjusted to make them equivalent to a

standard Aaa bond of at least twenty years' maturity; daily averages of yields on seasoned Aaa-rated corporate bonds; daily averages of yields on long-term Government securities (bonds due or callable in ten years or more) and on Government securities due in three to five years, computed on the basis of closing bid prices; Thursday averages of yields on twenty seasoned twenty-year tax-exempt bonds (carrying Moody's ratings of Aaa, Aa, A, and Baa).

Sources: Federal Reserve Bank of New York, Board of Governors of the Federal Reserve System, Moody's Investors Service, Inc., and The Bond Buyer.

FIGURE 9–2

SOURCE: Federal Reserve Bank of New York, *Monthly Review*, April 1973.

ment date and can be used at full face value for payment of tax on the tax date, or redeemed at maturity.[4] Most of these bills are sold in the second half of the year—when the Treasury needs more funds, as individual income tax payments help provide more funds in the spring. These bills are scheduled to mature in March and June. Some TABs mature in September. Finally, "strip" issues have been sold; in "strip" issues, bids are asked for an amount of each of a number of issues maturing in each of perhaps six or seven consecutive weeks. Because of the difficulty of determining appropriate bids, these have not been very popular.

Treasury bills are sold at auction, on a discount basis. Because the bills are worth face value at maturity, the interest is the amount of discount.[5] Noncompetitive offers may be made in an amount up to $200,000 by any one bidder. Thus small banks that may not have the sophistication to submit an appropriate bid can obtain Treasury bills. These are allotted first and carry a yield equal to the average yield on those competitive bids that are accepted. The rest of the bills are allotted to those offering the highest bid prices. The lowest accepted bid price is termed the stop-out price. Formerly, the smallest units in which bills were sold was $1,000 face value. But high yields on bills in the late 1960s led many individuals to withdraw their savings accounts and buy bills. So, the Treasury raised the minimum purchase to $10,000 in order to exclude the small investor from this market and prevent funds from being diverted away from the mortgage and housing market. The principal buyers of bills on initial issue are commercial banks, securities dealers, the Federal Reserve System, and government trust fund accounts.

A number of economists have argued that the Treasury could obtain more revenue from a competitive bidding auction in which all bids accepted would be accepted at one price—a price low enough, and hence a yield high enough, to result in sale of all bills offered. In the present type of auction, each bid accepted is accepted at the bid price. The argument is that a competitive bidding auction would probably have more participants, and hence probably higher prices and lower yields. One study showed that on the basis of a model of the demand for Treasury bills, as little as 1 percent increase in participation would result in more revenue. To obtain this result, noncompetitive bids must still be accepted, and noncompetitive demand must remain constant or at least not decline sharply. Noncompetitive bids account for about 20 percent of all bids,

---

[4]Commercial banks often buy large amounts of TAB issues, especially when issues carry the Treasury Tax and Loan Account privilege allowing banks to pay for them by crediting Treasury Tax and Loan Accounts. Commercial banks, however, often sell large amounts shortly after purchase; in effect, they perform an underwriting function.

[5]A 360-day year is used in calculating yields on Treasury bills. The formula for the discount or yield rate is

$$d = \frac{360}{n} \left(\frac{100 - P}{P} \right)$$

where d is the discount rate, n is the number of days to maturity, and P is the price. For the yield on a bond issue with the same maturity, the formula would be

$$i = \frac{365}{n} \left(\frac{100}{P} - 1 \right)$$

where i is the yield in percent.

and their elimination would mean a loss of participants who pay the average accepted bid price.[6] Although the results seem plausible, it is not certain that participation would increase if competitive biddings with all bids accepted at one price were used.

Government securities dealers make a market for all outstanding issues of Treasury bills, so that bills have a high degree of liquidity. Yields on outstanding issues tend to be higher when maturities are longer, but there have been times, especially in the late 1960s, when nine-month and twelve-month bills had lower yields than six-month bills. In addition to those purchasing new issues, corporations and state and local governments are significant holders of outstanding issues, buying them in the secondary market. However, ownership of more than half of the Treasury bills outstanding is not reported, so it is difficult to be sure which institutions are the major owners. With rising interest rates, corporations have attempted to reduce their cash balances, investing funds in Treasury bills, time certificates of deposit (CDs), and other liquid assets.

Short-Term Government Agency Securities

Government agency securities have recently become an important factor in the secondary money market. Most of these securities, when originally issued, could be classified as long-term or capital market securities; but as time passes, they become short-term in nature. Three types of securities are issued: (1) participation certificates, representing a "pool" of loans or other assets; (2) certificates of interest, similar to participation certificates, but issued for a maturity of fourteen months or less by the commodity Credit Corporation (CCC) and backed by a pool of loans made to farmers under the price support program; and (3) notes, bonds, and debentures. The notes, bonds, and debentures are often issued with intermediate-term maturities, although the practice varies among agencies. These securities are issued by the Federal National Mortgage Association (FNMA), the Federal Intermediate Credit Banks (FICBs) the Banks for Cooperatives (COOP), the Federal Home Loan Banks (FHLBs), the Federal Housing Administration (FHA), the Export-Import Bank, the Tennessee Valley Authority (TVA), and the Government National Mortgage Association (GNMA). The Federal Land Banks (FLBs) issue chiefly long-term securities, but some of these are always close enough to maturity to be classified as short-term.

Before 1969, participation certificates were treated in the federal budget as negative expenditures rather than as borrowings; it was decided at that time, however, that these certificates, if issued by wholly owned government agencies, should be treated as borrowing.

Conversion of a number of agencies to private ownership caused them to be removed from the federal government budget. It is generally believed that

[6]Steven Bolten, "Treasury Bill Auction Procedures: An Empirical Investigation," *Journal of Finance*, June 1973, pp. 577–85. His bibliography provides a guide to the various arguments.

the government would not permit default on these securities, and hence it does not make much difference from this standpoint whether they are included in the federal government budget or not. It *does*, however, make a difference from the standpoint of financial policy. Because they are not included in the budget, there is no review, in budget formulation, of the desirability of their issue. Thus securities that carry relatively low interest rates because of their nature as government or government-sponsored agency securities are not subject to review in the budget-making process. These securities are partially exempt from both private market discipline and budget scrutiny, leading some economists to argue that controls are needed over such borrowing. Others argue that budget review might result in inappropriate actions if fiscal policy is not timely and suitable.

Only GNMA and ExImBank participation certificates and FHA debentures are government-guaranteed, but the other securities have some sort of government backing. For some issues, purchase by the Secretary of the Treasury is authorized in case of need for market support; for other issues, agencies can borrow from the Treasury, if necessary, up to certain limits. Most agency issues can be used as collateral by commercial banks for Treasury Tax and Loan Accounts. Some agency issues can be used by member banks as collateral for borrowings from Federal Reserve Banks, and agency securities are sometimes purchased in open market operations by the Federal Reserve System. Most agency securities (except FHA debentures) cannot be called before maturity. Interest and capital gains are subject to federal income tax, but with a few exceptions they are not subject to state and local income taxes.

Some agencies issue chiefly long-term or capital market issues. Issues most relevant to the money market are the short-term or intermediate-term issues of the farm credit agencies—COOP, FICB, and FLB—and two of the housing agencies—FNMA and FHLB.

According to Treasury surveys, the most important owners of agency securities are commercial banks, state and local governments, United States government accounts and Federal Reserve Banks, mutual savings banks, savings and loan associations, business firms, and insurance companies. However, more than half of the total was listed as being held by "all other investors," so that the ownership picture is not complete.

In recent years, yields on agency securities have ranged from one basis point (1/100 of 1 percent or 0.01 percent) to twenty-five basis points (0.25%) above yields on Treasury securities.[7] The difference might be attributed to either risk or marketability, but it is likely that marketability is the more important factor, as risk difference is negligible. Treasury issues are more homogeneous and larger in amount. Regressions of yields against four variables that might influence such yields—issue size, issuing agency, maturity, and coupon rate—indicated that issue size is an important determinant, affecting yield inversely.

---

[7]Federal Reserve Bank of Cleveland, *Money Market Instruments*, 3rd ed., 1970, p. 40. These spreads may be compared with spreads of 25 to 75 basis points between yields on new agency *long-term* issues and yields on new Treasury notes and bonds.

Central Bank Liabilities: Federal Funds

Because the federal government, member banks and foreign banks, and certain other institutions have deposits in Federal Reserve Banks, it is not surprising that such deposits were traded by commercial banks as early as the 1920s. With the depression of the 1930s and the large amount of unused bank reserves, trading in Federal funds dried up, but in the post–World War II period and especially after 1955, Federal funds trading revived and grew in importance.

Commercial banks, agencies of foreign banks, and securities dealers now participate in the market. Securities dealers obtain bank loans in Federal funds in order to carry inventories of government securities. Some other institutions participate in minor ways. Because most trading is done by major banks, the Federal Reserve System confines collection of daily data to forty-six large banks.

The most frequent type of transaction is the one-day transaction, repayment being made the next day. Essentially, these transactions are one-day unsecured loans. Secured Federal funds transactions are used frequently by smaller banks. Purchasing (borrowing) banks place government securities in custody accounts for the selling banks for one day until repayment.

Most of the transactions are interbank transactions. Of course, banks could obtain funds, if needed to meet reserve requirements or for some other reason, by selling Treasury bills, but for one day or a few days, such sale could be costly. Turnaround costs for a bank that sold bills and then bought them back a day later would be perhaps as high as $1/100$ of one percent of the value of the bills, or 3.65 percent a year, plus the loss of interest on the bills.[8]

Because banks make heavy use of Federal funds to adjust reserve positions, those that have excess reserves early in a reserve period tend to sell funds toward the end of the period, thus reducing the rate on Federal funds.[9] Cyclically, the Federal funds rate tends to fall in recessions, when bank reserves rise, and to rise in periods of rising business activity. In recent years, some banks have borrowed Federal funds continuously, to maintain balance sheet

[8]See Federal Reserve Bank of Richmond, *Instruments of the Money Market*, 2nd ed., 1970, p. 19. Of course, if the funds were needed for a longer period, turnaround costs would, in most cases, be less as a percentage of the amount sold and repurchased.

[9]Bank reserve requirements must be met on a daily average basis over the statement week, which is Thursday through the following Wednesday. Thus banks with excess reserves tend to hold them Thursdays and Fridays, and to sell heavily on Wednesdays, frequently causing the rate to drop. Since September 1968, the reserves required during a given week are based on deposit balances and vault cash held (on a daily average basis) during the second week preceding the week for which requirements are computed. An excess or deficiency of reserves up to 2 percent of required reserves may be carried forward to the next week. Thus both banks and the Fed know what required reserves will be, although neither one knows how much reserves will be on hand to meet the requirements until the close of the period. There is an entertaining "diary" of the money desk of a large bank for a week in Wesley Lindow, *Inside the Money Market* (New York: Random House, 1972), pp. 97–103. Although reserves at the close were $1 million above requirements, the estimate at one point during the week was that they might be $240 million *below* requirements.

positions; of course, these banks recognize the cost of such borrowings and may find ways of lending such amounts of funds at rates higher than the cost of borrowing.

Also, because Federal funds are used by banks—especially major money market banks—to adjust reserve positions, the rate is very volatile. The Federal funds rate is thus quite useful as an indicator of pressure on bank reserves, and hence on the base for creating money (see Chapter 4), but it is not necessarily a good indicator of money market conditions generally, because its extreme volatility means that changes must be carefully interpreted.

The major suppliers of Federal funds are banks that have excess reserves, although Federal funds also arise from Federal Reserve purchases of government securities and from Treasury and foreign checks on balances held at Federal Reserve Banks. There is no primary market for Federal funds, as deposits are created without cost to the banks; any deposits in excess of required reserve amounts may be traded in the Federal funds market if banks so desire. In New York City, sale may be effected through an exchange of checks; the selling bank draws a check on its balance in the Federal Reserve Bank and this check is paid immediately, while the borrowing bank sends a check that is collected through the clearinghouse the next day. In other cases, notification is simply given to the Federal Reserve Bank to make the transfer of funds.

Bank Liabilities

Two types of bank liabilities are traded in the secondary money market, bank acceptances and negotiable certificates of deposit (CDs). Because bank acceptances and negotiable CDs are issued almost entirely by very strong banks, they have a low risk of defaults.

Bank Acceptances

A bank acceptance is a draft drawn on a bank by a drawer, often an exporter or other seller of merchandise, ordering the bank to pay to them or to another party a certain sum at some future date. Under a prearranged agreement these drafts are "accepted" by banks, indicating willingness to make such payments at the stated times. These bank acceptances, as the drafts are termed after being accepted, can then be sold in the secondary market until maturity, or held by the accepting bank itself. A substantial portion of these drafts arise in foreign trade transactions; exporters find less risk in drawing drafts on banks than in drawing drafts on importers. Arrangements are made under what are termed letters of credit for banks to pay the drafts, with provision for reimbursement by importers. Bank acceptances can also arise from acceptance agreements by banks with importers, to honor drafts by the importers, who will then reimburse the banks at maturity, usually from proceeds of sale of imported goods. Acceptances may be used to finance United States trade or to finance trade between other countries. The fact that drafts are accepted by major United States banks assures exporters of payment, provided they meet the specified conditions. Bank acceptances may also be used to finance domestic shipment and storage of goods.

When bank loan interest rates are very low, acceptances are less used, because it may be cheaper to obtain a bank loan. As loan interest rates rise, acceptance rates may not rise proportionately, for two reasons: (1) the fee for creating the acceptance, which is part of the cost, is a flat fee, seldom changed; and (2) because of the minimum risk on bank acceptances, rates on them may rise less than on loans. Thus in a period of high interest rates, such as the late 1960s, use of bank acceptances increases; there is also, of course, some secular trend increase with increase in world trade. Use of acceptance may also increase in a period of credit tightness because banks may have lent as much as they can, or as much as they wish, either to individual borrowers or to borrowers as a whole, but may still be able to accept drafts, perhaps selling the accepted drafts in the money market.

A very small amount of acceptances is created to provide "dollar exchange." Some countries, chiefly in Latin America, have marked seasonal fluctuations in exports. When exports are low, not many drafts are drawn and few bank acceptances are created, but the need for dollars to pay for imports may be strong. In such circumstances, it is permissible for United States banks to accept drafts for the purpose of providing dollars for the Latin American countries, with the understanding that the funds to pay the drafts at maturity can be provided from funds obtained from the more numerous drafts drawn when exports of the Latin American countries are seasonally large. This use of acceptances has diminished in recent years as industries in a number of Latin American countries have become more diversified, and is now of little importance.

Regulations governing creation of bank acceptances are strict because, since no funds need be paid out at the time of creation of acceptances, banks might otherwise be tempted to create too many acceptances.[10] Bank acceptances may be eligible for discount at Federal Reserve Banks or for purchase by the Federal Reserve System under certain conditions; regulations require evidence that the acceptances were used to finance import, export, storage, or shipment of goods, or to create dollar exchange.

Before World War I, "finance" bills were drawn by United States banks on financial institutions in London to obtain funds to pay for imports in the spring and summer. The United States banks were, of course, required to provide funds in London so that holders of accepted drafts could be paid when the acceptances matured. These funds were provided by selling documentary drafts drawn on London financial institutions pursuant to more plentiful United States exports in the autumn.[11] Recently, some large banks in money

---

[10]The rule has been that banks may not accept drafts for more than 10 percent of the bank's paid-up and unimpaired capital and surplus for any one borrower on an unsecured basis. Further, no bank may accept drafts for a total amount equal to more than 50 percent of its paid-up and unimpaired capital and surplus, except that with special permission from the Federal Reserve System a bank may increase the limit to 100 percent (but domestic acceptances in any event are limited to a total of 50 percent).

[11]Benjamin M. Anderson, *Economics and the Public Welfare* (New York: D. Van Nostrand Co., Inc., 1949), p. 19.

market centers have been accepting drafts drawn on them by customers who desired to obtain funds for working capital purposes.[12] Such acceptances are similar in many respects to finance bills and are not eligible for discount at Federal Reserve Banks. They enable business firms to obtain funds even when money is tight and loans from banks might be impossible to obtain. The accepted drafts can be sold in the money market; if they are not purchased by banks, bank funds are not used and remain available for other purposes. Nor are total deposits in the banking system reduced, as payment for the acceptances purchased, usually by check, reduces deposits in one bank but increases deposits in another bank. Because of this situation, the Federal Reserve System imposed a basic 5 percent reserve requirement on finance bills in June 1973, after business activity had been rising rapidly and money was becoming quite tight. An additional 3 percent reserve requirement was imposed on additional finance bills outstanding. Even with such control, finance bills may become more common as banks seek additional sources of funds.

Banks may buy their own acceptances at a discount that provides a yield. Banks are likely to buy their own or other acceptances when their reserves are relatively high, and to reduce holdings when reserves are declining and close to required levels. Because investors in foreign countries are familiar with bank acceptances and recognize their high degree of safety, high rates on bank acceptances may attract foreign funds for their purchase, thus providing additional funds for foreign trade and other types of business activity traditionally financed by bank acceptances, and also, in the future, for other financing.

The Federal Reserve System sometimes purchases bank acceptances as well as Treasury and agency securities, thus contributing to their liquidity. Although the technical requirements for creating bank acceptances are complicated and likely to prevent their rapid growth, it is probable they will grow slowly in volume and remain a money market instrument of some significance.

Negotiable CDs

Certificates of deposit, or time deposits made under specific agreement to leave the funds on deposit for a specific period of time, have existed for a long time. In 1961, however, banks began to issue certificates of deposit in negotiable form. This made it possible for a secondary market to be developed for them, and by 1968 outstanding negotiable CDs in denominations of $100,000 or more totaled over $24 billion. At that point they were the second most important money market instrument, followed by commercial paper, agency issues, and bank acceptances (Federal funds are not included in this comparison because the amount of Federal funds outstanding is not relevant. The relevant figure is the trading in such funds). By mid-1973, the volume of large negotiable CDs exceeded $60 billion, and government agency issues had become more important than commercial paper. Rapid growth of finance companies, which issue a large part of the commercial paper, and further issue of

---

[12]*Money Market Handbook for the Short-Term Investor*, 3rd ed. (New York: Brown Brothers Harriman & Co., 1970), p. 38.

commercial paper by bank holding companies and by some business firms, are likely to make commercial paper more important in the future—although the volume outstanding will probably fluctuate considerably because of its significant use in times of high business activity and "tight money."

Negotiable CDs may be issued in almost any denomination, and have been issued in denominations as small as $10,000 and as large as $10 million; however, most are for $100,000 or more, and denominations over $1 million are rare. Negotiable CDs are traded on a bond-yield equivalent basis (using a 365-day year) in contrast to Treasury bills, commercial paper, and bank acceptances, which are all traded on a discount basis (using a 360-day year). A Treasury bill discounted at 6 percent has a bond-yield equivalent of 6.18 percent.

Federal Reserve Regulation Q sets maximum interest rates that banks may pay on CDs. Higher rates are permitted on those with longer maturities and for denominations of $100,000 or over. Actual rates up to the permitted ceilings may vary through negotiation in the primary issue of CDs, and published rates are approximations. Rates obtained in the secondary market are, of course, not controlled, and may at times rise above rates set by Regulation Q. In May 1973, the Federal Reserve Board of Governors suspended Regulation Q ceilings on all CDs of $100,000 or more. Earlier it had imposed a 5 percent reserve requirement on CDs outstanding in mid-May; it imposed a rate of 8 percent on additional CDs outstanding thereafter, and also on bank-related commercial paper. Banks with a total outstanding of less than $10 million of CDs and bank-related commercial paper, combined, were exempted from the 8 percent marginal reserve requirement.

The argument for Regulation Q, which has been in effect in some form since the 1930s, was that banks might engage in "ruinous competition" unless prevented from offering unduly high interest rates to attract deposits. It was argued that if banks offered very high rates to attract deposits, they might make marginal loans, of doubtful safety, on which they could charge high rates. In the late 1950s, the Regulation Q ceiling was raised, and at the same time a sharp drop in yields on Treasury bills, accompanying the recession of 1957–58, induced nonfinancial corporations to increase their holdings of time deposits. The development of negotiable CDs in the early 1960s offered further inducement to corporations to hold time certificates of deposit, but they could always shift to open market instruments if ceiling rates limited their return to rates lower than those available in the market. Small holders of time deposits cannot easily invest in Treasury bills and a number of other market instruments because of minimum purchase limitations. Thus interest rate ceilings penalize small investors. This might be acceptable as a social objective if interest rate ceilings permitted a continuing relatively adequate flow of credit to smaller borrowers, such as small business firms, mortgage borrowers, and consumer borrowers. However, most economists argue that interest rate ceilings on time deposits are not a very efficient or effective way to influence the flow of credit. Removal of such ceilings is generally favored, but an appropriate time for removal of such ceilings has not appeared.

Business firms are the major holders of negotiable CDs, although, as indicated, they may at times shift to other market instruments when rates rise.

State and local governments, foreign governments and central banks, and individuals hold much smaller amounts.

There is a tendency for business firms to hold many of the CDs to maturity. Partly for this reason, as well as because of the limitations on rates on new issues, trading volume in CDs is much smaller than in Treasury bills. Dealers are reluctant to hold many CDs when interest rates are rising because capital losses may occur. The volume of CDs outstanding dropped sharply in 1969, from about $24 billion to about $11 billion. It has since increased as the relationship between ceiling rates and rates on other money market instruments has permitted issue of more CDs. Trading in CDs is not likely to be as important as trading in Treasury bills under any conditions, however, because of the lack of homogeneity in CDs—in issuer, maturity, rate, and other features.

Liabilities of Nonbank Financial Institutions and Business Firms: Commercial Paper

Commercial paper is the oldest of the short-term secondary money market instruments. Canada is the only other country that has a market for commercial paper, and its market is small. The United States market dates back to the early part of the nineteenth century. Most of the instruments were liabilities of business firms, as implied by the term commercial paper. During the Depression, however, the volume of commercial paper dropped to a very small amount; with interest rates on business loans very low (the prime, or lowest, rate was 1½ percent), there was little reason for firms to turn to the issue of commercial paper to obtain funds. At that time, however, finance companies began to issue paper, partly via the traditional method of sales through dealers, and partly through direct placement. The great growth of consumer credit after World War II caused finance companies to need more funds and resulted in the gradual acceptance of finance company paper. By the 1960s, direct placement was much more important than sales through dealers. Direct placement is used by finance companies that issue paper in sufficient volume to warrant using their own staffs to handle issues rather than paying commissions to dealers.

The volume of commercial paper outstanding increased greatly in the 1960s. This happened because of the great need for funds to finance a period of expansion in business activity, which continued for more than eight years; the rising cost of bank loans; and the fact that banks, in periods of credit tightness often were unable to satisfy demand for commercial loans. A supplemental factor causing increase in the use of commercial paper may have been the fact that its use enhances a corporation's "image": firms that issue commercial paper are understood to have excellent credit standing.

In the late 1960s, issue of commercial paper through dealers again became more important because a number of types of firms that had not previously used commercial paper began to issue it—firms such as public utilities, bank holding companies, insurance companies, transportation companies, and others. It has been suggested that this may have reduced the safety of commercial paper, as there were several defaults in the 1960s in contrast to many years without defaults. Commercial paper had up to that time been regarded as extremely safe and liquid. Although the secondary market was not very broad, commercial paper was not renewed at maturity. However, the bankruptcy of the Penn Central Transportation Company in the spring of 1970 led to a questioning of the quality of many issues. If firms had not been able to obtain bank loans, so that their financial position improved and so that they could meet issues of commercial paper as they matured, the liquidity crisis might have become much more serious. Ability of the commercial banks to make loans was in turn dependent on actions of the Federal Reserve System to increase their lending capability; this is referred to again in Chapter 16.

Issue of commercial paper through dealers has a seasonal pattern: it increases from the end of summer to a peak in November, increases again from January to March, and declines in the summer. Declines in outstandings also occur at corporate tax payment dates because some firms buy commercial paper issued by finance companies and scheduled to mature at or near tax dates so that the funds can be used by the firms to pay taxes.

For a long time banks were the chief buyers of commercial paper. In recent years, however, demand has also come in significant amounts from business firms and nonbank financial institutions. The position of banks is still very important because, in addition to being relatively important buyers, they act as agents in issuing the paper, holding it for safekeeping, and facilitating payment in Federal funds. They also provide lines of credit to firms that issue commercial paper. These bank lines of credit assure the firms of sufficient funds to meet payment of maturing issues of commercial paper.

Commercial paper, including finance company paper, is now one of the four largest money market instruments in volume outstanding. Maturity must be not more than 270 days, since beyond that term, registration under the securities legislation would be required for an issue, making it more costly. Dealers maintain inventories and are compensated by a commission, usually ⅛ percent on an annual basis, and also by any profit they may make from the difference between selling and buying prices. In direct placement, rates are usually quoted by the finance companies that issue most of the directly placed commercial paper. Buyers set the maturities between 3 and 270 days, usually to mature at a time when they need funds, for example, to pay taxes. Under this method, unless a finance company reduces its rate, the company may occasionally borrow funds it does not need; however, the larger finance companies need funds on a very regular basis. A National Credit Office (a subsidiary of Dun & Bradstreet) collects data on most companies that issue commercial paper, provides the names of principal banks used by such firms and unused lines of credit known to be available, as well as financial statement data, and assigns ratings to issues of commercial paper.

The rather weak secondary market, resulting from the fact that many buyers hold issues until maturity and other factors, means that rather substantial fluctuations in rates can occur. Nevertheless, the fact that commercial paper is one of the four largest secondary money market instruments in volume outstanding and the fact that this is the only secondary money market instrument representing business debt—and thus the only secondary market rate for such debt—give it significance.

Foreign Bank Dollar Liabilities: The Eurodollar Market

In international finance, certain currencies have importance as reserve assets held by central banks for final settlement of international debt and as vehicle currencies held and used by commercial banks and business firms to finance trade between the country concerned and among other countries. The wide use of the United States dollar, both as a reserve asset or reserve currency and as a vehicle currency, means that it has been in wide demand. Its generally greater stability than other currencies, evidenced by its devaluation only three times in this century—in 1933, in 1971, and in 1973, in contrast to the numerous and larger devaluations that have occurred for most other major currencies—makes it a desirable asset to hold.

"Eurodollars" is a general term used to refer to dollars on deposit in banks in countries other than the United States. A more accurate term for deposits denominated in currencies other than that of the country in which the deposits are held is "Eurocurrency," as most of the banks holding the deposits are located in Europe, but the currencies in which the deposits are denominated include German marks, Swiss and French francs, Dutch guilders, and Italian lire, as well as United States dollars. European banks holding such deposits agree to redeem the deposits on demand or at the agreed time *in United States dollars* or in the other designated currency. This is a significant departure from the usual situation, in which all of a bank's deposit liabilities are denominated in the currency of the country in which it is located. Whether these deposits are part of the money supply of the country in which they are held depends on the definition of money used (M_1 or M_2). Many Eurodollar accounts are time deposits, and even those that are demand or "call money" are not too frequently drawn upon by check.

Origin of the Market

In the 1950s, governments of Eastern European countries decided to transfer their dollar accounts to Europe, partly to avoid possible attachment of the accounts by United States claimants and partly to establish lines of credit in European countries. Banks were willing to accept such deposits because they wish to attract funds to increase their activity and profits; because European banks can frequently pay interest on demand deposits as well as on time deposits, it was possible for them to offer more attractive income to depositors than United States banks could offer. With the decline of the role of the pound sterling in financing world trade, as Britain's economic position was not as strong after World War II as it had been previously, British banks sought funds.

The United States had continued balance of payments deficits.[13] The result

[13]In any balance of payments, total debits equal total credits, as the balance of payments is based on double-entry accounting. Items below an arbitrary line are designated as "surplus" or "deficit" items. In present balance of payments accounting, losses of reserve assets, such as gold and dollars, together with increases in certain short-term

was an outflow of reserve assets and an increase in short-term liabilities; thus more dollars in the form of short-term liabilities of United States banks accumulated in the hands of foreigners. Foreigners found that often they could place such funds more profitably in European banks, as Eurodollar deposits, than in the United States money market. Thus there is a Eurodollar deposit interest rate, which must in general be above comparable rates paid by United States banks. There is also a Eurodollar loan interest rate, which banks charge borrowers for the use of such funds.

American investors have been discouraged from placing their funds in Eurodollar deposits by restraints under the balance of payments restrictions established since the early 1960s. Eurodollars may be borrowed by business firms, banks, and other institutions. Firms engaging in international trade, whether national corporations or multinational firms, are especially important borrowers. Rates on Eurodollar loans must be generally competitive with rates on loans obtained elsewhere.

On the deposit side, foreign central banks have at times encouraged the commercial banks in their countries to place funds in the Eurodollar market. When central banks were accumulating large amounts of dollars, they sometimes encouraged commercial banks to do this by making forward cover (future conversion of dollars into a bank's home currency) available cheaply. This presumably meant that the dollars lent by banks would not contribute to an increase in that country's money supply at that time, as they would have done if the country's central bank had to purchase and hold them, paying for the purchase by checks, which add to commercial bank reserves.

Significance of the Market

Because Eurodollars initially originate in the transfer of a demand deposit in a United States bank to a Eurodollar deposit in a European bank, payments to foreigners and transfer of foreign funds already on deposit in United States banks can create Eurodollars. Foreign holders of time deposits in the United States may switch them to demand deposits and then to Eurodollar deposits. The creation of Eurodollar deposits adds to the money supply in European countries.

Pyramiding of Eurodollar deposits may occur if banks that receive Eurodollar deposits make loans to business firms which redeposit the funds in other European banks. Even greater increase in the total money supply in Europe may occur if a bank that receives Eurodollar deposits places the funds on deposit in another European bank, in order to earn interest on the funds. A bank may do this if no suitable borrowers are applying for loans or if fluctuations

---

liabilities, are treated as deficits (inflows of gold or dollars and reductions in the designated short-term liabilities are surpluses). Losses of gold or dollars reduce a country's ability to meet its liabilities; an increase in liabilities means that more liabilities may have to be met by the holdings of gold and other reserves. For convenient explanations of the accounting problems, see Normal S. Fieleke, "Accounting for the Balance of Payments," Federal Reserve Bank of Boston, *New England Economic Review*, May–June 1971, pp. 2–15, and John Pippenger, "Balance of Payments Deficits: Measurement and Interpretation," Federal Reserve Bank of St. Louis, *Review*, November 1973, pp. 6–14.

in interest rates in different countries have made the rate in another European country slightly higher than the rate in which the Eurodollar deposits were originally placed. (The reader should keep in mind that in many countries in Europe little or no distinction is made between time and demand deposits, and interest is paid on both.) The bank in the second country may then use the funds to make loans; theoretically redeposit in a third or fourth country might occur. The money supply in the country in which the funds are originally deposited is increased when the funds are first deposited; transfer to an interbank deposit in another country increases the money supply in that country (because such deposits are treated as foreign deposits, and hence part of the money supply); and deposit of funds by borrowers and by those to whom borrowers make payments increases the money supply wherever this occurs. Thus there may be a considerable expansion of the total money supply in Europe, part of it occurring in each of a number of different countries.

Expansion ceases, however, when anyone who receives funds uses them to make payments to United States firms or residents. Deposits are returned to the United States. Some economists believe that leakages such as this prevent the size of the Eurodollar deposits from expanding very rapidly.

Accurate figures on the volume of Eurodollar balances are not available. By the end of 1969 the volume of Eurodollar balances outstanding was probably between $40 and $60 billion. By the end of 1972 it probably exceeded $100 billion on a net basis (excluding interbank deposits).

The rates usually quoted in publications are deposit interest rates; banks that have Eurodollar deposits set the spread between deposit and loan rates.

One special significance of the Eurodollar market with respect to United States financial markets is the use American banks decided to make of the Eurodollar market. American banks began to borrow Eurodollar deposits, especially from their foreign branches, and increased their borrowing when funds became tight, forcing them to look for another source of funds. The Eurodollars borrowed by American banks might be Eurodollar deposits already in the foreign branches or they might be created by the foreign branches. In creating these, the branch would do as any bank does in making a loan: debit loans (to the parent bank, in this case) and credit deposits (Eurodollar deposits, in this case). Incidentally, the borrowings added to the United States deficit in its balance of payments by one measure, referred to as the liquidity measure, because by this measure all increases in short-term bank liabilities to foreigners are counted as increases in the deficit. It did not add to the deficit by another measure, referred to as the official settlements measure, because by this measure only short-term bank liabilities to foreign *official* holders are counted as increases in the deficit. Consequently, although a rise in Eurodollar borrowings by American banks increased the deficit by the liquidity measure, repayment of borrowings resulted in an increase in the deficit by the official settlements measure, because repayment of the funds provided banks in Europe (branches of American banks) with more dollar balances than they wished to hold, and they sold these to central banks, in whole or in part, depending on their situation. Thus the United States balance of payments could (and did) show a deficit by one measure and a surplus by another measure. The reverse situation occurred in the following year.

In late 1969, the Federal Reserve Board of Governors imposed a reserve requirement of 10 percent against amounts borrowed by head offices from their foreign branches, above a certain minimum. This reserve requirement was increased to 20 percent in 1971 but was reduced to 8 percent in May 1973, at which time it was planned to eliminate the reserve-free base amount gradually, beginning in July 1973. The Federal Reserve Board Chairman also requested foreign banks operating in the United States to maintain similar reserves. It had become evident by 1973 that Eurodollar borrowings, issue of CDs, issue of bank-related commercial paper, and finance bills were all sources of funds for banks that were becoming too important to be ignored. Banks were certainly no longer limited to lending a fixed amount of deposits, if they ever had been so limited. The increase in these newly important sources of funds raises some further question concerning the appropriate definition of money, as they are included neither in M_1 nor in M_2. M_1 and M_2 were increasing in the first half of 1973 at much slower rates than such aggregates as the total of bank credit and bank reserves. Thus institutional changes such as the growth of the Eurodollar market and of other money market instruments were creating new problems.

The Eurodollar market is significant in several major respects. First, it tends to increase the forces causing differences among interest rates in different countries to be reduced.[14] Second, it makes funds easily available, from a source alternative to the domestic credit market, for borrowers such as multinational firms, operating in many countries and needing funds in each country where they operate. Third, because it has been subject to relatively few regulations, it is possible to transfer Eurodollar funds freely from one country to another and into other currencies, thus causing increased upward or downward pressures on values of currencies at times when movements of funds increase. Fourth, it may have been a factor of some significance—although it is difficult to estimate how much—causing an increase in the money supply in the United States to result in transfer of some funds to Eurodollar deposits, and thus to result in an increase in the money supply in Europe. To this extent, it may have aided in transmitting inflation in the United States to Europe.[15] Finally, the

[14]In early 1973, bankers were complaining that efforts to prevent a rise in the prime rate on bank loans in the United States were still succeeding—but that under the existing conditions, large firms could borrow at 6 percent in the United States and lend to foreign branches of United States banks, in the Eurodollar market, at 6½ percent. *Wall Street Journal*, February 2, 1973, p. 13.

[15]There is much controversy on this point. It might be assumed, especially if money were defined as M_2 (including time deposits in commercial banks), that the creation of Eurodollar deposits increased the money supply in European countries. It has been argued, however, that Eurodollar deposits do not serve as a principal means of payment, that only a small proportion of Eurobank deposits consists of call and overnight deposits, and that a large part of these are interbank deposits rather than deposits held by the public. Milton Friedman argued that a borrower could use a Eurodollar deposit to buy, for example, timber from Russia, and that Russia might keep the proceeds on deposit in a Eurodollar deposit in another London bank; see Milton Friedman, "The Euro-Dollar Market: Some First Principles," *Morgan Guaranty Survey*, October 1969, pp. 4–14. Fred Klopstock responded that this *could* occur, but that it was unlikely and that Eurobanks are likely to lose most of the funds withdrawn by check or otherwise from Eurodollar deposit accounts, as payments are made to those who deposit the proceeds in the United States. See Fred H. Klopstock, "Money Creation in the Euro-Dollar Market—A Note on Professor Friedman's Views," Federal Reserve Bank of New York, *Monthly Review*, January 1970, pp. 12–15.

development of the Eurodollar market has made the analysis of the balance of payments position somewhat more difficult. When one measure of deficit increases while another decreases, it is more difficult to determine what appropriate balance of payments policy should be.

RELATED SHORT-TERM FINANCIAL
ASSETS AND INTEREST RATES

Thus far we have discussed only short-term financial assets for which there is a secondary money market and hence a quickly fluctuating yield rate. There are, however, several short-term financial assets that are not normally traded in a secondary market, but are significant because yields in the money market are related to yields on these other short-term financial assets. Bank loans are made at varying interest rates, usually negotiated between the lending bank and the customer. For several decades, however, there has been an announced prime rate, granted to customers having the highest credit standing. Customers granted this rate may vary from time to time, but the announced prime rate is considered a floor for other loan rates. The Federal Reserve System makes discounts and advances for borrowing member banks at a specified rate, the discount rate. Securities dealers and other money market dealers borrow from banks at dealers' rates and obtain funds under repurchase agreements, selling securities to the banks and agreeing to repurchase them at agreed prices on a future date. Finally, rates on CDs that are not negotiable are related to those on negotiable CDs.

Bank Loans: The Prime Rate and Other Loan Rates

Bank loans are normally not traded in any secondary market; whatever liquidity exists in a loan portfolio must come from the fact that many business loans are short-term loans, so that a certain portion of the loan portfolio matures almost every day, and, unless loans are renewed, they are repaid. The interest rates on business and other loans are, however, significant for the money market for several reasons. First, some borrowers have the alternative of borrowing through issues of commercial paper, and some have the alternative of borrowing in the Eurodollar market. Second, the rate on business loans indicates the cost of short-term borrowing by business firms and thus is a useful indicator of demand and supply of short-term funds. Third, the publicity given to the prime rate has tended to focus attention on changes in that rate. Although the degree of attention may have been unwarranted, the rate could not be ignored.

An announced prime rate was first established in the 1930s to prevent interest rates from going too low. Banks had large amounts of excess reserves, business activity was at a low level, and it was feared that rates on business loans might go below the 1½ percent believed to be the administrative and servicing cost of business loans. This rate of 1½ percent remained as the prime rate until 1947. Since that time the prime rate has increased as interest rates generally rose and declined when they fell; adjustments were normally made in "steps" of at least ¼ percent at a time. Changes in the prime rate, with fluctuations in the commercial paper and Treasury bill rates for comparison, are shown in Figure 9–3.

When interest rates are high and credit availability is limited, a higher proportion of all business loans are made at the prime rate, although this may seem surprising. Customers who have been issuing commercial paper may turn to banks for loans when the rate on commercial paper rises significantly above the more slowly adjusted prime rate, and banks may accommodate such prime customers ahead of other customers.

The prime rate for some years was a lagging rate, being adjusted upward (or downward) only when banks were satisfied that the demand for loans had increased (or decreased) and was likely to remain at its current level or move further in the same direction. The prime rate was thus one of the last short-term rates to be changed. As the prime rate had become the base rate or anchor rate for other loan rates, this was significant.

Changes in the prime rate were usually initiated by a New York bank,

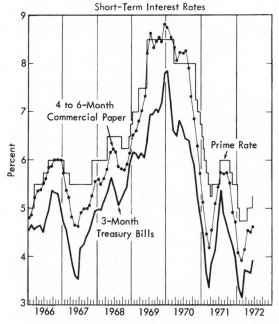

Note: Yields on three–month Treasury bills and four– to
    six–month commercial paper are monthly averages
    of daily figures. The prime rate is the interest rate
    posted by major commercial banks on short–term
    loans to their most creditworthy business borrowers.

FIGURE 9–3

SOURCE: Federal Reserve Bank of New York, *Monthly Review,* August 1972.

and an element of gamesmanship may have been present. Which bank would change its rate first? Would it suffer a loss of loan demand if others did not follow a rate increase? Would it receive a flood of loan applications if it lowered the rate? The prime rate remained unchanged from 1960 to 1965 but was changed several times a year in the second half of the decade of the 1960s. As might be expected, changes were generally upward from 1956 through 1969, as the prime rate followed the rising demand for funds in the latter stages of a period of rising business activity. Then in 1970 the rate was reduced rather drastically, raised briefly in 1971 for several months and then further reduced. In late 1972, it was raised again, as the increase in business activity became more rapid and the increase in demand for short-term funds, for inventory accumulation and other purposes, became stronger.

As might be anticipated, the increases in the prime rate in the late 1960s were both unpopular and distasteful for the banks. Being announced in newspapers and other media, they were especially evident to the public. Although they were simply following previous upward movements of other short-term rates, the attention given to them suggested to some banks the idea of using a "floating" prime rate, adjusted upward or downward in accordance with some rate in the secondary money market. The rate chosen was generally the commercial paper rate, because (1) it is a market rate, set by impersonal forces; (2) it is an alternative to bank borrowing, at least for some borrowers; and (3) the maturities of commercial paper are comparable to those of short-term business loans. One bank has also used the rate on 89-day CDs as a determinant of the floating prime rate. Bankers believed that by using the commercial paper rate as a determinant of the prime rate they could avoid outcries that they were unjustly raising loan rates, that they could make more frequent and more timely adjustments in the prime rate, and that they could raise the prime rate (and other loan rates) sufficiently to meet the costs of borrowing funds. The rate on CDs represents the cost of one part of borrowed funds. Because CD rates move with commercial paper rates and one bank used CD rates directly in its determination of the prime rate, loan rates should move reasonably proportionately with the cost to banks of borrowing funds. A floating prime rate would rise more rapidly and somewhat higher in periods of rising interest rates than the prime rate had in the past and would drop more rapidly and somewhat further in periods of falling rates.

In early 1973 banks were urged by monetary authorities not to raise the prime rate and to modify or abandon floating rate formulas that would have resulted in rate increases. It seemed that "floating" prime rates might disappear for a time. Obviously a rise in the announced prime rate was also undesirable from the viewpoint of those who feared that rising interest rates might revive or continue inflationary expectations and thus make the control of inflation more difficult.[16]

The Committee on Interest and Dividends, established by President Nixon

---

[16]It was reported that Bankers Trust Company, Mellon Bank, and Irving Trust Company suspended the use of automatic formulas to determine their floating prime rates, leaving only First National City Bank among large banks with a floating rate. *Wall Street Journal*, January 26, 1973, p. 13.

as part of the mechanism for control of inflation, pressured banks to establish dual prime rates: one, a rate, which might float, for large business borrowers; the other, which should be more stable, a rate applicable to small business and farm borrowers, mortgage borrowers, and consumers. The desire was to permit the rate charged to large business firms to rise consistently with the increase in the cost of borrowing by such firms from alternative sources such as commercial paper. Banks could thus charge rates on large business loans adequate to compensate them, in general, for the marginal cost of funds obtained through issues of CDs and/or commercial paper. At the same time, it was desired to restrain increases in interest rates charged small business firms, farmers, mortgage borrowers, and consumers, in order to avoid sharp cutbacks in funds available to them. As usual, in a period of business expansion, the most rapid rise was occurring in business borrowing, and it was desired to restrain this without necessarily imposing heavy restraint on other borrowing.[17]

The commercial paper rate is not necessarily the best guide for a "floating" prime rate. Sometimes the commercial paper rate is out of line with other secondary money market rates. At such times the floating prime rate, based on the commercial paper rate, will not adequately reflect the cost of funds borrowed by banks which have floating prime rates. With liability management as well as asset management an important part of bank portfolio policy, this is a significant feature.

Borrowing from the Fed:
Discounts and Advances and the Discount Rate

When the Federal Reserve System was first established in 1913, it was patterned to a considerable extent after the Bank of England. An important feature of Bank of England policy was use of the discount rate, the rate at which financial institutions could borrow to obtain needed funds. It was believed that the discount privilege and the discount rate would be the primary tools of the new central bank in determining how much, and at what cost, banks could borrow, and therefore how much credit they could create. Early critics of Federal Reserve policy, such as Benjamin Anderson, argued that the discount rate should be a penalty rate, above the prime loan rate, so that banks would discount at the Fed only if they badly needed funds.[18] Later, it was suggested—for example, by Robert Turner—that since banks could sell Treasury bills to obtain funds, it was only necessary for the discount rate to be above

---

[17]A succinct discussion may be found in the Federal Reserve Bank of San Francisco, *Business and Financial Letter*, April 27, 1973, pp. 1–3. See also "The Dual Rate Structure: A New Plan for the Banks," Chase Manhattan Bank, *Business in Brief*, April 1973, pp. 2–3.

[18]Benjamin M. Anderson, *Economics and the Public Welfare* (New York: Van Nostrand, 1949), pp. 58, 86. Anderson was economist for the Chase National Bank, and his argument was stated in *The Chase Economic Bulletin*, 1, No. 5 (July 20, 1921). Anderson did not believe that the central bank should undertake management of the money supply, but believed that it should simply serve as a "lender of last resort" in cases of emergency.

the Treasury bill rate for it to be a "penalty" rate.[19] In fact, the discount rate has seldom been a penalty rate in the United States; the discount rate has usually been lower than other rates it might logically be compared with.

Over the years, the task of the Federal Reserve System, as it was viewed by economists inside and outside the System, changed from primarily that of supplying funds in emergencies to that of controlling the money (and credit) supply. The role of discounts and advances also changed. Discounts and advances became a means of supplying funds to banks with temporary needs, sometimes because monetary policy actions had impinged too heavily on them. The discount privilege came to be regarded as a "safety valve," needed because, in a country of more than 13,000 separate banks, some were more likely to be adversely affected by monetary policy changes than others, and those so affected would need emergency funds.

Borrowing mechanics also changed. Most borrowing occurred in the form of advances with collateral rather than discounts, borrowing by banks on the basis of their own promissory notes rather than discounting notes of business firms already held by banks. The most common collateral is government securities. In the absence of "eligible paper" for discounts or government securities as collateral for advances, advances based on any collateral satisfactory to the Federal Reserve System may be made under a section of the law added in 1932, at a rate currently ½ percent above the normal discount rate. Documentation was made easier by execution of a continuing lending agreement, thus avoiding execution of new promissory notes and borrowing resolutions for a series of borrowings. Borrowing can be done by telephone, with immediate credit to the borrowing bank's reserve account.

In the 1960s, the Federal Reserve System made an extensive study of the discount mechanism and concluded that modifications were needed. It was suggested that banks should have a "basic borrowing privilege" that would vary with required reserves of banks; smaller banks would be able to borrow more, relative to their required reserves, than larger banks. A seasonal borrowing privilege was also suggested, to permit borrowing by banks, especially in rural areas, that experienced seasonal losses of deposits and seasonal increases in loans, both of which cause drains on reserves. The earlier philosophy had been that banks should be able to forecast such seasonal needs and could borrow only when needs were unexpectedly large. The proposals were deferred because of some opposition, and the proposal for a "basic borrowing privilege" had not yet been implemented in mid-1973. The proposal for a seasonal borrowing privilege was reannounced in late 1972, however, and implemented in April 1973. This facility was intended primarily to be of use to about 2,000 banks that have marked seasonal loan and deposit changes, most of these banks being not over $50 million each in deposits. Such banks, the Federal Reserve System officials concluded, have more difficulty in gaining access to the national money market to meet temporary needs. A decline in available funds (deposits minus loans) of 5 percent of the previous year's average deposits, for a period of at least eight weeks, is sufficient to qualify a bank

[19]Robert C. Turner, *Member Bank Borrowing* (Columbus, Ohio: Ohio State University Press, 1938).

for seasonal borrowing. In implementing this change, the readiness of the Federal Reserve System to lend in emergencies, even to nonbank financial institutions and to business firms, was restated.

Changes made in the discount rate have "announcement" effects in much the same way as changes in a fixed prime rate. It is not clear, however, whether these effects are always the same. An increase in the discount rate is usually interpreted as a signal that the Federal Reserve System intends to pursue a more restrictive monetary policy; but in fact such an increase may only indicate that the Federal Reserve System has adjusted the discount rate in line with other money market rates to prevent undue borrowing from the Fed by banks that could obtain funds in other ways. A rise in the discount rate can do little to slow the expansion of money and credit if at the same time the Federal Reserve System injects new funds into bank reserves by open market purchases.

Because the discount rate is determined administratively by the Federal Reserve System, it does not respond immediately to money market supply and demand.[20] The discount rate is significant for the amount of borrowed reserves, and therefore for the portion of bank reserves that must be repaid to the Fed in the near future. The role of the discount rate in monetary policy is less significant.[21] Suffice it to say at this point that the discount rate is of relatively minor importance in monetary policy but is of some importance in determining the role of borrowing from the Fed as a source of commercial banks funds and may be of some value as a lagging indicator of both general money market conditions and Federal Reserve System policy. In its suggestions for modification of the discount mechanism the Federal Reserve System proposed that the discount rate be changed by small amounts more frequently or otherwise become more flexible. In fact, the discount rate was changed quite frequently in the period from late 1970 to early 1973, but it was not "tied" in any specified way to money market rates.

Dealer Loans:
The Dealer Rate and Repurchase Agreements

Government securities dealers and other dealers in the money market make heavy use of borrowed funds to finance inventories of securities. These

[20]Some central banks have experimented with a "floating" discount rate. For example, late in 1956 the Bank of Canada announced that until further notice its minimum lending rate (discount rate) would be $\frac{1}{4}$ percent above the average Treasury bill rate, making the discount rate clearly a market-determined rate rather than a policy rate. See Peter G. Fousek, *Foreign Central Banking: The Instruments of Monetary Policy* (New York: Federal Reserve Bank of New York, 1957), pp. 18; 20. Also, see footnote 21.

[21]An indication of the declining importance of the discount rate in monetary policy is the abandonment of the traditional fixed "bank rate" (discount rate) of the Bank of England, a tradition for about 270 years. It was announced that a "last resort rate" would be based on the interest rate on Treasury bills. This policy officially recognized that the discount rate, or bank rate, is no longer a policy instrument, but simply a rate at which banks may borrow from the central bank, at somewhat higher cost than if they sold Treasury bills, when emergencies arise. The discount rate thus becomes a market rate rather than a fixed rate. See *Wall Street Journal*, October 10, 1972.

funds are generally obtained from commercial banks, but in some cases from corporations, either under dealer loans or what are termed repurchase agreements. Dealer loans are made to dealers by commercial banks at designated rates. These loans are usually made by banks in New York City, which post interest rates daily for dealer loans. Dealers obtain additional needed financing from repurchase agreements (RPs). RPs are also used by dealer banks to obtain financing not supplied by the banks themselves, in allotments to the securities or investment department. Dealer loans are collateralized by the securities being financed. The Federal Reserve System also makes repurchase agreements with dealers.

Repurchase agreements provide for purchase of securities by the lending bank, with payment usually in Federal funds by check on the bank's account at the Fed. Federal funds provide immediate cash, whereas a clearing-house check must be cleared, and the funds are not available until the next day. This *payment* in Federal funds should not be confused with borrowing and lending Federal funds, discussed earlier in the section on Federal funds.

Some repurchase agreements have fixed maturities; others have no maturity date. The latter may be terminated at any time; they are in effect "call loans," subject to call for repayment at any time. Dealers sometimes arrange reverse RPs, in which they agree to buy the securities and the other party to repurchase them later. Banks that make repurchase agreements could, alternatively, invest the funds in the Federal funds market, although Federal funds trading is usually in units of $1 million, so that an amount of funds less than $1 million might be difficult to invest in that market. Corporations could invest their funds in Treasury bills, commercial paper, or CDs, rather than in RPs, but RPs may be a very convenient form in which to invest extremely short-term funds. Because RPs are negotiated by the parties concerned, there are no regular data on RP rates, but scattered data indicate that rates on RPs are usually lower than rates on collateralized loans made by New York City banks.

Repurchase agreements are also made by the Trading Desk of the Federal Reserve Bank of New York, acting for the Federal Reserve System. These RPs are used for monetary policy purposes rather than for profit. The return is usually equal to the discount rate at the Federal Reserve Bank of New York. When the Federal Reserve System wishes to provide bank reserves on a long-term basis, it usually engaged in direct open market purchases. When it wishes to provide reserves on a temporary basis, it may use RPs. When RPs are used, participants in the market know that the transaction will be reversed in the near future. Hence it is believed that any decline in yields will be less than would accompany the same volume of open market purchases; thus the use of RPs may tend to stabilize yields.

Since 1966 matched sale-purchase transactions (or reverse RPs) have also been used.[22] It is agreed that the Federal Reserve System, in selling securities, will repurchase them within a short time. One reason for this type of arrangement rather than direct sales followed later by purchases is that banks may have acquired a large volume of temporary excess reserves. For example, an increase in the float that temporarily increases reserves may result when

---

[22]Sometimes these transactions are termed reverse RPs if arranged at the initiative of dealers, and matched sale-purchase transactions if arranged at the initiative of the Fed.

transportation facilities are halted by a snowstorm. The excess reserves may be temporarily reduced by reverse RPs.

CD Rates and Other Time Deposit Interest Rates

Negotiable CDs constituted in 1972 only about 10 percent of total time and savings deposits, although their volume increased sharply in 1973. In attracting time deposits, banks are competing in several different markets. Savings deposits and some types of other time deposits attract funds from individuals who might otherwise place the funds in other deposit-type institutions— primarily savings and loan associations and mutual savings banks—or in government savings bonds. Other time deposits, including nonnegotiable CDs, attract funds of individuals and corporations. Finally, negotiable CDs in denominations of $100,000 and over are issued mainly to corporations, and rates on them must be competitive with rates on other liquid market instruments. interest rates may vary from 4½ percent or less on some savings deposits to as much as 7½ percent on some large-denomination negotiable CDs.

Average rates actually paid are of interest to the Federal Reserve System because, as long as Regulation Q must be enforced, the relationship of rates actually paid to ceiling rates is significant. The public can invest in money market or capital market instruments rather than holding funds in time deposits. Hence, outflows of funds may at times occur on a large scale when other money and/or capital market rates significantly exceed time deposit interest rates. These outflows, called "disintermediation," may be quite important for monetary policy as they reduce time deposits and deprive both banks and other deposit-type institutions of funds. Disintermediation was of much concern in the late 1960s. Federal Reserve System authorities felt compelled to raise interest rate ceilings on time deposits to enable banks to compete for interest-sensitive funds and to avoid large outflows of funds from banks. At the same time, they worried about the effect of these increases on deposit-type institutions, which have difficulty paying interest rates much higher than those of recent past years because they are locked into holdings of long-term financial assets with specified yields, as explained in Chapter 6. Many economists believe that interest rate ceilings are undesirable because they discriminate against those who have insufficient knowledge and insufficient funds to invest in the money and capital markets directly.[23]

INTERRELATIONSHIPS OF SHORT-TERM INTEREST RATES

Since both borrowers and lenders in the short-term money market are primarily the Treasury, the central bank, commercial banks, corporations, finance

[23]For example, see Robert Lindsay, *The Economics of Interest Rate Ceilings*, New York University, Institute of Finance *Bulletin*, Nos. 68–9, December 1970. The history of rate ceilings was reviewed in Charlotte E. Ruebling, "The Administration of Regulation Q," Federal Reserve Bank of St. Louis, *Review*, February 1970, pp. 29–40.

companies, and government securities and other money market dealers, rates on different money market instruments are usually highly correlated with one another.

Normal Relationships

The most usual relationship is that Treasury bill rates are the lowest rates, with agency securities rates, bank acceptance rates, and commercial paper rates in ascending order. Negotiable CD rates have averaged somewhat above rates on government agency securities and slightly below rates on bank acceptances. Eurodollar rates have generally been higher than rates on CDs. Federal funds rates fluctuate widely because banks that borrow in the Federal funds market may urgently need funds and may be willing to pay a high rate. Until the mid-1960s, the Federal funds rate was seldom higher than the discount rate because banks could always borrow from the Fed as an alternative to borrowing Federal funds. In the mid-1960s, however, banks began to borrow Federal funds more regularly, and the Federal funds rate rose above the discount rate. The discount rate was lower than the Federal funds rate, but discounting was not used for regular borrowing because of Federal Reserve System regulations and the tradition against regular commercial bank borrowing from the Fed.

The announced prime rate is generally above the rate on commercial paper, although changes in the announced prime rate lag, and sometimes the commercial paper rate rises before the prime rate is raised sufficiently to equal the commercial paper rate.

As commercial banks can obtain funds either by discounts or advances from the Fed, borrowing in the Federal funds market, or selling Treasury bills, as well as in some other ways, it was generally believed that the discount rate and the Treasury bill rate would be relatively close together.[24] However, adjustments in the discount rate are frequently delayed for considerable periods of time. Thus in 1961 the discount rate was considerably higher than both the Federal funds rate and the Treasury bill rate, whereas in 1969 it was considerably below them.

Significance of the Treasury Bill Rate

If any single rate is to be selected as representative of money market rates, it should probably be the Treasury bill rate because this is the rate on the major money market instrument, and the market for Treasury bills is broad and sensitive.

Second, most open market purchases by the Federal Reserve System, and virtually all open market sales, involve Treasury bills. Prevailing conditions

---

[24]See, for example, National City Bank *Monthly Letter*, May 1954: "As a general rule, Treasury bill yields hold within ½ percent of the discount rate." This spread subsequently widened, becoming as much as 2 percent at some times in 1969–71.

in the Treasury bill market are considered in open market policy decisions, and open market operations affect Treasury bill yields.

Third, except for the Federal funds rate, which fluctuates widely, the Treasury bill rate is usually the lowest rate in the money market. Levels of other rates may be explained in terms of factors causing them to be higher than Treasury bill rates by varying amounts.

Role of the Federal Funds Rate

The fact that banks can quickly dispose of excess reserves and obtain reserves if they are deficient means that effects of monetary policy actions are transmitted through the banking system more quickly than they otherwise might be. If actions of the Federal Reserve System supply reserves to New York banks, such banks can normally quickly dispose of the reserves. Thus banks in the aggregate may remain more fully invested. The effect of a change in reserves in New York is quickly transmitted to banks elsewhere in the system.

When pressure for funds is strong, the Federal funds rate tends to fluctuate around the discount rate. Formerly, the discount rate was a ceiling rate for the Federal funds rate, but in recent years, as explained earlier, the Federal funds rate may rise to approximate yields banks can obtain on the loans for which there is heavy demand, or on certain investments that have high after-tax yields. When pressure for funds is slack, the Federal funds rate fluctuates more closely with the Treasury bill rate, as banks can obtain funds either by selling Treasury bills or by borrowing Federal funds.

The Federal funds rate is closely watched as a barometer of the money market, although its volatility and the fact that it may be associated with several other rates make interpretation of changes in it difficult. One approach is to determine the "basic reserve position" of the large money market banks— their excess reserves minus their borrowings from the Fed and their net purchases of Federal funds. This indicates how large excess reserves or reserve deficiencies would have been without borrowing from the Fed and without purchases of Federal funds. Because these are temporary means of adjusting reserve positions, large reserve deficiencies are likely to mean heavy demand for Federal funds; large amounts of excess reserves mean light demand. This analysis, combined with other information such as the strength of bank loan demand, is helpful in appraising money market positions of the key large banks and thus in interpreting movements of the Federal funds rate. As explained in Chapter 16, this and other information is used in determining appropriate discretionary monetary policy.

The Discount Rate, Dealer Rates, and Other Money Market Rates

The money market is the first point of impact in the transmission of effects of Federal Reserve System policy actions. Figure 9–4 indicates one view

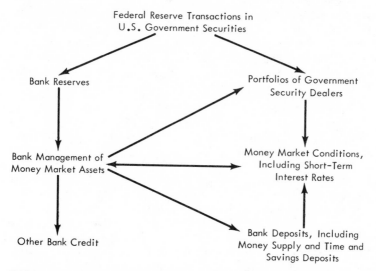

FIGURE 9–4   First Steps in the Monetary Process

SOURCE: Albert R. Koch, "An Approach to Monetary Policy Formulation," Federal Reserve Bank of Philadelphia, *Business Review*, February 1965.

of the first steps in this process.[25] Federal reserve transactions in United States government securities affect bank reserves on the one hand and portfolios of government securities dealers on the other. Bank reserve positions affect bank management of money market assets first, and of other credit somewhat later. Portfolios of government securities dealers affect money market conditions because dealers reduce or increase their borrowing as their inventories of securities rise or fall. Money market conditions are reflected in the level of Treasury bill rates, the level of the Federal funds rate in relation to the discount rate and to Treasury bill rates, the volume of Federal funds flows, and the volume of and rates on dealer loans. Money market changes in turn affect bank deposits, which are also affected by bank management of money market assets.

Since demand for money and bank credit is very volatile in the short run, it has been the Fed's aim for a long time to permit short-term changes in such demand to be accommodated. If this demand were not accommodated, money market conditions would be quite unstable. Such instability may, of course, be necessary, in the interest of other objectives, and this question is discussed in some detail in Chapter 16.

The key position of money market conditions may be appreciated by viewing, in bird's-eye fashion, some of the remaining steps in the monetary process. These are shown in tentative fashion in Figure 9–5. Although Figure 9–5 somewhat oversimplifies the relationship and although different economists

[25]Figures 9–4 and 9–5 are taken from Albert R. Koch, "An Approach to Monetary Policy Formulation," Federal Reserve Bank of Philadelphia, *Business Review*, February 1965, pp. 3–9; 12–15. A considerable part of the discussion is also based on that article, but the views expressed are those of the present authors.

emphasize in varying degrees specific relationships shown in the diagram, this bird's-eye view can be used as a framework for integrating various elements of the situation of the financial markets vis-à-vis the economy at any particular time.

FLUCTUATIONS IN MONEY MARKET RATES

Until 1965, wide fluctuations in money market rates were rather unusual. Rates might not change more than 25 basis points (¼ percent) from one month to the next, and rates on bank acceptances and finance paper might not vary for several months. Since 1965, there has been much greater fluctuation in rates. Monthly yield changes of 50 basis points or more are common. The reasons are varied and may stem from the variety of economic problems faced by the United States and accentuated by the economic pressures of the Vietnam War. There have been uncertainty about monetary policy and wide swings in rate of change in the money supply, uncertainty about fiscal policy and wide change in Federal budget deficits, uncertainty about the international monetary system and several crises involving sterling, marks, francs, and finally the dollar, and there has been uncertainty concerning the trend of many developments in society—inflation, productivity, desire for environmental improvement instead of increased output, and government corruption, among others.

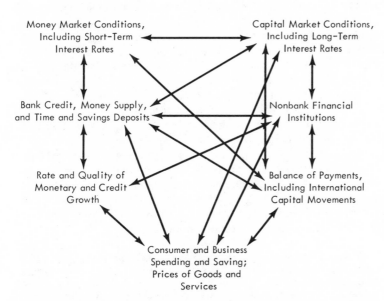

FIGURE 9–5 Major Remaining Steps in the Monetary Process—with Some of the Main Interactions Noted

SOURCE: Albert R. Koch, "An Approach to Monetary Policy Formulation," Federal Reserve Bank of Philadelphia, *Business Review*, February 1965.

Yield spreads also increased after 1965, both yield spreads between 3-month and 6-month maturities of the same type of instrument and spreads of yields on other instruments over yields on Treasury bills. Desire for liquidity may have been a significant factor explaining the first spread and perhaps the second. In connection with spreads of yields on other instruments over yields on Treasury bills, however, it should be noted that although the volume of Treasury bills increased sharply, the amount held by the Federal Reserve System and by government trust funds increased both absolutely and relative to amounts held by the public. Limited supply available to the public may have been a factor raising prices of Treasury bills and thus keeping yields lower than they would otherwise have been.

SIGNIFICANCE OF THE MONEY MARKET FOR THE CONTROL OF ECONOMIC ACTIVITY

The development and growth of the money market is especially significant for the control of economic activity for several reasons. (1) The money market is, as indicated earlier, the first point of impact of monetary policy actions. (2) Money market changes are frequently used as indicators of the impact of monetary policy and as guides for further actions. (3) The growth of the money market means a growth of substitutes for money; funds can be held in the form of money market instruments instead of money.

The significance of the third point requires some further elaboration. The development of instruments such as Treasury bills, commercial paper, and negotiable certificates of deposit tends to increase transactions velocity of money; that is, money is used to buy these instruments and is received by sellers or issuers. It also probably tends to permit an increase in the income velocity of money, that is, the turnover of money in income payments.[26] For example, an increase in commercial paper probably permits financing of purchases of goods and services that might not otherwise be sold. As Richard Selden has suggested, "to the extent that growth in aggregate spending is financed by rising velocity of money, the volume of demand deposits need not—indeed, *should* not—expand. In this manner, therefore, the growth of commercial paper in recent years, along with Treasury bills and other liquid assets, has tended to limit growth of bank deposits and earning assets."[27] If velocity rises, money supply need not rise as rapidly to finance a given rate of growth of the economy; hence a rise in velocity *may* cause the central bank to be more restrictive than otherwise in permitting increase in the money supply.

[26]There is no convenient measure of transactions velocity of money, payments/money supply, as there is no convenient measure of total payments. Bank debits (checks drawn on bank demand deposits and withdrawals from such deposits) may be used as a proxy for payments. A convenient measure of income velocity is GNP/money supply, shown in Figure 6-1.

[27]Richard T. Selden, *Trends and Cycles in the Commercial Paper Market*, Occasional Paper 85 (New York: National Bureau of Economic Research, 1963), pp. 88–89.

The recent trend in income velocity of money was shown in Figure 6–1, in Chapter 6. It is interesting that the upward trend accelerated in early 1972, but there is little firm evidence supporting any projection of the trend in velocity.[28] The general upward trend since World War II may be explained by two factors: (1) the increased efficiency in payment mechanisms that tend to reduce the amount of transactions balances of money needed for a given volume of payments, and (2) the gradual transfer of money balances held by business firms, and some balances held by households, into money substitutes such as time deposits, commercial paper, Treasury bills, and others. It seems reasonable to conclude that the second factor was induced in large part by the rise in interest rates: the rise in interest rates reduced the quantity of money demanded. Increasing safety of money substitutes may also have been a factor. This increasing safety is evidenced by the small number of defaults, except for commercial paper in 1970, and is supported by the existence and effectiveness of deposit insurance.

Total spending is the product of money supply times the velocity of money —MV in the well-known equation of exchange, $MV = PT$. (PT is the sum of all transactions, at the price for each transaction, and if only income transactions are counted, GNP may be used as PT). If velocity increases at 3 percent in a given year, while an increase in spending of 7 percent is desired, the needed increase in the money stock is approximately 4 percent. Thus changes in velocity are very significant for any attempt to fine-tune the rate of growth of economic activity through monetary policy. The trend in velocity of money gradually declined from the time of the Civil War until 1945; at that point, the direction dramatically reversed. The upward trend in velocity since that time had to be taken into account by those who believed in the effectiveness of monetary policy and a stable relationship of velocity to money supply.[29] What is even more disturbing to these economists is the fact that the rate of increase in velocity has not been constant, as is evident from Figure 6–1. If the rate of increase in velocity is not stable or does not have a stable relationship to the rate of increase in the money stock, no simple rule for increasing the money stock can be relied upon.

Monetary policy warrants more detailed examination in Chapters 15 and 16. At this point it is sufficient to establish the importance of velocity of money and the role of the growth of the money market and money market instruments in affecting velocity.

Finally, short-term interest rates have some impact on long-term rates. In many instances, a rise in short-term rates is accompanied by *some* rise in long-

[28]George Garvy and Martin R. Blyn, in one of the few direct research studies in this area, *The Velocity of Money* (Federal Reserve Bank of New York, 1969) conclude that because of possible developments in the more rapid transfer of payments, "judgments about the outlook for velocity are difficult to make" (p. 92).

[29]Richard T. Selden, "The Postwar Rise in the Velocity of Money: A Sectoral Analysis," *Journal of Finance*, December 1961, provided a detailed analysis of the rise, and Milton Friedman and Anna J. Schwartz, *A Monetary History of the United States, 1867–1960* (Princeton: Princeton University Press, 1963) devoted a rather long section to speculation on its causes; see especially pp. 673–75.

term rates. However, as a glance at Figure 9–1 indicates, in some years—for example, 1972—short-term interest rates rose sharply with no apparent upward effect on long-term rates. A forecast of the behavior of long-term rates is important because they affect investment spending, stock market prices, consumer spending (probably via stock market prices), and total business activity. Unfortunately, at this point caution is a virtue, and we shall find that even after our survey of interest rate theory in Chapters 12–14 we must admit that forecasts of long-term interest rates are hazardous.

SUMMARY

The money market refers to the market for short-term loans and investments, both the primary market in which short-term promissory notes and other instruments originate and the secondary market in which many of them are traded. Some short-term promissory notes do not have a secondary market: those arising from business loans made at the prime rate or at higher rates, dealer loans to government securities dealers, and loans to banks by the Fed. Many short-term instruments, however, are traded in the secondary money market: negotiable CDs, Treasury bills, bank acceptances, Federal funds, Eurodollars, short-term government agency securities, and commercial paper. Except for commercial paper, which does not have a very broad secondary market, all of these are liabilities of banks or of the central bank. Thus risk is minimal, and yield differences must presumably result from factors other than risk.

Although, as indicated later, long-term interest rates are probably more important in determining the general level of rates, the money market is significant as the market in which the Fed generally intervenes to implement monetary policy decisions. As the initial point in the transmission of effects of such actions, the money market is carefully watched by economists and financiers.

Major changes in the money market in recent years, such as the introduction of negotiable CDs and the growth in the volume of commercial paper, have caused shifts in analysis of the market. Introduction of a "floating" prime rate tied to the commercial paper rate or other secondary market rates and new relationships among the Federal funds rate, the Eurodollar rate, and the discount rate also have occurred.

With increase in the volume of money market instruments, which may be held as money substitutes, the money supply need not rise as rapidly as would otherwise be desirable. At the same time, more commercial paper, for example, probably means that more spending for goods is financed; increased spending means more rapid turnover, or velocity, of money. Rise in velocity and fluctuations in short-term interest rates, which have been unusually wide since 1965, make the selection of appropriate monetary policy actions more difficult. Yet an understanding of these factors is essential for effective monetary policy; otherwise we may be in danger, as Henry Wallich has commented, of finding that the monetary authority, "instead of controlling the heat . . . had merely been diddling the thermometer."[30]

QUESTIONS FOR DISCUSSION

1. Suggest some reasons for the more volatile behavior of short-term interest rates than long-term rates (shown in Figure 9–1).

2. Show why the money market is important in providing almost instant liquidity for short-term financial assets. What problems might arise if such liquidity could not be provided? Explain why the money market is important as the locus of the open market operations of the central bank. What do central banks do in countries that do not have well-developed, efficient money markets?

3. Compare two lists, one of borrowers and one of lenders, in the money market. Comment on the importance of banks, the central bank, and the government in the money market, and on the relative unimportance of the consumer and business sectors of the economy.

4. What were the reasons for the first issues of Treasury bills in the United States? Explain why, since 1929, they have become so important in government borrowing.

5. What is the importance of government-sponsored agencies to agriculture and housing? Does this constitute a subsidy to these sectors of the economy? Explain.

6. Do you foresee growth in "finance bills" in the coming years? Why or why not? Compare your forecast of growth in the volume of finance bills with your forecast for negotiable CDs, and explain. The volume of commercial paper outstanding increased greatly in the 1960s. Give some reasons for this, and discuss the possibility for growing importance of this market in the 1970s and 1980s.

7. How do Eurodollars complicate both the functioning of the money market and the use of open market operations as a tool of monetary policy? Do they also create some questions and uncertainties concerning the balance of payments? If so, how?

8. Do you think that a "prime rate" is necessary and useful? Why or why not? Is it possible, or likely, that the prime rate may disappear, leaving commercial loan rates without any well-publicized basic rate? Why or why not?

9. Why has discounting at Federal Reserve Banks, although it was important in the early years of the Federal Reserve System and has regained importance since 1951, become less important as a policy tool?

10. It was formerly argued by some economists that a "normal" range for income velocity of money in the United States was from two to four times a year. In 1973 the rate was nearly five times. What trend would you predict for the future, and why?

[30]Henry C. Wallich, "The Fed at the Crossroads," *Morgan Guaranty Survey*, October 1971, p. 10.

SELECTED REFERENCES

An interesting and lively discussion of the money market, with a very thoughtful analysis of prospective future developments, is to be found in Wesley Lindow, *Inside the Money Market* (New York: Random House, 1972). An equally lively discussion of the 1970 money market crisis is to be found in Adam Smith, *Supermoney* (New York: Random House, 1972), Chapter 2.

Two booklets, one entitled *Money Market Instruments*, issued by the Federal Reserve Bank of Cleveland, 3rd ed. (1970) and the other entitled *Instruments of the Money Market*, issued by the Federal Reserve Bank of Richmond, 2nd ed. (1970) are very useful. The Cleveland booklet is more detailed, with a number of useful references to writings on money market theory and practice; the Richmond booklet contains a section on the discount window.

On the prime rate, see "Floating the Prime Rate," Federal Reserve Bank of Richmond, *Monthly Review*, August 1972, pp. 10–14; Dwight B. Crane and William L. White, "Who Benefits from a Floating Prime Rate?" *Harvard Business Review*, January–February 1972, pp. 121–29; and Albert M. Wojnilower and Richard E. Speagle, "The Prime Rate," Federal Reserve Bank of New York, *Monthly Review*, Part I, April 1962, pp. 54–59, and Part II, May 1962, pp. 70–73.

Much information concerning the government securities market is available in the *Joint Treasury-Federal Reserve Study of the U.S. Government Securities Market* (Washington, D.C.: Board of Governors of the Federal Reserve System, 1969). See also the earlier *Study of the Dealer Market for Federal Government Securities*, U.S. Congress, Joint Economic Committee (Washington, D.C.: Government Printing Office, 1960).

The development of the Federal funds market is discussed in detail in Parker B. Willis, *The Federal Funds Market—Its Origin and Development*, Federal Reserve Bank of Boston, 3rd ed. (1968). See also Dorothy M. Nichols, *Trading in Federal Funds—Findings of a Three-Year Survey*, Board of Governors of the Federal Reserve System (1965).

Factors affecting the market for commercial paper are extensively analyzed in Richard T. Selden, *Trends and Cycles in the Commercial Paper Market*, Occasional Paper No. 85 (New York: National Bureau of Economic Research, 1963). See also George W. Cloos, "A Larger Role for Commercial Paper," Federal Reserve Bank of Chicago, *Business Conditions*, December 1968, pp. 2–12.

Useful detail on CDs is supplied by A. Gilbert Heebner, *Negotiable Certificates of Deposit: The Development of a Money Market Instrument* (New York: New York University, 1967). The complex issue of the desirability of interest rate ceilings (such as those imposed by Regulation Q and other restrictions) is thoroughly analyzed by Robert Lindsay, *The Economics of Interest Rate Ceilings* (New York: New York University, 1970).

On the Eurodollar market and questions of its significance, see Alexander K. Swoboda, *The Euro-Dollar Market: An Interpretation*, Essays in International Finance, No. 64 (Princeton, N.J.: Princeton University, 1968). For an exchange of views on monetary expansion via the Eurodollar market, see Milton Friedman, "The Euro-Dollar Market: Some First Principles," *Morgan*

Guaranty Survey, October 1969, pp. 4–14. (Reprinted in Federal Reserve Bank of St. Louis, *Review*, July 1971) and Fred H. Klopstock, "Money Creation in the Euro-Dollar Market—A Note on Professor Friedman's Views," Federal Reserve Bank of New York, *Monthly Review*, January 1970. See also Fred H. Klopstock, *The Eurodollar Market: Some Unresolved Issues*, Essays in International Finance, No. 65 (Princeton, N.J.: Princeton University, 1968), and Jane S. Little, "The Euro-Dollar Market: Its Nature and Impact," Federal Reserve Bank of Boston, *New England Economic Review*, May–June 1969, pp. 2–31.

For further detail on bank acceptances, see Robert L. Cooper, "Bankers' Acceptances," in *Essays in Domestic and International Finance*, Federal Reserve Bank of New York, 1969, pp. 63–71.

On the discount rate and the discount mechanism, see Board of Governors of the Federal Reserve System, *Reappraisal of the Federal Reserve Discount Mechanism*, 3 vols., 1971–72.

10

Capital Markets for Debt Securities

In examining long-term assets, we find that there are rates of return on real capital assets, corporate bonds, federal government bonds, state and local government bonds (termed "municipals"), mortgages, and equity securities (stocks). The first five are treated in this chapter. Because of its complexity, the market for equities is discussed separately in Chapter 11.

Individuals purchase all of these types of assets, but for some of the financial assets they hold only relatively small shares of total securities outstanding.[1] For example, in the mortgage market, it is estimated that individuals hold less than 10 percent of mortgages outstanding. On the other hand, they hold perhaps 20 percent of the corporate bonds outstanding, 30 percent of the municipals outstanding, 30 percent of the government debt outstanding, and nearly 25 percent of the federal agency debt outstanding. These figures include holdings of individuals as beneficiaries of trusts managed by trust departments of banks because statistics seldom indicate these separately. Thus the share held by individuals per se is quite small; this is also true of purchases of new issues. The market for debt securities is largely institutional. Hence, the policies of financial institutions are very important in determining the allocation of funds and relative interest rates. In contrast, it is estimated that individuals still hold nearly three-fourths of all outstanding equity securities (stocks).

Each type of financial institution has general characteristics that help determine the capital markets it will participate in, and each institution has financial policies that further direct its investment purchases and sales.

Major participants in the mortgage market are the savings and loan associations, the commercial banks, federal agencies, and the mutual savings banks. Other less important participants include the finance companies and life insurance companies, the latter holding large amounts of long-term mortgages.

---

[1]Data in this and the following paragraphs are drawn largely from Salomon Brothers, *Supply and Demand for Credit in 1973.*

The corporate bond market is much more diverse: significant institutional participants include life insurance companies, state and local government retirement funds, and private pension funds. Less important participants include mutual savings banks, property and casualty insurance companies, mutual funds, and commercial banks. Foreign investors also participate in this market, whereas they are insignificant in the mortgage market.

The only major institutional participants in the municipal bond market are the commercial banks and the property and casualty insurance companies; minor participants are life insurance companies, state and local retirement funds, and mutual savings banks. Business corporations also buy some of these securities.

All institutions buy federal government securities, although much of this debt is short-term. If holdings of United States agencies by trust funds and the Federal Reserve System are excluded, the remaining privately held long-term debt is about 60 percent of total marketable long-term federal debt. No institution may be characterized as a dominant holder of this debt, although commercial banks hold nearly half of those securities between one and five years to maturity and about one-third of those between five and ten years to maturity.

Of the $64 billion of federal agency debt outstanding at the beginning of 1973, approximately $16 billion were issued by the farm credit institutions, about $38 billion by the housing credit institutions, and the rest by miscellaneous agencies. Again, almost all institutions buy some securities, although commercial banks, savings and loan associations, and mutual savings banks are clearly the most important purchasers. These three institutions together hold more than half of the total privately held.

In order to understand the factors affecting particular capital markets, we analyze each of these separately. Before doing that, however, we examine the nature and efficiency of capital markets generally, and the role of the long-term rate of interest vis-à-vis the short-term rates found in the money market.

NATURE, ROLE, AND EFFICIENCY OF CAPITAL MARKETS

Capital markets are markets in which lenders and investors provide long-term funds in exchange for financial assets offered by borrowers or holders. We follow tradition in giving attention primarily to financial capital markets, but we must emphasize that the "market" for real capital assets is more fundamental. Returns on financial assets rest on the fact that these are claims on real capital assets; the rate of return on real capital assets is fundamental because it provides the basis for most of the demand for funds.[2]

[2]In addition to demand based on expected productive use of capital, there is of course some consumer demand for loans for immediate consumption and government demand based on factors other than expected yields from capital assets. Nevertheless, the major part of demand arises from the fact that a return or yield is expected from real capital assets, and funds are needed to acquire such assets.

Capital markets are those in which long-term financial assets are bought and sold, and the usual dividing line is that long-term assets have an original maturity of more than one year. On occasion, however, short-term securities may have a more restricted meaning.[3]

Primary and Secondary Markets

Capital markets and the "money market" involve both a market for new issues (a primary market) and a secondary market for trading in outstanding issues. In primary markets, borrowers and lenders negotiate the transfer of funds in exchange for some type of security—bonds, mortgages, shares of stock, or promissory notes or other specialized short-term financial assets. Secondary markets serve to provide liquidity for financial assets: if there were no secondary markets, anyone who purchased a security would generally have to hold it until maturity. If secondary markets were small and inefficient, holders might be able to sell securities after purchasing them, but perhaps only at significant losses. In the case of long-term financial assets, the market for outstanding issues is so important that it receives much more attention than the market for new issues. In this chapter, therefore, attention is devoted primarily to the secondary markets.

Capital markets originate as new issue markets; then as a considerable volume of issues comes into existence, trading in outstanding issues begins. Capital markets in which trading in secondary issues is rather "thin" exist in many countries. However, markets in many countries have not yet developed the volume of trading that makes it possible to regard long-term financial assets as liquid because they can be sold *quickly without significant loss*. Markets in which this is possible are said to have *breadth* when orders to buy or sell come from many different groups, *depth* when there are both buy and sell orders below and above the current market price, and *resiliency* when new orders come into the market in volume when prices fluctuate. Markets with these characteristics provide significant liquidity for assets that otherwise would not be liquid; investors are induced to hold these assets because risk is reduced or minimized, and borrowers find it easy to obtain funds.

Efficiency of Financial Markets

An *efficient* market not only provides liquidity but also functions to allocate resources to the most productive uses at the least possible cost. Approximately equal rates of return should be obtained on investments that are comparable in risk. One test is to compare rates of return on new issues with rates of return on the same (or similar) issues that have been outstanding. By this test, several studies indicated that, both for stocks and for bonds, any

[3]For example, short-term capital gains have been defined in the income tax law as gains obtained in holding securities not more than six months.

difference in yields between new issues and "seasoned" securities with the same investment characteristics tended to disappear relatively quickly.[4]

The costs of issuing new securities, "flotation costs," have tended to decline over a long period of time, indicating that capital markets are becoming more efficient in terms of lower costs.[5] Again, in making comparisons care must be taken to compare costs for similar issues. Trading costs such as brokers' commissions and dealers' price spreads do not show the same secular decline as flotation costs, and there may be elements of monopolistic profit in these fees. A "third market" in stocks traded on the New York Stock Exchange developed among large institutions because of lack of bidding by brokers for large transactions.[6] A substantial number of steps have been taken in recent years both to increase the safety of investors' funds and securities and to stimulate greater competition. It is not yet clear what the result of these actions has been, and the fact that small investors are selling more securities than they are buying suggests that they may fear a lack of safety or the presence of monopolistic elements or both.[7]

Allocational efficiency in a market such as that for stocks affects both the flow of new funds and the retention of earnings. If stocks must be sold at relatively low prices, flow of funds into such industries is discouraged. Similarly, if prices of stocks fall, stockholders will eventually refuse to permit retention of earnings; if stockholders do not receive dividends, they must be compensated by the expectations that earnings will be high enough to permit higher dividends in the future, and/or that earnings will be high enough to cause the price of the stock to rise, so that instead of dividends the investors in that stock will obtain capital gains.

Although efficiency of capital markets may be improved, it is generally agreed that capital markets in the United States are relatively efficient.

Long-term assets may be divided into real capital assets and seven categories of financial assets. Each category of long-term financial assets has a market with somewhat unique characteristics. These categories are government long-term securities (bonds and notes); long-term securities of the government-sponsored agencies, usually referred to as agency securities; securi-

---

[4]Irwin Friend and J. R. Longstreet, "Price Experience and Return on New Stock Issues," in *Investment Banking and the New Issues Market* (New York: World Publishing Company, 1967), Chapter 8; Joseph W. Conard, *The Behavior of Interest Rates* (New York: Columbia University Press, 1966), pp. 117–18; and Irwin Friend, "The Economic Consequences of the Stock Market," *American Economic Review*, Papers and Proceedings, May 1972, pp. 212–19. See also William J. Baumol, *The Stock Market and Economic Efficiency* (New York: Fordham University Press, 1965).

[5]Morris Mendelson, "Underwriting Compensation," in *Investment Banking and the New Issues Market, Ch. 7.*

[6]See Murray E. Polakoff and Arnold W. Sametz, "The Third Market—The Nature of Competition for Listed Securities Traded Off-Board," *The Antitrust Bulletin*, January–April 1966. The evidence of monopolistic elements is not firm. For some of the issues involved, see Murray C. Polakoff et al., *Financial Institutions and Markets*, Boston: Houghton Mifflin, 1970), pp. 590–606.

[7]Flow of funds data indicate that for a number of years individuals have been selling more stocks than they have been purchasing.

ties of state and local government units, referred to as municipal bonds; corporate bonds; mortgages; stocks; and the recently developed Eurobonds. Before examining each asset and market, we note the special importance of some representative long-term interest rate.

THE FUNDAMENTAL RATE OF INTEREST

Can we find a "representative" long-term interest rate which is determined by basic forces? From this rate, other long-term interest rates may differ only because of various special factors such as term to maturity, risk, marketability, and so forth. Two questions may be asked: (1) what causes interest to be paid or a return to be obtained on financial and real assets? and (2) what causes a return to be obtained on real capital assets and interest to be paid on financial assets other than money, whereas money may earn no interest?

Keynes addressed himself primarily to the second question. Because he had concluded that consumption is a function of income, saving (which is the difference between income and consumption) had to be a function of income also. Hence saving could not be a function of the interest rate—i.e., saving was regarded as interest inelastic, or, at best, as having very little interest elasticity. However, lending of funds already saved, and held in the form of money, was clearly dependent on the interest rate, he believed. Thus he regarded the demand for money as interest elastic. There has been considerable argument whether the consumption function or the interest elasticity of the demand for money was Keynes' single most important theoretical concept.

Sometimes theorists have treated the zero interest yield on currency as the fundamental rate. Interest rates on other types of assets are higher, it has been argued, because these assets are less liquid than currency. But, as Paul Samuelson has pointed out, this sounds as if interest depends solely on uncertainty and lack of liquidity—as if, if uncertainty could be eliminated, and all assets could be liquid, the rate of interest would come down to zero.[8]

There must be another reason for the payment of interest. The long-term interest rate is based fundamentally on the rate of return business firms believe they can obtain on real capital assets, with appropriate allowance for a differential between this rate and the interest rate they must pay for borrowed funds —a differential sufficient to compensate them for the risk taken in investing in real capital assets. Real capital assets are productive; using them, business firms can earn a return on their investment. Some economists have emphasized this rate as the fundamental rate of return or interest.[9] However, because that rate (often called the rate of profit) is difficult to measure with accuracy, because it is significantly affected by accounting procedures such as depreciation

[8]Paul A. Samuelson, "The Current State of the Theory of Interest Rates, with Special Reference to Mortgage Rates," *Proceedings of the 1960 Conference on Savings and Residential Financing* (Chicago: United States Savings and Loan League, 1960), pp. 11–29.

[9]James Tobin, "Money, Capital, and Other Stores of Value," *American Economic Review*, Papers and Proceedings, May 1961, pp. 26–37.

methods, and because it fluctuates quite widely from one company to another, analysts usually prefer to select the interest rate on long-term government securities or the yield on long-term corporate securities of some specified quality as the representative long-term rate.[10]

The Keynesian view of interest as something paid on bonds but not on money and an alternative view of interest as a rate of return obtained on real capital assets or equities may be illustrated in Figure 10–1, in which the alternative view is designated as the Tobin model.

The major yield difference to be explained in the Keynesian model is the difference between the yield on "bonds" (i) and the zero yield on money; the major yield difference to be explained in the Tobin model is the difference between the yield on real capital assets and equities (r) and the yield on bonds and money (the yield on money perhaps being zero because of institutional constraints). Thus in the Keynesian model, real capital assets are regarded as being similar to bonds, and the difference between the yield on bonds and on real capital assets is not stressed. The major basis for explaining interest rates is thus placed upon liquidity preference. As the yield on money is usually presumed to be zero, liquidity preference seems to be the major determinant of the rate of interest. In the Tobin model, on the other hand, bonds are deemed to be more similar to money than to real capital assets, and the major yield difference to be explained is that between the yield rate on real capital assets and that on bonds and money. Emphasis is therefore placed on productivity of capital as a major determinant of the long-term rate of interest. The Keynesian model implies that if money increases in amount relative to bonds and real capital assets, there will be a shift in demand toward the latter, thus presumably tending to reduce interest rates. The Tobin model implies that if there is an increase in the supply of money and bonds relative to the supply of real capital assets and equities, there will be a shift in demand toward the latter, presumably tending to reduce interest rates. Tobin treats the fact that zero interest is paid on money in the United States as an institutional accident, which may be true; there are some indications that interest may, in the future, be paid on demand deposits in the United States, as it now is in many other countries. Thus the difference between the short-term rate of interest on money and/or near-monies and money market instruments is less important

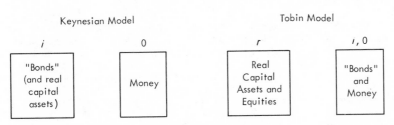

FIGURE 10–1   Keynesian and Tobin Models

[10]Frequently the rate used is the rate on some quality class of corporate bonds, such as Aaa bonds.

to him than the difference between the interest rates on money and bonds and the yields on real capital assets and equities.

Tobin suggested that a better model than either of those shown in Figure 10–1 would be a model in which major types of real and financial assets were designated, each with its own rate of return. Since it is impossible to explain in a basic theory each of the dozens of interest rates, and since it is likewise unsatisfactory to have simply a theory of "the" interest rate, an appropriate model might include six major rates of return, of which five are shown in Figure 10–2. The rates of return in the model are: (1) the rate of return on real capital assets that is just sufficient to induce wealth owners to hold such assets at their current prices (Tobin designates this rate as the "supply price" of capital); (2) a long-term interest rate, for which the rate on long-term government bonds may be used as a proxy; (3) the rate on private debt, for which a long-term corporate bond rate may be used as a proxy; (4) a short-term interest rate, for which the rate on short-term government securities (Treasury bills) may be used as a proxy; (5) an administratively fixed discount rate of the central bank (the rate at which commercial banks may borrow from the central bank); and (6) the zero rate of interest on currency and the rate of interest, if any, on demand deposits.[11] The rate of interest on demand deposits has been fixed at zero by law in the United States since 1933.[12]

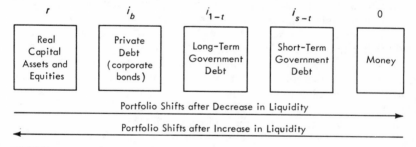

r i_b i_{1-t} i_{s-t} 0

| Real Capital Assets and Equities | Private Debt (corporate bonds) | Long-Term Government Debt | Short-Term Government Debt | Money |

Portfolio Shifts after Decrease in Liquidity

Portfolio Shifts after Increase in Liquidity

FIGURE 10–2 Major Assets in Yield Model

[11]James Tobin, "Money, Capital, and Other Stores of Value," *American Economic Review*, Papers and Proceedings, May 1961, p. 36; the order of listing has been changed. As Tobin points out, this model, in which real capital assets and money are the basic elements, may give different answers from the Keynesian model, in which "bonds" and money are the basic elements. In Keynesian analysis, for example, a smaller government debt would mean less bonds, therefore higher bond prices and lower yields, and hence a lower cost of capital, and more investment; reducing the government debt would, after some lag, be expansionary. The Tobin model, on the other hand, implies that a smaller government debt would not necessarily significantly reduce bond yields, as bonds and money are closer substitutes than bonds and real capital assets; with less liquid assets, wealth owners would require a higher yield to continue to hold the existing stock of real capital assets. With less liquidity in the economy, wealth owners would tend to shift from real capital assets and their proxies (stock or equities), and would demand more liquid assets, money as well as bonds. Demand for money as well as for bonds would prevent the interest rate from falling very far. Thus, retiring part of the government debt might be deflationary, reducing real investment, rather than expansionary.

[12]An interesting development, mentioned earlier, has been the offering by savings

When these complexities are added, the resulting model (Figure 10–2) seems little different from a Keynesian model; but because of the different origin, it may yield different results when used in analysis.

The rates of return to be explained in this model are r (the rate of return on real capital assets and equities), i_b (the yield on corporate bonds), i_{l-t} (the rate on long-term government bonds), and i_{s-t} (the rate on government short-term securities). Increases in liquidity through increases in the stock of money or government securities tend to cause portfolio shifts to private debt *and* to real capital assets and equities, whereas decreases in liquidity tend to cause portfolio shifts *out of* real capital assets, equities, and private debt, and into government securities and money. As r is also dependent upon changes in productivity, it may rise or fall independent of such portfolio shifts. The rate of interest on money may be zero because of institutional restraints, or, if interest can be paid on demand deposits and/or if time deposits are counted as money, it may be a positive rate. It is easy to see how inflation (a rise in prices of newly produced goods and services and of existing real goods) may tend to raise all interest rates, by shifting demand away from those assets shown in Figure 10–2 that either do not rise in price or cannot rise in price in the long run because they have fixed maturity values. If inflation is of a stop-and-go nature, as it was in the United States from 1946 to 1965, and perhaps was expected to continue to be, the shift may not be as marked as it might be under other circumstances. Holding stocks involves substantial risk if general economic and political conditions are uncertain, and holding real assets involves costs of some significance (insurance, taxes on real estate, and so on). Hence, if there is high or moderately high probability that inflation may slow down, shift into such assets may not be as rapid as under other circumstances.

A purely monetarist theory (such as the quantity theory of money) places great emphasis on one particular financial asset—money—whereas this model, although it could be used in a monetarist hypothesis, could also be used in a more general hypothesis in which the stock of money would be only one factor determining investment in real capital assets and hence affecting total output or GNP.

Before development of interest theory in Chapters 12–14, we examine in somewhat more detail long-term assets and the markets for them.

REAL CAPITAL ASSETS

Real capital assets (plant, machinery, equipment, and so forth) yield rates of return that constitute the fundamental determinant of demand for loanable funds for investment (the major determinant of supply is saving). These rates of return may be represented by an average rate, the rate of profit for the aver-

---

banks in some New England states of Negotiable Orders for Withdrawal (NOW), which may be used like checks, to order transfers of funds held by mutual savings bank depositors. If this and similar means of transferring savings deposits to third parties spread, the long-standing prohibition of payment of interest on demand deposits may be modified.

age firm. This rate must be high enough to induce wealth owners to hold such assets at their current prices; if wealth owners wish to hold more such assets, prices of the assets will rise; if they wish to hold less, prices will fall. The demand for these assets by wealth owners will depend on their portfolio choices among the various types of assets they can hold—including money, short-term government securities, long-term government securities, corporate bonds, and real capital assets.

The problem in analyzing the rate of return on real capital assets is, as noted above, that measurement of this rate is difficult because of the diversity in both types of real capital assets and the ways of measuring rates of return on such assets. Different accounting methods, especially for such things as depreciation, may result in quite different estimates of rates.

Presumably, the values of real capital assets owned by business firms are reflected in some manner in the values of the equities (stocks) that constitute claims on such assets, after creditors' claims are satisfied. We therefore return to the problem of yields on real capital assets and equities when we discuss the stock market in Chapter 11.

THE LONG-TERM GOVERNMENT SECURITIES MARKET

Under present conditions, government debt is an important part of the total of long-term securities. Because of their high degree of liquidity, government securities play an important role in portfolios of investors, particularly banks; in times of uncertainty, when desire for liquidity increases, they may be of great significance because of their convertibility into money to meet necessary payments. Some economists have emphasized the role of government debt in providing "ultimate" liquidity for the economy—that is, financial assets that would be liquid even if private institutions failed and could not redeem their debts (financial assets).[13] The key role of such liquidity is evident from a consideration of what might happen if numerous corporations and banks failed, as they did in the early 1930s, and people attempted to hold the remaining liquid assets, such as currency, thus reducing spending and causing a depression.

The Government Debt in Perspective

Government debt in the United States and in many other countries has increased greatly in wartime. In the period of World War I, government debt rose from a very small amount to more than $25 billion; in the period of World War II, it rose from about $50 billion to nearly $300 billion; in the period of involvement in the Vietnam conflict, it rose from a little over $300 billion to considerably more than $400 billion. However, in other periods the

---

[13]See, for example, Hyman P. Minsky, "Can 'It' Happen Again?" in Deane Carson, ed., *Banking and Monetary Studies* (Homewood, Ill.: Richard D. Irwin, 1963) and "Longer Waves in Financial Relations: Financial Factors in the More Severe Depressions," *American Economic Review*, Papers and Proceedings, May 1964, pp. 324–35.

growth of government debt was much slower than that of other types of debt. Although the growth of total debt approximately paralleled the growth of GNP in the 1950s and 1960s, government debt grew more slowly; mortgage debt and consumer debt rose especially rapidly, to finance housing and appliances that had not been available in the period of the Depression and World War II.

A substantial part of the total government debt is held by trust funds (such as that for social security) and by the Federal Reserve Banks. Essentially these holdings are not of concern in a discussion of the government securities market; what is most significant is the volume of publicly held debt. Of this, more than $50 billion consists of savings bonds and notes, which also are of only limited concern to a discussion of the government securities market; they are not marketable, but they may be redeemed, and if redemptions exceed new sales, the government must resort to additional sales of marketable securities even if its debt remains at the same level.

The significant figure for capital market analysis is the volume of long-term and intermediate-term marketable debt. The amount of such debt over one year to maturity was only about $135 billion in mid-1972. This may be compared with about $230 billion of corporate bonds outstanding and mortgage debt outstanding of approximately $500 billion.

A question often arises about the appropriate size of the national debt. This question involves both long-term and short-term debt, such as Treasury bills, and thus an answer cannot be given in terms of long-term debt alone. A view common among the public is that the debt should be reduced; but in terms of the analysis thus far, it should be evident that one factor affecting the appropriate size of the debt is that it should be related to liquidity needs of individuals and institutions, except insofar as such needs might be met by other instruments. If other forms of liquid debt, such as commercial paper or bank acceptances, become large in relation to liquid asset holdings, there would be less need to rely on the liquidity provided by government securities. Commercial banks need to hold large amounts of government securities for liquidity purposes, and deposit-type institutions also must keep significant amounts, though less in percentages of their portfolios because their liabilities are not as volatile as those of commercial banks. Insurance companies (especially nonlife insurance companies), state and local governments, and the federal government trust funds must also hold substantial amounts, and individuals may be expected to be holders. Thus any judgment of appropriate size of national debt rests partly on the need for liquid assets to be held by the various institutions and individuals; partly, it rests on considerations related to the size of interest payments on such debt as a part of total government expenditures. As the economy grows and financial institutions grow, the need for additional government securities for liquidity purposes increases.[14] It should be noted

---

[14]Procedure in projecting an appropriate amount of government debt may be: (1) project nominal GNP; (2) project total primary debt instruments, either on the basis of the past ratio of debt assets to nominal GNP of about 1.8 to 1, or with some adjustment of that ratio; (3) determine an appropriate ratio of government debt instruments as liquid assets in portfolios of individuals and institutions. If the expected rate of growth of government debt indicates a figure higher or lower than the projected appropriate value, liquidity may in the future be too great, or insufficient.

that under some conditions, such as those existing in the early 1970s, when the volume of long-term government securities is relatively small and the market for them relatively inactive, the liquidity of such securities may be reduced. However, they can always be used as security for loans from the Federal Reserve System to meet liquidity crises such as that in May 1970.

The Dealer Market

What is significant about the government debt is not so much its size as the fact that there is an extremely well organized, efficient market that assures the liquidity of these securities. The center of this market is a group of dealers, including some who specialize in trading in government securities, departments of several investment houses, and departments of several commercial banks. Telephone and teletype connections make possible instant communication, and absolute reliance on verbal agreements makes possible very rapid trading. Although many other financial institutions make markets in government securities for their customers—that is, they are ready and willing to buy or sell given amounts—the dealers at the core of the market are those with whom the Federal Reserve Bank of New York trades, in carrying out open market operations recommended by the Federal Open Market Committee. Dealers may apply to the bank for inclusion in the group, and the bank will decide on the basis of their reputation, financial situation, and apparent readiness, willingness, and ability to make a market in government securities.

Unlike brokers, who place orders and receive commissions, dealers buy and sell for themselves, maintaining inventories of various issues of government securities.[15] Thus they must be able to purchase these in large amounts and must often hold large amounts ready for sale. To do this they must borrow, as the amount of capital necessary would otherwise be too great.[16] If dealers did not have access to adequate financing, they would not be ready to take positions, and hence liquidity of government securities would suffer. If dealers were not ready to buy, a sudden item of news, announcement of government policy change, or economic forecast might cause sellers to become more vigorous, and prices to drop sharply. Of course, over a period of time, prices of long-term government securities may and do decline, as market interest rates rise and securities issued when rates were lower become less attractive. But sharp declines in short periods would be detrimental to liquidity. These have occasionally occurred, but efforts to maintain an efficient, broad dealer market have limited such occasions to a relatively small number.

Thus the basic reason for the dealer market in government securities is to

[15]The dealers generally deal in all maturities of government securities, although some of them restrict themselves to trading in certain maturities. They trade in short-term government securities as well as in bonds and notes, although at this point our concern is with the latter. For further details, see Ira O. Scott, Jr., *Government Securities Market* (New York: McGraw-Hill, 1965).

[16]The volume of trading in government securities by these dealers (including both short-term and long-term securities) may be as high as $2 billion or more a day. The reader may compare this, for example, with a 20-million share day, at an average price of perhaps $30 per share, on the New York Stock Exchange—a trading volume of $600 million.

maintain a high degree of liquidity because of the fact that government securities are largely held by financial institutions and other holders for liquidity purposes. An auction market, such as that on the stock exchanges, might at times lead to sharp price fluctuations, whereas in a dealer market, dealers can absorb demand by selling from their own inventories when demand is increasing and can buy for their own inventories when sellers are anxious to sell.

Dealers participate both in the primary market and in the secondary market for government securities. In the primary market, they subscribe to new issues and then resell them to the public, thus in effect underwriting large parts of the new issues. In exchange refundings, dealers buy large amounts of rights; and they are helpful in distributing securities in advance refundings. In cash refundings they are less active, as the Treasury aims to sell bonds directly for cash to private investors.

In the secondary market, dealers began early in the twentieth century to serve commercial banks, which were required to buy large amounts of government securities because at that time national bank notes had to be secured by government bonds. When these dealers demonstrated efficiency during World War I, most trading in government bonds shifted from the stock exchange to the dealers. Dealers make a market by quoting, in fractions of $\frac{1}{32}$ of a point, firm prices at which they will buy or sell; $100 represents par value. Dealers vary their inventories with fluctuations in interest rates because high rates make inventories expensive to carry (carrying is largely financed by borrowing). Moreover, rising rates mean falling bond prices, and dealers therefore suffer capital losses on bonds held at such times. In periods of widely fluctuating interest rates, as in the late 1960s, dealers' inventories may be low, and it may be difficult to execute large sales of bonds. Deterioration in the market for bonds at such times could be so great as to seriously undermine liquidity; those who need to sell bonds in order to pay maturing liabilities might find themselves unable to pay. Such a liquidity crisis could degenerate into a sharp decline in business activity, and therefore measures are taken to avoid such a situation.

New Issues of Government Securities

New issues of government securities are sold with the same concern for the effect on liquidity. When the government wishes to market a new issue, announcements are made by the Treasury through the Federal Reserve System, which acts as fiscal agent for the government. Decision must be made whether the new offering is to be for cash or in exchange for outstanding securities.[17] Because debt issues mature in time, refunding issues are needed sim-

[17]An exchange refunding is often used instead of a cash refunding. Holders may exchange for the new issue or redeem in cash; they may obtain cash directly or sell their "rights" to subscribe to the new issue to investors who want to subscribe. Holders may be offered either a new bond or a note, so that if they do not wish to buy a new long-term issue, they will be able to buy the intermediate-term note (which may have a maturity of from three to seven years). If the amount of "attrition" (securities turned in for cash) becomes great, as it may if interest rates are rising, so that investors hope to buy the new securities later at lower prices, cash refundings and cash sales may be used.

ply to maintain a given level of debt. If debt must increase because tax and other revenues are insufficient to meet spending, additional issues must be arranged.

One technique used is that of "advance refunding." New, long-term securities are offered to holders of outstanding issues that will mature some time in the future, in exchange. Yields on the new securities are slightly higher than both the yield to maturity on the outstanding issue and the present yields on other comparable government securities available in the market. The spread between the yield on the new issue and the current market rate for securities of comparable maturity has been, at least sometimes, about ¼ percent, thus providing a real incentive for investors to accept the exchange offering. Obviously, however, as pointed out by Ira Scott (see p. 43 in his book in the list of suggested references at the end of Chapter 8), terms of a refunding may vary depending on the Treasury's desires—to provide great incentive for exchange or little incentive.

Through this technique the Treasury lengthens the time to maturity of the debt because the new issue will mature later than the outstanding issue for which it is exchanged. The mere passage of time shortens the maturity of outstanding securities, and unless longer-term securities are sold, the gradual shortening of average maturity may mean that a great part of the debt must be refinanced each year, putting a burden on the market. In the early 1960s, aggressive use of advance refunding offset the decline in average maturity that had occurred previously. As indicated above, it has generally been difficult to do this in recent years because of the interest rate ceiling on government bonds and the fact that yields have generally been above this ceiling. In 1971 the Treasury was authorized to issue $10 billion in bonds without regard to the interest rate ceiling in order to enable the Treasury to issue long-term bonds and maintain the length of time to maturity of at least a very small portion of the debt.

The government usually does not wish to issue securities at a discount from par. In fact, it is common for a new issue to be sold at par or slightly above par and for the price to rise soon afterward, sometimes giving a "free ride" to purchasers of the new issue. Of course, at a later date, the securities may fall below par in price because if interest rates rise, bond prices fall.

The Federal Reserve System, as fiscal agent for the Treasury, handles the issuing of the securities. The Federal Reserve is also concerned, however, that its activities in the government securities market may cause difficulties in selling the new issue, thus damaging the liquidity of the government securities market. For a number of years the Federal Reserve System followed what was termed a "bills only" policy; it was argued that by buying and selling only Treasury bills in its open market operations, the Federal Reserve System would have less effect on prices and yields on intermediate-term and long-term government securities. Although the "bills only" policy was abandoned in 1961, most of the open market purchases and sales are still in Treasury bills.

Obviously, debt management actions by the Treasury, in issuing securities of certain types and maturities, are closely related to open market operations by the Federal Reserve System, in buying and selling government securities.

Appropriate policy coordination, discussed in Part V, could help in influencing yields on government securities of various maturities if such influence is possible.

It has sometimes been argued that the Treasury might use an auction technique for the sale of new issues of long-term government securities, just as it does for Treasury bills. In fact, that has been tried on several occasions. Auction of long-term government securities was tried in the 1930s, but results were not very satisfactory. In 1963, the auction technique was tried again, this time with competitive bidding by underwriter groups. The issues were allocated to the highest bidder for resale to the public. The first time, in January, the issue was quickly sold and went to a premium in price; the second time, in a less receptive market, the underwriters had some difficulty in disposing of the securities. Because, as stated above, the government does not feel pleased when new issues of government securities are difficult to sell or quickly go to a discount from par, the auction technique was not used again for some time.[18]

In late 1972, the Treasury announced 6¾ percent, twenty-year bonds for sale under a different ("Dutch") auction technique, in which bonds were awarded to all accepted bidders at the lowest accepted bid. It was suggested that pension funds, personal trusts, savings banks, and other institutions, which are not accustomed to bidding for Treasury bills as commercial banks are, might bid for bonds if they could expect to be awarded the right to purchase at the same price as other bidders, as long as their bids were within the range of accepted bids.[19] Immediate results did not indicate that this procedure was successful in attracting institutions other than commercial banks and investors outside the New York area. Almost all bidders were from the New York area; there was relatively few noncompetitive bids (only $72 million out of $625 million), and all bids of 99½ or more were accepted, so that the bonds were sold to yield 6.795 percent. They sold at several thirty-seconds below 99½ the first day.[20]

THE MARKET FOR GOVERNMENT AGENCY SECURITIES

Federal government agencies, discussed in Chapter 5, have sold debt issues since 1919, but the volume of such securities was not very large until the late 1960s. The agencies that issue long-term securities now include two agricultural credit agencies (Federal Land Banks and the Farmers' Home Adminis-

---

[18]Wall Street Journal, December 29, 1972, p. 2; Salomon Brothers, *Comments on Credit*, December 29, 1972, pp. 1–2.

[19]For more details about sales of Treasury securities in the 1960s, see "Managing the Debt of the 60s," Federal Reserve Bank of San Francisco, *Monthly Review*, January 1969, pp. 3–10.

[20]See Aubrey G. Lanston & Co., Inc., weekly letter, January 8, 1973.

tration), four housing agencies (the Federal National Mortgage Association, the Federal Home Loan Banks, the Federal Home Loan Mortgage Corporation, and the Government National Mortgage Association), the Export-Import Bank, the Tennessee Valley Authority, and the United States Postal Service. Many of these agencies are now privately owned, although they were originally established by the government. Federal Land Bank bonds, Federal National Mortgage Association debentures, Federal Home Loan Bank notes, and TVA bonds do not carry a United States government guarantee, but this appears to make little difference in their marketability. As there has never been any hint of default, the presence or absence of guarantee seems academic.

In some cases debt issues were issued by these agencies rather than by the Treasury simply to reduce Treasury borrowing at times when further Treasury issues would have been difficult to market or impossible because of debt limitation. A number of the issues are exempted from state and local income taxes on the interest paid.

New issues are marketed either through a network of securities dealers and banks or through underwriting syndicates. A fiscal agent makes arrangements for an issue, and the selling group is expected to place the securities with "true investors." One indication of the success of such placement is favorable price behavior in the secondary market—presumably if an issue is not placed with true investors, it may be quickly resold and price decline may result.

Agencies tend to market long-term issues in greater volume when interest rates are below their peaks. Coupon rates on new agency issues are above coupon rates on comparable Treasury issues, but below coupon rates on comparable corporate bonds.

Major purchasers of agency issues are commercial banks and savings institutions; state and local governments (including their retirement funds) are also significant buyers. Many agency securities are purchased by "other" investors, which may include trust departments of banks, individuals, foreign investors, nonprofit organizations, and nonbank securities dealers. The Federal Reserve System began buying agency securities in the secondary market in 1971, as part of its open market operations.

The secondary market is similar to that for government securities, and many dealers who make markets for government securities also make markets for agency securities.

Much of the increase in the volume of agency issues in recent years can be attributed to the fact that the mortgage market could not attract as much funds at prevailing high interest rates as it had previously, and agency issues were in many cases used to obtain funds that were then channeled into the mortgage market, as described later in this chapter. Early in 1974, a Federal Financing Bank was established to improve the efficiency of agency financing. Direct agencies included must ask the new FFB to borrow for if or obtain special permission from the Treasury, and the "guaranteed agencies," such as GNMA, which are outside the budget, may use it if they wish. The major privately owned agencies, such as FNMA and parts of the farm credit system, were not given access to the new bank and will continue to issue their own securities.

THE CORPORATE BOND MARKET

Yields on corporate bonds are always higher than yields on government securities, presumably because there is some risk of default on corporate securities. This risk may be negligible in the case of the best grades of corporate bonds, but its existence means that yields are at least slightly higher. Figure 10–3 shows relationships among corporate bond yields, federal government bond yields, and state and local government bond yields.

Unlike the government, which must market new debt issues whenever refunding is necessary and whenever expenditures exceed revenues and cash balances cannot be further reduced, corporations take the initiative in financing decisions. New plant and equipment purchases are planned with consideration of financing costs, and corporations may defer some investment plans if financing costs seem likely to be too high.

Although the corporate bond market is largely for the obligations of profit-making corporations, mention should be made of bonds issued to provide funds for building schools, hospitals, and churches. The interest to be paid on such bonds is usually covered by anticipated revenues, which can usually be projected with some assurance. These bonds have a good record, therefore, and are sold in the same manner as less-known corporate bonds.[21]

Corporations borrow through the issue of bonds when they do not generate sufficient funds internally to meet their needs. In years when needs are

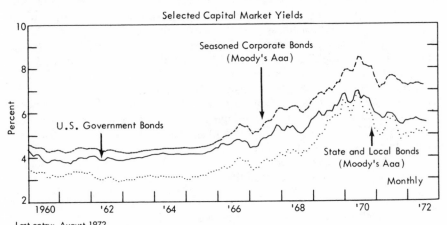

Selected Capital Market Yields

Last entry: August 1972
Source: Board of Governors of the Federal Reserve System

FIGURE 10–3

SOURCE: Federal Reserve Bank of Cleveland, *Economic Review*, August–September 1972.

[21]These are termed "church bonds" by one author; see Roland I. Robinson, *Money and Capital Markets* (New York: McGraw-Hill, 1964), p. 207.

low (in recession years), corporations in fact have sometimes used a small part of internally generated funds to pay back a small part of external debt. Hence there are substantial fluctuations in corporate bond issues. Because the supply of bonds fluctuates significantly, the market and yields fluctuate rather widely. Because the major purchasers of corporate bonds, as indicated in Chapter 5, are life insurance companies, pension funds, state and local government retirement funds, and individuals and nonprofit organizations, if these groups do not shift their funds to purchase more bonds in years of high business activity, bond prices inevitably fall, and yields rise.

Bond Prices and Yields

Corporate bonds are issued in denominations ranging from $100 to $10,000 or more, with $1,000 being the most common face value. They may be unsecured (debentures) or secured by mortgages (mortgage bonds), rolling stock (equipment obligations), or marketable securities (collateral trust bonds). Debentures are not actually unsecured but are backed by the general credit of the issuing corporation, and are issued, generally, by corporations with excellent credit ratings. Historically, secured issues generally have had more defaults than unsecured issues.[22] Some bonds contain promises to pay the principal, but not the interest if earnings are insufficient; these are termed "income" or "adjustment" bonds. There are also "assumed" bonds, assumed by a company acquiring another company in a merger, and "guaranteed" bonds, usually guaranteed by a company acquiring another company in a merger. Maturities usually vary from ten to thirty years. Most corporate bonds contain a call provision, permitting redemption before maturity; corporations may also set aside sinking funds to provide for retirement of bonds, and bonds may have provisions for retirement of a portion of an issue each year (serial bonds). Mention should also be made of convertible bonds, which can be converted under certain conditions into other securities, usually common stock.

Prices of bonds of the highest quality—for example, those rated as Aaa by Moody's investor service—are highest, and therefore the yields the lowest; yields for other grades of quality are higher, though differences may vary from time to time. The rates usually quoted and shown on charts are those for "seasoned" bonds—those that have been outstanding for some time. Yields on new issues are slightly different, as investors may not at first appraise them in the same way as they do later, when time for evaluation occurs.

Fluctuations in the Volume of Bond Issues

As indicated in Chapter 7, business demand for funds increases as business activity rises. At first, much of the demand may be for short-term funds, needed to increase inventories as rising sales reduce stocks of goods on hand. As a business recovery period progresses, however, business firms turn to long-term borrowing; recovery of confidence leads to planning for more capital investment, and the need for long-term funds becomes evident. Of course, there are firms, such as utilities, that must borrow at all times, because they must continue long-term investment to provide facilities for new customers as population and household formation increase.

It is significant that the amount of corporate bonds increased in the period 1965–70 as interest rates rose. In that period capital expenditures of corporations increased while the amount of internally generated funds rose very little after 1966. The growing need for external funds caused a large volume of new issues of corporate bonds at high yields; the share of corporate bonds outstanding rose while the share of long-term Treasury issues, the share of mortgages, and the share of state and local government all declined.

The key factor was the decline in retained earnings in a period of growing need for funds to meet planned capital investment. The increased supply of bonds drove yields on Moody's Aaa corporate bonds to a peak of over 8 percent yield in 1970, from a level of about 4 percent in the early 1960s. Bond buyers benefited from the higher yields, and the share of interest in national income, as compared to wages, rent, and profit, increased somewhat.[23] The rise in bond yields did not deter corporations from issuing bonds, and the share of bonds in the capital market continued to rise. The share of mortgages, municipal bonds, and long-term Treasury issues, on the other hand, declined as issuers were discouraged and the demand for such securities seemed to lessen. For mortgages, this occurred despite a rise in yields on FHA mortgages in the secondary market equally as great as the rise in corporate bond yields.

New Issues of Corporate Bonds—
Underwriting and Direct Placement

Corporations have two alternatives in the issue of bonds: public sale with the assistance of investment banks, or direct placement with one or a small number of institutions. In a public offering, a syndicate of investment bankers (one of them usually acting as manager) undertakes the marketing of the issue; arrangements vary from "best efforts" agreements to complete underwriting, in which sale of the securities is guaranteed by the investment banks that hold any securities they are unable to sell to the public. In a private or direct placement, the corporation may be aided by an investment bank, but an agreement is made directly with one or a small number of financial institutions for purchase of the securities, and the provisions of the agreement are tailored, by negotiation, to the desires of the two parties. In the late 1960s, the amount of corporate bonds privately placed declined somewhat, while

[23]From 1965 to 1970, net interest increased from 3.2 to 4.2 percent of national income; in the same period, corporate profits before taxes declined from 13.8 to 9.5 percent of national income, and the decline would be greater if the inventory valuation adjustment were included in the profit figures. In this period, interest received rose 81 percent while total national income rose by 41 percent.

public offerings greatly increased. Apparently as the volume of funds borrowed by corporations increased, some financial institutions, especially life insurance companies, reduced their commitments for private placement, partly because of their own reduced liquidity and partly because the yields on privately placed securities were less attractive relative to yields on publicly offered issues.

Growing concern over liquidity on the part of bond buyers in 1969 and early 1970 probably contributed to the shift away from privately or directly placed bonds to marketable bonds (directly placed issues are less marketable because they may contain special provisions, and in any event their market-ability has not been tested because they were privately placed). Until the decline in stock market prices in late 1969, inflation may also have been a factor inducing institutions to purchase stocks rather than privately placed issues of bonds.

The Secondary Market for Corporate Bonds

Corporate bonds are negotiable instruments; many are in bearer coupon form so that they may easily be transferred. Corporate bonds are traded on the organized exchanges, although the volume of trading is small compared to that in stocks. Corporate bonds are also traded in the over-the-counter market; volume of trading is small compared to that in government securities. The major purchasers of corporate bonds are life insurance companies, state and local governments—which purchase them because states often require their retirement funds to be invested partly in bonds—and private pension funds. As most bonds are bought by institutional investors, there is less need for sale for liquidity purposes than if bonds were largely owned by individuals. Commercial banks buy few corporate bonds because the increased risk and less liquidity, as compared with government securities, makes them unattractive—especially considering the transactions costs necessary because of the need for analysis of quality.

Because most bonds are now purchased by institutional investors, the secondary market is rather "thin." Institutions that purchase corporate bonds seldom need liquidity, except perhaps in a crisis, and hence need not often sell many bonds. Since institutions are not likely to sell high-quality bonds, the market for these is especially thin.

Because of the nature of corporate bonds, however, the secondary market could probably handle larger volume if necessary. The bid-and-ask spreads of dealers are not large, as they probably would be if a dealer were in a position to take advantage of a shortage of buyers or sellers. The relatively small corporate bond market could probably expand in size without difficulty. Thus lack of liquidity of corporate bonds is generally not likely to be a serious problem.

THE MUNICIPAL BOND MARKET

Municipal bonds are issued by about 25,000 out of about 80,000 state and local government units in the United States. They are available in varying maturities, are often issued in serial form to mature so much each year for a period of years, and the interest income on them is exempt from federal income tax. The after-tax income on these securities is higher for some investors than the yield on alternative investments.

"Municipals" and Their Purchasers

About three-fifths of municipal bonds are what are termed "full faith and credit" securities, based on the taxing authority of the government unit. State and local government units frequently have rather small limits, in their constitutions and elsewhere, on the amount of these bonds they may issue. For this reason and because of the increase in specific services, "revenue bonds" have been issued; payment of interest and principal is based on revenue to be received from sale of water, lease with an agency, highway and bridge tolls, and so forth. These securities are likely to carry higher yields than "full faith and credit" bonds.

Commercial banks are now the major holders of municipal bonds because they are interested in the tax exemption and the intermediate-term maturities, because they frequently underwrite general obligation issues and some types of revenue issues, and because they are frequently required to hold such bonds as collateral security for deposit of local government funds.

Issues of municipal bonds are underwritten by numerous firms, many underwriting issues of government units in their own areas. Bonds are frequently purchased by investors in the area as well. Underwriting bids for issues may be submitted by dealers and banks in the area, and bids are quite competitive for the intermediate-size and large-size issues.

"Thinness" of the Market

The same firms that underwrite issues maintain secondary markets for them. Investors are usually able to sell securities when desired, but the market is hardly very deep or resilient, as municipal bond issues are small and varied, many dealers are small, and the number of dealers able and willing to handle a given issue is small.

The continued need of state and local government units to borrow to finance capital expenditures and the limited groups of investors interested in buying these securities has led to some concern about the viability of this market in the future.[24] The thinness of the market is reflected in the fact that yields fluctuate much more widely than do yields on United States government securities (see Figure 10–3). At times, yields on state and local bonds

---

[24]See, for example, the address by Frank E. Morris, President, Federal Reserve Bank of Boston, "Restructuring the Municipal Bond Market," Federal Reserve Bank of Boston, *New England Economic Review*, January–February 1971, pp. 47–52. Morris discussed making municipal bonds fully taxable and providing some form of federal government interest subsidy, proposals such as Urbank, under which federal government instrumentalities would serve as a financing vehicle for state and local governments, and a federal government interest subsidy to pension funds in order to induce them to hold municipal bonds (they are the major bond-buying institution that might be attracted).

(Moody's Aaa) are almost as high as those on Treasury bonds; at other times, the yield spread is wide, perhaps as much as 1 percent or more.

The tax-exempt feature has limited purchases of municipal bonds almost entirely to commercial banks, high-income individuals, and property and casualty insurance companies.

High interest rates may halt bond issues by state and local government units because clauses in state constitutions prevent them from paying more than a specified maximum rate of interest. Some of these statutory interest rate ceilings were relaxed in the late 1960s after tight credit markets had curtailed borrowing.

THE MORTGAGE MARKET

The mortgage market is the largest debt segment of the capital markets. Moreover, real estate is a very large part of total real wealth; thus, although mortgages may be a high ratio of the value of properties recently purchased (whether new or old), it is a fairly small fraction of the total value of all real property.

A significant fact about mortgages as financial instruments is that those who purchase them tend to place more weight on the value of the real estate mortgaged than on the ability of the debtors to repay the mortgage debt. Whether they actually place more weight on the value of the collateral—and frequently they are urged to examine the debt repayment ability of the debtors—they certainly give this factor relatively more weight than in other segments of the capital markets. In the case of all types of bonds and stocks, relatively more weight is certainly given to the income-generating ability of borrowers.

Determination of Mortgage Rates and Fees

Down payments and maturities tend to be critical factors in mortgages. Especially in residential mortgages, individuals usually have difficulty in making large down payments, and the maturity is also critical because maturity determines the amount of repayment of principal and interest required each period. Fifty years ago, most mortgages were written to mature on a certain date, without amortization, but were usually renewed; the spread of the amortized mortgage loan has changed this situation. Loans may be made for periods shorter than those for which they are amortized, the loans being renegotiated before maturity, perhaps giving an opportunity to change the interest rate.

Another factor is that cost of making and servicing mortgage loans is fairly high. The cost of making mortgage loans is partly reflected in mortgage loan fees charged for "closing" mortgage loans. These are often substantial, although part of the total paid represents taxes of various types and fees charged by government offices. Cost of servicing is high because mortgage payments are made so frequently (usually monthly) and because it must be ascertained whether taxes and insurance premiums are being paid—otherwise value of the collateral may decline.

Mortgage interest rates themselves have two significant characteristics in comparison with other capital market yields: (1) they generally tend to be much less volatile, and (2) their movements tend to lag behind those of other rates. Yields on conventional and FHA-insured mortgages, in comparison with Aaa corporate bond yields, are shown in Figure 10–4. Mortgage rates are also typically higher than the other yields in the capital markets, but because costs of servicing mortgages are difficult to estimate, it is not clear whether rates are higher if this differential is removed. The cost of servicing single-family home mortgage loans has been estimated at about ½ percent per

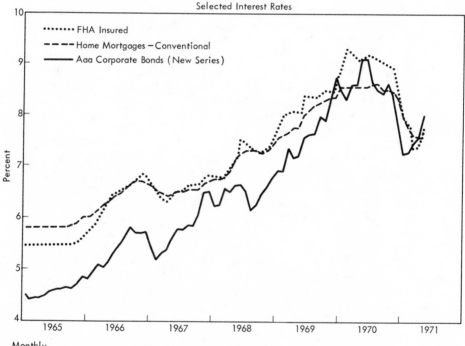

Selected Interest Rates

········· FHA Insured

– – – – Home Mortgages – Conventional

———— Aaa Corporate Bonds (New Series)

Monthly

Last Entry: May 1971

Note: Mortgage data based on FHA field-office reports for market areas of insuring office cities. For "conventional," average interest rates are for first mortgages on new homes. For "FHA-insured," weighted averages of private secondary market bid prices for certain new-house mortgages are converted to annual yield. Breaks in FHA insured series indicate periods of adjustment to changes in contractual interest rate. For corporate bonds, weighted average of new publicly offered bonds with at least 5-year call protection are used.

FIGURE 10–4

SOURCE: Federal Reserve Bank of Cleveland, *Economic Review*, July 1971.

year, and if this is so, mortgage loans may have earned slightly higher yields than high-quality capital market investments in many years.

Primary and Secondary Mortgage Markets

Individuals were at one time the principal mortgage lenders, but three groups of institutions now are the chief suppliers of mortgage money: savings and loan associations and mutual savings banks, commercial banks, and life insurance companies. A fourth group of institutions, mortgage companies, do not themselves hold large amounts of mortgage loans; instead, they make a number of mortgage loans and then arrange with another institution (usually a life insurance company) to purchase a block of mortgages. Advance commitments for such purchases assure the mortgage companies of liquidity and contribute to the lag in changes in interest rates and mortgage terms.

Building usually involves construction loans, often made by commercial banks. Thus there is an interconnection between the market for short-term loans and the mortgage loan market. Another interconnection appears when mortgage companies, and sometimes life insurance companies, "warehouse" mortgages with commercial banks—transfer them to the banks for a short period of time, to permit the mortgage company to make arrangements for placing them with a final holder, or because a life insurance company temporarily holds more mortgages than it wishes to or is able to hold in its portfolio.

Since the advent of FHA-insured and VA-guaranteed mortgages in the 1930s, the primary and secondary markets for mortgages have been divided between "conventional" mortgages and the insured or guaranteed mortgages. Ceilings on interest rates that could be charged on insured or guaranteed mortgages tended to dry up the market for these types of mortgages when credit became tight and interest rates high. Institutions have also differed in their policies in purchasing mortgages: mutual savings banks have sometimes held more than half of their total residential mortgage loans in insured and guaranteed loans, and commercial banks have held as much as one-third, whereas life insurance companies have usually held a much smaller fraction of their mortgage portfolios in such mortgages, and savings and loan associations an even smaller fraction. The reason for the very small fraction of insured and guaranteed mortgages in the portfolios of savings and loan associations is that these are generally local institutions, which make most of their mortgage loans in areas in which they themselves have some familiarity with the properties. The frequently higher yield on conventional mortgages and the lesser amount of "red tape" make savings and loan associations prefer conventional mortgages generally.

The growth of mortgage banks or mortgage companies as institutions probably is closely related to the growth of insured and guaranteed mortgages. Long ago, mortgage brokers and bankers did function in arranging mortgage credit. But the growth in the volume of insured and guaranteed mortgages and the fact that these could be purchased with some assurance of quality by institutions such as life insurance companies that had no offices in an area (for this purpose—although they may have had salesmen and agents who collected premiums) led to growth of mortgage companies. The mortgage companies sought commitments from the life insurance companies and other institutions, and assisted in arranging for construction loans from commercial banks, which could make construction loans with more assurance if they knew that the sale of the completed houses could be financed.

Improvements in the Secondary Mortgage Market

The small size and varying amount, quality, and characteristics of mortgage loans inhibited the development of a secondary market for mortgages. In order to encourage such development and to provide liquidity for mortgages so that institutions that hold them would have a degree of liquidity in that part of their asset portfolios, the government has established a number of agencies. The Federal National Mortgage Association (FNMA) was established in 1938, but served for a considerable time merely to acquire mortgages. It was reorganized in 1954, with the intention that one part of it, at least, would engage in both purchases and sales in an effort to create a significant secondary market. In 1968, the functions of holding and liquidating loans previously purchased were given to a new agency, the Government National Mortgage Association (GNMA, or Ginnie Mae). This agency has also subsidized and underwritten many of the programs developed by the Department of Housing and Urban Development (HUD) for low-income and other special housing.[25] GNMA has also developed what are known as "pass-throughs," packages of insured and guaranteed mortgage loans originated by a lending institution and approved (and servicing guaranteed) by GNMA.[26] FNMA was converted into a privately owned agency under 1968 legislation; it borrows by issuing short-term and intermediate-term securities, thus incurring higher costs when interest rates rise, while its return on assets in the form of mortgages remains relatively constant. Of course, GNMA is most needed to purchase mortgages when interest rates are high; at the same time, this is the time when its costs are high. FNMA now acquires mortgages by an auction procedure, in which FNMA offers a commitment to buy new mortgages, chiefly from mortgage companies; the mortgage companies need not sell to FNMA, but may, if interest rates fall and the prices of mortgages rise, sell them elsewhere.

[25]Under what is called the Tandem plan, Ginnie May buys mortgages from holders such as savings and loan associations at prices higher than private investors are willing to pay, and sells the mortgages to Fannie Mae at the going market price. In effect, Ginnie Mae was helping to pay the discount charges on mortgages in a market in which yields were high and/or rising, and in which therefore mortgages sold at discount. Otherwise, either home buyers or sellers would have had to absorb the entire discount, thus in effect reducing the prices at which sellers could sell homes, or increasing the cost of buying homes (mortgage costs).

[26]In addition to "pass-throughs," Ginnie Mae assists a similar program for sale of mortgage-backed bonds. Mortgages are packaged into blocks, and bought by Fannie Mae and Freddy Mac; bonds secured by pools of mortgages are issued and sold to private investors, and Ginnie Mae guarantees the bonds.

Because FNMA has thus become heavily engaged in buying mortgages from mortgage companies, Congress created in 1970 the Federal Home Loan Mortgage Company (FHLMC, or Freddie Mac) to sell securities to the public and use the proceeds to buy (and then sell) mortgages, primarily buying from savings and loan associations. Incidentally, FHLMC helps standardize documents, appraisals, and other features of mortgages to make them more easily saleable.

A related agency is the MGIC Mortgage Corporation (MGIC, or Maggie Mae), a private company that began business in the spring of 1972 to establish a secondary market for mortgages it insures. It also sells securities to the public to obtain funds for this purpose.

Thus four agencies are now engaged in creating a secondary market for mortgages. Originally this market was entirely for insured and guaranteed mortgages, but FNMA, FHLMC, and MGIC buy conventional mortgages (FNMA and FHLMC buy both types). The result is that the mortgage market is in a better position than it has ever been to compete for funds when credit is tight and interest rates high. The institutional structure of the mortgage market has become quite complex, as shown in Figure 10–5, but the credit crunches of 1966 and especially that of 1969 did not affect the mortgage market as adversely as they might have in the absence of these arrangements for liquidity for mortgages.[27]

Structure of the Residential Mortgage Market

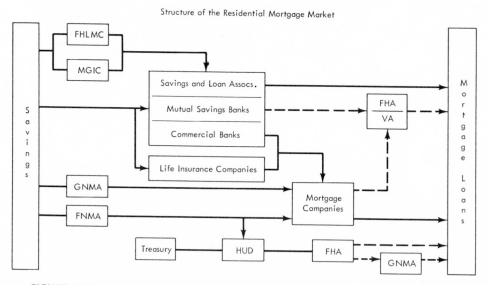

FIGURE 10–5

SOURCE: Federal Reserve Bank of Richmond, *Monthly Review*, September 1972.

[27]For an entertaining account of the activities of Fannie Mae, Ginnie Mae, and Freddie Mac, see Gurney Breckenfeld, "Nobody Pours it Like Fannie Mae," *Fortune*, June 1972, pp. 86–89, 136–47. The increased flow of loanable funds to housing may,

Government pressure to prevent high mortgage interest rates slowed the rise in rates on insured mortgages in the secondary market so that although rates rose to an unusually high peak, the spread between them and corporate bond yields narrowed (for a time in 1969, Aaa corporate bond yields actually exceeded yields on FHA-insured mortgages bought in the secondary market). The decline in housing in 1969–70 was less than in 1966, and the subsequent recovery—greatly aided by government programs—has been dramatic.

Although government activity in this area may be reduced somewhat by pressure to hold down increases in government budgets, it appears that government assistance to the secondary mortgage market will insulate housing from sharp declines in availability of funds, such as have occurred in the past and which became more serious when interest rates reached high levels.

Even so, the problem in providing enough financing for housing often extends beyond the need for additional funds to meet new demands for mortgage money. At times, there are not sufficient funds available in the mortgage market to cover mortgage commitments already outstanding, let alone new credit needs. Under such circumstances, such as occurred in the early fall of 1973, there will be a sharp decline in new commitments, which will reinforce the slowdown in residential construction imposed by high market rates of interest. Whether such a slowdown lasts very long depends, of course, on whether market interest rates remain high for a long time, or rather quickly decline somewhat from peak levels.

THE EUROBOND MARKET

A new market has developed in the past decade for what are termed Eurobonds. Eurobonds may be most easily defined as bonds denominated in a currency other than that of the country or countries in which most of the bonds are initially sold. Most Eurobonds are sold in Europe, in one or more countries, and most of them are denominated in United States dollars. Eurobonds are usually underwritten by an international syndicate of investment banking houses, and are sold simultaneously in several countries. They may be distinguished from foreign bonds, which are bonds issued by a foreign firm but denominated in the currency of the country in which the bonds are issued. Thus, a United States subsidiary in France might issue bonds in Italy in lire; these are foreign bonds. Or it might issue bonds denominated in dollars or marks, and market the bonds in Italy and perhaps several other countries in Europe (other than Germany). These are Eurobonds.

Most Eurobonds are publicly marketed, rather than privately placed, and most have maturities of ten to fifteen years. Convertible Eurobonds are not very common, but most are callable (or were when issued in years for which data are available). A few Eurobond issues have been denominated in several currencies, one part of the issue being denominated in each currency. A few

---

when demand exceeds supply at current interest rates, result in inability to obtain funds on the part of small businesses, consumers, privately financed mortgage borrowing, and state and local governments.

issues have had currency options—holders can ask for payment of interest and principal in one of several currencies. Some have been denominated in the European Unit of Account (EUA). The EUA was defined as a weight of gold, the weight being that contained at the time, by definition, in the United States dollar. Payment on these bonds was to be made in one of a number of currencies. The aim of these provisions was to eliminate the risk of holders receiving payment in currencies that had been devalued. In the case of bonds denominated in EUA, if a currency in the list were devalued, a bondholder who asked for redemption in that currency would receive a greater amount, corresponding to the current value of the EUA in that currency. At the end of 1970, an issue was floated in the European currency unit; holders could choose payment in any one of the Common Market currencies. A holder of EUA bonds could gain if his home currency were devalued, as he could ask for repayment in a currency not devalued. A holder of European currency unit bonds could gain if his home currency were devalued, and also if any of the five Common Market currencies (German marks, Dutch guilders, Italian lire, or French or Belgian francs) were revalued upward. Obviously, these various provisions have been designed to reduce risk of fluctuations in bond value.

Origin and Development of the Eurobond Market

The Interest Equalization Tax (IET), proposed in 1963 and enacted in 1964 retroactive to July 1963, increased the cost for United States residents of buying foreign bonds. This encouraged foreign borrowers, including foreign subsidiaries of United States firms, to issue bonds elsewhere; but because the United States dollar was still regarded as very sound currency, unlikely to be devalued, bonds were denominated in dollars. The voluntary foreign credit restraint program and mandatory controls introduced in 1968 further encouraged borrowing in foreign countries.

Eurobond issues were also encouraged by their freedom from the withholding of taxes on interest to bondholders, which would occur on ordinary bond issues sold in the United States.

Although Eurobond issues are publicly marketed rather than directly placed, the actual process is a mixture of the two methods. A group of managers of a bond marketing syndicate arranges to buy the issue from the issuing corporation. Then the underwriting group sells to an international selling group of houses, and they in turn sell to dealers, at successively smaller discounts. The bonds are then sold by dealers through direct contact with buyers; the public is not invited to buy such bonds.

Although there is no central collection of data on Eurobond issues, several agencies make estimates of the volume. It appears that by 1970 sales of new issues of Eurobonds totaled about $3 billion. There is apparently also a fairly sizable volume of secondary market trading in Eurobonds.

Yields on dollar Eurobonds have consistently been higher than yields on Aaa bonds of United States corporations; yields on deutsche mark Eurobonds were slightly higher for a time, and then fell below United States Aaa bond yields as upward revaluation of the deutsche mark was anticipated in 1969.

Present Status and Future of the Eurobond Market

The freedom from government control that has been characteristic of the Eurobond market is very appealing to issuers of bonds. Continued growth of a secondary market and the expertise and knowledge of the underwriters and distributing houses in this market may very well maintain the Eurobond market even if the IET, the original major cause of its development, were eliminated.

Probably about one-third of the total Eurobond issues have been issued by foreign subsidiaries of United States corporations. They have thus been able to borrow funds they probably could not have obtained in the United States in the recent period of controls on foreign investment and lending. These firms may in many cases continue to find it convenient to obtain funds in the countries in which they operate.

Flexibility in currencies of denomination and repayment may be an advantage if greater market flexibility is introduced into exchange rates and/or if devaluations and upward revaluations continue to be necessary from time to time. A gradual lessening of the role of the dollar as the "key" currency might also contribute to a desire for flexibility in currency designation.

If gradual relaxation of controls on foreign investment by the United States and by other countries occurs, the existence of the Eurobond market may contribute somewhat to reduction of international differences in interest rates among the major industrialized countries. As long as capital market controls continue to be important in European capital markets, the Eurobond market offers an alternative that, at least thus far, is subject to few controls.

From the standpoint of the United States capital markets, perhaps the major significance of the Eurobond market has been that it made it possible for foreign subsidiaries of United States firms to obtain funds in a period when balance of payments controls on foreign investment were deemed necessary by the United States government. Absence of this source of demand for funds from the United States capital markets in this period must surely have moderated somewhat the rise in interest rates, but there is no research thus far indicating the possible magnitude of moderation.

SUMMARY

Return on capital assets, both "real" and financial, is simply the increase in value of any asset held for a period of time, including capital gain or loss as well as interest or other income. Expressed as a rate per period and excluding capital gains or losses arising from price fluctuations, this increase is the interest rate.

The fundamental rate of interest is the rate of return on real capital assets. James Tobin has emphasized what he termed the "supply price" of capital, or the rate of return that just induces those who hold real capital assets to hold the existing stock of such assets at their current prices. This rate of return, unless it is below the cost of borrowing, determines the amount of investment, and thus constitutes a major determinant of the rate of economic growth.

Other rates are generally lower than this rate because of less risk involved in holding various financial assets. Yields in the corporate bond market are especially significant because they represent in general the marginal cost of long-term funds for corporations, except for those that resort to new issues of stock.

The market for long-term government securities is quite important because government securities provide much of the "ultimate liquidity" that is important whenever the possibility of substantial defaults on other obligations occur. As the long-term portion of the debt has been reduced, the importance of this market has also lessened somewhat, but other problems, including those of refunding large amounts of federal debt each year, have arisen.

Government agency securities have been growing rapidly in volume since 1965, and now constitute a significant part of the capital market. They are likely to continue to grow, and may become a source of liquidity comparable to Treasury securities.

The municipal bond market has limited demand because its special feature, tax exemption, appeals to a limited group of investors. This may give rise to a problem of financing construction activities of state and local governments if growth of such activities continues.

The mortgage market, especially the secondary mortgage market, has been aided and significantly improved by establishment and activities of government agencies and agencies initiated as such but later becoming private agencies. Nevertheless, even these efforts to channel funds into mortgages in periods when high yields in other markets prove more attractive have had only limited success.

The Eurobond market basically developed because various measures prevented foreign companies, including foreign subsidiaries of United States firms, from borrowing in the United States to the extent desired. The market has now developed a size and status that may enable it to continue to be of significance even if such controls on capital movements were eliminated. By meeting some of the demand for funds, the existence of this market may have moderated to some extent the rise in interest rates that occurred in the late 1960s.

In conclusion, capital markets provide liquidity for financial assets, thus making investors more willing to hold them. Improvements in information, functioning, and efficiency in capital markets improve this liquidity, and hence facilitate the flow of funds into investment. Fluctuations in rates in various segments of the capital markets tend to shift funds from one segment to another and may adversely affect particular types of activity for which funds are needed.

QUESTIONS FOR DISCUSSION

1. Develop a diagram showing the major connections between financial institutions and particular sectors of the capital markets for debt securities; show individuals also, where they are very important.

2. Why is the quick disappearance of differences between yields on new issues and those on comparable "seasoned" securities one indication of a relatively efficient capital market?

3. Discuss possible reasons for differences between the rate of return or yield on real capital assets and equities and that on corporate bonds; between that on corporate bonds and that on long-term government bonds; between government bonds and short-term government securities; and between short-term government securities and money (zero at present). Where would the yield on "near-monies" (deposits and similar accounts in deposit-type financial institutions) fall in this model?

4. Why is there a dealer market in government securities, rather than an auction market like that for stocks on the New York Stock Exchange?

5. Why did net new issues of government agency securities increase so rapidly in 1973? Is this characteristic of a year of rapid growth in business activity, or were other factors significant?

6. Why did the Federal Reserve System begin buying government agency securities in 1971?

7. Why was the spread between yields on seasoned corporate bonds and yields on United States government bonds so much wider in the early 1970s than in the 1960s?

8. Why did the spread between yields on United States government securities and yields on municipals narrow in the early 1970s?

9. Discuss the role played by the various recently-established government agencies in the mortgage market. What beneficial results has this activity had? Has it had any detrimental effects? If so, what and how?

10. Forecast the future growth of the Eurobond market (rapid growth, moderate growth, no growth, or decline), and explain your forecast in terms of characteristics of that market and changes anticipated in factors that affect the market. Discuss the probable effects that development of the Eurobond market has had on interest rates in the United States bond market and in Europe.

SELECTED REFERENCES

A series of articles in the *Economic Review* published by the Federal Reserve Bank of Cleveland provides useful information in brief form concerning recent developments in various segments of the capital markets: "Capital Market Developments, 1952–70," January 1972, pp. 12–23; "Corporate Bonds, 1960–68," September 1969, pp. 3–16; "Direct Placement of Corporate Debt," August 1970, pp. 18–32. "Federal Agency Issues: Newcomers in the Capital Market," February 1972, pp. 3–18; "The Secondary Mortgage Market," July 1971, pp. 14–32. "The Market for State and Local Government Bonds," August–September 1972, pp. 13–26; and "Eurobonds and the Eurobond Market," May 1971, pp. 3–17.

Trends in the bond market and price and yield data are conveniently presented in the weekly *Bond Market Roundup* and the *Quarterly Bond Market Review*, both published by Salomon Brothers. These are supplemented by an annual review. The Federal Reserve Bank of New York's *Monthly Review* contains a section reporting and analyzing developments in the capital markets.

Discussions of many institutions in the mortgage market, and of problems in that market, may be found in the Federal Home Loan Bank Board *Journal*, monthly. Of special interest are such issues as the Special Money Market Issue, September, 1971—see, for example, R. Bruce Ricks, "The Role of Federal Credit Agencies in the Capital Markets."

On origins and general nature of the Eurobond Market, see Gunter Dufey, *The Eurobond Market: Function and Future* (Seattle: Graduate School of Business Administration, University of Washington, 1969). Recent information is scattered, but *World Financial Markets*, issued monthly by Morgan Guaranty Trust Company, is useful, and such articles as Stanislas M. Yassukovich, "The Secondary Market in Eurobonds," *Euromoney*, June 1970, pp. 8–10, and "Eurobonds—Uneasy Peace in '71," *Euromoney*, March 1971, pp. 18–20, are informative. The Eurobond market as a force for capital market integration is examined in Morris Mendelson, "The Eurobond and Capital Market Integration," *Journal of Finance*, March 1972, pp. 110–26.

11

The Market
for Equities

Equities differ from debt securities in that they are ownership rather than creditor claims; creditor claims have priority. Although in case of financial difficulties creditors suffer losses, owners almost always suffer greater losses in such cases. Equities also normally have no maturity date. They may be outstanding as long as the company continues to operate. Hence a secondary as well as primary market for equities is essential for their liquidity. The secondary market is in fact a larger market, because the volume of securities outstanding is so great relative to the volume of new issues in any given year.

Equities are traded on exchanges, both regional and national, and in over-the-counter markets. No attempt is made in this chapter to cover the details of operation of these markets. Nor is any attempt made to develop methods of analysis of factors determining or affecting selection of individual equities for portfolios. These are topics covered in courses in investments.

Rather, our concern in this chapter is the fundamental basis for valuation of equities, the long-run trend of stock prices, the interconnections between the stock market and the markets for debt securities, and the relation of stock prices to business activity. We also give some attention, at the end of the chapter, to the efficiency of the market for equities and to some of the problems that are creating concern over this market as an integral part of the financial system.

Aside from efficiency, another aspect of the market for equities may give rise to concern. Heavy activity in this market can result in rapid increase in transactions velocity of money. This may lead to an increase in the income velocity of money, although the manner in which this occurs must be explained. The stock market is often cited as a barometer of business, and in fact stock market prices are one of the twelve leading indicators designated by the National Bureau of Economic Research as consistently rising in business upswings, falling in recessions, and changing direction of movement *prior to* a change in direction for business activity generally.

Whether this should be interpreted to mean that a stock market decline is a *cause* of a business recession—whether, for example, the stock market crash of 1929 was an important causal factor related to the Depression—is still debated. Perhaps the most common conclusion is that because the economy was vulnerable to unfavorable influences, the effect of the crash was much greater than it might otherwise have been. It caused a greater decline, once a decline had begun.

Let us first consider the nature of the market for equities, commonly referred to as "the stock market." This term covers a range of markets, including the New York Stock Exchange, the American Stock Exchange, a number of regional exchanges, and the over-the-counter market. Several thousand equity securities are listed on the organized exchanges, about half of them on the NYSE. Several thousand more corporations have more than 300 shareholders each, a level that leads the Securities and Exchange Commission to regard them as potentially being traded over-the-counter. Stock of companies with less than that number of shareholders is likely to be sold so infrequently that no regular market can be maintained for it. In the following discussion, the general term "the stock market" is used to apply to all secondary trading in equities. Although some reference is made to the well-known Dow-Jones Industrial Average as an index of stock prices, no attempt is made to give a detailed analysis of stock price averages and their relative merits as indicators. These details would require much more space than can be devoted to this subject. Nevertheless, a basic framework of analysis of the determinants of stock market prices and a foundation for analysis of the role of stock prices in affecting spending, discussed in Chapter 16, is essential.

EQUITIES AS CLAIMS ON REAL CAPITAL ASSETS

Because equities represent ownership claims, they are claims on real capital assets. The values of equities represent values of the real capital assets held by business firms. When values of equities are low, it is difficult for firms to raise capital through new equity issues, and a number of firms may be tempted to buy up shares of their own stock instead of investing in additional real assets. When values of equities are rising, it is easier to raise new capital through equity issues, and the rising values of real capital assets, reflected in the values of equities, tend to induce business firms to increase investment.

As is indicated subsequently, the market for equities is, of course, a market for claims on *future* earnings or dividends. As such, it is subject to more uncertainty than most capital markets, as earnings are more uncertain than bond repayment or refunding, and potentially at least, the earnings discounted may be far in the future. Hence it is not likely that a simple formula can be derived to explain stock prices; this is demonstrated later in this chapter. The short-run movements in equity values are likely to exhibit volatility and to respond to many factors that may be quite indirectly related to prospective earnings. Nevertheless, the importance of investment as a determinant of both full employment and economic growth is great, and the level of values of equities is an important factor affecting investment in the long run. For this reason, much more attention is given to long-run values of equities than to short-run fluctuations or cyclical variations.

THE STOCK MARKET

Four important differences exist between stocks and debt securities and the markets where they are traded. First, corporate stocks are in effect perpetual securities, with no maturity date. They continue to exist unless a firm goes out of business; when firms merge into other firms, stockholders in the merged firm are usually offered shares in the resulting firm, on some basis determined by relative valuations. Second, in large part because of the first difference, most of the trading is in the secondary market; relatively small amounts of new issues of stock are sold, especially in relation to the total volume of stock outstanding. This is even more true than it appears to be, because many new issues of companies that were privately owned and "go public" represent simply sale to the public of ownership equity already accumulated by the private owners. Third, trading in the secondary market is divided into two major segments, the over-the-counter market and the organized exchanges, whereas trading in bonds and mortgages is chiefly over-the-counter. The organized exchanges are widely publicized and attract interest and often purchases by a large segment of the public. Fourth, whereas bonds and mortgages have fixed interest rates and maturity values, so that their yields are affected by price changes occurring during their life, common stocks have no fixed yields.[1] Thus changes in prices of common stocks may result from either changes in yields (dividends or dividends plus capital gains) *or* changes in interest (discount) rates, the former usually being the more important.[2]

The Fundamental Approach to Valuation of Stocks[3]

These four differences constitute the keys to the fundamental approach to valuation of stocks. Whereas, since bonds and mortgages have maturity values, the formula for their value on a one-period basis is:

[1]Preferred stocks occupy a special position, as they have a specified fixed yield that must be paid before common stock dividends can be declared. The volume of preferred stock is relatively very small, but brief comment on their valuation is made later.

[2]It is useful to keep in mind that as the terms are used here, interest is simply the increase in value from the present moment to a future specified date, while discount is the decrease in value from that date to the present moment. Thus in the formula $PV \cdot i = Y$ (present value times the interest rate equals income), i is the interest rate; in the rearranged formula, $PV = Y/i$, i is the discount rate.

[3]The first systematic attempt to derive principles for valuation of common stocks is probably John B. Williams, *The Theory of Investment Value* (Cambridge, Mass.: Harvard University Press, 1938), although the basic idea was expressed at least as early as Edgar L. Smith, *Common Stocks as Long-Term Investments* (New York: Macmillan, 1924). The analysis was supported and extended by Nicholas Molodovsky in such writings as "Stock Values and Stock Prices," *Financial Analysts Journal*, May–June 1960. An interesting nontechnical review is Daniel Seligman, "Why the Stock Market Acts That Way," *Fortune*, November 1966, pp. 154–57; 234–38.

$$PV + PV \cdot i = Y + F, \text{ or } PV = \frac{Y + F}{1 + i}$$

In contrast, the formula for the value of a stock is basically:

$$PV = \frac{Y}{i}$$

In these formulas PV means present value; Y is the income; i is the rate of discount if one is looking at the discounting of a future value to the present; and F is the final maturity value.

Because stocks have no final maturity, only the yield need be considered in the basic formula. However, as soon as one views the yield over a number of periods instead of one period, the time horizon of investors becomes relevant. If, for example, investors look ahead only three years, although there is no final maturity value, there is a price at which the investors hope or expect to sell the stocks at the end of three years.[4] As this is an *expected* price (Fe) rather than a fixed price, it may vary substantially with investors' expectations. And because income (Y) in the case of stocks is also quite variable, there is significant basis for wide fluctuations in values of stocks.[5] Predictably, therefore, stock prices fluctuate much more than bond prices.

What determines expected prices of stocks at the ends of investors' time horizons? Basically, we must return to the formula above. Present value *at that time* will be equal to expected income divided by the discount rate:

$$Fe = Y_3/i$$

[4]In this case, the formula becomes

$$PV = \frac{Y_1}{1 + i} + \frac{Y_2}{(1 + i)^2} + \frac{Y_e}{(1 + i)^3} + \frac{Fe}{(1 + i)^3}$$

where Y_1, Y_2, and Y_3 are the expected earnings in each of the years to which the investor looks forward, and Fe is the final expected price of the stock at that time.

[5]The position taken in this section is that values of common stocks depend on both expected dividends and expected capital gains. This view is perhaps still somewhat controversial, although the definition offered by Benjamin Graham, David L. Dodd, and Sidney Cottle, *Security Analysis*, 4th ed. (New York: McGraw-Hill, 1962) included both. Writers such as Myron J. Gordon, *The Investment, Financing and Valuation of the Corporation* (Homewood, Ill.: Richard D. Irwin, 1962), especially Chapter 5, preferred to include only dividends. On the other hand, Franco Modigliani and Merton Miller went so far as to state that whether earnings are paid out in dividends or held as retained earnings "is a mere detail;" see "The Cost of Capital, Corporation Finance, and the Theory of Investment," *American Economic Review*, June 1958, pp. 261–97. Empirical evidence that retained earnings have been important was supplied by several studies, including Irwin Friend and Marshall Puckett, "Dividends and Stock Prices," *American Economic Review*, September 1964, p. 656–82, in which comparisons were made between prices for stocks of companies in "nongrowth industries" such as foods and steel and in "growth industries" such as electronics and chemicals.

Thus if a higher level of earnings were expected to continue, the value at that date would be that level of earnings discounted by the appropriate interest rate. This has led to the use, for present values of stocks at any time, of the expression "times earnings." If a discount rate of 5 percent were used for earnings, the present value of the stock would be 20 times earnings.

What determines the appropriate rate of interest or discount? On a bond or a mortgage, a coupon rate or interest rate is specified, but the yield may differ from the coupon rate. If more attractive opportunities for investment in similar securities become available, investors are likely to sell bonds, reducing the price but raising the yield for new investors. On the other hand, if a bond looks more attractive, investors are likely to buy bonds, raising their prices and reducing their yields for new investors. Similarly for stocks, the rate of yield may vary *if* other opportunities for investment, similar in quality, are found in the market. To the extent that stocks are similar to bonds, providing a relatively fixed income in the form of a steady dividend comparable to the steady rate of interest on bonds, the yield on stocks may be compared directly with yields on bonds. Since bondholders have priority over stockholders in claims on earnings, but no claim on earnings above a specified interest rate, the risk of *variation* in returns on stocks is greater. Yields which may be obtained may be much higher or much lower than those on bonds. To the extent that investors have an aversion to risk, yields they desire on stocks will be higher than on bonds. Therefore, if bond yields rise, for example in a period of inflation, the yield desired on stock rises, and the price/earnings ratio or "times earnings" ratio is therefore lower. The presence in the stock market of both very well informed investors, including large institutions and, at times at least, of large numbers of less informed investors, may create problems of information flow.

To recapitulate briefly: the fundamental approach to valuation of stocks tells us that stock values depend on (1) expected earnings over whatever time horizon is foreseen by investors; (2) the expected price at the end of that time horizon (which is based on a continuation of yields current at that time, in the absence of any reason to expect further change); and (3) the appropriate rate of discount, based on other opportunities for yield available in other capital markets.

Interconnections between the Bond Market and the Stock Market

To trace more precisely the influence of bond yields on valuation of stocks, let us focus attention on a group of stocks most similar to bonds in nature: utility stocks. Such stocks have rather regular yields because of regulation, and their earnings do not generally rise and fall rapidly, as may occur for the stocks of industrial companies. These stocks are as closely comparable to bonds as any we can examine. Thus if yields on bonds rise sharply, those who invest in utility stocks might be tempted to switch to bonds; if bond yields fall sharply, those who invest in bonds might be tempted to switch to utility stocks. Thus there will be a rather direct impact of changes in bond yields on the prices of utility stocks. Because purchase and sale of other stocks also may be influenced, there is likely to be some (but probably less) effect on their prices, and the effect may lag somewhat.

Thus the effect of changes in bond yields on stock valuations results from a change in the appropriate rate of discount to be used. If stocks had perfectly regular earnings, as is to some extent true of utility stocks, the change in the rate of discount would be almost directly proportional to the change in bond yields. Stock prices would fall as bond yields rose. This explains in part the decline and continued low level of prices of utility stocks after 1965, as bond yields rose and have remained relatively high.

The Role of "Technical" Factors

Changes in stock prices, especially short-term changes, depend on technical factors as well as on the fundamental factors that determine long-run levels of stock prices.[6] Because our attention in this book is on the role of capital markets in the economy rather than on the speculative fluctuations in day-to-day prices that are the subject of investments courses, only brief comments are made.

Technical factors include the important position of institutions (especially pension funds and mutual funds, and also trusts managed by trust departments of banks) in stock market trading, the effect of trends in stock market prices in influencing stock price expectations, and the short-run impact of orders to buy at specified prices and investors' desires to sell when significant profits have been made.

The growing role of institutions in stock market trading has tended to make stock prices more volatile. Individuals have been selling more stocks than they have purchased, and although, as indicated in Table 5–2 in Chapter 5, individuals still hold the majority of the total value of all stocks, individuals are not the dominant factor in buying and in the near future may not be the dominant factor in any market movements. Because institutions tend to trade in larger blocks than most individuals (sales of blocks of 10,000 or more shares are sometimes regarded as an indication of institutional trading), a simultaneous decision by a number of institutions to buy or sell particular stocks can quickly cause sharp fluctuations in its price.

Some financial economists argue that past stock market price trends have no effect on future stock prices; prices are assumed to be random fluctuations

---

[6]As John Maynard Keynes remarked long ago, "it is not sensible to pay 25 for an investment of which you believe the prospective yield to justify a value of 30, if you also believe that the market will value it at 20 three months hence" (*General Theory of Employment, Interest, and Money*, p. 155). Hence the investor (or speculator-investor) must concern himself with the developments likely to affect the views of other investors; individuals investing in the stock market must concern themselves with the groups of stocks likely to be bid up in price by other investors, as otherwise a particular stock, even though it has a potential long-run value much higher than its present price, may not be bid up for a considerable period of time. Institutions can afford to wait longer periods of time than most individuals, but even they tend to engage in "parallel buying."

from past levels—the "random walk" hypothesis.[7] On the other hand, market traders have numerous guides or rules which they believe can be used to predict future trends and patterns in stock prices on the basis of past trends. Rules such as that based on appearance of what are termed "head and shoulders" patterns and many others are believed to signal specific shifts in trends in stock prices. As these are in any event short-run changes, and as the issue between "random walk" theorists and "technicians" is by no means settled, we leave it at this point. Those who speculate in the stock market must make their own judgments about the validity of these rules.

Finally, investors frequently think in terms of buying securities when their prices fall to specified levels, on the ground that at those levels there is sufficient likelihood of rise in prices to justify purchase. Investors may leave specific limit purchase orders with brokers, or they may simply have price limits in mind. Similarly, investors who have accumulated significant profits may, unless deterred by potential capital gains taxes, sell when profits reach a point at which the likelihood of further increases in the prices of the stocks is relatively low. These facts aid in predicting the amplitude of short-term fluctuations in stock prices.

Because earnings of companies vary greatly, rates of growth of earnings vary, and investors' expectations of earnings may vary even more, no single price-earnings or "times-earnings" ratio can be applied to *present* earnings to obtain the present value of a given stock. Times-earnings ratios vary from 3 or 4 to more than 100. Is it possible, however, to apply a times-earnings ratio, under specified conditions, to the *average* of stocks traded on an exchange or a particular average of certain stocks, such as the Dow-Jones average? Because earnings vary much more than interest rates on bonds, there is obviously much more risk of price fluctuation and hence, possibly, of capital loss in investing in most stocks than in investing in bonds. The theory of effect of risk differentials on values is explored more thoroughly in Chapter 14, but at this point it may be noted simply that because of the greater risk, total yields on stocks, including capital gains, must usually be greater than yields on bonds. Hence times-earnings ratios for stocks, if based solely on past earnings, might be expected to be lower than such ratios for bonds. Times-earnings ratios on stocks are *not* based solely on past earnings, however; as described above, they are based on expected earnings for a period equal to the time horizon of the average investor, discounted at an appropriate rate. If earnings are expected to grow, the times-earnings ratio applied to present earnings must be higher. Based on postwar experience, this ratio has been about eighteen times earnings in periods when investor confidence was relatively high, and about twelve to fourteen times earnings for the Dow-Jones average when investor confidence was relatively low. In the absence of reasons for different ratios, these might be expected to prevail. Thus if confidence reaches a high level, as it is likely to do at peak levels of business activity, a times-earnings ratio of eighteen may be appropriate. When confidence is relatively low—either because it is believed that profit squeeze may threaten

---

[7]For some fairly recent studies of the "random walk" hypothesis, see the September 1968, special issue of the *Journal of Financial and Quantitative Analysis.*

profits, or that high interest rates resulting from inflation may cause a high rate of discount of expected earnings, or both—a times-earnings ratio of twelve to fourteen may be appropriate.

It is interesting to note that in late 1970, after the peak year of inflation in 1969 and a period of business recession in which profits had declined as a fraction of national income, the Dow-Jones index stood at approximately fourteen times the 1970 earnings on stocks included in that average, after recovery from the low at the time of the liquidity crisis of May 1970. It is likewise interesting to note that at the end of 1972 the Dow-Jones average stood at approximately sixteen times the level of 1972 earnings on stocks included in that average. Projections are always risky, but a forecast of the long-run level of stock prices should be based upon projections of GNP, of corporate earnings as a fraction of GNP and as specified amounts, of earnings on the stocks included in the Dow-Jones (or some other) average in relation to earnings of all corporations, and an appropriate times-earnings ratio. The interested reader may wish to use these basic projections to make his own calculations of a projected level of the Dow-Jones average for 1980 or 1985.

Institutional Trading and the Stock Market

The share of institutional trading in stock market activity has steadily increased in recent years. In 1961, institutions accounted for only one-third of all trading on the New York Stock Exchange. By 1971, institutions accounted for over 60 percent and individuals for only 40 percent. Commercial banks alone accounted for nearly 40 percent of trading; commercial bank trust departments are important in this respect because they manage noninsured pension funds and also trust funds. The New York Stock Exchange anticipates that the share of banks in trading will grow.

The growing role of institutions in stock market trading led to an extensive study of such trading by the Securities and Exchange Commission (SEC). The study, made on the basis of sampling during 1968 and 1969, found that although mutual fund trading was price aggressive (buying more when prices rose, and selling more when prices fell), bank trading was neutral—banks just as frequently sold when prices were rising, and bought when prices were falling.[8] It may be that banks have become more interested in "performance" since 1969, and now tend to contribute more to price changes. One investigation of "parallel trading" indicated that, although it could have been the result of chance, when it did occur, prices were positively related to it in the current month, and negatively related to it in the next month. Thus no firm evidence was found to support the need for restriction on trading activity of institutions.[9] Nevertheless, the rapid increase in block trading (trading of 10,000 or

[8]*Institutional Investor Study Report of the Securities and Exchange Commission,* Volume 4.

[9]Alan Kraus and Hans R. Stoll, "Parallel Trading by Institutional Investors," *Journal of Financial and Quantitative Analysis,* December 1972, pp. 2107–38.

more shares in one trade), from 3 percent of trading volume in 1965 to nearly 18 percent of total trading volume in 1971, indicates their potential impact on prices of particular stocks.[10]

Personal trust departments of commercial banks in 1971 held $224 billion in common stocks, as compared to $51 billion for mutual funds, $17 billion for life insurance companies, and $14 billion for property and casualty insurance companies.[11] These figures reflect a rapid rise in common stocks held in bank-managed pension funds (one-third increase in a single year, 1971) and a shift of assets in personal trust from bonds to stocks.[12] Trust departments of commercial banks are thus the largest single institutional holder of common stocks, holding in 1971 over 20 percent of the market value of all stocks outstanding. Because other institutions held about 8 percent, total institutional holdings were nearly one-third; individuals held about two-thirds, in contrast to over 70 percent in 1965.

Investment and brokerage houses have become concerned about the absence of many individual investors from the stock market since the market decline of 1969–70. The low level of stock prices in 1973, relative to current earnings of corporations, has led to a number of suggestions of measures to induce individuals, particularly small investors, to participate in the market. These suggestions range from changes in brokerage commission fees to suggestions for more favorable treatment for capital gains, including the suggestions that individuals be permitted to charge off against current income, for income tax purposes, as much as $5,000 a year of losses, instead of the current amount of $1,000 a year. The suggestion has also been made that the first $100,000 of capital gains for any individual, during his lifetime, not be taxed.

Obviously all of these suggestions are contrary to the demand, expressed by others, for heavier taxation of capital gains. The outcome is difficult to predict. But the fact that concern is now being expressed about the difficulty of corporations in obtaining new capital in the stock market indicates that an important new element—concern about economic growth—has been injected into the situation.

EXPLAINING AND PREDICTING STOCK MARKET PRICES

Explaining and predicting stock market prices are difficult tasks. In one study, an equation based on earnings and a rate of discount as the main variables

[10]Gertrude Mazza, "Growing Role of Institutional Investors on Wall Street," Federal Reserve Bank of Philadelphia, *Business Review*, August 1972, pp. 9–12. Statistical data were obtained from the SEC Statistical Bulletin.

[11]Board of Governors of the Federal Reserve System, Federal Deposit Insurance Corporation and Office of the Comptroller of the Currency, *Trust Assets of Insured Commercial Banks* (1970 and 1971).

[12]Edna E. Ehrlich, "The Functions and Investment Policies of Personal Trust Departments—Part II," Federal Reserve Bank of New York, *Monthly Review*, January 1973, pp. 12–19.

determining stock prices yielded moderately satisfactory results in terms of long-term trends, but the coefficient of correlation was only .26.[13] Stock market prices were much more variable than the predicted values based on the equation. A much better correlation (.47) was obtained when the money supply was added as a variable in the regression equation. Why? Here we have an interesting puzzle. Some have argued that individuals attempt to maintain constant proportions among holdings of various types of assets; hence, when the money supply is increased, individuals attempt to reduce money holdings by acquiring stocks, bonds, and other assets.[14] But this argument ignores the effect of yields on assets, and assumes that *fixed* proportions of holdings are desired. Some have argued that changes in the stock of money affect interest rates and thus affect stock prices; but why should the addition of the money supply to a regression in which an interest rate is already included improve the predictive ability?[15] A third suggestion is that the regression ignored the risk premium, because it is difficult to measure, and that although this may be legitimate during some periods when the risk premium remains constant, it is not useful when risk premiums change. High interest rates may cause the risk premium to increase because tight money increases the *variability* of corporate profits. Although this explanation has not been verified by conclusive tests, it seems plausible; even if it is correct, however, much remains to be done to provide a complete explanation of stock prices. As shown in Figure 11–1, stock prices deviated from the predicted trend for periods as long as two years or more when the money supply was not used in the equation, and for periods as long as a year or more when it was used.

Some final comments are appropriate on the long-run level of stock prices. In the years since World War II in the United States, stock prices have fallen in periods of inflation, and risen in periods when there was little or no inflation. Inflation is one of the causes of higher interest rates, and bond yields, which are one type of interest rate, thus rise in periods of inflation. If bonds thus seem somewhat more attractive to investors, they may shift funds from stocks to bonds.

It might be thought that, on the other hand, inflation would cause investors to avoid securities like bonds, which have fixed maturity values, and shift to stocks and other assets that can rise in price and thus provide a hedge against inflation. Perhaps if inflation were continuous over a long period, this would occur. But in the conditions in the United States, inflation was, as indicated earlier, intermittent, at least until 1965. Investors *may* have expected inflation to slow after a time; if so, investing in stocks as a hedge against inflation was less necessary than if inflation were expected to continue.

From late 1969 to late 1970, inflation was combined with a downturn in

[13]Stephen F. LeRoy, "Explaining Stock Prices," Federal Reserve Bank of Kansas City, *Monthly Review*, March 1972, pp. 10–19. The index of stock prices used in the study was Standard & Poor's index of 500 common stocks; the corporate bond yield was measured by Moody's Aaa corporate bond yield.

[14]Beryl W. Sprinkel, *Money and Stock Prices* (Homewood, Ill.: Richard D. Irwin, 1964).

[15]Michael W. Keran, "Expectations, Money, and the Stock Market," Federal Reserve Bank of St. Louis, *Review*, January 1971, pp. 16–31.

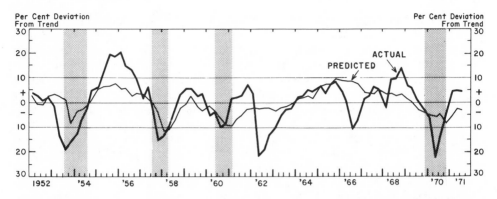

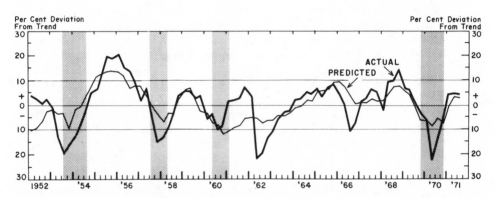

FIGURE 11–1   Actual and Predicted Stock Prices

SOURCE: Federal Reserve Bank of Kansas City, *Monthly Review*, March 1972, pp. 13, 15.

Note: In part (a) only corporate profits after taxes and the corporate bond interest rate were used in the regression equation. In part (b) money supply (M_1) was added to the regression equation.

general business activity. Government policy was intended to create a slow-down, if not an actual downturn, in general business activity, in order to reduce the rate of inflation. A reduction in the rate of inflation was not achieved as quickly as might have been desired; in fact, in 1973, inflation became an even more serious problem than previously. The reasons for the persistence of inflation in the face of a business downturn and higher unemployment and the rise in the rate of inflation in 1973 are not entirely clear.

In any event, past experience has indicated that periods of more rapid inflation were not periods of rapid rise in stock prices. Combined with this, a business recession is a period when profits normally fall more than most other categories of income and spending. Thus the decline in stock prices from 1968 to 1970 might have been foreseen on the basis of the decline in profits and also on the basis of past experience in inflationary periods if it had been foreseen that inflation would be persistent.

In the long run, however, the level of stock prices depends largely on what happens to profits as a share in national income. If profits return to a "normal" percentage of national income, whether inflation continues or not, in the long run earnings will rise significantly, as they must rise both absolutely and relative to GNP. If risk of fluctuations in profits is deemed great, the rate of discount to be applied may be higher than when less risk is anticipated, but if a period of relatively rapid growth in GNP continues, fears will tend to subside. Fears in early 1973 were twofold: (1) that profits might not return to "normal" levels in relation to GNP, partly because of controls on profits and partly because union labor power may cause wages to rise more rapidly than prices; and (2) that controls designed to curb inflation might prevent prices from rising as rapidly as wages and thus squeeze profits. Thus it could be anticipated that the first reaction to the announcement of removal of some wage and price controls would be some decline in stock prices, and that fears of a revival of the rate of inflation would lead also to some decline. If the rate of inflation does *not* increase significantly and if labor unions are *not* able to obtain wage increases in excess of the rate of price increases, stock prices could be expected to rise again.

What must be emphasized is that fundamental determinants of the long-run level of stock market prices are (1) the rate of inflation, which in turn affects bond yields; (2) the rate of increase in real GNP; and (3) the share of profits in nominal GNP. For the long-run investor, this understanding is quite relevant, although the short-run speculator may not find it very helpful in assisting him to find those stocks that may, in a short period, rise most rapidly in price.

In conclusion, no attempt has been made to describe or analyze the mechanics of trading in stocks, either on the organized exchanges or on the over-the-counter market. This is part of the subject of courses in investments. But an attempt has been made to show what factors are likely to influence average stock market prices in the long run. The reason for this is that, in an analysis of financial markets and the economy, the level of stock market prices is significant both for the flow of funds into financial and real investment and for effects the level of stock prices may have on other spending.

A continued flow of funds into stocks is vital to attract capital into investment, which in turn is an important determinant of economic growth. It is also vital, perhaps over a longer period, to retain funds already invested. Investors will not be satisfied to leave retained earnings in the hands of corporations unless such retained earnings are reflected in capital gains.

Second, stocks and real estate (and occasionally inventories of goods) are the chief assets held by consumers that fluctuate in value, usually with a rising trend in a growing economy. Thus if net worth affects spending, as some recent theories hypothesize, a rise in net worth from rising prices of stocks and real estate may be a second significant determinant of economic growth. The third major determinant, or group of determinants, of economic growth—productivity and the factors which affect it, such as education, innovations, and application of knowledge to production (improved technology)—should not be overlooked, but cannot be given much attention in this book.

EFFICIENCY OF THE STOCK MARKET

If profits are the key rate of return, and if the stock market functions to allocate funds to more profitable firms, as well as to assume a degree of liquidity for equity financial assets, the efficiency of the stock market is a matter of some concern. As pointed out at the beginning of the chapter, efficiency may be judged by two criteria: (1) does the market efficiently allocate funds to the most profitable uses? and (2) does the market have low costs of transactions?

Indirect tests of allocational efficiency have been made by attempting to determine whether the stock market responds quickly to new information. The studies supporting the "random walk" hypothesis—that past stock prices do not provide significant basis for predicting future price movements—have been interpreted by some as indicating that the market does respond quickly to new information. Tests have also been made comparing prices of stocks on which new information became available (for example, earnings announcements) with prices of those on which such information did not become available; these tests have indicated that such information is quickly reflected in stock prices.[16] A third type of indirect test has been studies to determine whether insiders, specialists trading on the exchanges, corporate officers and directors, and so on, have better-than-average trading profitability. The evidence seems to be that they do, but the interpretation of this evidence is in doubt: if a small group has monopolistic trading advantages, does this mean that the market is inefficient or simply that these groups are able to profit in the short period before the market adjusts to the new information?

More direct tests have attempted to determine whether risks perceived by investors correspond fairly closely to actual risks, on the presumption that investors have an aversion to risk. Studies have shown that the risk as measured by relative variability of return seems to be about the same for considerable periods of time, at least if groups of stocks are used for the test. Tests have also been made to determine whether return varies with risk of variability in return, which for stocks includes both dividends and capital gains or losses. The fact that over long periods of time returns on stocks have been about 9 percent compared to about 5 percent on bonds is some evidence that return varies with risk, but for stocks alone, the answer to the question is not so clear. A hump-shaped relationship has usually been found, but the location of the hump varies with the measures. That is, up to a certain point, return varies directly with risk; beyond that point, it varies indirectly. The location of the point depends on the use of arithmetic or geometric averages of returns.

Other studies indicate that new issues of stocks have not been particularly good investments over long periods, if it is assumed that new issues are somewhat more risky than seasoned issues and therefore should have higher returns.

Sometimes it is presumed that the return on a single stock should in gen-

---

[16]Eugene Fama, "Efficient Capital Markets: A Review of Theory and Empirical Work," *Journal of Finance*, Papers and Proceedings, May 1970, pp. 383–417.

eral remain in the same relationship (higher or lower) to the return on all stocks. It is also sometimes presumed that the trend in return on single stocks should rise directly as risk is greater, risk being measured by variation in return compared with variation in the return on all stocks. If these presumptions are made, results of tests indicate that the performance of the stock market has been better since World War II than it was before that, in meeting these conditions.

One study indicated that mutual funds performed very little better than the average investor, when the ratios of subsequent earnings to initial price were compared, and when ratios of trends in subsequent earnings and prices were compared.[17]

The authors of one study concluded that security analysts' forecasts were little better than past earnings growth in predicting future earnings. However, only five firms participated in the study, and the predictions were made for earnings growth over five years; perhaps a larger number of participants or a shorter period of forecasting would have given different results.[18]

A complete review of evidence from studies cannot be provided, but perhaps this is enough to indicate the basis for the general conclusion reached: evidence from studies indicates that the stock market is not very efficient as an allocator of resources, and this is confirmed by hindsight evaluation of unwarranted price changes. Moreover, there is extensive evidence of misrepresentation and manipulation.[19] However, it indicated that performance of the stock market has been better since World War II than before the war. These conclusions should not lead the reader to believe that the stock market is unnecessary. An allocational mechanism is certainly needed, and perhaps (except for manipulation) the stock market does about as well as can be expected, given the uncertainties of future earnings. The question that should be considered is whether significant improvements can be made.

One recent attempt at improvement has been regulatory action to make commission charges for buying and selling stocks on the New York and American Stock Exchanges competitive rather than fixed. Presumably the public would benefit from lower transactions costs (commissions). Commissions on large transactions (over $300,000) first were made negotiable; then in April 1974 competition was required for small transactions. It was expected that all commission rates would be competitive after April 1975. Losses in a "bear" (downward) market in 1973 caused concern that some brokerage houses might fail, as a number had in the 1970–71 period. It also seemed likely that brokerage houses, in an effort to reduce commission charges, would "unbundle" some of their services and establish separate fees for investment research or other services. Income from such fees might cushion a decline in income when a drop in market trading volume occurred. Whether the changes in brokerage

---

[17]Irwin Friend, "The Economic Consequences of the Stock Market," *American Economic Review*, Papers and Proceedings, May 1972, p. 218.

[18]John G. Cragg and Burton G. Malkiel, "The Consensus and Accuracy of Some Predictions of the Growth of Corporate Earnings," *Journal of Finance*, March 1968, pp. 67–84.

[19]Irwin Friend and E. S. Herman, "The SEC Through a Glass Darkly," *Journal of Business*, October 1964, pp. 382–405.

pricing practices will constitute a significant improvement in the efficiency of the market remains to be seen.

SUMMARY

Fundamentally, stocks are valued in the same basic way as bonds, on the basis of the discounted present value of expected yields. The general level of stock market prices depends basically on the level of expected earnings and the share of corporate earnings in GNP; this level of stock prices is important because stock prices reflect (although imperfectly) the underlying values attributed to real capital assets and thus help determine the level of investment and hence of economic growth. The level of stock prices is also important because capital gains (or losses) may be significant in determining the level of consumer spending—and hence may be a second important determinant (in addition to current income as measured in the national income accounts) of spending and economic growth.

Clearly, the factors that determine stock prices include the level and trend of earnings, the level of interest rates on alternative open market investments, and another factor, often loosely referred to as "investor confidence." Investor confidence seems generally to be increased when the stock of money increases, within limits.

In contrast to comments frequently made in the financial press, the stock market is probably not a very efficient market in terms of the second test, the level of transactions costs. But, as a wit might remark, "It's the only market we have." Efforts to reform the market to improve its efficiency in allocation or to minimize transactions costs should not create conditions that cause investors to lose confidence in the market; otherwise the continued gradual rise in stock prices, in line with expected or hoped-for rise in GNP, cannot occur.

QUESTIONS FOR DISCUSSION

1. If stock values are based on discounting expected future earnings, how can Levitz Furniture reasonably sell (as it did for a time) at 100 times current earnings?

2. If long-term interest rates on corporate bonds average 7 percent or more instead of 5 percent, what effect would this probably have on the prices of stocks?

3. Is it possible for a company to earn $1 per share one year, and $3 per share the next year, without significant changes in sales or operating costs? If so, how?

4. Make your own calculation of the possible Dow-Jones index in 1980, based upon a growth of the economy of 7½ percent a year in nominal GNP (4½ percent a year in real growth and 3 percent a year in inflation), profits at a "normal" ratio to GNP, profits on stocks in a DJIA at a "normal" ratio to profits in all corporations, and a "reasonable" multiple of the DJIA to earnings on stocks in the DJIA. Explain how you selected a "normal" ratio of profits in all corporations and a "reasonable" multiple of the DJIA to earnings on stocks in the DJIA.

5. Why should the stock of money be an important determinant of stock prices?

6. Why did inflation in the early 1970s seem to be a factor causing stock market prices to fall? What about the belief, generally accepted in the past, that stocks are a hedge against inflation?

7. Much evidence has been presented recently to indicate that few investors can do better, in the long run, than the Dow-Jones index. What can be inferred from such evidence, if it is valid?

8. Does the increasing dominance of institutions in *trading* on the stock market (not in volume of stocks owned) seem likely to be harmful? Why or why not?

9. Read the final chapter of *Supermoney* (see Selected References) and comment on "Adam Smith's" comment that "Something Else is Going On."

10. Explain (by some hypothesis) why stock market prices were so far below predicted levels in May 1970 (refer to Figure 11–1). How would you test your hypothesis?

SELECTED REFERENCES

John Kenneth Galbraith, *The Great Crash: 1929* (Boston: Houghton Mifflin, 1954) gives a very entertaining account of the crash and its impact upon the economy.

The generally accepted theory of the determination of stock prices is set forth in a relatively rigorous manner in Stephen F. LeRoy, "The Determination of Stock Prices," unpublished Ph.D. dissertation, University of Pennsylvania. A more easily accessible discussion by the same author is found in Stephen F. LeRoy, "Explaining Stock Prices," Federal Reserve Bank of Kansas City, *Monthly Review*, 1972, pp. 10–19. One view of the influence of money on stock prices is advanced by Beryl W. Sprinkel, *Money and Stock Prices* (Homewood, Ill.: Richard D. Irwin, 1964).

A comprehensive discussion of the market for equities is Sidney Robbins' *The Securities Markets: Operations and Issues* (New York: Free Press, 1966).

Everyone should read the irreverent but very relevant books by "Adam Smith," *The Money Game* (New York: Random House, 1967) and *Supermoney* (New York: Random House, 1972); the first of these was referred to by Paul Samuelson as "a modern classic."

The now rather extensive literature on the efficiency of the stock market is reviewed briefly by Irwin Friend, "The Economic Consequences of the Stock Market," *American Economic Review*, Papers and Proceedings, May 1972, pp. 212–19. The references cited by Friend and the studies he refers to provide a lengthy list, but somewhat inconclusive results.

Two stimulating, up-to-date discussions are found in James H. Lorie and Mary T. Hamilton, *The Stock Market: Theories and Evidence* (Homewood, Ill.: Dow Jones-Irwin, 1973), and Burton G. Malkiel, *A Random Walk Down Wall Street* (New York: W. W. Norton, 1973).

IV

The Level
and Structure of
Interest Rates

Institutions and markets dealing with loanable funds have been discussed in Chapters 3–11. We now focus our attention on the "price" of those funds, expressed as an interest rate. In Part IV we explore briefly two theories of the determination of interest rates at given levels of income and prices, and the general effect of inflation. Because different rates prevail on the myriad of different securities at any point in time, we also discuss reasons for interest rate differentials.

Chapter 12 contains a discussion of the basic economic theory of interest rate determination and some analysis involving uses of this theory. In Chapter 13, special emphasis is placed on the theory of the "term-to-maturity" structure of rates—that is, the theory explaining why interest rates on long-term securities differ from those on short-term securities. Finally, in Chapter 14, other factors such as risk, callability, taxability, and so forth that cause interest rate differentials are discussed.

12

The Determination
of the Level
# of Interest Rates

The study of interest rates and security prices is important because of the role they play in the allocation of economic and financial resources and thus the importance they have for the nation's standard of living over time. This chapter begins with definitions of interest rates as expressed in yields on securities. Following this is a brief outline of the classical and neoclassical views of interest and interest rates. One of the most important neoclassical models, that of Irving Fisher, is discussed in the appendix.

In the next section, two major approaches to interest rate theory are presented. These are the liquidity preference theory, discussed rather briefly, and the loanable funds theory, presented in more detail. Then we examine the role that price expectations are thought to play in the behavior of interest rates. We conclude with a section on interest rate behavior and an explanation of this behavior in terms of loanable funds theory.

DEFINITIONS AND RELATIONSHIPS
OF YIELDS AND PRICES

Under a contract, the issuer of a bond offers to pay an investor a fixed amount of interest. This amount is expressed as a percentage of the bond's par value. For example, if it is a $1,000 bond and the issuer pays $60 per year, the rate of interest (coupon rate) is 6 percent. The issuer also agrees to redeem the bond at par value at maturity.

As long as the market price of the bond equals its par value, the coupon rate equals the security's *yield*. But changing supply and demand for bonds bring about changes in market prices, and bonds may: (1) sell at a premium, in which case market price is greater than par value and the effective yield is less than the coupon rate, or (2) sell at a discount, in which case the market price is less than the par value and the effective yield is greater than the coupon rate. The redemption value, the ultimate obligation of the issuer of the bond, does not change, but the return (yield) to investors who buy the bond changes if the bond price differs from par value.

Bond prices and bond yields vary inversely. If a bond's market price rises, its yield declines; if the price declines, its yield rises. This inverse relationship is not one of cause and effect—price changes do not *cause* yields to change—but stems from the fact that the promised interest payment is fixed. Thus, the higher the price an investor must pay for a given amount of interest income, the lower his yield or rate of return. We observe this relationship in the market for debt instruments whenever supply of or demand for these securities changes. A period of falling bond prices occurs when the demand for bonds falls off or when the supply of bonds increases. Bond yields rise under these circumstances.

The formula:

$$PV = R/i$$

is the formula for the present value of a bond with equal annual interest payments of R dollars to be made forever—a perpetual bond or a Consol, that is, a bond with no maturity date.[1] Here, i is the "yield" or the "rate of discount." The inverse relationship between PV and i is obvious in the formula. The formula is definitional; that is, for a given present value of $1,000, and a given annual interest payment of $50, the rate of discount i must be .05 or 5 percent; the relation described in the formula defines the rate of discount, $i = R/PV$. Given any two of the three variables, the value of the third is fixed by definition—by the formula.

The formula for the present value of a bond of n periods to maturity with coupons payable at the end of each period is:

$$PV = \frac{R_1}{(1+i)} + \frac{R_2}{(1+i)^2} + \cdots + \frac{R_n}{(1+i)^n} + \frac{F}{(1+i)^n}$$

In this formula, PV represents present value, R is the amount of interest paid periodically, F is the face value to be redeemed at maturity, n is the number of periods until maturity, and i is the rate of interest.

Consider a two-year bond with a face value of $1,000, and a coupon yield of 3 percent so that R is $30; then,

$$\$1,000 = \frac{\$30}{(1+.03)} + \frac{\$30}{(1+.03)^2} + \frac{\$1,000}{(1+.03)^2}$$

Now assume that an increase in the demand for loans occurs, so that comparable bonds yield 4 percent. What price would one be willing to pay for this

---

[1]The term Consol is derived from the word consolidated. It refers to the consolidation of a number of outstanding British securities after World War I into perpetual bonds.

bond in order to realize a 4 percent return? That is, what would *PV* be if *i* were 4 percent?

$$PV = \frac{\$30}{(1.04)} + \frac{\$30}{(1.04)^2} + \frac{\$1,000}{(1.04)^2}$$

$$PV = \$28.85 + \$27.78 + \$925.93 = \$982.56$$

If interest payments are made semiannually, $15 appears in the numerator, and the denominator changes as shown for *n* semiannual periods.[2]

$$PV = \frac{\$15}{[1 + i/2]} + \frac{\$15}{[1 + i/2]^2} + \cdots \frac{\$15}{[1 + i/2]^{2n}} + \frac{\$1,000}{[1 + i/2]^{2n}}.$$

Readily available bond tables provide information on the variables in the equation so that the analyst does not have to perform the computations on each occasion. There are five variables:

1. *F*, face value to be repaid at maturity,
2. *PV*, present value,
3. *i*, the rate of interest (discount) or yield to maturity,
4. *R*, the periodic payment that indicates the value of a coupon, usually expressed as a percentage of face value,
5. *n*, the number of periods.

If we know any four of these, the fifth can be found from the formula.

A section taken from a bond table is shown in Table 12–1. A $100 face value bond (F = $100.00) with a 3 percent coupon (R = $3.00) that sells for

TABLE 12–1   Table Showing Present Values *(PV)* of Coupon Bonds
3 Percent Coupon, R = $3.00 Face Value, F = $100.00

i, yield to maturity percentage	*n*, years and months to maturity		
	9–10	*9–11*	*10–0*
2.90	100.85	100.85	100.86
2.95	100.42	100.43	100.43
3.00	100.00	100.00	100.00
3.05	99.58	99.57	99.57

Note: If the face value of a bond were $1,000 instead of $100, one would simply move the decimal point on *PV* to the right one digit.

[2]For quarterly interest payments R = 30/4 = 7.5 and in the denominator *i* would be divided by 4 as well. If interest payments are "compounded" continuously over time, the formula becomes: $A = PVe^{ni}$ where *e* is the mathematical constant 2.718 . . . and *A* is the amount to which *PV* will grow in *n* years at rate of interest *i*.

100.86 and has ten years to run to maturity will yield 2.90 percent; $PV = $ 100.86, $n = $ ten years, $i = 2.90$ percent. By knowing PV from the cells of the table, one can determine the yield to maturity in the left-hand column. Similarly, if one knows the yield to maturity, he can find the appropriate current price of the bond. Other tables not shown give PV and i when the bond carries a 3.25 percent coupon, a 3.50 percent coupon, and so forth.

An approximate method for determining the yield to maturity is found in the simple formula:[3]

$$i = \frac{\text{annual interest} + (-) \text{ average annual appreciation (depreciation)}}{\text{average investment}}$$

If an investor pays \$800 for a \$1,000 bond paying 5 percent each year and maturing in twenty years, then

$$i \cong \frac{\$50 + \$10}{\dfrac{\$800 + \$1000}{2}} = \frac{60}{900} = 6.67\%,$$

the approximate average *yield to maturity*. The *current* or market yield on this security is \$50/\$800 $= 6.2$ percent, but this calculation does not take into account the return to be realized because of the appreciation in value of this security as it approaches maturity or par value.

Differences in interest rates and yields on the variety of financial instruments are the subject of the two following chapters. For present purposes in looking at the "levels" of rates, we might let the average yield on default-free government bonds serve as a proxy for "the" rate of interest. The use of this rate avoids complexities caused by risk in corporate bonds, stocks, and real capital assets, and also avoids the difficult problems of measuring yields on stocks and real capital assets. We might use the average yield of a sample of Aaa-rated bonds as our representation of "the" interest rate, since risk is small. Whenever we refer to "the" interest rate or the level of rates, we have in mind a representative rate, and recognize that other rates differ from this rate for various reasons such as risk, maturity, tax status, marketability, and others.

THE CLASSICAL AND NEOCLASSICAL THEORIES OF THE DETERMINATION OF INTEREST RATES

The Classical Theory

Adam Smith, a classical economist, stressed the role of parsimony in fostering economic growth. Smith wrote:

---

[3]This formula is taken from William C. Freund, *Investment Fundamentals*, Americal Bankers Association, New York, 1966, p. 44.

> Capitals are increased by parsimony, and diminished by prodigality and mis-
> conduct.
>
> Whatever a person saves from his revenue he adds to his capital, and either
> employs it himself in maintaining an additional number of productive hands,
> or enables some other person to do so, by lending it to him for interest, that
> is, for a share of the profits. As the capital of an individual can be increased
> only by what he saves from his annual revenue or his annual gains, so the
> capital of a society, which is the same with that of all the individuals who
> compose it, can be increased only in the same manner.[4]

These sentiments carry through the writings of economists to this very
day, although not without qualification. If one has an income, by abstaining
from consumption—that is, by saving—one can purchase productive resources
so that his income in subsequent periods is increased. In this manner, standards of living rise.

For society to accumulate real wealth and capital, capital goods must be
produced, and resources devoted to production of capital goods cannot at the
same time be devoted to production of consumer services. Thus, people must
save, or refrain from consumption, if society's stock of wealth is to expand.
But the way saving occurs is more complicated than as envisaged by the classical spokesman.

Along with thrift, there must be productivity. Eugen von Böhm-Bawerk
stressed the concept of the "period of production" and "roundaboutness" in
the production process.[5] As an example, he suggested that one might imagine
himself living alone in a cabin by a lake, perhaps as Henry Thoreau once lived
near Walden Pond. One could walk to the lake for water whenever it was
needed. Or, one could devote time and effort to construct a bucket so as to
reduce the number of trips necessary for obtaining water. Or, one could spend
even greater time and effort and construct a trough from a spring, running it
past the cabin door so that water would be readily available whenever it was
desired. Thus, acquiring water for consumption can be done directly or in a
roundabout way. Roundaboutness in obtaining the water leads to a far greater
amount of water available for consumption with a given amount of effort than
the direct method of obtaining water. Thus, increasing roundaboutness in production of goods by using capital goods leads to greater productivity, increased
output per man-hour, and higher living standards.

The Neoclassical Theory

The neoclassical theory differs from classical theory in that it incorporates major amendments developed by later economists. These economists
stressed freedom of choice on the part of those who save or dissave, given the
interest rate that measures the reward. Individuals are thought to have a

---

[4]Adam Smith, *The Wealth of Nations* (1776), The Modern Library Edition, 1937,
p. 321.
[5]Eugen von Böhm-Bawerk, *Capital and Interest* (1922), translated by G. D. Huncke,
South Holland, Illinois, 1959.

"time-preference" for a consumption pattern over time. One may choose not to save but to dissave and perhaps go to school, travel, and so on. He may wish to consume today, realizing, of course, that his future income will be lower because of the interest he must pay. Others may wish to save. Businessmen may have investment opportunities that are productive in the sense that they yield increased real output in the future. The yield from investment allows them to pay interest out of future earnings. Thus, consumers sometimes supply savings and sometimes demand savings. Businessmen also supply savings and demand savings. Competition in the market for savings and for capital goods and consumer goods sets an equilibrium price on saving (interest yield) at which the amount of saving supplied equals that amount demanded. Thus, the neoclassical economist views the interest rate as the price that rations the available supply of saving to borrowers and that induces suppliers of saving to enter the market. They also recognize that the volume of saving depends not only on the interest rate but also on the income of society. The neoclassical position does not provide an answer to ethical questions on the virtue of saving or thrift, stressing instead the desirability of freedom of consumer choice, not only to choose among alternative goods, but also to choose a time-path of consumption by saving or not saving as one may desire.

In neoclassical economic theory, prices are determined by demand and supply. Goods have value only if there is a demand for them, but given a demand, costs help determine the supply at relative prices, and demand and supply together determine price. Because productivity of real capital assets is the basis for demand for investment funds, the fundamental "real" rate of interest is the rate of return on real capital assets, as stressed in Part III. This "real" rate of interest is reflected in the "money" rate of interest charged on loanable funds.

ALTERNATIVE APPROACHES TO THE DETERMINATION OF THE RATE OF INTEREST

Two alternative theories of the determination of the representative rate of interest are commonly used. In the liquidity preference theory, the rate of interest is determined by demand for and supply of money. In the loanable funds theory, the rate of interest is determined by demand for and supply of loanable funds. The former is a stock model requiring explanations of motives for holding cash balances and relating these to the stock of money existing *at* a given point in time. Loanable funds theory is commonly stated in a flow form in which demand is the amount which would be borrowed and supply is the amount (including newly created money) which would be loaned *during* a period.

In the economy as viewed here, individuals and institutions can do any one or a combination of three things—spend, lend, or hold money balances (barter is ignored). These activities are conducted in markets for goods and services, loanable funds, and money. At equilibrium in each market, demand for goods and services (spending) equals the supply of goods and services (receipts), amounts which lenders wish to lend equal amounts borrowers wish to obtain, and demand for money equals the supply of money. In a closed economy (that is, excluding foreign transactions for simplicity), if any two of these equalities exist, the third must also exist. Hence it is not a question of which theory is *right*, but of which theory is more *convenient* to needs.[6] This might be easier to visualize if liquidity preference theory were stated in a flow form: demand is demand for additional money created during a given period, and supply of money is additional money created during that period. It then is clear that if spending equals receipts and lending equals borrowing, any additional money created must be held as an addition to present holdings. Similarly, if spending equals receipts and any additional money created is added to present holdings, lending must equal borrowing.

This restatement is helpful in analysis of "hoarding." If the interest rate were higher than the equilibrium rate, demand for money would be less than supply of money—people would *try* to hold less money, by spending or lending. That is, they would dishoard. If the interest rate were lower than the equilibrium rate, the demand for money would be greater than the money supply —people would try to hold more money. That is, they would hoard. Thus dishoarding is just an increase in the velocity of money as people try to spend or lend more, and hoarding is just a reduction in the velocity of money as people try to hold larger money balances.

The restatement is also helpful in creating awareness that choice is possible between holding money and spending as well as between holding money and lending. Only the latter choice is suggested by liquidity preference theory —if the demand for money shifts, it is generally assumed that lending shifts in the opposite direction.

In any event, two models are used in interest rate theory. Which model should be used may depend partly on theoretical needs. The liquidity preference model fits well with the usual macroeconomic approach to the theory of determination of both interest rates and income. It may also depend partly on practical needs—the loanable funds model is easier to use if one wishes to obtain empirical data on supply and demand and to forecast interest rates. Choice of model may also be based on behavioral analysis: are people generally concerned with how much they wish to hold in money balances, or with how much they wish to invest in securities or loans?[7] In this book we stress the loanable funds model because it is the frame of reference used by most financial analysts. However, a brief outline of the liquidity preference approach is also desirable.

[6]This view was neatly expressed by Harry G. Johnson, "Monetary Theory and Keynesian Economics," *Pakistan Economic Journal*, June 1958, pp. 56–70; reprinted in Harry G. Johnson, *Money, Trade and Economic Growth* (London: Allen and Unwin, 1962) and in Warren L. Smith and Ronald L. Teigen (eds.), *Readings in Money, National Income, and Stabilization Policy* (Homewood, Ill.: Richard D. Irwin, 1965). For further discussion of the question of reconciling the liquidity preference and the loanable funds approaches, see: Frederick Lutz, *The Theory of Interest*, 2nd ed. (Chicago: Aldine Publishing Co., 1968).

[7]This and other more difficult questions are considered in Joseph W. Conard, *An Introduction to the Theory of Interest* (Berkeley and Los Angeles: University of California Press, 1959).

The Liquidity Preference Approach

The liquidity preference theoretical structure developed out of the writings of John Maynard Keynes in the 1930s as an integral part of his macroeconomic model of income determination. Readers of this text have already surveyed the Keynesian model of income determination in their introductory economics course; to examine it in detail here would be repetitious. It is appropriate, however, to mention briefly a few of the salient features of the model in order to note the connecting links between the various approaches to the study of interest.

Essentially, Keynes asked, as others before him had done, "Why do people bother to hold money—to keep money on hand?" As money is the most "liquid" of all assets, the question can be phrased, "Why do people desire liquidity?"—hence the reference to a "liquidity preference" function. His answer was that they hold money for transactions purposes, for precautionary purposes, and for speculative purposes. The amount held for transactions varies with the level of economic activity. The larger the volume of trade as measured, say, by GNP, the larger the quantity of money demanded to carry out this trade. The amount held for precautionary purposes is more or less constant and is not significantly related to other macroeconomic variables. The amount held for speculative purposes is inversely related to the level of interest rates.[8] If interest rates are high, people attempt to reduce the level of their idle cash balances and buy interest-earning bonds. They also expect that interest rates may fall, meaning that the price of bonds would rise and they could realize a capital gain. Thus, at high interest rates people economize on their cash balances, running them down to very low levels. If interest rates are low, people prefer to hold cash rather than interest-earning bonds; that is, they prefer having the liquidity of money rather than the interest return on the bonds, and they may expect bond prices to fall, as well, if and when interest rates rise. Thus the interest return on a bond is the opportunity cost of holding money—it is the cost of liquidity. If one holds money instead of an interest-earning bond, he gives up the interest return, and this represents an implicit cost to him.

The transactions demand for money is now thought to be sensitive to interest rates as well as to the level of economic activity as measured by income. This addendum to Keynesian theory was developed by Tobin and Baumol.[9] They noted that as income rises and interest rates rise, people begin to "economize" on their transactions balances; that is, they allow their transactions balances to fall, in relation to income. An individual who usually carries an average balance of $1,000 in his checking account when savings accounts pay only 3 percent may let his average checking balance fall to $500 and increase

[8]Subsequent development of theory elaborated on these motives, and in some analyses the precautionary and speculative motives are interrelated.

[9]See James Tobin, "The Interest-Elasticity of the Transactions Demand for Cash," *Review of Economics and Statistics*, August 1956, pp. 241–47, and W. J. Baumol, "The Transactions Demand for Cash: An Inventory Theoretic Approach," *Quarterly Journal of Economics*, November 1952, pp. 545–56.

his savings account by $500 when yields on savings accounts rise to 5 percent. There is not a great deal of income difference in this example, but corporate treasurers with $1 million in a demand deposit will find it profitable to put these funds into a time deposit account over the weekend. The higher the rate of interest, the greater the profit incentive to "manage" the checking account balance on a day-to-day basis. Thus, the transactions demand for money is held to be sensitive to interest rate levels.

By combining the parts of the puzzle, we can write $M_D = M(Y, i)$, which might be called either a liquidity preference function or a demand-for-money function. The equation reads that the quantity of money demanded, M, is related to income, Y, and the rate of interest, i. The relationship between changes in money and changes in income, $\triangle M / \triangle Y$, is believed to be positive, and the relationship between changes in interest and changes in money, $\triangle M / \triangle i$, is believed to be negative. The money supply in this model is assumed to be given, M_S. Thus, for a given level of income, the demand for money and the supply of money determine i at i_0 as shown in Figure 12–1. At any rate higher than i_0—for example, i_1—the demand for money is less than the supply of money, and people try to reduce their holdings of money. They try to do this by buying securities, driving up the price of securities and driving down the interest rate.

This, of course, is only part of the Keynesian model. The level of Y depends on the rate of investment spending, consumption spending, government spending, and net exports. Consumption and investment spending are related to i; therefore, i and Y are interdependent in the complete Keynesian model, as they are in the neoclassical framework. But here we have introduced the money supply as a partial determinant of the rate of interest. As the money supply rises, interest rates fall, and vice versa.[10]

Because Y and i are interdependent, we cannot have a complete theory of the determination of i without explaining the determination of Y as well, a project beyond the purpose of this book. But we can view the analysis as a

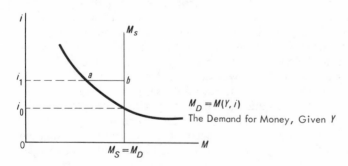

FIGURE 12–1

---

[10]In Hicksian *IS-LM* diagrams used in most macroeconomic texts, if the *IS* curve is positively sloped, an increase in M, which shifts the *LM* curve to the right, will lead to an *increase* in Y and in i as well.

partial equilibrium model and simply say that for a *given Y* and a *given* supply of money, *i* is determined.

Liquidity preference theory lacks realism because no explicit account is taken of the role of financial institutions and financial assets other than money and bonds. The choice between money and bonds is not the only choice available, because there are many types of "near-monies"—Treasury bills, commercial paper, certificates of deposit, and so forth. Also, there are real capital assets and stocks, which are claims on real capital assets.

The Loanable Funds Approach

This approach, like the liquidity preference approach, introduces the money supply explicitly, but is preferred by financial analysts because institutional elements can be handled more easily under it, and because it is more amenable as a basis for forecasting. As noted above, so far as can be determined the liquidity preference and loanable funds approaches are internally consistent with each other, although some concern remains about the strict logic of the matter.

The loanable funds approach is surely the simplest and easiest to understand. The rate of interest is determined by the supply of and demand for loanable funds, where these funds are flows into the market for securities representing loans and investments. Rather than analyzing why people hold the money they do at any point in time, as we do in the liquidity preference approach, the loanable funds approach asks why people lend or borrow for periods of time. It is perhaps a question of emphasis more than a basic difference. We have noted that the liquidity preference theory is a *stock* theory, while the loanable funds theory is a *flow* theory.[11] In the loanable funds approach, it is assumed that there is a downward sloping demand curve for funds and an upward sloping supply curve for funds, as in Figure 12–2.

Analyzing the supply curve first, we note that the supply of loanable funds is derived from three principal sources. First, funds are supplied by saving out of income. As in neoclassical theory, when interest rates rise, most savers lend more because their earnings are greater.

Second, the supply of loanable funds is increased whenever the money supply is increased; that is, whenever $\triangle M$ is positive. As described in Chapter 4, the money supply is increased through a complicated process. Money is created through central bank action, changes in bank reserves and currency (the monetary base), and the money multiplier. Changes in currency and in the money multiplier depend on portfolio decisions of various entities. This process eventually leads to an increase in the money supply, part of the supply of loanable funds, as noted in Figure 12–3, where S is the supply of saving and $\triangle M$ is the increase in the money supply. It is assumed that changes in the money supply are independent of the rate of interest, and therefore that the S

[11]This presents some problems in reconciling the two approaches, as the demand for and supply of money represent demand for and supply of the entire existing stock at a particular time, while the demand for and supply of loanable funds represent only the flow of amounts loaned and borrowed during a given period of time.

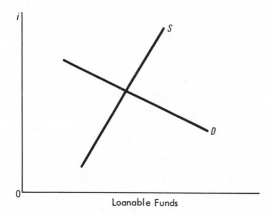

FIGURE 12–2

curve is simply shifted rightward by an amount, $\triangle M$, representing the increase in M. The $\triangle M$ represents an increase in demand and/or time deposits based on net new loans or securities purchased by the commercial banks.[12]

Third, the supply of loanable funds may be increased when individuals attempt to dishoard money, and decreased when individuals attempt to hoard. If, for example, the interest rate should rise, we note from Figure 12–1 showing liquidity preference that the quantity of money demanded would be less than the quantity supplied. Individuals would attempt to hold less money and would probably offer to buy bonds or other financial assets. Dishoarding would

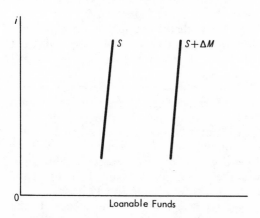

FIGURE 12–3

[12]If one believes that commercial banks may tend to increase the money supply somewhat more when interest rates are relatively high and that the central bank will permit this, the $S + \triangle M$ curve might slope a little more than the S curve.

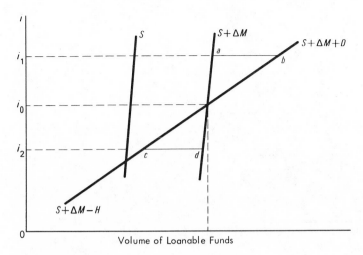

FIGURE 12-4

add to the supply of loanable funds. Thus, in Figure 12-3, to the total supply of funds would be added the amount of funds that would be dishoarded if interest rates were higher, as in Figure 12-4. The distance a–b in Figure 12-4 represents the distance ab in Figure 12-1. In case the interest rate should fall to i_2 in Figure 12-4, individuals would wish to hoard money and would sell bonds or other financial assets to add to their stock of money. Hoarding, represented by the distance cd, would reduce the volume of loanable funds.[13] This hoarding and dishoarding behavior is depicted in the curve labeled $S + \triangle M + D$ and $S + \triangle M - H$, where S stands for saving, $\triangle M$ stands for the increase in the money supply, D stands for dishoarding (or negative hoarding), and H stands for hoarding. This curve represents the total supply of loanable funds.

The demand for loanable funds is the result, first, of business demand to finance its capital and liquidity requirements. The long-term capital requirements are described by the investment-opportunity curve of the neoclassical model. The lower the money rate of interest, the larger the volume of funds demanded; hence in Figure 12-2 the demand curve slopes down and to the right. However, total demand for loanable funds also is meant to reflect demand by the federal government for funds as it seeks to finance its deficits by issuing bonds or other securities, and demand by state and local governments, which they express by issuing bonds to finance projects. Thus the total demand for funds is made up of business demand, federal government demand, and

[13]Note that dishoarding results in an increase in the rate of turnover (velocity) of money, while hoarding results in a decrease. Hoarding is often thought of in terms of money hidden under a mattress, but hoarding and dishoarding are slippery terms, and hoarding could not be measured in terms of the amount of money so hidden, even if that amount were known.

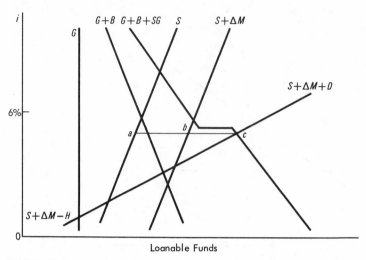

FIGURE 12–5

state and local government demand,[14] labeled *B, G,* and *SG* in Figure 12–5. (Foreign demand is temporarily ignored, and consumer demand is ignored because saving refers to net saving of the consumer sector (gross saving minus borrowing) plus gross business saving and government saving (if any).

It is widely held that the line indicating federal government demand, *G,* should be vertical. That is, unlike business demand, which is greater at lower interest rates, the quantity of funds borrowed by the federal government is insensitive to interest rates. State and local demand is sensitive to interest rates; indeed, state and local regulations sometimes prohibit borrowing at interest rates above (say) 6 percent. When the market interest rate on bonds exceeds this level, some local governments may be preempted from effectively demanding any funds at all. Thus total demand for funds may shift leftward at levels above the 6 percent legal maximum for certain state and local governments.

Figure 12–5 shows components of the demand and supply for funds that are nearly always considered by market analysts. However, the student should realize that many unmentioned factors affect these supply and demand schedules. For example, if new banks, savings and loan institutions, or finance companies are established, this may affect the supply of loanable funds. If international trade barriers are lowered, businesses may increase their demand for funds (the demand curve may shift to the right) in order to take advantage of their new found opportunities. Thus, these demand and supply curves are

---

[14]Consumer demand for loans is here omitted, being treated as a deduction from saving. Saving thus includes only net personal saving and not gross personal saving. Gross personal saving could be included in the supply of loanable funds and consumer borrowing in the demand for loanable funds if desired. In practice another category of demand is also included—the demand for mortgage credit—and foreign demand for loanable funds also must not be overlooked.

best thought of as abstract analytical frameworks useful to market observers as a frame of reference in which one can couch the many varied factors that affect the rate of interest and the volume of funds flowing into the market for loans.

The equilibrium point in Figure 12–5 (point *c*) is only a temporary equilibrium point. For at that point, there is dishoarding (in the amount of *bc*) and there is also an increase in the money supply (in the amount of *ab*). If increase in the money supply should cease next period, the supply curve would shift to the left. Furthermore, dishoarding in the current period would not be expected to continue in future periods. The current rate of increase in the money supply and the dishoarding that is taking place mean that the current supply of funds is increasing and current levels of interest rates are lower. Thus, we would expect investment and income to rise in the near future, leading to (1) a rightward shift in the *B* curve as businesses expand and borrow, and (2) a leftward shift in the *G* curve because higher income means higher tax receipts and a smaller budget deficit (less federal government borrowing), provided, of course, that government spending does not increase to offset this effect.

One defect of the loanable funds theory is that it normally shows only a partial or temporary equilibrium point. A final equilibrium point is not normally shown, because it depends on shifts in income, which are ignored in loanable funds theory as normally presented. The demand for and supply of loanable funds do not indicate what shifts in income will be. Hence the final equilibrium level of the interest rate, after all the interactions have been worked out, may be lower or higher than the point usually shown in a diagram —loanable funds theory does not by itself indicate the final equilibrium level of the rate of interest, but rather shows the current status of the financial market.

Thus care must be used in interpreting financial market development, using the supply and demand for funds framework. These supply and demand curves are *not* independent of each other, as is assumed for typical supply and demand curves for commodities. Factors influencing the supply of funds may eventually affect the demand for funds, and care must be exercised in interpreting the longer-run effects of shifts in either supply or demand.

In concluding, it is perhaps well to note that one may use either gross or net figures in the loanable funds approach, as long as he maintains internal consistency. For example, consumer dissaving (borrowing) can be subtracted from gross consumer saving to arrive at net consumer saving as the supply of funds from consumer saving. Alternatively, gross consumer saving could be used in the supply of saving curve, and consumer dissaving could be part of the demand for saving curve. The same is true of business saving. One may look at gross business saving (depreciation plus retained earnings) and gross demand for funds, or one may subtract depreciation and retained earnings from gross business demand for funds to arrive at net business demand for funds. One reason for using gross figures is that, as noted in Chapter 6, the net business demand for loanable funds depends in part upon the amount of internally generated funds that can meet part of the need for funds for investment.

PRICE EXPECTATIONS AND THE RATE OF INTEREST

In the theoretical explanation of determination of the level of interest rates outlined above, no explicit account was taken of the influence of price level changes (inflation or deflation) on the level of interest rates. It is clear that price level changes affect the real return that a lender receives from his loan and that a borrower must pay for his loan. If a contract is made under which the lender receives a return on a $100 loan of $8 at the end of one year, the nominal interest rate, i, is 8 percent. However, if on the date of maturity of the loan, the price level is found to have risen by 5 percent, then the real rate of earnings on the loan, r, would be only 3 percent. The borrower repays the lender with dollars that are less valuable in terms of purchasing power than the ones he borrowed a year earlier. In equation terms, we may write:

$$i = r + \dot{p}/p$$

where $\dot{p}$ stands for dp/dt or the derivative of the price level with respect to time, and p is the price level so that $\dot{p}/p$ is the percentage rate of change in the price level.[15]

---

[15]If prices increase from 100 to 110 in one year, then dp/dt is approximately $\Delta p/\Delta t = 10/1 = 10$. If the original price level, p, were 100, then $10/100 = .10$ or 10 percent, the rate of increase in p expressed in percentage terms so as to be consistent with the mode of expression for i and r. If $\Delta p/\Delta t = 30$ when the original p was 200, then the percentage rate of increase of p would be only 15 percent. A more exact formulation of the equation for discrete changes in i, r, and p would be:

$$(1 + i) = (1 + r) (1 + \dot{p}/p)$$
$$1 + i = 1 + r + \dot{p}/p + r(\dot{p}/p)$$
$$\text{or } i = r + \dot{p}/p + r(\dot{p}/p)$$

The last term on the right-hand side is the interaction term and is usually very small so that it is ignored in most discussions. If, for example, $i = 26$ percent, $r = 20$ percent, and $\dot{p}/p = 5$ percent, then

$$(1.26) = (1.20) (1.05) = 1 + .20 + .05 + .01$$

Omitting the interaction term would have made $i = 25$ percent instead of 26 percent. Thus, the error in omitting the term becomes significant if r or $\dot{p}/p$ or both are large. In the case of continuous functions rather than the discrete changes, the interaction terms drop out altogether. To illustrate, assume $i =$ nominal rate of interest, $r =$ real rate of interest, $p =$ price level, $V_n =$ nominal value of an asset, $V_r =$ real value of an asset, and

$$V_n = pV_r.$$

$$i = \text{the percentage change in } V_n = \frac{1}{V_n} \left(\frac{dV_n}{dt} \right)$$

$$r = \text{the percentage change in } V_r = \frac{1}{V_r} \left(\frac{dV_r}{dt} \right)$$

Irving Fisher used this formula as a basis for what is known as the "Fisher effect."[16] He argued that uniform expectations on the part of borrowers and lenders about future rates of inflation would affect the current nominal rate of interest. If borrowers believe that 5 percent inflation will occur during the year, they willingly pay this premium to borrow their funds,[17] and if lenders believe that 5 percent inflation will occur, they require a 5 percent premium to induce them to lend their funds. Thus,

$$i = r + (\dot{p}/p)^e$$

where the right-hand term no longer describes the *results* of *past* inflation but rather the *expected future* rate of inflation as indicated by the superscript *e*. If one believes that current expectations about future inflation rates are formed by the past history of inflation in a country, then one can construct a proxy for measuring $(\dot{p}/p)^e$. With a time series of data for the proxy and a series of observations on *i*, estimates of the real rate of return, *r*, can be calculated by simply subtracting $(\dot{p}/p)^e$ from *i*. If, on the other hand, one assumes that *r* is relatively constant, then variation in inflation-rate expectations would be the prime determinant of variations in *i*. From early 1930 to the mid-1960s, economists in the United States were not much interested in the problem of inflation, as it was not very serious domestically, except in war periods. But in the late 1960s and early 1970s, inflation proved to be much more of a problem. Numerous studies have been made that have focused attention on the "Fisher effect."[18]

Solving for *i*, find

$$i = \frac{1}{pV_r} \frac{d(pV_r)}{dt} = \frac{1}{pV_r} \left(p \frac{dV_r}{dt} + V_r \frac{dp}{dt} \right)$$

$$= \frac{1}{V_r} \frac{dV_r}{dt} + \frac{1}{p} \frac{dp}{dt} \quad \text{and therefore,}$$

$$i = r + \dot{p}/p \quad \text{for an infinitesimal unit of time.}$$

[16]Irving Fisher, *The Theory of Interest* (New York: The Macmillan Company, 1930), reprinted by Augustus M. Kelley, New York, 1961.

[17]The presumption is that as prices rise (and wages rise at about the same rate), profits and wages in money terms both rise. If, because of the existence of powerful unions, wages rise more rapidly than prices or if price controls are more tightly enforced than wage controls, profits may be squeezed and the statement above may have to be qualified.

[18]Recent studies include: R. A. Mundell, "Inflation and Real Interest," *Journal of Political Economy*, June 1967, pp. 280–83; W. Yohe and D. Karnosky "Interest Rates and Price Level Changes, 1952–1969," *Review*, Federal Reserve Bank of St. Louis, December 1969, pp. 18–38; W. E. Gibson, "Price Expectations Effects on Interest Rates," *Journal of Finance*, March 1970, pp. 19–34, and "Interest Rates and Inflationary Expectations," *American Economic Review*, December 1972, pp. 854–65; M. Feldstein, "Inflation, Specification Bias and the Impact of Interest Rates," *Journal of Political Economy*, December 1970, pp. 1325–39; Feldstein and O. Eckstein, "The Fundamental Determinants of the Interest Rate," *Review of Economics and Statistics*, November 1970, pp. 363–75; T. Sargent, "Commodity Price Expectations and the Interest Rate," *Quarterly Journal of Economics*, February 1969, pp. 127–40, and "Anticipated Infla-

The equation appears to be neat, but upon closer examination, use of it in economic forecasting could be fraught with pitfalls. We cannot examine these in depth, but we can briefly suggest their nature. First, when prices fell rapidly, as in 1930–32, recent price experience would have led to expectations of deflation, and if the real rate were constant, then, according to the formula, the nominal rate might have been negative; but it was not, and indeed it cannot, be negative, for lenders would simply retain cash holdings rather than lend at negative rates.[19] Second, a period of recent past experience without inflation could be upset by an outbreak of hostilities so that current expectations of future inflation would fail to be formed on the basis of past experience alone. Hence, the proxy variable for expected future inflation might fail regularly to predict significant turning points in expectations. Third, it is questionable whether "expectations of inflation" can ever be measured in a scientific way. By scientific, of course, we mean capable of being confirmed or refuted by reference to experience. If, for example, we asked everyone to declare their expectations, and if we observed the true i in the marketplace and the true r by looking at the technology of production and markets for commodities, and if the difference between i and r did *not* equal our observed $(\dot{p}/p)^e$, then we might presume that our measures were wrong—that we had *not* actually observed the true expected rate of price change. One can record a verbal expression of them, but one cannot *observe* people's opinions, and if their actions belie their words, the recorder of opinion may take the action as evidence of *what the true opinion must have been.*

After interest rates rise, financial analysts often simply rationalize this rise by reporting that investors are now expecting an increase in the rate of inflation. That is, rather than explain the rise in rates as having been caused by expected inflation, they explain changing expectations by inferring how expectations must have changed from the rise in rates. To use expectations as part of a theory to predict future changes in interest rates, one must be able to observe changes in expectations and test to see if these changes do lead to the theoretically predicted changes in rates. Until this happens, expectations may be only a rationalization, rather than a causal force in explaining changes in interest rates.

Thus, the equation showing the "Fisher effect" may be refuted because (1) it may not work at all in periods of deflation, (2) proxies for expectations are unreliable, and (3) direct observation of changing expectations, while tempting, may give us an untestable theory in a scientific sense.

It is tautologically true, for any investor who purchases a contract for which the unit of account (the dollar, say) is variable in real value, that his realized rate of return is less than the nominal rate:

$$r \equiv i - \dot{p}/p$$

[19] If the real rate were negative, as it might be when businessmen are very pessimistic, and the expected price level change were also negative, then nominal rates would have to be negative, according to the equation. But, of course, they never are, for any significant period.

where r is his ex post "realized" rate of return. But to proceed from this and attempt to explain i, and variation in i, through observation of $(\dot{p}/p)^e$ is quite another matter. Finally, to predict future i—the purpose of a theory of interest rate determination—one must observe not only *changes* in $(\dot{p}/p)^e$, but also changes in r.

Despite these problems besetting the "Fisher effect," the general framework expressed in the equation will probably continue to be used as a rationalization by financial analysts. Whenever supply and demand analysis fails to provide an adequate explanation for a change in i, they can always assume that changes in expected inflation must account for their error in forecasting.

Most economists would agree that the assertion "i will rise by the rate of inflation" is empirically true in the long run. But few would say that short-run fluctuations in i are explained by recent changes in the rate of inflation. Short-run fluctuations are best explained by examining the variety of forces of supply and demand for loanable funds in the context of the theory of interest rate level determination.

INTEREST RATE THEORY AT WORK

In the following two chapters we elaborate on some of the more important factors affecting the rate of interest on any particular security. In concluding this chapter we wish to indicate briefly how the theory developed so far provides the market analyst with a general appreciation of why interest rates rise or fall in the short run, in the long run, and among different regions or countries.

Interest Rate Levels in the Short Run

On a day-to-day basis, the short-term interest rates fluctuate in response to temporary and erratic forces affecting supply and demand for short-term funds. For example, the Federal Reserve float may fall unexpectedly and leave banks deficient in reserves. The Federal funds rate rises as a consequence. Cash may flow into circulation, and again there is upward pressure on rates. The demand for funds may increase if an announced Treasury security offering is larger than expected—again short-term rates may rise.

When supply and demand forces change as described, the Fed enters the market through open market purchases of government securities to help offset the rise in rates. Fed officials usually allow the rate to rise, but not by as much as it would have risen without intervention by the open market trading desk. Sometimes the Fed maintains an "even keel" for several days before and after a refinancing operation by the Treasury in order to ensure that the government securities market will not become "disorderly" and that the Treasury's issue will be well received.

Over a period of several months, however, longer-lasting forces interact to set the level of rates. These forces are related principally to changes in economic activity and the rate of inflation. In a period of economic expansion demand for funds on the part of business and private individuals tends to increase—the demand curve shifts to the right. This occurs as business firms expand their operations and borrow funds for inventories and working capital. For a time, expansionary monetary policy may contribute to an increase in the supply of funds, and higher incomes of wage earners also increase the supply of funds through the saving that follows. On the other hand, government demand for funds declines as tax receipts rise, reducing previous deficit levels in the federal budget. Thus the supply of funds shifts rightward, but the demand also shifts rightward, so that interest rates may not change perceptibly at this stage of the cycle in business activity.

However, as capacity utilization of fixed plant and equipment is approached, business firms begin to review and revise upward their heavy investment and construction requirements. The demand for large amounts of long-term funds is likely to begin to rise dramatically, pushing rates to higher levels, especially if monetary authorities begin applying brakes to the expansion in the form of a reduced rate of growth in the money supply. The velocity of money increases at higher interest rate levels because of dishoarding. As full capacity is approached and money income continues to rise, prices also begin to rise. Insofar as inflation occurs, nominal interest rates rise further. Thus, a booming economy is characterized by high and rising interest rates as the demand for funds exceeds the supply and as lenders require an inflation premium to induce them to buy debt securities instead of real assets or stocks. The rise in business activity in 1971–73 was an exception in one way because demand for stocks rose only moderately, and, in fact, was inadequate in 1973 to maintain stock market prices at the level attained at the beginning of that year.

We might characterize the analysis of nominal interest-rate levels by listing three types of effects: (1) liquidity effects, (2) income effects, and (3) inflationary effects. As the Fed increases the money supply, the initial effect is to push bond prices up and yields down. The liquidity position of the community has improved (the liquidity effect on interest rates). But more money and lower rates stimulate economic activity and increase income. This increase in income tends to offset the initial decline in yields and subsequently raise them (the income effect). If the economy is operating at or near capacity, the higher income is nominal and reflected heavily in inflation. Inflation pushes nominal interest rates up again (the inflationary effect).

In a downturn of the economy, the situation is reversed. Being uncertain of the economic outlook, consumers may increase the rate at which they save out of disposable income. As output is cut back and unemployment develops, this conservative consumption behavior on the part of the public is accentuated. The supply of funds derived from saving increases, and the demand for durable goods falls. At the same time, there is reduction in the demand for funds, as business firms begin programs of retrenchment (or reduce the rate at which they were expanding in the recent past). As income falls, this reduction in demand is accompanied by a reduction in saving and therefore in the supply of funds. With reduction in the supply of funds, interest rates do not fall as far as they might otherwise. But eventually, the leftward shift in demand overcomes the leftward shift in supply, especially if monetary authorities begin to increase the supply through expansionary policies. Thus interest rates fall.

The fall may lead to increased hoarding of money and a decline in the velocity of money, which also occurs as spending is reduced.

Interest Rate Levels in the Long Run

Over somewhat longer periods of time, monetary factors are less important than those stemming from thrift and productivity. Interest-rate levels may show long-term trends when the influence of short-run monetary factors is eliminated. For example, in countries that are developing their economies and are in the process of industrialization, demand for capital goods means high interest rates. These high rates attract foreign capital. This was true of the United States, which was a net importer of capital up until the 1930s. British funds were supplied to build much of the railway network in the United States in the late 1800s. These funds were attracted by the relatively high rate of interest to be earned.

When an economy matures and standards of living rise, the domestic supply of saving also rises, contributing to an increase in the supply of funds. Thus, interest rates tend to fall to more moderate levels if inflation is held under control.

International Comparisons of Interest Rates

A considerable amount of the difference in interest rates among countries can be explained by the different rates of inflation they experience. Several countries in South America seem to be able to live with almost steady rates of inflation of 10 or 20 percent per year. This makes nominal interest rates much higher in these countries than the rates for comparable securities in other countries with lower rates of inflation.

"Real" factors also affect interest rates. In some societies positive attitudes toward thrift are strongly entrenched, leading to relatively high saving rates, which add to the supply of funds. In others, people live from day to day with little in their culture that makes thrift a virtue. These differences explain differences in the supply of saving and thus in interest rates. Japan has been a prime example of a country where, for various reasons, people have maintained a relatively high rate of saving.

The natural resource bases of countries and the rates at which they are exploited *help* determine demand for funds and interest rates in particular countries. However, demand for funds may be strong in countries that have relatively meager natural resources—again, Japan is an example.

Finally, the political process that leads in one direction toward a welfare state or in the other direction toward less government activity also affects demand for funds on the part of government. The greater the degree of government activity in providing additional services, the greater its borrowing is likely to be because unpopular tax increases are not likely to keep up with increases in government expenditures.

SUMMARY

Before examining the theory of determination of the general level of interest rates, it is essential to keep in mind that the rate of interest (yield) on a security is inversely related to the price of the security, and that current prices depend on expected future yields discounted at some presumably appropriate rate.

Classical economists stressed the combination of productivity and thrift as the two principal determinants of interest rates. Neoclassical economists, while retaining the recognition of the importance of productivity and thrift, emphasized the desire for a certain pattern of consumption and saving over time. Thus, borrowing to increase current consumption (rather than to add to the stock of machinery, for example, as emphasized by classical thought) is also a determinant of demand for funds, and therefore of the level of interest rates.

A brief description of the liquidity preference approach indicates how demand for money and supply of money affect interest rates. If the money supply increases, the interest rate would be expected to fall, other things being equal.

The loanable funds theory of interest rate determination is the theory most often used by financial markets analysts. The supply of funds is composed of (a) saving, (b) changes in the supply of money, and (c) dishoarding. Demand for funds comes mainly from business and government.

Price level changes affect the "real" rate of interest realized from an investment. Expected price level changes also affect the willingness of borrowers and lenders to act, but a theory of interest based on expected inflation rates has several pitfalls.

In the short run, temporary and erratic factors affect interest rates. In the long run, productivity of capital and inflation are the major factors affecting interest rates, on the assumption that saving is a relatively stable proportion of income.

APPENDIX

The Fisherian Time-Preference Model

In neoclassical economic theory the pricing system allocates scarce resources among alternative uses. All prices are interrelated, and all are relative, indicating the rate at which one commodity will exchange for another at a point in time. An interest rate is a unique form of price—it indicates the rate at which a commodity can be exchanged for itself at *two* points in time. If I give you ten bushels of wheat today and you return eleven bushels to me one year from today, the real rate of interest is 10 percent. Therefore, interest rates serve to determine the time pattern of resource allocation. Individuals have preferences with a time dimension. A student may dissave now in anticipation of a higher income when he begins his career and earns income out of which he can repay his indebtedness. Middle-aged people may save today in anticipation of income falling when they enter retirement. In these cases, the individuals prefer to even out the time flow of their consumption. Furthermore, people may wish to borrow now in order to bring out productive investment.

To describe in a general way the forces giving rise to saving behavior, economists use "indifference curves." These are shown in Figure 12A–1, which is called Irving Fisher's two-period diagram.[20] An individual is assumed to have a time horizon of two periods. Income of the initial period, Y_0, is measured on the horizontal axis, and income of the subsequent period, Y_1, is measured on the vertical axis. The three indifference curves represent three levels of satisfaction that an individual may acquire from consumption during the two periods. If he consumes 100 each period he will reach the same level of satisfaction (be on the same indifference curve) as he would reach if he consumed 200 this period and only 50 next period (points a and b). But, he would reach a higher level of satisfaction if he could consume 200 each period (point c). There is, at any point on an indifference curve, a slope of the curve. At point a the slope of the curve S_1 is equal to the slope of the tangent to the curve (dashed line). The slope is defined to be Y_1/Y_0, and at a this is -1.

The slope of the indifference curve is called the marginal rate of time preference. At a, the individual is just willing to exchange a dollar's worth of this period's consumption for a dollar's consumption next period. However, if he is at point b the curve is flatter. If we measured Y_1/Y_0 it would be, perhaps, minus ¼. This indicates that his present consumption of 200 is

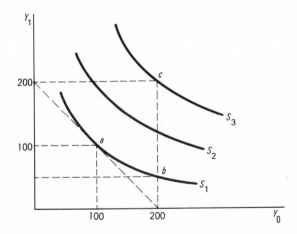

FIGURE 12A–1

[20]See Irving Fisher, *The Theory of Interest* (New York: Macmillan, 1930), reprinted by Augustus M. Kelley, New York, 1961.

high relative to next period's consumption and he would be happy to give up $4 of this year's consumption if he could only have another dollar's consumption next period.

Assume that the individual is at point a where Y_0 and Y_1 both equal 100. Assume also that the interest rate is zero. Then the dashed line represents the variety of ways he can consume his income of 200. He could consume all of it this period and none next period, or he could consume equal amounts each period, or all next period and none this period. Indeed, any point on the dashed line represents a possible pair of consumption amounts. We could call it his consumption-possibility curve. At a he is on his highest indifference curve.

Now assume he faces a positive interest rate. His consumption possibilities will now be different. They are reflected in the straight solid line in Figure 12A–2.

The slope of the solid line is $-(1 + i)$ where i is the market rate of interest. If $i = 20$ percent, the slope is -1.20. The horizontal intercept is $183.33, indicating that if the individual borrowed $83.33 today he could repay this amount along with $16.67 interest a year from today, by using his next period's income of $100. The intercept of the vertical axis is $220, indicating he might save all of his $100 and regain it with $20 interest and receive next period's $100 income as well. Thus, with a positive interest rate his possibilities have changed and he can now reach a higher indifference curve at point b by lending some of this period's income, and receiving his income and the repaid principal, along with earned interest, in the next period. A positive interest rate has induced him to save and lend, as noted in the diagram.

Another individual might have a preference map with a tangency point somewhere along the possibility curve below and to the right of point a, and

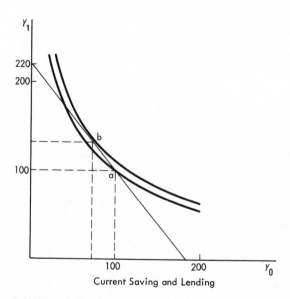

Current Saving and Lending

FIGURE 12A–2

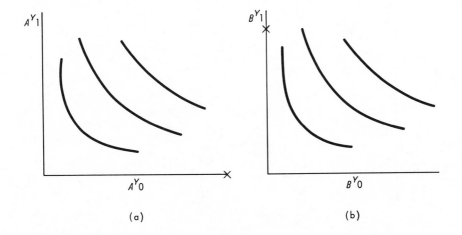

FIGURE 12A–3

he would be a borrower. In the economy as a whole all of the lenders would supply saving to the economy, and all of the borrowers would compete for this saving. The market rate of interest would be determined by competition among those who supply saving and those who demand loanable funds. In equilibrium the rate set in the market would be such that for each and every individual his marginal rate of time preference would equal $-(1 + r)$; that is, the slope of his indifference curve would equal the slope of the possibility curve. Every borrower and lender would be better off (in the sense of being on a higher indifference curve and realizing a higher level of satisfaction) when a market for saving and dissaving could be freely entered than they would be if such a market were denied existence.

To illustrate these propositions in greater detail, assume there are two individuals in an economy, each with a two-period time-preference function as suggested by Figures 12A–3(a) and 12A–3(b). In Figure 12A–3(a), individual A's income is given at point X—that is, he has income this period but unlike the case of Figures 12A–1 and 12A–2 he has *none* next period. Individual B has income next period but none this period. Using the Edgeworth box diagram technique, rotate individual B's axes by 180 degrees and superimpose the Xs. This appears in Figure 12A–4.

The indifference curves of A and B have points of tangency which, if connected, form what is called a contract line—that is, the set of all points for which A's marginal rate of time preference equals B's marginal rate of time preference. The size of the box represents total income of the two individuals in the two periods. At point a the marginal rate of time preference is the same for both A and B and also equals the slope of the line from the X point representing the original incomes of the two individuals to point a. The slope of this line equals $-(1 + i)$. Individual A lends to B the amount of current income as noted. This reduces B's next period income by an amount noted by "repayment of loan" and it increases A's second-period income by this amount as well.

If the amount of the loan were represented by point b, for example, at

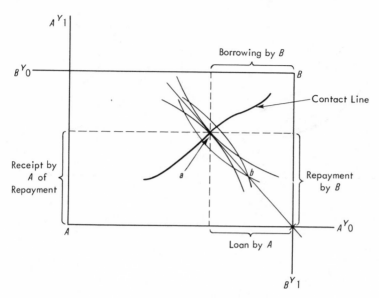

FIGURE 12A–4

this point A's marginal rate of time preference (the slope of his indifference curve) would be less (flatter) than would be B's marginal rate of time preference. This indicates that at this rate of interest B would be on a higher indifference curve if he could borrow more from A, and also that A would be on a higher curve if he could lend to B. Both A and B are better off if they move toward point a.

We can avoid thinking of A and B as particular individuals, but rather as representative groups of borrowers and lenders, who meet in the marketplace and supply and demand funds. This competitive interaction determines the market rate of interest at any point in time. Thus, the interest rate, which is a market clearing price for loanable funds, is determined, like other prices, by forces of supply and demand.

From Figures 12A–1 and 12A–2 we can see how a supply curve of loanable funds can be generated. A supply curve shows the interest rate on the vertical axis and the quantity of funds supplied on the horizontal axis. This appears in Figure 12A–5.

In Figure 12A–1, at point a the individual supplies no funds when interest rates are zero. This point is reflected in point a' in Figure 12A–5. From Figure 12A–2 we find the lender willing to move to point b, this is reflected as point b' in Figure 12A–5, which shows a positive amount of saving at a positive interest rate of 20 percent. (In this frame of reference we are making the simplified assumption that saving is the only source of supply of loanable funds.)

The supply curve as shown *may* bend backward to the left at high rates of interest, indicating that the volume of saving *may* fall rather than increase if interest rates reach very high levels. This, of course, is an "individual" supply curve. The aggregate market supply of savings curve would be derived simply by adding together the amounts that would be supplied at various rates of interest by all of the individuals in the economy.

The demand for loanable funds on the part of borrowers can also be derived in a similar way to that used to derive the supply curve. However, the demand for loanable funds is affected not only by the desire for different individuals to even out their income streams, but also, and more importantly, the demand for loanable funds arises because there exist real investment opportunities that provide a yield in the form of increases in income in the future.

Assume, for example, that the individual whose time-preference curves we are studying believes that by purchasing a $10 machine with a life of one year he can earn 100 percent return. That is, in a year's time he will realize an addition to his profit of $10, and beyond the $10 he pays in costs for the machine. The machine earns $20 so that at the end of the year the individual receives back his $10 principal on his investment and an additional $10 in "real" interest. This "real" interest rate is often called the "internal" rate of return. Now assume that a second machine, when employed along with the first, will yield a return of 50 percent. Finally, let a third machine yield a return of 20 percent. Thus, on the individual's two-period diagram, note the line from the X origin sloping up to the left in Figure 12A–6. The lower part of the curve shows the 100 percent rate on the first $10 machine, then the next segment of the curve shows the 50 percent return on the second $10 machine, and so forth.

The curve in Figure 12A–6 is called an investment-opportunity (IO) curve. Assume that the curve is smooth for simplicity, and superimpose it on the individual's map of indifference curves as in Figure 12A–7.

In the absence of investment opportunities this individual could move along the line from X to point a and reach a higher indifference curve than he would be on at point X. He could do this by saving part of his income and lending it at the interest rate of 20 percent. This line represents a set of possible options open to him for dividing his income among the two periods. With the IO curve he now expands his opportunities. He can move along the IO

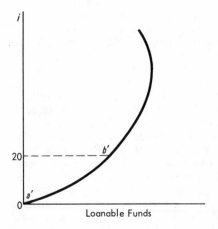

FIGURE 12A–5

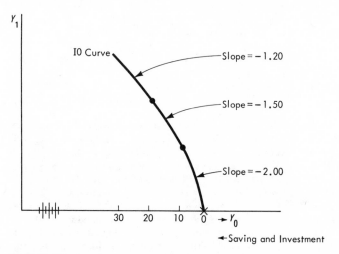

FIGURE 12A–6

curve to point b and reach a higher indifference curve because the investments will give him some income in period 1. But, if the market rate of interest is still 20 percent he may invest in the three machines a total of $30, but
then borrow $20 at the going interest rate of 20 percent and move down
along the new straight line to reach point c, a point on the highest indifference curve to him. Thus, he may invest (save) and borrow at the same time
to raise his current consumption above what it would be at point b. Most
individuals both invest and borrow simultaneously. The individual could, for
example, put up $10 of his own money and borrow the other $20 in order
to make the $30 investment. This is essentially what homeowners do with
their "down payments."

With investment opportunities, the possibility of increasing future income arises. Economic growth, in the sense of raising the income and consumption levels of the people, follows from investment. From the diagram
it is clear that lower interest rates lead to higher rates of investment spending
and to higher income next period. Of course, new technology leads to investment opportunity and is undoubtedly the root source of economic growth.
But investment made feasible by low interest rates is the proximate source
of higher living standards.

Thus, the neoclassical economic description of the savings-investment
process rests upon certain assumptions: (1) that people have time preferences
from which appropriate indifference curves may be derived; (2) that there
exists a technology such that investment will provide a positive return—that
is, a higher real income in the future than would be possible without it; (c)
that a competitive, free market exists where borrowers and lenders can meet;
and (d) that competitive forces will drive the rate of exchange between present and future income (the interest rate) to an equilibrium position where
$-(1 + i)$ equals the Marginal Rate of Time Preference for each individual
and also equals the Marginal Rate of Return on all the current investment
opportunities. At this equilibrium the market clears. The analysis turns on
the concepts of "thrift" and "productivity."

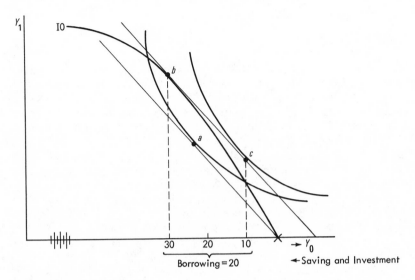

FIGURE 12A–7

QUESTIONS FOR DISCUSSION

1. Using the approximate method described in the text, estimate the yield to maturity if an investor pays $900 for a $1000 bond that pays 6 percent interest and matures in ten years. Now assume he pays $1200 for the same bond and estimate the yield to maturity.

2. The "roundaboutness" of production processes lead to efficiency in production. Imagine you wanted to make a single pair of eye glasses and speculate on how much roundaboutness you would have to engage in.

3. In what sense is the interest rate a "price"?

4. Draw a money demand curve like that in Figure 12–1 and draw two money supply schedules showing an increase in the money supply. Interpret the market process by which the increase in the money supply leads to a fall in interest rates.

5. List the principal components of the supply of loanable funds and of the demand for loanable funds.

6. Explain why the supply and demand curves are not independent of one another.

7. What is the relation between the nominal interest rate and the expected rate of inflation?

8. What are some of the difficulties with the "expected rate of inflation" theory?

9. From the Appendix, draw a time preference function showing Mr. *A* as a borrower. Note how the current market interest rate he faces is shown in the diagram. Would he borrow more or less if the interest rate were higher?

10. Redraw Figure 12A–7 for yourself and explain how most of us are *both* borrowers and lenders and why.

SELECTED REFERENCES

Most macroeconomic texts contain a thorough treatment of the theory of interest-rate determination at an elementary or intermediate level. In addition, most of the texts cited at the end of Chapter 1 provide coverage.

At a more advanced level of analysis is the discussion of interest-rate theory by the late Joseph W. Conard, *Introduction to the Theory of Interest* (Berkeley, Calif.: University of California Press, 1959).

The classic work of Irving Fisher, first published in 1930, still merits the attention of student and scholar alike. Fisher's *Theory of Interest* was reprinted by Augustus M. Kelley, New York, in 1955 and 1961.

A clear characterization and comparison of the classical, loanable funds, and Keynesian liquidity preference theories of interest is found in Alvin H. Hansen, *A Guide to Keynes* (New York: McGraw-Hill, 1953), Chapter 7.

For a concise discussion of various factors (including expectations) affecting the level of interest rates, see articles by Robert Eisner, W. E. Gibson, Thomas J. Sargent, and W. P. Yohe and D. S. Karnosky, in W. E. Gibson and George G. Kaufman, eds., *Monetary Economics: Readings on Current Issues* (New York: McGraw-Hill, 1971), Part IV. Also see W. E. Gibson, "Interest Rates and Inflationary Expectations," *American Economic Review*, December 1972, pp. 854–65, in which the author uses forecasts of price level changes collected by Joseph Livingston, a financial columnist, as a measure of expected rates of inflation, to help explain variations in nominal interest rates.

A clear, brief discussion of the role of expectations of inflation in determining nominal interest rates, and the controversy concerning this role, is found in Stephen F. LeRoy, "Interest Rates and the Inflation Premium," *Monthly Review*, Federal Reserve Bank of Kansas City, May 1973, pp. 11–18.

13

Rate Differentials: the Term Structure of Interest Rates

In earlier chapters we frequently referred to "the" interest rate or the "level" of interest rates as if there were only one rate or only one representative average of rates. It is now time to examine some important factors giving rise to interest rate differentials. These stem from the fact that there are many rates of interest reflecting the myriad types of loans and securities in financial markets. In this chapter we relate differences in yield to maturity on securities to differences in the length of time to maturity. We hold other factors constant by assuming that in all other respects the securities are homogeneous; they are alike with respect to credit risk, tax status, call provisions, and so on.

THE YIELD CURVE

We begin describing the term structure of interest rates by constructing a so-called yield curve. We first select a certain class of securities—for example, United States Treasury securities. These are presumed to be default-free, the risk of default at maturity being negligible. We may also exclude United States Treasury issues that have special tax provisions attached. Thus, we have a set of securities that is as homogeneous as we can find. We observe *on a particular day* (1) the yield to maturity, and (2) the length of time to maturity of these securities.

By measuring yield to maturity on the vertical axis and time to maturity on the horizontal axis, a set of points can be plotted as in Figure 13–1. The points shown are hypothetical, for illustrative purposes only. Each *x* represents a particular Treasury security, with the time until its maturity indicated on the horizontal axis and its yield to maturity (or to earliest call data if it is selling at a price above par) indicated on the vertical axes. The curve is drawn as of a specific date, say January 31, 1974. The shape of the curve may be slightly different on successive days.

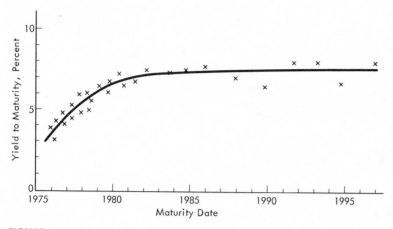

FIGURE 13–1

Most yield curves are drawn on the basis of data on United States Treasury obligations because these obligations are more homogeneous than, say, corporate securities or municipals (obligations of state and local government units), and the data are more readily available. Other yield curves are occasionally plotted by analysts especially interested in a particular market, although it is recognized that because these securities are less homogeneous than government securities, factors other than term to maturity probably affect the yield curves. For example, the *1973 Annual Review of the Bond Market,* by Salomon Brothers, includes yield curves for Federal agency, corporate, and municipal securities.

The Observed Behavior of the Term Structure

At various points in time yield curves have different shapes. In January the yield curve might assume its usual upward slope as in Figure 13–1. A month later, the curve could be nearly horizontal (termed a "flat" curve). Six months later it could be downward sloping instead of positively sloped. The purpose of developing a theory of the term structure of interest rates is to explain the shape of the yield curve and outline the reasons for changes in the shape over time. Figure 13–2 shows a set of four yield curves.

These four curves illustrate some of the variety of patterns that have occurred at various points in time. The yield curve for June 28, 1972, is somewhat more "typical" than the others. In recent decades short-term rates have frequently been lower than long-term rates. Humped curves, such as that for March 28, 1973, with peaks in the short-term maturity range are found fairly often but less frequently than those with a positive slope in the short-term and intermediate-term maturities. The upsloping curves prevail mostly during periods of moderate economic growth and periods of recession. Flat and downward sloping curves, perhaps with humps, are usually observed during periods of vigorous economic expansion and near peaks of business activity.

A comparison of yield curves suggests that as interest rates in general fluctuate up and down, short-term rates rise and fall relative to longer-term rates. Treasury bill rates, for example, fluctuate with greater amplitude than do bond yields. On the other hand, prices of long-term bonds are far more volatile than prices of short-term issues, *given the same percentage change in the yield*, and other things equal. This is a result of the mathematics of interest rates and security prices. Consider an example of a $1,000 consol and a $1,000 one-year security, each having a coupon rate of 5 percent and an initial market prices equal to par value. Assume that the market yield on each rises from 5 to 6 percent, at 20 percent increase. The price of the consol declines from $1,000 to $833.33 ($PV = R/i$, or $833.33 = $50/.06$). The price of the one-year security declines from $1,000 to $990.55 $\left(PV = \dfrac{R + F}{(1 + .06)} \right.$, or $990.55 = \dfrac{\$1,050}{1 + .06} \Big)$. Clearly, the consol's price declines far more than that of the one-year security. If yields were to *fall* instead of rise, say from 5 percent to 4 percent, the consol's price would rise by a greater percentage than that for the short-term security.

Alternatively, if the price of the consol fell by a given amount, say $100 (from $1,000 to $900), there would be only a slight increase in yield to maturity. A $100 decline in the price of a one-year security would imply a very large increase in its yield.

Time to maturity is, therefore, a major factor affecting the volatility of a

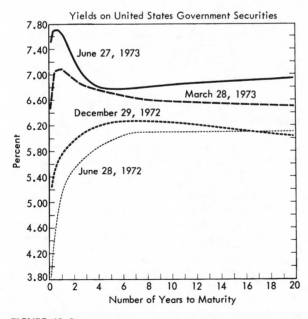

FIGURE 13–2

SOURCE: Federal Reserve Bank of New York, *Monthly Review*, July 1973, p. 167.

security's price. In general, volatility increases with maturity, although the incremental increases in volatility accompanying the lengthening of time to maturity by one more year become less and less as maturity lengthens.

The volatility of the price of a bond is also affected by the coupon rate. The lower the coupon rate, the greater the price volatility. In the formula

$$PV = \frac{R}{1 + i} + \frac{R}{(1 + i)^2} + \cdots$$

the Rs in the numerator affect the response of PV to a percentage change in i. The smaller the Rs, the greater the change in PV.[1]

Business Fluctuations and the Term Structure

During periods of economic expansion, interest rates generally rise and yield curves typically change from upsloping curves to flat curves; late in an expansion, the curve tends to become downward sloping or humped. An example of this upward shift in yield curves and the accompanying change in the form of the curves is illustrated in the yield curves shown in Figure 13–2, for the period of business expansion from June 1972 to June 1973. More generally, as market rates fluctuate over time, yield curves tend to oscillate in a range between a top and a bottom curve, as shown in Figure 13–3.

The range indicated in that figure as the "normal" range is the range within which the representative long-term rate usually fluctuates during the period under observation. This range may, of course, change with long-run trends in the underlying factors determining interest rates. During the Depression of the 1930s and during World War II, interest rates were much lower than in subsequent decades. Thus what is considered "normal" today is different from "normal" in those earlier years and perhaps from levels that will prevail in the future.[2]

Either or both theories of the term structure discussed in the following section may be used to explain the observable behavior of the yield curve—

[1] For a detailed description of the relation between yields and prices, see: Burton G. Malkiel, *The Term Structure of Interest Rates* (Princeton, N.J.: Princeton University Press, 1966), pp. 54–56; also see a discussion of Malkiel's theorems in Paul F. Smith, *Economics of Financial Institutions and Markets* (Homewood, Ill.: Richard D. Irwin, Inc., 1971), pp. 173–75; and Michael H. Hopewell and George G. Kaufman, "Bond Price Volatility and Term to Maturity: A Generalized Respecification," unpublished (Univ. of Oregon, 1972).

[2] This empirical description of yield curves should not be confused with the theory discussed below in the section on expected changes in long-term rates. The theory is based on the proposition that market participants have a general idea of what constitutes a "normal" level of long-term rates, so that if rates are significantly above that level, investors expect them to fall, while if they are significantly below that level, investors expect them to rise. Theories incorporating this hypothesis are found in Frank DeLeeuw, "A Model of Financial Behavior," in J. Duesenberry, G. Fromm, L. Klein, and E. Kuh, eds. *Brookings Quarterly Econometric Model of the United States Economy* (Chicago: Rand McNally & Co., 1965), and in Franco Modigliani and Richard Sutch's article, cited in footnote 3, this chapter.

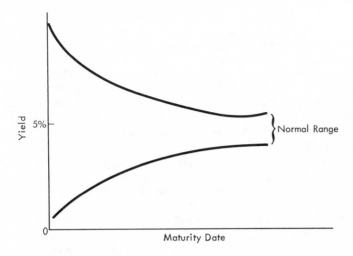

FIGURE 13–3

that is, to explain why (1) the short rate varies with greater amplitude than the long rate (this is not merely a matter of mathematics); (2) why sometimes the yield curve has humps; and (3) why there is a tendency for upward-sloping curves to rise rather steeply, whereas downward-sloping curves typically fall with a bit more gentle slope.

THE THEORY OF THE TERM
STRUCTURE OF INTEREST RATES

We have chosen to focus our discussion on two major theoretical approaches used to explain the term structure of interest rates: we refer to these as the "segmented markets" approach and the "expectations" approach. Sometimes economists attempt to synthesize various elements of the two approaches, but it is useful at the outset to dichotomize them in order to examine their differing characteristics. Occasionally a third approach, the "liquidity premium" approach, is mentioned, but it is most frequently viewed not so much as a separate approach but more as an addendum to either the expectations approach or the segmented markets approach.[3]

[3]There are several different views on this topic. For example, L. G. Telser, "A Critique of Some Recent Empirical Research on the Explanation of the Term Structure of Interest Rates," *Journal of Political Economy*, Supplement, August 1967, pp. 546–61, discussed the expectations theory and the liquidity-preference theory as alternatives and did not even mention the segmentation theory. Franco Modigliani and Richard Sutch, "Debt Management and the Term Structure of Interest Rates: An Empirical Analysis of Recent Experience," *Journal of Political Economy*, Supplement, August 1967, pp. 569–89, described their "preferred habitat" theory as "an adaptation of the expectational theory," while Reuben A. Kessel ("Comment," in the same journal issue, p. 592) regarded it as "another name for what the late Professor Conard referred to as market segmentation."

The Segmented Markets Approach

ʻUnder the segmented markets approach, the approach almost universally used by financial analysts, securities in different maturity ranges are considered to be imperfect substitutes. An increase in the supply of securities in one maturity range will lead to a decline in prices (rise in yields) of those securities. An increase in demand will lead to an increase in their prices. That is, we simply apply the usual supply and demand analysis we use in discussing determination of prices of commodities. Of course, "segmented" does not mean totally separate or independent. Indeed, all analysts recognize that the various markets for securities of different types may be highly interdependent. Three-month bills are very good substitutes for six-month bills, and six-month bills are good substitutes for nine-month bills. But three-month bills are seldom good substitutes for twenty-year bonds. Thus, the more distant different securities are from each other in the maturity range, the less substitutable they are for each other.

There is a tendency for firms to match the maturity of their assets with the maturity of their liabilities. Commercial banks have short-term liabilities; hence for liquidity purposes, they hold large amounts of short-term assets. Insurance companies, on the other hand, have liabilities that extend into the distant future and they hold large amounts of long-term securities in order to be sure the revenues they need will be available when the time arrives. Businesses with large inventories borrow short term to finance them, perhaps by pledging accounts receivable against commercial bank loans. Manufacturing firms constructing plants with an expected life of twenty years will sell twenty-year bonds to finance the construction. This tendency to match assets with liabilities is tantamount to "hedging" on a bet to avoid the risk of a sizable loss.

If a lender purchases a short-term security, the price of it will not change greatly while he holds it; that is, there is little risk of being forced to assume a capital loss in case he might wish to sell the security prior to maturity. Thus, short-term securities minimize the risk of capital loss. However, a lender who purchases a long-term security has greater certainty of a steady income flow over the extended period than does the one who makes repeated purchases of short-term securities over the years. Thus, long-term securities minimize the possibility of income variation. Persons wishing to avoid capital loss will buy short-term securities, and those wishing to avoid income variation will buy long-term securities.

Furthermore, short-term securities are more "liquid" than long-term securities. They are "closer" to money because they are (1) more readily marketable and (2) subject to less price variation because they are closer to maturity. Hence, it is generally assumed that lenders will be willing to pay a premium price for short-term over long-term securities, thereby pushing the yield on short-terms below those on long-terms. This *"liquidity premium" exists because lenders have a positive preference for liquidity, other things being equal.*[4]

_____

[4]The pervasive existence of a liquidity premium on short-term securities implies that the yield curve should generally be positively sloped—but this is not to suggest

Besides these institutional preferences for certain maturity ranges because of liquidity and risk preferences, there also exist certain legal restrictions that make securities of different maturities poor substitutes for each other. In some states, state-chartered commercial banks are allowed to count certain short-term securities as part of their legally required reserves, but long-term securities are not eligible for this purpose. A variety of other legal restrictions affect the demand for securities on the part of savings banks, insurance companies, and the managements of pension funds.

To summarize, the segmented markets approach treats securities of different maturities as related, but with unique characteristics. Short-term securities have liquidity and provide certainty of capital value, even for very short periods. Long-term securities have certainty of income flow. Legal restraints on investment activity also affect demand in the various maturity ranges. Therefore, different buyers have preferences for different maturities so that yields respond to changes in conditions of supply and demand in the different maturity ranges.

The Pure Expectations Approach

In this approach to the explanation of the term structure, expectations alone determine the structure of yields. Expectations concerning future interest rates determine the demand for securities, which in turn determines their yields, but relative supplies of securities do not affect their yields.

Assumptions and Inferences

The pure expectations theory of the term structure is based upon a number of simplifying assumptions:

1. that a large enough number of financial investors (or a smaller number who are well financed) hold uniform expectations about future values of short-term interest rates;
2. that no transactions costs exist, so that investors may enter and leave the market frequently without cost;
3. that no market imperfections inhibit interest rates from moving to their competitive level; and
4. that investors wish to maximize their holding period yield—that is, they wish to obtain the maximum income (profit) available over a given period of time.

In a world where these assumptions hold, the long-term rate will equal the average of short-term rates expected to prevail over the long-term period. To maximize holding-period yield, an investor may either invest in, say, a two-year security, or in two one-year securities, reinvesting at the end of each year. If a two-year security gives a higher return at the end of the two years

---

that negatively sloped curves would never appear, and indeed they do appear from time to time. For empirical evidence of the liquidity premium, see Kessel's monograph, cited in footnote 10 in this chapter.

than the same amount invested in two successive one-year securities, then the investor will, to maximize his income, purchase the two-year security. But, if the higher income will result from two successive one-year investments, then this is the course of investment he will follow to maximize his return over the two-year investment period.

For example, if he can purchase a current one-year security for a 3 percent return, and then a second one-year security for a 5 percent return, over the two years he will earn approximately 4 percent (the two-year average of 3 percent and 5 percent).

If R_1 is the current market rate of interest on a one-year security, and R_2 is the current market rate on a two-year security, and r_1 is the market rate on a one-year security that is expected to prevail one year from today, then in our example, $R_1 = 3$ percent, $r_1 = 5$ percent and

$$R_2 = \frac{(R_1 + r_1)}{2} = \frac{(3 + 5)}{2} = 4\%$$

This is the same as

$$(1 + R_2) = \frac{(1 + R_1) + (1 + r_1)}{2}$$

or

$$1.04 = \frac{(1.03) + (1.05)}{2}$$

In this example we have simply taken the arithmetic mean of the two short-term rates to find the long-term rate. However, the geometric mean is perhaps the more correct one to use, thus

$$R_2 \approx (R_1 \cdot r_1)^{\frac{1}{2}}$$

The exponent $\frac{1}{2}$ means we take the square root of the product of the two rates; or,

$$(1 + R_2) = [(1 + R_1)(1 + r_1)]^{\frac{1}{2}}$$

which is the more exact method of expression.

Thus, from these formulae it is clear that if a two-year bond is selling at a price to yield greater than 4 percent, the lender will choose it. But if the two-year security is selling to yield less than 4 percent, he will choose to invest in the current one-year security and reinvest at the end of the year in another one-year security to obtain a 4 percent yield over the two years.

The crucial element in the decision about which investment route to follow is the value of the one-year rate that investors *expect* to exist one year from today. If they hold this expectation with certainty (whether they prove to be right in the future or not), they will invest in a way that will bring the maturity pattern of rates into line with the expectations.

The slope of the yield curve would reflect these expectations. Consider, for example, the downward-sloping yield curve of Figure 13–3. If investors expected short-term rates to fall in the future—below the current level of long-term rates—then the combination of high yields on one-period securities today and low yields on one-period securities in the future will give a return equal to that of the current long-term security.[5]

Similarly, consider an upward-sloping yield curve. This will exist, according to the pure expectation theory, if investors expect future one-period rates to be above the current long-term rate.

Explaining Humped Yield Curves

The pure expectations approach is somewhat more cumbersome when it is used to explain the humped yield curve. If investors expect future short-term rates to rise *temporarily*, but to fall in a subsequent period, then a hump might arise in the yield curve. Thus, expectations of both rising and falling short-term yields must exist simultaneously in order to explain the hump. Even more complex sets of expectations could, according to the theory, give rise to yield curves with multiple humps—but such curves seldom if ever appear.

Formal Statement of the Theory

In order to generalize and formalize the theory it is necessary to introduce additional notation to set the time dimension of investment. We attach prescripts t, $t + 1$, $t + 2$, and so on to the variables R and r to indicate *dates* on which the variables are observed or are expected to be observed. Let $_tR_1$, $_tR_2$, . . . , and so on, represent the current yields on securities of 1, 2, . . . , periods to maturity existing at a moment in time, t, and let $_{t+1}r_{1,t}$, $_{t+1}r_{2,t}$, . . . , represent the yields on securities of 1, 2, . . . , periods to maturity that are expected to exist at a point in time, $t + 1$. Capital Rs represent *current* rates and the lower case rs represent *forward* rates, the rates expected to prevail in the future at time $t + 1$. The prescript to the R tells us what point in time we are observing current rates, the subscript tells the length of time to maturity of the security being observed. Because r represents forward rates, the prescript indicates the future date on which we expect to observe (estimate) the forward rate; the subscript, as in the case of R, represents the length of time to maturity. Thus, if $t =$ January 1, 1975, and the rate on one-year bills on that date is 5 percent, then $_tR_1 = 5$ percent or 0.05, and if on this same date, t, the

---

[5]There is a limit to the steepness of the negative slope of the curve, which is set by the opportunity for pure arbitrage. Assume, for example, that the one-year rate is 4 percent and the two-year rate is only 2 percent. Then one could borrow $1 million at 2 percent and invest it at 4 percent and at the end of one year he could have sufficient funds to repay at the end of two years—keeping as profit whatever he could earn from investing the $1 million for the second year.

forward rate, which is the rate that will exist on the future date $t + 1$ (or January 1, 1976), on a one-year security is 6 percent, then $_{t+1}r_{1,t} = 0.06$.[6]

This notation is complex, but becomes less confusing as we interpret the formula. Making the simplifying assumption that all coupon payments are accumulated and paid out upon maturity, then

$$(1 + {}_tR_2) = [(1 + {}_tR_1)(1 + {}_{t+1}r_1)]^{1/2}$$

This formula says that the yield on a two-year security will equal the geometric mean of the current (spot) rate on a one-year security and the forward one-year rate. As in our earlier example, if the spot one-year rate is 3 percent ($_tR_1 = .03$) and the one-year-forward one-year rate is 5 percent ($_{t+1}r_1 = .05$) then the spot *two*-year rate may be found from $\sqrt{(1.03)(1.05)}$ $= 1.039+$, or $_tR_2 = $ approximately 0.039.

As an investor, one has two choices: (1) he may purchase a two-year bond that yields 3.9 percent; alternatively (2), he may purchase a one-year bond that yields 3 percent and reinvest the proceeds at the end of one year at the forward rate of 5 percent so as to obtain an overall yield of 3.9 percent. Thus, if one plans to hold bonds for a period of two years (the holding period) and if he wishes to maximize his holding-period yield, then either course of action will give the same yield. If the current long-term rate happened to be above 3.9 percent, he would buy the long-term securities, and other investors would also buy them until the prices rose and the yield fell into line with the 3.9 percent. That is, anytime the rates in question were out of line with the formula, investors with sufficiently large sums to invest would bid for securities in a way that would return them to balance.

The examples we have provided thus far have used rates for only two periods, today's rates and rates expected to prevail one year from today. The formula can easily be extended several periods into the future. An investor may consider purchasing a ten-year bond at today's current yield, $_tR_{10}$, or a one-year security with current yield $_tR_1$, knowing the expected one-year yields for each of the following nine years, $_{t+1}r_1, _{t+2}r_1, \ldots _{t+9}r_1$. On the basis of these actual and expected values, an investor may choose either to buy the ten-year security or to make ten successive annual investments in one-year securities.

The relevant formula, for N periods into the future, is:

$$(1 + {}_tR_N) = [(1 + {}_tR_1)(1 + {}_{t+1}r_1)(1 + {}_{t+2}r_1) \ldots (1 + {}_{t+N-1}r_1)]^{1/N}$$

Thus, the current or spot yield on a bond of N years to maturity is equal to the Nth root of the product of the current one-year rate and all of the remaining forward-one-year rates (the geometric mean).

But an investor need not choose only between a ten-year bond and ten one-year securities; his range of choice is much wider. He may choose to buy

[6]The notation follows that suggested by David Meiselman, *The Term Structure of Interest Rates* (Englewood Cliffs, N.J.: Prentice-Hall, 1962).

a nine-year bond, hold it until maturity, and then buy a one-year security to complete a ten-year holding period. Or, he may purchase five successive two-year securities, or two successive five-year securities, or any of a variety of patterns. The general formula fits all patterns he may consider. For example, the yield on a ten-year security, $_tR_{10}$, is equal to the geometric average of the current yield on a nine-year security, $_tR_9$, and the yield expected to prevail on a one year security purchased nine years from today, $_{t+9}r_1$. This formula may be written in general terms by substituting $(1 + _tR_{N-1})$ for the first $_{N-1}$ terms within the brackets in the above equation so that the formula becomes

$$(1 + _tR_N) = [(1 + _tR_{N-1})^{N-1} (1 + _{t+N-1}r_1)]^{1/N}$$

If $N = 10$, this formula reads as follows: the current ten-year bond yield will equal the geometric mean of the current nine-year bond yield carried to the ninth power and the forward-one-year rate expected to prevail nine years from today.

Thus, according to pure expectations theory, today's long-term rate is determined by the geometric mean of the successive forward one-period rates, and one may purchase ten successive one-period securities or a nine-period security and a one-period security, or any combination of maturities for a ten-year period and realize the same earned income over the entire period. Indeed, the formula is constructed so that an investor wishing to hold a security for, say, two periods can purchase a ten-year bond and sell it at the end of the second period and realize the same holding-period yield as he would if he purchased a two-year security at the outset. Any combination of purchases is satisfactory if the equation holds true, and if it does not hold true, investors purchase securities in a manner so as to shift the current structure of yields into line with their expectations about future one-period yields.

Another view of the theory is gained by turning the formula around. By transformation of terms, place the forward yield on the left-hand side of the equation. For an example, return to our two-period equation:

$$(1 + _tR_2) = [(1 + _tR_1) (1 + _{t+1}r_1)]^2$$

square both sides to get

$$(1 + _tR_2)^2 = (1 + _tR_1) (1 + _{t+1}r_1)$$

divide by $(1 + _tR_1)$

$$\frac{(1 + _tR_2)^2}{(1 + _tR_1)} = 1 + _{t+1}r_1$$

or

$$_{t+1}r_1 = \frac{(1 + _tR_2)^2}{(1 + _tR_1)} - 1$$

In general notation for N periods, the formula becomes:

$$_{t + N - 1}r_1 = \frac{(1 + {}_tR_N)^N}{(1 + {}_tR_{N - 1})^{N - 1}} - 1$$

On the right-hand side, we have only the current interest rates that we observe in today's market place. By using these we can "estimate" the forward rate— that is, currently observable rates *imply* what the forward rate is expected to be.[7]

In this form the theory utilizes the currently observable yield structure to explain what current expectations of forward rates are; the theory does *not* use expected forward rates to explain the current level of the long-term rate, as appeared to be the case in the early formula. Thus, we set out to explain the term structure, and the expectations approach was to be one form of explanation; but in this form we find that we are explaining expectations rather than the term structure—the cart before the horse.[8] This is clearly not the proper form in which to couch the theory.

To recapitulate, remember that we assumed: (1) a world of no transactions costs, so that we can transfer into or out of a security at anytime cost-free; (2) that the securities we are looking at are all default-free and have no other characteristics that would lead one to differentiate among them, except time to maturity; (3) that there exists a sufficiently large number of well-financed investors who form uniform expectations (forecasts) about future (forward) one-year rates; and (4) that these investors are profit maximizers and seek to maximize their holding-period yields. Then from the formulas above, expectations on the part of these investors (along with the current one-period rate) will determine the current rates of interest on securities of 2, 3, 4, . . . , and so on, periods to maturity. If investor expectations are given and the current one-period rate is given, the *entire* yield curve is then explained by investor expectations. Note that nothing in this theory concerns the supply of securities unless the supply forthcoming should be so large that our well-financed investors would not have sufficient financial clout in the market to move the rates into line with their expectations. Thus, the relative supplies of securities in the various ranges of the maturity spectrum have no influence on the term structure, and we say that the expectations theory is a theory of the demand for securities because changes in supply exert no influence.

Liquidity Premium

The "liquidity premium" adjustment can be attached to the pure expectations approach. By recognizing a general preference for "liquidity," the de-

---

[7]In this form the equation can easily become a tautology; *r* is the forward rate people must expect if the current term structure gives us the *R*s.

[8]For example, see James C. Van Horne, *Function and Analysis of Capital Market Rates* (Englewood Cliffs, N.J.: Prentice-Hall, 1970), especially Chapter 4. He writes: "The unbiased expectations theory states that expectations of the future course of interest rates are the sole determinant [of the yield curve]. When the yield curve is upward sloping, this theory implies that market participants expect interest rates to rise in the future; a downward sloping curve implies that interest rates are expected to fall. . . . ," p. 97.

mand for securities based on expectations alone can be supplemented by an additional demand for the shorter-term maturities because of their greater liquidity. This liquidity premium suggests that lenders will bid more strongly for short-term securities, driving their price up and their yield down; thus, positively sloped yield curves should be more prevalent than negatively sloped yield curves—which fits the casual observation of yield curves. Throughout history yield curves have been more often positively sloped than they have been negatively sloped. Under the expectations approach, one supposes that roughly half the time investors expect future short-term rates to rise, and half the time they would expect future short-term rates to fall. Thus, roughly half the time the yield curve would be positively sloped and half the time negatively sloped. Because yield curves are positively sloped more frequently than they are negatively sloped, adding the "liquidity premium" to account for this improves the explanatory power of the theory.[9]

Reuben A. Kessel studied both the evidence and theory of the term structure, and found that addition of a liquidity premium to the expectations theory greatly enhanced its explanatory power. He argued that the short-term forward rate should be viewed not merely as an expected rate, but as an expected rate plus a premium for liquidity because short and long maturities are not perfect substitutes for one another. He found that expectations inferred from short-term portions of yield curves were biased upward, in comparison with the actual rates found in yield curves for succeeding periods. If bias were caused merely by error, why shouldn't the error be random—sometimes above and sometimes below actual future yields? Kessel stated, therefore:

> The joining of liquidity preferences to expectations explains the lack of symmetry in the movement of short- and long-term rates over the cycle. It explains why short-term rates do not exceed long-term rates at peaks by as much as they fall below long-term rates at troughs; why yield curves are positively sloped during most of the cycle; and why yield curves, when short-term rates are unusually high, never seem to be negatively sloped throughout their full length, but show humps near the short end.[10]

The yield curves of Figure 13–4 suggest the effects that Kessel refers to in this quotation.[11] Note that the bottom curve refers to the value of the liquid-

[9]Downward-sloping yield curves seemed to prevail during the early 1900s. This would appear at first glance to cast doubt on the liquidity premium hypothesis. However, during this period commercial banks operated under national banking laws that required them to hold certain long-term government securities as reserves against note issues. At the same time, the national debt was falling, and such bonds were being retired from circulation. In a sense, these bonds provided liquidity to banks, and the short supply of them meant higher prices and lower yields. Thus, the yield curve could have been merely reflecting this liquidity factor. See R. H. Scott, "A 'Liquidity' Factor Contributing to Those Downward Sloping Yield Curves, 1900–1916," *Review of Economics and Statistics*, August 1963, pp. 328–29; also see Jean M. Gray, "New Evidence on the Term Structure of Interest Rates, 1884–1900," *Journal of Finance*, Vol. 28, June 1973, pp. 635–46.

[10]Reuben A. Kessel, *The Cyclical Behavior of the Term Structure of Interest Rates*, Occasional Paper 91, National Bureau of Economic Research, New York, 1965, p. 98.

[11]This figure is adapted from Kessel, *Cyclical Behavior of Term Structure*, p. 88.

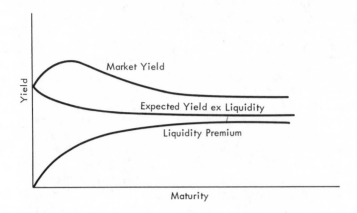

FIGURE 13–4

ity premium that an investor requires if he is to be induced to purchase a security. The middle curve indicates the structure of rates that would prevail, given only investors' expectations about forward yields. The top curve, showing the actual market yield, is the result of the addition of the liquidity premium to the expected yield. In this view, the hump in the curve is explained not by expectations but by a liquidity premium.

The expectations approach to the theory of the term structure has many intuitively pleasing aspects. Academic economists use the theory often, but financial analysts nearly always use the segmented markets approach. One reason why the theorists and practitioners differ so widely is the difficulty in observing "expectations."[12] Unless one can observe expectations so that one can observe changes in expectations from period to period, one can never use *observed* expectations to predict changes in the yield curve. And the purpose of any theory is to provide a framework useful in predicting future events.

In summary, the segmented markets approach regards securities of different maturities as similar in some respects, but sufficiently different that they are not perfect substitutes. Pure expectations theory, on the other hand, regards government securities of different maturities as being almost perfectly homogeneous. Expectations theory is frequently cast in such a form that one infers from yield curves what expectations *must have been*, rather than explaining yield curves by empirically determined expectations. Further analysis of the homogeneity assumption and further attempts to determine expectations empirically and to examine their relationships to subsequent yield changes are both desirable and probable.

[12]Hamburger and Latta compared methods of estimating "expected interest rates." See their article, "The Term Structure of Interest Rates: Some Additional Evidence," *Journal of Money, Credit, and Banking*, February 1969, pp. 71–83, and a reply by Richard Sutch and Franco Modigliani in the same issue, pp. 112–20.

Expected Changes in Long-Term Rates

The "pure" expectations approach is concerned with expectations about future short-term rates, but many observers suggest that expected changes in *long-term* rates have a very significant effect on term structure.

If, for example, interest rates are judged to be "high" by normal (historical) standards, then why should short-term rates be above long-term rates, as the evidence clearly shows they are at some times? The answer of some observers is that: (1) lenders buy long-term securities in the belief that yields will soon fall back to their normal level (prices of long-term securities will rise), and they avoid short-term issues; and (2) borrowers wish to borrow short, so they issue short-term securities rather than long-term securities because they believe long-term yields will soon fall back to their normal range.

If long-term yields are high, borrowers who normally would sell twenty-year bonds will "wait" until the long-term yields return to their normal range. To finance their current programs, however, they are willing to pay high yields on short-term issues, believing that they can "fund" their debt at a later time at lower interest rates. The attitude of lenders reinforces that of borrowers. Hence, the yield curve will be downward sloping because of a large demand for short-term funds and a slack supply and because of a large supply of long-term funds and slack demand.

In a period when interest rates are low by historical standards, the pressures on the yield curve are just the opposite. Lenders believe that interest rates will soon rise (prices of securities will fall), so they avoid buying long-term securities. Instead, they buy short-term securities, and this drives short-term yields down relative to long-term yields. Again, borrowers reinforce this by selling as much long-term debt as they can while yields are believed to be below their "normal" range.

Thus, it is argued that the cyclical pattern of interest rates reflects the normal response of profit-maximizing lenders and borrowers who have experienced the oscillation of yields in the past. In a booming economy, borrowers supply large amounts of short-term securities to the market, but in an economy during a recession they supply more long-term securities. Thus changes in supply and demand occur over a business cycle—changes that lead to the type of oscillation in the yield curve that we regularly observe.

Warren L. Smith expressed many of these considerations succinctly:

> . . . let us consider a situation in which the consensus of expectations on the part of borrowers and lenders is that interest rates are going to rise in the near future . . . lenders would have a tendency to eschew long-term securities, because they would expect to suffer capital losses on investments in such securities when interest rates rose and because they would feel that it was preferable to hold back and wait until prices of longer term securities fell before investing in them. Investors with this kind of expectations would tend to shift their flow of funds toward shorter term loans and securities. . . . Borrowers, on the other hand, would tend to make a reverse shift. To the extent that they felt that interest rates were going to rise, they would feel

that the present was an auspicious time to borrow at long-term in order to take maximum advantage of the existing relatively low rates. As a consequence of the shift of supply from the long- to the short-term market and the shift of demand from the short- to the long-term market, the long-term rate would tend to rise relative to the short-term rate, thus producing an upward-sloping yield curve. Under circumstances in which interest rates were expected to fall, precisely the opposite kinds of shifts would tend to occur. Supply would shift from the short- to the long-term market and demand from the long- to the short-term market, thus producing a rise in the short-term rate relative to the long-term rate and a downward-sloping yield curve.[13]

Warren Smith's explicit introduction of capital gains and losses necessitates some reference to the concept of "holding-period yield." Suppose that the short-term rate is currently 2 percent and is expected to rise to 4 percent in the next period, and to 6 percent in the following period. In the first period, the long-term rate would be approximately 3 percent, if the assumption of perfect substitutability held true. But if perfect substitutability exists, why should anyone accept 2 percent on short-term securities when he can obtain 3 percent on long-term securities? The answer is that if expectations are correct (or are believed to be correct), and the short-term rate does rise to 4 percent and then to 6 percent, the long-term rate will rise to 4 percent in the second period, and *holders* of long-term securities will suffer a capital loss. Their total yield (coupon yield minus capital loss) on a two-year security over a one-year holding period will be approximately the same as that obtained by the holder of one-year securities. The yield over a two-year holding period will be 3 percent coupon rate (or yield to maturity at the time of purchase) minus a capital loss, the amount of which would depend on the term to maturity. If the security were a two-year security, there would be no capital loss over the two-year holding period, but on any longer term security, there would be a capital loss, increasing with the length of maturity of the security. On a ten-year bond, the capital loss would be slightly more than 8 percent. This fact suggests that although securities with only small differences in length of maturity may be close substitutes, there is doubt about the substitutability of securities with great differences in maturity, for any holders who may have to sell before maturity.

Some Empirical Evidence on the Theory of the Term Structure

David Meiselman attempted to shore up the expectations theory by drawing certain implications from the expectations approach and testing these implications.[14] He proposed an "error-learning" model; that is, he suggested that if investors made errors when they forecast the forward-one-year rate they would revise their next forecast of the one-year rate by some proportion

[13]Warren L. Smith, *Debt Management in the United States*, Study Paper 19, materials prepared in connection with the study of employment, growth, and price levels for the Joint Economic Committee, 86th Cong., 2nd Sess., January 28, 1960, p. 82.

[14]Meiselman, *The Term Structure of Interest Rates*.

of the previous error. To test this theory, he ran statistical estimates of the following formula:

$$_{t + N}r_{1,t} - {}_{t + N}r_{1,t-1} = a + b({}_tR_1 - {}_tr_{1, t-1})$$

In this equation we have introduced a second subscript attached to *r*. This subscript designates the date on which the expected forward rate is assumed to have been anticipated. Thus, if today is January 1, 1975, then $t - 1$ is January 1, 1974. If N is 3, then $_{t + N}r_1, {}_{t-1}$ is the rate on a one-year security that, as of January 1, 1974, was expected to prevail on January 1, 1974. The left-hand side of the equation shows the difference between the expected one-year rate, expected to prvail at time $t + N$, and the one-year rate that a year earlier had been expected to prevail at this time $(t + N)$. Thus, the left-hand side of the equation depicts the revision of the forecast of the forward-one-year rate. The right-hand side of the equation shows the difference between the actual one-year rate today and the one-year rate that a year earlier had been expected to prevail today. Thus the right-hand side depicts the error in forecasting the current one-year rate.

All of the lower case *r*s were calculated from the capital *R*s; that is, the *r*s were calculated from the appropriate yield curve of spot rates. Thus, it was assumed that the *r*s were unbiased estimates of *R*s.

Professor Meiselman's equations had good fit to the data, and this was widely heralded as an indirect confirmation of the expectations theory. What was tested, of course, was whether *presumed* expected rates, revised on the basis of errors, could explain changes in the pattern of rates. Because expectations were not observed, the expectations theory was not tested directly.

Others have examined the expectations hypothesis directly by sending questionnaires to market participants. Malkiel and Kane selected a sample of 119 banks, 16 life insurance companies and 65 nonfinancial corporations. They received responses from 57 percent of the firms.[15] They asked for predictions of forward rates, among other questions. Without a detailed examination of their study—which merits the attention of the serious student—we wish to note their conclusions:

> Our various findings each support a single conclusion: that the demands for various maturities of debt are not infinitely elastic at going rates and, therefore, that changes in the relative supplies of different maturities . . . can alter the term structure. That expectations are not uniform but nevertheless influence investors' appraisals of market opportunities suggests that in order to induce investors to hold more of any maturity, it is necessary to accept a rise in the associated rate.[16]

Trudgian and Scott sent questionnaires to government securities dealers

[15]Edward J. Kane and Burton G. Malkiel, "The Term Structure of Interest Rates: An Analysis of a Survey of Interest-Rate Expectations," *Review of Economics and Statistics*, August 1967, pp. 343–55.

[16]Kane and Malkiel, *Review of Economics and Statistics*, August 1967, p. 354.

and asked about the formulation of expectations.[17] Only one of eleven dealers reported the formulation of expectations, but all respondents agreed that supply and demand factors were watched from minute to minute. Because they were concerned with dealers, not investors, their findings may not reflect the expectations of the final holders of securities. On the other hand, dealers are not brokers; that is, they hold blocks of securities for their own accounts. Therefore, they are extremely well-heeled investors, and in deciding to take sizable positions or not, they surely formulate expectations about future short-term yields if anyone does.

The Goldsmith-Nagan newsletter now from time to time reports on the forward rates expected by a group of market participants.[18] Some twenty-four to thirty market leaders whose names are listed are asked to forecast yields on various securities two and five months ahead. The securities are Treasury bills, notes, bonds, AAA utility bonds, federal bonds, Eurodollars, the discount rate, and so forth. An arithmetic average of the individual forecasts is reported. The first responses proved to fit the trend of rates that followed, indicating that forecasters who follow the market carefully can indeed forecast to some degree. Thus, attempts to observe expected forward rates directly will doubtless continue to be made by those who work in the financial markets.

There have been many tests of the impact of changes in supplies of Treasury securities on the level of yields and on the difference between short- and long-term yields. These tests, of course, were designed to see whether supply changes affect yields, as suggested by the segmented markets approach. Because, under the expectations approach, changes in supply are presumed to have no effect, any evidence of some effect would tend to refute the expectations approach and support the segmented markets approach.[19]

The controversy over the theory of the term structure provides an interesting example of a conflict in scientific theory. Practitioners seem to prefer the segmented markets approach; academics often prefer the abstract elegance of the expectations approach. The two approaches lead to divergent policy conclusions: the one suggests that monetary authorities can affect the yield curve by varying the volume of securities in the various maturity ranges; the other

[17]William Trudgian and R. H. Scott, "A Survey of the Maturity Pattern of Yields," *University of Washington Business Review*, Spring 1971, pp. 65–76.

[18]See the Goldsmith-Nagan "Bond and Money Market Letter," Washington, D.C., issues for October 4, 1969, December 27, 1969, and April 11, 1970, for the first three surveys.

[19]For a recent study, see Michael J. Hamburger and William L. Silber, "Debt Management and Interest Rates: A Reexamination of the Evidence," *The Manchester School of Economic and Social Studies*, December 1971, pp. 261–66. Also see Neil Wallace, "The Term Structure of Interest Rates and the Maturity Composition of the Federal Debt," *Journal of Finance*, May 1967, pp. 301–12; Burton G. Malkiel, *The Term Structure of Interest Rates: Expectations and Behavior Patterns* (Princeton, N.J.: Princeton University Press, 1966); R. H. Scott, "An Empirical Look at Debt Management," *1961 Proceedings of the Business and Economic Statistics Section*, American Statistical Association, pp. 130–37; Laurence Jay Mauer, "Commercial Bank Maturity Demand for United States Government Securities and the Determinants of the Term Structure of Interest Rates," *Journal of Financial and Quantitative Analysis*, March 1969, pp. 37–52; and Alex R. H. Weaver, "The Uncertainty of the Expectations Theory of the Term Structure of Interest Rates," *Western Economic Journal*, Spring 1966, pp. 122–34.

suggests that attempts to do so will surely fail. Testing for empirical verification of the two theories is fraught with difficulties—those relating to the selection of variables affecting supply and demand and those relating to the measurement (observation) of elusive expectations. As mentioned in the previous chapter with regard to expected rates of inflation, the use of expectations as a variable may be nonscientific because, if expectations as revealed fail to support the theory, an investigator may be led to reject his sample of expectations rather than to reject the theory itself. Theories with this characteristic are called nonoperational—the assumptions of the theory are such as to make it impossible to refute by empirical methods. Thus, persons who use the expectations hypothesis frequently end up with a rationalization of the current term structure rather than with an explanation. They argue that the currently observable term structure implies what expectations of future short-term yields must be—the very opposite of arguing that expectations determine the current term structure of rates.[20]

What is needed is a theory of the determination of expectations. To say that forward rates determine the yield curve is to beg the question; how are these expectations determined? If they are determined by supply and demand, then we are right back to the segmented markets approach. If they are determined by investors' appraisals of the current level of interest rates in relation to what they believe to be the "normal" or "typical" level of long-term rates, then further empirical study should be undertaken to discover how these beliefs come to be held.

One can understand that this subject is far too broad and deep to treat in detail in a few pages. Yield curves are fascinating to economists. They have important implications for policy, yet the two theoretical approaches used to explain them are conflicting. If any conclusion can be drawn, it is that economists have no completely satisfactory explanation of the yield structure at the present time.

THE THEORY OF THE TERM STRUCTURE AND ECONOMIC POLICY

Economists paid relatively little attention to the term structure of interest rates prior to the 1930s. They were concerned principally with the level of rates and the relation of this level of other economic variables. In recent years, the literature on the term structure has ballooned. This strong attention to a rather narrow, detailed subject grew out of a series of events, perhaps beginning with the writings of Keynes in the 1930s. Keynes did not believe that monetary policy could be very strong medicine to cure a depression, but that long-term

[20]For example, see footnote 8 above. See also "The Changing Structure of Interest Rates," Federal Reserve Bank of St. Louis, *Review*, June 1967, pp. 4–5; in this article, the authors, describing the downward-sloping yield curve of January 1967, state: "Such a relationship is consistent with market expectations of an approaching decline in interest rates. . . ." Consistent with, yes, but does it prove that this is what expectations were? The authors are using the yield curve itself to infer what expectations must have been.

interest rates should be kept low so as to encourage investment spending as much as possible. His principal concern was with long-term interest rates and long-term investment. When World War II began, the entire structure of interest rates was still low in the wake of the Great Depression. The Federal Reserve System "pegged" the market for United States Government securities at the prevailing yields. (In World War I, the Treasury had issued successive issues of securities, each at a slightly higher yield, so the market for securities dried up as everyone began to wait for the next issue. The Treasury did not want to see this situation repeated.) To "peg" the yield curve, the Federal Reserve simply bought any securities not bought by the private sector, at prices that maintained yields at fixed levels. In doing this, large volumes of reserves were added to the assets of commercial banks, and because loans were restricted principally to firms with legal priorities for activities related to war production, the banks' excess reserves were used to purchase government securities.

But the yield curve was positively sloped, with very short-term Treasury bills selling for ⅜ of one percent, and long-term bonds selling for 2½ percent. As the war continued, many portfolio managers recognized that long-term securities were just as "liquid" as short-term securities because of the (unannounced but finally recognizable) Fed purchasing policy. This meant that they did not buy low-yielding short-term securities, and the Federal Reserve's portfolio of short-term issues began to expand by large amounts.

Soon after the war came to an end, the Federal Reserve allowed the short-term rate to rise, but it retained the peg on long-term securities. There was much talk of a post-war recession, which never came about, but the Fed believed that low long-term rates were appropriate in a setting in which the war economy was winding down. After a slight recession in 1948–49, the economy began to boom again, and in June 1950, the Korean War broke out. At this point, Federal Reserve officials decided that a measure of restrictive policy might be desirable, and they discussed with Treasury officials their plan to allow long-term rates to rise. But Treasury officials had enjoyed a ready market for their issues at a very low interest rate. They were reluctant to give up this privileged position. In March 1951, the Treasury and Federal Reserve announced their *Accord*. President Truman had been asked to resolve the controversy, and he finally ruled in favor of the Federal Reserve. Thus, long-term interest rates were freed from the peg and began to rise.

In 1953, an ad hoc subcommittee of the Federal Open Market Committee reported on a study of the government securities market. It recommended that open market operations be confined to the market for Treasury bills, except that trading in long-term securities would take place in order to prevent or subdue any "disorderly conditions" that might develop among long-term issues. The bill market, it was argued, had depth, breadth, and resiliency, and was, therefore, the appropriate market to use to adjust member bank reserve positions. The Federal Open Market Committee adopted a resolution that became known as the "bills-only" policy.

When academic economists learned of this policy, some of them questioned its wisdom, and a considerable debate broke out. If, they argued, lower long-term interest rates were desirable, would bill purchases, adding to bank reserves, lead to lower long-term interest rates? Would they not simply lower bill rates, and only after considerable lag would trading along the maturity spectrum bring down the long-term rates? Would it not be a better policy if long-term rates were attacked directly by Fed purchases in the long-term range of maturities? If so, this would be more consistent with Keynesian theory.

The debate continued for several years. It was not until 1961 that the Fed abandoned the "bills-only" policy to engage in "operation twist." At that time, the economy was operating at less than full employment and it was considered desirable to lower long-term rates if possible, through expansionary monetary policy. But, it was also believed that the United States balance of payments required *higher* short-term interest rates because, if domestic short-term rates fell too far below foreign short-term rates, United States citizens would use dollars to buy foreign money and foreign short-term securities. Thus, the United States would "lose" dollars, adding to our balance of payments difficulties. The Fed wanted (1) to lower long-term rates, but (2) to avoid lowering short-term rates, which would tend to result from buying short-term securities to expand the money supply. Thus, it abandoned the "bills-only" policy and purchased some long-term government securities. In practice, the Fed still operates on a "bills-usually" policy, operating in the long-term market only on special occasions.

Thus, the Fed had pegged the rate structure during the war and was forced to continue the peg long after it was desirable to do so. In reaction, it responded by not only refusing to peg the structure, but also by not trading long-term securities at all. But, if long-term interest rates were important for economic stabilization, should it not operate in the long-term market? What is the relation between the long- and short-term markets?

The segmented markets theory suggested that changing relative supplies of long- and short-term securities outstanding, as might be done by Federal Reserve open market operations or by Treasury debt management, would affect the shape of the yield curve and could help achieve overall economic objectives. The expectations theory of the yield curve, on the other hand, suggests that changes in relative supplies have no perceptible effect on the yield curve and therefore that neither the Treasury nor the Federal Reserve should bother to take any action in an attempt to affect it. The controversy will continue until more convincing evidence in support of one of the two theories is provided.

USES OF YIELD CURVES IN FINANCIAL ANALYSIS

Financial analysts frequently draw a variety of yield curves as they keep track of the movements of interest rates on a daily basis. They observe the yields on individual securities over time, and they also compare yields of similar securities. With the yield curve, they can readily compare the yields of securities that differ in respect to maturity.

The first and most obvious reason to plot yield curves is to find an individual security that has a higher yield than other similar securities. If a single plotted point clearly lies above other points, then the analyst must decide whether it is leading the way to higher yields generally or whether its yield is simply out of line with others and will shortly fall into line again. In either case, the security represents a "good buy" in comparison with other similar outstanding securities.

A second reason to examine yield curves is to find a place in the time-dimension of outstanding securities that looks like a good place to float a new issue. United States Treasury officials look at yield curves, and they observe not only the yields but also the volume of outstanding securities in each maturity range. A combination of volume and yield indicates in which maturity range the market will most likely accept (digest) a new issue. Businessmen with a new issue for the market have the same interest in yield curves.

A third motive for drawing yield curves is to lay the ground for analyzing whether or not it would be profitable to "play the pattern of rates" or "ride the curve." Assume, for example, that short-term rates are low and that the curve rises from left to right, but that it levels off at a point about three years to maturity. If the analyst wishes to invest a sum for about six months and believes the yield curve is going to remain about this same shape for six months, he will buy that security situated at three years, at the corner of the decline. Then he will allow time to pass and "ride" down over the corner, selling his security in six months time. He will have earned more interest than he would have if he had purchased a six-month-to-maturity issue at the outset, *and* he will also have realized a capital gain that comes about when the price of the security rises concomitant with the decline in yield. Thus the chance for higher rates of return is increased if humps in the curve, or corners in the curve, are evident and are expected to remain.

If the yield curve is downward sloping from left to right and expected to remain in that position, then the buyer would want to purchase short-term securities. He would shift to long-term securities only if he expected the yield on long-term securities to fall in the near future. Thus the shape assumed by the yield curve may provide the frame of reference for establishing a strategy for buying the most profitable security.

SUMMARY

This entire chapter was concerned with one principal factor giving rise to interest rate differences—namely, the difference in term to maturity. The chapter began with description of the construction of yield curves and examples of a variety of yield curves and their behavior over time. Yield curves are usually positively sloped; downward sloping curves do occur frequently, usually at or near peaks of business activity.

Two theories can be used to explain (1) greater variability of the short-term rate, (2) humps in the yield curves, and (3) the tendency for upward-sloping curves to be steep and downward-sloping curves to be gentle. These theories are the "pure expectations" approach and the "segmented markets" approach. According to the expectations theory, the long-term interest rate equals the geometric average of the several short-term rates expected to prevail during the period to maturity of the long-term security. According to the segmented markets theory, supply and demand for securities in the various maturity ranges determine yields in various ranges. Although securities are substitutes, they are not perfect substitutes.

Some attempts have been made to test expectations theory by observing stated expectations and interest rate levels which follow. Tests have also been made to determine whether changes in supply affects security yields, but results are not conclusive in either case.

Some possible uses of the yield curve in economic policy and by financial analysts are to determine need for and success of attempts to shift yield curves, to aid in identifying securities with higher yields than those on many similar securities, to find the maturity of a new issue most likely to be "digested" easily by the market, and to analyze whether it is likely to be profitable to "ride the yield curve" in buying and selling securities.

QUESTIONS FOR DISCUSSION

1. Does "segmented markets" means "separated markets"? Explain your answer.

2. Distinguish between risk of capital loss and risk of income variability. On which type of security (long- or short-term) is each type of risk greatest?

3. Define the term "liquidity" as it is used in reference to securities. What is a "liquidity premium"?

4. List the four simplifying assumptions made under the pure expectations theory of the term structure.

5. Under the pure expectations theory, what determines the long-term interest rate? Give a numerical example using a simple average.

6. If long-term yields are thought to be above their normal range, what will be the shape of the yield curve? Why?

7. Briefly discuss some of the difficulties in measuring or observing expectations.

8. What was the Treasury-Federal Reserve *Accord* announced in March 1951?

9. Explain the "bills-only" policy of the Fed and its abandonment in pursuing "operation twist."

10. Explain how it may be profitable to "play the pattern of rates," or "ride the yield curve."

SUGGESTED REFERENCES

For a formal, classic description of the expectations theory with a liquidity premium, see Sir John Hicks, *Value and Capital*, 2nd ed. (Oxford: At the Clarendon Press, 1946), especially Chapter 11.

Burton G. Malkiel's book, cited in footnotes 1 and 19, contains an excellent theory presentation and a broad review of most research efforts devoted to term structure prior to 1966. Another fine description of term structure theory and evidence, tied to macroeconomic theory, is found in Jacob B. Michaelsen's book, *The Term Structure of Interest Rates: Financial Intermediaries and Debt Management* (New York: Intext Educational Publishers, 1973).

A challenge to the formal logic of the expectations approach is found in John H. Wood, "Expectations and the Demand for Bonds," *American Economic Review*, September, 1969, pp. 522–30. Also see comments on Wood's article by Richard Roll, A. Buse, and R. A. Kessel, and Wood's reply, in *American Economic Review*, March 1971, pp. 225–36.

The reader is also referred to studies mentioned in footnotes and bibliographies in those studies.

14

Rate Differentials: Factors Other than Maturity

In Chapter 13 we examined the relationship between yield and term to maturity of debt securities, with emphasis on government securities in order to avoid insofar as possible the influence on yield of other factors than term to maturity. It was assumed that these securities were homogeneous in all other major respects. In this chapter we relax that assumption and consider the influence on yields of other important factors including (1) risk of default, (2) callability, (3) tax status, (4) marketability, and (5) certain other characteristics generally of less importance, such as transaction costs, "seasoning," and so on. We also examine the nature of interest rate differentials on other specialized types of financial assets such as preferred stock and convertible bonds, and on mortgages, business loans, and savings deposits.

OBSERVED DIFFERENCES IN YIELDS

An elementary principle of scientific method that applies in economics as well as in physics and other "hard" sciences is that "no two things differ in but one respect alone." If we observe that yields on two securities differ, we are led by this principle to examine the securities more carefully in order to find other differences that might help explain our original observation. At the end of January 1974, a casual examination of some widely reported long-term interest rates showed the following: 7.41 percent on long-term Treasury issues; 6.50 percent on state and local Baa-rated bonds; 8.36 percent on Aaa-rated corporate bonds; 8.94 percent on Baa-rated corporate bonds; 8.75 percent on new mortgage loans with average maturity of twenty-five years; and so forth. Selected short-term rates at that time were: 8.75 percent on prime commercial paper; 8.75 percent on prime bank acceptances; and 8.22 percent on 3-month Treasury bills.

The difference between the yield on state and local bonds and on Baa-rated corporate bonds, both Baa-rated, was 2.44 percentage points; the difference between prime commercial paper and Treasury bill yields was .53 percentage points (often called 53 basis points). These yield differences tend to vary over time as business activity fluctuates. The sources of these observed differences in yields can be found in certain general attributes of securities, to which we now turn.

RISK

The term "risk" refers, in general, to the chance that the outcome of an action may vary. In purchasing bonds, there are several types of risk, each associated with the chance that the yield actually received may vary from that indicated on the bond. The most important of these is "risk of default." Three other forms of risk that are also important to prospective investors are described briefly, and somewhat more extensive consideration is then given to risk of default.

Types of Risk Other than Default Risk

First, there is the risk associated with inflation. The borrowing contract requires that a debtor repay a loan with certain nominal units of money; but inflation erodes the purchasing power of money, and debtors find that the real value of the repayment is reduced. One of the principal reasons that inflation in even moderate degree is held to be undesirable is that it leads to a redistribution of wealth away from creditors in favor of debtors.[1] This type of risk was discussed in Chapter 12 when we analyzed the effect of inflationary expectations on the nominal interest rate.

Second, a risk of capital loss arises if an investor decides that he must sell his securities before their maturity date arrives. As yields vary, market prices of securities also vary, and sales of securities prior to maturity may result in gain or loss. This type of risk is an important factor in considering the term structure of interest rates, because short-term securities carry less risk of capital loss than long-term securities do (see Chapter 13).

A third risk was also discussed in our analysis of the term structure of interest rates, the risk of variability of income. An investor may wish to realize a steady income flow from his financial investments. If he buys a short-term security rather than a long-term bond, his income may vary over the longer period. To obtain a steady or uniform income stream over twenty years, one might purchase a new 20-year bond with a 5 percent coupon yield even though 5-year bonds were selling at 6 percent yield. His choice of the lower yield is made because he does not wish to risk the possibility that at the end of five

[1] In spite of the importance of the subject, relatively little work has been done to evaluate the harm done by inflation versus the benefits of inflation. For a recent summary, see Edward Foster, *Costs and Benefits of Inflation*, Studies in Monetary Economics, No. 1 (Minneapolis, Minn.: Federal Reserve Bank of Minneapolis, 1972).

years the rate of return on bonds might be only 4 percent, which would mean a 33 percent drop in his income.

These kinds of risk and the relative strength of investors' desires to avoid them affect choices among the variety of types of security.

Risk of Default

To default is to fail to meet the terms of an agreement. To default on a bond is to fail to pay the interest when due or to fail to pay the full amount of the principal at maturity. It does not mean that the creditor receives nothing, although this is sometimes the case. Occasionally, the only loss to the creditor is a delay in receipt of payment. It is clear, therefore, that there are varying degrees of loss in defaults. United States Treasury securities are held to be default-free because the Treasury and the Federal Reserve System have the combined power to create whatever amounts of money are required to pay interest and principal when due. Thus, the difference between the yield on a Treasury security and that on a private security with identical provisions is often used as a measure of risk.

Two agencies in the United States that provide services to investors by examining various securities offered for sale and rating them according to the risk of default are Moody's Investors Service and Standard and Poor's. The highest-grade bonds are rated triple A. Although the risk of default on these securities is presumed to be negligible, they nevertheless carry a higher yield than that prevailing on default-free United States government bonds. The classifications used by the two rating services are described roughly in Table 14–1.

Studies made of the default experience of securities with the various ratings seem to support the conclusion that analysts working for the rating services do have the ability to discriminate among risk elements of different securities.[2]

TABLE 14–1 Investors' Services Rating Classifications

Moody's	General Description	Standard & Poor's
Aaa	Highest quality	AAA
Aa	High quality	AA
A	Upper medium grade	A
Baa	Medium grade	BBB
Ba	Lower medium grade	BB
B	Speculative	B
Caa	Poor standing (may be in default)	CCC-CC
Ca	Often in default	C for income bonds
C	Lowest grade (in default)	DDD-D

[2]W. Braddock Hickman, *Corporate Bond Quality and Investor Experience* (New York: National Bureau of Economic Research, 1958).

Lest the reader misinterpret this statement, we must clarify one important but subtle point. Assume that out of 100 securities, experience shows that only one of them was in default during its life. Then the probability of default is one in a hundred. This does not necessarily mean that a given security in this group has 1/100, or 1 percent, probability of default, because the 100 securities are not completely identical. If we knew the precise probability of default of each of the 100 securities, we could place each in the appropriate risk class, but reality forces us to group securities into heterogeneous classes according to a handful of general characteristics. For an analogy, consider fire insurance on homes. One home in 1,000 in a certain community may suffer fire damage in a given year, and the insurance company may establish your fire insurance premium on the basis of this suggested rate of loss, but a given home, because of the owner's excellent care with respect to fire protection, may be less likely to burn than the typical house in the group. Because it is impossible to reach the ideal situation in which each security would be in an exactly appropriate risk class, the best we can do is to establish broad risk categories. Thus, probability of default applies to a group of securities and not to individual securities within that group, and an analyst must look beyond the general risk class if he wishes to evaluate the merits of a particular security.

The concept of probability allows one to draw useful distinctions between certainty, risk, and uncertainty. If the probability that an event will occur is 1.00, then we say that this event is certain to occur. If we *believe* that this *event* will occur, then we behave as if, in this particular case, we lived in a world of certainty. On the other hand, past experience with classes of events and our knowledge based upon this experience allow us to attach probabilities between zero and one to the frequency of occurrence of an event. Given this probability, we can measure the extent of "risk"; we are uncertain of the precise outcome, but we are reasonably certain of the probability of the outcome. When we do not know the probability that an event will occur, we say we are uncertain of the outcome.[3] Thus, a "risk" situation differs from an "uncertain" situation; in the former the probabilities are known or believed to be of a certain level while in the latter even the probabilities are not known, nor can they be estimated with any degree of confidence.

Investors, aware of the possibility that a borrower may default, presumably estimate subjective probabilities of the possibility that default may occur, in order to judge the riskiness of an investment. These subjective probabilities are presumed to exist in the mind of the investor; they may be based upon highly objective data collected as a result of intensive study of a certain class of investments, or they may be the result of an investor's emotional response to a class of investments. They are called subjective probabilities because there is no way of knowing with precision how they were reached.[4] Undoubtedly

---

[3]Extensive development of these concepts may be found in Frank H. Knight, *Risk, Uncertainty, and Profit* (New York: Houghton Mifflin, 1921).

[4]Just as in the case of "expectations" as a variable in a model, "subjective probabilities" present the researcher with difficult if not impossible measurement problems. There is some question as to whether the concept of a subjective probability is operational, that is, whether it is refutable by experiment.

the rating services contribute to the formation of such subjective probabilities by the very act of rating bonds.

At the same time that the investor is assumed to have arrived at a subjective evaluation of the probability of default (risk), it is also assumed that he has formulated certain preferences concerning income from his investment and risk. It is generally assumed that most investors are "risk-averse;" that is, if faced with two choices of assets with the same expected yield and identical in all other respects, they will choose the one with the lower risk of default.[5] This implies that those borrowers who offer a security with a lower risk of default can also offer a lower yield. Similarly, if they offer a security with a high risk of default, they must offer a high rate of return to induce investors to purchase the security. Investors, then, balance risk against rate of return to fit their preferences and maximize their satisfaction from investments.

To achieve his desired balance between risk and return, an investor almost never places all his eggs in one basket; that is, he almost never invests in only one asset. Instead, he diversifies his portfolio. On the one hand, he may concentrate large proportions of his financial assets in Baa bonds and reach an optimum balance of risk and return; on the other hand, he may keep some funds in a relatively risk-free savings account and invest in a highly speculative stock at the same time and again reach an optimum balance between risk and return. The reason an investor diversifies his portfolio is to reduce the risk of default. To diversify means not only that he buys different securities in a given risk class and different securities in different risk classes, but also that he chooses securities whose returns have a low correlation with each other over time. Some firms prosper during economic booms; others prosper in recessions (producers of recap tires, for example). To diversify, one would not have a portfolio filled only with securities, all of which move up and down with gross national product, even though they may be in different risk classes. Portfolio decision theory is an integral part of all courses in financial management.[6] It is sufficient for our purposes to note the importance of risk in determining relative supplies of funds that flow to various financial markets.

The demand for funds is also affected by risk. The borrower of funds who supplies securities to the market is well aware that the risk on his securities affects the rate of interest that he must be willing to pay. If this rate of interest

---

[5]It is recognized, of course, that some people may receive psychic satisfaction from choosing a risky situation, as gamblers often do. An investor with such preferences would choose the more risky security even though it had the same expected yield as the less risky security.

[6]A large volume of readings in the theory of portfolio choice has developed in recent years. Basic among these are: Harry M. Markowitz, *Portfolio Selection: Efficient Diversification of Investments* (New York: John Wiley and Sons, Inc., 1959); William F. Sharpe, "Capital Asset Prices: A Theory of Market Equilibrium Under Conditions of Risk," *Journal of Finance*, Vol. 19 (September 1964), pp. 425–42; John Lintner, "Security Prices, Risk, and Maximal Gains from Diversification," *Journal of Finance*, Vol. 20 (December 1965), pp. 587–615; and Eugene F. Fama, "Risk, Return and Equilibrium: Some Clarifying Comments," *Journal of Finance*, Vol. 23 (March 1968), pp. 29–40. Some empirical evidence may be found in Robert M. Soldofsky and Roger L. Miller, "Risk-Premium Curves for Different Classes of Long-Term Securities, 1950–66," *Journal of Finance*, Vol. 24 (June 1969), pp. 429–45.

is high, he may decide that the potential return from the project he is considering is insufficient to warrant undertaking it. When a few borrowers at the margin reduce their demands for funds, the rate of interest may fall somewhat. In equilibrium, rates of interest on securities in each risk class are just sufficient to clear the market. Investors supply funds and absorb risks of default, and borrowers demand funds and offer securities with risks such that the rate of return on each class of risky security will just be sufficient to clear the market. Preferences of lenders and borrowers are satisfied at going market yields.

Given the attitudes of the investing public toward absorption of risk and the risks in investment projects that borrowers wish to undertake, the yield on risk assets will rise to an equilibrium position somewhat above the yield on assets that have no risk of default. The difference between these two yields is called the *risk premium*. The larger the risk premium, the larger the flow of funds into risky undertakings, as suppliers of funds shift from less risky assets to more risky assets, to take advantage of the higher return offered. Similarly, the lower the risk premium, the smaller the flow of funds into risky projects. On the demand side, the higher the premium, the less the quantity of funds that will be demanded, and the lower the premium, the larger the quantity of funds that will be demanded.

The results of our analysis can be summarized in the context of supply and demand for funds. In Figure 14–1, the market for default-free securities and the market for risky assets are shown. The solid lines represent the demand and supply for funds and their intersection point depicts the original equilibrium rates of interest at which funds are being traded in the two markets. The difference between R_r, representing the yield on risky funds, and R_d, representing the yield on default-free funds, represents the risk premium $(R_r - R_d)$. Assume, for example, that there occurs an exogenous reduction in risk because, let us say, of a general improvement in the business outlook. This leads to an increase in the supply of funds flowing into the market for risky assets, as shown by the dashed supply curve; there has been a shift in the supply curve, rightward. For simplicity, we ignore possible accompanying shifts in the demand curve. The likely source of this increased supply of funds is found in the market for default-free assets. (The demand-for-funds schedule in this graph is quite steep, indicating that it represents mostly demand for

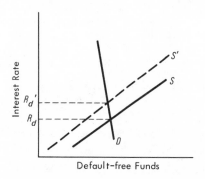

Default-free Funds

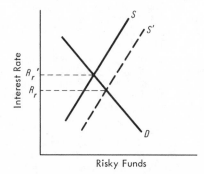

Risky Funds

FIGURE 14–1

United States Treasury securities.) In this market, the supply curve shifts to the left. In this way, shifting supplies of funds flowing to the two markets narrow the risk premium to $(R_r' - R_d')$.[7]

Cyclical Behavior of the Risk Premium

Risk premiums vary over the business cycle, as might be expected; they rise and fall inversely with the level of business activity. As economic conditions improve, yields begin to rise, and risk premiums decline as the difference in yield between default-free and risky securities narrows. But when business activity slows down and interest rates fall, the yields on default-free securities fall relative to those on risky securities, and the premium increases. This, at least, is the general pattern one would expect to prevail because bankruptcy rates are lower in an expansion and higher in a depression. However, the period from 1965 to 1970, generally held to be a period of expansion, witnessed increased premiums for risk. On the one hand, this could be the result of the inability of the Treasury to issue long-term securities because of the 4¼ percent ceiling set by Congress on the rate that could be paid on bonds. This meant that the supply of long-term United States government securities could not be increased and that their yields were also held down because demand for them continued to be relatively strong. The supply of corporate bonds, on the other hand, increased at a rapid pace, and their yields rose. Thus the differential between the rates on United States Treasury issues and on corporate issues may have widened because of supply changes and not necessarily because of increased risk differences.[8] On the other hand, a variety of troubles faced the nation during this period—the Vietnam conflict escalation, balance of payments problems, racial strife, and so on. Any one of these could generate apprehension on the part of lenders about the riskiness of financial assets.

Risk and the Term Structure

Three variables can be shown on two axes by plotting a set of curves, each one of the set representing yields at a different level of the third variable.

---

[7]Several studies have attempted to determine whether the risk premium is approximately the same as the loss suffered. Hickman, in *Corporate Bond Liquidity*, found that, for bonds he studied, realized yields were the same as promised yields because capital gains on called bonds and favorable conditions at the end of the period he studied offset losses from defaults. He also found that realized rates were higher for low-grade than for high-grade bonds. Higher losses were more than offset by higher yields. Other studies, such as Harold G. Fraine and Robert H. Mills, "Effects of Defaults and Credit Deterioration on Yields of Corporate Bonds," *Journal of Finance*, September 1961, pp. 423–34, used somewhat different measures and found that premiums in yields were greater than losses. Lawrence Fisher, "Determinants of Risk Premiums on Corporate Bonds," *Journal of Political Economy*, June 1959, pp. 217–39, found that earnings variability, length of time a company was solvent and creditors suffered no loss, and certain other factors explained much but not all of the risk premium.

[8]For further discussion, see Murray E. Polakoff et al., *Financial Institutions and Markets* (Boston: Houghton Mifflin, 1970) pp. 453–54.

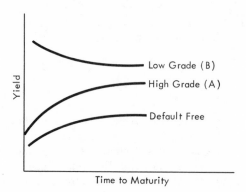

FIGURE 14-2

Thus, in Figure 14–2 yield is plotted on the vertical axis, time to maturity on the horizontal axis, and a set of yield curves is shown, each depicting yield on a different risk class of securities at any given point in time.

Intuitively one might expect that the *gap* between the yield on risky securities and that on default-free securities would be narrow when both have but a short time to run to maturity. If the firm has survived for years, as maturity approaches, the likelihood of default wanes. Empirically, this seems to be true for high-grade securities. However, especially in recession periods, the yield curve may be downward sloping for low-grade securities, even though government securities and high-grade corporate securities have upward-sloping yield curves. This is presumably the result of fear that the firm will be unable to redeem the outstanding securities at maturity, principally because of difficulties in obtaining refinancing privileges. R. E. Johnson refers to this as the problem of "crisis at maturity."[9]

A financial analyst, if considering recommending a particular security for a private portfolio, may wish to examine the term structure of rates on other securities of that class for purposes of comparing current yields to see whether the issue in question is a "good buy" relative to other issues. What appears at first glance to be a high yield for a short maturity may merely reflect the overall tendency for yields to be high on that particular high-risk class of securities.

CALLABILITY

In the event of changes in interest rates, borrowers may wish to pay the principal of a loan before maturity. Clauses may be inserted in the agreements to permit this or to provide a penalty for doing so. In the case of mortgages, the usual clause (if any) provides a penalty for prepayment. Yield differentials on mortgages may be related to such penalty clauses; borrowers may accept pen-

[9]R. E. Johnson, "Term Structures of Corporate Bond Yields as a Function of Risk Default," *Journal of Finance*, May 1967, pp. 318–21.

alty clauses if the interest rate to be paid is somewhat lower than would otherwise be required. For bonds, the usual clause is one permitting the corporation (borrower) to "call" the bond, paying the principal prior to maturity.

Call Provisions in Corporate Bonds

Corporate bonds usually carry call provisions that provide for possible retirement of the bonds at a variety of points in time over their life.[10] Just as in the case of mortgages, borrowers wish to be able to pay off loans if interest rates fall. Lenders, on the other hand, hope to tie borrowers to long-term commitments at high rates of interest. Thus, lenders desire protection against calls, and bonds with call provisions must carry a higher interest rate than similar bonds without them. However, because corporate bonds without call provisions are rare, it is difficult to test this presumption. Some bonds have an immediate call provision, while others have a deferred call provision. In one study, bonds with an immediate call provision had a premium of over ¼ percent in a period of high interest rates (1966–68), but no noticeable premium in a period of moderate interest rates (1963–65). This supports the presumption that the value of the call provision exists chiefly in periods when interest rates are high and therefore are expected to fall.[11]

Call Provisions in Government Securities

The United States Treasury also attaches call provisions to some of its securities. For example, the issue of 5/15/94–89 is callable on May 15, 1989. Its coupon rate is 4⅛ percent.[12] Whereas, in the case of corporate bonds, the purpose of a call provision is to make it possible to call the bonds and replace them with bonds at lower interest rates if rates fall, in the case of United States Treasury issues, the purpose is somewhat different. As noted in Chapter 8, the Treasury is forced to borrow whenever the budget deficit requires that new funds be raised, and cannot postpone projects and borrowing, as corporations can to some extent. The Treasury has less flexibility. However, it can adjust the maturity structure of its debt, within limits. Therefore, when the Treasury attaches a call provision to its debt, its main purpose may be to enable it to decide *when* to refund a debt issue. If the budget deficit is large and the demand for funds by the Treasury is likewise large, the Treasury will let a call date go by, not wishing to add to its fundings at that time. However, if the budget is balanced, in surplus, or has a small deficit, and a call date arrives,

[10]For example, a corporate bond may be callable according to its terms at $1,080 (for a $1,000 bond) at any time during the first year it is outstanding, for $1,070 during the second year, for $1,060 during the third year, and so forth. The interest coupon on this bond might be 8 percent. Had there been no call provision, the bond might have been salable at par with a 7 percent coupon. Thus, the premium for the call provision would be 1 percent in this example.

[11]Frank C. Jen and James E. Wert, "The Deferred Call Provision and Corporate Bond Yields," *Journal of Financial and Quantitative Analysis*, June 1968, pp. 157–69.

[12]This issue is also redeemable at par in payment of federal estate taxes.

Treasury officials may feel it is a good time for refunding. Of course, interest charges that must be paid by the Treasury are also relevant to a refunding decision. But because the Treasury must respond if deficits occur, considerations concerning call provisions differ somewhat from those faced by corporations.

TAXABILITY

Tax laws cause differences in yields on otherwise similar securities. Of particular importance in this regard are the tax on capital gains, estate taxes, and the income tax exemption on municipal securities.

Capital Gains Taxation

The law now provides that long-term capital gains are generally taxable at half of the rate applicable to short-term capital gains, with a maximum rate of 35 percent. A long-term capital gain arises when one buys a security, holds it for at least six months, and then sells it for a price higher than that paid for it. The difference between the purchase price and the selling price is the amount of capital gain, which is taxed at lower rates than other income.

To see how yield differentials can arise because of this tax provision, consider the following example. Assume that ten years ago the government sold a $1,000 twenty-year bond with a 3 percent coupon. If the current yield on 10-year securities is 6 percent, the present value of this outstanding 3 percent coupon issue would be in the neighborhood of $770. Now assume that the government sells a new 10-year bond with a 6 percent coupon. Thus, we have outstanding at the same time two United States Treasury securities, each default-free and with ten years to run to maturity. But the older bond will sell for more than $770 and carry a lower yield to maturity than the new 6 percent security. The older security is referred to as a "deep discount" bond, the term being a reference to its discounted price. The buyer of this bond will hold it to maturity and realize a capital gain of nearly $230. But this "income" is taxable at the 35 percent rate (or less, as 35 percent is the maximum).[13] Thus, individuals who are in tax brackets higher than 35 percent realize a greater after-tax income if they buy deep discount bonds than they would if they bought new 6 percent bonds. All of the 6 percent would be taxable as income, but only part of the roughly 6 percent yield to maturity of old bonds would be taxed as income; the remainder would be taxed as capital gain. This tax advantage would lead investors to prefer deep discount bonds; bidding for them would, to some extent, push their prices up and their yields down. Thus in the marketplace, with two similar bonds side by side, the deep discount bond usually carries a lower yield to maturity than the bond with the higher coupon.

[13]The actual rate of tax paid is much less than 35 percent, partly because 35 percent is the maximum tax, and partly because no tax is paid on capital gains unless they are realized. It has been estimated that only about one-fifth of the gains that accrue each year are realized by investors.

Estate Taxes and "Flower Bonds"

Estate taxes are another reason for yield differentials on bonds. The federal government has sometimes attached a provision to a bond permitting it to be used to pay estate taxes levied on the estate of the bondholder at his death. If this bond is selling at par value of $1,000, there is no advantage to the bondholder's estate and his beneficiaries. But if the bond is selling at (say) $800, then at death the Treasury accepts the bond in lieu of $1,000 of tax liability, and the inheritance is clearly higher than it otherwise would be. Thus bonds with estate tax eligibility that are selling at a discount have not only a capital gains element, but also an inheritance element that causes them to be preferred by investors. Yields on such securities are lower than those found on other comparable securities that do not carry the estate tax eligibility provision.[14]

Municipal Securities—Tax Exemption for Income

Exemption of interest income on bonds from income taxes has been provided in several cases, including exemption of interest income on U.S. government bonds from state income tax in some states and, in the past, partial exemption of interest income on certain federal government bonds. Today, however, the important exemption of interest income on bonds from income taxation is that for interest income on state and local securities (which are called "municipals").

Interest income on municipals was taxed before the Civil War, but later such taxation was declared unconstitutional. The Sixteenth Amendment to the Constitution permits the federal government to tax income "from whatever source derived," but Congress passed a law exempting income on municipals from federal government income taxation. The constitutional issue has not been tested; states seem to like the law, bondholders seem to like it, and it does not seem to deprive anyone of his rights and privileges. There has been little reason for a test.[15]

However, this tax exemption feature has come under the spotlight of public concern in recent years.[16] This is partly because of public knowledge that

[14]For example, on November 17, 1972, the estate-tax eligible bond of 2/15/80 sold to yield 6 percent before taxes while the noneligible bond of 8/15/79 sold to yield 6.14 percent. Of course, differences in maturity and coupon also affect the differential, but the rates noted are suggestive of the premium paid for estate tax eligible bonds.

[15]It should be noted that municipal obligations are subject to federal estate, gift, and capital gains taxes. The exemption from income taxation is derived from a series of Supreme Court decisions, reaching back as far as *McCulloch v. Maryland* (1824), in which it was held that a state could not tax bank notes issued by a bank established by the federal government because "the power to tax is the power to destroy." Gradually, through court decisions, both the immunity of state and local bond interest from federal government taxation and the immunity of interest on federal government obligations from taxation by state and local governments have become well established.

[16]For a review of a number of possible tax reforms being considered in late 1972, see Richard Armstrong, "The Right Kind of Tax Reform," *Fortune*, December 1972, pp. 86–89; 180–86.

certain individuals with millions of dollars of income each year have found a variety of loopholes so that they "pay no taxes" on their income. Often much of their income is derived from holdings of municipal bonds.

What is the real economic impact of this tax exemption? It is in effect a subsidy, partly a subsidy paid by the federal government to the state and local governments, and partly a subsidy to bondholders. The situation may be clarified by an example. Suppose individual A is in the 50 percent income bracket and that his income consists entirely of interest and dividends on securities. Now suppose that the yield on United States government bonds is 6 percent and the yield on similar municipal bonds is 3 percent. It is clear that A's after-tax income is the same whether he buys only United States bonds and pays no taxes on the interest at 50 percent or buys only municipal bonds and pays no taxes, except that in the latter case it is easier to fill out the tax form. Of course, the example is oversimplified; if the yield spread were less than 50 percent, which it usually is, then the taxpayer pays somewhat less taxes than otherwise. If the yield spread were only 30 percent, then someone in the 30 percent tax bracket would be just indifferent as to whether he held tax-exempt municipals or corporate bonds. But to say that the taxpayer *escapes* taxation is patently false. What is ostensibly a tax loophole is largely "closed" by the market, as yields on municipal bonds fall below those of other comparable securities. The state governments, on the other hand, may have construction projects to undertake and issue bonds to finance them. Without the tax exemption provision states would have to pay 6 percent (probably somewhat more because of other factors). Thus the property taxes out of which debt repayment is provided would have to be increased; with the tax exemption, these property taxes are lower. In essence, then, the principal real economic impact is simply to shift roughly half of the tax burden of the interest cost on state construction projects from the shoulders of state taxpayers and onto the shoulders of federal income taxpayers, including those who pay their taxes by accepting the lower income from municipal bonds.

The spread between yields on municipals and other securities is not estimated to be large enough to result in the total elimination of all tax advantage to the individual investor. Indeed, the marginal investor is at a point of indifference, but all other investors have presumably found that some tax savings can be realized through the tax exemption privilege. Just how much tax saving can be realized depends on many factors other than the privilege itself. Especially, investors in different tax brackets have different tax-saving potential. The higher the tax bracket the greater the potential saving. In one study, it was estimated that the average top-bracket private investor might receive a net after-tax yield on corporate securities (with 5 percent gross yield before tax) of only 1.5 percent, while these same individuals could realize a net after-tax yield of 3.6 percent on municipals; corporations would receive only 2.6 percent from corporate bonds but 3.6 percent from municipals, and so forth.

The spread between yields on municipals and on other securities tends to narrow in periods of tight money; that is, the yield on municipals rises relative to the yields on other securities as the economy moves on the upswing. One author attributes this phenomenon to the large role played by commercial banks in the market for municipals.[17] In periods of rising interest rates, banks are pressed to unload bonds from their portfolios to meet increased customer demand for loans. This has the general effect of pushing prices down and yields up. Because commercial banks are major holders of municipals, this sales pressure has the effect of raising the yields on municipals relative to yields on other securities. In any case, the narrowing of spreads does mean that that portion of the differential going to states as a subsidy falls, and that portion going to individuals or corporate investors as tax exemption rises in the business upswing.[18]

Some economists argue that the existence of a subsidy in the form of exemption of interest income from taxation may encourage financing of projects that can be financed by bonds, thus shifting the allocation of resources from what it might have been if the subsidy had not existed. For this reason they may favor elimination of the subsidy. Because the tax exemption provision enables some investors to escape from some part of their tax liability, others favor its elimination. Direct subsidy by the federal government to state and local governments would probably be a less costly way to achieve the same goal.[19] As the federal government has now begun a program of sharing tax revenues with state and local governments, the principal reason for subsidization by exemption of interest income from taxation now has less force. However, some groups will undoubtedly continue to voice strong support of the status quo for a variety of reasons.

MARKETABILITY

The term "liquidity" applies to a security that is readily marketable with negligible risk of loss. In a sense, the term "marketable" also implies that the security is salable with negligible risk of loss, and therefore the terms "marketability" and "liquidity" overlap extensively—they are nearly synonymous. In examining some of the factors that make one security more or less marketable than some other security, we find at the outset that marketability is improved when a security is traded in a market that has depth, breadth, and resiliency, as described in Chapter 10.

[17]Sidney Homer, "Factors Determining Municipal Bond Yields," United States Congress, Joint Economic Committee, *State and Local Public Facility Needs and Financing*, Washington, D.C., December 1966, Vol. II, p. 270; summarized in Polakoff et al., *Financial Institutions and Markets*, pp. 334–35.

[18]James C. Van Horne, *Function and Analysis of Capital Market Rates* (Englewood Cliffs, N.J.: Prentice-Hall, 1970), pp. 136–73.

[19]Roland I. Robinson, *The Postwar Market for State and Local Government Securities* (New York: National Bureau of Economic Research, 1960), p. 159. One recent study found that tax-exempt securities issued in 1969 will probably cost the federal government about $2.6 billion in lost revenues over the life of the bonds, while state and local governments will save only $1.9 billion because of lower interest rates on the bonds. Of course, these figures are based on estimates of the taxes not paid by holders of municipal bonds (which depend on their tax brackets). See Richard Armstrong, *Fortune*, December 1972, p. 89.

Specifically, marketability is increased whenever a security has a well-developed "secondary" market. That is, in selling an issue to a group of investors in a primary market, a secondary market is important for marketability— so that if the original investors wish to sell their holdings at a later time, they can do so.

The Federal National Mortgage Association (FNMA) and other agencies were established in order to provide such a secondary market for mortgage loans. Some states have now arranged for public fund investments in student loans. A state treasurer may purchase these from banks and savings and loan associations that have acquired a sizable portfolio of them. Managers may wish to sell some of them in order to acquire funds to offer *more* such loans to students.

Secondary markets have long existed for all readily exchangeable government and corporate securities, but a secondary market for mortgages was slow to develop. Governmental support for such a market was felt to be needed and has been expressed in many ways. The government's guarantee behind a mortgage or student loan greatly reduces the risk attached to it and tends to facilitate development of a secondary market.

The securities ratings applied to corporate and government securities by Moody's and Standard and Poor's also affect marketability by indicating a risk class to potential buyers.

Finally, the size of an issue is important. A small issue cannot be widely held, and there cannot be many market participants who hold large amounts of such an issue; therefore, general lack of knowledge about the issue makes its marketing more costly.[20]

Small amounts of an issue can be traded at the going market price, but large amounts often must be negotiated. Mutual funds, among other investors, have found that if they hold a large amount of one security, they will drive the price down by virtue of their own selling activity when they attempt to unload onto the market. Such securities lack a high degree of marketability— the market is said to be "thin" as opposed to "broad."

Thus, marketability is a general term for a wide variety of characteristics of securities reflecting the ease with which they can be sold. It is expected that readily marketable securities will sell for lower yields (higher prices) than other securities that are similar in all other respects; degrees of marketability give rise to varying yield differentials.

OTHER FACTORS AFFECTING YIELDS ON BONDS

One other factor causing differences in yields is differences in transactions costs, and several factors cause yields on newly issued securities to differ from those on "seasoned" issues.

---

[20]Lawrence Fisher used the market value of publicly traded bonds of a corporation as a proxy for marketability, in the study cited in footnote 7.

Transactions Costs

Arranging mortgages requires individual negotiation in most cases. State laws vary in requirements for deed certification and so forth. Fees charged in arranging mortgages reflect services provided, services necessary in making the loans. The services required for a $10,000 loan are often not much larger than those required for a $100,000 loan, certainly not ten times as large. Therefore, a service fee that is a fixed percentage of the dollar value of a loan is less profitable for a small loan than it is for a large loan.

Common stocks are usually traded in lots of 100 shares each. Anyone buying fewer than a "round lot" (usually 100 shares) is said to be trading in "odd-lots." Fees are charged by odd-lot houses, whose business it is to perform the paperwork necessary to break "round" lots into odd-lots.

Thus, there are a variety of transactions costs, usually covered by fees reflecting necessary services provided to effect the transfer of financial instruments. Often, however, the full cost of such services is not reflected in fees alone but may be reflected partially in the interest rate charged. The interest rate charged to a borrower may be higher when transaction costs are higher so that a differential in yields reflects the extent of transactions costs as well as risk, and so on.

A commercial bank is currently prohibited from paying interest on demand deposits, but it is allowed to service checking accounts without charging fees sufficient to offset the full cost of such service. Thus services are provided in lieu of interest, and, in fact, some imputed earnings (services which would otherwise have to be paid for) accrue to the depositor.

"Seasoned" versus New Issues

A seasoned issue, one that has been outstanding for some period of time, seems to be more acceptable to the investing public than a new issue of comparable standing otherwise. This is because of uncertainty over how the new issue will be received by the market; the uncertainty is reflected in the lower price and higher yield on new issues as compared with the higher price and lower yield on seasoned issues. On a few occasions, the yield on a new issue falls below comparable yields on seasoned issues, but such times are rare.

New issues of corporate bonds, unless privately placed, are sold through the market by investment bankers, who undertake commitments with issuers and are anxious to unload the greater portion of the bonds at the current market price in order to realize their profit before market conditions change. They are therefore likely to accept a slightly lower-than-market price to ensure the sale of holdings. This means that they are willing to "sweeten" the yield.

Of course, whether they are willing to sweeten the yield by lowering the price or not depends partly on their outlook concerning money market conditions. If they expect yields to rise in the near future, then the longer they hold an issue, the more likely it is that they will have to lower the price even further. This means they will suffer a capital loss and may not be able to realize a profit. Then incentive to unload is strong. If, however, they expect bond prices to rise in the near future, they will not be anxious to sell. Thus, in periods when yields trend upward, the differential between yields on new issues and those on seasoned issues tends to rise; and when yields trend downward, this differential tends to narrow.

When bond prices are low and yields are high—that is, in periods of tight credit and high interest rates—new issues typically carry high coupon rates. Seasoned issues may carry low coupon rates. Because low coupon issues carry tax advantages inasmuch as a substantial part of the earnings from them are subject to the lower tax rate on capital gains rather than the higher rate on interest income, investors are not willing to pay as high a price for new issues as for old ones. Therefore, charts showing higher differentials between the high yield on a new issue and the low yield on seasoned issues, occurring in periods of high interest rates, reflect the tax provisions rather than the date-of-issue characteristic alone. Presumably, if taxable-equivalent issues were compared, the new and seasoned issues would be much closer in yield.[21]

INTEREST RATE (YIELD) DIFFERENTIALS ON OTHER FINANCIAL ASSETS

In our analysis thus far, we have discussed both general and somewhat more specific characteristics giving rise to differentials in yields on securities. Our focus has been on notes and bonds, securities containing contractually fixed obligations as opposed to instruments of ownership represented in the market by shares of common stock. We have not attempted a comprehensive examination of the wealth of diverse types of clauses that can appear in loan agreements. This diversity is limited only by the imagination of the parties to such contracts. However, two general types of contracts that overlap fixed-rate obligations and ownership securities are quite common. These are preferred stock and convertible bonds. Both have characteristics that make them partly like bonds and partly like stocks, and differentials in yields are often observed because of these provisions. The other major types of financial assets—mortgages, loans, and savings deposits—are discussed briefly because many of the factors causing differences in bond yields also cause differences in yields on these financial assets.

Preferred Stock

The term "preferred" means that if dividends are declared, holders of preferred stock take precedence over holders of common stock; holders of pre-

---

[21]See Joseph W. Conard, *The Behavior of Interest Rates* (New York: National Bureau of Economic Research, 1966), especially pp. 113–15, where he reports a study of interest rate differentials.

ferred stock receive the full stipulated dividend before holders of common stock receive any dividends. A preferred stock carries an "interest rate" in the form of a specified number of dollars and cents per share. Thus, if earnings of $3 a share on total capital are realized, and management decides to declare these, or part of them, in dividends, holders of 6 percent preferred (par value, $100) will receive $6 per share, and common stockholders will receive nothing if there are equal amounts of preferred and common stock. As there is usually more common stock than preferred stock, common stockholders would usually receive something, but less than $6 a share. If earnings are $12 a share, holders of preferred stock receive only $6, while common stockholders receive more than $12 a share, unless, as occasionally is true, the preferred stock is "participating" preferred. This is rare; much more common is a provision for "cumulative" preferred stock; cumulative preferred stockholders receive all of their specified return before common stockholders receive any dividends, even if this means that common stockholders wait for years without any dividends.

Because declaration of dividends is a discretionary act of management, preferred stockholders not only may not receive dividends if there are no earnings or insufficient earnings; they may not receive dividends if these are not declared. They have no contractual claim on the firm's assets, as bondholders have. In such a situation bonds would be in default and bondholders could bring suit.

Thus one might expect that the effective yield on preferred stock would have to be higher than the yield on bonds of the same quality if the company were successful in inducing people to purchase the preferred stock. In general, this has been true. However, there are certain tax provisions which, as always, affect the "after-tax" yield. Only 15 percent of the dividends received by corporations that hold preferred stock of other corporations are subject to the income (profits) tax; the remaining 85 percent is tax exempt. Thus *corporate* holders find that preferred stock has some tax advantage; as corporations, including nonbank financial institutions, hold more stock, this leads to bidding up of prices and a corresponding lowering of yields.

Additionally, the corporate issuer of a bond can deduct interest payments from his income for tax purposes. But payments to preferred shareholders are not deductible. Therefore, there is less incentive for corporations to issue preferred stock than bonds, and the supply of new preferred shares has not been large in recent years. This restricted supply also leads to higher prices and lower yields. Thus there exists no large differential in yields between those on preferred shares and those on bonds, under present institutional arrangements, and in fact, since the mid-1960s, preferred stocks have sometimes yielded less than high-grade bonds.

Convertible Bonds

Some corporate bonds (and some preferred stocks) carry provisions that allow the holder to exchange them for the common stock of the company on prearranged terms. Because of this conversion privilege, these bonds have characteristics of both bonds and stocks. The purchaser of a convertible bond may share in any potential appreciation in value accorded to the company's stock by exercising his conversion rights, so that his investment resembles a stock purchase. On the other hand, if the company's profit position falters and this results in a decline in the price of outstanding shares of stock, the value embodied in the fixed obligation in the bond is retained by the investor. The convertible bond, therefore, has little downside risk of loss, while it is also capable of realizing gains.[22] For these reasons, the price of a convertible bond carries a premium over the prices of other bonds of similar quality, as buyers bid for the right to take advantage of any appreciation in share values while retaining the protection afforded the bondholder. Yields on convertible bonds are below those on other similar bonds.

Several other reasons for a yield differential between convertible and nonconvertible bonds have been suggested by market analysts. First, the option to convert to common stock usually has a fixed duration. Presumably, the longer the life of the option, the more valuable it is. Second, clauses in the bond's "fine print" may provide for restraint on the firm's ability to dilute its stock by issuing more stock. The stronger the antidilution clauses are, the more valuable the bond. Third, it is frequently the case that margin requirements on the purchase of convertible bonds are lower than those on stock. In early 1968, the requirements were 50 and 70 percent of market value, respectively. In early 1972, however, the percentages were 50 percent and 55 percent; the differential had fallen from 20 to 5 percentage points. In January 1974, the requirements were 30 percent and 50 percent, respectively. It is, therefore, less difficult for speculators to finance the purchase of convertible bonds than to finance the purchase of stock, but the extent to which this is true depends upon margin requirements set by the Board of Governors of the Federal Reserve System. Fourth, transactions costs connected with the trading of bonds are usually less than those incurred in trading a like amount of common stocks.

It is clear that in evaluating the desirability of investing in a convertible bond, many factors must be considered.[23] It is sufficient to note here that the conversion feature in general is an attractive attribute and leads to a premium price. Convertible bonds have a *bond-value* floor price, although this is not constant; if a company incurs losses, it may not even be able to pay interest on its bonds. Convertible bonds also have a *conversion value*, the value of the bonds if converted into stock at the current market price of the stock. It is common for convertible bonds to sell at premiums over both values; the convertible bond is worth as much as the stock into which it is convertible, and a little more because of the fact that it is less likely to decline sharply in value, as there is some protection because of the bond value floor price. If the pre-

---

[22]Of course, the market price of a bond can fall, as it will when interest rates rise; however, a convertible bond with the same timing, coupon rate, and so on, as a nonconvertible bond will fall in price no further than its counterpart. In this sense a "floor" to the fall in value is retained by convertible bonds.

[23]For a detailed statistical examination of the premium for the conversion privilege, see R. L. Wil, Jr., J. E. Segall, and David Green, Jr., "Premiums on Convertible Bonds," *Journal of Finance*, June 1968, pp. 445–63, and comments and a reply by P. D. Cretien, Jr., D. T. Duvel, and G. A. Mumey, *Journal of Finance*, September 1970, pp. 917–33.

mium of the market price over the bond value is large, there is usually only a small premium in the market price over the conversion value, and vice versa. This is because, when the premium of market price over bond value is great, it is usually because the price of the stock is high; investors may feel that it cannot go much higher, and therefore the premium of market price of the convertible bond over its conversion value is small. If the premium of market price over conversion value is large, it is usually because the price of the stock is rising, and conversion would enable the former bondholder to benefit from further rise in the price of the stock.

Firms issuing convertible securities must weigh these factors, for although the conversion feature may enable the firm to obtain funds at lower interest cost, there are costs to the firm in other ways. In particular, conversion to common stock, if profitable, dilutes the stock and presumably this tends to hold the price of the stock to a lower level than it otherwise might reach.

Mortgages

Interest rates on mortgages are generally higher than rates on high-quality corporate bonds. Mortgage rate levels are, of course, affected by many of the factors already discussed in this chapter.

Risk on a conventional mortgage, negotiated between a bank or savings and loan association and a homeowner, is greater than that on a comparable loan that has been insured by the FHA. Banks frequently require a larger down payment, perhaps 30 percent of the purchase price, in the case of a conventional mortgage loan, while insured and guaranteed loans, in some cases in the past, were made with no down payment (there was even at one time a "no-no-down-payment," in which some of the transactions costs were absorbed by lenders). The different treatment of down payments tends to absorb the risk differential so that interest rates as quoted to the public may appear the same. High down payments are like stringent collateral requirements, the value of the home under mortgage is the value of the "collateral" pledged in case of default. Moreover, the smaller the loan outstanding against this collateral, the lower the risk assumed by the lender.

Tax laws also have a significant effect on the demand for mortgage money and its supply. The Congress has often expressed a desire to see citizens well-housed; hence, they allow a homeowner to deduct from his income the amount of interest payments before computing his income tax liability. This is a form of subsidy to the homeowner that is intended to push mortgages rates higher than they might otherwise be and to induce more lenders to supply funds to the mortgage market rather than to other sectors.

Mortgages are not as readily marketable as bonds and many stocks. Again, to support the marketability of mortgages, the government formed FNMA, GNMA, and other agencies discussed earlier. It is difficult to know precisely what effect these programs have on mortgage yields. When these agencies tap the bond market for funds that are then channeled to the mortgage market, this tends to lower mortgage rates, but to push business loan and bond rates up. One wonders whether the new attractiveness of higher bond rates does not simply induce funds to flow out of the mortgage market to other sectors. However, the marketability of mortgages is enhanced, and there is probably some *net* lowering of mortgage yields.

Mortgages require considerably more servicing than business loans, and although some services are paid for directly through fees, services are probably partly paid for in somewhat higher rates charged on mortgages. Services include collecting mortgage payments, usually monthly, and checking to be sure that insurance premiums and taxes have been paid. Servicing costs are sometimes estimated at about ½ percent per year, and mortgage rates are sometimes shown with this (estimated) deduction from the quoted contract rate, which includes an amount sufficient to offset servicing costs. Sometimes service fees are paid directly to local institutions (such as mortgage banks or mortgage companies) by a life insurance company that does not wish to service loans it holds.

Mortgage rates tend to be less volatile than bond rates because lenders tend to increase or reduce rates by ½ percent or ¼ percent at a given time. The differential between mortgage rates over bond rates tends to be greatest when bond rates are relatively low, as mortgage lenders seem to be slow to lower their rates. They also seem to be somewhat reluctant (or fearful?) to raise them in periods of very high interest rates, and in these periods the differential may become quite small, as was shown in Figure 10–4.

Loans and Savings Deposits

A number of factors already discussed, particularly risk and transactions costs, explain differences in loan yields or interest rates. Interest on savings deposits differs for other reasons, discussed in part in Chapter 5, where it was pointed out that commercial banks appear to be able to pay lower interest than savings and loan associations, perhaps because of convenience of "one-stop" banking. In this section we examine two factors somewhat peculiar to loans—compensating balances and collateral requirements—that cause differences in interest rates charged; we also comment briefly on geographic factors affecting both loan rates and savings deposit rates.

Compensating Balances

Commercial banks often arrange agreements with borrowers to prevent deposit accounts falling below a certain level. That is, borrowers must keep on deposit a "compensating balance" of a certain sum as one condition for obtaining loans. This was described in Chapter 3, where it was noted that the effective interest rate is higher than the quoted rate when compensating balances are required because the borrower does not have full discretionary use of the funds. Size of compensating balances varies considerably—usually 10 to 20 percent of the original loan amount. Thus, effective yields vary directly with the compensating balances required, and nominal interest charges vary inversely with compensating balances.

The added cost to borrowers, however, depends on how much balance they *would have* maintained in the absence of the compensating balance requirement. When a business firm borrows, it frequently increases its sales, and with a larger volume of sales it needs larger working balances. As a matter of fact, it might be possible for banks to reduce compensating balance requirements somewhat, to charge borrowers slightly higher nominal rates of interest, and for both to benefit. This is because required reserves (on which earnings are zero) would be smaller with smaller compensating balances.[24]

Although compensating balance requirements increase effective interest rates, banks generally view them as a means of cementing bank-customer relationships and thus inducing customers to obtain future loans from the same bank and to use other bank services. An understanding about a compensating balance usually follows from a long-standing bank-customer relationship. A large business firm usually maintains a line of credit with its bank (or banks), enabling it to borrow whenever additional funds are needed, up to the limit of the line of credit, in exchange for agreement to keep a compensating balance. An individual not maintaining a compensating balance would pay a fee for establishing a line of credit; the fee is waived in exchange for the compensating balance.

Over business cycles, the size of compensating balances tends to vary. As monetary conditions become tight, banks require larger compensating balances in lieu of increasing nominal interest rates on loans. This applies principally to customers eligible for the prime rate, or a fixed rate above the prime rate, agreed upon in establishing lines of credit. In this way, commercial banks can introduce yield flexibility while keeping nominal rates fixed. In recent years four major banks introduced a "flexible" or "floating" prime rate, as noted in Chapter 9. With flexibility in setting the prime rate, it may be that variability in compensating balance requirements will no longer be necessary. But the future of a floating prime rate is uncertain at the time of writing this book.[25]

Collateral Requirements

It is clear that if a lender takes possession of a borrower's stocks or bonds, or acquires liens on his real property, the lender assumes less risk of loss from default by the borrower than he otherwise would. Thus, borrowers with collateral to pledge can usually obtain additional funds at a lower cost than otherwise. (If you have wealth, it is easier to borrow.) Indeed, in many instances such collateral is a necessary requirement to obtain funds at all from the lender.

[24]For further detail on some of these points, see Jack M. Guttentag and Richard G. Davis, "Compensating Balances," in *Essays in Money and Credit*, Federal Reserve Bank of New York, 1964, pp. 57–61.

[25]Under pressure from the government's Committee on Interest and Dividends in 1973, some banks suspended their "floating" prime rates because the rates would have risen under the formulas used. Later the government acquiesced in a rise in the prime rate, but suggested what became termed a "dual prime rate"—increases in the prime rate should be delayed and should be small, but if made, rates charged on loans to small business firms and consumers and on mortgage loans should not be increased unless absolutely necessary. See Federal Reserve Bank of San Francisco, *Business and Financial Letter*, March 2, 1973.

The "quality" of the collateral pledged is also often a factor that affects the yield. If warehouse receipts on inventories are pledged, the bank requires that such inventories be insured against fire and theft, and so on. The size of a down payment on a piece of property also may affect the lender's willingness to lend at a lower interest rate. The larger the down payment, the smaller will be the amount of the loan relative to the market value of the property, and therefore, the greater the assurance that the lender will be repaid from the sale of the property should the borrower default.

If a borrower owns a savings account, he may wish to withdraw cash from the account to pay for, say, a new automobile. The banker may suggest that he pledge his savings account as collateral and borrow the funds to purchase the car. The interest rate charged on such a loan would be very low compared to that charged if the car were mortgaged by the bank. But it would be higher than the rate earned by the savings account, perhaps 2 percent higher. Thus, if he earned 4 percent on his savings account and paid 6 percent for his loan, his net interest charges would be only 2 percent. However, by pledging his savings account, the borrower would relinquish the liquidity it gave him—the ability to withdraw funds from his savings account would be restricted. Thus, what appears to be a low 6 percent loan has its implicit costs, and these may make the "true" interest rate paid equal to the 9 or 10 percent or more, which is normally charged on automobile loans.

There are almost as many different kinds of collateral requirements as there are loans, and rates charged reflect this variety.

Geographical Differences

Some noticeable differences in yields have persisted in different geographical regions of the United States. Interest rates in the East are usually lower than those in the West and Southwest. These differentials are most pronounced in the mortgage market, and they are reflected in rates paid on savings deposits, inasmuch as these deposits provide the principal source of mortgage money for home building. Just why these rate differentials persist is not well understood. Of course, the mortgage market is principally a local market, and rates must be negotiated between lenders and borrowers. The market lacks the degree of perfection that the national securities markets have.

One may speculate that as means of communication improve and flexibility in portfolio management on the part of savings institutions becomes greater, these regional differences will be reduced or eradicated.

SUMMARY

Several factors other than term to maturity, the subject of the preceding chapter, affect the yield on securities: (1) *risk* and the risk premium that borrowers pay to lenders—presumably, the greater the risk of default, the higher must be the yield; (2) *callability*—call provisions on securities make them more desirable for issuers, but less attractive to investors, and hence securities with call provisions presumably sell for lower prices and higher yields than those without call provisions; (3) *tax status*—the reduced tax on long-term capital gains, estate tax provisions, and the income tax exemption for interest income on municipal bonds all affect yields; (4) *marketability* is a general term reflecting various attributes of a security that make it more or less marketable—presumably, the greater the marketability, the lower the yield; and (5) *transactions costs*.

Causes of differences between yields on *new* and on *seasoned* issues are related to holding costs of dealers as well as to risks of default.

Two hybrid forms of securities are preferred stocks and convertible bonds. In general, preferred stocks are less attractive than bonds issued by the same companies because preferred stocks do not contain fixed obligations to pay interest. Convertible bonds, on the other hand, are more attractive to investors than ordinary bonds, because they may appreciate in value if converted to stock that is rising in price.

Differentials in interest rates on mortgages result from such factors as servicing costs, while differences in rates on loans and on saving deposits result from compensating balance and collateral requirements and from geographical location.

QUESTIONS FOR DISCUSSION

1. What are the four kinds of risk that should concern students of financial markets?

2. Define the term "risk premium."

3. Explain the importance of a call provision to the buyer of a security.

4. Why might a deep-discount bond be expected to sell at a price giving a lower yield to maturity than a bond selling at par?

5. Present three economic effects of the income tax exemption on interest from municipal bonds. Do the rich escape from taxation when they buy these tax-exempt securities? Explain your answer.

6. What are compensating balances, how do they alter the "effective" interest rate on a loan, and what other purposes do they serve?

7. What category of investors might be especially likely to buy preferred stock? Why?

8. What factors increase marketability of securities? How would you test whether greater marketability is accompanied by lower yields?

9. Why may yields on new issues be quite high at certain times, in comparison with yields on similar "seasoned" bonds?

10. List some of the factors that may increase the attractiveness of convertible bonds especially at certain times.

SELECTED REFERENCES

A statistical study by Roy C. Fair and Burton G. Malkiel recently examined yield differentials that result from the relationship between the supplies of bonds outstanding and the anticipated level of new offerings. See "The Determination of Yield Differentials Between Debt Instruments of the Same Maturity," *Journal of Money, Credit, and Banking*, November 1971, pp. 733–49.

An analysis that integrates the effects of differences in tax treatment, call provisions, and default risk into the traditional yield-to-maturity formula is set forth in Timothy Q. Cook, "Some Factors Affecting Long-Term Yield Spreads in Recent Years," Federal Reserve Bank of Richmond, *Monthly Review*, September 1973, pp. 2–14

Because tax reform was under discussion in 1972–73, it is likely that changes may be made in some of the tax provisions discussed in the section on taxability. An excellent review of possible changes is found in Richard Armstrong, "The Right Kind of Tax Reform," *Fortune*, December 1972, pp. 86–89; 180–86. Tax provisions providing special rates and exemptions represent subsidies of one kind or another, and obviously opinions concerning the need for subsidies vary; neither the authors nor readers need agree with all of Armstrong's conclusions on what reform would be best. Also see, Peter Fortune, "Tax Exemption of State and Local Interest Payments: An Economic Analysis of Issues and Alternatives," *New England Economic Review*, Federal Reserve Bank of Boston, May–June 1973, pp. 3–31.

James C. Van Horne, *Function and Analysis of Capital Market Rates* (Englewood Cliffs, N.J.: Prentice-Hall, 1970), in Chapters 5, 6, and 7 (pp. 166–73) goes somewhat further in his discussion of the theory of risk than the authors of this book, as his book is entirely devoted to interest rates. Also see an excellent description of risk in Avery B. Cohan's "The Risk Structure of Interest Rates," a "Module" published by the General Learning Press, 1973, Morristown, New Jersey.

For more details on loan rates, see *Essays in Money and Credit*, Federal Reserve Bank of New York, 1964, especially "The Prime Rate," by Albert M. Wojnilower and Richard E. Speagle, pp. 47–56; "Compensating Balances," by Jack M. Guttentag and Richard G. Davis, pp. 57–61; and "Term Lending by New York City Banks," by George Budzeika, p. 67–71.

V

Monetary, Fiscal, and Debt Management Policies

We now turn our attention to policies of the Federal Reserve System and the Treasury and to the role these agencies play in financial markets. In Chapter 15, we examine the nation's major economic goals and policies used to attain these goals, and consider some arguments in support of different policy prescriptions. In Chapter 16 we outline the transmission mechanism by which monetary policy affects output, employment, and prices. We then discuss various strategies the Fed might follow in conducting its open market operations and some implications of different strategies for financial markets. We conclude the chapter with a section on policies and techniques used by the Fed in recent years. In Chapter 17 we discuss some of the ways Treasury operations impinge on financial and economic variables. Mostly, our attention is on the government budget, the composition of the federal debt, and the interrelationship between monetary, fiscal, and debt management policies, which are of vital concern to financial managers and financial analysts.

15

Economic Goals and Policies

MAJOR ECONOMIC GOALS

The federal government has the responsibility to promote the nation's economic welfare. The chief expression of this mandate is contained in the Employment Act of 1946, which provides that the government shall "promote maximum employment, production, and purchasing power." This Act also established the Council of Economic Advisers and the Joint Economic Committee to aid the President and Congress in achieving these objectives. Although there is no explicit reference to inflation nor to the balance of payments in the original Employment Act, it is widely accepted that government's goals should include (1) a high level of employment (often termed "full" employment), (2) reasonable price stability, (3) relatively rapid economic growth, and (4) an appropriate balance in the balance of payments.

It should not be inferred, however, that these are the only goals that are, or should be, sought through government policies. Some may wish to include additional goals such as a more equitable distribution of income and wealth, or economic freedom; others would prefer a different ranking of goals (in terms of priorities) than that presented above, and so forth. Nonetheless, these four goals would be included in most lists of national aims, although some argue that many goals should not be pursued by government, but should be left to individuals, expressing their own sets of preferences.

In this chapter we discuss the nation's major economic goals, then the macroeconomic policies for achieving them. The chapter concludes with a summary of the current debate over the appropriate roles of monetary and fiscal policies.

Full Employment and the Phillips Curve

Full employment is an ambiguous concept. Virtually no one interprets the term literally and seeks an unemployment rate of zero percent. Some degree of "frictional" unemployment is considered inevitable, and even desirable, in a dynamic economy where factors of production are free to respond to changing conditions in the product and factor markets. When unemployment, which had exceeded 7 percent of the labor force in the 1957–58 recession, nearly reached that level again in the 1960–61 recession, concern over this problem resulted in the selection in 1962 of an interim target of 4 percent as a goal of policy.[1] Nonetheless, the consensus was that the lower the rate of unemployment, the better, which seemed to imply that either the several goals were independent of each other or that the achievement of one would help assure the attainment of the others.

Prior to the mid-1950s, there was little empirical evidence concerning the relationship between unemployment and inflation. Serious inflation had seldom occurred in the United States except during and immediately following periods of mobilization for war. The inflation that did result was attributed to excessive aggregate demand and was expected only if and when unemployment was no longer a matter of concern. As a consequence, the likelihood of peacetime inflation was largely ignored and economists directed their attention to the prevention or elimination of high unemployment. Toward the end of the 1950s, however, the emergence of inflation at a time of slack demand when the economy was experiencing slow growth of output and rising unemployment led to new analyses of inflation and the relationship between inflation and the rate of unemployment.

In 1958, a study of the British economy by Professor A. W. Phillips offered evidence that the rate of increase in money wages and the rate of unemployment are inversely related.[2] Similar studies of the United States economy relating wage or price changes to the rate of unemployment, though far from conclusive, seemed to confirm this finding. This relationship, referred to as a Phillips curve, is shown in Figure 15–1, which relates various rates of inflation to hypothetical rates of unemployment.

There are several possible explanations of this inverse relationship be-

[1]The labor force is defined as persons sixteen years of age or over who are employed or looking for work. Unemployment as a percent of the labor force may rise if people lose jobs and also if new entrants or reentrants into the labor force cannot find work. The rate of unemployment has not been below the target of 4 percent since 1950 except in the Korean war period; on selection of the target, see *Economic Report of the President*, 1962, pp. 44 ff. Recently there has been discussion of the need for greater equality of incomes instead of, or in addition to, high employment and rapid growth. For some reasons why the goal of greater equality of income is not emphasized in this chapter, see Sanford Rose, "The Truth about Income Inequality in the U.S.," *Fortune*, December 1972, pp. 90–93, 158–72. A very perceptive note on additional complications in measuring inequality of incomes may be found in the letter to the editors by our colleague, Dean A. Worcester, *Fortune*, March 1973, pp. 65; 68. He points out that much of observed inequality in incomes is due to differences in *age*.

[2]A. W. Phillips, "The Relationship Between Unemployment and the Rate of Change of Money Wage Rates in the United Kingdom, 1861–1957," *Economica*, Vol. 25 (November 1958), pp. 283–99. See also P. A. Samuelson and R. M. Solow, "Analytical Aspects of Anti-Inflation Policy," *American Economic Review*, Vol. 50, May 1960, pp. 177–94, reprinted in W. L. Smith and R. L. Teigen, eds., *Readings in Money, National Income and Stabilization Policy*, 2nd ed. (Homewood, Illinois, Richard D. Irwin, Inc., 1970).

tween inflation and unemployment: the power of labor unions to push up money wages when unemployment is low; the emergence of bottlenecks in product markets; excess demand for labor, which bids up wage rates, and so on. Expressed differently, the downward-sloping character of the curve may be attributed to the presence of market imperfections, including elements of cost-push inflation. That is, if all markets were perfect and inflation was due solely to excessive demand for goods and services, the Phillips curve would be vertical at approximately full employment of labor; if cost-push were the only source of inflation, the curve would be horizontal at a rate of inflation corresponding to the difference between the annual rate of increase in money wages and productivity. In the latter case, the administration of prices by business or the power of labor unions to set wage rates independent of the rate of unemployment would rationalize the inflation during periods of recession.

The Phillips curve represents a menu of choices—the economically feasible combinations of inflation and unemployment—available to policymakers. The importance of this is that if such a relationship is typical and stable over time, "full" employment cannot be viewed as simply an absolute value of, say, 3 or 4 percent unemployment. Instead, full employment is that rate, which in combination with some expected rate of inflation, best satisfies the political preferences of society. This "trade-off" between unemployment and inflation means that to define full employment as, say, 3 or 4 percent unemployment implies a willingness to accept the rate of inflation that is expected to accompany it. That rate of inflation is the "cost" to society of achieving full employment.

Criticisms of the Phillips Curve Analysis

A number of economists have serious reservations concerning the validity and usefulness of the Phillips curve. One criticism is that the relationship is

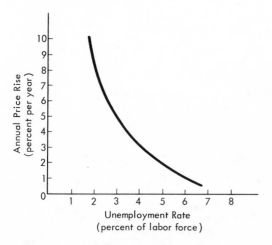

FIGURE 15–1   Phillips Curve

far too volatile to be useful as a policy tool.[3] A given Phillips curve implies a particular set of expectations concerning inflation: the higher the anticipated rate of inflation, the higher the curve lies, because workers will demand higher wages at any rate of unemployment. Now if expectations change, the curve shifts and the trade-off values are different. Only if expectations change slowly would the Phillips curve be a useful guide for stabilization policy.

A second, and related, criticism is that if the authorities try to secure a different pair of trade-off values from the "expected" combination shown on the curve, the entire curve will break down until expectations are reestablished. Many observers who oppose the use of the Phillips curve for policy purposes argue that except for very short-run periods the trade-off is an illusion. In the longer run, when people come to anticipate the actual rate of inflation, the rate of unemployment will settle at the "natural" rate, whatever the rate of inflation. In other words, the long-run Phillips curve will be a vertical line at a rate of unemployment determined by the real demand and supply for labor. In this view, an increase in aggregate demand may *temporarily* reduce the unemployment rate below the "natural" rate by increasing both the demand and supply of labor.[4] However, when workers become aware of the decrease in the real wage, they demand higher money wages, which reduces the quantity of labor demanded; unemployment increases, returning to the natural rate. Accordingly, we cannot "buy" full employment, except perhaps temporarily, with a given rate of inflation. Only by accelerating the rate of inflation over time can unemployment be maintained below the natural rate. This is not to say that these critics of the Phillips curve regard a high rate of unemployment as desirable. They would, however, seek to reduce unemployment by means other than expansionary monetary or fiscal policy, such as repeal of minimum wage laws, elimination of monopolistic practices of business and labor, and other measures designed to improve the mobility and skills of labor. Nonetheless, though most economists would favor such measures in order to shift the Phillips curve downward and to the left, and so reduce the cost of high employment, they continue to view the problem of goals as one of trade-offs. To accept the concept of a "natural" rate of unemployment goes against the grain of those who believe that economic policy *should* be used to achieve full employment and that monetary and fiscal measures are more likely to be effective than sole reliance upon reducing market imperfections, desirable though that may be.

[3]Martin Bronfenbrenner, "Nixonomics and Stagflation Reconsidered," *Economic Polices in the 1970s*, Alfred K. Ho, editor, Michigan Business Papers, No. 57, 1971, pp. 16–17.

[4]Milton Friedman, "The Role of Monetary Policy," *American Economic Review*, March 1968, pp. 1–17 (reprinted in Smith and Teigen, *Readings in Money, National Income and Stabilization Policy*). See also, Roger W. Spencer, "The Relation Between Prices and Employment: Two Views," Federal Reserve Bank of St. Louis, *Review*, March 1969, pp. 15–21. If the increase in aggregate demand is unanticipated, commodity prices typically rise faster than money wages, lowering real wages and increasing the quantity of labor demanded. If workers incorrectly anticipate higher real wages, they increase the quantity of labor supplied. For both of these reasons employment temporarily rises.

Empirical Evidence on the Phillips Curve

Since Phillips' study appeared, many other economists have sought further evidence on the relation for different time periods and different countries.[5] In recent years it appears that the curve as shown in Figure 15–1 has not been stable. In 1970, average unemployment was 4.9 percent, and the consumer price index rose by 5.9 percent from 1969 to 1970. Clearly such a pair of values would lie above and to the right of the curve in Figure 15–1. George L. Perry estimated two short-run curves: one for the mid-1950s and one for the period from 1967–70. These were flatter and above the one shown. He argues that part of the reason for this shift is the changing composition of the U.S. labor force. A larger proportion of women and youth, two groups with typically high rates of unemployment, are now in the labor force. Thus, the average rate is higher than formerly.

Eckstein and Brinner have also reported that the Phillips curve has shifted rightward.[6] They argue that as the rate of inflation increases, the Phillips curve will shift upward year by year. This is because inflation leads to expectations of more inflation, all of which feeds the inflation itself. Thus, the rate of inflation remains high even in the face of relatively large unemployment, and the Phillips curve is then held to have shifted upward.

The Council of Economic Advisers once constructed the relation as shown in Figure 15–2 in the belief that *changes* in the rate of unemployment and *changes* in the rate of inflation might be related with a lag. Note that the GNP "gap" is used as a measure of the rate of unemployment. This gap is the difference between actual GNP and what GNP would have been if the economy had operated at a full-employment level. The price index used to measure the rate of inflation in Figure 15–2 is the GNP deflator rather than the consumer price index.

Thus, the evidence on the Phillips curve is hardly uniform. The curve changes position from period to period and from place to place and it also changes depending on the choice of measures for rates of inflation and unemployment rates. We can hardly conclude, in view of the diverse estimates of the curve, that the Phillips curve represents any kind of empirical law. However, the evidence does give one the feeling that a curve of some sort does exist, although measurement of the trade-off at any point in time would be very rough indeed.

Price Stability

The goal of price stability is difficult to define and measure for reasons in addition to those mentioned above. First, several price indexes are used to value different goods and services, and their movements are not coincident.

---

[5]See G. L. Perry, *Unemployment, Money Wage Rates, and Inflation* (Cambridge, Mass.: M.I.T. Press, 1966); "Changing Labor Markets and Inflation," *Brookings Papers on Economic Activity*, No. 3, pp. 411–41, 1970; and Charles L. Schultze, "Has the Phillips Curve Shifted? Some Additional Evidence," *Brookings Papers on Economic Activity*, No. 2, 1971.

[6]Otto Eckstein and Roger Brinner, "The Inflation Process in the United States," Joint Economic Committee of Congress, February 22, 1972.

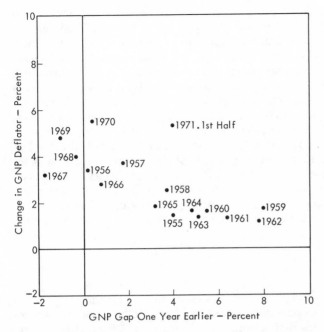

FIGURE 15–2 Relation of Change in GNP Deflator to Change in GNP Gap One Year Earlier

SOURCES: Department of Commerce and Council of Economic Advisers.

The Consumer Price Index, the Wholesale Price Index, and the GNP deflator may provide different answers to the question of how much inflation we are experiencing. In the four-year period 1967–71, for example, consumer prices rose at an average annual rate of 5.3 percent; wholesale prices rose at 3.5 percent; but the GNP deflator rose by 4.5 percent. Second, although it is widely recognized that product improvements and productivity increases occur over time, it is difficult to measure them, let alone incorporate them into the price indexes. This is especially evident in the case of services, like medical care, which have demonstrated dramatic increases in productivity as well as rising dollar costs. To the extent that increases in prices overstate the real costs to society of producing our goods and services, perhaps on the order of 1 to 2 percent per year, we might be willing to treat a modest degree of inflation as tantamount to price stability.

So far we have simply assumed that a stable price level is desirable, but a case can be made for gently rising or falling prices as a long-run goal. One argument for gradually rising prices is that a slight degree of inflation helps create an aura of prosperity and promote economic expansion and growth by rewarding the more venturesome, risk-taking elements of society.[7] On the other hand, declining prices (with stable or more slowly falling money wages)

---

[7] See Sumner H. Slichter, "On the Side of Inflation," *Harvard Business Review*, Vol. 35 (May–June 1957), pp. 15 ff.; and for a reply to his position see Neil H. Jacoby, "The Threat of Inflation," in the same journal, September–October 1957, pp. 15 ff.

provide a method of sharing the gains of productivity broadly, and benefit some segments of society that would otherwise suffer from reduced real income. However, neither a rising nor falling price level has found favor with most economists and policymakers. First, there are no safeguards to guarantee that gently rising (declining) prices will not become cumulative and lead to runaway inflation (deflation). Second, long-run inflation, for example, even if controlled, may seriously alter our balance of payments position vis-à-vis other countries, leading to chronic United States deficits or retaliation by countries adversely affected by lower prices in the United States. Third, our pricing mechanism is not sufficiently flexible, at least in the downward direction, to make such a goal institutionally feasible. It is doubtful that business or labor would welcome a regime of, say, falling prices and stable wages. As a consequence of these limitations, the consensus appears to be that the safest and most acceptable long-run goal is a stable price level, or one rising at a very modest rate, part of which may simply be the result of the statistical upward bias of the price indexes.

Economic Growth

One way for a nation to realize increases in output over time is to maintain full employment of its resources, including labor. To the extent that unemployment obtains, policies that restore full employment will provide a fairly rapid, one-shot increase in the production of goods and services, a process that closes the gap between the current and the potential levels of GNP. Once a full employment level is reached, output can increase at the rate of growth provided by a growing labor force and improvements in the nation's productivity. In this process, further increments in real output may only be realized by raising the economy's *capacity* to produce. Economists usually reserve the concept "economic growth" to refer to the latter process and measure growth in terms of the percentage increase in potential output or output per capita. In common parlance, however, the term is broadly used to include growth in actual *or* potential output, depending upon the particular context in which it is used. Unless otherwise indicated, we will mean by economic growth increases in capacity to produce additional output. This distinction is often important because some policy measures used to maintain or restore full employment, even though they increase current levels of GNP, may not raise the nation's long-run growth rate. For example, reductions in personal income tax rates or larger transfer payments by government may stimulate consumption and aggregate demand without increasing the rate of saving and capital formation. On the other hand, certain types of expenditures by government and investment by business firms may reduce unemployment and increase the potential level of output. That is, they may raise both actual output and the rate of economic growth.

Economic growth may be enhanced by: (1) more intensive use of capital; that is, more capital per unit of labor; (2) improved technology; (3) better education and training of the labor force; and (4) more effective management of resources. A national growth policy would consist of measures designed to increase the productivity of labor or capital. This might be accomplished by providing businessmen with incentives to add to the capital stock, to modern-ize existing facilities, to expand research and development, or to offer on-the-job training for their employees. In addition, direct government involvement in research programs or public works intended to raise capacity output might be undertaken.

The desirability of increasing the nation's output has been widely discussed and debated in recent years by economists, policymakers, and the public. Dur-ing the early 1960s and again in 1970–72, high unemployment has caused them to stress the need for expansionary policies to raise the level of aggregate demand. In addition, comparative studies have shown that during the 1960s, the growth rate of the GNP of the United States was well below that of a num-ber of major Western European countries, Japan, and probably the Soviet Union, although above that of countries such as Great Britain, and concern has been expressed over the implications of this development for the role of the United States in world affairs. On the other hand, not all are agreed that a higher rate of growth is desirable in today's world.

Many argue that it is time for the nation to recognize the costs as well as the benefits to society of more production. The more we produce, the fewer the natural resources available to future generations and the greater the pollution of our environment today and tomorrow. In this view, efforts to increase the GNP and the material wealth of the economy may reduce the quality of life and the average standard of living, contrary to earlier views, which at least implied the more the better. The rejoinder is that the problem of pollution can-not be solved by accepting a lower rate of output; we must increase our tech-nology and production in areas that will help provide clearer air and water, noise control, and so on. More important, while there remain substantial seg-ments of the population whose standard of living is unacceptably low, it is unconscionable to assert that we are producing too much.

Some economists, while not opposed to a relatively rapid rate of growth per se, believe that the decision to save, and thereby accumulate wealth, should be made by the individual citizen rather than by government. Accordingly, monetary and fiscal measures should not be used to determine the nation's growth rate. On the other hand, some economists accept economic growth as a proper goal of government but reject the notion that faster growth is easily attained and can be counted on to provide the output for every new claim on the nation's production. In this view, as expressed in the 1970 *Annual Report of the Council of Economic Advisers*, p. 72, "the basic full-employment growth path of an economy is not readily raised by any of the policy instruments that we now know about."

Suffice it to say, economic growth will probably continue to rank high on the list of national goals for the foreseeable future and policymakers will con-tinue to study the relationships among growth, unemployment, and inflation as they have in the past.

Balance of Payments Equilibrium

The fourth goal is an appropriate balance in the balance of payments, that is, the avoidance of large or chronic deficits or surpluses vis-à-vis the rest of the world. This is essential because serious imbalances disrupt trade with other countries, promote world-wide economic instability, and compromise other economic objectives. In a world of relatively fixed exchange rates, long-term deficits reduce a country's monetary reserves, exert deflationary or recessionary pressure at home, and encourage the deficit country to protect itself by erecting a system of controls in order to limit imports or restrict capital outflows. Surplus countries, on the other hand, gain reserves, develop inflationary pressures, and may therefore limit the inflow of capital from other countries. If a country responds to these imbalances by following severely restrictive or expansionary policies, the byproduct may be the export of unemployment or inflation to its trading partners, which invites retaliation and is counterproductive. If the United States is the deficit or surplus country, the disruptive effect is all the greater because of its importance in world affairs and the special role of the U.S. dollar in international financial markets. The dollar is widely used as a medium of exchange in the settlement of international debts and by the central banks of the world in maintaining the system of fixed but adjustable exchange rates, such as existed from 1946 to the spring of 1973. It is also an important asset in the portfolios of many central banks. Its role is, therefore, unique and imposes on the United States an obligation to avoid policies that would impair its ability to function as a world banker—a major source of the world's money and credit.

At the same time, the importance of the United States as a major source of the world's liquidity may require modest deficits as a means of assuring a net increment in the supply of international reserves. Increases in gold production and the use of Special Drawing Rights (credits created by the International Monetary Fund) may meet some of the need for monetary reserves, but for the foreseeable future some additional dollars may be essential to facilitate a rising volume of world trade and finance.[8]

With respect to the other goals, appropriate balance in the balance of payments may call for policies that are inconsistent with the achievement of domestic stability.[9] A serious recession in the United States indicates that expansionary monetary and fiscal measures are needed to restore full employment, but if we are currently running large deficits in our balance of payments, there may be a conflict between the domestic and international objectives: low inter-

---

[8]Negotiations are intended to determine the relative roles of gold, SDRs, dollars, and possibly other currencies as international reserve assets. It was hoped that progress could be made by the time of the annual IMF meeting at Nairobi in September 1973, but results at that meeting were disappointing. Urgent need for reform of the international monetary system was generally agreed upon, but agreement on specific answers to questions concerning reserve asset composition and other problems proved difficult to obtain.

[9]A succinct statement of the problem of reconciling domestic and international goals through monetary and fiscal policies is found in Robert A. Mundell, "The Appropriate Use of Monetary and Fiscal Policy for Internal and External Stability," *International Monetary Fund Staff Papers*, Vol. 9 (March 1962), pp. 70–9 (reprinted in Smith and Teigen, *Readings in Money, National Income and Stabilization Policy*); and an excellent graphical treatment of this subject may be found in Dwayne Wrightsman, "IS, LM and External Equilibrium," *American Economic Review*, Vol. 60 (March 1970), pp. 203–8.

est rates and increased spending will raise our imports of goods and services, and perhaps our imports of securities (that is, our lending or investing abroad). There will also be a conflict of goals if we simultaneously experience both inflation and a balance of payments surplus: restrictive policies may reduce inflation at home but will worsen our international position by cutting imports and by attracting capital (exporting securities). In the event that we face domestic recession *and* a surplus, or inflation *and* a deficit, the policies need not conflict: expansionary policies are indicated for recession and a balance of payments surplus; restrictive measures will help combat inflation at home and a deficit in our balance of payments.

The Dilemma of Policy

This brief discussion of economic goals should serve to underscore the importance and the difficulty of determining appropriate economic policy. If we are to enjoy a rising standard of living over the years ahead, it is imperative that widespread unemployment be avoided, and probably that inflation should be held to a rate not exceeding 2 to 4 percent per year. This will require a rate of growth in aggregate demand sufficient to provide for consumption of the output produced by a growing labor force, and by increased productivity; an excessive rate of growth in aggregate demand, however, is undesirable. If total spending rises too rapidly, inflation will result, as it may at less than full employment if cost-push factors are raising unit costs of production. Those responsible for monetary and fiscal policies then face the following dilemma: if steps are taken to reduce total spending, the rate of inflation may be lowered, but only by increasing unemployment. On the other hand, if policy is used to assure full employment, inflation will persist. Employers, when faced with excessive wage demands by union negotiators, will acquiesce to these demands in the belief that the Federal Reserve will have to permit the inflation or else assume the blame for the obvious inefficiencies in an economy with a high rate of unemployment.

In this view, inflation arises essentially because perfect competition does not exist in the markets for goods and the market for factors of production, or because prices are not sufficiently flexible to bring about a full employment equilibrium rapidly enough. One solution suggested by those opposed to implementation of contracyclical monetary and fiscal policies is that international trade barriers be lowered, unilaterally if necessary, in order to make America's markets more competitive. And they sometimes suggest that stronger enforcement of antitrust legislation would stimulate more effective competition.

Thus the policymakers are on the horns of a dilemma. They could pursue a policy of steady monetary growth over the long run, only to find that excessive inflation or excessive unemployment resulted, depending on whether the rate of increase in the money supply were too rapid or too slow. Or they may attempt to adjust its policy by basing its evaluation on several factors and find that the result may be somewhat more inflation and also somewhat more unemployment than desired.

MACROECONOMIC POLICIES

The types of policy available to the federal government to help achieve the economic objectives outlined above are often referred to as "stabilization policies." They are (1) monetary policy, (2) fiscal policy, (3) debt management policy, and (4) an incomes policy. These macroeconomic policies, which affect total spending and are in a sense financial in nature, are generally regarded as the major economic policies used to achieve the goals discussed previously. Especially in relation to some goals—for example, growth—other policies, such as antitrust activities, policies to promote labor mobility and to increase labor skills, and programs to enhance the general level of education may be important, but their discussion in any detail is beyond the scope of this book.

Monetary Policy

Broadly construed, monetary policy refers to those actions of the Federal Reserve that affect the behavior of monetary aggregates (for example, monetary base, M_1 or M_2 money supply, bank credit), interest rates, and the overall liquidity of the economy. Accordingly, a policy of monetary restraint would entail a slower rate of growth of the monetary aggregates and *tend* to raise interest rates and lower the liquidity of the economy as compared to a policy of monetary ease. This does not mean that whenever interest rates are high or rising that monetary policy is restrictive in an *absolute* sense, nor that it alone is responsible for the degree of credit restraint. Clearly the demand for funds, as well as the supply, affects the level of interest rates, and Federal Reserve policy is but one of several influences on credit conditions. When interest rates are rising over a period of weeks or months, as during a typical period of economic expansion, we attribute this development to a *relative* excess of demand over supply of funds at lower rates. Presumably, the Fed could moderate the rise in rates or even lower them, temporarily at least, if they increased the monetary base and money supply at a fast enough rate. Whether they could *maintain* lower rates over a longer period of time is a moot point—it would depend on the relative changes in the demand for and supply of loanable funds.

Conversely, low or declining interest rates, which occur during an economic downturn, cannot be said to be *caused* by Federal Reserve policy alone. A decline in the demand for funds *relative* to the supply of funds is the proximate cause of the observed decline in rates. These points are worthy of emphasis because all too often monetary policy is blamed or applauded for developments in financial markets through a failure to appreciate the meaning of Alfred Marshall's analogy that it takes *both* blades of the scissors of demand and supply to cut.

Our definition of monetary policy encompasses control over both money and credit. These controls may be divided into those that regulate the *volume* of money and credit (quantitative or general controls) and those that restrict the *uses* of credit (qualitative or selective controls). The two groups are shown in Table 15–1. Each was discussed briefly in Chapter 4 following the section on the monetary base and multiplier. They have also been referred to on numerous occasions in other chapters and it suffices here to make a few summary comments about their relative use and importance in monetary control.

The most important single control available to the Federal Reserve is open market operations. They have several advantages over the other measures, which explains why most observers identify monetary control with purchases and sales of government securities. First, as compared with the discount rate, open market operations are far more powerful, more flexible, and more precise in effect. With a portfolio of over $75 billion of securities and the ability to create monetary liabilities, the Fed can exert an enormous influence on bank reserves. Moreover, it can do so flexibly and at its own initiative. By comparison, the discount mechanism is a weak tool in that changes in the discount rate may or may not induce desired changes in bank borrowing, excess reserves, and deposits. Nor do changes in the discount rate signal changes in the posture of monetary policy in today's markets, in that the adjustments in the rate are usually made only after other market rates have already changed some weeks earlier—the discount rate is raised or lowered to bring it into "better alignment" with other rates. Second, compared with changes in reserve requirements, open market operations are again more flexible, more easily reversed, and perhaps more acceptable to member banks.

In short, the Federal Reserve can initiate changes in policy through purchases or sales of government securities; the quantitative effects on bank reserves can be estimated with reasonable precision; the operations can be adjusted or reversed easily and quickly; and member banks will be less apt to blame the Federal Reserve for the instability in their reserve position in the case of a restrictive policy if it results more from open market sales than from an increase in reserve requirements.[10] Against these important advantages it should be observed that open market operations may have some disadvantage in that their impact is not as immediate and uniform on all banks as the impact

TABLE 15–1　Monetary and Credit Controls

Quantitative *(General)*	*Qualitative* *(Selective)*
1. Open market operations 2. Changes in reserve requirements 3. Discount mechanism	1. Interest rate ceilings (Regulation Q) 2. Margin requirements (Regulations T, U, and G) 3. Consumer credit controls (Regulation W) 4. Mortgage credit (Regulation X) 5. Moral suasion ("Jawboning")

[10]For a fuller exposition of these points, see Thomas Mayer, *Monetary Policy in the United States* (New York: Random House, 1968), pp. 52–55.

of the other quantitative controls: the initial effect of open market purchases and sales is on banks in the major financial centers, and it takes time for these developments to be transmitted to the rest of the country.[11] Although the length of the lag is not known, it is now presumably less than in former years because of the increasing integration of financial markets and the development of new techniques for mobilizing reserves and deposits—for example, Federal funds, certificates of deposit, and repurchase agreements.

Fiscal Policy

Fiscal policy refers to federal government actions determining the size and composition of the budget, that is, expenditures and receipts. As usually understood, the term fiscal policy excludes state and local government budgets because these agencies have neither the responsibility for maintaining national prosperity nor the power to use their budgetary processes for that purpose. The major part of federal government spending is for currently produced goods and services; the remainder represents mostly transfer payments to individuals and grants-in-aid to state and local government. Receipts, on the other hand, consist mainly of personal and business taxes; contributions for social insurance make up most of the balance. As we shall see in Chapter 17, there are some reasons for arguing that the budget need not always be balanced and that a balanced budget at full employment *may* be the best objective.

A deficit results whenever receipts are less than expenditures. When a cash flow deficit occurs, the shortfall of receipts must be supplemented by drawing down cash or borrowing funds by issuing securities. Because of the need to maintain working cash balances, the deficit is financed almost entirely by borrowing from the public, the commercial banks, or, and only rarely, from the Federal Reserve System. A surplus budget, of course, means that receipts are currently in excess of expenditures. When this occurs, the federal government may increase its cash balances or reduce its outstanding debt. Again, the budget imbalance is normally reflected in a change in outstanding Treasury securities.

Fiscal policy, like monetary policy, affects the levels of employment, output, and prices by raising or lowering the level of money spending. But unlike monetary policy, which works via changes in monetary aggregates or interest rates, fiscal policy affects economic activity mainly by altering the level of disposable income available to the private sector. Changes in government expenditures produce initial changes in total spending because they are part of aggregate demand; they produce secondary changes in total spending to the extent that consumer spending changes are in response to changes in disposable income; that is, there are "multiplier" effects. Changes in tax rates, on the other hand, have only the secondary effect; they change disposable income but have weaker multiplier effects on total spending and income than do changes in expenditures, dollar for dollar. However, whether a deficit or surplus budget is the result of changes in expenditures or tax rates, economists are generally

---

[11]See Ira O. Scott, Jr., "The Regional Impact of Monetary Policy," *Quarterly Journal of Economics*, May 1955, pp. 269–84.

agreed that *at a given level of GNP*, deficit budgets are more expansionary than surplus budgets. This means also that the larger the deficit (the smaller the surplus), relative to GNP, the greater the fiscal stimulus. How a deficit budget is financed is a significant element in determining the impact that the deficit has on both the level of spending and interest rates.

The types of taxes and composition of federal government spending are also important. First, the distribution of income is apt to be different, depending upon the types of taxes used to raise revenue. Second, different tax structures, which affect private spending, and different expenditure programs will influence the composition of output and hence the allocation of resources. Fiscal policy, therefore, has effects on both the level and the composition of national output.

Debt Management Policy

Debt management refers to those actions of the Treasury and Federal Reserve System that affect the *composition* of the federal debt held by the public. The Treasury is responsible for issuing securities in order to raise funds when deficits are incurred, for seasonal requirements even though the annual budget is in balance, and to refinance maturing securities. On the other hand, if tax proceeds exceed expenditures, surplus funds are available to retire outstanding Treasury obligations. The decision to include the Federal Reserve's actions in the definition of debt management stems from the fact that the open market purchase or sale of government securities, in addition to its monetary effects, changes the *composition* of the public's holdings of these securities. The monetary authority, therefore, has a part in the debt management of policies of government.

To the extent that the structure of interest rates or the liquidity of the economy can be changed through debt management operations, stabilization of the economy might be enhanced by policies that would raise spending during recessions and restrict it when aggregate demand was generating inflationary pressures. Whether the government *should* manage the debt with this objective in mind or whether in this event such a policy would be likely to have significant effects on economic activity is subject to much debate. The question will be considered in Chapter 17.

Incomes Policies

Although it is widely agreed that monetary and fiscal policies constitute the main weapons in our arsenal of anti-inflation controls, many economists would supplement these conventional measures with "incomes policies." As usually understood, this concept includes government programs "aimed at securing restraint in labor demands regarding pay and in business decisions regarding prices."[12] Such programs might take the form of a zero-increase

---

[12]Thomas M. Humphrey, "The Economics of Incomes Policies," *Monthly Review*, Federal Reserve Bank of Richmond, October 1972, p. 3.

wage-price freeze—Phase I of the President's New Economic Policy implemented in August 1971—or the 5.5 percent wage increase guidelines and the
profit margin ceilings of Phase II—or an incomes policy with fewer or less
specific restrictions, along the lines of Phase III and Phase IV introduced in
1973. Whatever the precise form, incomes policies are intended to reduce inflationary pressure emanating from the cost or supply side of the market.

Proponents of incomes policies allege that cost-push inflation cannot be
satisfactorily dealt with through restrictive monetary and fiscal policies. In
this view, policies that restrain aggregate demand, though perhaps effective in
reducing inflation, do so only by raising unemployment to intolerable levels.
Because, the argument continues, this type of inflation derives from the monopoly power of unions to secure excessive wage payments and of business to
"pass through" these increased unit costs by raising prices, incomes policies
are the appropriate instruments to cope with this exercise of market power.

Incomes policies might also prove an effective means of dealing with the
problem of inflationary expectations as it relates to the wage-price spiral. If
wage demands are based upon expected rates of inflation, as well as on the
rate of unemployment, then price increases will induce wage increases, which
in turn exert subsequent upward pressure on prices, and so forth, generating a
spiral of inflation. Part of the rationale for incomes policies is that a program
that temporarily freezes prices and wages or establishes percentage guidelines
reduces the likelihood that inflationary expectations will be self-fulfilling.

The case against incomes policies is pressed by those who argue that such
policies (1) interfere with the market mechanism and misallocate resources,
and/or (2) are an ineffective means of combating inflation. Critics charge that
to the extent that such controls work, they do so by preventing the market
from clearing at equilibrium prices: resources will not flow into their highest
and best use, and such inefficiency reduces economic welfare. Second, those
who hold that inflation is due solely to excessive demand, rather than cost-push
factors, deny that incomes policies can prevent or combat inflation. In their
view, government is the real culprit, which, instead of controlling monetary
factors or the budget, seeks to blame labor or business for its own failure to
control aggregate demand.

Which view of the inflationary process is correct? Have incomes policies
been effective in curtailing inflation? Will incomes policies become a permanent part of our anti-inflation program? Unfortunately, there is no clear-cut
consensus on these or related questions. Most observers would probably agree
that, at times, inflationary pressures emanate from the supply side; but whether
such developments can be *sustained* at a critical rate in the absence of excess
demand is subject to much debate. As to the question of effectiveness, there is
no way to "prove" empirically that incomes policies have, or have not, worked.
The critical and unanswerable question is what would have happened if wage
and price controls had not been imposed. Furthermore, the actual behavior
of prices before and after the so-called guideposts of 1962–67 or before and
after the Phase I freeze of 1971 can be used to support either view of the effect
of incomes policies during those periods. In the earlier episode there was virtually no inflation in the year before the guideposts were introduced nor during
the first three years of the program. However, from early 1965 until the demise

of the guideposts, under pressure from escalation of the Vietnam War, prices rose at an increasing rate. There is a similar difficulty in interpreting the experience of 1971. The rate of inflation had been accelerating from mid-1965 until mid-1970, when consumer prices were advancing at an annual rate of 5.9 percent. Although still very high, the rate of inflation began to subside one year *before* the Phase I freeze, to an average rate of 4.3 percent for the period mid-1970 to mid-1971. It slowed further during the 90-day period of the freeze and through mid-1972 during Phase II.

Even though the evidence on effectiveness is inconclusive, many observers believe that *some* types of incomes policies will be employed from time to time in the foreseeable future. In a world where the goals of high employment, price stability, and economic freedom are difficult to reconcile, it seems a likely surmise that incomes policies will be regarded by many as the lesser of several evils.

THE MONETARIST-FISCALIST CONTROVERSY[13]

A debate has been in progress in the United States for some time as to what the government should do to help reduce unemployment and raise output without rekindling inflationary forces.

On the one side are the monetarists, who would place chief reliance on monetary policy, working through the system of markets in the private sector. Monetarists tout a modern form of the ancient "quantity theory of money," which holds that the quantity of money is the primary determinant of prices and income. On the other side are neo-Keynesian fiscalists who emphasize taxing and spending measures, perhaps supplemented by price and wage guidelines or controls.[14] Some monetarist-fiscalist differences reflect political judgments concerning what can or ought to be done; others stem from alternative models of economic behavior and interpretation of the results of empirical studies.

The Keynesian Revolution and the New Economics

The worldwide depression of the thirties and the promulgation of Keynesian theory in England and the United States caused a revolution in thinking about economic affairs. Indeed, the growing acceptance of Keynes' theories, in academic circles at least, followed from the failure of existing economic theory to provide a cogent rationale for the Depression, let alone a program for economic recovery.

The early Keynesian view was that equilibrium might occur at a level of

---

[13]This section is based on an article by William Pigott and Robert H. Scott, "The Monetarist Controversy in the United States," *The Banker*, October 1972, pp. 1259–66. We thank the editor of that journal for permission to use this material.

[14]Milton Friedman and Walter W. Heller, *Monetary vs. Fiscal Policy* (New York: W. W. Norton and Co., 1969).

employment considerably below "full employment." Moreover, expansionary monetary policy could not be counted on to restore full employment because:

1. an increase in the quantity of money might not reduce interest rates; and
2. even if market rates did decline a significant additional amount of investment might not be forthcoming.

The only remaining source of private spending, the consumer, was passive and unlikely to raise his expenditures in the absence of higher income and in the face of prolonged downturn.

Federal government deficit spending on a large scale was the Keynesian alternative to secular stagnation. By the end of the thirties many economists and many policymakers had accepted this doctrine; fiscal policy replaced monetary policy as senior partner in the program for economic stability. Those who favored a larger role for government and social planning also supported the concept of using the taxing and spending powers of government for social purposes.

The war that began in 1939 in Europe and America's subsequent involvement pushed our economy to full employment; the Depression was over and control of inflation became the prime concern. The problem of controlling inflation was magnified because Federal Reserve policy had been dedicated to pegging the market price of government securities at par for at least the duration of the war. Low and stable interest rates became the primary objective: low rates to minimize the Treasury's borrowing costs, stable rates to facilitate the sale of securities to the public.

The Depression and the war years convinced most observers that monetary policy was relatively impotent against depression and was likely to produce undesirable side-effects if used forcefully against inflation. Economic literature reflected this view of the world, and research efforts were focused on various elements of Keynes' basic theory: consumption-income relationships and budget multiplier models replaced work on money and its velocity, the stock-in-trade of macroeconomic researchers in earlier times.

With the advent of the Kennedy-Johnson administrations and the stewardship of Walter W. Heller as chairman of the Council of Economic Advisers, the "new economics," as neo-Keynesian theory was dubbed, became the conventional wisdom. The long period of business expansion beginning in 1961 and reinforced by the "magnificent tax cut" of 1964 ushered in a new period of prosperity without significant inflation until after 1965. Along with it came the new language of "full-employment surplus," "fiscal dividends," and "fine-tuning" which, if not household words, became part of the jargon of the financial press and the business community. The Keynesian revolution was complete.

The Monetarist Counterrevolution

But in the background there were signs of change, changing events and changing ideas. In the world of affairs, the rate of inflation began to increase in 1965; in the world of ideas, the reemergence of the quantity theory of money, dressed in modern garb by the new monetarists, raised serious questions for the new orthodoxy. On the one hand, the acceleration of inflation, in spite of fiscal restraint, and the failure of Keynesian economists to forecast the degree of inflation that occurred in the late sixties, led many observers to search for new answers. Second, the articulation of an alternative theory of money, prices, and interest rates advanced by monetarists received increasing attention. New studies offered a different, perhaps better, way of looking at government policies and their relationships to aggregate demand, prices, and financial markets.[15]

Since the mid-sixties, a strong vocal minority within the economics fraternity has achieved increasing acceptance by appealing to those who had become disenchanted with continual deficit spending and inflation and to those who always believed that monetary influences were of utmost importance. Although still not entirely persuasive to most economists, "the central issue that is debated these days in connection with macroeconomics is the doctrine of monetarism."[16] Monetarism must be recognized as an important alternative to Keynesianism, which had been largely unchallenged since the Great Depression.

Keynesian Doubts

A modern Keynesian's lack of confidence in monetary policy has three major bases. First, he believes that changes in the quantity of money are the *result* as well as a *cause* of changes in business conditions; changes in income and spending induce changes in money, as credit is granted and demand deposits increase. In technical terms, money is an "endogenous" variable. It follows that the policy of the monetary authority is only one of many factors determining the short-run behavior of money. Second, a Keynesian views securities rather than goods and services as close substitutes for money. He argues that *if* a change in the money stock *does* affect spending, it does so *indirectly* by changing credit conditions and interest rates. It is *not* expected that new money will be spent *directly* on consumer goods, at least not on a large scale. Finally, he believes that a change in the money supply, although it has some impact on interest rates, may not, say, lower the market rates of interest significantly, nor lead to significantly increased spending even if rates do fall.

Fiscal policy, on the other hand, has direct effects on income whether the deficits, say, are financed by new money created by the banking system or by the sale of securities to the public—that is, the "activation of idle balances." In the former case the multiplier effects will be larger, but either method will be expansionary. Today's Keynesians agree with the monetarists that money matters and that control over money (and credit) is necessary. The difference

[15]David I. Fand, "A Monetarist Model of the Monetary Process," *Journal of Finance*, May 1970, pp. 275–89; Leonall C. Andersen and Keith M. Carlson, "A Monetary Model for Economic Stabilization," *Review*, Federal Reserve Bank of St. Louis, April 1970, pp. 7–21.

[16]Paul Samuelson, "The Role of Money in National Economic Policy," *Controlling Monetary Aggregates*, Federal Reserve Bank of Boston, 1969, pp. 152–74.

between them is one of degree. If faced with serious unemployment or infla-tion, however, Keynesians look first at the budget, especially the surplus or deficit that would obtain at a full employment level of output. If both unem-ployment and inflation persist, a smaller "full-employment" surplus (or bigger actual deficit) should be coupled with a program of price and wage guidelines or controls.

Monetarist Rebuttal

Monetarists reject most of the above analysis concerning money and the relative roles of monetary and fiscal policies. For them the money supply can be, or is, a crucial variable, and its control is vital. Money in this view is con-trollable by the Federal Reserve; it is an "exogenous" variable. It is also a close substitute for real goods and services as well as for financial assets. *If, then, the money stock is increased, it will spill over into the market for con-sumers' and producers' goods as well as the market for securities and real estate.*[17] In this way the quantity of money has strong direct effects on private expenditure, not merely weak indirect effects via changes in the money and capital markets (and interest rates).

Because the public's desire to hold money is not highly sensitive to changes in the market rate of interest, hoarding and dishoarding do not occur on a significant scale. Thus, there will be no "activation of idle balances" to finance government deficits, but rather a "crowding out" of private expendi-tures when government borrowing drives up the cost of credit.[18] In short, the rate of interest is considered much more important in the decision to borrow and spend than in the decision to hold money or securities. Accordingly, the impact of fiscal policy hinges on the sources of finance. If no new money is forthcoming to finance, say, a budget deficit, the pure fiscal effect on the level of total spending, which Keynesians feel is strong, is expected by monetarists to be relatively minor.

Inflation, which helped give the modern quantity theorists a new lease on life, is judged by them to be a purely or mainly monetary phenomenon. The pronouncement that "at all times and in all places" inflation is associated with a rapid increase in the money supply leaves little doubt as to that point. De-mand-pull, not cost-push, factors are the source of inflation. To control infla-tion, control money; some would say that nothing more nor less is required; most would say that nothing else will do. The technique for control is rela-tively simple, in principle: the Federal Reserve should expand the money sup-ply at a fixed rate of growth per year regardless of the state of economic activ-ity. A monetary rule would replace the use of discretionary policy, the approach used since the inception of the Federal Reserve. The percentage

[17]Some suggest, for example, that open market purchases tend to lower interest rates and that this tends to raise stock market prices, thus increasing consumer wealth (through capital gains).

[18]Roger W. Spencer and William P. Yohe, "The 'Crowding Out' of Private Ex-penditures by Fiscal Policy Actions," *Review*, Federal Reserve Bank of St. Louis, Octo-ber 1970, pp. 12–24.

rate of growth would depend upon the definition of the money stock used, the expected long-run demand for money to hold, and the expected long-run growth rate of real output. For many monetarists this program would be far more likely to promote prosperity without inflation than any system of fine-tuning.[19]

Empirical Questions

There are a host of knotty empirical questions concerning the role of money and the effectiveness of monetary policies: What assets constitute the "true" money supply of economic theory? To what extent is money an endogenous/exogenous variable, however money is defined? What are the channels through which monetary influences operate on real income, prices, and interest rates? What kind of time lags affect the transmission of policy actions? How long and variable are these lags? How are monetary influences distributed between real and nominal variables, for example, output and prices? These empirical questions suggest the magnitude of the problem in assessing the usefulness and reliability of monetary controls. The most critical issue is the money-income nexus, the stability of the relationship between monetary changes and the level of income, and the direction of causation. If it can be shown that changes in the quantity of money *cause* regular, predictable changes in total spending, the collateral question of how this occurs would seem to be of secondary importance. For purposes of analysis, the channels of transmission of monetary influences are very important, but as a matter of policy the expected results, not its *modus operandi*, are of paramount concern. In brief, we would like to know (1) how much does money matter, and (2) in what ways does money matter. Most of the empirical work has been directed toward the first question.

Recent Research: Methods and Findings

Two main lines of research by monetarists have been used to present and support their position. One group of studies, exemplified by the pioneering work of Friedman, Schwartz, and Cagan, has examined the cyclical and secular relationship between the quantity of money and output, prices, and employment in the United States for as far back as 1867. Much of this work was done under the auspices of the National Bureau of Economic Research and led to the monumental study, *A Monetary History of the United States, 1867–1960*, by Milton Friedman and Anna Schwartz. Friedman's tentative conclusions were that:

> Changes in the quantity of money have important and broadly predictable economic effects. Long-period changes in the quantity of money relative to

[19]For an excellent summary of the rules versus authorities debate and the problem of lags, see Thomas Mayer, *Monetary Policy in the United States* (New York: Random House, 1968), pp. 200–10, 178–90.

output determine the secular behavior of prices. Substantial expansions in the quantity of money over short periods have been a proximate source of the accompanying inflation in prices. Substantial contractions in the quantity of money over short periods have been a major factor in producing severe economic contractions, and cyclical variations in the quantity of money may well be an important element in the ordinary mild business cycle.[20]

The conclusions are offered as "qualified" and "limited," and Friedman stresses the importance of interpreting the results obtained as representing average behavior, not applicable to every episode in our monetary history. He is also quick to point out that many factors other than the quantity of money are significant, perhaps dominant, especially in the case of long-run movements in real output, which depends on technological improvement and population growth. However, the finding of Friedman and Schwartz that in every one of the six major depressions during the past century—and at no other time—the money supply declined significantly and began to decline prior to the downturn in general economic activity is impressive evidence of the importance of money.[21] They stressed, moreover, that the change in the money supply in these cases resulted from what might be termed exogenous factors and could not be interpreted as feedback effects.

What then has been proved? Certainly that there is an important historical tie between money and economic behavior. But as Tobin and others have observed, it is one thing to demonstrate that "money matters;" it is quite another to conclude from this that "money is all that matters."[22]

The second empirical approach has been vigorously pursued by monetarists at the Federal Reserve Bank of St. Louis. It consists of using correlation analysis to test the explanatory power of monetary and fiscal variables. By relating changes in gross national product to changes in money (or the monetary base) and various measures or components of the budget, the St. Louis economists sought to measure the relative importance of monetary and fiscal actions in explaining the variations in economic activity. They concluded from their equations that the response of GNP to fiscal actions relative to monetary actions were not (1) larger, (2) more predictable, nor (3) faster. *In fact, the St. Louis studies find ". . . no measurable net fiscal influence on total spending in the test period," from 1952 to mid-1968.*[23] By implication, monetary actions explain more (nearly all) of the variance in GNP and are more powerful than fiscal actions.

The response was immediate. Economists at other Federal Reserve Banks

[20]Milton Friedman, "The Monetary Studies of the National Bureau," *The National Bureau Enters Its 45th Year, 44th Annual Report*, 1964, pp. 7–25.

[21]Milton Friedman and Anna J. Schwartz, "Money and Business Cycles," *Review of Economics and Statistics*, February 1963, Supplement, p. 34.

[22]James Tobin, "The Monetary Interpretation of History," *American Economic Review*, June 1965, pp. 646–85.

[23]The St. Louis study used changes in the high employment expenditures and receipts as measures of fiscal influence. Leonall C. Andersen and Jerry L. Jordan, "Monetary and Fiscal Actions: A Test of Their Relative Importance in Economic Stabilization," *Review*, Federal Reserve Bank of St. Louis, November 1968, pp. 11–24.

inclined to a more moderate view, and others with a more Keynesian orienta-
tion questioned the methods and the conclusions. Critics argued that the St.
Louis equations were spurious and incorrectly specified. Some contended that
the equations were not derived from any specific structural theoretical model
and therefore had no theoretical content. They were a weak substitute for the
specification of important behavioral relationships amenable to empirical verification. A clearly superior approach, it was argued, would be the specification
and testing of a complete model of the economy.[24]

Second, even if the equations used were legitimate, some reviewers alleged
that the proxy variables chosen to represent monetary actions were endogenous rather than exogenous. In other words, the question of feedback and
possible reverse-causation weakens or destroys the meaningfulness of the high
correlation coefficients obtained by the equations. Close association does not
prove causation.[25]

As might be expected, the controversy continues. Monetarists have been
much impressed with their own finding that money matters most, while other
economists want more convincing evidence. Both sides agree that earlier views
were extreme; the pendulum has indeed swung back quite a distance since the
Keynesian revolution, but much remains to be done to settle the dispute over
money and policy. Additional studies are necessary to reconcile the conflicting
evidence on hand concerning both the magnitude and timing of effects of monetary actions. We also need more information concerning the channels of
transmission of policy actions.

SUMMARY

Most economists and policymakers agree that the government should use monetary and fiscal policies to achieve high employment, price stability, economic
growth, and balance of payments equilibrium. There is less agreement on how
these goals should be defined and on whether they are compatible. The relationship between the rate of unemployment and the rate of inflation (Phillips
curve) and its implications for economic policy is one such area of controversy.

Although monetary and fiscal policies are widely regarded as the most
important anti-inflation controls, some would supplement these measures with

[24]James Tobin, "The Role of Money in National Economic Policy," *Controlling
Monetary Aggregates*, Federal Reserve Bank of Boston, 1969, p. 23. Large, multiple-
equation models of the economy were pioneered by Professor Lawrence R. Klein of the
Wharton School. These were followed by models constructed by Professor Dan Suits
of the University of Michigan, the Brookings-Social Science Research Council group,
and a group of economists from the Massachusetts Institute of Technology who worked
with the Staff of the Federal Reserve Board of Governors. Many other models also exist
today.

[25]Frank DeLeeuw and John Kalchbrenner, "Monetary and Fiscal Actions: A Test
of Their Relative Importance in Economic Stabilization—Comment," *Review*, Federal
Reserve Bank of St. Louis, April 1969, pp. 6–11. Also see, Henry A. Latané, "A Note
on Monetary Policy, Interest Rates and Income Velocity," *Southern Economic Journal*,
January 1970, pp. 328–30.

incomes policies to combat inflation, which they believe emanates from the supply side of the market. Others hold that incomes policies are not only unnecessary but unduly interfere with the market mechanism, thus disrupting the allocation of resources. Instead, critics would rely solely on monetary and fiscal measures to restrict aggregate demand.

An important current debate centers on the appropriate role of monetary and fiscal policies. Monetarists argue that changes in government expenditures and tax rates have uncertain or weak effects on income, employment, and prices and therefore they favor sole reliance on monetary controls. Fiscalists, utilizing an income and expenditures approach to economic analysis, are critical of the monetarists' empirical findings and support the use of budgetary changes to achieve economic stability and growth.

QUESTIONS FOR DISCUSSION

1. Explain what one means when he says that the Phillips curve represents a "trade-off."

2. How would expectations of inflation affect the position of the Phillips curve?

3. List the factors generally recognized as contributing significantly to economic growth.

4. Use examples to distinguish between "general" and "selective" controls exercised by the Federal Reserve System in the interest of economic stabilization.

5. What are the arguments in favor of and against imposition of a national incomes policy?

6. Briefly state the nature of the monetarist-fiscalist controversy.

7. What is the difference between the goal of high employment and the goal of rapid economic growth?

8. What are Professor Friedman's major arguments supporting his claim that changes in the quantity of money have a special importance in policy actions?

SELECTED REFERENCES

A useful review of the issues and an examination of several models constructed to explain the Phillips curve are found in Edward Foster, *Costs and Benefits of Inflation*, Studies in Monetary Economics No. 1, Federal Reserve Bank of Minneapolis, March 1972. A limited bibliography is also included.

In addition, the Samuelson-Solow article referred to in the text and several other references are of special interest:

Saul H. Hymans, "The Trade-Off Between Unemployment and Inflation: Theory and Measurement," *Readings in Money, National Income, and Stabilization Policy*, rev. by eds. W. L. Smith and R. L. Teigen. Homewood, Illinois: Richard D. Irwin, 1970, pp. 152–63.

Edmond S. Phelps et al., *Microeconomic Foundations of Employment and Inflation Theory.* New York: W. W. Norton and Company, Inc., 1970.

Almarin Phillips, (chairman), "Wage-Price Dynamics, Inflation, and Unemployment," Papers and discussion presented at the 1968 annual meeting of the American Economic Association and published in *American Economic Review*, May 1969, pp. 124–67.

U.S. Congress, Joint Economic Committee, *The Inflation Process in the United States* (A study prepared for the Joint Economic Committee by Otto Eckstein and Roger Brinner), 92nd Cong., 2nd sess., February 22, 1972.

Thomas M. Humphrey, "Changing Views of the Phillips Curve," *Monthly Review*, Federal Reserve Bank of Richmond, July 1973, pp. 1–13.

The student may find it illuminating to compare the views of three chairmen of the Council of Economic Advisers—two past and one current (1974)—on the monetary-fiscal "mix." See Walter W. Heller, *New Dimensions of Political Economy* (New York: W. W. Norton and Company, Inc., 1966, Chapter 2; Arthur M. Okun, "Rules and Roles for Fiscal and Monetary Policy," *Issues in Fiscal and Monetary Policy: The Eclectic Economist Views the Controversy*, ed. James J. Diamond, (Chicago: DePaul University Press, 1971), pp. 51–74; Herbert Stein, "Where Stands the New Fiscal Policy?" *Journal of Money, Credit and Banking*, August 1969, pp. 463–73.

A recent study by L. R. Klein compares three important models: (1) The Wharton Model, (2) the "academic" version of the Federal Reserve Board-Massachusetts Institute of Technology-Pennsylvania Model, and (3) the St. Louis Federal Reserve Model. Klein discusses the theoretical structure of the models and presents empirical evidence from tests with these models that bears on the monetarist-fiscalist debate. See Lawrence R. Klein, "Empirical Evidence on Fiscal and Monetary Models," *Issues in Fiscal and Monetarist Policy: The Eclectic Economist Views the Controversy* (Chicago: DePaul University Press, 1971), pp. 35–50.

A number of important issues in the debate over monetarism are discussed in Leonall C. Andersen, "The State of the Monetarist Debate," Federal Reserve Bank of St. Louis, *Review*, September 1973, pp. 2–8. See also the Commentary by L. R. Klein and that by Karl Brunner in the same issue, pp. 9–14.

The concept of unemployment and the methods used in collecting unemployment statistics for the evaluation of employment conditions are described in Sharon M. Haley, "Behind the Unemployment Rate," Federal Reserve Bank of Richmond, *Monthly Review*, October 1973, pp. 10–16.

The entire issue of the Federal Reserve Bank of Boston *New England Economic Review*, September/October 1973, was devoted to comparisons of the accuracy of macroeconomic econometric models for forecasting. Models that were "subjectively adjusted" were better in prediction than unadjusted models. See also Paul A. Samuelson, "Lessons from the Current Economic Expansion," *American Economic Review*, Papers and Proceedings, May 1974, pp. 75–77.

Another recent study of effects of inflation should be mentioned: Richard M. Young, "Inflation and the Distribution of Income: Are the Poor Really Hurt?," Federal Reserve Bank of Philadelphia, *Business Review*, September 1973, pp. 16–25.

16

Federal Reserve Policy and the Financial Markets

Our interest in Federal Reserve policy extends beyond the fact that what the Fed does strongly influences the course of economic activity. We are also interested in the Federal Reserve because in the conduct of its policies it participates directly in financial markets and produces important effects on monetary variables and credit conditions. Earlier we observed that the most important monetary policy tool, open market operations, impinges initially on commercial bank reserves and on the prices and yields of United States government securities. But the effects of policy are not limited to bank reserves and the market for government securities. They spread rapidly to other money and capital markets and, with a lag, to the markets for goods and services and thence to income, employment, and prices. However, thus far we have said little about *how* monetary changes are transmitted to other markets and sectors of the economy.

In the first section of this chapter we outline the transmission mechanism and indicate the channels through which monetary policy operates. Next, we look at the implementation process of monetary policy and discuss several alternative strategies the Fed could employ in its open market operations. The central issue in the selection of a potential strategy is the question of targets or guides: the variables that the Fed should seek to control in order to achieve its economic objectives. We examine some implications that different strategies have for the behavior of interest rates and the money supply.

MONETARY POLICY'S TRANSMISSION MECHANISM

The current status of monetary theory is such that it is not entirely clear how a change in monetary policy works its way through the financial and real sectors of the economy. Although economists agree that the initial impact is mainly on bank reserves, some emphasize subsequent changes in bank credit and interest rates and the influence they have on aggregate demand via spending for investment goods and consumer durables. Other analysts stress the importance of changes in the money supply and argue that these changes may directly affect spending for goods and services as well as indirectly through the prices and yields of financial assets. The disagreement is not so much over *which* variables enter the transmission process but over their *relative* importance in the linkage sequences.

However, most theories can be accommodated by viewing the transmission process as working through the following elements: (1) portfolio adjustment, (2) wealth effects, and (3) credit availability effects. Most theories interpret the process as working principally through portfolio adjustments, as spending units react to changes in the relative prices and yields of financial and real assets that are induced by a change in monetary policy.[1] As a result of these adjustments, the level of spending and income is altered; subsequent multiplier-accelerator effects reinforce the initial changes in spending; and all of these factors produce feedback on financial variables, including the money supply and interest rates.

Portfolio Adjustments

In order to trace the effects of a monetary change, let us assume that the portfolios of commercial banks and the public are initially in equilibrium: portfolios are optimal with respect to size and composition of assets.[2] Assume further that the Fed wishes to increase total spending in order to reduce the rate of unemployment and that to do so it buys Treasury bills from a government securities dealer. The immediate effect is an increase in demand deposits and reserves of commercial banks. The purchase also tends to raise prices and lower yields on Treasury bills. The following adjustments take place as banks and the public react to the change in reserves and to the new bill yields.

Commercial banks may repay borrowings from the Fed or add temporarily to their excess reserves. Thus, free reserves—excess reserves minus member bank borrowing from the Fed—initially rise, and the Federal funds rate declines. More importantly, the increase in excess reserves subsequently induces banks to expand their loans and investments. This is accompanied by a reduction in the rates charged bank borrowers and the yields on securities. The decline in bill yields makes other money market instruments more attractive and induces substitution into these assets, which raises their prices and lowers their yields—money market rates all tend to decline. Within a short

[1]See Maurice Mann, "How Does Monetary Policy Affect the Economy?", *Journal of Money, Credit, and Banking*, August 1969, pp. 538–48.

[2]This means that the actual rate of saving equals the desired rate and that the rate of return on assets cannot be increased by changes in the composition of assets within the constraints imposed by consideration of risk aversion, and so on. See Richard Zecher, "On the Content and Issues of Current Monetary Economics," *Money and Finance: Readings in Theory, Policy and Institutions* (2nd ed.), ed. Deane Carson (New York: John Wiley and Sons, Inc., 1972), pp. 259–69.

time, the process of substitution of higher- for lower-yielding securities and loans would be expected to spread to longer-term markets as lenders and borrowers adjust their portfolios of financial assets and liabilities. Corporate bond yields, as well as those on long-term Treasury issues, on municipal securities, and on mortgages, decline, reflecting the general easing of credit conditions in both the money and capital markets.

These interest rate effects tend to increase investment expenditures by business firms, spending by state and local government, and outlays by consumers for durable goods. Thus the main channel through which portfolio adjustments affect economic activity is the interest rate-investment channel.

With an expansion in bank credit, bank deposits rise. The public holds more deposits both as a direct result of the open market purchases by the Fed and as a result of the creation of deposits by banks. As new deposits begin to be held by consumers as well as by business firms (which constitute the major initial borrowers), consumers begin to adjust their asset portfolios. They may transfer funds from checking accounts to time deposits in commercial banks, to mutual savings banks, or to savings and loan accounts. As a result, additional loans may be made and the velocity of money tends to rise.

After a period of time, perhaps several months, following the initial monetary action, interest rates stop declining and begin to rise as the economic expansion exerts increasing pressure on financial markets. Just when this occurs depends upon the magnitude of the initial monetary stimulus and upon the response of borrowers and lenders in the money and capital markets to the changes in income and spending. But at some point rates rise. Further impetus to the upward movement is provided if commodity price increases build in a premium for expected inflation.

To summarize, monetary policy actions impinge initially on bank reserves and the market for government securities. Changes in other money markets and capital markets occur as a result of changes in relative prices and yields. These, in turn, induce further changes in the prices of existing goods and services. The increased relative profitability of consumer and producer goods opens up a gap between actual and desired stocks of real goods, which raises output and employment. Subsequently, prices of commodities increase as production is expanded; the rise in economic activity reverses the decline in market rates of interest, which rise toward new equilibrium levels. The process continues until output, prices, and interest rates reestablish equilibrium in the portfolios of market participants—until prices and quantities of financial and real assets again satisfy the preferences of asset holders.

Wealth Effects

Many economists, while interpreting the above process in terms of portfolio adjustments, suggest that monetary policy also operates through a "wealth effect"—through a change in the *size* as well as the composition of assets. Thus, changes in wealth are expected to alter spending-saving decisions with consequent effects on output, employment, and prices. In economists' jargon, an increase, say, in the public's wealth will produce an upward shift in the consumption function. Similarly, a decline in wealth will lower consumer spending.

The wealth effect is induced by a change in interest rates resulting from Federal Reserve open market operations. When, for example, the Fed buys government securities, market rates tend to decline, and the prices of securities rise. As noted, these changes spill over into the markets for other securities and real assets. Thus, an expansionary monetary policy, the argument runs, lowers a broad range of capitalization rates by which investors value expected income; this is reflected in higher market values of stocks, bonds, real estate, and other forms of wealth. The predicted effect is an increase in consumer spending because of this increase in wealth, and thus an increase in aggregate demand, which induces higher levels of output, employment, and prices.[3] For example, in the Federal Reserve—MIT—Penn model of the economy, a major portion of the effect of monetary policy on economic activity derives from the effect of policy on the stock market. Moreover, in this model the introduction of the stock market-wealth effect link significantly speeds up the response of changes in nominal GNP to changes in monetary measures. It reduces the lag in effect of policy from 3 years (the lag without the wealth effect) to 5 to 6 quarters.[4]

Some have questioned this line of reasoning by pointing out that although wealth holders experience an immediate increase in the market value of their assets when capitalization rates decline, the lower level of yields may require more saving in the future in order to maintain the same level of income. In short, although the wealth holder's present need for saving is reduced, his future requirements may be increased by the decline in yields, and the longer-run effect on spending may be uncertain.[5] However, most economists have come to accept the hypothesis that current consumption is a function of "life cycle" or "permanent" income and the implication of that hypothesis that increases in net worth, including capital gains, cause an increase in consumption spending. It should be noted that this is classified as a wealth effect rather than an income effect because capital gains are not treated as income in national income accounting, in which income is defined as the revenue earned in a period as a result of the production of goods and services during that period.

---

[3]Some economists argue that Federal Reserve operations produce wealth effects *directly* as well as through changes in interest rates. There is considerable doubt about the validity of this view, and most models limit the wealth effect to the mechanism outlined in the text. See Warren L. Smith, "On Some Current Issues in Monetary Economics: An Interpretation," *Journal of Economic Literature*, September 1970, pp. 768–69.

[4]See Franco Modigliani, "Monetary Policy and Consumption: Linkages Via Interest Rates and Wealth Effects in the FMP Model," *Consumer Spending and Monetary Policy: The Linkages*, Federal Reserve Bank of Boston, June 1971, pp. 9–58.

[5]Henry C. Wallich raises this point in his discussion of Warren L. Smith's "A Neo-Keynesian View of Monetary Policy," *Controlling Monetary Aggregates*, Federal Reserve Bank of Boston, 1969, pp. 130–31. A further consideration that weakens the influence of the wealth effect of debt securities is that most long-term government debt, where the potential for price changes is the greatest, is not held by consumers nor nonfinancial business firms. Moreover, many bond holders, especially financial institutions, carry these securities at par rather than market value.

The Availability of Credit

If all markets were perfect and prices and yields adjusted rapidly to changes in supply and demand, the full effects of monetary policy would be transmitted promptly through changes in relative prices. However, many financial markets are characterized by imperfections and institutional factors that do not allow prices to equate supply and demand. For a period of time, prices may fail to clear the market, and an excess of demand or supply must be accommodated by nonprice factors—there are changes in the "availability" rather than in the price of credit.[6] The most important examples of how monetary policy works through changes in the availability of credit are found in the markets for bank loans, mortgages, and savings deposits. Although changes in the availability of credit may signal a shift toward monetary ease or restraint, the following discussion will be limited to the effects that might be expected to obtain during a period of restrictive monetary policy.

It has been observed in earlier chapters that commercial bankers employ certain devices such as compensating balance requirements, standards of creditworthiness, or the pledging of collateral as part of loan agreements. If these nonprice elements are used to restrict loan demand, the volume of credit outstanding may be restrained without immediate or appreciable changes in rates of interest. In this regard it is often charged that credit rationing discriminates against small businesses, in that these firms, having virtually no access to capital markets, are heavily dependent upon bank loans. If, then, the argument runs, the lending capacity of banks is restricted by monetary policy, bankers continue to lend to their regular (presumably larger) customers and curtail their loans to smaller, less creditworthy borrowers. On the other hand, there is some evidence that small firms obtain some additional bank credit indirectly during such times in the form of trade credit extended by the larger firms, which continue to receive bank financing. In this way small business firms may be able to carry additional inventories and accounts receivable financed by the larger firms rather than directly by commercial banks. In this view, credit restraint impinges on business firms in general rather than solely on small business. But in either case a program of monetary ease or restraint may be effective even though loan rates are slow to adjust to equilibrium levels.

For somewhat different reasons, the mortgage market and the construction industry may also be affected by changes in Fed policy that work through changes in the availability of credit. Legal restrictions on interest rates charged mortgage borrowers or paid to savers may reduce the flow of funds into new mortgages and hence restrict construction spending, as during the "credit crunches" of 1966 and 1969, with the result that monetary restraint impinges severely on these markets as compared to other markets in which prices are flexible and competitive.

[6]Changes in the availability of credit are usually stressed in the context of restrictive monetary policy. An analysis of the arguments that changes in the availability of credit may be an effective aspect of monetary control is provided in Thomas Mayer, *Monetary Policy in the United States* (New York: Random House, 1968), pp. 126–37.

Similarly, state and local governments may reduce their borrowing and their spending during periods of monetary restraint, not only because the cost of credit is high and rising, but also because of restrictions on the rate of interest they are allowed to pay for borrowed funds. Such restrictions result from ceiling rates established by bond referenda, statutory law, or constitutional provisions. They effectively preclude borrowing when market rates rise above the rates permitted, as occurred during the credit crunches referred to earlier. For essentially the same reason, the federal government has often been denied access to the long-term capital market because of the 4¼ percent limitation on the rate it may offer investors on securities having a maturity in excess of seven years. When the yields on corporate securities, municipals, and mortgages rise to levels that more than compensate for the risk of default, the United States Treasury finds it necessary to restrict its new issues to the shorter-term markets.

Thus, the availability of credit effects are especially important because of the selective impact they seem to have on various sectors of the economy. Although the evidence is by no means conclusive, it appears that a policy of monetary restraint imposes a special burden upon small business, state and local governments, and the mortgage market and construction industry.[7] Although some of the restrictiveness is due simply to the fact that the cost of credit is higher during such periods, part of the restraint results from certain nonprice elements, including legal restrictions imposed by government regulations and laws, business practices in oligopolistic markets (bank lending practices), and information costs that delay interest rates adjustments.

Nonetheless, most of these restrictions on the flow of credit are temporary, and when interest rates do subsequently rise and perform their functioning as a rationing device, the only lasting impact of monetary restraint results from the changes in market rates and prices.

The Problem of Time Lags

One of the most important problems inherent in programs aimed at maintaining high employment without inflation over a considerable period is that of time lags. Briefly stated, the problem is that it takes time for policymakers to recognize that economic conditions have improved or worsened (the recognition lag), to take corrective steps to restore the desired level of economic activity (the administrative lag), and time for these measures to have effects on the levels of output, employment, and prices (the impact lag). These time lags are shown in Figure 16–1.

If the lags were always short in duration or highly regular in timing, they

[7]There have been many studies of the impact of monetary policy on various sectors of the economy. A survey of recent econometric studies and an extensive bibliography is found in Michael J. Hamburger, "The Impact of Monetary Variables: A Survey of Recent Econometric Literature," *Essays in Domestic and International Finance*, Federal Reserve Bank of New York, 1969, pp. 37–49, reprinted in W. L. Smith and R. L. Teigen, eds., *Readings in Money, National Income and Stabilization Policy*, 2nd ed. (Homewood, Ill.: Richard D. Irwin, Inc., 1970). See also the arguments on both sides of the question of whether monetary restraint effectively discriminates against certain borrowers in Thomas Mayer, *Monetary Policy in the United States*, pp. 164–74.

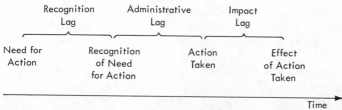

FIGURE 16–1 Lags in Monetary and Fiscal Policies

could either be ignored or, in the latter case, incorporated into the policymaking process. In these circumstances, lags would not interfere significantly with macroeconomic policies. Long and variable lags, on the other hand, increase the risk that policies designed to achieve our economic goals may in fact destabilize the economy by accentuating fluctuations in spending and income emanating from the private sector. The problem of lags is especially troublesome for "discretionary" as opposed to "automatic" policy, because the former institutes changes in policy only after the need for action has become evident, rather than automatically when economic conditions themselves change. Although estimates differ as to the average length and variability of these three lags, the consensus seems to be that: (1) the recognition lag is the same for monetary and fiscal policies, (2) the administrative lag is longer for fiscal policy, and (3) the impact lag is longer for monetary policy.

Recognition and Administrative Lags

The recognition lag results from the fact that the monetary authority is unable to predict turning points in the level of economic activity with precision. Thus, it must collect and interpret data to confirm that economic conditions have changed. This may require several weeks, even months, because there are many economic series, and often these data give conflicting information about the direction of the economy.

Once the monetary authority has ascertained that policy should be changed, the necessary steps can be taken very quickly because the decision-making power is concentrated in the hands of the twelve members of the Federal Open Market Committee, a meeting of which can be convened on short notice.

Lags in the Impact of Monetary Policy

The crucial question for monetary policy concerns the impact lag—the time it takes policy actions to affect final spending decisions. Much of the disagreement over the length and variability of this lag relates to the choice among the variables used to represent monetary policy, for example, bank reserves, money supply, bank credit, or interest rates. When, for example, can it be assumed that a change in monetary policy has taken place—when reserves have changed, or the rate of growth in M_1 or M_2, or credit conditions and interest rates?

Some disagreement also centers on how to measure the appropriate changes in whichever policy variable is selected and in the real variables that are the objectives of policy. Richard G. Davis notes that it makes a great deal of difference how this is done:

> If, for example, the rate of change in the money supply is replaced by deviations in the level of the money supply from its long-run trend, the average lag between monetary peaks so measured and peaks in general business apparently shrinks from the sixteen months previously cited to a mere five months. Alternatively, it can be plausibly argued that the appropriate measure is the lag between the rate of change in the money supply, and the *rate of change* rather than the level of some measure of business activity such as gross national product (GNP) or industrial production. When peaks and troughs for money and business are compared on this basis, the lead of money over business appears to be quite short.[8]

Though most estimates of the average length of the impact lag are in the neighborhood of six to nine months, the empirical evidence is sketchy. More importantly for monetary policy, the question of the variability of lags remains unresolved as well. Some hold that the lag is both long and variable; they therefore favor a monetary rule such as that proposed by the monetarists. Others find shorter and less variable lags in their studies of the transmission mechanism, leading them to support the continuation of discretionary monetary control. In between are those who assert that though the impact lag is relatively stable it is longer than the standard estimates suggest.

To summarize, monetary policy is intended to raise or lower the level of spending by the private sector, and it operates through (1) portfolio adjustments, (2) wealth effects, and (3) credit availability effects. Most economists agree that monetary policy influences are transmitted primarily through portfolio adjustments that occur as a result of a change in the Federal Reserve's holdings of government securities. Wealth holders, including commercial banks, are induced, by changes in the money supply and the yield on financial assets, to alter their relative holdings of various types of financial and real assets. Thus the prices of existing real assets rise when the money supply is increased, and this, in turn, induces an increase in newly produced goods and services, with subsequent effects on the level of employment and on prices in general. At the same time, these changes in economic activity have feedback effects on the financial system, so that financial and real variables interact, moving the economy toward a new equilibrium position. Figure 16–2 shows the major effects of monetary policy. Financial yields, shown at the left, affect the components of aggregate demand on the right through the three channels discussed above. In this diagram the feedback effects are not shown, nor are

---

[8]Richard G. Davis, "The Role of the Money Supply in Business Cycles," Federal Reserve Bank of New York, *Monthly Review*, April 1968, p. 71. Italics in original. The reference to the 16-month lag is to Milton Friedman's estimate. See "The Lag Effect in Monetary Policy," *Journal of Political Economy*, October 1961, p. 456. More recently Friedman seems to have revised his estimate to 6–9 months. Milton Friedman, "How Much Monetary Growth?" Morgan Guaranty Trust Company, *The Morgan Guaranty Survey*, February 1973, pp. 5–10.

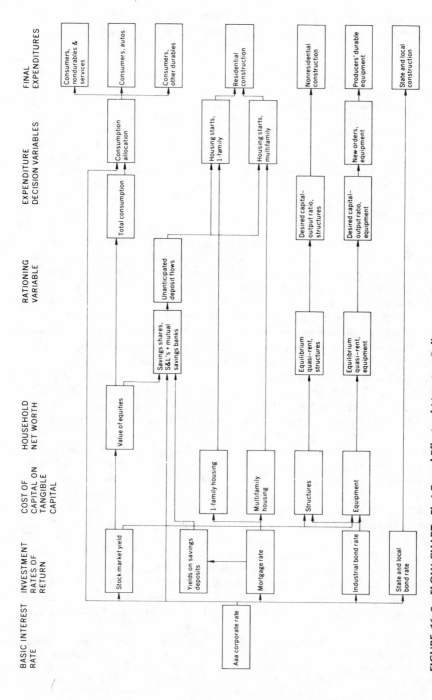

FIGURE 16-2 FLOW CHART: First-Round Effects of Monetary Policy

SOURCE: *Federal Reserve Bulletin*, June 1969, p. 484.

the initial effects on the money markets, described earlier in this chapter and at the close of Chapter 9.

THE IMPLEMENTATION OF MONETARY POLICY

Even though most economists agree that monetary policy works through the effects described in the preceding section, they differ as to the specification of the transmission mechanism—as to the relative importance of money, credit, and interest rates in the transmission of the effects of monetary policy. As a consequence, there are differences of opinion over *how* the Federal Reserve should manipulate its policy instruments so as to achieve the desired movements in output, employment, and prices. This is the implementation problem of monetary policy.

Our discussion of the implementation of monetary policy was begun in Chapter 4, in which we presented a simple framework within which the Fed acted on the money supply by altering the so-called monetary base. This framework was used for expository purposes: it was intended to show how the money supply is determined by the portfolio decisions of commercial banks, the public, the Treasury, and the Fed. It also served as an introduction to the policy instruments used by the Federal Reserve System.

The monetary base-money supply formulation is *one* approach the Federal Reserve could use in implementing its policy. Indeed, many economists especially those who take a monetarist view of the transmission mechanism, argue that such a procedure is more likely than most to satisfy our economic objectives. However, there are a large number of strategies that could be used, and it is useful to consider a few of them, including, of course, approaches used by the Fed in recent years. In this section we indicate the need for policy guides; we examine various strategies available to the Federal Reserve; we explain why the Federal Reserve has adopted certain approaches over recent years, and we look at the implications that different policies have for the financial markets.

The Need for Monetary Policy Guides

The way monetary policy changes are transmitted to the rest of the economy is imperfectly understood: there are variable lags in the effect of policy; changes in income and employment are related to nonmonetary factors; there is continual interaction between real and financial variables. What all of this means to the Fed is that it cannot be sure whether its current policy is expansionary or restrictive—and therefore appropriate in terms of its objectives—by simply observing *current* changes in, say, GNP, prices, or the rate of unemployment. These ultimate target variables are too remote from the impact of open market operations to serve as reliable guides to policy; their movements may mislead the monetary authority instead of providing it with useful information about the current thrust of policy.

The Fed needs a guide, a variable located somewhere in the transmission mechanism that will provide this information. The "ideal" guide to policy is an important linkage variable that changes only in response to actions by the Federal Reserve, that is, is not influenced by other factors, including changes in the ultimate target variables. That is, the ideal guide would be unaffected by "feedback" from the real sector of the economy. If, for example, the money supply met these requirements, the Fed could manipulate its open market operations with a view to changing the money supply and hence the level, say, of GNP with confidence that the money supply would reflect only the impact of its policy actions. The money supply would serve as both the guide and the target of policy.

Unfortunately, the money supply does not fully meet these requirements, nor for that matter does any other variable in the transmission process. Those variables that are closely related to GNP, such as the money supply, interest rates, and bank credit, are importantly affected by other factors, including changes in GNP (through changes in the demand for money and credit). This makes it difficult for the monetary authority to distinguish between the effects of its policies (supply factors) and the effects of other influences (demand factors). If the guide is used as the day-to-day operating target, then the short-run influence of these other, nonpolicy factors causes it to transmit misleading information about the day-to-day effects that policy actions are having on the intermediate-term behavior of the indicator.

Thus the Fed needs two guides to provide it with two pieces of information: (1) an "indicator" to provide information about the current thrust of the entire financial sector, including Federal Reserve actions, on future movements in the ultimate target variables; and (2) an "operating target" to tell the Fed whether or not its policy actions are the probable cause of the current changes in monetary and credit conditions. For example, the Fed needs to know whether current monetary conditions are becoming more expansionary, remaining unchanged, or becoming more restrictive. They also need to know whether these developments are the results of their actions or of other influences, such as changing demand for credit. This latter information allows the Fed to judge the appropriateness of its current policy position.

The indicator variables link the operating targets with the ultimate target variables. The most widely used indicators are the money supply, bank credit, long-term interest rates or some variant of these. The operating targets are variables the Fed can readily control through day-to-day open market operations, for example, money market interest rates, bank reserves, and so on. The relationships between these three classes of variables are illustrated in Figure 16–3. Because economists disagree over the information content of alternative variables, there are several possible strategies including: (1) a "money supply" strategy, so-called because the money supply is the variable which is alleged to determine GNP; (2) an "interest rate" strategy; and (3) a "bank credit" strategy.

Each strategy is based upon a different hypothesis about the way open market operations are related to the ultimate targets—about the transmission mechanism. They all imply that the relationships between variables are suffi-

FIGURE 16-3

Policy Instrument	Operating Target	Indicator or Intermediate Target	Ultimate Targets
Open market operations $\longrightarrow$	Monetary base $\longrightarrow$	M_1 money supply $\longrightarrow$	GNP, prices, employment
Open market operations $\longrightarrow$	Free reserves $\longrightarrow$	Interest rate $\longrightarrow$	GNP, prices, employment
Open market operations $\longrightarrow$	Nonborrowed reserves $\longrightarrow$	Bank credit $\longrightarrow$	GNP, prices, employment

ciently stable that the monetary authority can determine with reasonable accuracy the effects of its policy actions. How can the policymaker choose between them? Which strategy should he follow? The choice between them is an empirical question: which will best predict the actual results? Let us consider the kind of information necessary to predict these effects by looking at what is required if the policy action is to be successful.

1. The Fed must be able to *control* the operating target on a near-term basis.
2. A change in the operating target must be followed by a *predictable* change in the indicator over a somewhat longer period of time.
3. A change in the indicator must have a *predictable* influence on the ultimate target.[9]

In much of the following discussion of these criteria, we restrict our attention to strategies in which a reserve aggregate serves as the operating target and a monetary aggregate is the indicator. We do so because this type of approach is currently the basis of Federal Reserve open market operations. More importantly, most of the problems of monetary control can be illustrated by reference to these aggregates and the relationships among them. Moreover, much of the current empirical work concerned with implementing policy has been undertaken within this kind of framework.

The Problem of Controlling the Monetary Aggregate

Let us suppose that the Fed has decided upon the desired rate of growth in, say, the M_1 money supply. Assume further that it views the monetary control process in terms of the monetary base-money supply hypothesis outlined earlier. What sources of difficulty are there in such a procedure?

[9] A useful discussion of these criteria and of interest rate and money supply strategies is found in Albert E. Burger, "The Implementation Problem of Monetary Policy," Federal Reserve Bank of St. Louis, *Review*, March 1971, pp. 20–30.

The main difficulty is in predicting the effects that a given change in the monetary base may have on the money multiplier, m. We recall that

$$m = \frac{1 + k}{r(1 + t + g) + k},$$

in the definition of multiplier used in Chapter 4. In essence, the problem is that a change in the base may induce subsequent adjustments in the portfolios of the banks and the public which, by changing the value of the money multiplier, partially offset the effects of the change in the monetary base on the money supply.

If, for example, the Fed buys government securities in order to increase the growth rate of the monetary base, interest rates on these securities tend to decline. If the fall in rates induces commercial banks to hold additional excess reserves rather than increasing their loans and security holdings, the money multiplier declines as the ratio of reserves to deposits, r, rises. In the same way, if the decline in market rates induces the public to raise its time deposit/demand deposit ratio, t, the multiplier declines. In both cases the decline in the multiplier offsets some of the expansionary effect of the larger base. These changes in the multiplier are referred to as "feedback" effects; they occur because the multiplier is a function of the base, that is, $m = f(B)$. The problem for monetary control is that the magnitudes of these effects, which depend upon the interest sensitivity of the demand for excess reserves and time deposits, are difficult to predict. It may also be true that a rise in the base induces a shift by the public toward larger currency holdings and time deposits because of rising income. If so, the multiplier will decline. However, these effects due to changes in income and economic activity occur somewhat slowly and for that reason do not interfere unduly with short-run monetary control.

Similarly, a restrictive monetary policy means a slower rate of growth in the base. But open market sales of securities by the Fed tend to raise market interest rates; this rise may induce banks to reduce their holdings of excess reserves. Also, the public may decide to increase its holdings of market instruments and reduce its time deposits. In these cases, where r and t decline, the money multiplier rises. Thus a major issue in the money supply control procedure is the interest elasticity of the uses of the base. How predictable are the interest rate effects on the distribution of the base between, say, demand deposits, time deposits, and excess reserves?

Considerable empirical research has been aimed at measuring the interest elasticity of the money supply. Much of this work was undertaken in the process of constructing large-scale econometric models of the United States economy. These studies differ in a number of significant ways, including the specification of demand functions for excess reserves, currency, deposits, the time period from which the data are taken, the extent of disaggregation of data, and so forth. For these and other reasons the studies reach somewhat different conclusions. There is a wide range of estimates of interest elasticity, which are difficult to reconcile. However, one review of these studies concludes that "the available evidence suggests quite conclusively that the short-run feedbacks through interest rate changes, which would be generated by policy changes in reserve aggregates, are very weak and should cause little, if any, difficulty for the implementation of policy actions aimed at controlling the money stock through the control of a reserve aggregate."[10]

Changes in Treasury deposits at commercial banks also affect the money multiplier. The g-ratio, where g = government deposits/demand deposits, rises and falls reflecting changes in Treasury receipts relative to expenditures and Treasury decisions concerning the proportion of its balances it wishes to hold at commercial banks rather than at Federal Reserve Banks. If, say, tax payments by the public or loan proceeds from the sale of government securities are credited to the Treasury's tax and loan accounts at commercial banks, the money multiplier declines. This means that the money supply may be subject to rather abrupt short-run changes that the Fed must try to anticipate if it is to achieve its target rate of growth in M_1.

The second problem in monetary control relates to changes in the size of the monetary base itself. Without doubt the Fed can control the behavior of the base over a period of several months, but shorter-run control is made difficult because of unexpected changes in such items as float, member bank borrowings, United States Treasury deposits at Federal Reserve Banks, and adjustments due to changes in reserve requirements. In some cases, the changes are due to random developments; at other times cyclical or seasonal changes occur, such as in the case of float or United States Treasury deposits, which do not conform with previous experience. Errors in sampling or reporting of data, or simply information lags, cause the actual rate of growth to deviate from the desired rate. The significance of this is that the Fed is unable to predict these changes in operating factors on a daily, weekly, or perhaps monthly basis. Instead, they must aim for control over a longer period and thus accept wider swings in the money supply than desired. However, the evidence is quite clear that the quarter-to-quarter changes in the base—those important for control over economic activity—can be controlled through open market operations if the Federal Reserve wishes to do so.

A final problem is the accurate measurement of the money supply itself. Revision of money supply statistics in early 1974 indicated that both M_1 and M_2 increased at more rapid rates during 1973 than had been shown by the previous data. A significant factor was the relatively more rapid growth of nonmember banks, mentioned in Chapter 3. Since data on deposits in these banks are available only several times a year, the nonmember bank deposit component of the money supply must be estimated for interim periods. The growth in the share of total *private* deposits held by nonmember banks, from about 18 percent in the early 1960s to about 25 percent in early 1974, has increased the difficulty of measuring the money supply accurately. To the extent that the money supply increased more than was indicated or desired in 1972 and 1973, this may have been one cause of the speedup in inflation.

[10]See Robert H. Rasche, "A Review of Empirical Studies of the Money Supply Mechanism," Federal Reserve Bank of St. Louis, *Review*, July 1972, pp. 11–19; see p. 19.

The Selection and Control of the Operating Target

The monetary base may be suitable as an operating target for purposes of monetary control, but it is not, of course, the only reserve aggregate available to the Fed. Other reserve aggregates besides the base are member bank reserves and RPDs. One of these, RPDs, has not yet been defined in the text. They are reserves available for private nonbank deposits; that is, RPDs equal total member bank reserves minus those reserves used to meet legal requirements against United States government deposits and net interbank deposits.

The Fed must choose its operating target on the basis of two considerations: (1) which is the easiest to control in its day-to-day operations, and (2) which has the most predictable relationship to the intermediate target, that is, which has the most stable multiplier relating the reserve aggregate (operating target) to its monetary aggregate (intermediate target)? A problem arises in making its choice because it is easier for the Fed to control some reserve aggregates than others, but those reserve aggregates that are easiest to control may have the least stable multiplier so that predicting the effect of changes in the reserve aggregate on the monetary aggregate is less certain. Thus the Fed in its choice faces a trade-off between its ability to control the reserve aggregate and its ability to predict its monetary target. The information requirements are illustrated in Figure 16–4, which shows the relationships among three reserve aggregates.

The boxes across the top of the illustration show the "uses" of reserve aggregates. Each "use" influences either (1) the relationship between open market operations and the reserve aggregate or (2) the relationship between the reserve aggregate and the monetary aggregate. Let us assume for the moment that the monetary base is given—determined by open market operations. In order to predict the relationship between the monetary base and the money supply we must predict the six "uses" of the base—how it will be distributed among the items shown in the six boxes. If all the "uses" of the base were known with certainty, the relationship between the rate of growth of the base and the rate of growth of the money supply would be determined, allowing the Fed to achieve the desired growth rate in the stock of money by appropriate open market operations. This information would provide the value of the "money multiplier" in our earlier formula,

$$m = M/B.$$

The "uses" of the monetary base reflect the portfolio decisions of the public, the commercial banks, and the Treasury.

If total member bank reserves are used as the operating target, the rate of growth in this variable necessary to achieve a desired rate of growth in the money supply depends upon the "uses" shown in boxes 2–6. It would be necessary to predict those "uses," that is, to estimate the "multiplier" relating total member bank reserves to the money supply. In order to *achieve* the bank re-

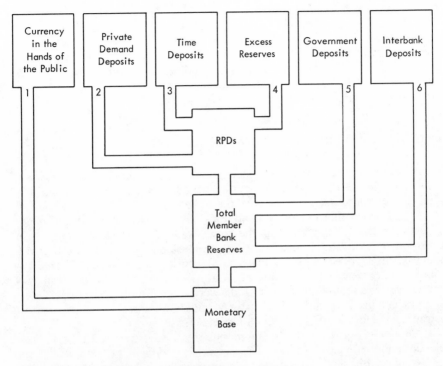

FIGURE 16–4   Uses of Reserve Aggregates

Note: A widely used variant of the monetary base is the net source base, which equals the monetary base minus reserve adjustments and borrowings from the Federal Reserve.

SOURCE: This figure and discussion of the "uses" of reserve aggregates as operating targets are taken from Charlotte E. Ruebling, "RPDs and Other Reserve Operating Targets," Federal Reserve Bank of St. Louis, *Review*, August 1972, pp. 2–7.

serve target, the Fed must have knowledge of the monetary base and of its division between bank reserves and currency in the hands of the public.

The use of RPDs as the operating target requires predicting the "uses" shown in boxes 2–4. This should provide the "multiplier" linking RPDs to the money supply. It is also seen that in order to achieve the target rate of growth in RPDs, the Fed would need information about 1, 5, and 6, currency in the hands of the public, government deposits, and interbank deposits.

Thus the information necessary to specify the required rate of growth in the reserve aggregate depends upon the reserve aggregate selected as the operating target. Different information is also needed to control the various reserve aggregate targets. It would appear that the easier it is to control the operating target, the more difficult it is to predict the appropriate reserve aggregate multiplier. That is, one might expect, for example, that the monetary base, which should be easier to control than, say, RPDs, would have a much less stable multiplier to use to predict a change in the money supply than the one associated with RPDs. However, the evidence is not totally clear on this point. One study that tested for stability of the multiplier relationships did not ". . . provide any basis for conjecture that there has been a more stable relationship between the money stock and RPDs than between the net source base and money."[11] But as the study noted, the findings are inconclusive; they are based upon a particular control procedure and special assumptions about the information available to the Federal Reserve System.

The Choice of the Indicator or Intermediate Target

Whether the Fed uses the monetary base, total member bank reserves, RPDs, or other variables as the operating target, it must also select an indicator. If the money supply is used as the indicator, an increase in its rate of growth is a signal that monetary conditions have become more expansionary (or less restrictive); a slowdown in the growth rate of the stock of money is an indication that monetary forces are less expansionary (or more restrictive). Similarly, an increase in bank loans and security holdings—bank credit— would be interpreted to mean that monetary factors were more expansionary than formerly; a reduction in bank credit would signal more restraint. If interest rates are used as indicators, a rise would be interpreted as evidence of restraint; a decline would be a sign of monetary ease.

Empirically, however, different measures of, say, money or of interest rates may move in opposite directions, making it difficult to say what "the" money supply or "the" interest rate is currently doing. That is, M_1 may grow faster while M_2 grows at a slower rate than in previous periods. In the same way, money market rates do not always rise or decline together nor move in the same direction as capital market rates from day to day, week to week, or even from month to month. For example, during 1972 short-term and intermediate-term rates rose continually through the first eight months, while longer-term rates remained relatively stable at first and later declined during the same period.

More importantly, over periods of several months changes in money (M_1 or M_2), bank credit, and interest rates in general are typically in the same direction. That is, with the exception of cyclical turning points, at which differences in direction and rates of change may be observed, money, credit, and interest rates generally increase during periods of economic expansion and decline during periods of economic slowdown and recession. Thus, monetary and credit aggregates may signal a policy of monetary ease, while interest rates indicate a program of restraint. However, we know that all three sets of variables are affected by and reflect factors other than monetary policy—both supply and demand are important. The choice between these indicators poses a

---

[11]Albert E. Burger, "Money Stock Control," Federal Reserve Bank of St. Louis, *Review*, October 1972, pp. 10–18. The results of this study are shown in detail in the complete version of the paper published in *Controlling Monetary Aggregates II: The Implementation*, Federal Reserve Bank of Boston, September 1972, pp. 35–55.

number of problems at both the theoretical and empirical levels. Those who argue in favor of interest rates as the indicator do so on the grounds that interest rates provide more information about future income changes than do money or credit. In this view, the demand for money function is either elastic or unstable or both, so that changes in money do not predict income with an acceptable degree of certainty. Those who favor money over interest rates allege that the demand for money is highly interest inelastic and stable, whereas the demand for goods and services is unstable. In this view, essentially the monetarist position, changes in the stock of money best predict the behavior of income. In this framework, the empirical question concerns the relative shape and stability of the demand function for money, on the one hand, and the demand for goods and services on the other.

Money Market Conditions Strategy

Thus far, we have restricted our attention to strategies in which reserve aggregates serve as the operating target and money, credit, or long-term interest rates are the indicators. However, money market conditions may also provide the basis for open market operations, either in conjunction with these aggregates or in an independent strategy. Indeed, during the 1950s and 1960s, money market conditions played several roles in Federal Reserve policy. We discuss the reasons for the Fed's concern over money market conditions later in this chapter. But at this point we emphasize two ways in which money market conditions could be used in open market strategy: as an operating target or as the indicator.

First, money market variables, for example, the Federal funds rate or free reserves, may serve as the day-to-day operating target. In such an approach, open market operations are aimed at a certain value or range of values for, say, the Federal funds rate, in order to achieve a desired rate of growth in the money supply or bank credit, or a desired change in long-term rates of interest. Used in this way, the money market variable is an alternative to the monetary base, bank reserves, RPDs, and so on. On the other hand, money market variables could be used in conjunction with various reserve aggregates, provided only that the control period be different for each target in the linkage between open market operations and, say, GNP. Professor Jack Guttentag has suggested such an approach, which he refers to as a "complete strategy," because it relates the day-to-day target to those having longer control periods and thus to the Federal Reserve System's ultimate objectives. His example illustrates such a procedure.[12] In this rather sophisticated approach, money market conditions are a low-order target, which are changed by the Fed so as to produce subsequent changes in the more remote targets as shown in Figure 16–5.

[12]See Jack M. Guttentag "The Strategy of Open Market Operations," *The Quarterly Journal of Economics*, February 1966, pp. 1–30. See, especially, his discussion of the importance of money market conditions in Federal Reserve policy during the period 1951–60, pp. 3–20.

FIGURE 16–5

	Day	*Week*	*Month*	*Quarter*	*Quarter*
Open market operations $\longrightarrow$	Money market conditions	Free reserves	Total reserves	Money supply	GNP
	$\longrightarrow$	$\longrightarrow$	$\longrightarrow$	$\longrightarrow$	$\longrightarrow$

Second, money market conditions can be used, not as a stepping stone to other more remote goals, but as a goal of policy itself.[13] In this case, free reserves, the Federal funds rate, or some index of money market conditions might be used instead of money, credit, or long-term interest rates as the indicator the Federal Reserve seeks to control. On the other hand, money market conditions *and*, say, the money supply might be deemed equally important objectives of policy. In either instance, control over money or credit would be more difficult to achieve than when money market conditions are simply a lower-level target. This is because it is difficult to determine the relationship between money market conditions and GNP, and in the absence of knowledge about this linkage, *stable* money market conditions tend to become the goal of policy under the implied assumption that this should promote stability of GNP and also prevent undue fluctuations in the financial markets. In short, if little is known about what money market conditions ought to be, there is an understandable temptation to assume that they ought to be stable.

IMPLICATIONS OF VARIOUS STRATEGIES FOR FINANCIAL MARKETS

The particular strategy used by the Fed in its open market operations may have important implications for the financial markets. It seems likely, in the short run at least, that interest rates will fluctuate somewhat more under a money supply or bank credit strategy than under those aimed at money market conditions or interest rates. This follows from the fact that the Fed cannot simultaneously control both money and interest rates. Thus if the Fed aims at a week-to-week or month-to-month growth rate in the stock of money, it must allow changes in the demand for money to be reflected in interest rate movements. On the other hand, the Fed may be able to maintain relatively stable interest rates in the short run if it is willing to allow whatever changes in the money supply are required to equate supply and demand for money at those rates.

Figure 16–6 is used to illustrate this short-run trade-off between changes

[13] A summary of papers relating to Federal Reserve procedures that elaborates on this point is found in Thomas Mayer, "The Federal Reserve's Policy Procedures—a Review of a Federal Reserve Study and an Ensuing Conference," *Journal of Money, Credit, and Banking*, August 1972, pp. 529–50.

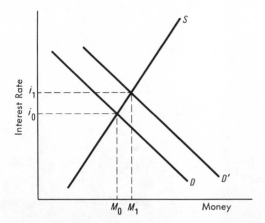

FIGURE 16-6

in interest rates and changes in the money stock.[14] We use the term "money stock" to denote the quantity of money determined by the interaction of the demand and supply *schedules* (functions or curves) for money. The demand schedule for money (D) is assumed to depend upon both the rate of interest and the level of income. The supply curve for money (S) depends upon both the rate of interest and the monetary base (or reserves). The initial equilibrium rate of interest is i_0 and the money stock is M_0.

Let there be an increase in the demand for money, as might occur during a period of economic expansion. The demand schedule shifts right to D', and the interest rate rises toward the new equilibrium rate, i_1. The money stock rises to M_1 as the rise in the interest rate induces the banks to reduce their holdings of excess reserves and expand their loans. Under a money supply strategy the Fed would permit the rate of interest to rise. If the accompanying increase in the money stock were deemed excessive, the Fed could reduce the monetary base (bank reserves), with the result that the interest rate would rise above i_1. In Figure 16-6 this would be shown by a shift to the left in the money supply curve. But if the money stock increase were relatively small and consistent with current policy objectives, the base would not need to be reduced; the result would be as shown.

But suppose now that the Fed aims at stable money markets or stable long-term interest rates rather than stable monetary growth. In this case, illustrated in Figure 16-7, the rise in the interest rate to i_1 requires an increase in the monetary base—a shift in the supply curve to S'—in order to restore the initial target rate of interest, i_0. The money stock increases in this case to M_2. As our illustration shows, the Fed is unable to control both the money stock

[14]An analysis of recent Federal Reserve policy that takes this approach is found in Albert E. Burger and Neil A. Stevens, "Monetary Expansion and Federal Reserve Open Market Committee Operating Strategy in 1971," Federal Reserve Bank of St. Louis, *Review*, March 1972, pp. 11–31, especially pp. 16–19.

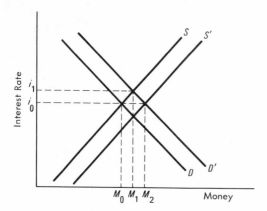

FIGURE 16–7

and the rate of interest, where changes in the latter are demand-induced. Of course, the situation is quite different if the initial rise in interest rates resulted from a reduction in the monetary base, perhaps because of unexpected reductions in float or member bank borrowings. In this instance, the rise in interest rates would be supply-induced and would be accompanied by a reduction in the money stock. Under *either* a money supply or an interest rate strategy, the Fed would increase the monetary base in order to lower interest rates *or* to increase the money stock to the equilibrium position.

Thus far, we have assumed that the Fed can stabilize interest rates, if it wishes to do so, through appropriate open market operations. This seems a reasonable assumption for the short run. But in the long run, the monetary instability that such a policy would produce might cause large swings in income; the demand for money would therefore also change, with the result that interest rates might be highly unstable. In short, monetary policy aimed at stable money market conditions or stable longer-term interest rates might in the longer run be self-defeating. The longer-run behavior of interest rates, wide swings or relative stability, depends in part on how successful monetary and fiscal policies turn out to be in maintaining high levels of income and employment without significant rates of inflation. In this regard, the jury is still out on the important empirical question: how can economic stability be achieved and maintained?

In the meantime, the Fed faces a dilemma: should it try to control the growth of money or temporarily offset demand-induced changes in interest rates?[15] There are arguments for both courses of action. Abrupt changes in interest rates and money market conditions are apt to interfere with Treasury

[15]For a clear statement of the nature of the dilemma and the Federal Reserve's attempts to resolve it see David P. Eastburn, "The Future Role of Interest Rates in Open Market Policy," Federal Reserve Bank of Philadelphia, *Business Review*, January 1973, pp. 3–7.

financing operations; high market interest rates may occasionally lead to "credit crunches," as in 1966 and 1969, with severe impact on certain markets and sectors of the economy. This raises questions of equity among various groups of income earners and spenders: what are the discriminatory effects of tight monetary conditions? should interest rates (and returns to lenders) be allowed to rise at a time when controls over wages and other prices are employed, as in Phase II-, III- or IV-type incomes policies? More importantly, because there is considerable uncertainty about the role of money, credit, and interest rates in economic affairs, it can be argued that wide fluctuations in in-interest rates are apt to be destabilizing and procyclical in effect. Perhaps money market conditions and interest rates should be controlled.

On the other hand, many economists believe that the social benefits of stable money market conditions or interest rates are negligible compared with the costs of such policy. Moreover, they believe that the Treasury's financing problems and "credit crunches," for example, are the product of rigidities in the financial structure, such as, interest rate ceilings on long-term government securities, ceilings on rates paid on time and savings deposits at financial institutions, fixed-rate mortgages, and so on. In this view, these problems should be resolved by eliminating these restrictions or altering the institutional framework in other ways that introduce more flexibility. More importantly, those who stress the importance of control over monetary aggregates believe that this is the primary responsibility of the Fed and that credit markets should be allowed to ration the available supply without interference from the central bank. Let us turn now to the approaches taken by the Fed as it has sought to cope with these and other problems in recent years.

RECENT FEDERAL RESERVE OPEN MARKET STRATEGY

During the period since World War II, the Federal Reserve's open market strategy has incorporated several sets of guides: money market conditions, the level and structure of interest rates, and monetary and credit aggregates. The relative importance of these variables has changed over the years, reflecting changes in economic and financial developments and in monetary theory. In general, there has been increased emphasis on the behavior of monetary and credit aggregates; the structure, as well as the level, of interest rates has become a matter of concern; and money market conditions have become somewhat less important. Moreover, the role of money market conditions in Federal Reserve policy has changed in recent years. It is believed by most economists that the greater attention currently being paid to money and credit is a constructive change, one that has been long overdue. At the same time it is recognized that efforts to control the growth rate of the money supply and credit may at times conflict with other objectives of policy such as the maintenance of orderly money markets and reasonably stable interest rates. In the discussion that follows, we outline the major changes that have taken place with respect to open market strategy.

The Importance of Money Market Conditions

The money market has always been an area of great concern to the Federal Reserve System. First, it is the point of contact between the Fed and the financial community; open market operations have traditionally been conducted in the short-term government securities market, and the Fed has felt a responsibility to help maintain "depth, breadth, and resiliency" in this market to ensure the effectiveness of its monetary policies. Second, the Treasury enters the market on numerous occasions during the year to finance its deficits, refinance its maturing securities, and to meet seasonal discrepancies between tax receipts and expenditures. At these times the Fed typically follows an "even keel" policy, one of maintaining relatively orderly conditions in the market or at least correcting disorderly conditions should they develop. Third, the Fed has sought to prevent undue, sharp fluctuations in money market conditions in general—at least fluctuations likely to be self-correcting—because such abrupt changes might destabilize other financial markets. They might be misinterpreted by market participants as a signal of longer-run changes in credit conditions or monetary policy.

Changes in the Role of Money Market Conditions

During the 1950s and early 1960s, money market conditions played a dominant role in Federal Reserve policy and served as the primary guide to open market operations. In the earlier part of this period much emphasis was placed upon the free reserve position of commercial banks and the Fed's "feel of the market." In more recent years, the Federal funds rate has become the principal proxy for money market conditions. Along with this shift in attention toward the Federal funds rate, there has come a *relative* decline in the importance of money market conditions vis-à-vis the monetary aggregates.

The "feel of the market" measure of money market conditions is a rather vague, imprecise concept. It seems to mean the "gut feel" that experienced Federal Reserve officials develop by looking at the reserve positions of money market banks, the financial position of government securities dealers, and money market rates, and from daily contact with participants in the money and capital markets. Money markets are said to be "tight" or "easy" if the Fed's officials detect a certain "tone" or "color" from daily examination of the market. The obvious weakness of such a measure is its lack of empirical content; it is an almost purely subjective element, which makes it virtually impossible to evaluate or compare policies.

The free reserve position of member banks was often used as one basis for determining the "feel of the market" or as a proxy for money market conditions. In its latter capacity it served as the operating target, and perhaps the only target, of open market operations. Without exploring the limitations of the free reserve target in detail, because it has long since been deemphasized in setting open market policy, it should be noted that the main weakness of this guide is that it may provide misleading information about the direction of monetary policy. A simple example will illustrate this point.

Suppose the Fed decides to shift to a slightly more expansionary policy and that to do so the free reserve target is raised from, say, $700 million to $800 million. Open market purchases are undertaken, with the initial result that bank reserves rise and the free reserve figure of $800 million is achieved. If banks respond to these changes by expanding their loans and deposits, required reserves rise, excess reserves fall, and the free reserve position declines from the $800 million level to a somewhat lower figure. To restore free reserves to the desired target level, additional purchases of securities are made; required reserves rise as additional loans replace excess reserves, and deposits rise, with the result that free reserves again decline. It is easily seen that what appears to be a slightly more expansionary policy—raising free reserves from $700 million to $800 million—in fact may lead to continual increases in money and credit. The behavior of free reserves misleads the monetary authority and induces changes in monetary and credit conditions that are neither desired nor expected. The reverse operations when policy is aimed at more restraint produce continual declines in money and credit so long as a particular free reserves position is the primary target. This is not to say that free reserve changes cannot be used to provide information about the expected impact of policy. Rather, they should not be used as *the* guide to open market operations. Some have argued that free reserves were used as the main operating target by the Fed during the 1950s and most of the 1960s.[16]

In early 1966, a sharp increase in credit and money induced the Fed to modify its open market procedure and use a so-called proviso clause in the Federal Open Market Committee directive (discussed below). In essence, the proviso clause acts as a constraint by setting a limiting value on some variable with which the Fed is concerned. For example, if open market operations are conducted with a view "to maintaining the prevailing firm conditions in the money market, *provided, however,* that these operations shall be modified if bank credit declines significantly," then the behavior of bank credit acts as a constraint, as per the proviso clause, on open market operations. The importance of the proviso clause is that it allows consideration of more than one high-level or intermediate target—for example, bank credit *and* money market conditions. At the same time, if the two or more variables whose behavior is to be controlled have the same control period—for example, average monthly values of both—the proviso clause may require that one target be compromised in order to achieve the other. In our example, a significant decline in bank credit forces the Fed to disregard, temporarily at least, the order to maintain the existing degree of restraint in the money market. In effect, the proviso clause sets a limit on a policy of restraint or, in other cases, a policy of ease.

In terms of the historical changes in Federal Reserve policy, the proviso

---

[16]See Allan H. Meltzer, "The Appropriate Indicators of Monetary Policy," Part I, *Proceedings of the 1969 Conference on Savings and Residential Financing,* pp. 11–31. Some reservations concerning the studies by Brunner and Meltzer are found in Guttentag, *Quarterly Journal of Economics,* February 1966, p. 17.

clause indicated a shift in emphasis away from money market conditions and toward monetary and credit aggregates. From mid-1966 to mid-1969 the proviso clauses were generally specified in terms of bank credit.

1970: A Shift toward Monetary and Credit Aggregates[17]

In 1970, a further step was taken which signaled the rise in importance of money and credit in Federal Reserve policy. First, instructions regarding open market operations specifically called for actions aimed at *money* and credit rather than money market conditions and credit, as before. Second, these references were made directly, rather than indirectly through a proviso clause. For example, in the instructions issued on March 10, 1970 the Federal Open Market Committee said:

> . . . it is the policy of the Federal Open Market Committee to foster financial conditions conducive to orderly reduction in the rate of inflation, while encouraging the resumption of sustainable economic growth and the attainment of reasonable equilibrium in the country's balance of payments.
>
> To implement this policy, the Committee desires to see moderate growth in money and bank credit over the months ahead. System open market operations until the next meeting of the Committee shall be conducted with a view to maintaining money market conditions consistent with that objective.[18]

The reasons for the policy change in 1970 were essentially the same as those that led to the use of a proviso clause: it became increasingly evident during the late 1960s that money and credit were not under sufficient control. Their annual rates of growth were often excessive, and there were wide swings in growth rates of both series on a monthly and quarterly basis.[19] No doubt the increasing respectability of the monetarist view that "money matters much" (most?) was an important element, too, in the decisions to stress money as well as credit and to keep an eye on both aggregates rather than primarily on money market conditions.[20]

However, although monetary and credit aggregates received more emphasis in Federal Reserve thinking in the late 1960s and in 1970–71, the strat-

[17]The following discussion draws upon the more complete presentation of the reasons for these changes in open market policy found in "Monetary Aggregates and Money Market Conditions in Open Market Policy," *Federal Reserve Bulletin*, February 1971, pp. 79–95.

[18]"Record of Policy Actions of the Federal Open Market Committee," *Federal Reserve Bulletin*, June 1970, p. 512.

[19]From January 1967 to January 1969, M_1 grew at an annual rate of 7.6 percent; after that the rate declined to 2.9 percent until February 1970. During the same period, M_2 grew at 10.3 percent and later at 0.7 percent per year; the growth rates for bank credit were 11 percent and 6.3 percent.

[20]See Andrew F. Brimmer, "The Political Economy of Money: Evolution and Impact of Monetarism in the Federal Reserve System," (Paper delivered at the Eighty-fourth Annual Meeting of the American Economic Association, New Orleans, Louisiana, December 27, 1971), pp. 344–52.

egy used during this period retained money market conditions as the operating target. The change had been an important one, but it did not change the focal point of day-to-day open market operations.

The Use of RPDs as an Operating Target

In February 1972, the Federal Reserve took a further step and selected as its immediate operating target reserves available to support private nonbank deposits, RPDs. The precipitating factors were:

1. The Federal Reserve's projections that real GNP would continue to grow at the current high rate of about 6 percent through the first half of 1972, with consequent upward pressure on prices.
2. The fact that total reserves had grown from December to January at a seasonally adjusted annual rate of about 21 percent.
3. The sharp rise in the M_2 money supply and in the adjusted bank credit proxy.

In view of these developments, the FOMC concluded that "in the present environment it was desirable to increase somewhat the relative emphasis placed on reserves while continuing to take appropriate account of money market conditions."[21]

RPDs were chosen as the operating target rather than the monetary base or total reserves because the Committee felt that it is appropriate for system open market operations to accommodate the changes that occur in government and interbank deposits—that these changes are not of major significance for policy (see Figure 16–4 for the relationship between these measures and uses of reserves).[22] The RPD growth rate target was set for a two-month time period with a 4 percent spread—a practice which was altered slightly in 1973 to permit more flexibility in the target rate of growth of RPDs.

It should be noted that the Fed has not been prepared to adhere rigidly to the RPD target to the exclusion of other considerations. If the growth rate of monetary aggregates deviates significantly from the expected rate, the RPD target range will presumably be adjusted as it may be if the Federal funds rate should move outside of the (unspecified) desired range. Treasury financing and capital market developments continue to be taken into account in the conduct of open market operations.

Experience with RPDs as an operating target has been limited, but thus far the results have not been overly encouraging. First, during the first year of its use the target was elusive: the actual rate of growth in RPDs deviated more than might have been expected from the target range, as shown in Figure

[21]"Record of Policy Actions of the Federal Open Market Committee," *Federal Reserve Bulletin*, May 1972, p. 459.

[22]The Federal Open Market Committee also stated that RPDs are a better target than, say, total reserves because of the difficulty of predicting short-run fluctuations in government and interbank deposits. But see the discussion in connection with Figure 16–4 where we argue that such information is required to achieve the target rate of growth in RPDs.

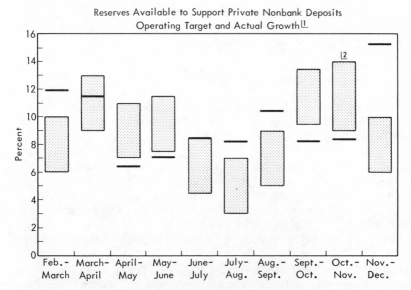

Reserves Available to Support Private Nonbank Deposits
Operating Target and Actual Growth [1]

[1] The dotted areas indicate FOMC target growth range for RPDs; the bars indicate actual growth achieved. The actual RPD growth rates were computed using the RPD series prior to the February 1973 revision. The figures represent simple annual rates over the two-month periods indicated.

[2] The original RPD growth range of 6 – 11 percent was modified to 9 – 14 as a result of changes in Regulations D and J.

Note: The actual figures for November and December were adjusted in order to compensate for changes in Regulations D and J.

FIGURE 16–8

SOURCE: Federal Reserve Bank of St. Louis, *Review*, March 1973, p. 19.

16–8. More importantly, the monetary and credit aggregates continued to fluctuate widely from quarter to quarter. Although it may not be important or feasible to control, say, week-to-week or perhaps even month-to-month movements in monetary and credit aggregates, the erratic behavior during 1972 was somewhat discouraging. If these fluctuations continue to characterize monetary developments in the years ahead, they will pose a serious problem for the Fed in its efforts to maintain economic stability.

However, to the extent that the RPD target range is set by considerations of money market conditions and interest rates rather than by the behavior of money and credit, the "experiment" with RPDs may be in jeopardy not because the approach is faulty but because the underlying dilemma remains: should we control money and credit *or* money market conditions and interest rates?[23] Although it *may* be desirable largely to ignore market conditions and

[23]There is further evidence that recent Federal Reserve policy has been greatly concerned with high interest rates: the use of "moral suasion" in forcing a (temporary) rollback of the prime rate in early 1973; the long lag between the sustained upward

interest rates and concentrate solely on money and credit aggregates, it is unlikely that such a change will be made in the foreseeable future.

HOW MONETARY POLICY IS CARRIED OUT

Open market operations are carried out by the Federal Reserve Bank of New York under the direction of the FOMC.[24] About every four weeks the FOMC meets in Washington to assess the current economic and financial outlook and to decide what changes if any should be made in current policy.

The FOMC

Prior to each meeting FOMC members are kept apprised of current economic and financial developments; the Board of Governors and the Reserve Bank presidents receive a continual flow of reports on business and financial trends from their research departments and a daily account of open market operations and conditions in the money markets. Each group is briefed by their respective staffs as to the financial and economic implications of the alternative drafts of the policy directive that the FOMC will give to the Manager of the System Open Market Account (SOMA) at the next meeting. Committee members also are provided by the Board's staff with estimates of the range of interest rates and money supply figures expected to result from the adoption of various versions of the directive to the Manager.

At each meeting, senior officials of the Board of Governors and the Federal Reserve Bank of New York, including the Manager of the SOMA, report further on international and domestic markets and on business conditions since the last meeting.[25] The economic and financial data reviewed include those for: industrial production, retail sales, unemployment, wholesale and retail prices, market interest rates, money supply, bank credit, and bank reserves. Periodically, the Board's staff presents detailed projections of economic activity over the next few months. Included are estimates of GNP and its components and of the monetary and credit conditions implied in these projections.

After the staff reports are presented and discussed, each member of the FOMC gives his views on the current outlook for the economy and the financial markets and at times comments on the conduct of monetary policy since the last meeting of the Committee. He also expresses his preferences (or reservations) concerning alternative drafts of the directive to be voted upon at the

---

movement of money market rates and subsequent increases in the discount rate in 1972–1973.

[24]We have relied upon the description of FOMC meetings provided in Paul Meek, *Open Market Operations* (3rd ed.) Federal Reserve Bank of New York, 1973.

[25]The Special Manager, SOMA, is in charge of the Foreign Department of the Federal Reserve Bank of New York. He reports on recent foreign exchange operations undertaken on behalf of the Treasury and the FOMC. Semiannual reports of these operations are in the March and September issues of the *Federal Reserve Bulletin*.

end of the meeting. In the days of the chairmanship of William McChesney Martin, the chairman of the FOMC, who is also Chairman of the Board of Governors, customarily gave his views last and then summarized what he viewed as the "consensus," and put before the committee a directive. Under the chairmanship of Arthur Burns, since February 1, 1970, Burns is likely to participate more actively in discussions.

When the directive is adopted, by majority vote, and transmitted to the Federal Reserve Bank of New York, it guides the Manager of the SOMA in conducting open market operations during the period until the next FOMC meeting.

Directives of the FOMC

The directive of the FOMC to the Federal Reserve Bank of New York consists of a two-to-four paragraph statement that (1) summarizes major economic and financial information reviewed at the meeting, (2) states the policy consensus of the FOMC, and (3) sets forth the operating instructions to the Manager of the SOMA.[26] The policy consensus and operating instructions of a recent directive are as follows:

> In light of the foregoing developments, it is the policy of the Federal Open Market Committee to foster financial conditions conducive to sustainable real economic growth and increased employment, abatement of inflationary pressures, and attainment of reasonable equilibrium in the country's balance of payments.
>
> To implement this policy, while taking special account of the effects of possible bank regulatory changes, developments in credit markets, and international developments, the Committee seeks to achieve bank reserve and money market conditions that will support more moderate growth in monetary aggregates over the months ahead.[27]

The first paragraph expresses the policy consensus; it is stated in broad terms, and may be repeated from one meeting to the next or changed if the FOMC determines that economic conditions warrant it. The second paragraph sets forth operating instructions, also in general terms. Any special factors the Committee believes should be taken into account, such as forthcoming Treasury financing, liquidity crises, capital market developments, or uncertainties in the foreign exchange markets, are usually specifically noted in the operating instructions. The details surrounding these special factors may or may not be included in the written directive. In any event, they have been discussed in the

[26]The directive, a digest of the meeting, and the votes on the policy decisions made at the meeting are released approximately ninety days following the meeting as the "Record of the Policy Actions of the Federal Open Market Committee." They are published in the *Federal Reserve Bulletin* as well as in the Board of Governor's *Annual Report*.

[27]This economic policy directive is from the meeting held in September, 1972. It is published in the *Federal Reserve Bulletin*, December 1972, pp. 1022–23.

meeting and provide important background information to the Manager, which helps him translate the directive into specific actions taken on behalf of the System account. In addition, it is important to note that if and when operating instructions are given in terms of specific target variables, including a desired range of values for those variables, they are promulgated during the meeting but are not included in the directive itself. In brief, the operating instructions contained in the directive are stated in very broad terms and must be interpreted in the light of what was discussed and decided upon at the meeting from which the directive emanated.

The minor shifts that occur in policy directives may be illustrated by quoting from the directive adopted at the meeting of November 19–20, 1973:

> In light of the foregoing developments, it is the policy of the Federal Open Market Committee to foster financial conditions conducive to abatement of inflationary pressures, a sustainable rate of advance in economic activity, and equilibrium in the country's balance of payments.
>
> To implement this policy, while taking account of international and domestic financial market developments, the Committee seeks to achieve bank reserve and money market conditions consistent with moderate growth in monetary aggregates over the months ahead.

It may be noted that the above directions gave first priority to "abatement of inflationary pressures" and made other minor changes to reflect modifications in the conditions that constituted the background for the policy.

The Mechanics of Open Market Operations

The Manager is responsible for open market operations undertaken by the Federal Reserve Bank of New York at the direction of the FOMC. He presides over the Trading Desk, where a small staff of securities traders is linked by telephone to the twenty or so primary dealers in government securities. The Desk's traders are in continual contact with these dealers, thus obtaining up-to-the-minute quotations on the prices and yields at which government securities are being exchanged. When the Manager decides to buy or sell a certain amount of, say, Treasury bills, the quotations from a "go-around" of the market provide a basis for placing orders with those dealers offering the most attractive terms.

Throughout the trading day, the Manager receives the latest information on developments in the financial markets—including current figures on bank reserve positions and market rates and on changes in bank deposits and bank credit—as they become available. Of special interest are data on the basic reserve position of money market banks, the Federal funds rate, member bank borrowings, and the inventory position and borrowings of the government securities dealers. Conferences between dealers and officials of the Securities Department of the Federal Reserve Bank of New York occur daily and provide those responsible for the conduct of open market operations with a better "feel of the market." The Manager or his deputy exchange views with Treasury officials early each day concerning the outlook for Treasury cash balances at the Federal Reserve Banks and the proposed schedule of "calls" the Treasury will make on its Tax and Loan Accounts at commercial banks across the country. Lastly, the Manager consults with senior officials on the staff of the Board of Governors in Washington and one of the Reserve Bank Presidents currently serving on the FOMC. This daily telephone conference is to apprise these officials of current developments and the Manager's plan of action as well as to enable the Manager to gain additional clarification of matters discussed at the last FOMC meeting.

During the course of an average day, the Desk's purchases and sales of securities amount to several hundred million dollars, a large figure even in a market in which total transactions often run over $2½ billion. Occasionally the Fed buys or sells coupon issues (Treasury notes or bonds) and also buys small amounts of Federal agency issues and bankers acceptances, holding them until maturity, but the bulk of its transactions are in Treasury bills. These purchases and sales of government securities are made on an outright basis or through repurchase agreements (RPs) or reverse repurchase agreements entered into with the dealers. As Table 16–1 indicates, both techniques have been used in recent years.

These repurchase agreements are undertaken at the initiative of the Fed when it wishes to inject funds into the market (RPs) or withdraw them (reverse RPs) for short periods of time. Desk RPs are transacted only with nonbank dealers, usually at the discount rate, and may carry maturities up to fifteen days, although the Fed or the dealers can terminate the agreement at any time before maturity. Reverse RPs, on the other hand, more accurately described as "matched sale-purchase" transactions, are entered into with both nonbank

TABLE 16–1   Federal Reserve System Open Market Transactions 1962–72

Year	Outright (purchases plus sales) (billions of $)	Repurchase Agreements (purchases plus sales) (billions of $)
1962	16.6	12.0
1963	13.3	18.1
1964	15.9	18.0
1965	14.1	30.0
1966	25.9	19.2
1967	16.2	34.1
1968	51.2	31.8
1969	62.9	47.6
1970	41.9	67.9
1971	47.6	88.4
1972	63.3	63.1

Note: U.S. Government securities only and excluding redemptions.

SOURCE: *Federal Reserve Bulletins.*

and bank dealers and at a competitive price rather than at the discount rate.[28]

From the standpoint of monetary policy, RPs add to bank reserves and are undertaken when the Fed's projections indicate the need for a short-term easing of reserve positions and money market conditions. RPs also provide the dealers with temporary financing and thus are thought to contribute to the smooth functioning of the market for government securities. When RPs run off, deposits and reserves are automatically replenished. Thus an advantage of RPs and reverse RPs is that because the effect on reserves is known to be temporary, money market rates tend to decline or rise less than they would have had outright purchases or sales been made by the Desk. For this reason, especially, reverse RPs have been used instead of sales in order to curtail the growth of bank reserves during periods of high interest rates such as during the "credit crunches" of the later 1960s.[29]

SUMMARY

Most monetary theories specify a transmission mechanism in which monetary policy works through portfolio adjustments, wealth effects, and credit availability effects. Changes in supply schedules and prices (yields) of financial assets induce a substitution of real assets for financial assets, and subsequently these changes are transmitted to aggregate demand and the levels of output, employment, and prices. Changes in the availability of credit result from market imperfections and governmental restrictions on the flow of credit, and although these effects are mostly short-lived, they do have an important and selective impact on various sectors of the economy. It is also recognized that monetary policy is subject to certain lags, whose average length and variability is not precisely known.

Because there are different interpretations of the transmission mechanism, economists are divided over the question of how monetary policy should be implemented. Some argue that a money supply strategy is necessary to achieve the ultimate goals of policy. Others emphasize the role of credit conditions and interest rates in economic affairs and favor these variables as indicators of monetary policy. Even so, most agree that the operating target should be a quantifiable variable—for example, monetary base, total reserves, or RPDs—rather than some proxy for money market conditions.

Whatever procedure is used by the Fed to achieve its macroeconomic objectives, money market conditions are likely to remain an important element in the implementation process. Concern over "disintermediation" and "credit

[28]The Fed sets the sales price and dealers submit bids on the price at which they are willing to sell the securities back to the Fed a few days later. The Fed then sells to the dealers offering the lowest resale prices.

[29]In the second half of 1966, matched sales-purchases totalled more than $4 billion. In 1967 the total declined to $1.3 billion as market pressures eased, but rose to more than $17 billion in 1968 and about $30 billion in 1969. See "Repurchase Agreements: Their Role in Dealer Financing and Monetary Policy," Federal Reserve Bank of Cleveland, *Money Market Instruments*, 1970, pp. 42–52.

crunches," with their attendant effects on financial institutions and markets and hence on certain sectors of the economy, can be expected to play an important role in Federal Reserve policies. Thus credit market stability and interest rates themselves—independent of the part they play in the linkage between open market operations and aggregate demand—are goals of policy. This poses a dilemma for Federal Reserve officials when monetary restraint makes high and rising interest rates virtually inevitable. Should the Fed try to control the monetary growth rate or promote money market and interest rate stability?

It is evident that how monetary policy should be conducted is not completely agreed upon. Nevertheless, it has gradually been agreed that monetary policy is very important in its effects upon the level of economic activity. The manner in which the dials should be turned in order to achieve the desired objectives is being clarified as more research is conducted, but monetary policy, and therefore determination of the level of economic activity, is still an art as well as a science.

QUESTIONS FOR DISCUSSION

1. Briefly trace the transmission mechanism from an open market purchase by the Fed by way of interest rates to an increase in income.

2. How would changes in wealth be expected to change aggregate spending?

3. What is meant by the term "credit availability"?

4. How do we classify the lags in effects of monetary policy?

5. Describe how an increase in the reserve base may affect the value of the money multiplier.

6. Why are changes in income, employment, or prices unreliable guides in the daily conduct of monetary policy?

7. What are RPDs? Evaluate their usefulness, from the brief experience with their use as an operating target.

8. If the strategy of the monetary authority is to keep interest rates constant, would one expect the money supply to fluctuate widely, and vice versa? Explain your reasoning.

9. What are "net free (borrowed) reserves"? Give an example showing how they might provide misleading evidence about the direction of monetary policy.

10. Some argue that control over the growth rate of money should not be the sole aim of the monetary authority. They believe that interest rates and money market conditions are also important. Why might these be a matter of concern?

SELECTED REFERENCES

A useful introduction to econometric models and the role of money in alternative transmission mechanisms is provided by Joseph M. Crews, "Econometric Models: The Monetarist and Non-Monetarist Views Compared," Federal Reserve Bank of Richmond, *Monthly Review*, February 1973, pp. 3–12.

A brief summary of recent empirical work on various aspects of the transmission process, including time lags and sectoral impacts is found in Maurice Mann, "How Does Monetary Policy Affect the Economy?", *Journal of Money, Credit, and Banking*, August 1969, pp. 538–48. An extensive bibliography is included.

Several conferences on targets, indicators, and the implementation of monetary policy have produced many important papers and reviews of the conferences' discussion. See especially the following:

Board of Governors of the Federal Reserve System, *Open Market Policies and Operating Procedures—Staff Studies*, 1971.

Federal Reserve Bank of Boston, *Controlling Monetary Aggregates*, 1969.

Federal Reserve Bank of Boston, *Controlling Monetary Aggregates II: The Implementation*, 1973.

Karl Brunner, ed., *Targets and Indicators of Monetary Policy*. San Francisco: Chandler Publishing Co., 1969.

Two sources that offer comprehensive coverage of the theory and practice of monetary policy are:

Thomas Mayer, *Monetary Policy in the United States*. New York: Random House, 1968.

George G. Kaufman, *Current Issues in Monetary Economics and Policy: A Review*. New York University, Graduate School of Business Administration, *The Bulletin*, No. 57, May 1969. An extensive bibliography is included.

For an interesting treatment of personalities and procedures in Federal Reserve policymaking, see Lawrence Malkin, "A Practical Politician at the Fed," *Fortune*, May 1971, pp. 148–51, 254–64.

17

Fiscal
and Debt Management
Policies

Without taking a strong position in the monetarist-fiscalist debate, we devote the first part of this chapter to fiscal policy and show how fiscal policy decisions have profound effects in financial markets. One may debate whether fiscal policy ought to be used or not, but everyone recognizes that fiscal actions *do* significantly affect financial markets and institutions, whatever their other merits or demerits. Debt management policy, a poor cousin to fiscal and monetary policy in terms of strength of its impact, is discussed briefly at the end of the chapter, as day-to-day analysis of conditions in financial markets would be incomplete without attention to the Treasury's debt management posture.

It was noted in discussing the "loanable funds" theory of interest rate determination (Chapter 12) that the federal government's demand for funds is a significant component of overall demand for funds. If the federal budget is in deficit because of an increase in Treasury spending, the Treasury must in general sell additional debt instruments to finance the excess of expenditures over revenues. This additional demand for funds pushes interest rates up, *other things remaining equal.*

An increase in the deficit may also occur if national income falls and Treasury tax revenues fall concomitantly. The decline in national income leads to a decline in demand for funds by private individuals and firms, and to this extent there is downward pressure on interest rates. But because the Treasury's budget is in deficit, the increased demand for funds by the Treasury places upward pressure on interest rates so that they do not fall as much as they otherwise would. It is clear that all of the factors affecting yields must be considered simultaneously by the financial market analyst. It is also clear that federal budget requirements are one factor of primary importance; whether the budget is in deficit, balanced, or in surplus, it cannot be ignored. Because the federal budget balance depends upon both revenues and expenditures, both aspects must be considered in evaluating fiscal policy. To these considerations we now turn.

THE NATURE OF FISCAL POLICY

For an economy, income and output are two sides of the same coin. What is produced (output) is also received by some individual or group (income). For analytical purposes, income is separated into classes. Total income is the sum of consumption spending, investment spending, government spending, and net exports. Because government spending is part of income, if government expenditures rise, there is a direct impact on total spending. Because the level of employment is highly correlated with the level of income, when resources are underemployed, one way to stimulate employment and raise income is to increase the level of government spending.

Of course, the relation between government spending and income is not simply one of addition. Increased income may lead to increased consumption expenditures and further increases in income. However, if interest rates rise as income rises, the level of private investment spending may decline and partially offset the original expansionary influence of increased government spending on income, and so forth. It is sufficient here to note that an increase in government spending is thought to be expansionary, although the magnitude of its impact is the subject of debate. Similarly, tax revenues are held to be contractionary; they reduce the purchasing power of individuals and businesses and lead to a reduction in demand and a cutback in production. Thus, a combination of lower taxes and higher government expenditures (leading to a budget deficit) stimulates the economy, and a combination of higher taxes and reduced government spending (leading to a budget surplus) dampens economic activity. Government spending and taxing decisions combine in the resulting budget to form the nation's fiscal policy.

When Congress appropriates funds for a program, its purpose is to provide a socially desirable service. The criteria for a spending decision are generally independent of the level of economic activity, although in the Great Depression of the 1930s it was sometimes argued that spending was desirable in and of itself if it led to increased employment. In general, however, government spending is undertaken for specific projects that Congress recognizes to be appropriate for government; hence, the level of government spending should be determined by the desirability and cost of those projects—by something other than the general level of income and employment.

Taxing, on the other hand, is for the purpose of diverting resources away from the private sector in favor of the public sector. If the economy is fully employed, an increase in government spending cannot occur without causing inflation unless some purchasing power is diverted to government. Taxes are used for this purpose. However, if the economy is underemployed, there no longer exists a justification for collecting taxes equal to the full amount of expenditures.

In the 1930s, Keynes argued that governments could more easily vary the level of spending than they could the level of taxing, simply because the latter is politically explosive. He suggested, therefore, that as a practical matter variation in government spending should be used to ensure full employment. However, in 1962, spokesmen for the Kennedy administration proposed that Congress authorize the President to vary the income tax rate by 5 percent in either direction. The 20 percent tax bracket could be raised to 21 percent ($1/20 = 5$ percent) or lowered to 19 percent, for example. The changed rate was to have been effective for a six-month period and the President would then have had to present to Congress the reasons for his decision. He could then have asked Congress to approve an extension of the change for another six months, and at the end of this period the tax rate would return to its original level and remain there with no Congressional act required. The details of the proposal were extensive and need not detain us here, but it is likely that future administrations will continue to search for ways to introduce greater flexibility into taxation, so that variation in tax rates may more readily assist in achieving the objectives of fiscal policy.

AUTOMATIC STABILIZERS

Because the amount of income taxes an individual or business firm must pay is some percentage of income or profits, it follows that tax receipts rise as national income rises. Furthermore, income tax rates are graduated so that the average rate of taxation also tends to rise as income rises. In an economy with rising income, therefore, existing tax rates and the rate structure lead automatically to a larger amount of tax collections. These additional taxes help hold the lid on the expansion; and if the economic boom is accompanied by inflation, these tax collections help restrain inflation. If the economy moves downward with falling income and rising unemployment, the tax receipts fall off, leaving more purchasing power in the hands of consumers than they would have had if tax collections were a constant amount. Swings in income and employment are smaller in amplitude than they would be in the absence of this automatic stabilization device.

Certain kinds of transfer payments by government also come into operations automatically under the law: unemployment compensation payments and certain types of welfare payments. These portions of government expenditure move in a contracyclical direction; as income falls and unemployment rises, there is a rise in unemployment compensation payments, which tends to prevent consumer purchasing power from falling as much as it otherwise would. Again there is a tendency for the amplitude of swings in business activity to be below what it would be in the absence of this automatic variation in government expenditures.

Because business and consumer saving, taxes, and transfer payments vary with swings in economic activity, it is difficult to estimate the net effectiveness of automatic stabilizers. In one study, it was estimated that automatic stabilizers may reduce the size of changes in the level of national income to roughly half of what they would be in the absence of automatic stabilizers.[1] Of course,

[1]Peter Eilbott, "The Effectiveness of Automatic Stabilizers," *American Economic Review*, Vol. 6 (June 1966), pp. 433–64.

since stabilizers only *respond* to variation in income, they are never able to *prevent* variation in income. Therefore, to prevent variation in income and supplement the effects of the automatic stabilizers when desired, discretionary fiscal policy actions may be necessary.

Some elements of the federal budget respond automatically in a procyclical way. These might be called automatic *de*stabilizers. In an expansion, interest rates rise, so that government expenditures for interest on the national debt also rise and are to some extent inflationary. The retirement programs for civilian and military personnel now have automatic cost-of-living adjustment provisions that contribute to inflation unless monetary policy or other actions offset this.

Built-in automatic stabilizers help keep an economy that is near full employment at this position. But they cut two ways. If an economy is considerably below full employment, then automatic stabilizers help *restrain* an expansion once it has gotten under way. On these occasions the existence of automatic stabilizers increases the need for discretionary policy actions.[2]

DISCRETIONARY FISCAL POLICY ACTIONS

Tax revenues are affected by the level of economic activity, but they are also affected by the rate of taxation levied by Congress. Any change in tax rates is a discretionary act of fiscal policy. Furthermore, changes in the types of taxes imposed—income taxes, excise taxes, import duties, and so on—affect the extent of fiscal impact. Most government expenditures are also discretionary, and both increases and reductions in spending are sometimes undertaken overtly for the purpose of economic stabilization. President Nixon's vetoes of certain spending bills in 1973 are an example of restraint for this purpose.

Tax Changes

In 1964 President Johnson asked for, and Congress approved, a large cut in taxes. Not only were there reductions in each of the income tax bracket rates, but also there were reductions in many federal excise taxes. The tax cuts had been proposed much earlier, and it was a long time before Congress finally passed this legislation. With this act, however, Congress for the first time approved a reduction in taxes for the explicit purpose of stimulating economic activity. The expansion that followed seemed to validate the action.

By 1965, United States government spending to support military involvement in Vietnam was rapidly accelerating. Government spending for domestic programs also increased, and inflationary pressures grew. In an attempt to slow the rise in prices, an income tax surcharge was imposed in the middle of 1968.

[2]For a discussion of the way changing patterns of federal expenditures in recent years have changed the strength of automatic stabilizers, see Nancy H. Teeters, "Built-in Flexibility of Federal Expenditures," *Brookings Papers on Economic Activity,*" Vol. 3 (1971), pp. 615–57.

This represented a discretionary attempt to implement counterinflationary fiscal policy. In the wake of this tax increase, however, consumption and income continued to rise, and many analysts felt that the failure to stop the inflation showed that fiscal policy actions were weak in their effect. Interpretations of the data vary. Because many factors change simultaneously, it is extremely difficult to isolate the relative importance of a single factor. Perhaps consumption and income continued to increase because of other factors, and perhaps they were significantly lower than they would have been if the tax surcharge had not been imposed. That this is probably true can be seen by observing personal income (the sum of personal consumption, saving, and taxes), and noting that the ratio of personal consumption to income fell after the tax increase; that the ratio of personal saving to income also fell; and that the ratio of personal taxes to income rose as expected in the wake of the tax surcharge. The tax surcharge affected both saving and consumption; to the extent that consumption was held down by the increase in taxes, it is safe to conclude that the tax *did* help dampen the overheated economy.[3]

Changes in types of taxes, as well as changes in the overall level of tax rates, can be used as discretionary fiscal policy tools. Examples are the investment tax credit and accelerated depreciation allowances.

The investment tax credit allows a business firm to deduct a certain percentage of its expenditure of fixed plant and equipment from its tax liability. This amounts to a direct subsidy to the firm, inasmuch as by this means the effective cost of purchasing equipment is lowered (by approximately 7½ percent on long-lived items). The purpose of the tax, when it was first introduced in 1962, was to stimulate employment and output of the capital goods industries. The tax has been rescinded and reintroduced on occasion since then. If it is announced that the tax credit will be allowed for one year (say), then businessmen may wish to purchase capital goods before the tax is removed. In this way the tax has certain "announcement effects" that the simple change in the effective price of equipment does not reflect. Although it has been considered an effective policy measure, it can be criticized on a variety of other grounds. Businessmen find that it is difficult to plan when the tax is an on-again off-again policy. Besides, the tax distorts the relation between the prices of some equipment and of other factors of production for certain firms. Distortion of relative prices tends to induce a misallocation of resources; thus, this tax credit has some unfortunate side effects.

Accelerated depreciation allowances have also been used as a policy tool. A firm may deduct depreciation expenses from its income for tax purposes. If a piece of equipment has an expected life of twenty years, depreciation takes place over this period. Under accelerated depreciation, the firm may deduct all of its depreciation allowances over the first five years of the life of the equipment. This means, of course, that after five years have passed, the firm will no longer have this accounting expense item, and its tax payments will then be larger than they would have been if depreciation had occurred evenly through-

---

[3]Murray L. Weidenbaum, "Fiscal Policy for a Period of Transition," *Review*, Federal Reserve Bank of St. Louis, November 1970, pp. 8–13.

out the full twenty-year period. For this reason, it is sometimes said that accelerated depreciation allowances represent, in their effect, an interest-free loan by the government to firms in the form of delayed tax liabilities. Most firms do take advantage of this allowance when they can, but it is difficult to estimate whether these allowances stimulate significantly the total level of investment spending undertaken by private business. Nevertheless, arguments for increasing and decreasing the degree of acceleration (as measured by the time period over which the full amount of depreciation is allowed) usually allude to the overall impact on business activity of changing such allowances.

Expenditure Changes

Discretionary changes may be made not only in the level of taxes, but also in the level of government spending for stabilization purposes. President Kennedy asked for and received limited discretionary authority to contribute to expansionary spending for public works—mostly on a matching-funds basis for fire stations, libraries, and so on, purchased or built by state and local governments.

In 1973 a debate with significant political implications spread throughout the United States. It concerned the propriety of President Nixon's decision to cut spending by simply refusing to spend money for certain programs Congress had appropriated funds for. One might call these discretionary spending cuts. It represents a type of veto power that would effectively thwart congressional mandates even though a majority vote were large enough to override a formal veto. It is a direct challenge to the authority of Congress. Needless to say, it strikes at the heart of the political concept of the separation of power among the three branches of government: legislative, executive and judicial. On the other hand, Congress has often freely delegated its authority to the executive branch and has written legislation designed to provide flexibility in the implementation of its programs. The issue will doubtless have to be resolved by public opinion and perhaps in the courts, over the years to come.

Although it is true that government expenditures can be varied by discretion, the extent to which it is practical to change the level of government spending is limited. This is partly because some legislation automatically appropriates budget authority on a recurring basis. Social security benefits, Medicare benefits, interest on the national debt, the highway trust fund expenditures, and the unemployment insurance trust fund expenditures are major types of permanent spending authority. Figure 17–1 indicates the relative magnitude of current and permanent authority to spend. At the bottom, the extent of the permanent authority to spend is shown. Upon entering the fiscal year 1973, previous authority existed for $266.7 billion, $98.3 billion of which was slated for 1973. This, together with $151.7 billion of current authority, gave a total 1973 budget of $250.0 billion. Thus the appropriations process makes a substantial portion of the budget inflexible. Furthermore, even current programs are often based upon earlier policy decisions and are entrenched. We must conclude, therefore, that the extent of discretion in implementing

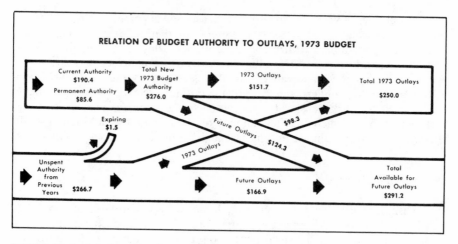

FIGURE 17–1   Relation of Budget Authority to Outlays, 1973 Budget

SOURCES: The Budget of the United States Government, Fiscal Year 1972 and Mid-Session Review of the 1973 Budget.

stabilization policy through government spending is quite limited, and will remain so in the absence of future institutional changes that would permit greater flexibility.[4]

THE HIGH EMPLOYMENT BUDGET: A GUIDELINE FOR FISCAL POLICY

Budget concepts vary. The reader will recall the discussion of the unified budget, the national income accounts budget, and Treasury cash flows in Chapter 8. Budget concepts now differ principally because of the different treatments given to time of payment for goods and time of delivery (cash vs. accrual). In general, the financial analyst must carefully examine Treasury cash flows in order to assess the prevailing demand for funds by the Treasury. However, he must also understand policy positions in order to interpret the likely evolution of the budget.

    The national income accounts budget reflects the macroeconomic impact of tax and expenditure policies. At one point in the development of national income theory, economists believed that a deficit in this budget represented an expansionary fiscal policy, a surplus represented a restrictive fiscal policy. In order to stabilize the economy, it was argued that a deficit should exist in a recession, and a surplus should exist in a boom period, so that over a cycle in

    [4]Glenn Picou, "The Federal Budget: Retrospect and Prospect," *Monthly Review*, Federal Reserve Bank of Richmond, December 1972, pp. 1–8; and George E. Garrison, "Federal Budget—Patterns Already Set Limit Choices to Be Made," *Business Review*, Federal Reserve Bank of Dallas, January 1973, pp. 7–11.

business activity the budget should roughly balance. Thus the deficit or surplus was taken as an indicator of the fiscal policy that was actually in effect at any given time.

But it soon became clear that a serious problem arises when the actual budget surplus or deficit is used as an indicator of fiscal policy. This is because the budget not only affects the level of national income but is also affected by *changes* in the level of national income. If income falls because of a decline in investment, tax receipts fall and the budget turns to deficit. But this deficit does not reflect the posture of fiscal policy—it does not indicate that fiscal policy is expansive; rather, it indicates only that a recession is under way. Similarly, a budget surplus does not necessarily indicate a restrictive fiscal policy if the surplus arose because of an investment boom and an expansion in income and tax revenues.

In comparing the strength of fiscal policy in one recession with that in another, one might find that a $5 billion deficit occurred in both periods and conclude that fiscal stimulus was the same in both. But in one instance the deficit might have been merely the result of the decline in income, while in the other a deliberate tax cut may have brought on the deficit. Thus, the size of the actual deficit or surplus is an imperfect measure of the impact of fiscal policy.

In order to arrive at a better indicator for fiscal policy the concept of a "high-employment" or "full-employment" budget was developed. It was formally set forth by the national administration in 1962, when the Council of Economic Advisors stressed the concept in its *Annual Report*.

The high-employment budget is an estimate of the way the national income accounts budget would appear if the economy were operating at full employment instead of at its actual level. It is a hypothetical budget. When "full employment" exists, it should be identical with the national income accounts budget.

To illustrate the concept in abstract terms, remember that tax revenues are related to income. As income rises, income revenues also rise. If government spending remains unchanged, then variation in income results in variation in tax revenues and the variation in the size of the budget deficit or surplus. To appreciate this phenomenon, consider Figure 17–2.

On the vertical axis, the state of the budget (surplus or deficit) is measured. On the horizontal axis, national income is measured. Two levels of national income are noted. Y_F is the level of income that it is estimated would prevail if the nation's economic resources were fully employed; and Y_A is the current actual level of income. (It is assumed that government expenditures are fixed.) The straight line from the origin labeled t_A shows the relationship of tax revenue to income with a given tax structure. The t_A line intersects the horizontal representation of a balanced budget at point a. This indicates that the current budget is balanced. However, if the economy were operating at full employment so that income equaled Y_F, tax revenues would be larger, and the budget would be in surplus by $10 billion, as indicated by point c. The surplus is represented by the distance cd. Because the full-employment budget is in surplus, it is argued, there is justification for lowering tax rates so that the dashed tax line t_F would prevail. Accordingly, the current actual budget would be in deficit by an amount indicated by the vertical distance from a to b. At this new tax rate, the stimulus of a deficit would tend to raise income and employment. If this stimulus were to push income up to Y_F, then the budget would be in balance as indicated by point d. The distance from c to d can be used as a measure of "fiscal drag." It is taken as an indicator of the extent current tax rates are holding back economic activity. This, then, is a rationale for reducing tax rates and running a deficit in the hypothetical current period.

A chart showing one measure of the high-employment budget for 1963–72 appears in Figure 17–3. The large gap between the actual national income accounts budget and the high-employment budget beginning in the second half of 1969 and continuing through 1972 reflects the high unemployment level, low income, and low tax revenues in the economy over this period. Generally, the high-employment budget lies above the actual national income accounts budget, although in 1966 and again for a brief period in 1968 their positions were reversed. However, from mid-1966 to the end of 1968 the full-employment budget was in deficit along with the actual budget. Consideration of this deficit played a role in arguments for the imposition of the tax surcharge in 1968.

The high-employment budget may, therefore, be used as an indicator of the current and projected status of fiscal policy. In general, if the high-employment budget is in surplus, this indicates that a certain fiscal drag is levied on the economy by high tax rates even though the actual budget is in deficit. A policy to lower taxes would be appropriate. Similarly, if the high-employment budget were in deficit, this could be interpreted as a stimulative fiscal position even though the actual budget were in surplus. In this sense the high-employment budget is thought to be a better guide or indicator of the extent fiscal policy is stimulative or restrictive than is the actual national income accounts budget.

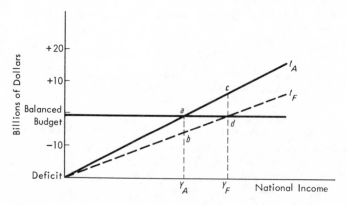

FIGURE 17–2

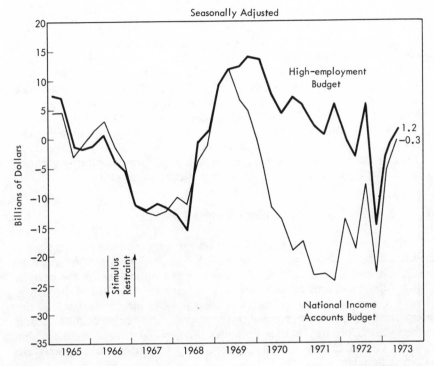

FIGURE 17-3   Fiscal Measures (+) Surplus; (−) Deficit Quarterly Totals at Annual Rates

Note: Latest data plotted, 2nd quarter estimated.

SOURCES: U.S. Department of Commerce, Council of Economic Advisers, and Federal Reserve Bank of St. Louis.

Calculation of the High-Employment Budget

Many detailed steps are involved in actual calculations of the high-employment budget, but in general there are six broad calculations.[5] First, the growth rate of real GNP must be estimated. Second, to this hypothetical growth rate of real GNP there is attached a measure of the rate of inflation; the current rate is extrapolated into the future. This gives an estimate of what the full-employment level of money income would be. Third, this level of income is allocated among the principal components of income, for example, personal income, corporate profit, and so on, according to the ratios that usually obtain when the economy is operating at full employment. Fourth, the

[5]For a thorough discussion of the methods used by the Council of Economic Advisers see Michael Levy, *Fiscal Policy, Cycles and Growth*, Studies in Business Economics No. 81, National Industrial Conference Board, New York, 1963.

tax levies that, on the average, apply to each of the components are used to give an estimate of what tax revenues would be under full employment. Fifth, current expenditure levels are adjusted, principally by estimating the reduction in unemployment compensation expenditures that would be expected to take place if the high level of income were achieved, and then reducing the actual level of government expenditures by this amount. Sixth, the result of the tax revenue estimate and the expenditure estimate, when taken together, provide an estimate of the full employment budget surplus or deficit.

The Nixon administration has used the concept of the full-employment budget as a justification for some sizable deficits from 1970 to 1972.[6] But, in 1973 the full-employment budget turned to deficit, and this may partly account for the President's determined antiexpenditure stand in that year.

Limitations of the High Employment Budget Concept

Limitations of the high-employment budget concept are becoming more widely recognized.[7] Problems with its use are related to assumptions made in the estimating procedure. For example, the rate of inflation used is the current rate; if a different rate of inflation actually occurs, the estimates of the deficit may vary considerably. The estimates of the shares of income realized by the different national income components are also the subject of dispute among fiscal analysts.[8] Corporate profits estimates are especially troublesome in this regard. Of course, in any estimating procedure, the various assumptions are always questionable.

Estimates of the full-employment budget have been made not only by the Council of Economic Advisers, but also by the Federal Reserve Bank of St. Louis (shown in Figure 17–3), and by Arthur Okun and Nancy Teeters of the Brookings Institution.[9] Insofar as these sources use different assumptions, the estimates of the surplus or deficit vary and probably represent a source of some confusion to fiscal analysts. However, the concept will surely prevail and does seem to represent some improvement over the previous concept of a

[6]In the *Budget for 1973*, the President stated:

> The full-employment budget concept is central to the budget policy of this Administration. Except in emergency conditions expenditures should not exceed the level at which the budget would be balanced under conditions of full employment. The 1973 budget conforms to this guideline. By doing so, it provides the necessary stimulus for expansion, but is not inflationary. (p. 14; italics omitted)

[7]Michael J. Prell, "The Full Employment Budget—Its Uses and Limitations," *Monthly Review*, Federal Reserve Bank of Kansas City, April 1973, pp. 3–12; James R. McCabe, "The Full-Employment Budget: A Guide for Fiscal Policy," *Monthly Review*, Federal Reserve Bank of Richmond, May 1972, pp. 2–8; and George Terborgh, "Phantom Budgets and Fiscal Policy," *Morgan Guaranty Survey*, Morgan Guaranty Trust Company, New York, November 1972, pp. 7–10.

[8]Nancy H. Teeters, "Estimates of the Full-Employment Surplus, 1955–64," *Review of Economics and Statistics*, Vol. 47 (August 1965), p. 309.

[9]Arthur M. Okun and Nancy H. Teeters, "The Full-Employment Surplus Revisited," paper delivered at the First Conference of the Brookings Panel on Economic Activity, April 17, 1970, Washington, D.C.

"cyclically balanced budget," which suggested that deficits during depressions should be made up by surpluses in times of prosperity so that the size of the national debt would remain more or less constant over the cycle. With the use of the concept of a full-employment balanced budget, the national debt will probably increase, as deficits will occur at levels below full employment, and surpluses would only occur if employment were higher than the rate accepted as "full employment."

The Initial Stimulus Indicator of Fiscal Policy

In view of the difficulties associated with the estimating techniques required to arrive at figures for a full-employment budget, other measures of fiscal impact have been developed. One of these, constructed by economists at the Federal Reserve Bank of New York, is called the "initial stimulus" measure.[10] The construction of the initial stimulus measure involves three steps. First, quarter-to-quarter changes in federal expenditures (national income accounts basis) are recorded. This expenditures variable is based on the implicit assumption that all federal outlays are acts of discretionary fiscal policy, even expenditures associated with changes in spending for unemployment compensation. (It will be remembered that unemployment compensation payments are deducted from expenditures in computing the full-employment budget, so that the treatment of these expenditures differs in the two measures.) Second, the initial dollar impact of discretionary tax changes is recorded. The value of this impact is zero in all quarters except those where a tax is changed. Also, these tax data are reversed in sign; that is, tax increases are given a negative sign to represent a dampening effect, and tax reductions are given a positive sign to represent a stimulative effect on economic activity. Third, the two impacts, of expenditure changes and of tax changes, are added together to arrive at a measure of the "initial stimulus" of fiscal policy.

The initial stimulus measure has some advantages over the full employment budget concept. It is easier to construct because it involves fewer estimating procedures. And, in one study, it showed greater power in contributing to the explanation of changes in GNP than the full-employment budget measure showed.[11]

Budget Concepts and the Financial Analyst

Under the dictates of an active countercyclical fiscal policy, financial analysts learned to expect that a recession would be followed by an expansion

[10]See "The Initial Effects of Federal Budgetary Changes on Aggregate Spending," *Monthly Review*, Federal Reserve Bank of New York, July 1965, pp. 141–49. Also, William H. Oakland, "Budgetary Measures of Fiscal Performance," *Southern Economic Journal*, April 1969, pp. 348–58, and a comment by E. G. Corrigan in the same *Journal*, April 1970, pp. 470–73.

[11]E. Gerald Corrigan, "The Measurement and Importance of Fiscal Policy Changes," *Monthly Review*, Federal Reserve Bank of New York, June 1970, pp. 133–45.

in the size of the federal debt and an increase in the volume of new Treasury securities entering the market. As a recession develops, interest rates tend to fall, but the added Treasury demand for funds would be expected to offset partially, or even fully, the decline in interest rates.

Because national administrations have adopted the full-employment budget concept, it is likely that the size of a deficit that is politically acceptable is even larger than it was before. The full-employment budget might be in surplus even if the actual budget were in deficit. Therefore, taxes might be lowered and the actual budget deficit enlarged. Because of this, the financial analyst should expect even larger variations in Treasury demand for funds than he would have expected if policymakers had not accepted the full-employment budget concept as an indicator of the posture of fiscal stimulus or drag.

LIMITATIONS OF DISCRETIONARY FISCAL POLICY

In the discussion of the monetarist-fiscalist controversy in Chapter 15, we noted that monetarists argue against the use of countercyclical fiscal policy. As part of their position, they refer to the "crowding-out" effect: if a deficit is financed by the sale of debt, this drives up interest rates and crowds out an equal amount of private investment that otherwise would have taken place. Thus, in this view, the net impact of a debt-financed government deficit on the level of aggregate demand would be negligible. If the economy is fully employed, this certainly would be true, for by definition spending in the private sector must be crowded out by higher interest rates as full employment implies that the capacity to produce is fixed at current levels of production. It also implies that government deficits are *not* inflationary—a charge that conservatives have leveled at Keynesian proponents of deficit spending. However, if slack exists in an economy, then an expansion of government spending through debt financing *may* not push interest rates up; instead, it may generate employment and production and raise the real standard of living by stimulating economic activity without forcing a reduction in other private spending.

Having already examined the arguments in some detail earlier, we do not do so again here. But we wish to emphasize that any financial market analyst must be concerned with the volume of debt coming into the market, whether or not fiscal policy is effective in stimulating employment. The crowding-out effect implies significant movements in interest rates even if it does not affect aggregate demand. Thus, even the monetarists, who do not believe in fiscal policy as a tool, would recognize the importance of fiscal policy to the financial markets.

Another limitation of discretionary fiscal policy is that it takes effect only with a lag. Just as in the case of lags in the effect of monetary policy, there is for fiscal policy a recognition lag, an implementation lag, and an impact lag. The recognition lag is presumably the same for both fiscal and monetary authorities. But, taxes and expenditures are changed only by the slow and cumbersome legislative process. Thus, the implementation lag is longer for fiscal policy than it is for monetary policy. However, unlike monetary policy, the impact lag of fiscal policy is short. Once taxes are cut and increased expenditures begin, the impact is almost immediate. But the total lag in effect of fiscal policy is sizable, and the effectiveness of discretionary monetary policy is limited to that extent.

DEBT MANAGEMENT POLICY

It seems likely that in the years ahead the federal debt will continue to grow. How much it increases will depend upon a host of economic and political considerations including the state of the economy, attitudes toward government spending and taxing, and the relative roles of federal versus state and local governments. We do not wish to examine in detail the question of whether this prospect is desirable or not. The issue is a complex one and charged with emotion. Some economists prefer to retain balance in the budget and even pay off the existing debt. They argue that there are adverse "distributional effects" when tax revenues are transferred to those who hold the debt. They also allege that interest rates are distorted from what they would be in the absence of the debt.

Some economists, on the other hand, believe that great concern over a domestically held debt is unwarranted. Indeed, some argue that not only does economic growth require a growing money supply over time but that a growing federal debt is a useful means of increasing the nation's stock of liquid assets. Moreover, financial institutions prefer to hold some of their portfolio of assets in default-free securities. In this view, continued growth in the federal debt is both necessary and desirable.

Defining Debt Management

Earlier in the text, we defined debt management as those actions of the Treasury and the Federal Reserve System that affect the composition of the federal debt held by the public. This definition distinguishes debt management policy from fiscal policy which has to do with the *size* of the budget deficit or surplus. It also limits monetary policy actions to those which change the amount rather than the types of securities bought or sold by the Federal Reserve System in its open market operations. Although these definitions are arbitrary they help underscore the interrelation between fiscal, monetary, and debt management policies. Moreover, all three have important implications for financial markets.

Debt Management Operations

Treasury and Federal Reserve operations change the maturity structure of the marketable component of the debt. In order to isolate the effects of debt management, assume the total amount of marketable government debt is constant. The Treasury, then, can shorten or lengthen the debt by changing the mix of securities in the hands of the public. In the former case the Treasury issues bills or notes and buys or retires bonds. To lengthen the debt the Treasury refunds the debt by replacing maturing bills with longer-term securities.

The Federal Reserve also engages in debt management when it carries out an open market operation that alters the maturity structure of the publicly held debt. If the Fed were to, say, sell $500 million of long-term securities and buy the same amount of short-term securities, the reserves of banks would remain the same but the publicly held debt would be lengthened. If the Fed exchanged short-term for long-term government securities the maturity of the debt held by the public would be shortened.

The marketable component of the public debt is the important one for debt management. It consists of Treasury bills, notes, and bonds. Nonmarketable issues, those that must be held until maturity or redemption by the Treasury, include savings bonds and notes, foreign issues, and special issues. Table 17–1 presents the types of securities that made up the public debt at the end of October 1973.

Because these various types of securities have been discussed in earlier chapters, little needs to be said about them here. Suffice it to say, the Treasury has primary responsibility for managing the debt and Treasury officials make day-to-day decisions concerning the marketable debt held by the public. They decide on the types and maturities of securities to be issued; the yields on coupon issues; special features such as call provisions, ownership restrictions, and allotments that might attach to these obligations, and so on.

Before turning to questions of the economic impact of the debt and appropriate debt management policy let us look at the ownership of the debt and its maturity distribution. Table 17–2 shows that over two-fifths of the debt was

TABLE 17–1   U.S. Government Public Debt, October 31, 1973 (billions of dollars)

Type of Security	Amount	Percent of Total
Marketable		
Bills	101.6	22.1
Notes	120.7	26.2
Bonds	41.8	9.1
Total Marketable	264.0	57.4
Nonmarketable[1]		
Savings bonds and notes	60.5	13.2
Foreign issues	27.8	6.0
Convertible bonds	2.3	0.5
Special issues	105.1	22.9
Total Nonmarketable	195.7	42.6
Total Public Debt[2]	459.7	100.0

[1]Includes $900 million of depository, retirement and other bonds not shown separately.
[2]Excludes non-interest bearing debt (of which $619 million on October 31, 1973, was not subject to statutory debt limitation).

SOURCE: *Federal Reserve Bulletin*, December 1973, p. A42.

TABLE 17–2 Ownership of Public Debt, October 31, 1973 (billions of dollars)

Held by	Amount	Percent of Total
Nonbank private investors		
Individuals	76.9	16.6
State and local governments	28.0	6.1
Corporations	13.5	2.9
Foreign and international	57.5	12.4
Insurance companies	5.6	1.2
Mutual savings banks	2.0	0.4
Miscellaneous investors	17.5	3.8
Total nonbank	201.1	43.4
Banks		
Commercial banks	55.4	12.0
Federal Reserve Banks	78.5	17.0
Total bank	133.9	29.0
U.S. government agencies and trust funds	127.4	27.6
Total public debt	462.4	100.0

SOURCE: *Federal Reserve Bulletin*, December 1973, p. A42.

held by nonbank private investors. Among these, individuals were the largest holders; foreign holdings were next, and up sharply compared to the pre-1971 period, the rise due to foreign central banks' purchases with dollars accumulated in foreign exchange markets. Commercial banks and Federal Reserve Banks held a little less than one-third; government agencies and trust funds held more than one-quarter of the debt.

The maturity distribution of the marketable debt on October 31, 1973 is presented in Table 17–3. Nearly one-half of these securities were due or callable within one year, eighty percent within five years. Clearly, most of the marketable securities were short-term. These include bills and those notes and bonds that have been outstanding for a period of time. Some of the notes and bonds were securities whose original maturities may have been intermediate or long-term but whose time until due or callable has been reduced with the passage of time. From the portfolio managers' point of view, a bond whose original maturity was, say, ten years is considered a short-term liquid instrument if it is due within one or two years.

Economic Impact of Changes in Debt Structure

In one view, changing the maturity structure of the debt may alter the maturity structure of interest rates: lengthening the debt means more long-term debt and less short-term debt. This increased supply of long-term securities should lead to higher long-term interest rates, and the reduced supply of short-term securities should lead to lower short-term interest rates. Thus, the

TABLE 17–3 Maturity Distribution of Marketable Securities, October 31, 1973
(billions of dollars)

Due or Callable	Amount	Percent of Total
Within 1 year	130.9	49.6
1–5 years	80.5	30.5
5–10 years	31.1	11.8
10–20 years	15.3	5.8
Over 20 years	6.2	2.3
Total	264.0	100.0

SOURCE: *Federal Reserve Bulletin*, December 1973, p. A43.

yield curve should be more positively sloped after a debt lengthening operation than it was before. There is some evidence that this is the case.[12]

Higher long-term rates dampen the willingness of businessmen to engage in long-lived investment, and long-lived investment is below what it otherwise would be. Thus, lengthening the debt should help restrict a boom in investment and dampen an overheated economy. Lower short-term rates might encourage some forms of investment, specifically investment in inventories. Most economists feel, however, that long-term investment projects are more sensitive to interest rate charges than is inventory investment. Thus, if long-term investments are significantly restricted but inventory investment is little changed, the net effect of lengthening the maturity structure of the debt would be restrictive.

Another view, consistent with possible interest rate effects, is that the "liquidity" of the public's portfolio can be changed by debt management. Thus, if the Treasury shortens the debt and issues more short-term securities, these securities will, because of their liquidity, be good substitutes for money. Therefore, people will demand less money and lower their cash balances by purchasing goods (and perhaps bonds). This will increase the velocity of money, and the increased spending will be expansionary. The reverse will occur when debt maturity is lengthened.

Thus, by changing the liquidity of the public's portfolio, not only do interest rates change, thereby indirectly changing investment spending, but spending also changes directly as the desire to hold cash balances is affected. In these ways some economists believe that debt management can significantly affect the overall level of economic activity.

[12]R. H. Scott found that the difference between long and short yields increased by thirty-four basis points when the average length of time to maturity of the federal debt increased by one month. However, both long and short yields increased, and this led some critics to discount the findings, for presumably the long yield should increase and the short yield should decrease. But, that both increased can be explained by the general upward trend of interest rates during the period the data were analyzed. See his "Liquidity and the Term Structure of Interest Rates," *Quarterly Journal of Economics*, Vol. 79 (February 1965), pp. 135–45.

Holding Interest Charges Down

Treasury officials are pressed by political forces to minimize the interest charges on the debt in order to appease taxpayers. Because the duties of the Secretary of the Treasury seem similar to those of a corporate treasurer, it is typical to find Treasury officials behaving like corporate treasurers. They handle the government's accounts in the best way they can in order to minimize expenses. Unfortunately, when it comes to management of the debt, these cost-minimizing policies may lead to perverse economic effects. To understand why this is so, consider the following facts:

1. The government, because it creates money, could immediately retire all outstanding interest-bearing indebtedness by issuing currency. Interest payments would cease. This would reduce the taxpayers' burden, but it would also produce a disastrous inflation. If taxes are insufficient to provide the funds that government wants to spend, the government must borrow rather than print money if it wishes to contain inflation. Thus, interest charges on the national debt do not represent some rate of return on an investment program of the government, as interest charges on the national debt are completely independent of the government's investment programs.
2. The size of the government's debt is so large that debt managers could, if they wished to do so, manipulate yields. That is, they could speculate against dealers and other speculators; they could sell debt, drive the price down, and buy it back at a lower price.
3. Treasury officials do not do these things because they do not wish to manage the debt for government "profit," as a corporate treasurer might. They do not wish to because it is not in the public interest.
4. However, in the past it has been typical for Treasury officials to lengthen the debt in periods of low interest rates and slack economic activity, and to shorten the debt during periods of high interest rates and strong economic activity. To minimize costs to the business, a corporate treasurer should do this: fund debt at low interest rates and borrow short in periods of high rates, in anticipation of lower long-term yields in the near future. In this way interest costs are lowered over the life of the debt, and corporate profits will be improved. But, when the federal Treasury does this, it lengthens the debt precisely when stabilization policy calls for shortening the debt. The Treasury absorbs funds that otherwise would flow into the corporate bond market to be used for expansion. The reverse occurs when contractionary policy is called for and the Treasury issues short-term liquid assets and thereby contributes to expansionary pressures.

Of course, part of the reason for the Treasury behavior is the ceiling that Congress has placed on the interest rate that can be paid on Treasury bonds. This law prevented the sale of bonds when market yields rose above the ceiling (see discussion in Chapter 8), precisely when the Treasury should have sold long-term securities for policy purposes.

Effectiveness of Debt Management

Nearly everyone agrees that for stabilization purposes debt management policy is less powerful than either monetary or fiscal policy. However, it is a liquidity policy that can either support or work at cross purposes with the other policy tools. In general, if a policy direction is called for, it would seem best if all policy tools were coordinated, so as not to thwart each other.

If debt management were completely ineffective as a policy tool, then for stabilization purposes it would not matter whether the Treasury sold long-term or short-term securities. Because short-term rates are generally lower than long-term rates, turning over the debt with regular issues of weekly bills would keep interest charges low. Why would any pressure to lengthen the debt be warranted? On the other hand, if perverse management of the debt can *interfere* with monetary policy, then it follows that it is a policy tool with noticeable effectiveness, and should be handled accordingly. The issue, then, is largely empirical—just how powerful is debt management policy?

Opinion among economists seems to be divided. Of 125 economists with interest in these issues, some 71 replied to a questionnaire sent out by the House Committee on Banking and Currency.[13] One question was, "Given the goals of the Employment Act, what can debt management do to help their implementation?" Answers of about 55 who commented on this question were summarized by the House committee staff. About 20 percent of those answering, or 11 persons, recommended pursuing debt management policy aggressively, but about 75 percent ". . . would appear to agree that the important contribution debt management can make to economic stability is simply not to interfere with other stabilization policies. This majority consisted of those who stated that debt management has no potential as a stabilization policy yet recommended keeping the age mix of the debt constant, and those who concluded that debt management would be destabilizing if used to minimize carrying costs and recommended that it definitely not be used for this purpose."[14]

[13]House of Representatives, Subcommittee on Domestic Finance, Committee on Banking and Currency, *Compendium on Monetary Policy Guidelines and Federal Reserve Structure*, December 1968, 90th Cong., 2nd sess.

[14]House of Representatives, *Compendium on Monetary Policy Guidelines*, p. 19. Dudley G. Luckett wrote:

> Debt management policy . . . probably has little or no role to play in economic stabilization. Not only is it apparently a weak policy instrument in its own right, but it seems unlikely that it is capable of doing anything different than could be accomplished by a slightly stronger monetary policy.

Four sentences later he concluded,

> Thus, the role of debt management should be viewed as essentially passive, and coordination should consist simply of holding debt management *interference* with monetary policy to a minimum (p. 413; italics are this author's).

But, if debt management policy actions are weak, why bother to worry about interference?

It there any past experience that could give us a hint as to the strength of debt management policy? "Operation Twist" took place in 1961. The Fed abandoned its "bills-only" policy and bought bonds to hold bond yields down in the interest of domestic expansion, while selling bills to push bill yields up into line with international bill yields so as to discourage the outflow of funds and mitigate balance of payments problems. Did the program work? Yield differences did not respond significantly, but perhaps this was because the Treasury issued considerable new long-term debt through advance refundings, and so on, at the same time the Federal Reserve was buying long-term debt. Furthermore, it was during this same period that the market for negotiable certificates of deposit was developed by commercial bankers. Thus, the "experiment" was impure because other forces affected the securities markets at the same time. The real question is, what would the pattern of yields have looked like if the Fed had not purchased those long-term securities it did? Controlled experiments are required to answer questions such as this with confidence.[15]

Milton Friedman stated that he believed the influence of small changes in maturity structure to have only a slight effect on the demand for money.[16] He noted, however, that when bond prices were unpegged after the Federal Reserve-Treasury Accord of 1951, securities that formerly were effectively demand obligations became long-term securities in fact as well as in name. This was a drastic increase in the "effective maturity" of the debt, and he argued that this loss of liquidity led to an ". . . increase in the demand for money by something like 2 or 3 percent."[17]

It is fair to conclude that debt management, if *aggressively* pursued, *could* become an effective stabilization tool. But other considerations, mostly political, suggest that orderly management of the debt, keeping the structure more or less constant and allowing the Fed to carry out monetary policy without interference from perverse debt management policies, would represent an appropriate division of responsibilities, especially from an administrative point of view.

FINANCIAL ANALYSTS AND THE FEDERAL DEBT

Financial analysts are vitally interested in current and prospective developments in the money and capital markets. They therefore examine carefully any factors which affect the supply of and demand for credit, including, of course, fiscal and debt management policy actions. A thorough review of all official budget documents is the first step in projecting government demand for funds during the forthcoming period. Analysts may use the government's estimates of the budget as set forth in these documents as the basis for their projections

[15]For a discussion of "operation twist" see James R. Schlesinger, "The Sequel to Bills Only," *Review of Economics and Statistics*, Vol. 44 (May 1962), pp. 184–89.

[16]Milton Friedman, *A Program for Monetary Stability*, Fordham University Press, New York, 1959, p. 61.

[17]Friedman, *Program for Monetary Stability*, pp. 107–8.

or they may modify them to conform with their own appraisals of the outlook for tax revenues, expenditures, and changes in the amount and structure of the federal debt. The next step is to estimate the private market financing of federal debt. The net volume of private market financing of Treasury debt is arrived at by subtracting from the total amount of credit required the amount of purchases expected to be made by the Federal Reserve System and the trust funds.

In early 1973, for example, one estimate of the year's expected increase in Treasury debt was $24.5 billion. The deficit was expected to be larger during the first half of the year than during the second half, because overwithholding of taxes would require tax refunds in the spring and a consequent drain on Treasury cash. However, in order to provide an increasing money supply, the Fed was expected to purchase about $7 billion. Trust funds were expected to acquire $10.7 billion. This left $6.8 billion to be absorbed in the marketplace. It was anticipated also that federal agencies would need to raise $16.2 billion from private investors, so that the total demand from the federal sector would amount to $23 billion.[18]

Official budget projections, of course, often have political dimensions. If military appropriation bills fail to pass Congressional review, then expenditures later in the year reflect this, and realized budgets differ from those projected at the outset. After taking as many of these considerations as possible into account, estimated Treasury demand for funds is pooled with corporate demand, mortgage demand, and so forth in order to arrive at overall demand.

Sometimes unusual circumstances require a revision of estimates. For example, when the dollar was devalued in 1973 by 10 percent in terms of its official gold content, the value of the gold held by the Treasury increased by 10 percent. This enabled the Treasury to deposit gold certificates with the Fed in that amount in exchange for an increase in the Treasury's deposit account. This raised the cash position of the Treasury and enabled it to avoid having to borrow roughly a billion dollars that it otherwise would have had to borrow.

The Treasury bill market is also subject to special pressures before and after a devaluation. Holders of dollars used these to purchase German marks in anticipation of dollar devaluation. The Deutsche Bundesbank issued marks and accepted dollars; with these dollars it purchased U.S. Treasury bills, thereby keeping bill prices higher and yields lower than otherwise. After the devaluation, one would normally expect a return flow of marks and a demand for dollars. To obtain dollars, the Bundesbank would sell Treasury bills with the general effect of an upward pressure on yields.

Thus, international as well as domestic developments impinge upon the market for government securities and thus upon the market for other securities. Financial analysts must be sensitive to changes in economic affairs, the political climate, and actions of the monetary authorities, and to international financial changes, if they are to keep abreast of changes in financial market conditions.

[18]These estimates may be found in *Supply and Demand for Credit for 1973*, by Henry Kaufman, James McKean, and Albert Cross, Salomon Brothers.

SUMMARY

Fiscal policy refers to federal government spending and taxing policy. Although there is disagreement over whether fiscal policy actions have important effects on the level of economic activity, there is a consensus that deficits or surpluses in federal budgets have profound effects in financial markets.

Automatic stabilizers such as the progressivity of the personal income tax and the unemployment compensation program tend to dampen swings in economic activity. Discretionary changes in tax rates and in expenditures have also been used for stabilization purposes.

Because the current federal government budget not only affects the level of national income but is affected by changes in income, it is often a misleading guide to the thrust of fiscal policy. Many economists use the "high employment budget" or the "initial stimulus" measure of the budget to determine the direction of fiscal influence.

Debt management policy includes Treasury and Federal Reserve actions that affect the composition of the debt in the hands of the public. By shortening or lengthening the maturity of the marketable debt, policymakers seek to change the relative levels of interest rates in the term structure or, more broadly, the liquidity of the economy. Many economists believe that these changes significantly alter the overall level of economic activity. However, many believe that debt management is much less powerful than monetary or fiscal policy actions. Some believe that the goal of debt managers should be to minimize the cost of the debt. Nonetheless, financial analysts must take note of changes in Treasury budgets and monetary policy actions in evaluating the situation in the money and capital markets, in forecasting interest rates, and in determining appropriate actions in borrowing and in managing financial portfolios.

QUESTIONS FOR DISCUSSION

1. Give an example of an "automatic stabilizer," and explain how it works.

2. "In essence, accelerated depreciation allowances amount to an interest-free loan by government to business." Explain.

3. How does the "high-employment" budget differ from the national income accounts budget reflecting federal government spending?

4. Draw a figure similar to that shown in Figure 17–2 and show the situation in which, instead of "fiscal drag" we have fiscal stimulus. That is, show that tax receipts at full employment would create a deficit rather than a surplus.

5. Describe the "initial stimulus" measure of fiscal policy.

6. Explain what is meant by "debt management for economic stability."

7. What responses should one expect if he argues that the Treasury should "minimize the interest cost of the national debt"?

SELECTED REFERENCES

A witty, interesting history of fiscal policy from the 1930s to the late 1960s may be found in Herbert Stein, *The Fiscal Revolution in America* (Chicago: University of Chicago Press, 1969); in 1973, Mr. Stein was Chairman of the President's Council of Economic Advisers. Various views on fiscal policy may be found in Lester C. Thurow, ed., *American Fiscal Policy* (Englewood Cliffs, N.J.: Prentice-Hall, 1967). The issues related to tax policy are quite thoroughly reviewed in Joseph A. Pechman, *Federal Tax Policy* (Washington, D.C.: The Brookings Institution, 1971).

A number of research studies on specific aspects of countercyclical fiscal policy are summarized in Albert Ando, E. Cary Brown, and Ann F. Friedlander, *Studies in Economic Stabilization* (Washington, D.C.: The Brookings Institution, 1968). Current studies on nearly all aspects of fiscal policy may be found in the periodical, *Brookings Papers on Economic Activity.*

An excellent review of debt management up to 1960 is Tilford C. Gaines, *Techniques of Treasury Debt Management* (The Free Press of Glencoe and the Graduate School of Business, Columbia University), 1962. The relation between debt policy and monetary policy is discussed in Milton Friedman, *A Program for Monetary Stability* (Fordham University Press, 1959). For other readings related to debt management, see the references to studies of the term structure of interest rates in Chapter 13.

For a defense of the high employment budget concept, see Henry N. Goldstein, "In Defense of Phantom Budgets," *Morgan Guaranty Survey*, April 1973, pp. 6–9.

Epilogue

Financial institutions and markets of the future will differ significantly from those studied in *Financial Markets and the Economy*. We can expect changes in the types and means of providing financial services, in the roles played by various types of financial institutions, and in the structure and operations of money and capital markets. This surmise is supported by past and current developments.

The history of the financial system attests to its capacity and requirement for change. It has grown and developed in response to needs of the economy; it has reflected changes in the nation's social goals; and it has adapted to, and even overcome, obstacles presented by various kinds of government regulations. Based upon past performance, there is every reason to suppose that the financial system will continue to exhibit a high degree of flexibility and innovativeness.

Technological changes are altering the nation's payments system and moving us rapidly toward what many call the "checkless" society. One aspect of this development is that some elements of an electronic funds transfer system (EFTS) are already operational, and others are expected to become so within a short time.

Institutions and markets of the future will also reflect actions taken by Congress, state legislatures, and the financial institution regulatory authorities. Recently, the Administration urged enactment of legislation for fundamental reform of the nation's depository financial system. Much attention was given to these proposals and to implications of their adoption for commercial banks, the thrift industry, and the markets they serve.

Recent trends and developments in financial institutions that may be recalled from the text include the emergence of negotiable certificates of deposit; disintermediation because of the widening gap between market and ceiling rates on time deposits in the 1966, 1969, and 1973 credit crunches; formation of bank holding companies that could issue commercial paper and, through

431

subsidiaries, engage in a large number of activities related to banking. Other trends include the extension of international banking and rapid growth in retail banking and other consumer services by both banks and thrift institutions since 1960. "Retail banking" may broadly include establishment of limited facility branches and satellites, and increased services by mutual savings banks and savings and loan associations including limited transfer (payment) facilities and NOW accounts providing expanded services.

Other developments illustrating the adaptability of financial institutions to changes in market conditions and government regulations are the variable rate mortgage, the floating prime rate, equipment leasing by commercial banks, and numerous others. Changes that have indirectly, but perhaps more significantly in the long run, affected financial institutions are the shift toward greater flexibility in exchange rates, the growing involvement of government in the mortgage market, changes in the implementation of monetary policy, the use of an incomes policy, and changes in the structure of the banking system, to name a few. A particularly important coming development is the emergence of an electronic funds transfer system (EFTS) with the probability that at some point thrift institutions will participate generally in the payments system.

How the financial system evolves in the future will depend not only on technology but also on changes in the regulatory environment and, at a more basic level, in the economy. In August 1973 the Administration, in a special message to Congress, urged enactment of legislation for substantive changes in the regulation of financial institutions. These proposals were very similar to those of the Hunt Commission, whose broad objective was ". . . to move as far as possible toward freedom of financial markets and to equip all institutions with the powers necessary to compete in such markets." This was to be accomplished by providing more competition among financial institutions, less regulation of their activities, and more uniformity in reserve requirements and taxation.

Among the more important proposals were those permitting more diversification of assets and liabilities of thrift institutions, including authority to offer checking and NOW accounts to consumers; extension of NOW account authority to commercial banks; a phase-out of interest rate ceilings on time deposits; substitution of a tax credit on mortgage loans for special tax treatment of thrift institutions; and identical reserve requirements for thrift institutions and commercial banks on any demand deposits (including checking accounts and NOW accounts). It was recommended that these proposals be adopted as a "package" rather than piecemeal.

The Hunt Commission was established in 1970, after a period of considerable unrest in the financial markets. Periodic "credit crunches" and disintermediation had plagued the mortgage market and housing industry. State and local governments and small business firms were faced with financial crises, while larger borrowers were able to continue to obtain funds by borrowing directly in the securities market. Commercial banks were tapping nondeposit sources of funds, establishing holding companies, and experimenting with elements of an EFTS.

The Commission did not deal explicitly with all of these problems; instead, it focused mainly on ways to permit freer competition between banks and thrift institutions and on mortgage and housing markets. The Commission's Report was designed with a view to making its proposals politically acceptable and as a basis for legislative action.

Not unexpectedly, the Report was criticized on a number of grounds. Some savings and loan officials, for example, argued that if the recommendations were adopted as a "package," many S&Ls would be forced to convert into commercial banks, and the housing industry would suffer. They favored retention of differential interest rate ceilings and lower effective tax rates on thrift institutions. But they supported broader authority for S&Ls in consumer and real estate financing.

In general, the banking industry was more receptive to the Commission's recommendations, on condition that they would be adopted in toto. Many bankers felt that competitive equality would be denied if, say S&Ls were permitted to accept checking accounts or make consumer loans without being subject to the same reserve requirements and tax status as banks. Some alleged that elimination of Regulation Q would give large money market banks an unfair advantage in the competition for savings. Like many in the thrift industry, some bankers feared ruinous "rate wars."

Some financial observers charged that the Report did not get to the heart of the disintermediation problem. In one view, control of inflation, not the elimination of rate ceilings, would minimize the disruptive effects of high or fluctuating interest rates on the housing industry. More broadly, the Commission was faulted for failure to address itself to the problem of establishing priorities for social goals, the appropriate mix of monetary and fiscal policies, or monopoly power in banking. Finally, some critics found the recommendations inconsistent: removal of rate ceilings on savings but retention of the prohibition of interest payments on demand deposits; competitive equality but a tax credit on mortgages, which benefits mostly thrift institutions; and so forth.

At the time of writing (early 1974), it seems doubtful that the Commission's recommendations, at least in toto, will be enacted into law within the near future. There has been little public concern over the issues involved, no unequivocal endorsement by any powerful segment of the financial community, and considerable opposition from the thrift industry. Moreover, congressional attention has turned toward more pressing problems occasioned by the energy crisis, a resulting desire to achieve self-sufficiency in energy, and the problem of continued inflation. Inflation has continued not only during rapidly rising business activity (1970–73), but in the subsequent period of slower growth. Combating "stagflation" has become a matter of real concern. Perhaps, as some critics argued, it will take a financial disaster to produce fundamental reform of the financial system.

Technological developments will change the financial system in ways that are not yet clear. At some point, a consensus may be reached—as it was before enactment of the National Banking Act, before the establishment of the Federal Reserve System, and at the time of reforms in the 1930s—that an overhaul of the regulatory framework is badly needed.

Index

436